Shadow Warriors

ALSO BY TOM CLANCY

THE HUNT FOR RED OCTOBER

RED STORM RISING

PATRIOT GAMES

THE CARDINAL OF THE KREMLIN

CLEAR AND PRESENT DANGER

THE SUM OF ALL FEARS

WITHOUT REMORSE

DEBT OF HONOR

EXECUTIVE ORDERS

RAINBOW SIX

THE BEAR AND THE DRAGON

NONFICTION

SUBMARINE:
A Guided Tour Inside a Nuclear Warship

ARMORED CAV:
A Guided Tour of an Armored Cavalry Regiment

FIGHTER WING:
A Guided Tour of an Air Force Combat Wing

MARINE:
A Guided Tour of a Marine Expeditionary Unit

AIRBORNE:
A Guided Tour of an Airborne Task Force

CARRIER:
A Guided Tour of an Aircraft Carrier

SPECIAL FORCES:
A Guided Tour of U.S. Army Special Forces

INTO THE STORM:
A Study in Command
WITH GENERAL FRED FRANKS, JR. (RET.)

EVERY MAN A TIGER
WITH GENERAL CHUCK HORNER (RET.)

SHADOW WARRIORS

INSIDE THE SPECIAL FORCES

TOM CLANCY

WITH GENERAL CARL STINER (Ret.)

AND TONY KOLTZ

SIDGWICK & JACKSON

First published in the United Kingdom 2002 by Sidgwick & Jackson
an imprint of Pan Macmillan Ltd
Pan Macmillan, 20 New Wharf Road, London N1 9RR
Basingstoke and Oxford
Associated companies throughout the world
www.panmacmillan.com

First published in the United States of America 2002
by G. P. Putnam's Sons
Published simultaneously in Australia and New Zealand
by Sidgwick & Jackson

ISBN 0 283 07283 0

Book design by Lovedoy Studio USA

9 8 7 6 5 4 3 2 1

A CIP catalogue record for this book is available from
the British Library.

Printed and bound in Great Britain by
Mackays of Chatham plc, Chatham, Kent

Dedication

This book is dedicated to all the great soldiers, sailors, airmen, and marines with whom and for whom I have been privileged to serve during my thirty-five years of service.

Among these, an elite brotherhood of warriors deserves the highest possible recognition—our nation's Special Operations Force, past and present.

To those who have sacrificed their lives in the defense of our freedoms, we owe our deepest respect and gratitude. And to their families, we offer our deepest sympathy and prayers for their future.

—General Carl Stiner (Ret.)

Contents

AUTHORS' NOTE   XI

I.   MONDAY, OCTOBER 7, 1985   1

II.   PIONEERS   35

III.   WARRIORS' WARRIOR   67

IV.   COUNTRY CARL   99

V.   FEW ARE CALLED,
        FEWER ARE CHOSEN   127

VI.   VIETNAM   161

VII.   BETWEEN THE WARS   205

VIII.   THE LEBANON TRAGEDY   227

IX.   THE *ACHILLE LAURO* STRIKE   265

X.   PANAMA: OPERATION BLUE SPOON   297

XI. PANAMA: OPERATION JUST CAUSE   341

XII. SHADOWS IN THE STORM   395

XIII. BULLDOG AND HIS PACK:
       AN INCIDENT IN THE WAR   451

XIV. THE FACE OF THE FUTURE   469

XV. TUESDAY, SEPTEMBER 11, 2001   501

APPENDIX I:
THE UNITED STATES SPECIAL
OPERATIONS COMMAND: A BRIEF HISTORY   511

APPENDIX II: LEADERSHIP   523

ACKNOWLEDGMENTS   531

BIBLIOGRAPHY   535

INDEX   539

Authors' Note

During any given week, an average of more than 3,500 Special Operations Forces (SOF) are deployed overseas in some sixty-nine countries. Their missions range from counterdrug assistance and demining to peacekeeping, disaster relief, military training assistance, and many other special mission activities. As such, they function as instruments of U.S. national policy, and develop relationships with the militaries and governments of the host nations in a way that best serves our national interests now and in the future.

In the writing of this book, we have attempted to include all the information possible about the capabilities of these unique forces, the sacrifices that they make, and the mission areas of their responsibility, as well as just tell some good stories. Needless to say, however, some of these missions and capabilities are sensitive and cannot be revealed for national security reasons. Likewise, the names of some of the personnel, as well as family members, must be protected for personal security reasons. We know the reader will understand that there are some details that are not appropriate for discussion here, and will pardon any necessary omissions.

—*Tom Clancy and General Carl Stiner (Ret.)*

I

Monday,
October 7, 1985

Brigadier General Carl Stiner, the commander of the Joint Special Operations Task Force, was returning from his morning run at Fort Bragg, North Carolina, when his J-2 intelligence officer, Colonel Mike Flynn, met him at the gate. "A cruise ship has been hijacked in the Mediterranean," Flynn told him coolly, but with urgency, "and Americans are very likely on board."

No other organization had the capability to recapture a ship on the high seas, and Stiner knew they would certainly be called in, and soon.

Stiner was a slender man of six feet, with a crisp but not rigid military bearing and a comfortable, easy look. At the same time, he had always been driven by an underlying intensity and a deep competitiveness. It wasn't just that he wanted to be the best, or to lead his troops to be the best—all officers want that—but that he had time and again figured out ways to make it happen.

As he and Flynn hurried toward the headquarters building, Stiner was already processing the news. He knew that Flynn's sparse information was all that was then available, or else Flynn would have told him more. Even so, he had to begin initial actions based on that slender thread. Through long hours of intense planning, training, and rehearsal, JSOTF had developed force packages for virtually any anticipated crisis situation; these were always ready to go within a few hours, as long as there were airplanes available to haul his men. Based on the planning and rehearsals, Stiner focused on what he had to work out right away: "It's a tough target . . . got to get more detailed information," he thought to himself. "We'll have a long way to go and have to get on the road as soon as possible . . . must order up airlift now. And we must find out the location of the ship."

As these thoughts went through his mind, he remained calm. When Special Forces have a job to do, the job must be done fast, accurately, and efficiently. It is likely to be extremely complex, with many lives at risk, and many unknown variables. Facing those conditions, people in these units do not waste their time and effort expressing feelings. They are businesslike, always focusing on the mission at hand—looking especially for vulnerabilities that can be exploited to solve the problem in the cleanest, most complete way possible.

Once he reached the headquarters, he went without pausing to the Joint Operations Center (JOC), a high-tech war room, complete with computer workstations and secure communications to all JSOTF units, the Pentagon, and major commands throughout the world. There he would review the latest intelligence and learn firsthand everything anyone knew about the incident in the Mediterranean. His staff principals had already assembled, waiting for his guidance.

The Task Force maintained its own twenty-four-hour intelligence center, complete with "watch officers"—military officers and civilians expert at picking out intelligence indicators of an impending crisis—analysts, and databases covering every known terrorist organization. Terminals connected the command with all major news networks, including Reuters and the BBC—the first indication of a developing incident often appeared as a news item. JSOTF also had its own people resident in all U.S. intelligence agencies—always looking for indicators of terrorist activities, as well as already existing information that had not seemed important to analysts in those agencies.

In most cases, the headquarters learned of terrorist incidents early, and they usually had the most complete information about them.

Stiner knew that all available intelligence information had already been transmitted by the staff to the units that would be involved. This also meant that all his units would have begun to ready their forces for deployment, while anticipating further guidance from him. They always made maximum use of the time available. In this business, time was a most precious asset.

BEFORE Stiner had taken this command, previous tours in the Middle East had taught him a lot about terrorists and how they operated. For instance, while he had been the chief of training for the modernization of the Saudi Arabian National Guard from 1975 to 1977, he had had a chance to take the measure of Yasir Arafat and his chief lieutenants. Along with other dignitaries from the region, the Palestinians had been invited to a graduation dinner for an officer candidate class by King Khalid and Prince Abdullah, the commander of the National Guard.

Arafat's lieutenants were impressive, no doubt about it. Most of them had advanced degrees from American universities. They were all well-dressed, very sharp, well-spoken, and knowledgeable about world affairs. Arafat was obviously the leader—and clearly an intelligent and remarkable man—but the lieutenants who made things work struck Stiner as truly formidable. In years to come, that impression proved terribly accurate.

Later, in 1983, Stiner was assigned to Lebanon. There he got a firsthand experience of terrorism and its effects—a U.S. ambassador had been assassinated; while he was there, more than sixty people at the American Embassy, and later more than two hundred U.S. Marines, were killed by bombs.

In those days, Beirut was not only an armed camp with many hostile factions, but a place where fighting might break out anywhere at any time. No one was safe, and death was an ever-present risk—from snipers, crossfires between factions, ambushes, and indiscriminate shelling by heavy artillery and rocket fire. The shelling sometimes involved thousands of rounds, which reduced entire sections of the city to rubble in half an hour.

It was not an easy assignment. Yet, for Stiner, it proved to be rewarding. It offered a chance to learn lessons he could get nowhere else.

- ✪ You learned how to survive. Or you didn't.
- ✪ You learned whom to trust in a life-or-death situation—and whom, by faction or religious motivation, you could not trust.
- ✪ You learned to think like a terrorist.

THE EVOLUTION OF JSOTF

The traditional function of wars is to change an existing state of affairs. In the early 1970s, a new form of warfare, or maybe a new way of practicing a very old form of warfare, emerged—state-supported terrorism. Nations that were not militarily powerful learned to use terrorist tactics to obtain objectives and concessions they could never win through diplomatic or military means.

When this new form of warfare broke out, the United States quickly showed itself unprepared to cope with it. It had neither a national policy nor intelligence capabilities aimed at terrorism, nor any military forces adequately trained and prepared to respond to terrorist provocations. Although the United States was the most powerful nation in the world, its military capabilities were focused on the Soviet Union and not on something like this.

In 1972, Israeli athletes at the Munich Olympics were massacred by Black September terrorists. This outrage might have been avoided if German snipers had had the ability to hit the terrorists as they led the hostages across the airport runway to their getaway plane.

The Israelis took this lesson to heart, and on July 4, 1976, eighty-six Israeli paratroopers landed at Entebbe Airport in Uganda. Their mission was to rescue the passengers from an Air France airliner hijacked eight days earlier. In a matter of minutes, the paratroopers had rescued ninety-five hostages and killed four terrorists—though at the cost of the lives of two hostages and the paratroop commander. News of the raid flashed all over the world—and pointed out even more sharply America's inadequacies in fighting terrorism.

This truth had already been brought out in May 1975: Forty-one American Marines were killed in an attempt to rescue the thirty-nine crewmen of the American merchant ship *Mayaguez* after it had been seized by the Cambodian government. The rescue attempt had failed.

These incidents clearly indicated that the United States was unprepared to deal with terrorist-created hostage situations.

To correct this shortfall, in the mid-70s, three farseeing people began lobbying for the creation of a special "elite" unit to deal with this unconventional threat: Lieutenant General Edward C. "Shy" Meyer, Director of Operations for the Army; Major General Robert "Bob" Kingston, Commander of the Army's Special Forces; and Robert Kupperman, Chief Scientist for the Arms Control and Disarmament Agency, who was managing the government's studies on terrorism.

The three initially made little headway. Scant support for the "elite" unit could be found among the services, and even within the Army, even though it was devastatingly clear that the technology in which the Army was investing so heavily—tanks, helicopters, air defense missiles, armored personnel carriers, and all the other machinery of the modern-day battlefield—was of little use against terrorists. The opposition stemmed primarily from two sources: a bias against elite units as such—elites have never been popular in the U.S. Army—and the perception that the unit would rob resources and available funds from the existing force structure.

On June 2, 1977, Lieutenant General Meyer presented the concept of this special mission unit to Army Chief of Staff General Bernard Rogers.

This unit was to be the premier counterterrorist force. Because it was expected to deal with the most complex crisis situations, it would have capabilities like no other military unit. It would be organized with three operational squadrons and a support squadron; and it was to be composed of handpicked men with demonstrated special maturity, courage, inner strength, and the physical and mental ability to react appropriately to resolve every kind of crisis situation—including imminent danger to themselves.

On November 19, 1977, the Army officially activated the unit, but it took another two years to develop the tactics and procedures required for the unit's projected mission.

The unit's final exam and validation exercise was held at Hunter Army Airfield at Fort Stewart, Georgia, and ended in the early-morning hours of Sunday, November 4. It was now certified for its special mission requirements.

IRONICALLY, just as the exercise was taking place, a mob was invading the American Embassy in Tehran. Moments later everyone inside—fifty-three people—became hostages to the new religious-led Iranian revolutionary government.

The crisis of the next 444 days challenged the United States as it had never been challenged before, and proved a horribly painful lesson in effective response to terrorist incidents. The nation was faced with risks, quandaries, contradictions, legal issues, other nations' involvement, and sovereignty issues; and there were no easy solutions. We were presented with what was in fact an act of war, yet this "war" was on a scale that made the use of heavy weapons either impractical or overkill. And besides, there were hostages. We wanted to do something to turn the situation to our advantage.

But what?

In terms of shooters and operators, the unit was probably the most capable unit of its kind in the world, but it did not yet have the necessary infrastructure to go with it—no command organization, no staff, no combat support units. To make matters more frustratingly complex, the intelligence infrastructure necessary for support of rescue operations did not exist in Iran, either.

Meanwhile, President Jimmy Carter—sitting very uncomfortably between a rock and a hard place—decided that an operation to rescue the fifty-three hostages had to be attempted. Army Special Forces had to be the centerpiece of any rescue in Iran.

The obvious model was the Israeli raid on Entebbe. A brilliantly planned, led, and executed operation . . . yet only a marginally useful model. The difficulties of a raid into Tehran were incomparably larger. The Entebbe raid was made against an airfield. The raiders could land there quickly, and make their move against the terrorists almost before they themselves had been detected. Tehran was a major metropolis, with a population in the millions, and it was hundreds of miles inside a vast and hostile country. Getting inside Tehran and into the embassy undetected and with sufficient force to do any good presented many problems.

Major General James Vaught was picked to head the rescue operation. He had a capable Special Forces Unit, but that was all he had. He literally had to begin from scratch to create an effective headquarters for command, control, and intelligence support functions—to select and train a competent staff, develop a plan, select the support units, and train the force for the mission.

If Special Forces could get to the U.S. Embassy in Tehran, they were certainly capable of conducting the rescue operation, but getting them there and back was the challenge. It meant the establishment of staging bases in countries willing to support American efforts and of a support infrastructure within Iran itself. This required, first, an airfield for transloading the rescue force from C-130s to helicopters, which would then take the force on to a landing site near Tehran and back; and second, trucks in waiting near the landing site.

Also required were C-130s and crews that were capable of flying "blacked-out missions" into sites in the desert at night, and a reliable helicopter unit that could take the rescue force from the transload site to Tehran and back.

No units capable of performing this mission existed in any of the services. Jim Vaught had to form, equip, and train them.

It was a daunting challenge to develop in very little time the individual- and unit-level proficiency required to accomplish the job—for example, flying with night-vision goggles had never been done before—and Jim Vaught was the right man for the mission, but the units, equipment, and crews available were at best only marginally capable of taking it on.

Even more difficult was the establishment of an intelligence and support mechanism inside Iran. Vaught did this partly with CIA support, but primarily by using his own assets, sending his own people into Iran to prepare the way. His plan called for establishing an intelligence support infrastructure in Tehran whose function was to verify that the hostages were being held in the Chancery, a ninety-room structure on the Embassy compound, and to arrange for trucks to be waiting near the helicopter landing site for transporting the unit, and later the hostages, back and forth between the landing site and the Embassy compound. This mission was accomplished by Major Dick Meadows, three Special Forces NCOs, and two agents provided by the CIA.

On April 1, 1980, a one-legged CIA pilot in a small two-engine plane flew Major John Carney into Iran at night. Carney's mission was to locate and lay out a 3,000-foot landing strip on a remote desert site in Iran called Desert One. This was to serve as the transload site for the shooters, as well as the refueling site for the helicopter force that would join them after they had been launched from the aircraft carrier Nimitz. The force was composed of eight Navy Sea Stallion helicopters—not the right aircraft for the job, but the best available in terms of range and payload.

Carney laid out the strip with the help of a small Honda dirt bike he brought on the plane. Once the field was established, he installed an airfield lighting system that could be turned on remotely from the cockpit of the lead C-130 (a duty he himself performed on the night of the landing).

On April 24, 1980, 132 members of the rescue force arrived at a forward staging base on Masirah Island near Oman. There they transloaded to C-130s for the low-level flight to Desert One.

That night, the C-130s made it to the Desert One area with no unusual problems, but the helicopters did not arrive as scheduled. Of the eight Sea Stallions, six operational helicopters finally arrived at the desert landing strip an hour and a half late, after an encounter with a severe unforecasted sandstorm. The other two had had mechanical problems before reaching the sandstorm and had returned to the Nimitz. Six Sea Stallions were enough to carry out the mission—but only barely. If another was lost, then some part of the rescue force would have to be left behind, which was not a good idea. All of the force was essential.

Meanwhile, that hour-and-a-half delay made everybody nervous. The helicopters had to leave in time to reach the secluded landing site near Tehran before daylight.

The mission's luck did not improve. During refueling, one of the six remaining helicopters burned out a hydraulic pump. And now there were five—not enough to complete the mission—and it was too late to reach the hide site.

At that point, the decision was made to abort the mission. It was a choice no one wanted to make, but no other choice was possible.

And then came tragedy.

After refueling, one of the helicopters was maneuvering in a hover in a cloud of desert dust, following a flashlight to a touchdown location. The helicopter pilot thought the man with the flashlight was a combat ground controller, when in fact he was not. He was simply a man with a flashlight—possibly a C-130 crew member checking out his aircraft. Meanwhile, the helicopter pilot expected the man with the flashlight to be holding still. In fact, he was moving, trying to get away from the dust storm thrown up by the helicopter's blades. This combination of mistakes resulted in the helicopter veering so close to a C-130 that its blades clipped the C-130's wingtip and ignited the fuel stored there, instantly setting off a flaming inferno. In moments, five men on the C-130 and three men on the helicopter were killed.

The commander of the helicopters then elected to abandon all the helicopters rather than risk further disasters. Everyone who wasn't then on a 130 scrambled aboard, and the best America could muster abandoned the Iranian desert site in shocked disarray.

THE nation suffered a devastating humiliation. Burned and abandoned American equipment littered the desert. Eight Americans had died. The American hostages remained locked up in Tehran. America's enemies laughed.

This failure weighed heavily on the troops who had trained so hard and risked their lives in Iran, all of whom believed that if they could have gotten to Tehran, they could have done the job they'd been sent to do. The failure had in no way been their fault, but the fault of the men who had thrown them together so unprepared and underequipped.

The consequences of the Desert One failure included two key actions that would greatly transform the U.S. special missions capability in the future. First, two days after the failed mission, President Carter ordered the Pentagon to prepare a second rescue mission. Carter additionally ordered the Secretary of Defense to make sure that this time the mission had all the resources it needed. Second, the Secretary of Defense appointed an investigative panel, chaired by the former Chief of Naval Operations, Admiral James L. Holloway, to examine the Iranian hostage rescue attempt, and to make appropriate suggestions for improving future capability. The panel would recommend that a standing joint task force be established as a national-level asset, with its own headquarters, forces, and necessary capabilities for effective and responsive operations.

In August, Major General Richard "Dick" Scholtes became commander of a new organization, the JSOTF, and was given the mission for the second attempt at rescuing the hostages, code-named HONEY BADGER. The planning and training were soon underway, and featured serious improvements over the previous attempt. For example, modified Army Blackhawks would now fly the mission, with much greater reliability and range than the Navy RH-53 Sea Stallions that had been used before. Several operational options were worked on, though again with a scarcity of solid intelligence (it was later learned from released hostages that on the date planned for the rescue attempt less than five percent of the hostages were where the intelligence community thought they were).

On President Ronald Reagan's Inauguration Day, January 20, 1981, the final rehearsal was being conducted at the training site in Texas when it all suddenly became moot. Word came in that the hostages had been released. The mission was no longer needed.

The United States military had had nothing to do with it. Rather, Iraq's invasion of Iran on September 22, 1980, had persuaded Iran that its national survival was at stake—and that it needed the $12 billion in assets frozen by the Carter administration (including major weapons systems purchased by the Shah) more than it needed the hostages. Iran made the initial moves to free the hostages—timing it to become a political issue in the upcoming election, because they expected a better deal from a Reagan administration. It worked. Though they did not get all $12 billion, the $8 billion they did get was not milk money.

Meanwhile, the training and preparation for Operation HONEY BADGER had greatly improved the readiness and capability of the units involved. Its cancellation would now allow Dick Scholtes to devote his full time and attention to future readiness.

In the days ahead, readiness and capabilities would grow enough for them to begin responding effectively to mission taskings from Washington. For example, an intelligence report that a prison camp in Laos still contained a number of American POWs from the Vietnam war sparked preparations for a covert rescue operation that would require the development of specific tactics, techniques, procedures, and special equipment.

These were developed and rehearsed as part of a very complex plan, involving the seizure of an airfield in a friendly country, from which the rescue would be launched. Before the launch, however, Dick Scholtes, a cautious man and a realist, asked for "U.S. eyes on the target" to validate the intelligence report. Not only did he want U.S. eyes, he wanted his own people to accompany the CIA's people. This did not happen. Instead, the Agency sent a bunch of their guys (none of them American) into Laos. Though they came back with hundreds of pictures, none showed anyone who could be verified as American. Scholtes continued to insist on sending his own people in to recon the site, but permission for this could not be obtained, and the mission eventually went away.

Even so, efforts were not wasted. Once again, not only was the training useful, but the tactics, techniques, and equipment that had been developed specifically for the mission would remain useful.

Later, unwittingly looking forward to October 1985, the Norwegian government, concerned about the emerging terrorist threat and the possible vulnerability of its cruise liner industry, wondered if the United States had the expertise to "take down" a large luxury liner at sea. To find out, they provided the cruise liner *Norwegian Princess* as a training aid.

JSOTF expertly demonstrated they knew how to perform the task with panache—and in darkness.

ON October 25, 1983, JSOTF took part in Operation URGENT FURY—the invasion of Grenada—in association with a larger force under the command of CINCLANT (Commander in Chief, Atlantic). URGENT FURY's overall mission had three goals: to rescue American students at Grenada's Medical University just outside the capital, St. George's; to rescue the former governor general, who was being held under house arrest by the new Cuba-backed leftist regime; and to prevent the use of the island by the Cuban or Soviet military. The mission included taking over the entire island. It was not a well-run operation.

Though JSOTF was committed to URGENT FURY, the commitment came very late—too late to plan, prepare, and train appropriately. This problem was compounded by intelligence foulups.

As Dick Scholtes recalls: "Changes in command and control and in missions over the course of the days immediately before H-hour (the time of the attack) drove us very close to a major catastrophe on that island.

"At the start, on Thursday the twentieth, we were to run the mission unilaterally. Then, on Friday, CINCLANT was put in charge, with only a JSOTF involvement. Then, on Sunday, the Marine barracks in Beirut was blown up, a giant blow to the spirit of the Marine Corps, and this led again to major changes: During a command briefing at the Pentagon, the Commandant of the Marines announced to the Chairman (of the Joint Chiefs of Staff) that unless the Marines joined the attack on the island, the Corps would never recover.

"Less than forty-eight hours before H-hour, the Marines had become involved in URGENT FURY, which meant that a totally new overall commander had to be appointed, Admiral Metcalfe. Three major command-and-control changes had been made in as many days.

"Mission changes came just as fast and furious.

"On Monday, at the final briefing for Metcalfe, the Department of State (DOS) reps present announced that it was critical to seize the Richmond Hill Prison at H-hour—even though the DOS could not tell us who was in the prison, who we were to secure, and whether the guards were the good guys or the bad guys. 'That doesn't make sense,' I told them. 'Since we can't ascertain who is in the prison and who are the good guys and the bad guys, we will make it a follow-up target.' They insisted, so I asked for a twenty-four- to forty-eight-hour delay to give us time to gather better information. The delay was disapproved. (We had also been asking for an 0200 nighttime H-hour, but with little success. Everyone would be landing in daylight rather than darkness.) We now had a major change in mission for one of our major assault units—and without adequate intelligence. This meant, among other things, that we had to change the Blackhawk loading on the C-5s that were already at Pope Air Force Base—not easy to do in the time we had.

"Later, we learned why no one would accept our request for an 0200 H-hour or for a twenty-four- to forty-eight-hour delay. The DOS and the CIA had written a detailed plan for the seizure of the island. This plan included a seven-nation assisting force, which was to land at H+3 and then come under JSOTF control. These nations knew nine days before JSOTF was informed of the mission that the island would be invaded at 0500 on Tuesday, the twenty-fifth. There was no way we could have changed that.

"There were other intelligence mix-ups.

"For example, the intelligence community told us that all the medical students were located at the University's True Blue Campus, which we targeted. They were not. More than half were at Grand Anse, about two miles away on the other side of the island. And to top it off, the president of the university had been visiting the DOS two days before we started the planning, and no one thought to ask him where to find the students.

"Another example: The intelligence community claimed there were only two 40mm AA (antiaircraft) guns on the island. The truth was, the enemy had about six mixed 40mm and two quad 50s at the airfield. And at Fort Frederick, which overlooked the helicopter approach to Richmond Hill Prison, there were an additional two 40mms and two quad 50s.

"Another problem: air support. Without our AC-130 gunships, the entire mission would have been an even greater failure. And then Admiral Metcalfe had the audacity to warn me that no close air support would be available to us. I told him I was using only my organic assets, and I guess he never understood.

"Considering the challenges of this demanding operation, compounded by the half-baked command and mission changes, together with the risk of conducting such complex operations against heavily defended targets in broad daylight with little or no accurate intelligence information and without the correct support of conventional commanders, JSOTF somehow brought off the missions we'd been assigned and made lemonade out of a lemon."

ONE glaring example of the kind of problem Scholtes mentions was a mission performed by the Navy SEALs. At first light, the SEALs planned to airdrop a reconnaissance team with boats—called a night boat drop—and to observe and report activities at Salinas Airfield in preparation for a Ranger assault to secure the airfield. As it turned out, this SEAL team had never made a night boat drop, the two C-130 crews assigned to conduct the drop had never made a boat drop at all, and the drop did not take place at first light but in total darkness in a sudden and unforecasted squall. The waves were much higher than expected; one plane dropped its SEALs two miles from the other; and in the end, four SEALs drowned. Their bodies were never recovered.

Two other targets assigned to the SEALs were the governor general's mansion and the radio station approximately seven miles away. Even though they had trained to operate at night, in order to take advantage of the darkness, both SEAL teams were inserted in daylight. The SEAL team tasked with securing the governor general's mansion had the added complication of bringing in a three-man State Department radio team, which carried a portable broadcast radio with them to allow the governor general to broadcast to the nation that he was okay and still in charge.

As soon as they hit the ground, the SEAL team that was supposed to secure the radio station became involved in heavy fighting with an armed guard force. They were outmanned and outgunned. After the team leader and one of his men were wounded, the team was forced to withdraw back to the coast until they could be picked up at night.

The team securing the governor general's mansion fared better, but their operation was not without problems, either.

As their helicopters approached the mansion, they found no place to land, a consequence of poor intelligence preparation; the terrain was too steep and covered with large trees. That meant the assault team had to slide down a seventy-five-foot rope in order to get on the ground and clear a landing zone for the helicopter carrying the State Department radio team.

As the helicopter moved around the mansion's grounds, it began taking heavy antiaircraft fire from a nearby hill. Though the helicopter was hit several times and the copilot was severely wounded, the pilot did a magnificent job of keeping the helicopter from crashing (he later made it back to the operation's flagship, *Guam,* which had hospital facilities onboard).

Meanwhile, the SEALs had secured the facility, and had the governor and his wife well in hand, and in good spirits, when suddenly three armored personnel carriers appeared at the mansion's gate. The SEALs quickly got control of the situation, however, by calling in an AC-130 gunship. The gunship blasted the APCs just as they were swinging their turrets toward the mansion.

The SEALs did very well, considering what they had to work with. But there were failures above them.

DURING Operation URGENT FURY, Carl Stiner was in Beirut. Even so, he was able to monitor the battle on a SATCOM radio connection he shared with the Chairman of the Joint Chiefs of Staff, General Jack Vessey. Vessey had given Stiner the frequency of his private channel, so he could communicate directly with the Chairman, but it also allowed him to listen to all the reports coming in during URGENT FURY.

Because Stiner and Scholtes had been friends and neighbors at Fort Bragg, where Stiner had been Assistant Division Commander for Operations of the 82nd Airborne Division before he was sent to Lebanon in August 1983, listening to the SATCOM reports was a disheartening experience. "I could really feel how Dick Scholtes must have suffered," he observes. "All caused by factors over which he had no control."

For the next ten months, Dick Scholtes worked day and night to make sure such things would never happen again, and to develop the best capability possible for counterterrorism and other unanticipated special mission requirements. In August 1984, when Stiner himself assumed command of JSOTF, he received from Dick Scholtes the best trained and most competent joint headquarters and the finest special missions units in the world.

Stiner's mission "was to make it even better by making sure the United States was never so caught by surprise that it had no forces appropriately prepared to deal with the situation. When a Joint Special Operations Task Force is committed, all other options for solving the problem have either proved inappropriate or inadequate. Thus the stakes are high."

But no matter how superbly trained and prepared you are, operations can fail, even when you make all the right moves. Sometimes the terrorists operate within secure sanctuaries, such as Beirut, where they can't be hit. Sometimes delay and indecision from above prevent you from taking timely action to seize the best opportunities.

Both elements would haunt the command in June 1985, just four months before the events aboard the *Achille Lauro*.

TWA 847

On Friday, June 14, 1985, at 10:00 A.M. local time, TWA Flight 847 took off from Athens Airport headed for Rome, with 153 passengers and crew on board, 135 of whom were American. The plane, a relatively short-range Boeing 727, was piloted by Captain John Testrake; its copilot was First Officer Phillip Marsca; and Christian Zimmerman was the flight engineer.

According to information later provided by Greek authorities, the day before three young men in their twenties had traveled from Beirut to Athens, spent the night in the Athens terminal, and then tried to make reservations on the Athens-to-Rome leg of Flight 847. Their intent: to hijack the aircraft. It was a full flight, however, and only two of them, traveling under the code names Castro and Said (and later identified as Mohamed Ali Hamadi and Hassan Izz-al-din), were able to get seats. The one who had to stay behind in Athens would later be identified as Ali Atwa, and held by Greek authorities, as soon as his part in the hijack became known. The three of them, as it now seems, belonged to Hezbollah, a radical, revolutionary, terrorist faction with ties to Iran. The hijack was a Hezbollah operation, though other factions active in Lebanon would also make their presence felt as the event played out.

Once they were on board, Castro and Said took seats in the rear of the plane near the lavatory, where the weapons used in the hijacking had been stashed, most likely by airport employees. One of them took a small carry-on bag into the lavatory and secured the weapons—two pistols and hand grenades.

As soon as the plane reached flight altitude, the two terrorists went into action. They leapt from their seats and ran to the front of the plane. When they got there, they pushed the flight attendant, Uli Derickson, to the floor, screaming all the while in Arabic and broken English, "Come to die. Americans die." They then tried to make their presence known to the cockpit crew by knocking Uli Derickson's head against the cockpit door. After they'd shoved a grenade in her face and a gun in her ear, she somehow managed to get to the intercom and inform Christian Zimmerman that a hijacking was taking place.

Captain Testrake immediately ordered the door of the cabin to be opened, and the two hijackers shouted their first demand: They wanted to go to Algeria.

This was not possible. The 727 didn't have enough fuel on board, so the Captain recommended Cairo instead. This suggestion made the already jumpy terrorists even more upset. "If not Algeria, then Beirut," they shouted. "Fuel only."

Captain Testrake changed course and headed toward Beirut, which was seven hundred miles away and only just barely within range.

Meanwhile, Castro ordered all the passengers in the first-class section to move to the rear of the airplane. Since there were not enough seats available, some of them were forced to sit with other passengers. He then directed Uli Derickson to gather all the passports so he could tell which passengers were American and/or Jewish. Once the passports had been collected, Castro ordered Uli to pick out the Israelis, but it turned out that no Israelis were aboard. He then told her to select the Jews, but that also proved impossible, since American passports do not show religion. Growing more impatient, he had her read the passenger list for him. When she came to what sounded like a Jewish name, he ordered her to find that passenger's passport. Seven people fit this category.

Castro next shifted his attention to military ID cards (servicemen usually travel on their ID cards rather than passports). Aboard the plane were an Army reservist named Kurt Karlson and six Navy divers returning from an underwater job in Greece. Castro and Said forced the divers to move to widely separated seats, yelling, "Marines! The *New Jersey!*" The battleship *New Jersey* had recently fired on Beirut, and 1,500 Marines had been stationed at the Beirut airport.

Then Castro ordered all passengers to sit with their heads between their legs without looking up.

When TWA 847 reached the Beirut area, it was very low on fuel. Even so, Beirut control denied the aircraft permission to land. Since this did not please the hijackers, one of them, who was in the cockpit at the time, pulled the pin of a hand grenade and threatened to blow up the airliner. Captain Testrake decided he had no choice but to bluff his way in.

That worked, and they were able to set down safely and park. They then waited for refueling. The terrorists still intended to fly to Algeria.

As they touched down, the cockpit crew couldn't help but notice the wreckage of a Jordanian airliner blown up two days earlier by the PLO.

Because the Lebanese were far from eager to get involved in the ongoing crisis, they ignored the request for fuel. That meant that the terrorists were again displeased. To make clear their determination, they tightly bound the hands of Navy diver Robert Stethem with a bungee cord, dragged him to the front of the airplane, beat him savagely enough to break all his ribs, then dumped him moaning and bleeding in a seat near the front of the plane.

When the captain radioed the tower, "They are beating the passengers and threatening to kill them!" the Lebanese authorities were persuaded to send a refueling truck to TWA 847.

Because it was a long flight to Algeria, Testrake had to take on all the fuel the plane could hold, making the plane some 15,000 pounds overweight with a full load of passengers—and unsafe for takeoff. In view of that, the hijackers agreed to let seventeen women and two children go (they left by sliding down the emergency escape chutes). Releasing the passengers not only made the plane safer, it reduced the number of people that the hijackers had to control—and provided access to a source of intelligence about what was happening on the plane.

Predictably, considering the delay and indecision that marked the whole sequence of events, it was several hours before the released passengers could be flown to Cyprus, a hundred miles away, where they could be interviewed in detail by American officials.

Meanwhile, word of the hijacking did not reach Washington officials until about 4:00 A.M., Washington time. JSOTF learned of it shortly thereafter, from news reports picked up by its Reuters and BBC monitors. Crisis-management teams started gathering at the Federal Aviation Administration, the Pentagon, the State Department, and the White House Situation Room, but none of them had more than sketchy details.

At 6:30 Friday morning, Washington time, TWA 847 cleared the runway in Beirut and headed for Algeria, 1,800 miles away.

By that time the gears in Washington had started to grind into motion. The Pentagon had been ready to respond immediately—it operates twenty-four hours a day—but no one with sufficient rank to make a decision had been available at the White House or State Department. The Administration's terrorist incident working group did not meet until approximately 10:00 that morning.

Meanwhile, at Fort Bragg, JSOTF had already alerted its own forces in anticipation that Americans could be on board the hijacked aircraft, as well as the Military Airlift Command, since lift assets would be needed soon, and the J-3 (Operations) officer of the Joint Chiefs of Staff, requesting Pentagon authority for immediate deployment. The forces that would take part in the operation would come primarily from Army Special Forces and an Army special operations helicopter unit. They expected to fly first to Sigonella, a NATO base on Sicily operated jointly by the United States and Italy, and therefore strategically located at the midpoint of the Mediterranean.

Since only two lightly armed terrorists were in charge of the airplane, excellent conditions existed for a takedown—if, as seemed to be the case, Algeria was in fact TWA 847's destination, and if it was possible to persuade the Algerians to hold the plane on the ground.

With this scenario in mind, JSOTF requested USEUCOM (European Command) to authorize two C-130 Combat Talon aircraft, capable of low-level flight and landing in total darkness to be prepared to deploy from Mildenhall, England, to Sigonella. JSOTF had additionally requested another TWA Boeing 727, identical to the hijacked aircraft, to join the Task Force at Sigonella.

Since JSOTF maintained a detailed database covering every airfield in those regions of the world where terrorist incidents were likely to take place, it was aware of all the characteristics of the Algerian airfield to which the hijacked plane would most likely head. Thus JSOTF had two takedown options: Combat Talon aircraft carrying the rescue force could land blacked out at night. Or the second TWA 727 could be used as a Trojan horse.

All the while, valuable time was being wasted. The Force had been ready to go soon after learning of the hijacking but, as was the case in the past and as would be the case later that year in October, neither airlift nor crews qualified to fly these missions were available. Rounding them up consumed valuable time . . . time the terrorists used most efficiently to stay ahead of JSOTF's reaction time.

When the Administration's terrorist incident working group finally met on Friday morning, they recommended that the Task Force be dispatched immediately.

If airlift had been readily available, Stiner and his forces (including the Combat Talons from England and the TWA 727) could have been arriving at Sigonella at about the time TWA 847 was approaching Algeria. However, the Pentagon was reluctant to launch the Task Force until TWA 847 settled down wherever it was going.

BY midday Algerian time, during (as it happened) the Muslim holy season of Ramadan, TWA 847 was approaching Algeria.

While en route there, Castro made a broadcast in Arabic over the plane's radio, detailing the terrorists' demands: He wanted more than seven hundred Shiites released from prison in Israel, seventeen other Shiites freed from a prison in Kuwait, two other Shiites released from Spain, and two others from Cyprus. Additionally, he wanted Israel to withdraw from southern Lebanon, the United States to admit responsibility for a recent car bombing in Beirut, and the world to condemn America for its support of Israel.

These demands were, of course, impossible to meet.

As the aircraft was approaching the airfield in Algeria, the State

Department passed on to Ambassador Michael Newlin a directive from President Reagan. He was to contact Algerian president Chadli Benjedid and make two requests: first, to make an exception to Algeria's policy that hijacked aircraft not be allowed to land; and second, to keep the plane on the ground and not permit it to take off again after landing.

Looking back over the entire TWA 847 affair, it is possible to see that the United States had only one real opportunity to rescue the hostages without high risk of bloodshed. It was during that first stopover in Algeria. That opportunity was blown, however.

Instead of doing everything in his power to make direct contact with President Benjedid, as he'd been instructed, Michael Newlin settled for subordinates, and then he allowed the Algerian subordinates to pretty much call the shots.

As he later reported, most of his own staff was unavailable (having already taken off to Mediterranean beaches for the weekend), and he found few members of the Algerian government who would take his calls. Newlin did manage to get hold of Benjedid's chief of staff, however, and forty-five minutes later, he called back to say that TWA 847 would be permitted to land "on humanitarian grounds."

By this time, TWA 847 was already requesting permission to land, and had less than thirty minutes of fuel remaining.

After landing, the terrorists decided to return to Beirut to pick up reinforcements, causing another problem with refueling, which meant that another American serviceman, Army Reservist Kurt Karlson, was beaten. Again, though, that facilitated matters (though the flight attendant, Uli Derickson, had to pay for the fuel with her Shell credit card, since TWA didn't have landing facilities in Algeria; she was later billed for six thousand gallons of jet fuel at a dollar a gallon). On the other hand, the terrorists released another twenty-one passengers—eighteen of them American.

Once the refueling was completed, TWA 847 took off again and headed back toward Beirut. The Algerian government made no move to hold the plane on the ground.

Meanwhile, an Air Force C-141 was launching from Andrews AFB just outside Washington, D.C., with the twenty-man Emergency Support Team (EST), headed by a senior State Department official, Ambassador David Long. Joining him were a senior CIA official (formerly a senior station chief), representatives from the Defense Intelligence Agency, communications and technical personnel, selected members of the White House

National Security Staff, and a couple of senior Special Forces officers who would act in an advisory and coordination role. The EST's mission was to precede the Task Force, assist the Ambassador and his staff, and interface with JSOTF, the State Department, and National Intelligence Agencies. After some indecision about the best place to go, the team decided to land at Sigonella.

IT was after 2:00 in the morning when TWA 847 began its approach for its second landing in Beirut.

The runway marker lights were out. The airport was blacked out. Once again the Beirut control tower refused permission to land, and once again Captain Testrake was desperate: "I have no more than twenty minutes of fuel left," he explained to the tower. "I'm coming in even if it means landing next to the runway."

When Testrake broke out of the clouds 500 feet above the airport, he could see vehicles blocking the runway. He radioed to the tower: "We're in deadly danger. I implore you to open your airport and let us land."

The controller replied, "Unfortunately, my superiors do not care about your problems."

"If we try to land, we'll crash," Testrake told the hijackers.

"Good," one answered. "That will save us the trouble of blowing it up."

"Prepare the passengers for a crash landing," Testrake told Uli Derickson. He then made an announcement to the passengers: "We are low on fuel and have to land. We have fuel for only one approach. We're going in. Prepare for a crash landing. If they do not remove the obstacles, we will land on the ground beside the runway. Otherwise, we will have to land in the water."

But with three miles to go, the runway lights flashed on, the vehicles were removed, and the tower told Testrake he was clear to land.

Another gut-cruncher. . . . These were getting to be a habit.

Once the aircraft was on the ground, the hijackers ordered Testrake to stop in the middle of the runway, far from any buildings. Castro and Said then began talking to the tower in Arabic, their voices increasingly angry. They were demanding that reinforcements be allowed to board the plane, and the Lebanese authorities were resisting their demands.

"I don't want to talk to you," one of them screamed at the controller. "I only talk to the Amal." Amal was an armed Shiite faction in Beirut, headed by a lawyer named Nhabbi Barri, with ties to Syrian president Hafez Assad. Amal was somewhat more moderate than Hezbollah. As later became apparent, Assad was working behind the scenes with Amal and Hezbollah's Iranian masters to resolve the situation, but on terms that would be to his political advantage.

"You are trying to gain time," the terrorist continued. "You don't believe me. We'll kill this Marine." He meant Robert Stethem, the Navy diver who had been beaten during the first landing in Beirut.

Castro then dragged Stethem, screaming in agony, to the open door of the aircraft, placed a pistol to the back of his head, and fired. Then he dumped his body onto the tarmac.

"He has just killed a passenger," the pilot reported.

As he spoke, Castro snatched the microphone and said, "You see. You now believe. There will be another in five minutes."

At this point, Castro ordered Testrake to taxi to the refueling points.

The terrorists never forgot that time was precious. The longer they stayed in one place, the greater the window for a takedown attempt. Thus they bounced back and forth from one place to the other.

"As I began moving down the runway," Testrake later remembered, "I turned the wheel sharply to avoid running over the young serviceman's body."

As all this was going on, everyone on the plane had fallen silent—horrified at the violence—until one of the terrorists started singing a song. "It was a song of celebration," Uli Derickson recalled.

Meanwhile, the terrorists chose their next victim: Clinton Suggs, another Navy diver.

"The hijacker came back where I was," Suggs recalled, "and he was kicking me and hitting me and calling me American pig. I thought I was dead. I prayed and asked the Lord to receive me in his arms."

All of a sudden, the back door of the plane opened and ten or twelve heavily armed militiamen carrying automatic weapons rushed onto the plane, screaming and shouting. The terrorists had succeeded in getting their reinforcements . . . and multiplying the difficulty of a takedown.

One of the twelve, who identified himself as Gihad and spoke fluent English, was in fact one of Lebanon's leading terrorists, Imad Mugniyah. Mugniyah had once been a member of Amal, but at this time he was with Hezbollah—their "enforcer." Muginayah now took charge of the operation.

After the aircraft was refueled, six Americans, including Kurt Karlson, Clinton Suggs, and three other Navy divers, were ordered into seats in the last two rows of the plane. Shortly after that, the six were rushed down the back steps of the plane into a waiting enclosed truck. A few moments later, a second group of five passengers—another Navy diver and four of the seven with Jewish-sounding names—were also taken off the plane, loaded into another truck, and whisked away.

Flight 847 then took off again, headed for Algeria. This second Algerian episode would last until Sunday.

It was now daybreak Saturday.

ROBERT Stethem's body had already been dumped on the tarmac in Beirut before Carl Stiner was given authority to launch with his JSOTF. Six to eight more hours of flying time were required before they could be in position to resolve the situation.

While Stiner was en route, the State Department had directed Ambassador Newlin to ask the Algerians for permission to bring in Long's EST, who by then had reached Sigonella.

According to Newlin, however, the Algerians refused. They could not permit a rescue mission, and that's what the EST, with its Air Force C-141, seemed to be.

Unable to bring in his aircraft or his entire team, Long did the best he could. He pared his numbers down by a third and flew this smaller group by commercial air to Algiers by way of Marseilles.

Meanwhile, JSOTF and the rest of the support team had arrived at Sigonella, having planned the rescue operation en route. Soon after landing they linked up with the TWA 727 and the two Combat Talon aircraft from England. All the pieces were now in place for a rescue operation, and sufficient darkness remained to reach Algeria and conduct the operation before daylight. However, a rescue operation would be a different ball game now. Instead of the pair of lightly armed terrorists that had been on board the first time the plane landed in Algeria, there were now fourteen heavily armed Hezbollah militiamen on the plane, some armed with machine guns.

The only thing the Task Force team could do now was wait in the hangar for further developments.

TWA 847 landed once again in Algeria early Saturday morning, and they would remain there this time for just over twenty-four hours. During the just-completed Beirut to Algiers leg of the 847 odyssey, the hijackers had systematically robbed everyone else on the plane.

Soon after the aircraft landed, the hijackers made another demand. They wanted the Greek government to release Ali Atwa, their accomplice who had been arrested at the Athens airport the day before. If he was not released, the hijackers promised, they would kill the plane's Greek passengers. If he was, the Greek passengers would be freed. The Greeks caved in, and that afternoon, an Olympic Airways jet took off from Athens bound for Algeria with Ali Atwa on board.

The Algerians, however, managed to use the release of Atwa to extract a few more concessions from the terrorists, who agreed to free everyone on the plane except the American male passengers and crew. According to Michael Newlin, the Algerians negotiated a brilliant deal. "They were absolutely superb," he said. "They made the terrorists pay for everything."

What the terrorists "paid for" was not obvious to Stiner. The terrorists had been in total control all along—and still were.

Newlin later recalled that when he left the airport early Sunday morning, he was certain that the Algerians and the International Committee of the Red Cross would resolve the crisis without further bloodshed. Armed with that conviction, he went to sleep.

A few hours later, an Embassy officer called him: The hijackers were again demanding fuel.

Newlin then called the Secretary General of the Algerian Presidency, the Algerian executive's chief administrative officer, and reiterated the American position: "Everything possible should be done to keep the plane on the ground," he told him, "even if it means shooting out the tires."

Moments later, the Embassy officer reported to Newlin that TWA 847 was taking off. Newlin again got on the phone with the Secretary General.

"We had to let them go," the Algerian told him. "The hijackers threatened to blow up the plane." Later, the Algerians offered a second excuse: "The hijackers undoubtedly heard radio reports that U.S. Special Forces were on the way," they explained.

That statement was disingenuous. Whether or not the hijackers had heard such reports (most of which were, as it happened, inaccurate), their actions had proved they were worried about a rescue attempt from the very start. They didn't need a news report to tell them that they'd been on the ground too long in Algeria.

In the meantime, the U.S. government had failed to gain Algerian approval of a rescue operation, but even if they had gotten it, the situation had become agonizingly complex. Unlike the first time TWA 847 had landed in Algeria, the terrorists were clearly in control. Not only had their numbers grown, but they'd unloaded a total of thirty-one hostages in Beirut, at least nineteen of whom had been disbursed among the heavily armed militias holed up in the labyrinthine southern suburbs of Beirut. It was now impossible to rescue all the hostages in a single attempt.

TWA 847 took off for Beirut shortly after 8:00 A.M., after spending more than twenty-five hours on the ground in Algeria. A half hour later, an Air Alger plane arrived from Marseilles, carrying David Long and five members of his emergency support team, too late to affect the outcome of the TWA 847 hijack drama. TWA 847 was gone from Algiers forever.

Meanwhile, as TWA 847 was winging once again toward Beirut, Captain Testrake managed to listen in as the terrorists were making further plans. Their new idea was to take on more fuel in Beirut, then move on (he thought) to Tehran. That was definitely not what Testrake wanted. Once they landed in Beirut this time, he decided, he would see to it that they did not take off again. Testrake and Zimmerman, the flight engineer, then worked out a plan of their own, and when the plane touched down in Beirut, Zimmerman shut off the fuel valve and switched off the electrical power to one of the engines. Lights began flashing like mad on the instrument panel.

"TWA 847 can't go anywhere," Testrake explained to Mugniyah, "until a new engine can be brought in from the States."

It was now Sunday afternoon in Beirut, Sunday morning in Washington.

BY this time, Carl Stiner had reached the conclusion that the two Combat Talons and the TWA 727 were no longer useful, and with Pentagon approval, released them. He then loaded up the rest of the force and headed to Cyprus, where he was later joined by David Long and his emergency support team. Stiner still had sufficient capability to conduct a rescue operation—and he still hoped that as this thing played out, an opportunity might present itself.

This was going to be far from easy. Beirut was a much tougher nut to crack than Algeria. Thirty passengers remained on the plane. Their location, at least, was known, but the nineteen taken off the plane earlier were almost impossible to locate. The armed militias that controlled south Beirut were now holding them in separate locations there (mostly in basements).

They might as well have been at the bottom of the sea.

Reliable intelligence information was scarce in Beirut in those days: U.S. national overhead systems (satellites) could not, for example, intercept militia communications, since they communicated by handheld, low-level frequency radios or by messenger. Far worse, the American intelligence network had been tragically blown after the recent kidnapping and torture of the CIA station chief, William Buckley. The U.S. had no choice but to assume that Buckley had revealed his network of agents and that they had all been "neutralized."

As soon as Stiner reached Cyprus, he called Reggie Bartholomew, the American ambassador in Lebanon, brought him up to date, and asked how JSOTF could help.

Though the two men had not seen each other in over a year, they knew each other well, having been together in 1983 and early 1984 when the heaviest fighting had taken place in Beirut. The two men had been on the receiving end of many shellings and had met many times with the factional leaders now holding at least nineteen of the TWA 847 hostages. These experiences had built up considerable mutual respect.

"What I'd like you to do," Bartholomew told Stiner, "is fly over here with a couple of your people and a couple of people from the EST. Once you're in Beirut, we'll decide the best course of action. Then you can go back to Cypress and set things up."

Stiner immediately loaded Lieutenant Colonel "Pete," the two ranking members of the EST team (one from the State Department and one from the CIA), and a SATCOM radio and its operators onto a helicopter and set off for Beirut. TWA 847 was clearly visible on the Beirut International Airport tarmac as they made their final approach to the landing pad near the Ambassador's residence.

Bartholomew's first priority, not surprisingly, was to keep TWA 847 under surveillance.

"We have a superb surveillance capability with us," Stiner told him. "As soon as I get back to Cyprus, I'll send it to you."

Meanwhile, the rest of the team Stiner had brought with him from Cyprus, including the SATCOM and operators, stayed in Beirut with the Ambassador, so there'd be constant communication.

The surveillance team Stiner sent back to Ambassador Bartholomew consisted of four people, bringing with them day and night long-range surveillance capability. An hour after their arrival in Beirut, he had them positioned in a house on a ridge overlooking Beirut International Airport.

For the next several hours, this team was the sole source of intelligence on what was happening on TWA 847. But that night, the Amal militia downloaded the remaining hostages and crew and dispersed them within the south suburbs. There was no longer any way to know where any of the hostages were.

AT this point, though they waited on Cyprus for an additional two weeks, Carl Stiner and JSOTF's role in the TWA 847 affair ended. Now it was up to negotiations between Syria, Iran, and the factional leaders (Washington also produced a number of diplomatic initiatives, but these also seem to have had little effect on the final outcome). Finally, Hafez Assad struck a deal, and the hostages were released to travel to Damascus, where they would be passed over into the hands of the American Ambassador.

It was a prestigious victory for Assad—at least in the Arab world—and a humiliating experience for Stiner and his companions.

In his words:

> Watching the Red Cross vans carry the hostages out of Beirut towards Damascus was a bitter experience. We could not get out of our minds the certainty that we'd had the capability to do a rescue operation that would have been a piece of cake. But we failed to bring it off. We just never had the opportunity.
>
> If only three factors, all beyond our control, could have been changed, this situation might well have been different:
>
> One, we needed dedicated aircraft maintained at the same alert standard that we were.
>
> Two, we should have been launched as soon as we'd learned of the hijacking.
>
> Three, we needed the Algerian government to hold TWA 847 on the ground . . . and then to allow us to conduct a rescue operation.
>
> With all that in mind, as we flew back home, I decided to speak straight in the debriefing I'd very soon be giving to the Chairman and Joint Chiefs of Staff.
>
> The next day in the Pentagon I gave my debriefing. After going through the story in detail (which they were all pretty much aware of from my constant communications), I concluded with something like the following:
>
> "Gentlemen, we should all be embarrassed by the failure we have just struggled through. In my mind, the consequences of failure of this nature are just as devastating as losing a major battle, especially politically.
>
> "We ought to be able to figure out that the terrorists understand better than we do the timing of the decision-making process here in Washington

*and the time required for launching and getting to where they have perpe-
trated their action—and that they are operating within that cycle.
Consequently, we are always chasing our tail—and we always will be unless we do something about this situation.*

*"We are the most powerful nation in the world, and if we cannot give
this mission the appropriate priority—with dedicated lift assets—then we
ought to get out of this business and quit wasting the taxpayers' money."*

*I realized that these were mighty big words for a person of my rank to be
saying in this situation, but I felt I owed it to them and to my people in the
Task Force.*

*I also felt that General Vessey, the Chairman; General Shy Meyer, Chief
of Staff of the Army; and General P. X. Kelley, commandant of the Marine
Corps (whom I had worked for as his Chief of Staff of the Rapid
Deployment Joint Task Force, and whose Marines in Beirut had not long
ago been killed by a terrorist with a truck bomb) understood clearly what
I was recommending. I felt certain that they would, with the support of the
other service chiefs, make it happen.*

And they did.

*Within the next months, C-141s, double-crewed, were placed on the
same alert string as we were (though too late to affect the outcome of the
events of October).*

*This initiative, together with the latitude and authority already given to
the Command to establish relationships and provide assistance to friendly
nations who desired them, have proved very beneficial in the war against
terrorism.*

THE MEETING IN THE JOC

October 7, 1985: It was time to test the new initiatives.

Soon after Stiner arrived at the JOC, he learned the identity of the hijacked ship. It was the Italian cruise liner *Achille Lauro*. The information
came by way of a tantalizingly brief emergency message from the ship,
which had been received by a radio station in Göteborg, Sweden. According
to the message, a group of armed men had taken control of the liner off the
coast of Egypt. And that was it. It was very little to go on, but enough to be
able to figure out what forces would be required to "take the ship down"—
and to know that they needed to launch instantly.

Because this was a complex target, and because no one knew whether the takedown would be in a port or somewhere on the high seas, Stiner instructed J-3 (Operations Officer) Colonel Frank Akers to notify the commanders to prepare the following units for immediate deployment (Akers had already given them a heads-up):

- ✪ SEALs: Required assault teams, sniper teams, and special boat detachments. Since this was to be primarily a maritime operation, the Navy SEALs would play the leading role.
- ✪ Other selected personnel and special units: leaders, planners, and intelligence operators. Approximately twenty-five personnel.
- ✪ The Army special helicopter package: ten Blackhawks, six Little Bird gunships, and four Little Bird lift ships (this was the standard alert package that had been developed over time; it was adequate for the mission and would fit in available jet transports).
- ✪ Air Force special tactics operation: for airfield control and pararescue.
- ✪ The Task Force Command Group: Necessary operations and intelligence staff officers, communications, and medical personnel.

Though the SEALs were expertly trained in takedowns, and could do the job in a matter of minutes, a cruise ship is the toughest of targets. First, the takedown must be done at night while the ship is under way, because nobody has yet figured out a way to stop a ship without damaging it; then, once the SEALs are aboard, they have to take out all the terrorists they can on their initial sweep, control the passengers and crew, and search at least a thousand rooms, nooks, and crannies and clear them of hidden terrorists . . . and possibly explosives.

Once the force package had been designated, Stiner instructed his deputy commander, Brigadier General Frank Kelly, to begin working the Military Airlift Command for the long-range strategic lift aircraft needed, but with capabilities designed specifically for special operations needs. It was a much larger force than was normally required, but this would be a very complex and challenging target.

Airlift, Stiner knew, would be the long pole in the tent, since it was under the control of the Military Airlift Command and outside his authority. Although the Task Force had a readiness requirement to be wheels-up in two hours, the necessary lift was not maintained on the same alert status—especially the C-5s. Additionally, the specially trained SOLL II crews (Special Operations Low Level crews fly blacked-out, low-level, and in all weather conditions) had to be rounded up to fly the planes. The terrorists were not dumb. They knew our reaction time, based upon the distance that had to be traveled and the time the Washington decision-making cycle usually took, and they operated inside these times. Every minute counted.

The JSOTF's standing request was to launch immediately after first notification of an incident. If it turned out no U.S. interest was involved, then the planes could be turned around over the Atlantic and brought home, but if there was a threat, the Task Force would be way ahead of the game.

Meanwhile, Stiner had to check with Washington for further intelligence, and since approval authority for launch and execution came from the Secretary of Defense and the President, he had to see about that as well, working through the Chairman of the Joint Chiefs or his assistant, who communicated with the Defense Secretary.

At about 0900, Stiner called the J-3 of the Joint Staff, who, like Stiner, was available twenty-four hours a day, to see if he had any further intelligence, and to request permission to launch his liaison teams. The J-3 would then take the request to the Chairman, Admiral William Crowe, who had taken over the job only three weeks earlier.

The three-man liaison teams were always on standby. Each team—an operations officer (a colonel or lieutenant colonel), an intelligence officer (a major), and a SATCOM radio operator—gave Stiner immediate access to any key people who might be players during a crisis. The liaison teams always knew what he was thinking and doing, and were authorized to speak for him.

The J-3 assured Stiner that he would get back to him *soon* about sending the liaison teams. "Information is sketchy and incomplete," he continued, "but the ship seems to have been hijacked near Alexandria, Egypt, after dropping off most of its passengers for a tour of the Pyramids. There are indications that Americans are among the remaining passengers, but it's not known how many got off for the tour and how many remain on board."

"Good news," Stiner answered. "That means a lot fewer to sort and control . . . but all the more reason to launch right away."

"You'll be glad to know, then, that the OSG will be meeting soon," he replied. The OSG would influence the launch decision. "We should have some decision from them shortly."

The U.S. interagency crisis team, also known as the operational subgroup (OSG), or terrorist incident working group, was chaired by the National Security Adviser, Bud MacFarlane, but since MacFarlane was out of town accompanying the President on a trip to Chicago, his deputy, Vice Admiral John Poindexter, was running the meeting. Its members included from the State Department, Ambassador for Counterterrorism Robert Oakley and Assistant Secretary of Defense Noel Cook; Charles Allen from the CIA; Oliver "Buck" Revell from the FBI; Fred Fielding from the White House staff; and Oliver North from the NSC staff. The group's mission was to monitor crisis situations and coordinate interagency support as appropriate for the situation. Though the group had an operational role, it was not in the chain of command, but did make appropriate recommendations to the National Security Council.

It was already early afternoon when Stiner called the J-3 again to inform him that, except for the airlift, the Task Force was ready to go and to please emphasize this to Admiral Crowe.

"We have to take the ship down during darkness," Stiner told the J-3, "which means it's imperative that we get at least as far as Sigonella come daylight tomorrow"—Tuesday, October 8. "This will give us options we would not otherwise have."

Though this was Admiral Crowe's first crisis since becoming the Chairman, his Assistant, Vice Admiral Arthur "Art" Moreau had done that job for a couple of years. He knew the ropes, had worked previous crises, had personal relationships with several key allies, and could make things happen quickly.

Special operations forces had been back and forth through Sigonella so many times during 1985, reacting to terrorist incidents and setting up planning and liaison for the future, that Stiner had stationed a permanent liaison team and SATCOM there as an extension of the U.S. commander's operations center. This team was Stiner's eyes and ears throughout the Mediterranean, and it operated twenty-four hours a day, collecting operational and intelligence information and coordinating JSOTF's requirements for passing through Sigonella.

Sigonella was a vital base as far as JSOTF operations were concerned, and the commander of the U.S. side, Navy Captain Bill Spearman, knew how to make things happen. Spearman always took care of JSOTF's needs, no matter what they were, but also had very good relations with his Italian counterparts (though on one occasion, as luck would have it, Stiner and Spearman had worked out plans, should the need ever arise, for Spearman to take control of the airport control tower from the Italians, who normally ran it. . . . The plan actually had to be put into effect later that week).

Sometime during midafternoon, word finally came from Washington approving the launch of Stiner's liaison teams. They all departed in civilian clothes, traveling by commercial air.

Colonel "Dave" headed the team that would set up at the Embassy in Rome. Another team flew to Stuttgart, Germany, home of the U.S. European Command (USEUCOM). Another team went to Gaeta, Italy, Vice Admiral Frank Kelso's Sixth Fleet Headquarters. And one went to the Military Airlift Command at Scott Air Force Base in St. Louis, Missouri.

During the afternoon, Stiner had a conference call with the commanders of his task force to coordinate their actions. Each command had already exchanged liaison officers, which was normal operating procedure—and it was the same people each time.

Every hour or so, he talked to Washington, pressing for airlift and the decision to launch. . . . Time was passing!

Meanwhile, additional intelligence began to trickle in, but the actual whereabouts of the *Achille Lauro* was unknown, though reconnaissance planes from the USS *Saratoga* were looking for it.

At long last, at about 1700 hours, Stiner was informed that approval had finally been given to launch the Task Force. The airplanes would be arriving shortly. Everyone moved quickly to their departure airfields and prepared for outloading. All the required equipment (helicopters, special boats, etc.) had already been made ready, and now it was just a matter of loading, which would not take very long once the planes arrived.

Soon after that, a call came to Stiner from a member of the National Security Council staff, wanting to know why they were taking so long to get under way.

"We've been ready most of the day," Stiner told him. "Maybe you can help by calling the Pentagon to speed up our airlift."

The airlift arrived at about midnight—twelve to fourteen hours after Stiner had hoped to be in the air. During the loading, special hatch-mount antennas were installed on the airplanes, both for plane-to-plane communications en route and for communications with any major commands that might be involved with the operation. The airplanes were also quickly configured inside with working tables and communications modules, for operational planning.

On Stiner's plane, in addition to the battle staff of colonels, lieutenant colonels, and majors engaged in operational, intelligence, air operations, and the like, there were Air Force combat controllers and communicators, about twenty operators/shooters, and the medical-surgical suite (an operating table had been set up on the tailgate). Major Dr. Darrel Porr, the task force's chief medical officer, had procured state-of-the-art medical equipment from all over the world, and had assembled a stable of specialist surgeons who could, if necessary, perform emergency surgery on the tailgate of the plane.

At about 0100 on October 8, the aircraft began lifting off for Sigonella. Since the *Achille Lauro* still had not been located, Stiner's plan was to stop there briefly and drop off a small team of SEALs and a pair of Little Bird gunships. This was a precautionary measure, in case they were needed later. They were.

Then he planned to continue quickly on to a military base on Cyprus, which was strategically located in the eastern part of the Mediterranean and within helicopter range of most potential targets. The Task Force was familiar with this base, and had used it several times before. But using it came with conditions. Because of Soviet Intelligence Satellite (SATRAN) passes, JSOTF aircraft had to arrive during darkness, get all their equipment off-loaded and into hangars, and get their transport planes out of there before daylight. They'd be dispersed to other bases in the region, but close enough to react if the teams had to move quickly.

As they flew over the Atlantic, Stiner took time to process the latest intelligence information. A picture was taking shape about the challenge they faced: There were four heavily armed terrorists, ninety-seven passengers of several nationalities (some of whom were U.S. citizens), and a ship's crew of 344. The ship's location was still unknown. It had gone into "radio silence" immediately following the hijacking, headed north, and was presumed to be somewhere in the eastern Mediterranean.

THERE was nothing more to be done now. The plans were in place, and would be updated as soon as any more information came in. Once they hit the ground, his units would start to put the plans into effect, but for now it was a rare moment of peace.

As the plane vibrated around him, Stiner's thoughts drifted back to what had brought him to this time and place, to all the training and missions that had come before, to the hot and often desolate places he had been. And he thought of the men who had come before him, who had created the kind of warfare in which he was now engaged.

Commando raids, deep reconnaissance, sabotage, guerrilla bands—these had all existed as long as men had clashed violently with other men. But what was now called "unconventional warfare" had not become officially recognized as a proper activity for "real" soldiers until World War II.

During World War II, they wrote the book on special warfare. . . .

II

PIONEERS

0200. August 11, 1944. Central France.

A lone, low-flying British Stirling bomber winged over the German-occupied Department of Correze, south of the Loire in the Massif Central. It had taken off three hours earlier from a base in England and joined the bomber stream of Stirlings and Halifaxes destined for Germany. Over France it had faked an abort and looped out of the stream, turning west toward England, all the while descending. When it was low enough to become invisible to German radar, it had made another turn, this time to the southeast.

This particular Stirling was not fitted out with bombs. Packed tight within its narrow fuselage were a ten-man French SAS reconnaissance team, parachute-equipped cargo pods, and a three-man OSS Jedburgh team, code-named "Team James." The SAS troops were commanded by a Captain Wauthier. Team James consisted of an American lieutenant, Jack Singlaub; an American technical sergeant, Tony Dennau; and a French army lieutenant, whose *nom de guerre* was Dominique Leb.

Singlaub, the team commander, was a Californian who had come to the OSS out of the 515th Parachute Infantry Regiment, at Fort Benning, Georgia (he was also demolition-qualified, having trained for it after he'd broken an ankle and needed something useful to do).

Dennau was a Sinatra-sized ball of fire from Green Bay, Wisconsin, who actually enjoyed jumping out of airplanes in the dark and then hiking through hostile countryside. He was the radio operator, but was also a terrific shot.

The Frenchman was a Breton aristocrat whose real name was Jacques Le Bel de Penguilly. Since Nazi reprisals against Free French officers' families were common, Maquis officers often concealed their true identities. Jacques (Dominique) was a necessary part of the team. His French was of course more fluent than the Americans', but even more important, he had a far better sense than Singlaub of the intricacies of the French political scene. The Free French were fiercely divided into contending factions, all hoping to lead the nation after the war—with Monarchists on the far right, Communists on the far left, and the followers of General de Gaulle in the center. With the notable exception of the Communists, the factions kept their differences out of the struggle with the Nazis. The Communists, no less than the others, wanted to kick the Nazis out, but they were as much interested in achieving an end state after the war that favored their cause. They cooperated when it suited them. Jacques was a Gaullist.

Singlaub was jammed against the Stirling's forward bulkhead, bent under the weight of his parachute. Though Dominique and Dennau were close by (similarly hunchbacked), there was no conversation. The roar of the engines and the wail of the slipstream made talk impossible. They all wore British camouflage smocks and para-helmets. On his chest, Singlaub carried a musette bag containing codebooks and 100,000 French francs. A leg bag held extra ammunition and grenades. He was armed with a Spanish 9mm Llama pistol, a weapon chosen because of the relative availability of 9mm ammunition in occupied Europe.

The engines changed tone and the aircraft slowed.

Aft, the tough, highly trained SAS troops gathered around a rectangular hole in the aircraft's rear deck—the jump hatch, or Joe hole, as it was called. Soon, they were dropping through the hole, one by one. Then a crew member pushed their cargo pods after them.

The Jeds were next.

They proceeded aft toward the dark, howling rectangle.

"About three minutes," the RAF dispatcher shouted into Singlaub's ear.

They hooked up their static lines. Then each man checked the snap-clips of his teammates on the deck ring, and double-checked his own. Looking down through the hole, Singlaub could just barely make out the dark masses of forests and the lighter blotches of fields. No lights were visible, and few roads.

Three orange signal flares lit the night below, the Maquis drop-zone signal. Meanwhile, Singlaub knew, a Maquis controller was flashing a preset
code letter to the pilot. If the code letter was correct, they'd be dropping
through the hole before they started another breath.

"Go!" the dispatcher shouted, smacking Singlaub's helmet. And the
young lieutenant went feet first into the dark, 800 feet above the countryside, ankles and knees together, hands tight against the wool of his trousers.
He hurtled through the dark for a moment, then the chute opened with the
familiar whomping sound he knew so well. (Unlike American chutes, which
burst open the moment the static line went tight and could easily malfunction, British chutes didn't deploy until the suspension lines went taut—
a much safer system. On the other hand, American paratroopers carried a
small reserve chute on their chest; Brits did not. If their chutes failed, that
was it.)

Singlaub checked his canopy, noting two more canopies above him—
Dominique and Dennau. Behind them, four smaller canopies also opened:
their cargo pods.

HE had trained long and hard for that moment.

It had begun on an October morning in 1943 in Washington, D.C., in an
office in the Munitions Building. He'd gotten there after answering a call
for foreign-language-speaking volunteers who were eager for hazardous duty
behind enemy lines (he spoke fair French). The outfit issuing the call was
the OSS—Office of Strategic Services—about which Singlaub knew very
little, except that it was involved in secret intelligence and sabotage operations overseas and was commanded by the legendary General "Wild Bill"
Donovan. That seemed pretty good to Singlaub.

A grueling interview determined that he might have what the OSS
needed, and he was ordered to show up in the headquarters parking lot the
next morning for transportation to the Congressional Country Club. The
name was not a joke. At one time, congressmen *had* actually gone there to
drink and play golf, but the war had turned it into an OSS training camp.
It still retained its congressional luxuries however: crystal chandeliers,
leather chairs, oil paintings in expensive frames, good china.

In fact, training at the Congressional Country Club did not seem dis-
cordant to the average OSS volunteer. Before Franklin Roosevelt had picked
him to run his new intelligence organization, Donovan had been a Wall
Street lawyer with the kind of blue-blood, Ivy League connections that

were common at the time. It was only natural that he had built his OSS out of the same privileged, clubby extended family. Most senior officers came from Ivy League–dominated professions, as did many who were present for the orientation with Jack Singlaub that October morning. To his immense relief, however, it wasn't only the social elite he saw there. Also present were hardened-looking airborne lieutenants like Singlaub who'd come out of OCS or ROTC, as he had (the war had cut his college career short).

The welcoming colonel made instantly clear what they'd be facing:

"You've been brought here," he said, "to evaluate your suitability for combat duty with resistance groups in enemy-occupied areas. . . . I'm talking about guerrilla warfare, espionage, and sabotage. Obviously, no one doubts your courage, but we have to make certain you possess the qualities needed for a type of operation never before attempted on the scale we envision.

"Guerrillas move fast, operating mainly at night, then disperse into the countryside and reassemble miles away. The skills required of a guerrilla leader will be the same as those shown by the best backwoods fighters and Indian scouts." Singlaub brightened when he heard this. He had always loved outdoor sports—hunting, fishing, camping—more than the regimentation of playground and team sports. All during high school and college, he had spent whatever time he could trekking the High Sierras. He was happy in the woods and the wilderness.

"We aren't looking for individual heroes," the colonel concluded, "although your courage will certainly be tested in the coming weeks. We want mature officers who can train foreign resistance troops, quickly and efficiently, then lead them aggressively. If we are not completely satisfied with your potential, you *will* be assigned to normal duties."

Over the next weeks, Singlaub and his companions learned, and were tested on, the basic skills of guerrilla warfare—how to move stealthily at night (over grassy fields that had once been manicured fairways); how to take out targets like railway switches, power transformers, sentry posts, and bridges. But most important, they were tested on how well they could handle what they'd be up against psychologically. Behind the lines they'd be on their own. How well would they hold up? How well could they handle the inevitable crises and screwups? How well would they handle men who were incompetent or overaggressive or nuts?

To that end, ringers from the training staff were inserted into teams in order to screw things up. How well the team handled this subordinate was often more important to their final evaluation than how well they placed demo charges on a railway trestle.

Once they had successfully passed over these hurdles, the OSS candidates were sent to what was called Area B-1. This had once upon a time been a boys' camp in western Maryland, and later FDR's weekend retreat, Shangri-la. After the war it became the presidential retreat now called Camp David.

Here the training emphasized tradecraft, and especially hand-to-hand combat.

For that they had probably the best instructor in the world, the British Major William Fairbairn, the inventor of the world-famous Fairbairn double-edged fighting knife (the commandos' close-in weapon of choice) and the developer of the hand-to-hand training course for the commandos. Fairbairn's philosophy was simple: You trained for months with a wide variety of Allied and enemy weapons until you handled any of them as instinctively as a major-league ballplayer swung a bat.

And so from early morning until late at night, that's what they did—not to mention the morning runs, the labyrinthine and dangerous obstacle courses, the nighttime crawls through cold, rain-soaked woods to plant demo charges, or the hours practicing encryption and clandestine radio procedures.

In December, Singlaub sailed for England on the *Queen Elizabeth*. There, his training continued, now under the auspices of the British Special Operations Executive (SOE, the umbrella organization that managed all the British unconventional warfare groups). The SOE ran clandestine training sites around the world, as well as squadrons of airdrop and reconnaissance aircraft, speedboats, and submarines; and it maintained enough forgers and mapmakers to keep several companies of James Bonds busy. SOE espionage and sabotage teams had worked in occupied Europe for some time, but now OSS liaison teams had been placed in France and had joined the covert effort. Soon, OSS teams would be given a much larger role.

The training in England was no less grueling than that in Virginia and Maryland. Initially, the focus was on parachute training and live-fire exercises; but there was also increasing emphasis on real-life situations the teams might run into—clandestine tradecraft and living cover stories. Men who failed these tests were sent back to regular units.

After a time, three-man teams were formed—an American or British officer, a French counterpart, and an enlisted radio operator. These teams were to be air-dropped into occupied France, where they would help organize, train, and lead Maquis resistance units in support of the Allied invasion. It was hoped that by then Maquis troops would number in the tens of thousands, and that the occupying Nazi army would find itself attacked on two fronts—Americans, Brits, and Canadians driving west from Normandy, and Maquisards making life hard for the Germans in their rear areas.

In order to minimize Nazi reprisals against civilians, it was essential that the major Maquisard offensive not break out until after the invasion had been launched. And then Maquis objectives and timetables had to be coordinated with overall Allied goals. This would require considerable psychological, political, and military acuity—in a fiercely high-stress, high-threat environment.

The operation was named JEDBURGH, after a castle in Scotland, and the teams were called Jedburgh Teams.

SINGLAUB landed in waist-high brush, rolled to the ground, then picked himself up and, as he gathered his chute into a bundle, made sure that Dominique and Dennau had come down safely fifty yards away.

Darkened figures emerged from the trees, calling out softly in French. Some separated from the rest in order to grab the cargo chutes. Most of the others spread out into a periphery defense. A single figure approached, their contact, a British SOE officer named Simon. They had landed about three kilometers from a village called Bonnefond, he explained, and about twenty kilometers from a German garrison in the town of Egletons.

After months of training, Jack Singlaub was at last in occupied France. He was twenty-three years old.

Soon the three newly arrived Jeds were ready to go. The heavy radio was stowed in Dennau's rucksack; Singlaub had slid a magazine into their submachine gun and readied the weapon; they had disposed of their chutes and shouldered their rucksacks; and Simon and the Maquis were leading them off into the night-shrouded woods. As they went, Singlaub noted with professional satisfaction that the Maquis troops were both well-trained and well-armed. They kept a good interval in their column, there was a point squad ahead, and flankers were on the sides.

HERE was the situation they faced: At that time, 8,000 Maquisards of the Force Francaises d'Interieur (FFI) operated in the region. Of these, 5,000 belonged to the well-trained and well-armed Gaullist Armée Secrete (AS), while most of the rest were Communist Franc Tireurs et Partisans (FTP). Though there was little love or cooperation between the two, Maquis attacks on German garrisons and convoys had grown since D Day.

Meanwhile, a breakout seemed near out of the Normandy beachhead. Once it came, Allied armies would race west along the Loire. An increasingly likely second Allied invasion—from the Mediterranean coast up the Rhone valley—would put further pressure on the Germans.

The Loire rises in the south of France, flows vaguely north and west to Orléans, about a hundred kilometers south of Paris, then turns west and flows into the Atlantic. The major artery passing through Correze, Route Nationale 89, connected Bordeaux on the coast with Lyon on the Rhone (which is east of the Loire and flows south into the Mediterranean). Route 89 was the main German logistics—and escape—route from southwestern France. For that reason, German forces along the highway remained potent: Better than 2,000 veteran artillery and armor-equipped troops were divided among four heavily fortified garrisons along the highway (at Tulle, Brive, Egletons, and Ussel), while specially trained mobile anti-Maquis troops, equipped with light armor, trucks, and spotter planes, continued at the ready to sweep up Free French units. The Germans intended to keep Route 89 open.

On the other hand, the terrain gave a big advantage to the Maquis. The Massif Central was rugged, offering plentiful choke points. Both road and rail lines through Correze ran along narrow valleys. There was God's own plenty of bridges, viaducts, culverts—lots of targets. And to make matters more interesting, an Allied breakout from Normandy would cut off the Germans in southwest France, while an Allied sweep up the Rhone would close the box and trap them. The time was growing ripe for a major Maquis uprising in the Massif.

Airdrops had equipped the Maquis with modern weapons. They wanted—and needed—more, but it was a good start. Team James's job was to train the Maquis units in the use of those weapons and to be the liaison between the Maquis and Allied headquarters for further weapons drops. They would also be involved in sabotage and ambush operations as needed. And, not least, they'd be expected to lead the Maquis troops against the Germans, in whose eyes the Jedburghs were spies and not soldiers. If captured, they could expect torture and execution. (Poison pills had been issued to those who wanted them. Singlaub did not.)

As they marched to the farmhouse that would become their first command post, or PC—*poste de commandement,* as the Maquis called it—(it was the practice to move PCs frequently), Simon pointed out landmarks and explained the current situation to the three Jeds: "All the local German garrisons are surrounded," he said. "They won't come out at night for fear of ambush. But Egletons is a tough nut—a reinforced company of Hun infantry, with at least a platoon of SS, occupies a commanding position over the Correze valley. The proper lot of machine guns, several antitank guns, and maybe some mortars. They've also got a wireless, so they're in contact with their division HQ in Clermont-Ferrand." Clermont-Ferrand was the base for one of the Wehrmacht specially trained anti-Maquis units. "The German garrisons at Brive and Tulle are larger than the one at Egletons," Simon continued, "but we have more Maquis companies surrounding them; they don't have a wireless; and we've cut all the phone and telegraph lines." He grinned in the moonlight. "Poor buggers don't know what we're up to."

It was an interesting situation for guerrillas. The enemy was reeling, nervous, vulnerable, yet far from defeated, and still very deadly. The time was ripe for forceful actions, yet overconfidence could ruin everything.

Soon after dawn, there was a war council. Present were Jack Singlaub, Dominique, Simon, Captain Wauthier (he and his SAS troops had arrived earlier after a long hike through the woods, somewhat more lightly equipped than they'd hoped, having lost through various mishaps four of their cargo pods), and the local Maquis commander, a tough, smart, and very professional former French regular army officer whose *nom de guerre* was Captain Hubert. Hubert had arrived not long after Wauthier, driving an ancient Renault whose better days long predated the war, and commanded a 3,000-strong Gaullist AS unit called the Corps Franc de Tulle.

Once the SAS guys and several squads of Hubert's Maquis set up perimeter defense around the PC, the council began. Hubert in particular had important matters to discuss, chiefly:

His troops were poorly armed. Only about a third of his men carried weapons—captured German Mauser rifles, Schmeisser submachine guns, and a handful of British Sten guns and pistols. The best-armed Maquis in the Correze were the troops of the region's AS commander (whose *nom de guerre* was Patrick). An enormous American airdrop, with more than seventy B-17s taking part, on Bastille Day, July 14, had provided Patrick with enough rifles, Sten and Bren guns, grenades, pistols, and a few bazookas and British Piat antitank weapons to equip his own 2,000-man unit, but had left few leavings for Hubert.

Nevertheless, Patrick had put these forces to excellent use. His unit had set up permanent ambushes at three points along Route 89, had completely surrounded the German garrison at Brive, and blocked the southwest approach to the Correze valley, while a smaller but equally well-armed AS unit had blocked the valley's northeast entrance.

Not only did Hubert's troops crave a piece of this action, but many of them, he added pointedly, had been waiting for weapons for three years, ever since they'd escaped the Nazi Blitzkrieg. "My men are ready to fight the Boches," he said. "But we cannot do it with naked hands."

When Dominique asked him for detailed requirements, after which contact would be made with London, Hubert (ever the professional) instantly produced a typed list, which he had already long ago prepared. And then he continued, turning even more serious: "There is another matter," he said carefully. "The FTP has recently come into this neighborhood in force, especially south of the highway, in the hills around Egletons—the area which has been my own operational area. They are commanded by a onetime schoolteacher and army corporal who calls himself Colonel Antoine. Antoine commands 3,000 well-armed troops," having received their weapons during the massive American Bastille Day airdrop. "Previously, they operated in the Department of Lot-et-Garonne to our south. But now they are here.

"Antoine is not at all interested in cooperation with us," Hubert continued, not hiding his scorn. "He is very *political*. Yes, he wants a public victory over the Boches. But he certainly does not want to share the victory with us."

Hubert's implication was simple and ominous. If Hubert's troops weren't brought up to the armed strength of Antoine's, the Communists had a good chance of gaining the credit for liberating central Correze, in that way setting the stage for their postwar political agenda. Many FTP soldiers were good, brave, and dedicated, and had fought hard and taken many casualties, but they were poorly trained—more an armed rabble than a well-disciplined fighting force. Even if they wished to coordinate operations with the AS, which they showed little inclination to do, coordination with them would not come easy. Needless to say, relations between the Communist FTP and the Gaullist AS were tense.

Meanwhile, Hubert went on, word had come from higher up that

General George Patton's Third Army had at last broken out from Normandy and was driving east at full throttle between the Loire and the Seine. That meant his southern flank was exposed—a situation that typically left Patton unconcerned: "Let the other son-of-a-bitch worry about flanks," he told an aide. Be that as it may, his right flank *was* exposed, and the FFI had been given the job of protecting it. Specifically, their mission was to blockade the German forces south of the Loire and west of the Massif Central.

Meaning: The political strain between the FTP and AS had instantly turned dangerous. The blockade would require carefully coordinated actions. But if groups like Antoine's maintained an independent, politically motivated strategy, and continued to resist cooperation, the Germans could crush each center of resistance in turn, like beads on a string. This would also inevitably mean bad news for civilians because of savage Nazi reprisals.

Just after D Day, a pair of over enthusiastic Maquis botch-ups had brought on Nazi massacres in the towns of Oradour-sur-Glane and Tulle. In Tulle, the Nazis hanged nearly a hundred men from lampposts. In Oradour-sur-Glane, the SS jammed hundreds of men into barns and garages and hundreds more women and children into the town church, then machine-gunned the men and set fire to the barns, garages, and church. No one inside—men, women, or children—survived the flames. After that, they looted the town and killed the few people who'd tried to hide in cellars. They left behind a ghost town.

No doubt about it, Hubert had made a powerful case—military, political, and humanitarian—for getting weapons for his troops. Dominique and Singlaub promised to do what they could.

Later that morning, word came that an OSS operational group had blown up a rail bridge on a northern spur to the east-west line connecting Bordeaux with Lyon, while another band of saboteurs had taken a hydro-electric plant out of action. This cut off power both to an arms factory in Tulle and to the electrified rail line between Correze and Bordeaux. Other Maquis commanders had their eye on Route 89 bridges and were asking for explosives.

This presented Lieutenant Singlaub with a problem. Though the bridges were legitimate targets, closing the highway was not a good idea. The Route 89 corridor through Correze was terrific ambush country, while a closed Route 89 would simply drive the German traffic north toward the more open country near the Loire—and expose Patton's flank. Conclusion: It was best to keep pressure on the German garrisons along Route 89 but to leave the bridges intact and keep the highway open. This decision soon became the first Team James operational order to the Maquis.

OVER the next days, Dominique and Singlaub reconnoitered, paying special attention to the German garrisons at Brive, Tulle, Ussel, and Egletons—heavily defended, with sandbagged windows, barbed-wire entanglements, and machine-gun emplacements. Well-trained and disciplined Maquis forces had isolated each of these garrisons; barricades and roadblocks had been set up. Soon there would be coordinated attacks.

Meanwhile, seven of Antoine's FTP companies, together with two of Hubert's AS companies, were laying siege to what was to prove the hardest nut to crack, the garrison at Egletons.

Unhappily, this "joint" arrangement was working no better than previous FTP-AS acts of "cooperation." As ever, the Communists intended to go their own independent way.

This situation grew more complicated a day or so later, when Patrick's regional intelligence officer, who called himself Coriolan, passed on disturbing news: Informants within Antoine's FTP units had warned Coriolan that on the previous night Antoine had pressed the attack against Egletons, and had done it without informing Hubert of this operation, or bothering to coordinate his attack with the AS companies taking part in the encirclement.

Worse, the poorly trained FTP troops screwed it up. Instead of catching the Germans off guard, their attack was so inept that the Germans had managed to retreat in good order back into a fortified and practically impregnable refuge in the École Professionelle, a three-story stone-and-concrete complex on a ridge at the edge of town. Because they were in radio contact with their regional headquarters and defended by heavy machine guns and a 37mm antitank gun, they were as comfy as rats in a sewer. Before long, an armored column would come to relieve them. And air support wasn't far away.

The choice was clear. The Jedburghs had to go to Egletons (where they would join Hubert, who was already there), do what they could to salvage the situation, and prepare to ambush the German relief column. Since collaborators and spies were everywhere, the three of them (and a ten-man AS escort) had to hike over backcountry Maquis trails—maybe twenty-five kilometers point to point, but closer to fifty on the ground. It took them a day.

That evening they linked up with Hubert, who had set up his PC on the ground floor of a stone house with a walled garden, perhaps 500 meters from the northwest corner of the École Professionelle. His two companies had taken positions in neighboring houses and along a sunken road, while the FTP troops were in pockets ringed around the other three corners of the school compound.

After Hubert's briefing and a quick look around, Dominique and Singlaub tried to link up with the FTP and conduct the kind of reconnaissance needed for a realistic attack plan, but quickly decided to put that off until daylight after they were warned off by FTP sentries, whose hostility was palpable.

The next morning, the Communists' suspicion and hostility was little diminished, but nevertheless, the two Jedburgh officers managed to talk their way into the FTP area.

Once again Singlaub was struck by the indiscipline of the FTP troops, who were firing Bren guns sporadically at the stone facade of the school, to no real effect except to send stone chips flying. Uncoordinated fire is like an unfocused lens—a waste.

When Dominique and Singlaub asked for directions to the FTP commander, sullen Communists pointed out a bullet-pocked house near the school. The way there was dicey, since much of the street was in view of the school, and there was so much glass and rubble underfoot it was impossible for the two Jedburghs not to make noise and call attention to themselves. This was made worse by the FTP soldiers they passed en route, all of whom seemed bent to point them out and challenge their presence.

Bent low, they raced down the street, then passed through a garden and burst through the back door of the house closest to the school. While Dominique stayed behind to guard his rear, Singlaub climbed up to the slate-roofed attic to see what he could learn. A small, square window opened onto the school, two hundred meters away. He opened it and stealthily raised his face to look outside.

Some of his OSS training in England came in handy just then—how to make quick, accurate recons. It was like a meditation technique: The idea was to clear your mind of conscious thought, focus your gaze like a camera, and let what passed before you register as though your mind were photographic film. Singlaub panned his eyes across the school courtyard across the road and the school walls and windows, noting the timber barricades, overturned concrete slabs, and heavy furniture blocking the windows. Shadowy figures moving in the shrubbery probably indicated a machine-gun crew.

At that moment, angry shouts came from below. And he could hear Dominique cursing. Meanwhile, off to the side he could see FTP soldiers down in the street stupidly pointing fingers in the direction of his own attic window, effectively spotting him for the German gunners. In OSS school, they'd had to go through what were called "bungler exercises," in which the trainees would be subjected to unexpected, frustrating, and often stupid annoyances to see how they would react. This was different. It was the real thing. The German gunners quickly got the point and started spraying the window from at least two machine guns, but not before Singlaub had scrambled down the stairs and out the back door. By then, the machine guns had opened up on the front windows. Dominique was waiting for him, his face white with fury—not so much at the Germans as at their own supposed friends.

"Let's get out of here," Singlaub said to him, "in case the Krauts have got a mortar over there."

There came then a loud crack and a deep-throated metallic clang, as the 37mm antitank gun blew a hole through the slate roof under which Singlaub had just been hiding. Slate fragments showered down as he and Dominique scuttled away.

A little later that morning, they were set to meet Antoine (they had so far never set eyes on him), for a tactical conference in a stone barn on the other side of the sunken road. But the Communist leader was proving to be elusive ("He's been called away on urgent operational matters," it was explained), and his chief of staff showed up in his stead.

By then it was clear to the Jeds that taking the school with the weapons they had—Bren guns, Sten guns, rifles, pistols, and hand grenades—was not going to happen. Their alternatives: a long siege (a bad idea, in view of the Germans' ability to send help to their Egletons garrison from their headquarters in Clermont-Ferrand), or a quick, perfectly coordinated attack, supported by mortars and bazookas.

Antoine's intention, relayed by his chief of staff, was to continue the siege indefinitely. "There are SS inside! We will pin them down." In other words, Antoine was happy to engage in a silly operation in order to reap the political benefit derived from making a few of the hated SS troops moderately miserable.

And so Antoine ordered the siege to continue.

Meanwhile, word had come that Captain Wauthier had received an airdrop the night before. Now the strength of his SAS unit had grown to thirty men, and he had mortars and British Piats (which were like bazookas). With this added firepower, Dominique and Singlaub reasoned that it ought to be possible to break the siege at Egletons in a few hours . . . and rake in the Germans' heavy machine guns and antitank guns, which were badly needed.

A runner was dispatched to Wauthier with the request.

And then, at 0900, the Nazis in the Egletons garrison got *their* help, in the form of three Luftwaffe Heinkel-111 medium bombers. The Heinkels swooped down low for bomb runs, one after the other, while Hubert's Maquis and the Jeds dived for cover.

The first plane dropped a stick of 100-kilo bombs that blasted the row of houses facing the school. The concussion shook everything nearby, and the red-flickering tailgun swept up afterward.

When the second Heinkel lined up on FTP positions, several brave—or recklessly foolish—Communists raced into the center of the road and fired rifles and Sten guns at the plane, braving machine-gun fire from both the school and the Heinkel's nose gunner. Two bombs dropped out of the plane into somebody's garden. They exploded moments later.

A time delay! Singlaub realized. So the low-flying bombers could escape the blast. If properly coordinated, he quickly reasoned, Bren guns, which fired the same .303 round as a Spitfire fighter, might throw off the bombardiers' aim and take the pressure off the Maquis front-line positions.

Dominique grabbed four Bren gunners from the FTP units, while Singlaub rounded up four from Hubert and set them up in the sunken road. Singlaub gave instructions and Dominique translated. The Heinkels were now making single bomb passes that took them directly overhead. As a bomber approached, he and Dominique would estimate its speed and altitude and hold up fingers to indicate how many plane-length leads the gunners should allow when they fired—one finger equaled one lead, two fingers equaled two, and so on. A clenched fist meant no lead.

A Heinkel was now coming in below 200 feet, lined up directly above the sunken road. The Bren gunners crouched at the ready. Singlaub could clearly see the pilots in their leather helmets. He took a breath and stepped out, with one finger raised. "Fire!"

But then the pilot saw them, and at the last minute banked right. So the rounds that hit only raked his left wingtip.

Better luck next time, Singlaub hoped.

The next Heinkel drove in from Dominique's direction, and Dominique was standing there, clearly visible, his fist beating against the sky. "No lead!" Singlaub yelled. The Brens coughed and rattled as one, with accurate, coordinated fire, hosing the green-painted bomber with a Spitfire's firepower at point-blank range. Shards of glass scattered from the nose, holes appeared in the belly and right engine nacelle, and you could see oil streaming along the base of the wing.

The pilot banked hard left, aborting the bomb run, and limped away on one engine. His right engine was out and throwing clouds of smoke. He slowly lost altitude as he staggered north over the Correze valley. Singlaub later learned that the Heinkel had crashed and burned a few kilometers away.

The Maquis screamed and howled, wild with the ecstasy of the kill. And Singlaub was no less thrilled. "My heart thudded in my throat and temples," he recalled later. "My breath was ragged. I was caught up in the rage of battle."

At 1300 Captain Wauthier and his SAS platoon sprinted into town under a rain of bullets. The Heinkels had been replaced by three Focke-Wulf 190 fighter-bombers, which were strafing anything that moved, and punctuating that with fragmentation bombs. The superbly trained SAS troops seemed indifferent to all this, and looked very glamorous in their red berets.

Soon SAS NCOs had taken charge and were preparing mortar positions. The plan was to lay down a mortar barrage on the school courtyard. It was hoped this would drive the German troops indoors and allow the Maquis to push their Bren gun positions forward and dig them in. Singlaub decided to act as forward observer and direct the mortar fire.

In the meantime, Dominique would try to track down the elusive Antoine and do what he could to convince him to allow his forces to join the attack, or at least to lend troops for ambushes north of town.

Singlaub returned to his early-morning observation position in the attic of the house near the school. This time, FTP troops he passed on the way included Bren gunners who'd fought the Heinkels with him that morning; they greeted him with welcoming smiles. He was no longer *persona non grata* among the Communists.

He made his way carefully up the stairs of the now-much-damaged house. The roughly planked attic floor was littered with slate fragments and splintered wood from the 37mm shell. Entrance and exit holes in the steeply raked roof indicated the shell's path. He crouched low, slithered across the floor, and took up a position he hoped would be invisible.

Moments later, the first SAS mortar round arced into the courtyard, driving German soldiers out of shallow foxholes in a hedgerow into the cover of the school. Singlaub shouted down to a young FTP sergeant, who was acting as his relay, "Correct fire twenty meters right, and then forward." The next round dropped on a timber barricade near the school's administration wing. Another covey of enemy troops raced into the school. Singlaub was beginning to feel good. Now they were getting even for the heavy air attacks they'd faced that morning. A few rounds later, the mortar rounds had nicely bracketed all of the German outside positions, and it was time to drop a few rounds onto the school itself. Since several machine gunners had set up positions in the school attic, Singlaub directed fire onto the roof (like the local houses, slate-and-timber), with the aim of driving the Germans down to lower floors. For this job, Wauthier added phosphorus to the high-explosive rounds. Soon, fires were burning merrily in the attic.

Things were going so well that Singlaub forgot where he was—and that the Germans would be looking hard for the forward observer—or that he was silhouetted against the 37mm exit hole as he crouched beside the circular entrance hole. His carelessness did not go unnoticed. In a flash, steel-jacketed machine gun rounds were clattering against the slate, spraying the entrance hole, and madly ricocheting about the attic.

He was hit.

The next thing he knew, he was sprawled on his back. "My skull [was] ringing like a gong," he said. "It was as if someone had thrown a bucketful of rocks in my face. I felt the blood, warm and salty, on my right cheek, then saw thick, dark drops raining on the floor. My hand went to my ear and came away sticky red. There was blood all over my para-smock now. The pain began after the initial shock, hot and persistent. I got control of my breathing and took stock. My head moved all right on my neck, and there was no spurting arterial blood. So I must have been superficially gouged by slate and bullet fragments."

The side of his face wasn't pretty, but he was not seriously hurt. What came upon him then was a tightly focused rage.

When the machine gun turned its attention to the house's lower floors, Singlaub took one last glance at the school, and there he noticed for the first time the barrel of the 37mm gun swiveling beneath camouflage netting in the hedgerow seventy meters away. The crew was wearing camouflage gear and had leaves threaded onto their helmets, but from his angle, they were clearly exposed.

This was too good a chance to pass up.

Almost without thinking, he dashed down the stairs and out into the back garden. When they saw the bloodied side of his head, the FTP soldiers rushed forward to give Singlaub aid, but in fact the injury looked far worse than it was. And besides, at that moment he was practically unstoppable. Without offering more than a mumbled explanation in his uncertain French, he grabbed their Bren gun and a spare thirty-round magazine, and without looking back, made his way to the edge of the garden, then raced thirty meters down the street to the cover of a bomb-blasted plane tree, which, at sixty meters from the hedgerow, was in easy range of the gun's position.

By the time he reached the tree, most of the bleeding had stopped—not that *that* mattered much in his current frame of mind. He worked his way quickly around the trunk, leveled the Bren, and sighted on the hedgerow and the Germans. Four long bursts, and the magazine was empty. In went the fresh one. The soldiers around the gun jerked into activity, intending to turn the gun toward this mad attacker, but they were toppling over satisfyingly before they could reach it. A German soldier trained his rifle toward the plane tree but then was flung backward, his arms flying.

The second magazine exhausted, Singlaub raced back to the shelter of the garden. As he ran, he was aware of someone shooting at him, but he wasn't hit.

Back in the garden, he gave up his Bren gun to the awed, wide-eyed FTP troops. He'd been possessed by a god; they weren't used to that. One of them took a cloth, dipped it in a bucket, and reverently washed his wound. Then the young American lieutenant sat down with his back against the fieldstone wall, lifted his face to the sun and billowing afternoon clouds, and let his pounding heart grow quiet.

The attack was going well: Most of the Germans in the courtyard had been driven back into the school buildings. Wauthier's SAS Bren teams had moved forward along the school's left flanks to a commanding position over the courtyard, and though Dominique had had no success locating Antoine, his company commanders had agreed to work under Wauthier. That night, Wauthier radioed a request to London for an air strike the next afternoon. The plan was to again pin down any Germans in foxholes with mortars and Piats, or better, to drive them again back into the school. Then, just before the air strike was scheduled, the French would pull back a couple of streets, and British Mosquito bombers would dive-bomb the school.

The catch: Maquis operations were not exactly top Allied priority just then. Hubert had yet to receive his promised arms drop, for instance. And besides, there were more pressing preoccupations, such as the invasion of southern France earlier that morning by Allied armies under General Alexander Patch. All the Maquis units in south and central France were expected to support the invasion, which meant all of them were requesting more of everything.

During the night, the Germans in the school tried to push back into positions in the courtyard. And by morning the Focke-Wulfs came back, with a full array of strafing, fragmentation bombs, incendiaries, and high-explosives.

That afternoon, the time approached for the planned Mosquito attack. Mortar shells again ripped into the courtyard. SAS troops moved close in and fired their Piats. It all went swimmingly. The Germans pulled back into the school. But no Mosquitoes. The only planes in the air were Focke-Wulfs and Heinkels. There was nothing to do but keep down and wait.

DURING the night, Coriolan brought heartening news: First, the Maquis had breached the defenses of the German garrison in Ussel, and the garrison had then surrendered. Second, the more powerful garrisons at Tulle and Brive, besieged by Patrick's forces and Hubert's remaining companies, had agreed to surrender—but with a condition. They'd been promised that an American officer would accept their surrender.

That meant Singlaub, who set out in a *gazogene* farm truck to take care of that chore. At Tulle and Brive, Singlaub produced an ornate document, which he had signed, promising the German commanders full protection of Supreme Allied Headquarters, and the German companies laid down their arms. It was a good haul—rifles, machine guns, cases of grenades, and a 75mm field gun. The weapons from Tulle went directly to Hubert's men, and were most welcome.

As soon as the ceremony was over, Hubert and Singlaub climbed into the *gazogene* truck for the return journey to Egletons.

There optimism remained low, despite the surrender of three German garrisons. The Luftwaffe was strafing everything that moved (Singlaub and Hubert had to hike the final few kilometers into town), and Luftwaffe bombs had turned much of Egletons into rubble, most notably the barn they had been using as a PC. Even so, Tony Dennau, their radioman, had stayed at his post in a corner of the building, sending messages to London even as the barn took direct hits. In the walls and ceiling all around him were numerous shrapnel scars. *"Il est formidable,"* Wauthier beamed, indicating the radioman, when Singlaub and Hubert entered what was left of the barn.

Dominique was at Antoine's command post down the street. And so, surprisingly, was Antoine, a tough little guy with a commanding, intelligent voice. When Singlaub arrived, Antoine and his staff were all atwitter with rumors that the troops of the Tulle garrison had not surrendered, but had broken free and were on the way to break the siege at Egletons, threatening the Free French forces' rear.

Though Singlaub carefully explained that he had been present when the entire Tulle garrison had surrendered, that information did not satisfy Antoine, who was in the process of sending teams from his already tightly strained companies out along the road to Tulle to establish ambush positions.

Meanwhile, Coriolan had arrived with news that the German relief column was finally moving out of Clermont-Ferrand—2,000 heavily armed men in 150 trucks, defended by a pair of armored cars with automatic weapons.

Tulle, it should be noted, was west of Egletons, while Clermont-Ferrand was east. Diluting the strength of the forces in Egletons chasing phantom Germans could make the situation in Egletons perilous. Even more important, a terrific opportunity was presenting itself to ambush the relief column on the road between Ussel and Egletons. Antoine's troops were essential to add strength to that effort and to maintain pressure on the Egletons garrison. But Antoine would have none of that. It was an article of faith that Germans from Tulle were on the way to attack his rear. He would stop them.

By nightfall, the town was quiet. Dominique and Wauthier had left to set up ambushes on the highway. The civilians were abandoning the town, and carrying with them the Maquis wounded. Remaining behind, for the moment, were Singlaub and Dennau, and the remnants of Hubert's and Antoine's troops. But as soon as all the civilians had been reported out of danger, Singlaub ordered the FTP and AS forces to fall back into the forest. Though he knew Dominique and Wauthier would damage the German relief column, there was no way they were strong enough to stop them with the forces at their disposal.

Singlaub and Dennau grabbed their codebooks, their radio, a few emergency rations, their bundles of one-hundred-franc notes, and some spare Sten gun magazines and marched with the Maquis through the still-burning streets of Egletons. Soon they were passing through upland pastures and then forest trails. As they hiked through the darkness, they could just hear the distant rumble of land mines and the rattle of heavy machine guns—Dominique and Wauthier ruining the Germans' evening.

THE next day, Singlaub linked up with Dominique and Wauthier in a ruined church. The ambushes, as expected, had not stopped the Germans, but had delayed them. And they had knocked out an armored car and six trucks, and killed at least twenty-five enemy soldiers.

The relief column arrived in Egletons at dawn, loaded up the entire garrison onto the trucks, and rumbled off to Tulle, where they hoped to do the same thing. But of course they were a day late for that. Then they turned back toward Clermont-Ferrand.

That afternoon, eight camouflaged Mosquitoes showed up (the war's most beautiful warplanes), and elegantly swooped and dived, dropping bombs that flattened the school buildings. But the horses were out of the barn. The École Professionelle had been emptied of Germans.

They were disappointingly late, but by then, the capture of the Correze garrisons, the siege of Egletons, the sabotage, the surrender of thousands of troops along with the seizure of their weapons, and the aggressive ambushes on the highways, had put the fire out of the Germans in Correze. The area was effectively liberated—not that there was a letup during the next weeks.

Route 89 was kept open, in the expectation that the German First Army Group still garrisoned in southwest France would continue to use it as an avenue of escape. Dominique and Singlaub trained Antoine's and Hubert's troops in the use of the captured weapons, while sending out demolition teams to destroy the bridges on the side roads. Hubert's ambushes along the highway continued.

Hubert, meanwhile, came up with a scheme to use a fleet of trucks and scout cars he had captured to create a mobile attack force that would harass the retreating German columns to the north, between Correze and the Loire, and keep them too occupied to pose a danger to Patton on the other side of the river. The Free French command authorized this plan, even though Hubert had not yet received the arms shipment he had long ago requested (thousands of tons of munitions, officially destined for the Maquis, sat in warehouses in England, a typical wartime foulup; Maquis demands during the uprising were so many and so pressing that the distribution system cracked under the strain). Hubert had to strip some of his ambush teams of weapons in order to equip his mobile force. Dominique and Singlaub helped by getting hold of a fast 1939 front-wheel-drive Citroën and setting off on a series of lightning reconnaissance missions for him. The Germans staggered their convoys to protect them against Allied air attacks, but they staggered them at predictable intervals. The Jeds simply waited for an interval and then cruised blithely between them. The results were gratifying. Hubert's force made life hell for the Germans for weeks.

Antoine's FTP, meanwhile, pulled out of the war to devote themselves to the political fight that would break out after the German surrender. The Communists took over the town of Tulle, with its arms factory, and got the factory running again (they had to force the technicians and engineers to work for them). The commissars above Antoine wanted weapons for the revolution they hoped to ignite after the war. That was more important than further participation in the liberation of France.

On September 26, with Paris and most of France liberated, Team James returned to England for further assignments. For Jack Singlaub, that was to mean a mission to Southeast Asia—a story for another time.

JACK Singlaub's Jedburgh experience is certainly a compelling yarn, but it offers more than that. The story offers a model for the elements of unconventional warfare, as well as for the skills needed by special forces soldiers. It's one of the primary texts in what might be called the Special Forces Bible.

These are some of the more outstanding elements and skills it illustrates:

❂ The special soldier can expect to operate in areas deep beyond the official lines of battle, where the zones controlled by one side or the other may be indistinct, or even meaningless. Likewise, he may have a hard time telling good guys from bad guys, and the official names or political pedigree of a leader, group, or faction may also not tell him much about who and what he is facing.

❂ He can expect to operate in a high-threat, high-stress environment, with little or no support from his parent organization.

❂ He'll need to be expert in all the basic soldier skills, not only as a military practitioner but as a teacher. He also needs to be familiar with a wide range of foreign weapons and systems, and he should be expert in various forms of hand-to-hand combat.

- ❂ He needs to be reasonably proficient in the language of the country in which he's operating, and knowledgeable about the culture, political situation, and physical conditions of the people.

- ❂ Since he'll be operating behind the lines, he must be able to live a cover story and handle other aspects of the tradecraft of the secret world.

- ❂ He must have the psychological strength to handle the stresses with which he'll be faced: living on his own, the absence of support, the inevitable screwups of others, inevitably magnified by the absence of support.

- ❂ He must be endowed with considerable resourcefulness, flexibility, and ingenuity. More important, he must demonstrate a high level of psychological, political, and military acuity. He must be able to sell, persuade, cajole, browbeat, and convince people who dislike him, distrust him, and are doing their best to con him. His best weapon in this conflict will often be his ability to do his job so well that his adversary/friend can't help but come to trust him.

- ❂ The stakes he faces are high. He and his team represent on their own the policies of their country. They will often have to make choices on how to implement these policies with little or no guidance from above. They have to be competent to make the right choices. At the same time, their choices directly affect not only the lives of the guerrillas or partisans with whom they are working, but—perhaps more important—the lives of both "innocent" and "involved" civilians.

Each of these elements and skills comes more alive within a historical context—which brings us to Colonel Aaron Bank, who learned them at the same school as Singlaub, and later became one of the founders of U.S. Special Forces. Aaron Bank is on every Green Beret's shortlist of Great Ones.

Aaron Bank

Aaron Bank, another Jedburgh, parachuted into the south of France in 1944 and operated in Provence, where his experiences closely mirrored

Jack Singlaub's: attacks on strategic facilities and convoys, guidance and instruction of Maquis, conflicts with Communists. Following the liberation of France, Bank, who spoke passable German, and who was by then a major, was asked by his OSS superiors to create a special operations company of dissident German soldiers. Their mission—personally assigned by Bill Donovan himself—was to capture Hitler alive, in the event he and his henchmen attempted to barricade themselves in what the Nazis chose to call their National Redoubt in the mountains of Bavaria. The European war ended, the Redoubt proved to be a myth, and Bank's mission was aborted. Later, Bank was sent by the OSS to Indochina, where, among other things, he spent a pleasant day or two traveling with Ho Chi Minh, as well as several fascinating months increasing his knowledge of peoples' wars and guerrilla operations.

The OSS was disbanded in September 1945, and Bank was brought back—somewhat reluctantly—into the main body of the Army. There he sorely missed the old Jedburgh thrill of always being on the edge of the action, and the Jedburgh freedom of operating on his own behind the lines (though he knew some traditionalists were uncomfortable with giving people like him so much leash—they called it lax and unmilitary). But he was himself a good soldier, and went where he was sent without public complaints.

Far more important: He was certain the Army was losing something essential when it did not pick up the capabilities abandoned with the dissolution of the OSS Jedburgh teams and operational groups (the latter were teams of thirty men that could be split into two teams of fifteen—precursors of the twelve-man Special Forces A-Detachments). During World War II, operational groups were inserted behind the lines in Europe and Asia (primarily Burma), where they performed direct-action combat roles, such as sabotage, or linked up with guerrillas and partisans, as the Jedburghs did.

Bank believed that the postwar Army required similar units, but ones that were even better trained, equipped, prepared, and staffed. In his view, special operations forces designed to organize, guide, and equip indigenous resistance or guerrilla movements could turn out to be as essential as any of the conventional combat arms in the U.S. arsenal.

IN 1947, the CIA was formed, with a mission to re-create the intelligence operations of the OSS. It was also given a covert, special operations role, to deal with resistance movements and guerrilla organizations, but it was never comfortable with it. Even after the creation of the CIA, Bank continued to feel a strong need for the Army to take on the entire task once performed by the Special Operations branch of the OSS.

This conviction was not shared by the majority of the Army. Conventional soldiers tend to see unconventional warfare primarily as a sideshow, peripheral to the *real* action—that is, regular infantry, airborne, tanks, artillery—and more than a little outrageous. "To the orthodox, traditional soldier," Bank writes in his memoir, *From the OSS to Green Berets: The Birth of Special Forces,* "it was something slimy, underhanded, illegal, and ungentlemanly. It did not fit in the honor code of their profession of arms."

Over the years, U.S. soldiers have been especially vulnerable to this attitude. As noted before, our army is traditionally nervous about elites. It's a citizens' army—ordinary folks. Superior soldiers and superior units are welcome, but they aren't expected to call much attention to themselves. Special forces, by their nature, call attention to themselves. A few years later, after the formation of U.S. Special Forces, assignment there was not thought to be a lucky career move.

The U.S. Army is no more friendly to oddballs and reformers than it is to elites. It is bound by rules, nervous about innovation, slow to change. Revolutionaries need not apply. Yet, as Aaron Bank knew, the Army is not a monolith. It's a very large house with hundreds of rooms. Reformers aren't exactly encouraged, but smart, politically savvy, courageous men who are patient, do their homework, and are willing to risk their careers have a shot at making their changes stick—especially if an inspired few others share the dream.

Meanwhile, during the years between the dissolution of the OSS and the outbreak of the war in Korea, Bank did his homework. Specifically, he read all he could find about unconventional warfare. What is it? How does it differ from "conventional" war? What does history say about it? Why do we have operations called "special"?

Unconventional Warfare

Unconventional warfare is hard to pin down, but over the years, a working understanding has developed. It is far from complete, and is blind to many nuances, but it's not a bad place to start:

Unconventional warfare primarily involves operations different from the conventional fires and movement of massed troops, armor, artillery, and airpower. Normally, unconventional warfare is performed by small, highly trained units, takes place behind regular lines of battle, and involves such activities as reconnaissance, sabotage, raids, raids in force, assassination, and, above all, the training and support of friendly guerrilla forces. This comes under the overall title of direct action.

One prime example of direct action was a blowtorch-violent joint U.S./Canadian ranger unit, called the First Special Service Force (FSSF), that so distinguished itself in World War II that it has been designated an official ancestor of today's Special Forces. The FSSF was formed to make lightning raids on targets such as the Germans' heavy-water production facilities in Norway and the Romanian oil fields, but was used primarily to crack through mountain fortifications in Italy (where it took heavy losses).

But unconventional—"special"—warfare also has other facets, as every Jedburgh knew: Screwing with your enemy's head is one. Helping people in trouble—with medical aid, organizational advice and counsel, assistance in building bridges and roads, and getting clean water—is another. "Screwing with your enemy's head" is called psychological operations, or PSYOPs (in Aaron Bank's day: psychological warfare).

"Helping people" usually comes under the rubric of civil affairs (CA), a tool that's been in the special operations kit nearly as long as PSYOPs. There are many justifications for CA, including simple goodness, but its main military one is this. A population that is friendly to you and has experienced your kindness is not likely to feel kindly to—or give help and support to—your enemy.

The debate has raged over which is the purest model for "special" units— larger units such as Rangers and commandoes, which tend more to direct action or smaller teams such as Jedburghs and A-Detachments, which specialize more in teaching and training indigenous forces.

Here, as it turns out, "purest" is a blind alley, and the best answer is "all of the above."

HISTORICALLY, there is no clean division between conventional and unconventional wars. The historical roots of both go back equally far. At the time of Jesus, freedom fighters fought a long, drawn-out guerrilla war with the occupying Romans. A thousand years later, Vikings launched commando-type raids from seas and rivers. During Napoleon's occupation of Spain in the early nineteenth century, Spanish guerrillas forced the French army to regret their conquest (and Spaniards gave this form of warfare its name: *guerrilla* in Spanish means "little war"). Robin Hood and his men were guerrillas. T. E. Lawrence was a kind of semi-freelance special operations officer guiding indigenous Arabs in their struggle to break free of an oppressive occupying power.

Traditionally, resistance, insurgent, or guerrilla movements spring up from people who are otherwise powerless to gain liberation from foreign occupation or to gain freedom from their own oppressive or tyrannical government—a prime instance of Carl von Clausewitz's most famous insight, in *On War*, published in 1832, that war is simply another form of politics.

Though von Clausewitz's insight has never been lost on the more thoughtful of military men, military planners don't normally give the political aspects of a problem serious consideration when they develop their strategy and tactics. They mostly see civilians as either encumbrances, props, or potential threats ("Get the damned civilians out of my way!").

Recent times have seen a change in these attitudes, a change that is reflected in the currently fashionable expression, "end state"—as in, "What end state do we want and how can we achieve it?" "End state" reflects both the military *and* political situation hoped for at the end of a conflict. Yet it still remains true that most military leaders do not normally consider how those under their command can affect a political situation that can in turn have a bearing on the outcome of a war.

Such is not the case with practitioners of unconventional war. Special soldiers have to be conscious of both the political implications of their military actions and the military implications of political actions—in fact, they have to be conscious of anything they do or say that could have an impact on the people they have been assigned to help and guide. Success lies far beyond the obtaining of military objectives.

This is why psychological operations and civic affairs* have always been part of the special warfare toolkit. It is also why flexibility, resourcefulness, and political savvy were so important to Jack Singlaub, Aaron Bank, and the other Jedburghs. It is also, finally, why governments have come to find more and more uses for military forces that have these and associated capabili-

---

*At one time, CA was thought of as an adjunct to military police—useful once the battle was over and order was being restored. After a war, more than police protection was needed. Later it was realized that CA could be useful during a conflict (Carl Stiner used his CA resources to great effect during the Panama invasion) or even before a conflict begins, *to prevent it*.

ties. They are precision instruments, while tanks, artillery, and the other major combat arms are, by comparison, blunt—though far more powerful.

To put it another way: Special operations are conducted against strategic and operational targets that can't be attacked in any other way. A strategic and operational target generally has to do with the center of gravity of an enemy (another term from Clausewitz), and that center of gravity can be physical, psychological, or economic. If conventional weaponry can't deal with it . . . special operations can.

When a nation finds it has a recurring need for these kinds of forces, then they form them into a special operations branch. During World War II, for example, the British knew they could never slug it out toe-to-toe with the German armies. Their special operations branch was intended to give them a lever that might even up the score.

By way of contrast, the Germans did not institutionalize special operations, and it's a mystery why. It is equally mysterious that, when their armies were defeated, they did not organize guerrilla and partisan resistance to counter the Allied occupation of their country. Though they had extensive experience with partisans in the USSR, France, Yugoslavia, Greece, and elsewhere, and knew personally how partisans could make an occupying power suffer, the Germans did not themselves choose to organize such movements.

It is especially puzzling because German commando exploits were among the most daring and resourceful ever conducted. In 1940, for example, the fortress of Eben Emael, in southern Belgium at the junction of the Meuse River and the Albert Canal, was the most powerful fortress in Europe—heavily armored gun turrets above ground, the rest in hollowed-out underground galleries, and manned by 1,200 men. None of the Maginot Line fortifications came close to it. If the Germans hoped to attack west, toward the channel ports, or south, toward France, they had to overcome Eben Emael.

After six months of training in glider operations, as well as on a replica of the fortress itself, eighty German engineer-commandos, commanded by a sergeant, landed on the roof of Eben Emael in nine gliders and launched a carefully orchestrated attack—highlighted by the first-time-ever use of shaped charges in war—that resulted in the capture of the impregnable fortress thirty hours later. Shaped charges focus blast effects in order to penetrate armor, and are now very common in all kinds of anti-armor and deep-penetration-type weapons.

But then when the operation was over, the engineer-commandos went back into the Wehrmacht war machine. The Germans saw no recurring need for a standing special operations capability.

In 1943, after the Allied invasion of Italy, the Italians kicked Mussolini out of power and placed him in exile, under heavy guard, at an isolated mountaintop hotel, where it was believed no conceivable force could rescue him. The only access was by funicular railway. On September 13, however, another daredevil band of German glider commandos, led by one of the greatest of special operators, the Austrian Otto Skorzeny, landed a hundred yards from the hotel, overwhelmed the *carabinieri* guards, brought in a small Fieseler-Storch aircraft, and spirited the Duce away in it.

The commandos then returned to their regular units.

IN THE WILDERNESS

From 1946 to 1951, the Army maintained an interest in rebuilding an unconventional-warfare capability, and conducted many studies, but not much actually happened. Since there was a Ranger precedent, one study looked at the possibility of starting up a Ranger group that could carry out both a Jedburgh-like teaching-and-training mission and Ranger-type raids. Another study proposed creating a special operations force using refugee soldiers from Soviet satellite countries in eastern Europe, many of whom had extensive unconventional warfare experience fighting the Nazis. These men could join up under the provisions of the Lodge Act, which allowed foreigners to join the U.S. military services and, after two years, be granted citizenship. It would be a kind of American Special Forces Foreign Legion.

Unfortunately, there were at most 3,000 men available for such a unit, which was not enough to do the job (though Lodge Act volunteers later did become a major component of early Special Forces).

Nothing came of any of these proposals.

Like all Jedburghs, Aaron Bank had some familiarity with psychological warfare techniques, such as spreading rumors to build up civilian morale or enemy fears, or to spread false information. However, Bank never imagined he himself would be assigned to a psychological warfare unit. He simply was not trained for it.

Yet that was what happened, early in 1951. Bank, a colonel by then, was with a combat unit in Korea, the 187th Airborne Regimental Combat Team, when he received orders to go back to the States and report to the

Psychological Warfare staff in Washington, under Brigadier General Robert McClure.

McClure, a remarkable man, had run psychological warfare (more accurately, created it out of nothing) in Europe for Eisenhower and, after the war, had directed the de-Nazification program for the Allied military government in Germany. The outbreak of the Korean War had pointed up to him the necessity for rebuilding a psychological operations capability.

As Eisenhower's man in charge of psychological war, McClure had often coordinated his operations with the OSS staff, and had thus come into contact with the OSS Special Operations Branch. He had been impressed with what he saw, and when the time came for him to restart psychological operations, he successfully argued that special operations be included in his team. To that end, McClure teamed Bank with still another remarkable man, a brilliant and highly energetic lieutenant colonel named Russell Volckmann. Their job: to bring special operations back into the Army.

When the Japanese captured the Philippines during the early days of America's involvement in World War II, Volckmann became one of those intrepid Americans who did not surrender. He joined Filipino soldiers and a few other Americans on the island of Luzon in organizing guerrilla resistance to the Japanese. In Bank's words, "When General MacArthur said, 'I shall return,' Russ, who was then a captain, echoed, 'I shall remain'—with MacArthur's blessing." After three years of fighting, their initially small force had grown to something near 15,000 strong—roughly division strength—and had killed or captured many thousand Japanese. When the moment for the Japanese surrender finally arrived, the Japanese commander, General Yamashita, gave it not to MacArthur but to the guerrilla force.

To honor the guerrilla contribution to victory, MacArthur granted Volckmann—now a colonel—a place at the formal surrender table.*

BANK, Volckmann, and McClure pooled their experience and research, and sat down to try to resolve the many issues that had long occupied special warfare experts: the Ranger versus special operations/guerrilla support

---

* Another well-known Philippine guerrilla, Colonel Wendell Fertig, who had gallantly fought the Japanese on Mindanao, later joined Bank and Volckmann's staff. A pretty good movie was made in the 1950s about Fertig, and you can read about him in our friend W. E. B. Griffin's novel *Behind the Lines*.

model; problems of command and control, staff, logistics, and field operations; the question of how to use Lodge Act aliens, and so on. These matters would continue to occupy special warfare experts over the next five
decades.

Meanwhile, the Army itself took the Ranger issue off the table for the
time being by deactivating the Ranger units then in existence, and setting
up a Ranger School, where combat and other selected personnel could receive Ranger training and then return to their home units. This was good
news to Aaron Bank, who was partial to the OSS and not the Ranger model
for special operations. Since the Army still required deep-penetration, long-
term operations, the deactivation of the Ranger units would free up personnel spaces for them.

Shortly thereafter, Bank and Volckmann were authorized to put together
a Table of Organization and Equipment (TO&E), the final step needed for
the creation of a military unit. The questions now were: How did you make
military units that would operate flexibly and resourcefully in nonstandard
situations? How big should the operational teams be? How should they be
composed?

Bank's preference was to put together a pool of highly trained men who
could be formed into units purpose-built for specific missions. For various
Army bureaucracy reasons, however, that was not a workable option.
Meanwhile, the OSS offered two already proven models: the three-man
Jedburgh team and the thirty-man operational groups. Though not as flexible or as "stealthy" as a Jedburgh team, the OGs were capable of conducting direct-action raids against difficult targets far behind the lines, or
guerrilla actions in areas where there were no indigenous guerrillas. The
ability of OGs to be split into fifteen-man teams, for greater flexibility, gave
Bank another idea: Why not create a core SF field unit that was somewhat
larger and more capable than the small Jedburgh team, but somewhat
smaller than the OG direct-action strike units? Out of this thought came
the Special Forces A-Detachment (or A Team). These were initially fifteen-
man half-size OGs, but soon turned into the twelve-man units of today's
Special Forces. A captain commanded, with a lieutenant as his number
two (later a warrant officer), while the balance was made up of experienced
NCOs. Everyone was to be highly specialized, but—for flexibility and re-
dundancy—these specialties were to be paired. There would be two
weapons specialists, two communications specialists, two medics, and so
on. Everyone would also be cross-trained, not as specialists, but able to

handle the other jobs in a pinch. Everyone was also to be airborne and Ranger-qualified, and, in the early days, a few people on the teams could speak fluently the language of the country in which the team would operate. Later, every Special Forces soldier received extensive and very high-level language and cultural training.

The A-Detachment was (and is) a tiny unit, which did not by itself throw a lot of firepower, but it jammed into a diminutive package a lot of rank and experience. It was also a highly flexible arrangement: Cut one in two and you had something very close to a Jedburgh team. Put two A-Detachments together and you had an OG.

The A-Detachment would operate in the field somewhere in a target country. A B Detachment, usually commanded by a major, assisted by two other officers and nine NCOs, would run three A-Detachments, usually from some central location such as a major town or regional capital.

A C-Detachment, with the same complement of officers and NCOs, would run three Bs, usually from the target country's national capital. The C was to be commanded by a lieutenant colonel, who would have a major as his executive officer.

Three Cs made a group, which was commanded by a colonel. The groups had (and still have) a regional orientation.

The Special Forces mission, as defined by the TO&E, read (in essence): "to infiltrate by air, sea, or land deep into enemy-controlled territory, and to stay, organize, equip, train, control, and direct the indigenous potential in the conduct of Special Forces Operations." Special Forces Operations were defined as: "the organization of resistance movements and operation of their component networks, conduct of guerrilla warfare, field intelligence gathering, espionage, sabotage, subversion, and escape and evasion activities."

All these people would need a place to lay their heads, and space for offices, classes, and training. They also needed a center where special operations and unconventional warfare theory and practice, policy and doctrine, and techniques and tactics could be studied, debated, and developed. If Aaron Bank and Russell Volckmann had had their wish, there would have been a facility dedicated to this purpose—a Special Warfare Center and School. However, since Special Forces were for the time being a component of the Psychological Warfare Branch, the Special Warfare Center and School would have to start out as an adjunct to a projected Psychological Warfare Center, which Brigadier General McClure planned for Fort Bragg, North Carolina. This center was approved in March 1952. It was to be, temporarily, under Bank's command. He would also, more permanently, become commander of the first unit to be activated, the 10th Special Forces Group, which was to have a European focus.

Next came recruiting, which in the early days was aimed at airborne troops, Rangers, and Lodge Act volunteers. The Green Berets still aim their recruiting primarily at airborne and Ranger forces.

On June 19, 1952, Bank activated the unit and assumed command. "Present for duty," he writes, "were seven enlisted men, one warrant officer, and me, making a slim morning report."

The numbers quickly grew.

Later that year, the 10th Group was moved to Bad Tolz, south of Munich, in Germany, but not before it was split in two. The half that stayed behind became the newly organized 77th Special Forces Group.

McClure, Bank, and Volckmann—together with many, many others who'd helped, advised, and supported them—had well and truly launched U.S. Special Forces.

It was, however, still a small and—yes—peripheral organization in those days. Until the day in 1961 when the U.S. Special Forces had its defining moment.

III

WARRIORS' WARRIOR

The Army is a tremendous place for an oddball like me, if you can stay alive and keep from being relieved of your commission while you're trying to get along. In the Army there's a place for every kind of intellect. There's an un-limited field for exercising ingenuity and imagination. Yet the Army, being an institution on which the welfare of the nation rests, is not going to jump lightly from one side to another because some guy comes along with a new idea. It re-ally has to be pushed to accept the new—and sometimes by two or three gen-erations of people.

— LIEUTENANT GENERAL WILLIAM P. YARBOROUGH (RET.)

That defining moment took place on October 12, 1961, at the Rod and Gun Club near McKellar's Pond at Fort Bragg, North Carolina. Present that day were the new Special Forces commander, the recently promoted Brigadier General Bill Yarborough; President John F. Kennedy's military aide, Major General Chester V. (Ted) Clifton; President Kennedy himself; and assorted other dignitaries.

Kennedy had ostensibly come down to Bragg for two purposes. One was to observe an Army division, the 82nd Airborne, drawn up on Simmons Airfield with guidons flying and all of its supporting weapons and equip-ment—Clifton had felt the young President would benefit from watching an entire Army division spread out before him. The other reason, however, was the real purpose of the trip, as Clifton, the President, and Bill Yarborough were well aware: It was to let Kennedy experience what Special Forces could do.

Kennedy was already favorably inclined toward special operations. In his eyes, they were glamorous, and Kennedy was always favorably inclined toward glamour. But far more important to him, Special Forces had the potential to do things that he very badly wanted done.

Back then, Kennedy had a vision that few of the nation's leaders shared. He saw the likelihood that the United States would soon find itself entangled in a new kind of conflict that would pose a new kind of threat. In his words, we faced "another type of war" than we were used to, one that challenged our normal ways of waging war, "new in its intensity, ancient in its origins—war by guerrillas, subversives, insurgents, assassins; war by ambush instead of by combat; by infiltration instead of by aggression, seeking victory by eroding and exhausting the enemy instead of engaging him. It requires, in those situations where we must encounter it, a whole new kind of strategy, a wholly different kind of force."

A vivid, exciting, and properly staged Special Forces show, Clifton and Yarborough agreed, would surely demonstrate for their commander-in-chief that the Army already possessed the kind of soldier and force needed to prevail in this new arena. It was far from fully formed and developed, no one would deny that, but Yarborough thought he could demonstrate that he had the core needed to build it.

As an added boon that day, for the first time at an official function, the Special Forces troops wore their far-from-official but much-cherished headgear—the green beret. At that time, wearing green berets as an item of uniform was strictly forbidden. The Army of the 1960s did not allow a distinctive uniform for "elite" troops like Special Forces or paratroopers. The name of the game was uniformity and homogenization. Even so, all Special Forces troops kept a green beret somewhere, and wore it on field maneuvers in remote areas, or when no one who could do anything about it was looking.

Bill Yarborough and Ted Clifton had been classmates and close friends at West Point, and remained lifetime friends. Before Kennedy's trip to Fort Bragg, Clifton and Yarborough had debated the wearing of the beret for the President. On the downside, they were putting their military careers at risk. On the upside, they felt that the Special Forces needed to be recognized as extraordinary by their military colleagues and the public. To Yarborough, a man profoundly sensitive to symbols, the beret was not simply a distinctive piece of clothing, but an emblem.

"I think the President would like to see your guys in their green berets," said Clifton.

"So do I," Yarborough replied. "But, of course, they're not authorized."

"Well," Clifton said, "you tell them to come out wearing it."

"What happens after that?"

"Whatever it is, we'll fix it."

And so on the twelfth of October, green berets of a grand variety of shades and textures, some of them veterans of dozens of field exercises, emerged from every kind of hiding place. The men wearing them that day stood proud in a way they had never been allowed to before. And the smiling young president was delighted.

Later, even as the Uniform Board of the Army tried to grapple with this outrage, a telegram from the White House came to Brigadier General Yarborough, indicating that the President had given his approval to the beret as a symbol of excellence. From that moment on, the green beret was officially sanctioned.

Since then, berets of many varieties have become official headgear for U.S. Army units—first for recognized elites such as Rangers (black berets) and paratroopers (red-maroon). More recently—amid considerable controversy—the entire Army has been given the privilege of wearing black berets (the Rangers will now wear tan).

Be that as it may, the wearing of the berets was not the main event back on that warm autumn day forty years ago. The main event was the "Gabriel Demonstration," named after a Special Forces soldier named Gabriel— though the name's associations with the announcing angel Gabriel were not forgotten. The idea was to display the variety, flexibility, and resourcefulness of the A-Detachments as played off against some of the more significant challenges they might be expected to face. Normally, they would have taken the President around to various locations where the teams were in action, but that would not work here, partly because of the nature of special forces, which operate in widely separated areas and in clandestine and covert situations, making observation difficult—but mostly, Ted Clifton informed Yarborough beforehand, because Kennedy's bad back didn't allow him much movement.

Instead of bringing the President to the show, they would have to bring the show to the President.

To that end, Clifton and Yarborough worked out a system in which Special Forces skill groups would pass a reviewing stand on floats (or using floats as props) mounted on flatbed trucks. Each one would stop in front of the President, and that element's activity would be revealed. There was little emphasis on equipment, gear, and weapons. The emphasis was on people.

One float, for example, showed an enemy guerrilla base like those in Laos, South Vietnam, and elsewhere in Southeast Asia. Such bases were hard to find, fix, or destroy, since they moved in fluid fashion and were concealed in swamps, jungles, or mountain hideaways. Finding and destroying such bases, the President was told, required highly trained, specially equipped, light mobile combat units. Special Forces A-Detachments could perform in these roles, but more appropriately, they could train others to do so.

Another float showed how the language and cultural training possessed by A-Detachment troops allowed them to train and assist native forces. Another showed how Special Forces civic actions (such as medical help) supplemented their combat functions, benefited ordinary folks who might otherwise help the bad guys, and helped drain away the seas where enemy guerrillas swam.

Others showed Special Forces psychological and communications skills—by broadcast, loudspeakers in villages, or leaflets. Thousands of leaflets fell out of the sky that day to reinforce the point. Others showed more traditional special operations—such as training friendly guerrillas to operate against enemy convoys and supply dumps deep within enemy territory.

The show worked.

Shortly thereafter, presidential approval came for a much larger Special Forces—more groups, more men, and much more money.

This growth came at a price. The "big" Army was not comfortable with Special Forces, and the presidential blessing did not increase their comfort. Before Bill Yarborough had taken over as commander, Special Forces had been minor and marginalized, though perhaps useful in a protracted conflict. Members of Special Forces could not expect long army careers or fast promotions. It was a dead-end unit.

Much of the army leadership in the Pentagon would have been happy if Special Forces stayed that way.

Before Kennedy's visit, Bill Yarborough got this message loud and clear from more than one friendly and well-meaning superior. For example, the commander of the XVIII Airborne Corps, a three-star general, told him: "You just got your star, Bill, but I'm going to tell you straight. You're trying to pull off something that nobody much likes and that nobody's going to accept unless the President is dead sold on it. I mean, he has to be *dead sold on it,* because those guys there at the Pentagon are going to go after your ass if he's not."

On the other hand, it would be wrong to paint the "big" Army as totally obstructionist.

When Bill Yarborough took over the Special Warfare Center* in 1961, one of his first directives to his staff was to work out the philosophy that would shape the center according to President Kennedy's aims—a difficult job made more difficult by the "big" Army's failure to understand the problems Kennedy was trying to address. However, important elements in the Army did in fact try very hard to carry out the President's desires in the counterinsurgency arena.

For instance, a Special Warfare Directorate was created within the office of the Army's Deputy Chief of Staff for Military Operations. In January 1961, this directorate initiated the first courses of instruction in counterinsurgency at the Special Warfare School.

Then, early in 1962, a board of thirteen general officers chaired by General Hamilton Howze gathered at the Special Warfare Center. The Howze Board recommended that all Army officers from colonel through four-star general, as well as all the Army divisions in the United States, should be educated and trained in counterinsurgency. The Board also recommended doubling Special Forces from the then-2,300 to 4,600. By mid-1968, this level had been raised to eight Special Forces groups totalling more than 9,000 men.

MEANWHILE, the show Yarborough and Clifton put on for the President that October day was really the culmination of three entwined, but not (at that time) totally recognized or understood, forces.

First—and he did not know this—Bill Yarborough had been handpicked by Kennedy for the command of Special Forces, with help and advice from

_____

*On December 10, 1955, Brigadier General McClure's Psychological Warfare Center had become the Special Warfare Center and School.

Ted Clifton. The President had told the Army Chief of Staff that he wanted Yarborough, so Yarborough he got. This token of executive preference was inevitably resented by "those guys there at the Pentagon," who liked to be in charge of picking who went where. They didn't like it when the President took that power away from them, and this meant that Yarborough started with strikes against him.

Second, Bill Yarborough knew that Special Forces was the only U.S. military concept oriented toward the "new form of warfare" that so worried the President, but he also knew that this would be a very tough sell to the Army without Kennedy's help. The Army had continued to fight World War II— a firepower and massed-forces war—for decades after that war was won. It meant that Yarborough would have to sail close to the wind in order to promote and sell Special Forces. He would have to convince the president and the American public. As Ted Clifton had known well when he passed Yarborough's name to Kennedy, Yarborough was a master promoter— "Showbiz" to his friends. He was the man for the job.

Third—and this is the primary reason why that October day was Special Forces' defining moment—now that he had been empowered by his commander-in-chief, Bill Yarborough began to transform Special Forces, making it over in his own image. Yarborough was a creature of many dimensions. And that was what Special Forces became.

In leaving that legacy, he proved through his genius, his vision, and his actions that the Clifton-Kennedy laying-on-of-hands that had brought him to Fort Bragg was the correct choice. Before Yarborough, U.S. Special Forces had been a career backwater. The Special Forces that exist today, with the help of hundreds of other great men, are largely his creation.

In the beginning, Yarborough had been far from pleased to take on the Special Forces job. When he was told to report to Fort Bragg, he was a high-level counterintelligence operative in Europe—commander of the 66th Counterintelligence Corps Group, headquartered in Stuttgart, Germany, where he was charged with providing security for all of the U.S. Army in Europe. His counterintelligence teams worked through field stations throughout Germany, as well as in Italy, Switzerland, and Paris, and they also worked closely with German, British, and French security agencies. It was a job that he adored and hated to leave. He loved its international character, its record of successes—they identified, captured, or "neutralized" an amazing number of enemy agents—and its dynamic of intrigue and labyrinthine complexity. It was a terrific job for a highly intelligent man.

Trading all that in for command of what seemed to be a static operation didn't look like fun, nor did it seem to offer much scope or excitement for a man like Yarborough.

"I couldn't have been more wrong," he says now.

Where he was wrong, in fact, was not in his early characterization of his new command, but in not yet seeing what John Kennedy already knew, that a new kind of force was needed to fight a new kind of war. Aaron Bank's Special Forces had preserved in amber his vision of the OSS and Jedburgh World War II glory days. What was needed now was to transform the soldiers that Bank and Volckmann had trained to rampage behind the lines into fighting men who were far more highly skilled, imaginative, flexible, culturally sensitive, and resourceful. Yarborough produced men capable of handling missions that were far more complex than those he had encountered as an intelligence officer in Europe—and did so with style, finesse, and precisely focused force (when necessary).

It wasn't what Special Forces had been that was important; it was what they would become—that was the creation of Bill Yarborough.

SHOWBIZ

An army career is not exactly the expected choice of profession for a self-described oddball with an affinity for new ideas. Even stranger, Bill Yarborough was an army brat; his father, a decorated veteran of World War I combat in Siberia and a Russian linguist, retired as a colonel. He had no illusions about army life. Worse, he was a sensitive and highly intelligent young man with artistic tendencies. He loved to draw and paint. Such people tend to have trouble with the Army's sometimes numbing regulations, thickheaded bureaucracy, and paucity of vision.

On the other hand, young Bill Yarborough recognized that, despite the occasional institutional silliness, his father's calling was a noble one, that the life could be both fulfilling and fun, and that, most important, he himself was a warrior.

Yarborough joined the Army as an enlisted man in 1931, an experience that gave him invaluable insight into the folks on the ground. He later put that to good use when he commanded Special Forces.

He won an appointment to West Point a year later. At the Academy, he and his classmate Ted Clifton came to run a school publication, the *West Point Pointer*. Clifton was editor and Yarborough managing editor; he wrote feature articles and drew cartoons—a practice that has stayed with him all his life.

Yarborough graduated in 1936, received his commission as a second lieutenant from the hands of General John J. Pershing, and was assigned to the 57th Infantry, Philippine Scouts, stationed at Fort McKinley on Luzon. In the period before he left for the Philippines, he wooed and married another army brat—though that was not all that Norma and Bill Yarborough had in common: They both shared a lifetime love of the Far East and of the art of Asia (their home in North Carolina is filled with it).

After a three-year tour in the Philippines, Yarborough characteristically found his way to the cutting edge of the new Army, which in the early 1940s meant jumping out of airplanes with a parachute (a not-very-well-developed device). He was among the first to volunteer for and test this new and very dangerous form of warfare.

Paratroopers gave armies greatly increased mobility, but at a cost. The air transports that flew them were vulnerable, and paratroopers couldn't carry much in the way of support or firepower with them. In their early days, in other words, airborne units operated more like Special Forces teams than regular infantry.

Meanwhile, as he learned the jump trade, his Airborne superiors offered him a chance to exercise his love of symbols.

It's easy for outsiders to miss the point of the Army's wealth of institutional symbols. Qualification badges, ribbons, decorations, unit patches—even special hats or boots or songs—have a big place in a soldier's sense of identity and pride. They're certainly not essential, but they are more than gaudy decoration. Strong men will choke up now and again when they are put in the presence of some particularly meaningful piece of colored cloth.

This is not to say that there is no place for flamboyance and swagger in a soldier's outfit. You want dignity, but you don't want a soldier to *look* timid. A modicum of flair doesn't hurt here. Yarborough has always been conscious of these truths. "A distinctive uniform," he writes, "enhances an individual's pride, makes him a man apart, makes him special."

Not surprisingly, his paratroop superiors were aware of his knack for drawing and design, and so he was asked to create the first airborne qualification badge, and then to have a silversmith produce enough of them to award the first group of qualifying paratroopers. Airborne forces still wear the wings Bill Yarborough designed.

His talents were not limited to airborne wings. He had a further knack for designing specialized clothing: the first airborne jump boots, for instance—jump boots have had the same kind of meaning for paratroopers that green berets have for Special Forces—and he would later create other pieces of military clothing, some of which found their way into the catalogs of outdoor-clothing specialists such as L.L. Bean.

Early on in his command of the Green Berets, he argued for the use of the Bowie knife, both as a weapon useful in hand-to-hand combat and as a symbol of accomplishment. At one time sabers had satisfied that kind of need, but the Army had taken away sabers. They were no more practical in the twentieth century than horse-mounted cavalry. To Yarborough, the Bowie knife seemed like a splendid replacement, rich in frontier tradition and heroic resonance.

Yarborough's dream was to present a Bowie knife to each new member of his Special Forces, together with the green beret. The knife would have an inscription on each side: on one the soldier's name, and on the other the Special Forces motto, *de oppresso liber* ("to free the oppressed").

The Army never approved the idea—but Bill Yarborough kept coming up with others.

Like the movies, for instance.

Back in 1941, Bill Yarborough had become a leader of the new breed of airborne warrior, and he had learned an important lesson about selling a cutting-edge-but-maybe-somewhat-suspect military unit to both the Army and the American public.

Hollywood helps.

In 1941, RKO made a movie called *Parachute Battalion* about three young men, played by Robert Preston, Edmund O'Brien, and Harry Carey, who go through parachute training. Since it would not do to have big stars risk their lives jumping out of airplanes, Bill Yarborough and his paratroop companions stood in as stunt doubles. It was not a memorable movie, but it did glamorize airborne forces, and made both the "big" Army and the public take more notice of them.

Later, Yarborough grabbed a similar opportunity when the writer Robin Moore presented himself at his doorstep with an idea for a novel about Special Forces. Yarborough liked the idea so much that he became a kind of muse in the writing of *The Green Berets*, which later became the hit John Wayne movie.

The Green Berets turned out to be the Special Forces "Gabriel Demonstration" for the American public.

But Yarborough didn't stop there.

As far back as his service as an enlisted man, he'd loved military bands. He loved the way the old marches and military hymns stirred the heart. Later, as Special Forces commander, he felt strongly that the Green Berets deserved a heart-stirring military hymn of their own. First, he got the bandmaster at West Point to write a Green Beret march. Then one day, totally out of the blue, a young SF sergeant named Barry Sadler came into Yarborough's office and started playing a song he'd written called "The Ballad of the Green Beret."

> *Fighting soldiers from the sky,*
> *Fearless men who jump and die. . . .*

One thing led to another, and before long, Sergeant Sadler, still on active duty, appeared on *The Ed Sullivan Show* to sing his ballad. The public was knocked out; the song was a hit; it was translated into many languages; affection and respect for U.S. Special Forces mushroomed—and Bill Yarborough not only had a hymn, he had another huge public relations success for his Green Berets.[*]

Now he had his Special Forces novel, his Special Forces movie, and his Special Forces hymn. He needed only one more further component: a Special Forces prayer—some nondenominational words that would express and define the way Special Forces soldiers might relate to their God (there being no atheists in foxholes). It had to be something that would relate to all of his men, whatever the race or creed. And this is what he wrote:

> *Almighty God, who art the author of liberty and the champion of the oppressed, hear our prayer.*

> *We, the men of Special Forces, acknowledge our dependence upon thee in the preservation of human freedom.*

> *Go with us as we seek to defend the defenseless and to free the enslaved.*

---

[*]An unexpected but gratifying endorsement came from the Soviet censors, who banned "The Ballad of the Green Beret" in the USSR.

May we ever remember that our nation, whose motto is "In God We Trust," expects that we shall acquit ourselves with honor, that we may never bring shame upon our faith, our families, or our fellow men.

Grant us wisdom from thy mind, courage from thine heart, strength from thine arm, and protection by thine hand.

It is for thee that we do battle, and to thee belongs the victor's crown.

For thine is the kingdom and the power and the glory forever. Amen.

Meanwhile, back in World War II, Yarborough continued to jump out of airplanes, but now in combat—in the invasion of North Africa in November of 1942 (the first use of American parachute troops in combat) and in later operations in Tunisia. The parachute battalion he commanded for the invasion of Sicily lost twenty-three airplanes to "friendly" antiaircraft fire. His paratroop battalion later fought at Anzio, and one of his troops, Sergeant Paul B. Huff, was the first parachute soldier to win the Medal of Honor. Later, his battalion dropped into southern France and fought along the French Riviera to the Maritime Alps. As the war was ending, he received a battlefield promotion to full colonel and was given command of an infantry regimental combat team that fought along the rugged Italian coast to Genoa. During the process, he won a Silver Star.

Previously, however, he had come close to shooting his military career in the foot.

Always outspoken, Yarborough had openly questioned his division commander's handling of the massive airborne assault into Sicily that had resulted in many transports getting shot down, with great loss of life. His commander, then–Major General Matthew Ridgeway, was not pleased with his subordinate's outburst and relieved him of his command. Fortunately, Ridgeway's superior, then-Lieutenant General Mark W. Clark, the 5th Army commander, liked Yarborough and saw promise in the rash young man. Clark gave him a temporary staff job, and later another fighting command.

In time, Yarborough and Ridgeway became good friends, and in fact, Yarborough came to realize that Ridgeway had done what was necessary when he'd ordered the assault. It was like with Eisenhower and D Day. The attack had to be so overwhelming that it would prevail despite the staggering losses. It is every commander's nightmare—but it was a powerful lesson for young Yarborough.

After the war, he was sent to Vienna as the provost marshal of U.S.

forces in Austria and provost marshal in Vienna. The job resembled a police chief's, but also involved cooperation with the equivalent officers of the
three other occupying powers: England, France, and the USSR. It proved
to be Yarborough's first introduction to what was later called "civil affairs."

Since the official mission of the four occupying powers was to restore
civil order and the rule of law, Yarborough grew interested in how the occupying troops might be disrupting that process—by, for example, criminal
activities. To that end, he initiated a statistical study showing the nationalities responsible for the greatest number of crimes and the nature of those
crimes. He then published regularly a booklet showing the curves of murder, rape, theft, arson, black market, and so on.

The results were fascinating. The Russians committed by far the most
crimes, followed by the French, the Americans, and then the British.

There were a lot of factors. For one, the nationalities that had suffered
most under the Germans and Austrians were hardly eager to protect
German or Austrian legal rights. But it was equally true that the *kinds* of soldiers in occupation had a lot to do with how well they conducted themselves. The American troops that had been in combat were fairly
well-behaved and responsive to discipline, but when their replacements
began to arrive to take over the occupation, discipline began to collapse and
crime rates began to rise.

The Russians, it seems, screened their soldiers not at all. In fact, as
Yarborough learned from his Russian counterpart, who became a good
friend, it was doubtful if many of the Russian commanders even knew where
their people were. Their comings and goings made a mockery of regulations.

Yarborough tried to fix the American part of this situation several times.
In his view, Vienna was not just an occupied capital; it was a major, politically charged test case, the success or failure of which could determine the
future political direction taken by a great part of Europe. It seemed to him
the United States should send representatives who would present the country in a good light, people who would create positive psychological leverage.

However, when he went to his superiors with this suggestion, he was told
in no uncertain terms to forget it. He'd have to take his share of people with
everybody else—the Army way—and leave the rest to leadership. This was,
as he put it, "the old answer."

A new answer was needed: Only picked men should be allowed in that
kind of arena. In years to come, he took this insight to other politically
charged environments such as Vietnam, Laos, Cambodia, and Thailand.

In Vienna (and later in Southeast Asia), civilians had high expectations for the Americans who had appeared among them. They had status and stature. They represented a vast, powerful country; they were there to help. If these expectations were going to be realized, then the old Army way wasn't going to work.

"Ordinary" soldiers were not up to the job at hand. "Special" soldiers were needed.

Bill Yarborough lost that battle. But the point lodged in his mind.

His next years followed the normal, and not very exciting, path expected of midlevel Army officers. He graduated from the British Staff College in Camberley, England, in 1951, then spent the next two years as a staff officer in London representing the U.S. Joint Chiefs of Staff on the project to construct the framework for the North Atlantic Treaty Organization. There he met and befriended a man who would come to have a large influence on Special Forces, Roger Hilsman. Another West Point graduate, and a World War II guerrilla fighter with Merrill's Marauders in Burma, Hilsman later became the State Department's head of intelligence, then Assistant Secretary of State for Far Eastern Affairs during the Kennedy years, and one of Kennedy's chief foreign policy advisers. More than anyone else, Hilsman was the Kennedy adviser responsible for his interest in irregular warfare.

After leaving England, Yarborough attended the Army War College and remained there on the faculty for two years after graduation. During that time, he made a study of the various forms future wars might take, including guerrilla war. In connection with that study, he visited the Special Forces at Fort Bragg, then under the command of Lieutenant Colonel Edson D. Raff, another pioneer paratrooper and veteran of the 1942 North African invasion. At Special Forces Headquarters, Yarborough got a VIP briefing on their mission and capabilities, but despite Raff's enthusiasm, he was not much impressed with what he saw: During a big war, he concluded, Special Forces might have some influence on guerrillas and orient them to our cause, but it would be a mere sideshow.

In 1956, he was sent to Cambodia, as Deputy Chief of the Military Assistance Advisory Group, where he spent a great deal of time in the field with Cambodian troops—another enlightening experience (he loved Cambodia). He was impressed, first of all, with the physical difficulties of waging conventional war in that environment, and then with the Cambodian soldiers' ability to exist and thrive in that environment nevertheless.

He tells about it:

In 1956, General Ciccolella and I, serving on the MAG there, made several trips to the eastern provinces. At one time we went all the way from Phnom Penh over to Ban Me Thuot, and through a road the French had carved out, now overgrown. The rusting machinery was still there, and along the border areas the forces on both sides [Communist and anti-Communist] had met and recoiled, I guess, because there was no evidence of military activity along the border between Cambodia and Vietnam; but when one got inside the boundaries of Vietnam, fortifications looked over most logical approaches.

The going in those two provinces was very difficult, especially in the rainy season. On one of our trips, we got caught in torrential rains.

We had with us a small contingent of Cambodians, a three-quarter-ton truck, two jeeps, and a trailer. Darkness fell, quickly, as it does in the tropics; and the road we were on began to disappear under water. On each side of us was nothing but flat land, and I began to feel desperate. Not only was it possible for us to drown, but we could also flounder around in this flooded and featureless landscape and get completely lost, which was not acceptable either.

So what to do?

Well, just before the last vestiges of light were gone, we found a little mound—a small hill—and we pulled our equipment up onto it as the rains continued to pelt down on us. Then we deployed our sleeping bags under what cover we could find and tried to get a little rest. Next morning we'd see what else we could do.

About three in the morning, we heard sounds from the direction we'd just come from. Soon we could make out blinking through the rain—a flashlight here and there—and the sounds a mule train might make, coming up the road.

About half an hour later a young Cambodian lieutenant came up, wet to the skin; he saluted and then asked: "Est-ce que je peux vous aider?"— Can I help you out?

And we said: "Well, who are you? Where are you going? How did you get here?"

"We're going to the border post along the frontier," he said, "and we're just moving through the mud."

"How are you doing it?"

He showed us:

What they were doing was using a winch on the front of a three quarter ton truck. They'd attach a line onto a tree and winch forward about twenty-five or thirty feet. And then they'd repeat the process. They'd moved all the way along the road this way.

"Are you going to stop here for the night?" we asked. "Or wait until the rain stops?"

"Oh no, there's a much better place on up ahead. We'll go on up there." And then he said, "Can we pull you along?"

"No, we'll wait for dawn," I said.

So when dawn came, we moved out. The waters had receded a little bit, and you could see where you were going.

About ten miles ahead, we came to the encampment where the Cambodian lieutenant had by now laid out his command post gear. By that time, the Cambodian officers had taken off their uniforms and changed into their "sampots"—a wrap-around garment—and the soldier orderlies were serving them. They were completely at home in that environment . . . really good jungle and frontier soldiers.

Some time later, we finally got to the frontier post that was our destination. It was like a fort in our Old West. It had sharpened stakes around it to keep out the primitive hill tribes they called the "Mnongs" and the Vietnamese called the "Montagnards." In the morning, the bugle would sound, the flag would go up, and the Khmer soldiers would go out on the town (which was nearby), trading with zircons, just like our frontier soldiers trading with the Indians. At night they came back inside the fort.

Well, my feeling was that Cambodians would make superb irregular warfare soldiers, the guerrilla warfare type.

The seed of another Special Forces mission was planted.

In 1957, Yarborough took command of the 7th Infantry Regiment and moved it to Germany from Fort Benning, Georgia. From there he was sent to Counterintelligence in Europe . . . and then to Fort Bragg, to command Special Forces.

A NEW FORM OF WAR

John Kennedy's thoughts on unconventional warfare were a response to very real worries back in the 1950s and '60s—the seemingly relentless and insidious spread of the "Communist Empire" and the sudden collapse of colonialism.

Colonialism—the rule by Western powers over Third World peoples for the sake of their economic exploitation—had lasted several centuries. Its death (except in the Soviet version) took approximately two decades, the years following the end of the Second World War.

Sadly, the departure of the old colonial masters brought few blessings to the newly independent Third World nations; the old masters left behind very few capable indigenous leaders and very little for them to work with. The "white man's burden" was a never-delivered promise. In most newly decolonized Third World nations, the infrastructures necessary to maintain a society as a going concern were lacking—transportation, education, health care, banks and investment, and most of all, enforceable laws and an effective justice system to protect them. More often than not, the emerging Third World leaders were primarily interested in personal aggrandizement and wealth rather than in the long, hard toil needed to build a viable nation.

The citizens of those nations, meanwhile, wanted what everybody else wants—better lives for themselves and their children. "We've thrown the old masters out," they argued, sensibly (and often after long, hard struggles, pain, and sacrifice). "Now we deserve to see the fruits of our victory."

When the fruits didn't immediately appear—and in fact seemed to recede ever further into a future ever more squalid and rotten with corruption—it's not hard to imagine their dismay, nor to see how quickly their mood turned nasty.

Naturally, this potentially explosive situation became a major arena in the battle between the Communist powers and the West. At stake were power and influence over a great part of the world's population, as well as control over a vast wealth of natural resources.

The more ideologically driven Communists started out with a number of advantages in this contest: They had no link with the old, discredited colonial powers, and they promised heaven on earth . . . and soon. The Chinese, in particular, had also developed effective techniques for transforming the dismay, discontent, and rage against the failed or failing Third World governments into mechanisms that seriously threatened those systems.

The Western powers (the United States in particular, as their leader) started fighting with serious disadvantages. Communism represented the bright and shiny future. The democracies, and capitalism, represented the discredited past. Nor were the democracies especially skillful in the

PSYOPs part of the struggle. Democratic capitalism and the rule of law, adapted to the cultural requirements and traditions of each society, remains the best hope for most of the world's people. The West did not do a very good job selling that truth.

Meanwhile, Mao Tse-tung's victory in China showed the way for others: Dismay and discontent can be transformed into dissent and dissidence. Dissidence can be transformed into subversion and terrorism. Subversion and terrorism can be transformed into active insurrection. Insurrection can be transformed into guerrilla war. And in time, guerrilla war can be transformed into conventional military action—but only when the guerrillas feel totally confident that the outcome favors them.

Each stage in the process supports actions aimed at exploiting the ruling system's weaknesses. The aim is not direct confrontation, but to cause a rotting from within. Agents corrupt or "turn" politicians. Other agents take over labor unions, student groups, farmers' collectives; they infiltrate the media, the military, and the police—all as vehicles for propaganda and subversion.

The revolutionaries do not expect to destroy the system in a single blow or series of blows. Any weakness will do—economic, political, psychological, physical. In fact, the greatest vulnerability of any system is often psychological—will. As a result, eroding the will of the enemy to continue the struggle is always a chief aim of the underground opposition. This can take a very long time—years, even decades. The subversive leadership, as Mao has taught, must always remain patient.

It follows that each stage is supported by the ones before it, and each stage remains active even as new ones arise. At the same time, the various elements and stages of the subversive underground are protected from detection by means of a complex cell structure. Chop off a finger, but the body remains, and a new finger grows.

It follows as well that all of these elements depend on near-flawless intelligence, and on the whole they get it. Their eyes are everywhere; they know whatever the people know.

It follows, finally, that the more active stages depend almost totally on the support of the people—for supplies, intelligence, money, and recruits. Very often this support comes at great risk and considerable cost. The governing bodies—like the Germans in occupied France—look for payback opportunities, or else simply for ways to send a strong message. The more threatened they become, the more likely they are to flail about violently—to the psychological advantage of the revolution.

Of course, standing up under such assaults requires strong, highly motivated people.

From this comes Mao's famous sea and fish image. The people are the sea; the revolutionaries are the fish. The sea supports the fish. It also hides them from predators. The revolutionaries only want to show themselves when they are not themselves vulnerable. Then they fade back into the sea, or the mountains or the jungle.

Of course, the revolutionaries almost always received support from one or another Communist power. It was a war by proxy.

Meanwhile, all too often, Third World leaders sold their services to the highest bidder, or to whichever bidder was handy at the moment.

This was President Kennedy's new kind of war. It went under many names—revolution, peoples' war, subterranean war, multidimensional war, slow-burn war, war in the shadows. All of these names were useful, and described a significant aspect of the struggle.

The focus on concealment and complexity, however, points to a hard but basic truth: The old way of fighting wars simply did not work. You couldn't just send in the cavalry, or an armored corps. You could bomb a people back into the Stone Age, and their children would come out of their holes, throw stones, and vanish back into the holes.

Where's the enemy? Who are we actually fighting? When we take a piece of territory, do we hold anything worth holding?

The President had it right: A new kind of fighting force was required. This force had to know guerrillas inside and out—how they lived, how they fought, how they swam in the sea of the people. The Bank-Volckmann-McClure Special Forces had no problems there, but skill at behind-the-lines sabotage and running around with guerrillas was far from enough. For the early Special Forces, guerrillas and partisans were expected to be our friends. A reorientation was needed when guerrillas became our enemies. It wasn't a gigantic reorientation, but attitudes had to change and new skills had to be learned.

For one thing, you couldn't begin to uproot guerrillas without at the same time understanding and attacking the shadowy mechanisms that spawned and sustained them—the vast network of subversion, terror, support, and intelligence. But doing so without utterly wiping out the very freedoms that the United States was trying to preserve and promote was a daunting task.

Nor was it easy to go into somebody else's home and set their house in order. Sovereign states consider internal subversion a very touchy matter.

They are not eager to give foreigners access to the mechanisms that support it. In fact, the governments of these states are often themselves diseased. The cure proposed by the revolutionaries may well be the wrong cure, yet their cause may be just.

This meant that if American Special Forces were going to do any good at all in a counterinsurgency situation, they would have to be able to walk a very thin and risky line. They would have to act toward the local government with great care and finesse, based on the direction they'd been given by their own commanders and government, while developing more than a skin-deep rapport with the native peoples.

In view of this very sensitive psychological and political environment, it became evident to Bill Yarborough that the criteria for Special Forces would have to include far more than just expertise in guerrilla warfare. Personal character became extremely important—the judgment, maturity, self-discipline, and ability to work harmoniously with people who were culturally very different from Americans.

What kind of soldier operates effectively in such an environment?

First of all—and this is as true now as it was in 1961—it is one who thinks in ways that conventional soldiers are not expected to. Like all soldiers, Special Forces men work under a chain of command, but unlike the others, they may not always have direct or even regular communication with their superiors. That means that at times they need to act on their own, which means they inevitably make decisions on their own—though based, it is hoped, on a clear understanding of their commanders' and their nation's intent. At times these decisions have an impact far greater than those that more conventional soldiers may be called on to make. They may not only radically change lives or lead to deaths, they may also affect policy decisions going all the way up the chain of command to the President.

At the same time, tough problems come up that only Special Forces soldiers can solve. Many of these problems are practical—a Special Forces soldier might be required to deliver babies, extract teeth, or design a bridge and supervise its construction. Others are psychological—Special Forces soldiers may well need to persuade, cajole, or manipulate a not-very-friendly local leader to work for goals that may be in the United States' interest but not obviously in his. Either way, the problems are typically unexpected, complex, and open-ended, and there is no guarantee of help from above.

In addition, Special Forces soldiers cannot focus their individual tactics, techniques, capabilities, and thinking on a few specifics. They can't simply rely on well-honed soldier skills. They are taught, and are expected to think, in the broadest terms. When they work a problem, they are not merely trying to solve it in the best way for their team but in the best way for the United States. They need to be able to see and handle such problems in all their complexity.

Soldiers are called "special" in part because they can be trusted to make such decisions.

EMPOWERED though he was by the President to make those soldiers, Bill Yarborough had a big job ahead of him. He had to take the "old" Special Forces and turn it into the "new" Special Forces—and not all of the "old" wanted to become "new." He had to grow the small and marginal outfit into a force of significant size with greatly increased output, yet bring into the force the very best recruits. This meant "raiding" the rest of the Army for people nobody in the rest of the Army was willing to give up (he was empowered to do so, but at the cost of much resentment). He had to weed out those who did not make the mark, while educating and training to the very highest standards the picked and tested men who remained, and then he had to fill these men, individually and collectively, with pride and self-esteem. Meanwhile, he had to study the nature of the enemy and the ways others had learned to combat such an enemy; he had to do it to a depth rarely—if ever—accomplished by a military organization; and he had to find ways to make his Special Forces not just learn these insights, but incorporate them into their blood and sinews. And finally, he had to continue to sell his always fragile and vulnerable Special Forces to the "big" Army and to the American people.

A NEW KIND OF FIGHTING FORCE

Bill Yarborough faced a big job, but first he had to clean house—which involved raising the bar.

Not long after he took over Special Forces in 1961, Yarborough came to realize that a significant portion of the SF old-timers did not measure up to the standards his new fighting force required. These old guys were a rough lot—fire-breathers and flame-spouters. They were extraordinary soldiers, but not all of them could be counted on to operate well in politically and psychologically sensitive situations.

"The ones I was especially anxious not to retain in the Green Berets,"

Yarborough remarks, "were the 'old jockstrap commandos,' the Ranger types. And I must say there were considerable numbers of those in Special Forces.

"I'd fought with Rangers during World War II, and I had known and admired them for their best qualities: They were gallant 'bloodletters.' They were fighting machines. They were anything but diplomats, and rejected any suggestion that they ought to be. And they paid little attention to what we might call the more humane qualities, like compassion, pity, and mercy. If such things suited the occasion, all right; but if they didn't, that was all right, too. They were there to cut a swath. Wherever you turned the Rangers and commandos loose, boy, there they would go. There wasn't any question about it.

"Well, some of my Army colleagues in key positions in the Department of the Army continue to look upon Special Forces as a kind of commando. They have never been able to understand why we had to get rid of so many of the old jockstrap guys, or why later we had to have such a high attrition rate in the Qualification Course. They couldn't understand the attrition rates for judgment, or for inability to understand humanity. . . . A guy who wouldn't get down on his belly alongside a Montagnard and show him the sight picture [in aiming a weapon] was no use to me.

"We continually got called to task about our high attrition rate, but as long as I had anything to do about it, we didn't bend one inch, and I would back to the limit every man who came out of that cauldron, out of that system."

Some of the old SF guys were a rough lot off-duty as well as on—and that presented Yarborough with yet more problems.

Because Special Forces was a marginal outfit where promotions were scarce, the best officers tended to avoid the assignment if they could. In those days, the level of SF training for officers was also low; the Q Course, for example, could be waived for field-grade officers, and often was.

For various reasons, the future for good Special Forces NCOs was brighter, and NCO quality tended to be higher. The NCOs' expertise also tended to be high (many of them were World War II and/or Korea veterans with considerable experience in the field; most had been shot at), and Yarborough wanted to make the most of their expertise in teaching his younger soldiers. But they also tended to act as though they had carte blanche to do things pretty much as they pleased. They tended to run a bit wild when they were out there with the younger guys.

They had to be reined in.

The officers, though, were a bigger problem. There were outstanding exceptions, but too many officers looked at the assignment as a place to park and have macho fun—drinking, wild parties, womanizing, playing around with other guys' wives.

That had to stop.

Early on in his command, Yarborough took his officers—captain and higher—out into the pine woods on the base and told them straight what he expected of them. He was not gentle.

The event was long remembered as Yarborough's "Talk in the Woods."

"As long as I'm in charge of Special Forces," he told them, "the rules are going to change. There'll be a new start.

"First, there will be no womanizing, no drunkenness, no wild parties, no adultery. There'll be no troublemakers. No wild men. From now on all that stuff is out—and there will be no deviations. There will be moral standards, there will be disciplinary standards, there will be appearance standards.

"Second, all officers will go through the Q Course. No exceptions. No matter what his rank.

"Third, everything I'm saying applies to all ranks. No exceptions. So you're going to make it all clear to every one of your NCOs.

"Finally, if you don't like it, you can deal with it in two ways. You can end your career. Or you can come to my office and request to be transferred out. Otherwise, if you want to stay in this unit, there will be big changes."

The worst got out. The best stayed. And Yarborough moved on to the real work that remained.

Meanwhile, Special Forces officers and NCOs began to find promotions coming their way. If you got into Special Forces, and you could cut it, you could expect to get promoted very quickly and look forward to a long Army career, if you wanted it.

So Special Forces stopped being the end of the road for wild men, misfits, and has-beens. It became the place you wanted to be. It was the place where the action was.

Soon after the Kennedy administration had identified "counterinsurgency" as an official instrument of United States foreign policy, it became clear that some of the major weapon systems needed for counterinsurgency would have to be forged from among the resources specific to the behavioral and social sciences—psychology, anthropology, political science, economics, history, and international relations. The problem would be to integrate these disciplines with more direct military functions to produce an effective instrument in the murky environment of actual counterinsurgency campaigns.

The Special Warfare Center had to explore this new field.

Bill Yarborough was himself a scholar and an intellectual, and his experience in intelligence and counterintelligence had taught him a great deal about how to go about understanding one's adversaries (and one's friends). He knew where and how to look for sources of knowledge and inspiration.

He went first to Roger Hilsman, who had already played a major role at the State Department and White House in promoting the concept of counterinsurgency and the convoluted world of irregular warfare. Hilsman came down to the Special Warfare Center on several occasions, and provided Yarborough and his staff and students with background information and insights.

Yarborough and his staff also studied positive and negative examples: Positive in the case of the British, whose triumph in Malaya pointed the way toward a workable counterinsurgency doctrine—a combination of sophistication about native cultures and a willingness to be uncompromisingly brutal in infiltrating local insurgencies and then uprooting them from the people. Negative in the case of the French defeat in Indochina and their phony victory in Algeria.

Others who regularly gave him counsel included experts like Charles M. Thayer, the head of the U.S. military mission to Yugoslavia during World War II and who later headed the Voice of America; Dr. Jay Zawodny, then professor of political science at the University of Pennsylvania, who had fought with the Polish underground in Warsaw during the Second World War and later authored numerous works on irregular warfare and psychological operations; and several others of equal expertise.

Some of the sources consulted and studied were controversial. Yarborough was not afraid to shock his students. Conventional thinking was not going to get the job done.

The left-leaning French soldier-writer Bernard Fall, for example, was a frequent lecturer at the Special Warfare School's irregular warfare classes. The author of the now classic history of the French war in Indochina, *Street Without Joy*, which was used as a text at the school, Fall was sharp-tongued, abrasive, and contemptuous of American efforts in Southeast Asia, and more often than not sparked heated reactions from his soldier audiences.

"On his side," Yarborough writes, "were facts, figures, history, and personal experience. On the students' side were usually emotional distress stemming from hurt pride and an inadequate database."

Eventually, Fall's contempt for American policy in Vietnam brought his appearances at Fort Bragg to the attention of "those guys there in the Pentagon." This brought Yarborough a telephone call from Washington: "The Frenchman Bernard Fall is no longer welcome at the Special Warfare School," he was told. But when Yarborough demanded that this order be put in writing, the demand was withdrawn, and Fall's catalytic presence continued to shake up the young Green Berets at the school.

Another controversial source of insight on irregular warfare was a larger-than-life Air Force colonel named Edward Lansdale—a real-world character who had seemingly leapt out of a spy novel. His story, in fact, inspired more than one novelist; he was the model for Graham Greene's *The Quiet American* and Lederer and Burdick's *The Ugly American* (their character also contains elements of Roger Hilsman). Though controversial—his conduct in Vietnam was questionable—his accomplishments were real. During the '50s, Lansdale was loaned to the CIA and assigned to the Philippines, where he gave the Agency its greatest victory against Communist insurgents there, called the Huks.

He did this in several ways. First, he promoted an undeniably great man, Ramon Magsaysay, as an alternative to the Communists. Magsaysay, arguably the Washington and Lincoln of the Philippines, became president of that country, but was killed in an air crash after too short a time in office. Second, Lansdale had a kind of mad genius for the art of what later became known as "black" psychological operations—lies that damage an enemy. For example, he had the rumor spread in rural villages that men with evil in their hearts would be food for the local vampire. He then had his people drain the blood out of a dead Huk, punch holes in his neck, and leave him in the middle of a well-traveled road. Word got around very quickly that the Huks were vampire bait. But third, and most important for Bill Yarborough's delvings into the heart of irregular and political warfare, "Ed Lansdale made me understand," he writes, "the relationship between what we clumsily call Civic Action and the ability of a regular army to function among the people. This insight was responsible to a great degree for the effectiveness of the counterinsurgency operation in the Philippines. It made the people feel that the military were not oppressors. Rather, the man in uniform represented the government; and, if they were eager to assist and help the people, then the government must be of the same frame of mind." The good acts of the men in uniform argued to the benevolence, right intentions, and honor of the government.

"Later on in my research," he continues, "I discovered that Ed Lansdale was not the author of this concept . . . but Mao Tse-tung. Mao was the greatest modern proponent of this philosophy.

"In studying Mao's campaigns leading to the expulsion of Chiang Kai-shek from mainland China, I found that, in the beginning, the Nationalist armies were very much greater numerically than the Communist forces. But as Mao withdrew along the route of his long march, his soldiers treated people very generously and kindly, and with great respect. And so instead of fleeing to get out of the way of the Communists, in the normal way of civilians and armies, the people welcomed them.

"This behavior goes back to Mao's Nine Rules of Conduct, which his Red Army troops were made to memorize (they were even set to music and sung daily). These rules were strictly enforced. A man who violated them was severely punished, perhaps executed."

Here's a sample:

- ✪ There shall be no confiscations whatever from the poor peasantry.
- ✪ If you borrow anything, return it.
- ✪ Replace all articles you damage.
- ✪ Pay for everything that you purchase.
- ✪ Be honest in all transactions with the peasants.
- ✪ Be courteous and polite to the people and help them when you can.

This meant practically, Yarborough continues, "that the ordinary rules soldiers were used to in the field did not apply. Civilians were not kicked out if they got in the way. A soldier was encouraged to share his last crust of bread with a peasant. If a door was taken off a house for a soldier to sleep on, the custom in China, it would be replaced before the troops left. The best place for a gun position might be in the center of a tomb. Even so, the Red Army would respect the people and place the gun somewhere else.

"In consequence, the Red Army swelled, while Chiang Kai-shek's forces lost the confidence of ever greater numbers of people."

Careful study of Mao, as well as other Communist authorities such as Che Guevara and the Vietnamese Vo Nguyen Giap and Truong Chinh, rounded out further the picture of multidimensional warfare. (It should be noted that such study was not exactly encouraged by "those guys at the Pentagon.") Their brand of irregular warfare, Yarborough's studies revealed, featured the following ingredients:

- ✪ Patience to withstand protracted conflict. "Time works for us. Time will be our best strategist."—Truong Chinh.
- ✪ Political awareness on the part of all ranks.
- ✪ Intensive wooing of all the "little people" to the side of the insurgent.
- ✪ The weakening of the enemy's morale by constant propaganda and terrorist harassment.
- ✪ Constant offensive action against enemy personnel and sensitive points, but only when tactical advantage is on the side of the irregulars.
- ✪ The avoidance of pitched battles with equal or superior forces.
- ✪ Defense only when it is essential to survival or to aid another element to withdraw.
- ✪ The consideration of the enemy's supply system as your own—making him haul the matériel to dumps, then seizing it from him.
- ✪ Constant striving to grow undercover forces into regular forces, ones capable of meeting the enemy on his own ground when the time and circumstances make victory certain.

With these studies as a guide, the new direction of Special Forces became clear.

If their job was to teach armed forces of a threatened nation how to combat a local insurgency, then their first task there was to demonstrate carefully thought out and executed military and nonmilitary actions that would allow those forces to win and maintain the support of the people. All of this would require the highest level of discipline on the part of not only the Green Berets but also the local forces. Such discipline would ensure a high level of conduct and moral behavior among the people in politically sensitive areas.

Though conventional soldiers don't normally concern themselves with the civilians who find themselves caught up in the tides of war, when it became obvious that the political and psychological fallout from this lack of concern could negate a brilliant battlefield victory, military leaders had to seriously adjust their thinking. In the U.S. Army, the Special Forces were the first to be taught this lesson officially and put it into practice as a principle of war.

Before long, Green Berets, using an American version of Mao's "Rules for Conduct," began to have a powerful impact on the lives of "little people" in Third World nations living in remote, often jungle, areas. Previously, such people did not much figure in the overall scheme of military maneuver. And for their part, the "little people" tended to be suspicious of foreign soldiers in their midst. However, a combination of personal qualities and soldier skills soon began to increase cooperation and mutual trust, and these came to grow into admiration and friendship.

The Green Berets paid attention to all kinds of little things that other soldiers rarely cared about. For example, they helped a villager increase his water supplies by showing him a simple well-digging technique. They worked side by side with him to build a log bridge that would save a half-mile trudge around a swamp to reach his primitive patch of farmland. They showed him how to dig an irrigation ditch. They gave him seeds that grew into better vegetables than he had ever imagined possible. But strangest—and most heartwarming—of all, they paid attention to the villager as an individual. They could speak to him in his own dialect—maybe not fluently, but enough. And they shared the lives of the village people. They ate their food and drank their drink; they sat around their fires in the evening and chatted with them; they slept in huts like theirs.

Once friendship had been established, the military task of defending the village began. Green Berets traced village fortification outlines, and villagers placed row on row of sharpened stakes in the ground, angled toward approach routes. With Green Beret help, they dug protective shelters inside the village perimeters. They set up an alarm system, using an old tire rim or an empty artillery shell case, to warn of attack. During all this time, Green Berets worked alongside the villagers, and when attack came, they fought side by side with them.

Green Beret A-Detachments have always featured medical expertise—two highly trained medical specialists, with each of the remaining eight troopers cross-trained in medical skills.

The justification for this expertise came out of the original Special Forces mission, which was to organize and train guerrilla and insurgent forces. During their early days, guerrillas are exceedingly vulnerable. To protect themselves while they grow in strength, they must hide in difficult-to-reach areas such as jungles, swamps, or rugged mountains. Under such conditions, day-to-day survival is often a triumph in itself. If a guerrilla is sick or wounded, he has no outside help on which to rely.

Here is where Green Beret medical skills enter the picture. Green Beret medics could provide the medical knowledge to keep guerrillas going as functioning fighters.

Those skills were put to similar use in the villages, which were scarcely less isolated than the guerrilla bases, and provided even more reason for friendship and trust. Often for the first time, villagers had access to basic dental care, prenatal care, antibiotics, vaccinations, and nutrition and disease-prevention advice.

Training for these missions was intense, difficult, and as realistic as possible. Green Berets returning from foreign missions were sucked dry of information, and they helped train the men replacing them. Replicas of villages were constructed, accurate to the finest detail. In order to prepare for a mission, the Berets lived exactly as they expected to live in the field—food, shelter, work, language, everything.

As a training aid, Yarborough had a portion of a Vietnamese guerrilla village constructed at Fort Bragg, complete with artifacts, livestock, and escape tunnels. On one of his later trips to Vietnam, Yarborough was both amused and gratified to find a replica of his replica village being used by the Vietnamese army at their Infantry Training Center.

Bill Yarborough's devotion to intense Special Forces preparation also included uncommon (for the Army) attention to specialized personal equipment, such as clothing, medical kits, and rations. Predictably, the "big" Army monolith had a hard time handling this.

Bill Yarborough takes the story from here:

I have always felt that equipment for a Special Forces soldier was primarily for the purpose of keeping him alive and it had little to do with weaponry. The health of the soldier was what counted, and we could best take care of this by making sure he had the best clothing, field medical gear, and rations. As a matter of fact, I felt that if the American had a superior weapon when he was out among indigenous forces who had to make do with something more basic, his own credibility suffered. I was not convinced, for instance, that the M-16 should be a Special Forces weapon; a survival weapon was more the kind of thing an SF soldier wanted. Or else,

*if he didn't have the right weapon for particular conditions, he'd take it
from the enemy or improvise.*

To this end, the training system at Fort Bragg included an extraordinarily
wide variety of weapons collected from worldwide sources. A Special Forces
soldier was expected to be familiar with all of them and be able to assemble and use them.

I didn't see the Special Forces soldier as a direct combat instrument. I saw
him as a catalyst who could gather around him those whom he could then
train and lend help to lead, and what weapon he carried was secondary.

So I put an enormous amount of time in personal equipment and special uniforms, even though such things were not looked on kindly by the
Quartermaster Corps and others, who looked at such views as overly ro-
mantic, and that in the Army, the essential thing is to give a soldier a good
weapon, enough ammunition, clothes on his back, shoes on his feet, and
transportation.

In 1961, I went to the Quartermaster Depot at Natick, Massachusetts,
to see what kind of tropical gear we had in stock for the guys who were
going to Southeast Asia. When I got there, I was in for a shock. They didn't
have anything suitable for jungle action. All the World War II experience
fighting in the jungle and the tropics was apparently down the drain.

I did find in the Quartermaster Museum what they called "tropical fatigues." But these had the same imagination as ordinary dung shovelers' fatigues. No utility whatever. There was a shirt and pants. The shirt had two
small breast pockets and no lower pockets. The pants had ordinary pockets, no cargo pockets. The cloth, though, was okay. It was the kind of cloth
that was close-woven enough to make it impervious to mosquito bites.

So I said, "Well, let's see. The cloth is good. We can start with that." And
I went from there. "Send me one of those down," I told them, "and we'll doctor it up a bit and see what we can do about making it a little more worthy for combat." So I took what they were calling "tropical fatigues" and put
cargo pockets on the trousers and two large pockets with bellows pleats on
the shirt. I angled the upper pockets on the shirt to allow easier access
when web equipment was worn, added epaulets, and also buttoned tabs at
the waist to allow the blouse to be gathered. The sleeves were designed to
be rolled up, if there were no mosquitoes around and weather permitted.

Little by little, with our help, the Quartermaster had a jungle uniform for
Vietnam—even though they never admitted they had a requirement for one.

Yet making it happen was a hard thing. The paperwork alone for the issue of the jungle uniform weighed many pounds. And with the first batch of uniforms came orders that they would only be worn in the field, and only by Special Forces.

That of course changed.

It was most fortunate for the United States Army, he concludes with masterful understatement, *that when U.S. troops were eventually sent to Vietnam in huge numbers, the tropical field uniform we designed for Special Forces was available for general use.*

Meanwhile, as Bill Yarborough was forging his new breed of soldier, the "big" Army continued on its more traditional paths, casting an ever-colder eye on the oddball operation in North Carolina, with its presidential favor, its substantial funding ("What they get, I lose"—the military has always operated in a zero-sum mode), and its license to raid the best units for their best men—especially their best NCOs—and "take them out of the Army," as one four-star general put it.

Generals, as generals will, began to murmur among themselves against the Green Beret upstarts and Bill Yarborough's "private army." The talk never became public, but a consensus was building in favor of the tried and true: "They've been feeding soldiers Laotian food down there at Fort Bragg. What the hell for? Firepower wins wars. Not lousy food." Or more generally: "They're going their own way down there. They don't respect the rules. They do things their way and not the Army way."

Some of these charges were not without substance. Though Yarborough never actually broke regulations, he bent them; and where there were holes, he slipped through them. A strict interpretation of regulations would not have been kind to him.

In his defense, he was never dishonest. When you have to improvise, you almost inevitably find yourself slipping between rules. In fact, it's hard to imagine how else to build an organization the rules never foresaw.

The negative currents came to a head soon after John Kennedy's assassination. General H. K. Johnson, the Army's very conventional-minded new chief of staff (he took over from General Maxwell Taylor when Taylor became ambassador to South Vietnam), was one of those generals who simply did not understand the new breed of soldier. He was terribly bothered by what Yarborough was doing. He was just getting away with too much.

Johnson's solution: He had to show Bill Yarborough who was the boss.

The Army had several layers between Yarborough and the President. In Johnson's view, Yarborough had ignored them.

Johnson was, in fact, a good and honorable man, and a hero—he'd been a Japanese prisoner during World War II. Before he moved, he visited Yarborough's operation—and he left very impressed. "I'll tell you," Johnson told another general friend, "he's put together a heck of a fighting team."

Even so, Yarborough had to go. And besides, he had been on the job for four years. It was time to move on.

By then, Yarborough had gotten his second star, as major general, and he was sent to Korea, where he represented the UN command as the Senior Member of the Military Armistice Commission at Panmunjon. There he dealt with the North Korean and Chinese negotiators in a way that only his experience in Special Forces could have prepared him for. The job called not only for negotiating skills, but also for PSYOPs and propaganda skills. Most observers called him the toughest negotiator the Communists faced at Panmunjon.

From Korea, he served at the Pentagon, where his most important job was to run Army Intelligence (his official title was Assistant Chief of Staff for Intelligence). He was later (in 1966) promoted to Lieutenant General and given command of I Corps Group in Korea, and then in 1969 he moved on to Hawaii as Chief of Staff and Deputy Commander-in-Chief of U.S. Army, Pacific. He retired in 1971, after thirty-six years of active service.

DURING Bill Yarborough's tenure as commander of Special Forces, his Green Berets not only carried out their mission in Southeast Asia but were also active in a number of other parts of the world.

From a base in Panama, several teams were sent to the countries of Central and South America, always at the invitation of those countries. In Colombia, for example, ten years of insurgency, called "La Violencia," had yielded something like 300,000 deaths. Green Berets and Colombian security officials worked together to produce the first comprehensive plan—based on civic action to help the local economy, health, and education—to deal with the terror. Though Colombia was to suffer from later terrors, La Violencia ended.

Green Berets in arctic gear worked their way by dogsled, snow weasel, and airplane around the northernmost perimeter of the United States, bringing medical and dental care and planning skills.

Other Green Beret teams worked in the Pacific on islands of the

American Trust Territories, building roads, schoolhouses, and recreational facilities. Others worked in the Philippines. Still others worked in Ethiopia and Congo (later Zaire, later Congo again).

When Bill Yarborough took command of Special Forces in 1961, he presided over four years of metamorphosis and explosive growth, and left as a major general. No matter how often and how badly he'd ruffled the feathers of his superiors fighting for his beloved Green Berets, his career had prospered.

DURING those four years of ferment, a great many warriors joined the now-transformed U.S. Special Forces. One of them was a young captain named Carl Stiner. It is now time for his story.

IV

COUNTRY
CARL

C arl Stiner grew up on a hundred-acre farm in rural northeast Tennessee, eight miles from the nearest town, La Follette. In the 1930s and '40s, the divide between town and country in that part of the world was vast. The main roads were paved; the rest were dirt or gravel. There were occasional trips to town, but people still mostly shopped in country stores. There were few cars, and electricity was scarce, finally reaching the Stiner farm in 1948. People made their own entertainment. For boys, most of that was outdoors—hunting or hiking in the nearby Cumberland Mountains, and swimming or fishing in Norris Lake, the big TVA project built in 1936.

It was a God- and country loving community. Everybody went to (mostly) Baptist churches on Sunday, and every able-bodied young man served his country.

A bus line ran twice a day between La Follette and nearby Middlesboro, Kentucky. Stiner still has vivid memories of looking out across the fields at age six or seven and watching older boys walk toward the highway to catch the bus to the induction center in La Follette during World War II. Whether they'd been drafted or volunteered, they all went. Later, he listened with respect as the returning boys, now men, recounted their combat experiences—the dread, discomfort, and pain, but the fun, too, and the joy of parades through newly liberated towns. The sacrifices had a purpose that even a ten-year-old could recognize.

When the time came, he knew he owed his country no less service than these men had given.*

Like most folks in rural Appalachia, the Stiner family's roots in America went far back.

The Steiner (the original spelling) family came to this country from Germany around 1710. Five Steiner brothers settled in Pennsylvania, then Steiners moved to Virginia and North Carolina. In 1820, Henry Stiner (the spelling had simplified by then) crossed over into East Tennessee, looking for land. He found what he was looking for at the Great Bend of the Powell River. The soil along the river was rich, the woods were full of deer, the river was abundant with fish, and only four other families were living nearby. Henry purchased 1,000 acres and then went back to North Carolina to collect his family. Several other families returned with them to the Powell River Valley. By 1889, the settlement had three stores, a steam sawmill, and a gristmill; living there were twenty-seven families, including more than a hundred children; there were thirty-five dogs and sixty-five horses.

Later, in 1936, the rising of Norris Lake displaced the community at the Great Bend of Powell River. Among those forced to move were Emit Stiner and his family. Emit was Carl's father.

Carl Stiner remembers his family this way:

Starting in 1936, my father worked as a diamond drill operator and powder man for the Tennessee Valley Authority, constructing Norris Dam as well as some of the other TVA dams that were built in the thirties and forties. He drilled foundations for the dams and set the charges for blasting out rock or spillways. By the time the war started, he already had several children, which meant he was not drafted, but was instead taken into service for the construction of the Oak Ridge nuclear plant (a few miles from La Follette).

When he was not building dams and nuclear plants, my father farmed. But during the war, Oak Ridge took precedence.

The plant was started in 1942 (though its existence was not officially known until President Truman announced production of the atomic bomb

---

*Because of his background, some of his Army friends later came to call him "Country Carl": a friendly nickname, not a derisive one. Stiner has always loved his origins, and anyone mistaking Stiner for a rube is likely to discover his own mistake with rich embarrassment.

in August 1945). It was a crash program, and security was very tight. The facility was protected by a high Cyclone fence, armed security guards patrolled on horses, and construction workers had to live like army forces in a barracks on the plant complex (where they were often kept busy seven days a week). But occasionally my father could get loose and come home on the weekends. When he was away, my mother, Hassie Stiner, supervised the farm and took care of the family.

I was the oldest of five—three other brothers and a sister. And my paternal grandparents also lived with us.

We all worked hard. Counting leased land, we farmed about two hundred acres, raising tobacco, grain crops, and cattle—and that was before tractors. Horses and mules did that job. About the time one of the boys turned six, he went to the fields to work; and during the growing season (when we weren't at school) we worked sunup to sundown, weather permitting, six days a week. Even if it rained, there was something to do, like pitching hay, or grinding feed for the cattle.

It was hard, but our life was not harsh. There was time off on Sunday for church, friends, and play. Since there was only one car per family, which wasn't used much for recreation, our friends would congregate at a common place, which was as likely as not our farm. Fifteen or twenty boys might gather there on Sunday afternoons for ball games or boxing.

The boys liked our farm because of its central location, its large level field for our ball games; and there was plenty of livestock, in case we decided to do a little rodeoing (but never when my dad was around, because he didn't like you messing with the livestock). Sometimes we ended the day by choosing sides and fighting a corncob battle among the barns. One of these could last for a couple of hours. Getting hit on the side of the head with a wet corncob is an experience that's not easy to forget.

There was also plenty to enjoy up in the mountains (they call it hiking these days; we called it climbing)—cave formations, waterfalls, spectacular views; and the copperheads were an ever-present but exciting challenge. Nearby Norris Lake always beckoned for swimming, boating, and fishing. It was a beautiful lake, nestled in the mountains, narrow, deep, and huge, with lots of jags and branches running up into the hollows—more than eight hundred miles of shoreline. We'd go fishing on a Friday or Saturday night, build a big fire, and sit there and fish until the next day. In season we went hunting.

My dad was a superb hunter, and he always owned a pair of splendid bird dogs. From the time I was old enough to recognize what a shotgun was for, I wanted to go with him. He started letting me do it about the time I started to help him work the farm. Not that I was old enough or big enough to carry a gun or shoot. But I could stalk thickets and brush piles, and flush birds out; and I could learn weapon safety from him, as well as all his hunting tricks.

I was thirteen when I was given my first shotgun. It was a single shot, and I couldn't load it until a dog was actually pointing. That way I'd have a chance at hitting the bird, but wasn't otherwise dangerous. If I missed the bird, my dad still had time to shoot it himself.

When I was older and had learned everything he felt I needed to know about hunting, I was allowed out on my own. In high school, a bunch of my friends and I would always go out on Thanksgiving Day, rain or shine, for our annual quail hunt (for safety purposes, there were never more than four in a single hunting party). We'd be out all day, without stopping to eat. And then our mothers would put out the big turkey meal in the evening.

It was a great place to be young. We found adventure in everything we did. If it wasn't there already, we made it that way. We went out and found things to do that gave us enjoyment, and learned to see the good and the purpose in whatever we were doing—even the heavy, manual farm labor. This meant it was pretty hard to be bored and frustrated.

I always enjoyed what I was doing and took a lot of satisfaction from it. And this has stayed with me. I live and farm there still. Something just clicked in me, I guess. I left just after college, and spent most of my life away. But I had to go home and make whatever contribution I could for what my community had given me in my younger days.

Looking back on those days, I feel very fortunate to have been reared in a home where discipline, love, respect, and adherence to principles were the standards by which we were raised.

The most powerful influence on me, without a doubt, was my father. He was tough—hard as the concrete he used to work—but fair, and expected every person to pull his own weight. He was a man of high principles, and required us kids to conform to them. Yet he was not rigid. He cared deeply for everyone in his family, and wanted us all to be (in the words of the old Army ad line) "all we could be." He would have made a good first sergeant.

It's worth mentioning some of his principles that have stayed with me and that I have tried to apply in my own life:

- Always respect other people, unless they give you reason not to.
- Don't run with sheep-killing dogs, unless you are willing to suffer the consequences of being caught up with them.
- Anything that is worth doing is worth doing right. Nothing good ever comes without hard work.
- Don't ever accept less of yourself than you are capable of.
- You've got to set the example for anybody who works for you. Don't expect them to do anything you wouldn't do first. (For us kids, he expected us to do more work than any man he could hire.)
- Look beyond the end of your nose, and work toward what you want to become.

My father had few illusions. He never wanted us to follow in his footsteps and bend our backs to a lifetime of brutally tough construction and endless farm work. He understood what education would give us (though he himself only got through eighth grade). The older we grew, the harder he and my mother pressed us to get the best education we could. "You don't want to do what I'm doing for the rest of your life," he kept telling us. "Your back won't hold out forever, and you will never be able to give your children what they need to prepare them to support their families." I will never forget his charge when he and my mom dropped me off at college (it was my first time there; I'd never visited the place before I was accepted). He said: "Boy, get an education, or don't come back."

His advice bore fruit. All but one of the children ended up with college degrees, and most went on for advanced degrees.*

There was another big education motivator in those days. Before the war, college was not in the cards for most young men from Appalachian Tennessee. But the postwar period saw GI Bill–trained doctors, lawyers, and other professionals bringing their expertise back to our Eastern Tennessee communities, and this brought us all long-term benefits. Those who didn't seek college were still able to take advantage of the technical skills and

---

*My brother Tom served in the army for twenty-nine years, retiring as a colonel. He was elected County Executive six years ago, and still serves in that position. A second brother, Glen, died at age forty-one. My third brother, Emory, is an executive with Burlington Industries. My sister, JoAnn, the youngest, is a registered nurse.

training opportunities they had gained in the army and other armed services to become skilled tradespeople—electricians, mechanics, plumbers, and the like.

It was amazing to see how all this skill and expertise began to grow our community. And it wasn't hard to apply these lessons to ourselves. So my objective was to go directly into college after high school. I applied to two or three, and all of them accepted me.

In those days, we didn't have high school counselors to steer us, and in any case, I didn't know much except agriculture. At the same time I was strongly aware of the obligation to serve my country after college (and felt it would be better to go in as a commissioned officer). For those reasons I elected to go to Tennessee Polytechnic Institute, called Tennessee Tech, which was the only one of the three colleges I applied to that offered both a degree in agriculture and an ROTC program. Tennessee Tech was in Cookeville, Tennessee, eighty-two miles north of Nashville.

Though Tech offered only Army ROTC, that was not a problem for me, since I never considered another service. I guess it was partly because of the influence of the boys I saw going off to the Army and fighting the war, and partly because I grew up outdoors in the country with lots of friends. The Army offered a continuation of that life. And truth was, I didn't know that much about the other services.

On my graduation day, June 30, 1958, I was commissioned a second lieutenant in the infantry. This was a reserve commission; I was offered a regular army commission two years later. Though my mom and two of my brothers attended the graduation and commissioning ceremonies, there was no time for celebration, because I had to report for active duty the same day. I set out within the hour for Fort Benning (near Columbus, in southwestern Georgia), and drove without stopping, so I could report in before midnight without being AWOL.

Fort Benning is a vast military base, primarily infantry—and called "The Home of the Infantry." Housed there are the Infantry School, the Airborne School, the Ranger School, the basic and the advanced officer courses, as well as officer candidate school. Many combat brigades were stationed at Benning, as was the 10th Mountain Division, which had just returned from Germany. I was initially assigned there as an assistant platoon leader.

My first duties were as "pit" officer (running the targets up and down) for a known-distance rifle range, and officer in charge of a 106mm recoilless rifle range. And at least two afternoons a week the officers taught general education subjects to the NCOs to help them get their high school GEDs.

I loved the Army from day one—even though my jobs then weren't especially challenging, and I hardly had much responsibility. I liked everything about it: the people, the structured environment, the training, the responsibility, and the opportunity for growth by using my own talents, capabilities, and initiative.

After approximately six months, I took the Basic Officers Course, followed by Jump School and Ranger School. All were completed within eighteen months.

The Basic Course took up where the ROTC program left off. We mastered more advanced skills and developed technical competence in leadership, weapons, and tactical subjects that qualified us to lead an infantry platoon in combat operations. For example, we studied map reading in much greater detail than we had in ROTC; we learned how to effectively employ every weapon that was organic to a platoon; we learned patrolling and tactics at the platoon level, integration of fires, and how infantry should function with armor.

My other big learning experience in those early days at Fort Benning was meeting Sue, who became my wife.

Understand that just as Fort Benning is called the Home of the Infantry, Columbus is known as the mother-in-law of the infantry, because so many Columbus girls marry the new second lieutenants that come into town. It certainly turned out that way for me.

When I drove into Fort Benning on that Friday night after I graduated from college, it was 10:00 P.M. I signed in at Division Headquarters, was assigned a BOQ room, and was instructed to return by 9:00 A.M. Monday.

I had no idea what to do for the rest of the weekend, and I had never been to Fort Benning.

The next morning, as I was looking for a place to eat, I ran into First Lieutenant Jim Smith, who was also living in the BOQ and who knew a good place to go for breakfast—if I had a set of wheels (he had wrecked his car). What we could do, he said, was go eat breakfast, and then in the afternoon drive over to the officers' club, where his girlfriend and one of her friends were waiting for him, and we could all go out together.

That sounded pretty good to me. So we did that. The friend turned out to be Sue.

Jim Smith's girlfriend, Ann Scott, met us at the Officers' Club swimming pool. After I was introduced, Ann pointed to her friend, Sue, who was in the swimming pool, and called out to her to come over. After the introductions, the next order of business was the evening's activities. "Wouldn't you all like to go to dinner with us tonight?" Jim asked Sue and me.

In view of Sue's good looks and her bright and pleasant personality, I certainly welcomed the opportunity, but I knew that his motivation was my means of transportation. I think Sue might have been a little leery, but we were both caught in a bind with the two of them standing there looking so plaintively at us. Sue and I sort of shrugged and said okay, and then we all went to dinner that night at the Patton House on Fort Benning.

Over dinner, I learned that Sue was nineteen, employed as a secretary to the president and vice president of Burnham Van Service, and enrolled in night classes at the Columbus Center of the University of Georgia. It also turned out she was the reigning "Miss Georgia Air Reserve" (somebody else had obviously thought she was as good-looking as I did).

In her family were five sisters and a brother (almost the exact reverse of mine). Her brother, the oldest of the children, had fought in World War II and then become a lineman with the Georgia Power Company, where he was tragically electrocuted. Her dad worked for Bibb Manufacturing Company (a textile mill in Columbus), and her mother kept the home.

From the beginning, I liked Sue a lot, and as I got to know her family, I liked them also. I'm not so sure that she thought as much of me as I did of her, but we started dating occasionally, and I continued to do my thing, soldiering as a young lieutenant.

Meanwhile, I became friends with a service station owner named Kirby Smith, who also owned a pair of modified stock cars. Although he did not drive himself, Kirby sponsored his mechanic in stock car racing. I liked racing and would go with them on the weekends, and after a time I started driving myself. We would usually go to Valdosta, Georgia, and race there on a Friday night, then on to Montgomery, Alabama, and race Saturday night, then to Atlanta for Sunday night racing, and then back to Columbus in time for me to stand reveille on Monday morning.

I liked the racing—the challenge, the competition, the risk, and living on the edge. I guess I have always been that way—and the Army has afforded similar satisfaction in most of my assignments.

Sue and I dated for eighteen months, and in August 1959, we became engaged. Three months later, we were married in her church, the Porter

Memorial Baptist Church in Columbus, Georgia. Proposing to Sue, though, put an end to my racing career. When I popped the question, she gave me an ultimatum. "It's either your racing, or me," she said. "You make the choice." It didn't take me long to sort out my priorities.

As I look back over the forty-one years of our marriage, Sue has proved the best companion and wife any man could ask for—my closest friend and toughest critic. She has been a role-model mother, raising two outstanding daughters, while taking care of the family and wifely responsibilities in every command I held. Marrying her was the soundest decision I ever made.

JUMPING OUT OF AIRPLANES

Clancy: Jump and Ranger Schools came after the Basic Course. For Stiner, Jump School came almost immediately. He graduated from the Basic Course on Friday, had Saturday off, reported to Jump School on Sunday, and started training on Monday morning.

Parachute and Ranger training are tough! Few people enjoy jumping out of airplanes. The risk is always there, rushing up at you; parachutes don't always open; and even when they do open correctly, bones can break when a trooper lands.

However, it's also not much fun to spend a couple of hard weeks in a swamp in summer or in the mountains in winter, with little or no sleep, having to live off the land when food is not available while conducting training as stressful and physically demanding as real combat. Ranger experience puts a soldier up against the absolute limits of mind and body.

On the other hand, soldiers who successfully make it through these ordeals have a right to feel good about themselves. The best soldiers are usually Airborne- and Ranger-qualified; and Airborne or Ranger units are usually thought of as elite.

All of this notwithstanding, in the 1960s every officer had to go through either Jump or Ranger School, and officers who expected to be assigned to a combat unit, whether infantry, armor, or artillery, had to go through both. The Army expected officers to be versatile. It wasn't enough to serve effectively in their own technical specialties; officers had to have all the skills necessary to lead a unit in combat, and the broader perspective that gave. Even officers who weren't in combat branches, such as quartermaster, ordnance, or signal, were expected to handle specialized combat-oriented tasks and challenges.

Every officer served at least two years in a combat unit before going to the branch in which he was commissioned, and to the basic officer qualification course in that branch. For those in noncombat branches, this was not only valuable experience in itself, but helped them later in serving and supporting the combat units.

This is no longer the practice in the Army, partly because the shortage of officers has meant that the services can no longer afford the luxury, and partly because of the way the Army has evolved over time. Now the Army is run the way business is, where most people are specialists. Forty years ago, everyone outside of the technical branches was seen as a generalist. The perception was that it didn't matter who you were on the battlefield, you were a better leader if you had a core of basic officer skills that enabled you to take care of your men under all circumstances.

In most ways, today's Army is a better-prepared and more effective force than the Army of forty years ago, but the discontinuation of combat unit training and experience for all officers is a real loss.

THE objective of Jump School has always been to teach a soldier how to put on his parachute and equipment properly, then how to exit an airplane, descend, and land safely. Mental alertness, confidence, and the ability to react automatically to just about anything that might happen during a jump are critical.

The course normally took four weeks, but the Army was testing to see if compression could save training time and money without affecting performance, so for the 1958 class of infantry lieutenants, the course was compressed to three weeks. The instructors were all handpicked NCOs, all master jumpers—and they were professional and tough.

The program of instruction consisted of a ground week, tower week, and jump week—all punctuated with an extensive physical training program and a very stringent personal inspection each morning, especially during the first two weeks.

Following the in-ranks inspection by the Black Hats (the Airborne cadre), daily training started with a one-hour session of rigorous physical training: push-ups, squat jumps, sit-ups, pull-ups, deep knee bends, squat thrusts, and a three-mile run in combat boots. The Black Hats' favorite technique for teaching alertness was to bark: "Hit it!" This could be directed at an individual or at the whole group. The instant anyone heard the words, he immediately had to hop up about six inches off the ground and go into the correct position for exiting an aircraft—that is, chin on chest, forearms and fingers extended as if grasping the reserve parachute, elbows held tight to the sides, and counting: "one thousand, two thousand, three thousand, four thousand," representing the seconds it takes a parachute to open. Once in the exit position, he'd start jumping up and down with knees bent and toes pointed to the ground. Anyone who was slow to react and/or did not do any of this correctly could expect to hear "Give me twenty," or however many push-ups the Black Hat wanted to lay on.

Their favored "weapon" for ensuring conformity and mental alertness was push-ups or squat jumps for every infraction or mistake in training—no matter who committed it—so on any given day, a trainee could find himself doing two hundred or more extra push ups.

During the first week, Stiner and the others were taught how to perform parachute landing falls from any direction (left front, right front, left side, right side, left rear, right rear). They started by standing on the ground in the sawdust pit and hopping up and then falling in whichever direction they were told to. After they'd mastered this skill from the ground—maybe a hundred or more parachute landing falls (PLFs)—they moved up to a PLF platform, a wooden structure five feet off the ground. They continued falling from there until they were proficient in every kind of PLF.

Each time anyone made a PLF, he had to simulate a "prepared to land" position—that is, he'd reach up and pull down on the two front risers of his (simulated) parachute, with elbows tight to the side, chin tucked to the chest, knees slightly bent, feet and knees held tightly together with toes slightly pointed toward the ground. When he touched the ground, he'd roll in the direction that would most cushion his fall.

After PLFs, they advanced to the "swing landing fall trainer," a circular steel frame suspended by a cable that hangs over a six-foot-high platform. The student, wearing a parachute harness, attached his risers to this frame, then stepped off the platform and began to swing free. The instructor on the ground controlled the swing and determined when and how the student would hit the ground. As often as not, it was when he was in the most awkward position for landing. This device realistically replicated the kinds of falls a jumper was likely to make under actual conditions. Since most injuries occur upon landing, it was vital for the student to master them all.

During the second week, they worked on the thirty-four-foot tower, which provided a rough likeness of the sensation of jumping out of an airplane, except there was no 125-knot wind blast. According to the experts, thirty-four feet is the optimum height for creating the greatest fear: Anyone who falls from that height without a parachute has a chance to survive. Above that height, it's all over anyhow.

On top of the tower was a boxlike structure replicating part of an airplane fuselage. A steel cable extended from inside this "fuselage" at a slight angle downward for approximately 150 feet, and then it was anchored about eight feet off the ground. The student hooked his risers to a pulley that rode on this cable. Upon the command "Stand in the door," the student took a position in the door. Upon the "Go" command, the student leapt up and out, and then immediately assumed a tight body position and began his count. By that time, he had fallen to the length of his risers, approximately eight feet, and could feel the jolt of the cable (in an actual jump he would have fallen approximately 200 to 250 feet by the time his parachute opened). When he felt the jolt, the jumper checked his (imaginary) canopy to make sure it was fully deployed, with no more than four broken suspension lines and no tears larger than his helmet. He did that by comparing his rate of fall with that of the other jumpers in the air; if he was falling faster than they were, he considered activating his reserve parachute.

During descent, the jumper kept a sharp lookout in order to avoid other jumpers, and then began his preparations for landing when he was approximately fifty to a hundred feet above the ground. By this time, he had reached the end of the cable. Once there, he was critiqued by a Black Hat and told to recover and jump again. About fifteen to twenty exits were required from the thirty-four-foot tower before a trainee got a "good to go."

The last two days of the second week, Stiner and his comrades worked on the 250-foot towers. There, a trainee wore a special type of parachute, which was attached to a ring equal to the circumference of an actual parachute canopy. He was then pulled up to an extended arm on the tower. At the top, his parachute was released and he was allowed to float to the ground. He would then land as hard as if he'd jumped from an actual plane.

The third week was devoted to jumping. Also included were instructions on actions inside the aircraft, which were conducted in mock-ups. The Black Hats performed the duties of jumpmasters and would put everyone through the jump commands. These were: "Twenty minutes," meaning: "Do a preliminary check of your own equipment; helmet tight, etc." At ten minutes came "Get ready," meaning: "Unbuckle your seat belt and prepare to stand up." Next came "Outboard personnel, Stand up," meaning: "Jumpers seated closest to the skin of the aircraft stand first." Then "Inboard personnel, stand up," meaning: "All the other jumpers, stand up." Then "Hook up," meaning: "All jumpers hook their snap fastener." This was attached to the end of the static line, and hooked to the anchor line cable. Then "Check equipment," meaning: "Each jumper checks his own equipment, plus the static line of the jumper to his front." Then "Sound off for equipment check." The count started in the rear of the stick (the line of jumpers), with each sounding off loudly, "Okay," and slapping the buttocks of the man in front of him. The count was passed forward by every man in the stick. The last man to receive the count then signaled the jumpmaster, "All okay, jumpmaster." One minute out from the drop zone, the loadmasters (part of the plane's crew) opened the jump doors. The jumpmaster looked out to verify that they were in fact over the drop zone, then looked to the rear of the aircraft to verify that no following planes had dropped below the altitude where his paratroopers would be exiting. Once he had verified that it was safe to jump, he pointed to the first jumper and commanded: "Stand in the door." The jumper shuffled to the door, assumed an exit position, and watched for the green light. When it lit, the jumpmaster commanded, "Go," and slapped him on the buttocks. The jumper exited, and the stick followed at one-second intervals.

This procedure was followed before every jump, and it is still followed by airborne units today, no matter how experienced they are.

All jumps were made from C-119 aircraft (the old twin-tail flying boxcars), and the guys were ready "almost to jump without a parachute," Stiner observes, "to get relief from rolling around in that sawdust pit and doing push-ups all day.

"The first jump was the easiest," he continues, "at least for me. But that 125-knot blast of wind was something that none of us had experienced. On the ground, Black Hats with bullhorns were yelling at the students who weren't doing it right; they gave strong personal critiques of each landing.

"We jumped four times that week, all during daylight. The fifth jump was with equipment, which included our load-bearing equipment and M-1 rifle.

"Saturday was a big day. Graduation! Families and girlfriends were allowed to attend and to assist in pinning on our wings. Everyone in my group graduated, except a few who'd been injured. We all felt very proud and privileged to wear the jump wings.

"Some people claim to love jumping out of airplanes. That may be so. But not me. Though I spent most of my career in airborne units and made 189 jumps, practically all at night with combat equipment, I was never crazy about jumping out of airplanes. After I had gained the confidence afforded by Jumpmaster School, however, I got to where jumping didn't bother me.

"Airborne units are unique in the capability they provide—that is, 'forced entry' operations. It's not just the jumping, it's the type of people that comprise the ranks of airborne units which makes the assignment so special."

SWAMPS AND MOUNTAINS

Carl Stiner graduated from Jump School on Saturday and reported into Ranger School the next morning. That afternoon, he and his companions received orientations and drew equipment. They began training at daylight Monday morning.

Ranger School has two principal aims: to prepare small-unit leaders for the missions and situations they are likely to face in combat, and to teach skills that are necessary for survival in enemy-held territory. It is the most physically demanding school in the Army for non–Special Operations soldiers.

Though Ranger School is normally nine weeks long, for Stiner it lasted eight weeks—October to December 1958. (Nothing was deleted but the sleep.) It consisted of three phases: two weeks at Fort Benning, Georgia; three weeks in the Okefenokee Swamp at Eglin Air Force Base, Florida; and three weeks in the mountains at Dahlonega, Georgia.*

Carl Stiner continues:

ONCE a soldier has completed the Ranger Course, he knows down to the tips of his fingers what his capabilities and limitations are. He has not only mastered the skills required of a small-unit leader in combat, but he also has the confidence and skills necessary to survive there. I have always trusted a Ranger-qualified officer or NCO to lead patrols for me in combat or any other tough situation, because I knew he had the skills necessary to accomplish the mission and would "take care" of those entrusted to his leadership in the right way.

These experiences do not only apply to junior officers, they become the

---

*Over the years, Ranger School has changed to meet the needs and challenges of the times. Long before the Gulf War, a desert phase, conducted at Fort Bliss, Texas, was added to the program of instruction. It greatly benefited the young leaders who fought in Operation DESERT STORM.

essential underpinnings of competence through all the ranks and assignments of an Army career—particularly command. They give an understanding of a man's capabilities and limitations that comes in no other way, and they develop self-confidence in ways not otherwise possible.

You have to be made of the right stuff to do it successfully. In practice it means that you go day and night; you get very little sleep; you are exhausted; you may get shin splints; you're strung out; you are in swamps; you're in mountains; you're cold; you're wet; you might be exposed to frostbite or hypothermia; or else you're hot; you're thirsty; you learn to live off the land and eat what's available. You learn to depend on each other. Although each man is expected to master individual skills, and in all field operations you usually operate in squad- and platform-size units, you take care of each other. From day one you are assigned a "Ranger buddy." In other words, if your buddy should fall out, you are expected to carry him—or fall out trying.

Under these conditions, there's no place for the limp-wristed or faint of heart.

THE FORT BENNING PHASE   The basic objective of the Benning phase was to learn the fundamentals of patrolling: the essentials of planning; operations orders; selecting primary and alternate routes, assembly areas, rallying points, passage of lines, actions at the objectives; and above all the value of rehearsals. You did it over and over until you got it right.

The first two weeks were focused on heavy-duty physical training—log drills, endurance runs, hand-to-hand combat, the bayonet assault course, and the obstacle course. It was also during this phase that we were introduced to a new form of PT—"rope football." We played this in a sawdust pit of not more than sixty feet in diameter. The class was divided into two teams of about fifty men, who'd go down in a football stance facing each other about three feet apart. In between the teams was dropped a knotted ball of cable rope that weighed something like fifty pounds. The object of the game was to move the ball to the other side of the pit. Anything went. There were no time-outs, no fouls or penalties for unsportsmanlike conduct. You scratched, clawed, climbed over, or did whatever else you had to do to win. The penalty for losing was seventy-five or a hundred push-ups.

We also did a lot of rope work—learning the different knots and how to build different kinds of rope bridges—and we did a lot of rope climbing. There were two objectives here: to learn the different ways to climb a rope, and to build upper-body strength.

Another important element was advanced land navigation. Soldiers have to be expert navigators—to be able to get to where they are going when they are not familiar with the territory—and they have to do it quickly under the worst circumstances. Nowadays we have global positioning systems to make navigating easier, and these do give us an enormous advantage, but there is no substitute for a map in the hands of a good map reader and a compass in the hands of a good navigator. If you have these, and if all the electronic wizardry fails, you still have all you need to find out where you are and to keep you on course.

Also critical to the team is a good pace man, who keeps an accurate count of how much distance you have covered. He has to be able to consistently step a yard or meter with each normal step. Then he keeps count of the pace. One way to do it is by moving a small stone from one pocket to another every time he has gone a hundred paces. Another technique is to tie a knot in a string for each hundred paces. There are any number of techniques, of course, but the point is the same: You have to have a system to ensure that the count is not lost (or forgotten) should the patrol be ambushed.

Finally, we were taught every fundamental about patrolling: the different kinds of patrols (reconnaissance, combat, raids, ambushes, etc.), the organizations of each type of patrol, the patrol order, selecting routes, actions at danger areas, and action upon reaching the objective. During the Benning phase, we rehearsed many times over our patrolling techniques.

THE FLORIDA PHASE   We left Fort Benning early on a Saturday morning in October on buses headed to the Florida Ranger Camp on Eglin Air Force Base. Few of us remembered much about the trip, which took most of the day, because we slept as much as we could.

Near the Florida state line, a member of the Ranger cadre woke us up to put us in the right frame of mind. He read us a "general situation": "The United States is at war," he told us. "And we have entered a mythical country"—I've forgotten its name—"as a replacement unit." From here on out, everything was to be a tactical simulation of real war—*tactical* twenty-four hours each and every day.

When we reached our Florida destination, our accommodations were austere—tents that accommodated twenty-four men each, canvas cots, no floors, a World War II–type mess hall, a small arms room, and a small aid station manned by a single medic. This didn't bother me; it was obvious that we wouldn't be spending much time there (and this would be luxury compared with where we were going).

About half an hour after we arrived, we were given an alert order to be prepared to move out within two hours on our first reconnaissance patrol. Our mission: to reconnoiter a possible enemy missile site. When we moved out, we moved directly into the swamps into water up to our waists. We were there for the next three days and nights.

This turned out to be the norm for the entire training—constant patrolling, constant raids, constant ambushes . . . and always wet and cold. You don't normally think of Florida as cold. But in October, that's what it can get if you are constantly wet, even in Florida.

As a part of the Florida phase, we were given special instructions on "survival": how to catch and prepare food; what to eat and what not to eat (which wild plants and berries were safe, which weren't); and we were given chickens, rabbits, alligators, opossums, raccoons, and snakes that we had to prepare for some day's "feast."

We learned a lot about snakes. They were all over the place, particularly coral snakes and water moccasins. One day the cadre brought out what seemed to be a wagonload of snakes (nonpoisonous!) and passed them among us (we were sitting on logs). They started with one or two at a time, but that soon turned into armloads of six or eight. We got familiarized with snakes in a hurry.

Another challenge was the confidence course—an inverted crawl on ropes hanging forty feet above murky, over-our-heads water, with explosives in the water going off constantly. At some point on the rope, we'd be told to drop into the water and swim to dry land about a hundred feet away—with the explosives still going off.

During the three weeks, we only saw base camp, our tent, and the mess hall about four or five times. At other times we ate food provided by "partisans" (that is, if we linked up with them at the designated place and time—we didn't always do that); and it was usually live chickens, rabbits, or even a goat.

We didn't get much sleep either. I was one of the designated "sleep keepers." That meant I had to keep a record of whatever sleep I was able to get that was more than thirty minutes. As I recall, at the end of seventeen days, my records indicated it totalled eight hours and ten minutes.

I've always loved the outdoors. I really enjoy the wilderness and its challenges. So, acute discomforts aside—the constant wet and cold and lack of sleep—I really enjoyed the Florida phase. I had never been in a really big swamp, especially one as treacherous and challenging as the Okefenokee. The Yellow River runs right through it—very swift, deep, and dangerous. You can easily blunder into it, especially at night, without knowing it. That is, you can be wading up to your waist in standing swamp water, and then *bam,* you're in the river, swift, strong, and deep, cutting right through the still water. It's dangerous!

When the three weeks were over, most of us who'd started were still hanging in and looking forward to the next phase, though some had been eliminated—for attitude, lack of motivation, physical failure, or whatever; the rest of us never really knew why. You knew somebody'd been elimi-nated when you saw a student standing out at the end of Flight Strip Number 7, which was located near our base camp, with his bag packed, waiting for the plane from Fort Benning, which came about every three days. He stayed there by himself until the plane came. I can't imagine how humiliating this must have been. At least it would have been terrible for me.

THE MOUNTAIN PHASE   We came in from our last patrol in Florida at midafternoon on a Saturday, finished our patrol debriefings, and began to clean and turn in the weapons and equipment that would remain at the campsite. After a big meal in the mess hall we hit the sack somewhere around midnight—dry for a change—for much-needed sleep.

At about 0300 Sunday morning, the Ranger cadre came running through the camp yelling: "Formation in ten minutes. Fall out with all your gear, pre-pared to move out."

We jumped out of the sack (having slept in our fatigues), quickly put on our dry pair of boots, rolled up our sleeping bags (which stayed with the cot), put on our Ranger web gear (harness), and fell in at our appointed place in a company formation. The camp commander, a major, positioned himself before the formation and announced, "There has been a major enemy breakthrough in the northern part of the operational area."—north-ern Georgia—"You are to move out immediately as much-needed rein-forcements in that sector of the combat zone." Buses arrived ten minutes later, and we set out for northern Georgia.

I don't remember much about that trip, because we slept most of the way. But I do remember that at about noon the buses pulled into a Howard Johnson's restaurant somewhere in central Georgia (no doubt arrangements had been made in advance), and an announcement was made: "We will be here one hour. This is your last chance to eat before arriving at the front."

I will never forget the surprised look of the families there, obviously just out of church services, when we stormed into the place wearing our camouflage paint and fatigues. It did not take them long, though, to recognize who we were, especially when the Ranger lieutenant accompanying us announced, "Rangers, you have fifty minutes until you go back on the buses."

I don't know how it was possible to serve so many in such a short time, but the restaurant staff managed it, and we were all well fed.

Back on the buses and back to sleep again.

At about 1600 hours, the buses pulled off the highway where a gravel road ran off into the woods and several empty two-and-a-half ton trucks were parked. A Ranger captain was standing in the middle of the road. As soon as we'd dismounted and formed up in front of him, he advised that it was not safe to take the buses any farther because of enemy infiltration teams in the area. We would have to take the trucks. He also indicated that the beds of the trucks had been sandbagged and that we should be prepared for ambush. Since we didn't have any weapons, we were glad to see two armed guards with each truck. Even though we didn't have our individual weapons, we had rehearsed counterambush drills from a truck or convoy many times, so we knew what to do.

We had probably gone no more than five miles until we were ambushed by a platoon of dug-in "enemy." Of course, it was all explosives and blank fire, but they really shot us up good. We quickly dismounted and dived in a ditch alongside the road. When the smoke had cleared, we were assembled back on the road and told that our trucks had been destroyed and that we would have to run the rest of the way—about five miles and mostly uphill.

At the base camp (it was in a beautiful spot, as it happened), we were fed a great evening meal—all we could eat. Then we drew our weapons and individual equipment and squared away our sleeping tents. As in Florida, we wouldn't see much of them for the next three weeks.

The next morning started with rappelling instruction, which was conducted under Master Sergeant Stinchcomb, who knew more about rock climbing and rappelling, and about ropes and how to use them, than any man I have ever met.

First we learned how to tie every knot needed for Ranger-type operations. Then we trained in rappelling until we'd mastered all the rappelling techniques—first on the lower cliffs (thirty to fifty feet) and then on higher ones (sixty to eighty feet). Finally, we were required to rappel with our Ranger buddy hanging on our back.

After the rock work, there was instruction in the mountain adaptations to already learned skills, such as land navigation, wilderness survival, and operational survival.

Though the basic land navigation techniques still applied, keeping track of distances traveled in rugged mountainous terrain is more complex and challenging than on level ground. You can never be sure of the length of your pace, for example.

Then came instruction on wilderness survival. In the mountains, the snakes are different than the ones in Florida—copperheads and rattlesnakes rather than water moccasins and coral snakes. And in the mountains you don't find the same edible plants and berries that you do in the swamps.

We also got instruction on avoiding detection. We were taught to stay away from danger areas, such as roads and built-up areas (towns, houses, etc.), and how to cross danger areas (open fields and roads) without being observed.

We also patrolled, day and night, just as in Florida. But the rough terrain and heavy loads (like machine guns) some patrol members had to carry made a big difference, requiring more careful planning of patrol routes and more time for reaching the objective.

As was the case throughout the entire Ranger instruction program, every patrol had to be planned and rehearsed in every detail to ensure that it would go right, and every student had to know every detail of the plan. Although a patrol leader and assistant patrol leader were designated in advance, you never knew when you may be called on to be the patrol leader—most usually in the most demanding situations, such as the middle of a firefight. A member of the Ranger cadre (called a lane grader) accompanied every patrol. This was usually a first lieutenant or a senior NCO, but sometimes both, depending on the size of the patrol. Their job was to evaluate the performance of every member of the patrol, and to be present in case of an emergency or life-threatening situation.

Meanwhile, the aggressors (the bad guys) were all over the place, knew the terrain better than we did, and had co-opted most of the civilians that lived in the area, which meant we could not trust anyone.

The weather became a major factor in early December.

Our last patrol was to be a long-range combat patrol to simulate the "blowup" of the Toccoa Dam, which was about fifty or sixty miles from our base area. Before we left there'd been reports of bad weather coming in—all the more reason to go.

Our platoon-size patrol (about forty men) was infiltrated late one evening by helicopter to a landing zone about three miles south of the Toccoa River and thirty miles upstream from the dam. As we moved quickly to the river, night was falling and the temperature was dropping rapidly. Because of the cold, the patrol leader decided that we would construct and cross on a three-rope bridge, and that way keep dry.

Though the water was up to his neck in some places and running pretty fast, the designated swimmer waded to the other side without incident, dragging the main rope as he went. He attached it to a tree and came back for the two smaller ropes that would serve as the handrails. Once he had dragged these over, it did not take us long to make the bridge ready to go, and we began to cross.

Maybe ten people had made it to the other side when we were ambushed by a squad-sized enemy element from the far side of the river (no doubt the aggressor had been given the location of our crossing site). This was the most vulnerable position we could possibly have been in. We had very little ability to defend ourselves.

The only safe thing the patrol leader could do was order everybody into the water and have them quickly wade to the other side.

The firefight didn't last long, but most of us were wet by then, and it was snowing—really coming down. As the patrol regrouped and we headed out on our route, the wind picked up, the temperature dropped even more, and somewhere around midnight, our clothing began to freeze. At this point, the Ranger lane grader (a staff sergeant) told the patrol leader to start running the patrol in order to minimize the possibility of hypothermia—a wise decision!

An hour or so later, the snow was maybe four inches deep, and a few of the students began to lose it, my buddy among them. He dropped down in the snow and started begging for someone to knock his brains out with an entrenching tool. He was a strong, determined officer, and I knew he didn't mean what he was saying. And besides, we weren't even carrying entrenching tools.

I had a notion to try to carry him, but I instantly realized that wouldn't work, because I already had the .30-caliber machine gun to lug. I slapped him to try to bring him back to his senses, and he came out of it enough to raise himself to his knees. But that wasn't enough. The patrol was running off and leaving us. I knew I had to get him moving somehow before they got too far ahead of us, so I gave him a good kick in the rear. He got up, staggered, mumbled something, started trotting, and then started running again. I kept him in front of me, prodding him, until daybreak, when he snapped out of it. Though he went down two or three more times, the same treatment worked each time. (Later he had no recollection of that night.)

Other students had similar problems, but the other buddies did what they had to do to keep going.

At daylight, it was still snowing hard, the ceiling was down to the treetops, and most of our compasses were too fogged up to read. Fortunately, enough of them worked to keep us on course.

All that day we trudged through the mountains, still on course. By midafternoon the snow had drifted so deep that the patrol had to rotate its strongest members to the "point man" position to break the trail.

At nightfall, we were supposed to rendezvous with a partisan band to get our supply of food. We arrived at the rendezvous point, set up security, and waited for an hour; but no partisans came, and of course there was no food.

At that point, the lane grader decided that since we were so deep in the enemy's rear and the weather was so bad, it might be safe enough to begin moving on roads. The road he brought us to was a welcome sight, and it was obvious that no one had traveled it since the snow had begun. So we were able to move more rapidly, to make up for lost time.

Around midnight I began to have problems of my own. I didn't exactly lose it, because I kept moving ahead—I kept walking and walking. But as I trudged along, I had no idea who I was or where I was going. I just knew I had to keep going, and stay with the other guys. I guess I was in this delirious state for three to four hours.

Come daylight, we left the road and continued moving about 500 yards into the woods and parallel to the road. But when night fell, we were back on the road again. Though the snow had stopped, what was on the ground was knee deep; and it was *cold*—I'd guess it was near zero. We hadn't eaten since we'd launched a couple of days back, and people were getting pretty hungry.

About 2200 hours, we came upon a farmhouse and heard some hogs. The word came back asking if anyone knew how to kill and dress a pig. "I can," I said, and went forward. But when I saw that the "pig" weighed about two hundred pounds, I knew I would have to have some help—three more men. One guy had to grab him by the snout to keep him from squealing. One guy had to grab him by the ears to steady his head. And one guy had to grab him by the tail and hold on, to keep him from swishing his body around and throwing the rest of us all over the hog lot.

Though no one else in the patrol had any experience with hogs, everyone was so hungry it didn't take long to scare up the three volunteers. I appointed each to his duties (snout man, ears man, and tail man), gave them a quick briefing about what to do (we all had to act simultaneously), and we entered the hog lot. This was going to be a challenge, I knew, but we had to accomplish the mission if we wanted to eat.

Meanwhile, the patrol leader went about establishing a security perimeter around the farmhouse.

We climbed over the fence into the hog lot, skirted another hog house, which contained a pair of hogs that were bigger than the one we'd picked, and jumped on our hog. At that point, the ears man did his part right and hung on; but the snout and tail men didn't do so well, and the hog started squealing and thrashing about. The only thing I could do was jump on him myself and stick him in the throat. He and I rolled around in the hog manure (which was not all frozen) for a couple of minutes, but after a time the hog went limp. Then I quickly gutted and quartered him so we could carry our dinner more easily.

Meanwhile, all this commotion had brought the farmer running out onto his snow-covered porch, but a machine gun opened up (not to hurt him, but to catch his attention), and he dropped flat on his back and did a "crab walk" back inside the house. I felt kind of bad taking his hog, but learned later that the Army had an agreement with the farmers to reimburse them for anything the Ranger students took for food.

Once I had the hog quartered, we grabbed our food and headed deep into the woods, then built a fire and had roasted pig. A welcome feast!

We continued on the rest of the night and the next day.

At about 2200 hours that night, we arrived at our attack position, about a mile from the Toccoa Dam. A reconnaissance patrol sent out to scout for enemy positions returned around midnight and reported that an enemy position with a campfire was about 100 meters north of the dam and close to our planned route. For that reason, the patrol leader decided to change our route and send out a six-man patrol to neutralize the enemy position (I was on that team). We would do that when the rest of the patrol was in place to attack the dam.

H-hour was to be 0500 hours. After the attack, we were supposed to make it to a clearing about a mile away, and at 0600 hours, helicopters would extract us from there.

The entire patrol set out from the attack position at about 0300 hours—moving very cautiously. An hour later, my team split off and headed for the enemy position north of the dam. As we approached it, we could see the fire and at least two aggressor guards near the ditch line on the far side of the road. They were in a cut, and the bank behind them was about ten feet high. We crossed the road and circled behind them, using the bank as cover, then crawled the last couple hundred yards until we were directly above them.

At 0555 hours, the message came over the radio that the rest of the patrol was in position to launch the attack. Moments later, four of us jumped off the bank, right on top of the bad guys, and slammed them to the ground. Before they knew what happened, we had them bound and gagged.

About that time, we heard the rest of the patrol launch the attack on the dam—although there wasn't much shooting, maybe ten rounds or less. This sounded a little strange (we normally put out a great volume of fire), but we had been using our weapons as pikes in order to climb the steep, ice-frozen slopes, and the end of most of our rifle barrels had been too plugged with ice to fire.

Meanwhile I took advantage of the fire the bad guys had built and turned my back to it. I stood that way for what couldn't have been more than a couple of minutes—but that was long enough for me to doze off and fall over backwards into the fire, igniting my field jacket. Thank goodness for the snow. Needless to say, I woke up in a hurry, and managed to roll over and put it out—though the entire back of my jacket was burned out.

I didn't have much time to reflect on that. It would soon be daylight, and we had to get over to our pickup zone before dawn.

We began to run.

By then the weather had begun to clear, and although the weather had delayed the completion of our mission a couple of days, the helicopters were coming for us. And as we approached the clearing, we could hear the roar as they approached. Then snow was blowing everywhere as they set down—the most beautiful sight I had seen in seven weeks.

WE flew back to the Ranger Base Camp at Dahlonega, where we were met by quite a reception. The Ranger department commander, a colonel, was there, along with a team of doctors and a chaplain. The docs checked us all, but found nothing major (there was a little frostbite—ears, fingers, and toes). Next came a hot meal—all we could eat. Then we were put on the buses and sent back to Fort Benning.

On the way back, I learned from one of the Ranger instructors that the two men we had pounced on by the fire had actually been civilian members of the waterworks fixing a busted water main. They had not been "bad guys" at all.

The next morning we had a company formation to find out who had earned the Ranger Tab. No guests were invited. When your name was called, you stepped forward. When the calling was done, approximately twenty men were left behind who'd gone all the way through the training, but for some reason had failed to earn the tab. I felt sorry for them, but that's the way it is. The standard has to be met.

TRAINING

Carl Stiner has always been known in the Army as an expert trainer, and many of his Army assignments directly involved training. Here are some of his thoughts on that experience:

EARLY in my career, I realized that military training offers a unique opportunity—not only for preparing men for combat, but for preparing them for the most important of life's values: personal attributes, principles, ethics, motivation for the right reasons, love of country, and self-respect—in other words, the values that should be manifested in every citizen of our great nation. No other institution in our society can possibly provide the same kind of environment, together with the caring and dedicated leadership, for molding and shaping the young men and women who elect to serve their country. Not every soldier will turn out as we hope, but the great majority certainly will, and they will always be grateful for the opportunity and the caring that gave them a greater perspective on life.

In my judgment, training is the essential element for the readiness of any unit in any service. The very best equipment is great to have, and I'll never turn any down, but well-trained *people* win wars. No impersonal piece of equipment or technology can ever replace a well-trained soldier, sailor, airman, Marine, or Coast Guardsman.

In our army, the objective of training must be to maximize the competency and proficiency of every individual and unit.

To that end, a commander must be personally involved in the development and structuring of his unit's training program. This must be based on a detailed analysis of the unit's mission requirements. From this is derived the Mission Essential Task List (METL); and then from this METL, all subordinate units at every level develop a METL of their own.

Next comes an analysis to determine the specific tasks inherent in the METL for successfully accomplishing their respective mission, and under what "conditions" and to what "standards" each must be performed successfully.

These critical elements, "METL, tasks, conditions, and standards," are the "core" element of the training program. This is the Army system, and I know of no better system in any army in the world.

Once the training program has been determined, we must turn to the way training is conducted. *That* is what makes the ultimate difference between soldiers who will survive and win in combat and those who don't.

I, myself, have always enjoyed tough, realistic training, and have made it my number-one priority in all the units I have commanded. Of course, "taking care of your people" ranks equally; the two are inseparable and synonymous. I have never had a soldier complain about too much tough, realistic training. Soldiers understand its value when it comes time to lay their life on the line.

Each soldier, therefore, should be required to *fully* perform every task to the standard expected of him for success in combat. This kind of training builds confidence at the individual and unit level—the kind of confidence and teamwork between the soldiers and within the unit that allows them to fully perform their mission without fear of being killed by friendly fire. No "simulation" or technology can ever take the place of this.

Realistic scenarios developed from unit war plans and other contingency requirements should serve as the basis for all training. Training should then always be conducted under the most demanding and realistic conditions possible—simulating nothing except for the safety of the participants. In other words, all training, particularly at the small-unit and combined-arms levels (battalion and below), should be live fire, and conducted at night. If this is not possible, then MILES devices, which are lasers, accompanied by receiving devices on each soldier, should be used to let soldiers know when they have screwed up and been hit.

Here are a few training principles that I have tried to live by:

✪ A commander should always have his unit ready to go to war, *without* any required train-up period. If he has been given the resources he needs, there is no reason why his unit should not be ready at all times. If some reason is beyond his control, he should have identified it a long while back and brought it to the attention of his commanders, so something could be done about the problem.

✪ A commander must be in the field personally supervising and evaluating training. Otherwise, he will never know the true status of the training readiness of his unit, and how to structure future training for correcting both unit and individual weaknesses.

Neither can a commander make an honest judgment on what his unit can or cannot do unless he knows the unit's training readiness—inside and out.

✪ *Time* is a commander's most crucial asset, and it should never be wasted—not a single minute.

A training opportunity exists in everything a unit is required to do—no matter if it is mission-related or not—and it is the leader's responsibility to look ahead and identify these opportunities and take advantage of them. It could be guard duty, police call, burial details, or many other administrative activities. These should be performed by squads and conducted in a way that allows each individual and the unit itself to emerge better trained and feeling good about their performance.

For example, if transportation is scarce, many training opportunities—such as counterambush drills—are available during tactical foot marches to the designated training areas.

Every officer and NCO in the chain of command must always have "hip-pocket training" ready for his unit in order to take advantage of unprogrammed and unanticipated time that could become available for training. For example: "The trucks that were supposed to show up will arrive thirty minutes late. Let's get in some mortar practice." Oftentimes, small-unit leaders fail to recognize and plan appropriately for these opportunities—a situation that requires leader training by the commander.

Time lost can never be recovered.

- ✪ If a unit fails to meet the standard for a given training event, then the commander should adjust the schedule to keep the unit in the field until they get it right—no matter how long it takes. Don't ever say, "We'll correct the deficiency next time out." There may not be a next time before they are committed to battle.

- ✪ The responsible commander (brigade, battalion) should never be satisfied with "just" meeting the standard. He should keep "raising the bar," with an ultimate goal of maximizing the technical and tactical proficiency of every individual. For example: Every soldier in an infantry squad should qualify for the Expert Infantry Badge, every medic should qualify for the Expert Field Medical Badge, every mortar crew member as Master Gunner, and so on. A great ancillary benefit also comes from this—unit pride, cohesion, and individual early promotions.

- ✪ Cross-training between skills is also very important, especially within crews of crew-served weapons that are vital to unit effectiveness in combat. Replacements are not always readily available on the battlefield.

Nothing I have said is new to any successful commander. We have lived by these principles and tenets in fulfilling our responsibilities for preparing those entrusted to us—the cream of America's youth—for success in battle. This responsibility is a sacred trust, directed not only toward success in battle, but also to the lives of the men and women we command. This includes bringing them safely back to their families, and having them feel good about themselves for what they have done for our nation.

Soldiers will unhesitatingly lay their lives on the line because of this trust in their commander and their fellow soldiers. They have no one else to look to.

This means, finally, that a commander's unit, no matter what kind it is, will be only as good as he is, a direct reflection of his principles and values, and of his dedication, his motivation, and his love and respect for his troops. A commander must therefore give it whatever it takes. No one else will do it for him.

During most of my Army career, I have been fortunate to serve in combat units where training and preparedness for no-notice contingency operations were an imperative—and for having had this opportunity I indeed feel privileged.

V

Few Are Called,
Fewer Are Chosen

September 1964. Fort Jackson, South Carolina.

Army posts are predictable places. Most of the time, you know what to expect—reveille in the morning, taps at night, squads, companies, battalions, PT, drills, marches, orders, regulations, tightly scheduled intense training, "sirs" and salutes—and wildlife management.

Most Army bases in the United States have game-conservation programs. On selected fields and training areas, corn, millet, sunflower, winter wheat, and other feeds are planted so that doves, quail, grouse, turkeys, deer, and all manner of other wild creatures can mature and receive cover and protection from predators. As an added benefit, these same fields offer soldiers who like hunting splendid sites for game shooting. Every Saturday in season, you can find soldier-hunters out on some wildlife conservation area.

This particular Saturday, Captain Carl Stiner was at Fort Jackson, where he'd been assigned after completing the Advanced Infantry Course at Fort Benning, Georgia. He had served there for sixteen months. It was bright and warm, a fine day for dove hunting. Suddenly, out of the blue, a jeep came roaring up, blasting its horn and making a god-awful mess of the shooting. A pair of MPs leaped out and headed right for Stiner.

"Sir," the senior MP said, hustling up with urgency in his voice, "you have orders, sir, for reassignment, and you need to get back in to look at them. Right now, sir. You're going to have to move this weekend."

That was very unusual, so Stiner asked, "What's the nature of the orders?"

"We don't know, sir. We were told they're classified, and you need to come back in."

"Who sent you out here?" Stiner pressed.

They named a warrant officer assigned to the training center headquarters.

"Well, that explains it," Stiner said to himself; he knew the man well. The warrant officer was a famous trickster.

He said to the MPs, "Well, I'm not going back in right now. I'll come back after a while. Just tell him not to worry about it." So they left . . . with visible misgivings. And Stiner stayed at the dove shoot.

Still, the MPs' message couldn't help but gnaw at his brain. He continued to agitate over what had just happened, until, some time later, the jeep returned. This time the MPs had no hesitation. "Sir, you have got to go back in. They're classified orders, and the post is preparing to move you and your family this weekend."

At which point, Stiner thought, Maybe nobody's playing a trick on me after all.

The reassignment was to Fort Bragg, North Carolina. He had a building number where he was supposed to report, but the MOS (Military Occupation Specialty) was indeed classified. Stiner had no idea what he was about to get into, but whatever it was, the Army had told him to move, so that afternoon, he and his wife, Sue, began to get themselves and their infant daughter, Carla, ready.

The next day they checked into a rental trailer near Fort Bragg, since no quarters were available, and on Monday Stiner reported in at the building he'd been given. When he showed up, a line of maybe fifty officers, most of them captains, but also a few first lieutenants, was there, all of them in the same boat. They had all been pulled in on short notice, and none of them had any idea what was going on.

Welcome to the Special Forces.

WHEN Stiner was called into Special Forces, he knew very little about who they were or what they did. Their secretive, closed nature extended to the rest of the army. He did know the Special Forces were highly selective and highly trained, and that as army units went, they were small (in 1964, approximately 17,700 people, including PSYOPs and Civil Affairs). And he knew they were unconventional in their thinking, their organization, and their mission—even their headgear was unorthodox: green berets. The rest he would have to find out as he went along.

At the lineup, Stiner was assigned to A Company of the recently activated (because of the Vietnam buildup) 3rd Special Forces Group, and told to check in with the company XO, a diminutive major by the name of LeBlanc, who was wearing—Stiner couldn't help but notice—a Bowie knife strapped to his leg.

When Stiner walked smartly into LeBlanc's office, the major looked up and frowned. Stiner was wearing the standard flat-topped green service hat with a bill, and the XO wasn't pleased. "That will never do," he announced. "But I'll get you straightened out before you see the old man.

"The first thing you are to do is get that flying saucer thing off of your head, and don't let me see it back on your head again as long as you are in this outfit. For if you do, I'll have to stick it where the sun doesn't shine.

"What you're going to do is go down to the supply room and draw you two berets. Understand you're not authorized to wear the flash yet." The flash was his unit colors, and showed he was a *real* Green Beret. "But you can wear the chocolate bar," a little bar that represented the colors of what would be in the big flash when he earned it. "You'll wear that until you are Prefix Three–qualified," which meant he had successfully passed the Special Forces Qualifying Course (called Q Course). This normally took ten weeks.

From there, the XO got down to the real business at hand. "What you're here for is you're going to be an A-Detachment commander. That means two things are imperative. One is you've got to learn to send and receive Morse code at the rate of six words a minute. If you can get faster, that's better, but six is the minimum. And you will have to take your turn on the radio and the generator just like each member of the team does."

Though a captain commanding a conventional unit—normally a company of 100-plus men—is expected to be proficient on such equipment as the radio, he is not expected to be an operator in the field. Special Forces A-Detachment captains are different. There are only twelve people on the team, and because there's only so much twelve people can do, especially when they are miles behind enemy lines, everybody has to take a turn at many of the jobs, with no discrimination because of rank. The primary means of field communication in the early '60s was by Morse code on ancient ANGRA-109 radios (pronounced "Angry"). These were powered by a heavy, hand-cranked generator (there were no batteries), and it took two men to operate them. One man strapped the key to his leg so he could send and receive, while the other one sat nearby and cranked the generator.

LeBlanc went on: "The second imperative is that you have to learn the Last Rites of the religion of every man in your detachment, because there won't be chaplains with you most of the time, and you'll have to be able to do them. You can expect there'll be three or four religions and beliefs in your twelve-man detachment, twelve counting yourself."

And that was the extent of his guidance.

"Now go down and get your equipment."

Next came the "old man," the company commander, Lieutenant Colonel Perry. Stiner made sure he was wearing the green beret by then.

"When was the last time you jumped?" Perry asked.

All Special Forces soldiers had to be parachute-qualified. Some obtained the qualification after joining Special Forces, while a few others might not have jumped in some time when they arrived at Fort Bragg.

"It's been about six years," Stiner answered.

"Well, we've got a different kind of parachute now than you used, so you'll have to have a little refresher training. We've also got a policy around here: Your first jump is usually at night—and you will enjoy jumping at night. It's the closest thing to going to bed with your wife."

And then, "The last thing you need to know is we get together every Friday afternoon at four o'clock for happy hour. You're expected to bring your wife; and you're expected to have a 3rd Special Forces Group mug—which I just happen to sell for three dollars." In fact, he had a case of them underneath his desk, and Stiner shelled out for one. "You can either bring it with you when you come," Perry announced, as he handed Stiner his, "or else display it on the wall behind the bar down at our officers' club annex"— a one-story World War II building.

This little ritual of happy hours and mugs might jar people in these politically correct times, but that was simply the way the Army was back then—rougher around the edges, more freewheeling. The social culture in the Army as a whole was far less structured than it is now, and a far greater range of behavior was tolerated. Socializing tended to center on gatherings where everyone drank; Friday-afternoon "happy hours" were the norm, and there were those who drank too much. Today, an officer who gets a DUI might as well hang up his career. Back then, the Army was far more forgiving. "Officers' clubs were anything but bastions of decorum," Stiner notes. "I was never surprised if a fight broke out; there were crap and poker games, and all kinds of teasing, strutting, and showing off—male stuff. It was pretty much the accepted culture.

"I'm not saying that Army life centered on all this. Far from it. It was a very small part of our lives. When we were on duty, we worked long and hard hours, we trained hard, we respected each other and looked out for each other's lives, just as we do now. But we also played hard.

"Remember that we're talking about only a few years after the end of the Korean War. The Army was not as sophisticated or professional as it is now. For example, in those days commanders were not nearly as involved in the training of their soldiers or in the taking care of families. That culture did not really begin evolving until the draft was done away with and we became a volunteer force. After that, the training of officers and NCOs became much more formalized and institutionalized—as did off-duty social events. Except for large unit-level social events, social life doesn't center on the officers' clubs anymore. In fact, very few military installations have even been able to retain centralized officers' clubs owing to financial management parameters legislated by Congress. Instead, commanders tend to host dinner parties at home for the officers and their spouses. It's relatively relaxed and informal, and drinking is limited.

"There are pluses and minuses in all this. We probably don't have as much spontaneity in today's Army as we did back then, and that's a loss; but fewer make fools of themselves, and that's a gain."

TRAINING

Now Stiner had to learn how to be a Special Forces soldier.

In 1964, the Special Forces mission was primarily focused on unconventional warfare (UW), and the chief threat was Soviet expansion in Europe. The entire Special Forces 10th Group was stationed in Europe, and money, weapons, and supplies had been cached in Eastern Europe and in the parts of Western Europe that might be overrun by the Soviets. In the event of a Warsaw Pact invasion, A-Detachments could be dropped behind the lines, or else they could hide and reappear after having been passed over by invading forces, then link up with friendly guerrillas and partisans. Their mission: sabotage, subversion, and organizing and equipping resistance movements. All of this required a high level of independence, analysis, and decision-making.

The Leadership Reaction Course was one of the ways they trained and tested for these qualities. It emphasized teamwork, imagination, resourcefulness, ingenuity, and, of course, leadership, and started with a physically and intellectually difficult puzzle. For instance, imagine a moat in which the water is eight or ten feet deep and the distance from one bank to the other is twelve feet. A team in training is provided with a fifty-five-gallon drum of gasoline and three pieces of timber, two of them ten feet long and the third eight feet. The team's job is to get the barrel (and themselves) across the moat using the materials provided. If the team has what it takes to become Special Forces soldiers, they'll work out a way to do it.

Another method of training was by sensory deprivation. Operating on their own behind the lines in enemy territory puts extraordinary demands on soldiers. One of the most difficult of these is the absence of emotional support. Friendships, trust, and confidence belong to a soldier's makeup as much as obedience, and readily available support provides a powerfully counterbalance to the uncertainty in a soldier's life. Many excellent soldiers stay up to speed primarily because they are praised. They need the certainty that comes from knowing somebody above them considers them to be a good and solid performer.

That is not the case with Special Forces soldiers, who must operate in environments in which every kind of support is minimal, absent, or transitory. Some soldiers have the spirit and will to handle that situation, but many others don't.

The Special Forces sensory-deprivation training program is designed to find who has what it takes. Soldiers are not told the goals or the standards they are expected to reach, or whether they're doing well or badly. A soldier might be told one day: "You show up at this road junction at 0600 hours in the morning with your rucksack." When he arrives, an NCO will be waiting with a piece of paper that contains his next instructions, which might be: "You are to move from this point to this point"—say, twenty-five miles. And then he's left on his own, with no help other than a map and a compass, no idea of how long he has to get from point to point. When—or if—he shows up at the appointed location, his presence is simply acknowledged. He is not told whether he passed or failed, or if he made the journey in the correct time. Success in this exercise comes not only from accomplishing a difficult task, but from doing it totally out of his own internal resources.

Much of Special Forces training is conducted according to similar "rules."

IN the meantime, the Special Forces soldier must also train for specific skills. As previously noted, in an A-Detachment, soldiers not only have to handle their own specialty, but be prepared to handle everyone else's.

SHADOW WARRIORS ★ 133

When Stiner met the A-Detachment that he was to command for the next eight months, he was impressed. The members of his detachment were all professional Special Forces soldiers with considerable experience. Most were years older than Stiner, and maybe half were Lodge Act volunteers originally from Eastern European countries. They were already proficient in unconventional and covert warfare and spoke one or two other languages. At the same time, they were more or less new to one another, having been reassigned within the Special Forces following the forming of the 3rd Group, and so had not trained together as an A-Detachment. During the weeks Stiner was taking the Q Course, his A-Detachment was learning what it needed to know to function as a group.

In the '60s, everyone in an A-Detachment was trained in the following skills:

Each soldier had to be an expert marksman on his individual weapon (a pistol) and his M-16 rifle, and be familiar with weapons, such as AK-47s, that he might encounter in the part of the world in which he might be employed. He had to be able to shoot them with reasonable accuracy, and to take them apart and maintain them. In the case of larger weapons such as mortars and machine guns, he had to be able to emplace and employ them properly so they could provide the protection and support they were designed to give.

Each soldier was trained in explosives. He learned the kind of charge, the shape, and the placement for bringing down a bridge or power lines, for cratering charges or breaching, for getting inside a sealed and defended building with the minimum damage to the structure or to hostages who may be inside. If he had no explosives of his own, he was taught how to obtain what he needed to make them from local sources.

Each soldier received communications training—sending and receiving Morse code, and code writing. If a team was actually working behind enemy lines, they'd only come up on the radio at preappointed times every day or two, when the communications sergeant would get up on his telegraph to send his message. Everyone on the team, however, was capable of operating any kind of communications gear they might be using.

Each soldier received advanced first-aid training.

Each soldier learned how to conduct clandestine and covert operations; how to establish intelligence nets and escape and evasion nets; how to conduct resupply operations at night; how to set up a field for landing airplanes and bring them in, and how to set up parachute drop zones. He learned clandestine infiltration and exfiltration techniques, land navigation, and special (or deep) reconnaissance, in which he would operate in total stealth, in order to put eyes directly on anything an enemy might not want him to see. Often this meant living for days in hide sites—holes in the ground a team would dig and then cover over with dirt, branches, or other concealment.

Each soldier was provided with a working knowledge of the principal language in his group's area of focus—German, say, for members of the 10th Group in Europe, or Swahili for the 3rd Group. Later, language proficiency was increased enormously, and Special Forces soldiers were expected to devote as long as six months or a year, full-time, to attaining fluency in their language. In 1964, fluency was not required, but soldiers were expected to communicate in a simple and rudimentary way.

Similarly, each soldier was provided with cultural training, as appropriate, so that when he went into a country, he knew how to behave in ways that would win friends and not alienate the people he was there to help, and thus harm the mission.

Finally, although each A-Detachment commander had an operations sergeant and a weapons sergeant, it was an officer's responsibility to know indirect fire support—artillery fire and mortar fire—and how to employ it most accurately and effectively. He had to know how to plan defensive fires, or call in air or naval gunfire, if these ever became necessary.

EVERY Q Course is a mixture of classroom instruction and field training, but with a heavy overbalance toward the field. For Carl Stiner and those fifty or so other officers who were called in with him, it was—once again—an accelerated program, seven weeks rather than the more normal ten. Today the Q Course is even longer.

In the '60s, most classes were conducted at the Special Forces headquarters complex in the Smoke Bomb Hill area of Fort Bragg, in rickety World War II–vintage converted weatherboard barracks or, less frequently, in smaller single-story orderly-room-type buildings. Air-conditioning was not even a dream. Guys didn't go there expecting comfort.

After a week of primary instruction, everyone moved to the field for another couple of weeks to practice the techniques studied in the classroom. This sequence was the norm throughout the course.

Field instruction and practice were conducted in training areas on Fort Bragg and neighboring Camp MacKall, and in the Uwharrie National Forest fifty miles away in western North Carolina. In later years, Camp MacKall was transformed into a well equipped training facility for Special Forces, but in those days, the Camp MacKall training facility did not exist, and there was nothing out there except the remains of a World War II training airfield for the gliders of the 82nd Airborne Division and the concrete foundations of torn-down buildings.

Finally, all the instruction and training were brought together in a major exercise, at the time called Gobbler Woods, and now called Robin Sage, in the Uwharrie National Forest area.

Gobbler Woods worked like this: The student-officers would be formed up into simulated A-Detachments deployed to a fictional country (often, for the sake of the game, called Pineland). There they were expected to contact indigenous Pineland natives and to turn them into guerrillas. These were normally played by soldiers from support units at Fort Bragg (maybe 250 of them), who dressed and acted like civilians.

The A-Detachment's job was to work with the guerrilla chief (who always made it a point to be difficult), mold his followers into guerrilla units, and get them to do what the A-Detachment wanted them to do—blow up bridges, blow down power lines, set ambushes, and perform other unconventional warfare–type tasks—as well as civil affairs work aimed at winning the hearts and minds of the local people.

Soldiers who did this successfully were rewarded with the flash on their green berets. If not, they were given the opportunity to take another Q Course or they'd be sent back to the conventional forces. Of those who took the course with Stiner, most passed.

That is not the case today. Today there are more washouts, partly because standards are higher, and partly because Stiner and the other officers with him had been carefully selected for assignment to Special Forces. The Army wanted them there. Today, Special Forces is a totally volunteer force—"a three-time volunteer force," as Stiner likes to point out, "once to join the Army in the first place, second to get parachute-qualified, and third to join Special Forces."

Then or now, it wasn't easy. Those who successfully completed it could be proud of the accomplishment. More important: *They could be counted on by everyone else.*

AFTER the Q Course came still more training. For example . . .

CLANDESTINE ENTRY   There are several ways to get into a country where American soldiers are not wanted. They can come in covertly—as tourists, workers, or businessmen—or clandestinely—by submarine, boat, or aircraft—or they can drop in by parachute, which is more often than not the way it gets done.

That means Special Forces troops spend a lot of time jumping out of airplanes.

Carl Stiner talks about the way they did it in 1964:

WHEN a lot of people are dropping out of a formation of large aircraft, the first priority is getting them all down safely. Conventional airborne units jump with a standard (not maneuverable) parachute in order to minimize the risk of midair entanglements—a good way to get seriously hurt, or killed. The other priority is keeping them together in some kind of order, so thousands of soldiers are not scattered all over the countryside. This priority is handled by a technique called "cross-loading": squads, platoons, and crews are loaded on each airplane so that they exit near where their mission is to be accomplished on the ground. This minimizes assembly time after landing and maximizes the fighting effectiveness of the units.

On a jump mission, the pilot flying the airplane is in charge overall, but the jumpmaster in the back is responsible for all the jumpers. That means he has to know where he is at all times. And he does that by communicating with the pilot, by studying the map, and by plotting checkpoints on that map—points on the ground such as rivers, bridges, or natural features that he can recognize from the air en route to the drop area.

Meanwhile, since the pilot is up in the cockpit where he can see more, he helps by calling out, "We have crossed such and such a river," or, "We're approaching such and such a terrain feature."

When you were inserting an A-Detachment into what we called denied territory (territory where we weren't welcome and where it could be dangerous to be an American soldier), you wanted the team to be able to land as close to each other as possible.

By that time, Tojo parachutes had replaced the older, simpler parachutes on which I had originally trained. In those days, the Tojo parachutes were steerable to a degree. Not steerable enough for you to aim at a point on the ground and hit it, but enough to permit the detachment to assemble in the air and then come down in the same immediate area.

The Tojos looked like your regular umbrella canopies, but they had a twenty-square-foot orifice in the back in the shape of an oval, and out of this would come thrust of about eight knots. The chute had a system of slip risers on rollers that you activated after you exited the airplane. By tilting the canopy one way or another, that allowed you to direct that thrust.

When you jumped, the slip risers were secured to your harness with forks. Once you were in the air, you pulled the forks out, and the risers were released to slip on the rollers. Then if you wanted to turn to the right, for example, you'd reach back with your right hand and grab the right rear riser, and with your left hand you'd grab the left front. Then you'd pull the right rear down and push the left front up. That would tilt the canopy so you would turn to the right. When you got turned around as far as you wanted to go, then you'd center them again and you'd straighten out. . . . Or you tried to, because you never really kept going in that direction.

The big problem for the jumper was orienting the chute to face the wind as he was coming in for his landing. (If a jumper came in running with the wind, he would hit the ground at the speed of the wind, plus the eight knots of thrust coming out of the chute's rear orifice.) The tendency of the parachute was to turn and run with the wind, which meant that jumpers had to work at the risers constantly to keep themselves properly oriented. Since most Special Forces jumps were at night, the best indication of wind direction was the sensation of it on a jumper's face.

If everything was going right, the team would leave the airplane as a chalk or string. The lead jumper would normally face into the wind and hold until everybody else could assemble on him by steering their parachutes. They'd try to work it so they'd be about a hundred feet apart. Fifty to a hundred feet was the normal separation distance for experienced jumpers. That way, all of the detachment had a better chance of landing close to each other and defending itself upon landing. You're vulnerable on the drop zone!

The separation distance was very important, because if chutes became entangled there was a serious risk of a canopy collapse. This was especially true of the Tojo chutes, because these chutes tended to push each other.

Each jumper also had a reserve chute that was good as long as you were more than 500 feet up. Should it become necessary to activate your reserve, you would pull the handle with your right hand while holding your left hand in front of the reserve in order to catch it when it popped out of its container. Then you worked your right hand underneath the skirt of the reserve and threw it down and to your left as hard as you could to facilitate inflation.

If this didn't work, you would have to try again. Sometimes the reserve would just go up partially inflated and wrap around the main chute, which was not fully inflated. People who get hurt jumping usually get hurt when they land. But when you get an entanglement, you're looking at real trouble.

Nowadays, reserve parachutes are much improved. These are equipped with a cartridge that propels the canopy far enough out to give you a much greater percentage for inflation, regardless of the malfunction with your main chute.

A jumper was also taught not to look for or reach for the ground on a night parachute jump. Rather, he was trained to look for the silhouette of the tree line, which would tell him he was thirty to fifty feet from the ground and could start preparing to land by making sure he was facing into the wind and by holding his feet and knees tightly together, which allowed the jumper to roll instantly in the direction of drift, and thus minimize the risk of a broken leg.

After everyone had assembled on the lead jumper, he would aim as best he could to drop into the drop zone—there was normally not much space, maybe a small opening in the trees, a clearing perhaps two or three hundred yards wide. Once he was on the ground, the other jumpers, who by now have stacked themselves above him, could aim directly on him and could usually land within a circle of a hundred feet.

After you were down, the first order of business was defending yourself as a team, but you had to do something about the parachute, and you had two options. You could take it with you or you could bury it. You could never leave it lying where you landed, because if you did, it could be spotted either from the ground or from the air.

Of the two options, taking your parachute with you was the least desirable choice. It was a lot of extra weight and volume to lug around. The best solution was to move off the drop zone, find a secure location in a gully or wooded area, and bury it so it couldn't be found.

Either way, you wanted to get out of the drop site almost immediately, carrying the parachute. Once you had reached a concealed location, you could usually bury your parachute in about fifteen or twenty minutes.

And from there you moved out in accordance with your plan for accomplishing the mission.

LAND NAVIGATION　*Finding your objective was far from a given. It was nighttime; the terrain was unfamiliar, the people potentially hostile, and in*

*those days there were no night-vision goggles or GPS satellites to help you find
your way. The teams had to be expert at land navigation and find their objectives the old-fashioned way—the way they'd probably learned to do it in Ranger
training—by relying on maps, compasses, and the stars.*

*They had to be dead-certain expert map readers, they had to be equally pro-
ficient using compasses, and they had to know how to count their pace.*

Carl Stiner continues:

AN important part of the preparation for a mission involved studying the
maps of the area where we'd be operating. We had to make ourselves absolutely familiar with that territory. Not only was there very little room for
error in linking up with our objective (which might be a guerrilla band or a
place where we could hide while we set up for our larger mission), but we
also had to avoid blundering into one of the many places where we were not
welcome. That meant we memorized everything we might need to know—
all the landmarks—rivers and streams, dams, bridges, roads, crossroads,
transmission towers, power transmission junctions, and other infrastructure
elements, as well as towns, villages, police, and military facilities.

When we were in the field, one man would keep track of the compass,
while two pace men working in conjunction with each other would keep
count of the pace. And anybody in the team could handle these jobs. The
detachment commander usually kept himself free to manage and orchestrate the operation. The important thing was to keep an accurate count no
matter what happened (so we'd have two men counting). But we also had
to make sure that we didn't lose count if we ran into an ambush or some
other event that might cause somebody to forget the count.

Meanwhile, even though we had memorized the map and had confidence in our compass reading and pace counting, every once in a while it
was a good idea to make sure we were still on track. And that meant checking our map—not an easy thing to do in the dark when you can't show any
light.

The way we did it was to use our GI flashlights and get under a poncho.
Our GI flashlights had a series of filters that were kept in the cap that covered the battery compartment. One of these was a red filter, and that was the
one we used, because red light has less effect on your night vision. While
everyone else in the team circled around the poncho and stood guard, the
commander, his second (whoever would take over if something happened to
him), the compass man, and the pace man would get under the poncho and

study the map to determine if they were exactly where they should be. If they had deviated, then they'd work out the adjustments they had to make.

It was also possible to navigate by the stars, if, for example, something had happened to our compass. But we preferred the compass, because it was not weather dependent. Still, we had to learn the basic constellations—the Big Dipper, Orion, the Scorpion, in the Northern Hemisphere; Cassiopeia in the Southern. We learned that the two corner stars of the Dipper point to the North Star, which lies five times the distance separating the two pointer stars. So if we could see stars, we could find our way.

One final aspect of planning our route was to identify rallying points. That way, if we got ambushed or ran into some other enemy action, we could break contact and split up, and everybody would reassemble at the next rallying point, or the last one we had passed—depending upon whichever the commander designated.

There is a myth that Special Forces soldiers itch for firefights—that they are all Rambo-like killing machines with nothing better to do than waste enemies. There is zero reality in this myth. Special Forces soldiers are not killing machines; their value lies elsewhere. They are simply too highly trained, too valuable, to be placed in greater risk than is absolutely essential. That means they avoid fights when they can. They fade away into the woods rather than stand up and prove how macho they are. In fact, the Special Forces selection process selects against those types. No Rambos. No Tim McVeighs. Special Forces soldiers are fighters, and they can call upon that energy and skill to kill when they must; but they are expected to focus that fighter energy in a laser-sharp, mature way.

RESUPPLY   *Surviving in a covert or clandestine environment doesn't come easily. Living conditions are apt to be paleolithic. Food comes from wherever you can scrounge it. Water is more often than not contaminated. And a significant portion of the population is apt to have a desire to torture or kill the "American invaders," even if another significant part of the population is glad to have them around.*

Meanwhile, living off the land has limits. Despite their best efforts, the team may not find enough food to keep going. They may run out of ammunition or medical supplies. Wounded may have to be evacuated. And there you are, with many hostile miles separating you from the supply chain.

Demands for supplies can grow especially strong when forming or aiding a guerrilla band. Guerrillas may welcome them, tolerate their presence, or pre-

fer to do without them, but they always crave the American bounty they are convinced the American soldiers are there to shower on them—food, medical supplies, uniforms, electronics, weapons, and ammunition. Showering such bounty is not a primary mission, yet often enough, the guerrillas may be more interested in the supplies than in the fight—thus yielding an opportunity for an A-Detachment to exercise its thinking and negotiating skills: "You do what we think is best, and we'll provide you with food and weapons."

In any event, the team has to know how to get in resupply. In rare circumstances, a team will be in a situation that permits a submarine delivery. Far more regularly, supplies are air-dropped or flown in.

Carl Stiner tells how this was done:

WHEN you needed supplies, you sent out a list of your requirements by tapping them out in code on your ANGRA-109 radio. How the supplies would be delivered—whether dropped or flown in—depended on the nature of the situation.

If you were going to be resupplied by parachute, you would have selected a place where you wanted the supplies dropped—a clearing in the woods, the edge of a field, an empty section of a road, an open hilltop. This drop zone information, together with the code letter you'd use to signal the pilot (formed by small flaming cans), would be included in the resupply request. Then a day or two later, you'd learn when you could expect the delivery. This was always at night, at a particular time. Let's say 0330 on April 17.

On the seventeenth of April, you'd set up at the drop zone with your team and with the guerrillas you might need to secure the area and carry the supplies to the camp (if you were working with guerrillas). A few minutes before drop time, you would mark out the drop point with flame pots you'd make by filling C-ration cans (or any metal cans) with sand and gasoline. You would light these so they'd be visible two minutes prior to the designated drop time, and you left them lit for two to three minutes, but no more. If the plane wasn't there by then, you put them out.

A single plane would usually be flying this mission. The pilot had to penetrate enemy airspace, come in low enough to avoid radar, set a course, and then find these little points of light during that five-minute window, drop, and then continue on the course he'd set, so no enemy who might be looking could track where the drop had been made (or *if* it had been made).

Naturally, if he didn't find you during the five-minute window, you got no resupply. And you had to try again later.

The minute the plane was overhead, you put out the flame pots and pre-pared to grab the bundle that was parachuting down. Usually it came equipped with a tiny flashing light attached so you could see where it was coming down and start moving to where it was going to hit.

Once you had recovered the bundle, you had to recover the parachute and the cargo net the bundle was dropped in, then distribute the load among your carrying party (which might be just your team or it might be guerrillas), and sanitize the area so nobody could tell later that you had taken an airdrop there. This was all accomplished in the shortest possible time in order to avoid detection and compromise.

It was always interesting to find out what you were actually getting. Food, for instance, often came in the form of living animals. Sometimes you'd learn they had dropped a live animal when you heard moos coming from out of the sky. When that happened, you knew you had a problem. And if you had farm experience, you were grateful for it. Cows are never easy, and they aren't trained to jump out of airplanes; and if they hit the ground and broke a leg, you had a real problem. But even if they came down unin-jured, they were often not gentle enough to be led off easily. Either way, they often started bellowing and making all kinds of noise, so you had to kill them right there, and then quarter the meat on the spot, so your carrying party could carry the edible parts and bury what you couldn't use.

Sometimes you might get a goat, a pig, or chickens. And on the whole, we preferred these to cows. They're easier to come by, relatively easy to han-dle, they don't weigh that much, and one person can usually carry them.

Eating out there in the woods was where I learned the value of hot sauce. Every Special Forces soldier carries a bottle of hot sauce in his rucksack. Once we got animals or birds back to camp and butchered them, well, you don't do the best job of cooking in the world out there, so a little hot sauce covers a lot of errors—Louisiana hot sauce, Texas Pete, or Tabasco—it sure helps the taste. It also helps regular rations, which we often had dropped in.

Of course, the A-Detachment part is not all there is to know about the resupply story. Let's look at it from the headquarters side:

Let's say we had a mission to resupply an A-Detachment in the field. The mission would go to the NCO who was the S-4 (logistics) of the C-Detachment to which the A-Detachment belonged. It was his job to put it all together. If it was a goat, pig, cow, or chickens, he had to go buy it from some farmer (funds were provided to pay for it), and he had to build a cage for it.

Among the other details he had to know would be the kind of airplane that would fly the mission, including most crucially the dimensions of its exit door, since you couldn't get anything in or out that was larger than the door. In other words, he had to take the size of the door into consideration in choosing an animal to air-drop and building a cage to contain it.

The NCO would then fly the mission, and he'd be the one who made the drop. While the pilot flew the course over the drop zone, the NCO had to put the animal, the cage, or the bundle out through the door at the right time to make it hit the drop zone that the A-Detachment had illuminated on the ground.

One time, while I was the S-3 of the C-Detachment, an A-Detachment had called in for resupply, and we had set up a drop that was to fly in on an Army U-10 Helio Courier. The U-10 was a high-wing, single-engine turbo-prop that was both very rugged and a super-short-field airplane, which could take off and land in a matter of yards (every time you landed in one, you thought you'd crashed, because you hit the ground so hard). Though it was technically a four-place aircraft, we usually took out the rear seats to make room for cargo.

The night this resupply mission was to be flown, I decided I was going to go along to see how it went. When I got to the airfield, I found the supply sergeant there getting ready to load a crate full of white Leghorns—both chickens and roosters all mixed together—onto the U-10, and the crate was about twice as long as the inside dimensions of the aircraft. So about half of it was sticking out. In fact, so much was sticking out that the sergeant had to ride on top of the crate and the parachute all the way out to the drop to keep it from getting jerked out the door.

When we cranked up, feathers started flying. The force of the prop was blowing them off the chickens. But I didn't say anything; it was his show, not mine. And I kept quiet when we took off from the airport, although there was a cloud of feathers big enough to almost hide the plane.

From then on, things went pretty smoothly, and we went out and made a good drop.

The next morning, I went out to the swamp where the A-Detachment had their base camp area set up to check on how they were doing, and the first thing I saw was this one naked rooster, with a piece of heavy-duty cable looped around his leg, which was all they could find to tie him up with. The only feather on him was a tail feather sticking up, about three inches long, and it was broken.

When I asked them what in the world they were going to do with that rooster, they said, "Well, we haven't decided yet, but we have decided one thing, and that is that he ought to live. Anything that went through that flight and lived deserves to survive for a while longer."

DEALING with airdrops kept us busy, but we had a lot more to do when we had supplies delivered directly by aircraft. We had to know how to select and set up an airstrip, mark it, and then bring in an airplane at night. This was especially tough because we did all this totally on our own. We had no Air Force Combat controllers with us. We had only the members of our own detachment and the guerrillas, if we had guerrillas with us, to organize it. Then, when he came in, the pilot had to trust our judgment absolutely. He had never seen the airfield before. It was a blank to him.

In those days, we had several different kinds of aircraft available for this mission, all of them fixed-wing, because helicopters didn't have range enough for it. The Army had U-10s and Caribous, which were both capable of landing on dirt fields. But we also had available larger Air Force C-123s and C-130s, which had to be landed on roads, and there were even a few C-47s still around. And from time to time, leased indigenous aircraft would be made available for covert operations.

What you'd do then is work out the length your airfield had to be, whether it was on a dirt field, a dirt road, or a paved road; you'd walk every inch of that length to make sure it wasn't too rough or rutted; and you'd get rid of rocks, power lines, and other obstacles. You'd check out the trees nearby and compute the approach glide path the plane would have to come in on, so it didn't hit any of them. You (and the guerrillas, if they were available) would then lay out flame pots so that the length of the runway was marked out. Once all that was taken care of, you'd radio in all the data associated with the airfield—its location, its dimensions, and so on—and your mission would be scheduled. That is, your headquarters would work out the particulars of the mission and get back to you with them, something like: "The plane will be there on 23 June, at 0330," which usually meant a window of five or ten minutes. "And it will be approaching on a certain azimuth."

When the window itself approached, you wouldn't have any radio communication with the pilot. He would land on your visual signal.

About the time the pilot was five minutes out, the flame pots would be lit. Meanwhile, whoever was running the airfield—officer or NCO—would take a flashlight with a colored filter on it (blue or green, usually—something pretty hard to see) and lie down on the approach end of the airstrip and wait.

The first thing the pilot would see was the flicker of the flame pots. When he saw those, he knew it was safe to land. That is, he knew not only where the field was and that you had laid it out, but that you had secured the area, and there was no enemy in the neighborhood. The next thing he'd see was the flashlight on the end of the runway, and he would then aim his left wheel at that light (because he was sitting in the left seat) and glide in about six feet above it. That meant that if you were the one holding the flashlight, you lay there absolutely still as he approached, seeming to come right at you, and stayed cool as several tons of airplane (if it was one of the big Air Force ones) lumbered in at man height over you. It was a hairy experience.

Once he had landed, we'd off-load the cargo and he would take on anything or anyone you had for him to bring out, and then he would turn around and take off in the opposite direction.

We practiced all that many times.

SURVIVAL AND ESCAPE-AND-EVASION   *Special Forces soldiers had to be expert at survival, escape, and evasion. They had to know how to live off the land, how to set up snares and traps to catch their food, what was edible and what was not. And they had to be expert swimmers.*

Carl Stiner continues:

IN Vietnam, sometime in 1964–65, two NCOs drowned trying to swim a river while they were trying to evade capture. As a result, the requirement was established that we all had to be able to swim (I think it was a mile). And we had to be able to swim at least half a mile with our boots and combat gear on.

If you were carrying a rucksack and it was essential that you had to keep it, you built a raft out of your poncho for the rucksack and other heavy equipment and supplies, including your weapon. Then you towed this raft as you swam.

You also had to know how to assist your rescue in whatever way possible. Specifically, you had to know how to set up pickup zones, and how to signal searching aircraft with mirrors.

The officers were taught special code writing, in the event we were captured. It was a very complex and sophisticated system that involved the positioning of letters that were included in specially designated code words. That way, if we were allowed to write letters, we could include codes that would indicate where we were being held.

Detachment commanders must also have the technical expertise to set up and operate an escape-and-evasion net. The infrastructure available is, of course, critical—safe houses, drop points, and the transportation network. But even more critical is selecting the right people to operate the net (which means you need a system for vetting them to ensure that they continue to be people you can trust), and establishing compartments (cells), so that if one of your operatives or compartments is compromised, the remainder of the mechanism is not. If a cell system is established and operated properly, one cell does not know who is in the next cell.

Your transportation system must be organized and compartmented in the same way. If the plan is to take people from here to there and drop them off at a point where they can be picked up by someone else and taken to another cell's safe house, only the detachment commanders should know the complete operation of the whole system.

Meanwhile, the "precious cargo" that enters this net has no say-so over their own security and destiny. Nor would they usually have any means of self-protection: Their lives depend absolutely on the people that make up the net.

DURING the time I was undergoing survival, escape, and evasion training, intelligence reports began to indicate—and in vivid detail—the horrific conditions and torture undergone by U.S. military prisoners held by the Viet Cong and North Vietnamese. As a consequence, another special area, resistance training, was added to our program of instruction.

Although what we got was not nearly as intense and realistic as the training given today, it was still pretty tough, considering that we were getting a start-up program and didn't have much available time left in our course. It was of great benefit to each of us.

Today—now that we have the experiences of those prisoners who endured and survived—nineteen days of intensified training have been added to the Special Forces Q Course, called SERE (Survival, Escape, Resistance, and Evasion). During this training, students are placed in the role of prisoner and subjected (short of personal injury, and under the close watch and care of appropriate medical professionals) to the conditions and treatment they could expect if taken captive. SERE training brings them to the absolute limits of their mental and physical endurance, and is fundamental to survival in captivity.

Up until the time I went through SERE training, I had been satisfied that I had received the best training possible to develop me technically and tactically as a leader of men in combat. However, I had not yet actually experienced combat.

The Q Course, and particularly the SERE experience, prepared me for the *real* experience of combat in ways that everything I'd learned up until then had not. They revealed to me that in order for a leader to possess and project the courage expected by his men in combat, he himself must find the means to be at peace with himself. For me, this strength comes from an abiding faith in my relationship with God. This strength allows a person to live one day at a time without fear of death. I have never known an atheist in combat, and I do not ever expect to find one.

I do not believe that this is a revelation discovered only by Carl Stiner. Based upon my experience, it is a belief that serves as the inner strength and motivation of the greatest majority of all combat leaders, both officer and enlisted. I do not know of a substitute for this.

THE GRADUATION EXERCISE: GOBBLER WOODS/ROBIN SAGE

The graduation exercise, an unconventional warfare field-training exercise, which is conducted approximately seventy-five miles northwest of Fort Bragg in the Uhwarrie National Forest and surrounding communities and lasts approximately three weeks, is the culmination of the Q Course. During this period the Special Forces students, now organized as A-Detachments, put into practice the skills they have learned in their training.

For the purposes of the Gobbler Woods exercise in which Stiner participated, the training area became the fictional country, Pineland, which was run by a corrupt leftist government, backed by a larger Communist country. An insurgency was striving to overthrow the government and bring in democracy, but they needed help. The Communist country had meanwhile pledged to send forces to help the Pineland government crush the insurgents.

The exercise was made as realistic as possible. For example, local civilians played various parts, and provided support to both sides. The counterinsurgency force, usually an active-duty brigade, and the guerrilla force, approximately 100 to 150 soldiers, were drawn from various support units at Fort Bragg.

The fledgling Special Forces soldiers were evaluated on their specialties, tactical skills, and overall performance within their A-Detachment.

Carl Stiner continues:

I have participated on both sides of this exercise, both as a student and as a guerrilla chief. This is a particular exercise from 1964:

After they'd been given the mission, the A-Detachment entered an "isolation area" to begin their preparation (the isolation area is part of the preparation for every Special Forces mission). While there, they saw no families, friends, or anybody else who was not involved in preparing them for their mission. For the Gobbler Woods exercise, the isolation period lasted about a week; for a real-world mission, it could last up to six weeks. During this time, they developed their operations order and studied every aspect of the operational area where they would be inserted—the government, terrain, climate, personalities, the guerrilla force, the people, the culture, and anything else appropriate. They were assisted in this by a pool of experts with advanced degrees who provided instruction in specific areas.

The final phase of isolation was the briefback, usually to the Group Commander and his staff. This covered—to the "nth" degree—every detail of the mission and how it would be accomplished. This had all been committed to memory. No orders or paperwork were carried by any member of the team. After the briefback, the judgment was made whether or not they were ready to go. If that decision was a "yes," they moved directly from the isolation area to the departure airfield ready for launch.

While the A-Detachment was making its preparations, the guerrilla chief (usually a Special Forces major or captain) had moved to the operational area and begun working at winning the hearts and minds of the local people in order to establish a support infrastructure for the guerrilla force.

When I played guerrilla chief, the most effective technique I found was to drive up on a Sunday morning to Albemarle County (in Pineland) with Sue, and spend the day meeting people. I would visit country grocery stores and restaurants and any other gathering I could find. I was looking for people who needed some kind of help.

At one stop, for example, I learned that a man with a large dairy operation was having a rough time getting his cows milked on time and was way behind getting his crops in, mainly because his wife was in bad shape with cancer.

I went to see him, explained who I was, and told him about the training exercise that was about to take place. Though he'd heard of it, he told me, he hadn't participated in the past. I also told him that I grew up on a farm in Tennessee and was well aware of the challenges he was facing working a farm and taking care of a sick wife.

"In a couple of days," I said, "I'm going to have about 150 soldiers, all wearing civilian clothes, who're going to serve as my guerrillas. I'll be glad to pick four or five farm-raised boys out of this group and let them live and work with you. You can let them bunk in chicken houses, or the dairy barn, or wherever you want them, and they are yours to work to help bring in the crops and to help with the milking, or whatever.

"All I ask is for you to protect them if the counterinsurgency force"—the 101st Airborne, in this case—"comes around trying to police up my guerrillas. If they do, I just want you to say, 'I don't know anything about that. I don't fool with these things. And I don't want you running over my fields with your trucks.'

"All I ask in return is for you to let me use one of your trucks, maybe a couple of nights a week, to haul fifteen or twenty of my guerrillas over to simulate blowing up a bridge or some similar target."

"That's fine with me," he told me. "And I appreciate very much the help."

"That's wonderful," I said. "But how about talking to some of your friends to see if some of them also need some help?"

He told me he'd do that, and he did.

I then reminded him about how important it was for us to trust each other. "If we don't," I said, "we stand to lose all of our guerrillas and then we won't be able to help you or your friends."

He told me he understood that, and he did.

And so, with this farmer's help, I was able to establish other contacts that ultimately became a key part of my infrastructure throughout the community.

I also contacted local pastors to find out who in their congregations might need some help, and they offered me good sources that provided protection and support for small groups of my guerrillas.

It's amazing how you can organize people for our kinds of causes. They all want to get in there and support—sometimes more than you really want.

I USUALLY brought my guerrillas out a week before the Special Forces students jumped in, in order to allow time for blending with the local people and getting our operating base set up properly. On the day they arrived, I selected those who'd be going out to work for and live with the contacts I'd made, like the dairy farmer.

But before they did that, I laid down the law about standards, principles, and conduct: "There is to be absolute integrity," I told them. "Respect for the human dignity of each and every person; respect for property; no abuse (verbal or otherwise); no hanky-panky; and no incidents that would degrade your morality and our ability to live and operate among the people. We are here to help them, and they will help us if we do. We cannot survive without their protection and support. One bad incident from you, and you are gone—and so is your career. And by the way, no alcohol!"

I would also tell them, "Go to church, sing in the choir if you can, and get to know everybody in that church. If you blend into that community and cause them to respect you, they will protect you and we'll have their cooperation in everything we do."

I always tried to put my guerrillas in key parts of the community. They and the people that support them were my intelligence network. That way I always knew what was going on all over the county.

A COUPLE of days before the A-Detachment was to jump in, my guerrillas would come together in order to organize our "base camp" and develop plans for the linkup and reception of the A-Detachment. There was also a rehearsal for securing the drop zone.

After the jump, the assistant guerrilla chief (a Special Forces NCO) usually made the linkup and guided the detachment to the base camp. Once there, they were told they would meet the guerrilla chief the next morning. The A-Detachment spent the rest of the night in the base camp, usually guarded by the guerrillas.

At the morning meeting, which usually took about an hour, the guerrilla chief always played hardball. He made his initial demands as tough as he could, so it would be close to impossible for the A-Detachment commander to meet them. We did this in order to evaluate the A-Detachment commander's ability to establish rapport and gain enough of the confidence of the guerrilla chief to accomplish the mission.

After the meeting, the guerrilla chief presented a list of the supplies and materials he wanted and gave a rundown of the capabilities of his force and the training assistance they needed.

The A-Detachment commander, having done his homework during the detachment's isolation back at Bragg, then presented his training plan for the guerrillas.

The initial phase of formal training usually started the next morning. While this was under way, the A-Detachment assessed and validated the training readiness of the "G" (guerrilla) force for conducting operations. Meanwhile, the detachment commander and the guerrilla chief formulated an operation plan together, with specific targets for accomplishing the overall strategic objective.

In addition to the tactical aspects of the plan, psychological operations and civil affairs played a vital role to ensure the support of the people. The entire effort *had* to be truly integrated, with the parts supporting the whole.

Of course, I had already started civil affairs work within the community by providing selected guerrillas to work with people like the dairy farmer whose wife had cancer. But more could be done—such as medical assistance missions, for example, where our medic treated minor illnesses in the more remote parts of the county where medical help was scarce. We also had guerrillas (free labor) clean up playgrounds and cemeteries and the like. And to widen and strengthen my intelligence net and base of support, I provided guerrillas (in pairs) to the city and county maintenance departments.

The A-Detachment itself had been augmented with a psychological operations specialist, who (among other things) could produce leaflets (though in a very rudimentary way compared with what we can do today). Nevertheless, we produced and distributed leaflets designed to degrade the will, loyalty, and combat effectiveness of the counterinsurgency force, and to bolster and widen our support among the people.

We distributed our leaflets by airdrop at night, or by hand; and they were amazingly effective, especially in inhibiting the counterinsurgency force. For example, landowners and farmers would prevent them from using or even crossing their land—while at the same time harboring us and providing support.

I guess this was the beginning of my understanding of the real power of psychological operations. If you can influence and control people's minds, then you are well on the way to winning, while keeping the loss of lives to a minimum.

By the end of the first week, the training of the guerrillas was going well, and they were hitting one point target (a bridge, for instance) each night. Meanwhile, local farmers, bread-delivery distributors, and the county maintenance department were providing trucks for our transportation—and were even scouting some targets for us. By the end of the second week, the guerrillas had progressed to platoon-size (thirty to forty men) raids on larger targets. By the third and final week, they were making even larger raids.

Throughout all this activity (while operating in a community we had never known before), we didn't lose a single man to the counterinsurgency force—although they chased us day and night. Nor did we have a single bad incident from either our A-Detachment soldiers or the guerrilla force. Nobody did anything we would not be proud of.

As a result of our operations, the leftist government of Pineland was overthrown and replaced by a democracy.

Was it now time for the A-Detachment to go home? Not quite yet.

An important aspect of unconventional warfare is bringing it to closure. Quite simply, no new government can exist for long without the support of the force that helped to bring it to power, nor can they risk having a formidable armed band running around out of control. The best way to deal with these possibilities was for our guys to work out a plan to disarm and disband the "G" force. And they had to do it before they could go home. (In real life, the smoothness of this operation usually depended on concessions made by the new government to the guerrilla leader.)

And so ended the Q Course of 1964. I'm proud to say that all the SF students who participated earned the "flash" that made them fully qualified as Green Berets.

Special Forces Training Today

In recent years, Special Forces mission areas have expanded. As this has happened, so has the scope of the selection process and the training program. Thus today, the initial phase of formal qualification training lasts between twenty-four and thirty-six months, depending on the MOS of the student.

Applicants are all volunteers. They must be airborne-qualified, in good physical condition, and have nothing in their backgrounds that would prevent a security clearance to at least the SECRET level.

The Special Forces Qualification Course breaks down as follows:

- ✪ *Phase I (Camp MacKall): SF Assessment and Selection—25 days*
- ✪ *Phase II (Camp MacKall): Land Navigation, Small-Unit Training, Live Fire—48 days*
- ✪ *Phase III (Fort Bragg):   MOS Training:*
  - *18B (Weapons)—2 months*
  - *18C (Engineers)—2 months*
  - *18D (Medic)—12 months*
  - *18E (Commo)—4 months*
- ✪ *Phase IV (Camp MacKall): Training to include Robin Sage (2 weeks)—39 days*
- ✪ *SERE: Survival, Escape, Resistance, and Evasion (Camp MacKall): 19 days*
- ✪ *Graduation: Flash Awarded*
- ✪ *Language Training: 4–6 months*

The toughest part physically is the SF assessment and selection phase, during which soldiers are continuously assessed to determine whether or not they have what it takes. The first week is designed to evaluate a soldier's emotional and psychological makeup, mainly by means of written and practical tests. The second week is structured to test the soldier's endurance, strength, will, and mental toughness. It involves a complete range of physical tests, including timed runs, obstacle courses, rucksack marches, day and night land navigation, and swimming wearing uniform and boots. During this week, the soldier's ability to function effectively in a high-stress environment is also evaluated by means of sleep deprivation and more psychological testing. The third week evaluates his leadership abilities as an individual and as part of a team.

At the end of the three weeks, a board of impartial senior officers and NCOs reviews each candidate's performance record and makes the final determination about his suitability for Special Forces training. The board also recommends a military occupational specialty for each soldier.

The Assessment and Selection course is conducted eight times a year. In the past, the average selection rate has averaged about twenty-nine percent. Recently, however, the rate has risen to fifty percent. A more stringent preliminary screening process and better-quality applicants have meant that the higher rate has been accomplished without sacrificing quality. Soldiers who fail to make the selection are sent back to their units with a letter of commendation. Some are allowed to try again, and some of them will make it on the second go.

Meanwhile, those who were selected will enter the Q Course (Phase II), where they must satisfactorily complete whatever their MOS requires (including Robin Sage and SERE training).

After graduation and award of the "flash," each soldier is assigned to a unit, but before he joins his A-Detachment, he must complete six months (or more) of language training (depending on his unit's area of orientation).

Now he has mastered the basics, but as a member of a team his training continues for the rest of his career. His next formal course of instruction (which comes very soon) will likely be military free-fall (parachute) or combat diver (scuba) training. Additionally, he will begin to receive intense formal instruction in the culture of his area of focus.

CARL STINER, GREEN BERET

During the two months after graduation from the Q Course, Stiner attended Jumpmaster School (two weeks at Fort Bragg) and continued to improve the proficiency of his A-Detachment in field-training exercises in the Uhwarrie National Forest.

In January 1965, and for the next six months, he was commander of a B-Detachment in A Company, 3rd Special Forces Group. More field training followed, and on a larger scale.

ONE exercise I particularly remember (modeled after "Gobbler Woods") involved two B-Detachments—mine in a counterinsurgency role against Captain Charlie Johnson's in a UW role. This exercise was conducted in an area of Florida, bounded in the north by the city of Titusville, in the south by the city of Melbourne, in the west by the St. John's River, and in the east by the Atlantic Ocean. All of this was civilian-owned land, and virgin territory for military training activities. A large segment of the civilian populace was organized and trained by one or the other B-Detachment, and they participated enthusiastically. Army aviation was used extensively in support. Air boats were also used by both sides (great preparatory training for Vietnam!).

At the conclusion of the exercise, and in an effort to desensitize and reunite our civilian friends who had participated (some had gotten a little *too* involved—they actually wanted to keep fighting their "enemies," some of them with guns), we hosted a barbecue supper—and military demonstration—for the entire community. This worked. Peace was restored.

As we were flying back to Fort Bragg the next day, I noticed a commotion up near the front of the airplane.

Some NCOs had been trying to smuggle a four-foot alligator back as a company mascot. When I checked out the commotion, I discovered that the alligator had gotten loose, and they were trying to subdue him. They eventually did, binding him with rope from one end to the other.

When we landed, we were met by our commander, Lieutenant Colonel Hoyt, and Sergeant Major Arthur. The sergeant major immediately detected the smuggling operation, and took the four smugglers, along with the gator, to the company area and had them spend most of the night digging the gator a pond. They secured him there with leg irons so he would not get loose and eat the real company mascot, a dog.

It didn't stop there. The NCOs allowed that the gator had to be "airborne"-qualified, especially since the dog was. So they connived with the riggers into making him a harness and a special parachute. About a week later, during a scheduled jump on St. Mere Eglise Drop Zone, they threw the gator out of an aircraft and followed him to the ground. He made it down just fine, but when they got to where he'd come down, all they found was the harness and chute. He'd eaten his way out of the harness and disappeared.

Thirteen years later, the Fort Bragg game warden discovered a seven-foot alligator in the swamp at the western end of St. Mere Eglise Drop Zone, the only gator ever at Fort Bragg—and it remains a mystery to this day how he got there.

Soldiers, and especially Special Forces soldiers, are always looking for imaginative ways to entertain themselves, and there is nothing wrong with it, so long as it is legal, ethical, and no one is hurt.

IN July 1965, following the training exercise in Florida, I became the Company S-3 (Operations Officer), responsible for the training and readiness of the company. I remained in that position until the spring of 1966, when I left Special Forces to attend the Command and General Staff College at Leavenworth, Kansas.

During this period, when all the services were undergoing the buildup for Vietnam, large numbers of draftees were being brought into the Army, and the training centers were filled to capacity.

In August, the entire company, which consisted of the headquarters and two B-Detachments (the third B-Detachment was on mission to Ethiopia), had deployed to the Pisgah National Forest in western North Carolina for training in the higher and more rugged parts of the mountains. This had been ongoing for about a week, when I received a call on my FM radio from Lieutenant Colonel Hoyt, who, I could tell, was in a helicopter, asking me to meet him at a road intersection about ten miles away from our base camp.

I jumped into my leased pickup truck and headed for the intersection, thinking as I went that it was unusual for him to fly this far (more than a hundred miles). Whatever the reason, it must be important.

I arrived at the intersection before he did, and marked a landing zone in a small clearing beside the intersection with the orange panels that we always carried.

When he landed ten minutes later, he came running up to me (the helicopter did not shut down). "How long will it take you to get the company back to Fort Bragg?" he asked—the first words out of his mouth.

"It'll take a while," I answered, "because they are spread out all over these mountains in various operating areas, and we don't have enough transportation to move the entire company in one lift. I guess with the vehicles that we have, and with what they can come up with through their local civilian contacts, we could all close Fort Bragg sometime during the night."

"Good," he said. "Go back and get them organized and moving."

Then he explained: "The training centers have overflowed, and just this morning we received the mission to conduct basic entry-level training for approximately five hundred new infantry draftees that will arrive at Bragg within three to four days.

"Group is working on where to house them," he went on, "and what parts of the training might be done more efficiently by committee"— weapons training and the like—"and this should be pretty well finalized by the time I get back.

"You have more training experience of this nature than anyone else in the Group," he continued, "and the Group Commander"—by then Colonel Leroy Stanley—"and I want you to lead a group of selected cadre to Fort Jackson, departing at six in the morning, to observe how they conduct Basic Combat Training"—in this case he meant the first eight weeks—"and bring back all the lesson plans you can gather up."

"No problem, sir," I answered. "I'll get the company moving right away. As for the basic training part, I've got this cold, from beginning to end, and can teach all the subjects blindfolded. But we'll have to give our cadre some preliminary training to get started, and I can do that in a couple of days, and continuing as we progress through the training cycle.

"What you can do, sir, to facilitate organizing for training," I told him, "is to go back and begin to pick and structure the cadre for a training battalion that will consist of three companies." And then I laid out how the structure ought to work: "These should be commanded by captains, with a sergeant major or master sergeant as first sergeant; four platoons per company should be commanded by a lieutenant, with a master sergeant or sergeant first class as platoon sergeant; and each platoon should consist of four squads, each led by a staff sergeant or sergeant." I also told him that it would be very beneficial if I could take to Fort Jackson with me our three company commanders and one representative (officer or NCO) from each platoon (a total of fifteen), to observe firsthand how it is done.

"Okay," Hoyt said. "You'll be commanding one of the companies. And while you're putting your guys together out here, I'll go back and ensure that the right people are ready for the trip to Fort Jackson."

On my way back to our base camp, I was thinking, "Man, what an opportunity to turn out the best-trained and -motivated battalion ever. With all of these outstanding NCOs, there's no limit to what we can do for these new men."

At the same time, I couldn't help but contrast the performance of our Special Forces guys in a training situation with what I'd had to handle in my last training company at Fort Jackson: It was me and an outstanding first sergeant (Ned Lyle, to my knowledge the only man in the Army authorized to wear the bayonet as a decoration), a Specialist 4 company clerk (who was pending charges for hoarding mail and possessing pornographic materials), four NCOs (all possessing medical profiles that precluded their making the morning twenty-minute run; instead I kept them posted at strategic locations where they could police up the stragglers while I ran the company), a mess sergeant who was addicted to paregoric, and a supply sergeant I didn't trust. This was all that I had to work with, and I thought we did a good job—considering.

During one period at Jackson, I had two companies of more than two hundred trainees each in cycle at the same time: One company was in its seventh week of training, and the other was just beginning its first week. We managed the training so that one NCO stayed with each company at all times. The two other NCOs and I would train one company from 4:00 A.M. to noon, and the other from 1:00 to 9:00 P.M.

In other words, considering the talent and caring leadership we were about to bring to bear on this mission, it would be a piece of cake and a very rewarding experience for us and the new recruits.

After Lieutenant Colonel Hoyt left, I called base camp and instructed my radio operator to have all detachment commanders standing by for a conference call when I arrived.

During the conference call, I advised the commanders of the new mission, then instructed them to move their units by "infiltration," so as to close on Fort Bragg by midnight. "Infiltration" means authority to move by individual vehicle over multiple routes, rather than by convoy over a single route. I didn't tell them how to do it, because I knew they would figure out the "how."

This was about 3:00 P.M.; they had nine hours to get back.

The next morning at 5:00, I met Lieutenant Colonel Hoyt at the company headquarters. He had followed through on his part. Not only had the names of personnel been slated against the battalion structure I had recommended, but the group selected for the visit to Fort Jackson was standing by and ready to go.

Before we left, I asked him for one other thing: "In order to bring these new troops on right, we need to have the barracks ready in advance, including having the beds made. The sooner we can get this done, the more time we'll have available for training the trainers before the new troops arrive." I knew that some of the older NCOs would probably bitch about making the beds, but I also knew that before the training cycle was over, they would see it was a wise move. This would be reflected in the attitude and motivation of the new troops, who'd have realized they were fortunate to be in the hands of caring professionals.

The day at Fort Jackson proved very worthwhile. We observed the training in action, talked with the cadre, and gathered up all the lesson plans to bring back with us.

After our return to Bragg, we spent the next three days getting organized and putting our common training areas in order. Then we went through a two-day train-the-trainer program, which took us through the first couple of weeks of the training cycle.

And then at 4:00 P.M. on the fourth day after notification, we received about five hundred new inductees straight from civilian life.

The next eight weeks proved a memorable and rewarding experience both for our cadre and the trainees. The cadre demonstrated incredible professionalism and caring, and the training battalion responded with incredible receptivity, motivation, and esprit.

Even though the trainees eventually ended up in Vietnam as individual replacements, many chose to make the Army a career, and some found their way back to Special Forces as outstanding NCOs. Others—the better-educated ones—ended up as commissioned officers.

VIETNAM was also demanding ever more from Special Forces. Especially important at that time were trained B-Detachments, and this became our priority mission. For my final seven months in the 3rd Group, we organized, trained, and deployed three B-Detachments to Southeast Asia (to Thailand and Vietnam).

Since increased emphasis was now being focused on counterinsurgency and advisory activities in Vietnam—organizing, training, equipping, and employing Montagnard tribesmen for thwarting the infiltration of North Vietnamese Army (NVA) units; MIKE force reaction units; and advisory activities for South Vietnamese Army units—the main thrust of the tactical training was focused on tactical operations at battalion and lower levels, including the employment and integration of fire support, aerial as well as artillery.

I was in fact scheduled to deploy with each of the three units we sent over. But then, about a month prior to their deployment, I was told that I had not been cleared to go by the office of Officer Personnel Operations (OPO). The reason, I finally learned from OPO, was that I had been selected to attend the Command and General Staff College, and then I'd go to Vietnam (though this was not specifically stated, I understood that I most likely would not be assigned to a Special Forces unit there).

I left A Company, 3rd SFG, in late May 1966.

VI

VIETNAM

Special Forces had a long history in Vietnam.

In 1954, the French defeat at Dien Bien Phu by Ho Chi Minh's Viet Minh ended French colonial rule in Indochina. Vietnam was separated into independent northern and southern halves, and Laos and Cambodia also gained independence. In 1959, North Vietnam adopted a new constitution, based on Communist principles and calling for the reunification of Vietnam. From the end of French rule until that year, the North had supported the Viet Cong insurgency in the South, though not as wholeheartedly as in the decade to come. The insurgency had nevertheless grown ever stronger in the countryside during that time, owing in part to Viet Cong success in persuading the country's people that their cause was better than the government's, and in part to the South Vietnam government's seeming indifference—or blindness—to security outside the cities.

In May 1959, however, the North's support of the Viet Cong took a big leap forward: The North Vietnamese Central Committee deemed the moment ripe to increase military efforts against the South. Corollary with that decision was a plan to construct a logistics network through southern Laos and parts of Cambodia (and bypassing the demilitarized zone then separating North from South Vietnam). This network came to be called the Ho Chi Minh Trail.

Its construction proved to be the decisive act of the war in Southeast Asia.

Meanwhile, in July 1959, twelve U.S. Special Forces teams (from the then 77th Special Group—later the 7th), together with a control team, arrived in Laos to help the French* organize and train the lackluster Laotian Army. This was a clandestine operation—primarily because the French were not eager to lose face yet again in Southeast Asia. The Green Berets arrived as "civilians," wearing civilian clothes and carrying "civilian" identification cards; and they were paid out of "civilian" (that is to say, CIA) accounts.

No obvious connection exists between the decision to build the Trail and the arrival of Special Forces troops in Laos, yet the two are intertwined. The continuing association between U.S. Special Forces and the Ho Chi Minh Trail turned out to be a major factor in the part Special Forces played in the war in Southeast Asia. The link took many forms—direct and indirect—and a few of them will be mentioned here.

The Trail itself was not a trail, of course, but a communications-and-transportation network, a command-and-control structure, and a system of troop-staging areas. Its facilities and capabilities—especially in its early days—were primitive, yet also astonishingly robust. One of its strengths was its very primitiveness. A freeway not only represented a vast expenditure of capital and labor, it was an easy target. A dirt road could support a much smaller volume of traffic, but most damage could be easily repaired by men or women with shovels. The traffic volume problem was easily solved by constructing a network of many roads—and by patience. And since these roads were virtually invisible under the cover of the tropical rain forest, it was hard to discern a definite target.

That was the real strategic significance of the Ho Chi Minh Trail—its security. Throughout the war, the North Vietnamese were able to use Laos and Cambodia as sanctuaries. Though such sanctuaries were never total or absolute, U.S. and allied forces were severely limited in their ability to attack them.

In fact, the best opportunity for putting a cork in the Trail was probably early in its existence. Its presence was beginning to be recognized by 1961 and 1962, but it hardly seemed a factor in the war. Perhaps 1,500 North Vietnamese troops a month filtered down into the South, an insignificant number compared to the tens of thousands per month (including tanks

---

*The French Army continued to advise the Laotian Army even after Laotian independence—though unenthusiastically. The absence of serious French interest in the enterprise led to U.S. Special Forces involvement.

and other heavy weapons) that later used the Trail. As a result, few in authority took it seriously, and that generally remained the case until it was too late to do anything about the Trail without committing massive forces—and by then political considerations had ended any chance for such a commitment. It was a big mistake. Another one was the belief held by most American military commanders that the war would be decided by slugging it out with heavy firepower and conventional forces. The Viet Cong and the North Vietnamese never bought this concept. To them the war was at times a conventional war, at times a "people's" war, and at times a guerrilla war; they chose the mode of combat that best suited their advantage—and our disadvantage.

It is credible to argue that if the United States or South Vietnam had found some way to permanently block the Ho Chi Minh Trail in 1962 or 1963, then the massive American intervention three or four years later might not have had to happen—and perhaps the war in Vietnam would have turned out more happily.

WHITE STAR

In 1961, early in his brief presidency, John Kennedy was faced with a mess in Laos—part Communist-backed insurgency, part dynastic struggles between competing princes, and part power grabs by military leaders. All of which was made more complicated by virtue of the complex ethnic makeup of the country. In addition to ethnic Laotians, the backcountry was inhabited by semiprimitive Kha and Meo tribes, who were both disliked and distrusted by the Laotians. Though the tribesmen were often superb soldiers, the Laotians were not eager to arm or train them.

The initial power struggle in Laos followed close on the heels of the Geneva Conference of 1954, which gave Laos independence. On one side was the Royal Laotian government, officially headed by a titular king but in reality led by neutralist Prince Souvanna Phouma. On the other side were the Communist insurgents, the Pathet Lao, led by Souvanna Phouma's half brother, Prince Souphanovong, and supported by the North Vietnamese (though they were always more interested in South Vietnam). Until 1959, the Pathet Lao occupied the two northern provinces, but worked to expand on that base. From 1959 until 1961, amid coups and countercoups, the situation grew even more complex, with the emergence of a right-wing power base under General Phoumi Nosavan, who seized power in December of that year. Meanwhile, the neutralists had lost U.S. backing (which went to General Nosavan) and threw in with the Pathet Lao, while at the same time begging the Soviets for help. The Soviets were ready to give it—though predictably most of their assistance went to the Communists.

According to the classic "Domino Theory," "We had to do something about Laos." If Laos fell to the Communists, could South Vietnam, Cambodia, and Thailand be far behind? Though history has proved the Domino Theory wrong, it made a lot of sense then.

Earlier in 1961, following the withdrawal in 1960 of the French Military Mission to Laos, U.S. Special Forces were officially admitted into Laos— their presence was no longer clandestine; they could wear U.S. uniforms, including their green berets—and were designated by the newly established U.S. Military Assistance Advisory Group Laos (MAAG Laos) as White Star Mobile Training Teams.

These teams performed many tasks: Some became instructors in recently opened Laotian military schools. Others went into the field with the Laotian Army as conventional operational advisers. Others provided medical assistance or coordination and communications services; gathered intelligence for MAAG Laos; or worked closely with the minority hill peoples, where among other things they formed, equipped, and trained Meo and Kha military companies.

It was in this last mission that the White Star teams made their lasting mark. In the hills of Laos, Bill Yarborough's vision of Special Forces was tested and proved. Here also the Special Forces organization and leadership learned the lessons they brought with them not long afterward, when they were assigned to take on the mess in Vietnam.

The White Star teams were fortunate in their leadership.

One commander, for example, Lieutenant Colonel John T. Little, had learned the Bill Yarborough lesson well: that only part of the Special Forces mission in Laos was to show indigenous soldiers how to march, shoot, and communicate. In a message to the troops in Laos, dated September 22, 1961, and titled "Civil Assistance," Little laid down the parameters that were to guide the White Star teams. These are extracts:

> In an insurgency situation, the guerrilla is dependent on a sympa-
> thetic population. Counter-guerrilla operations must, therefore, have
> as one objective winning the population's cooperation and denying the
> enemy their sympathy.

An imaginative program of village assistance, properly backed by the military and civil authorities, is one form of psychological operation which will contribute significantly both toward this objective and toward the achieving of U.S. goals in Laos.

You are not in competition with other U.S. agencies . . . you are the spearhead and focal point for the injection of these activities until Laos civil assistance teams are trained and operational.

Upon arrival in the village, pay a courtesy call on the Chao Muong [the district political boss]. Do not talk shop on the first meeting. Just make friends.

Deal directly with the Chao Muong. Do not work through his subordinate. Always work through one man—the chief.

Make a statement on graft. Let the Chao Muong know that under no circumstances will you tolerate graft, and if you detect it, your aid will stop. If corruption starts, the villagers will tell you. You do not need to search for it.

Always make the villagers share the workload. Let them know that all these projects are village projects, not U.S. help for the helpless. Once you do one project all by yourself, the villagers will forever after expect this from your team. Do not give them something for nothing. For example, a good approach could be: "I will try to get a tin roof for your school house if you will build the school and furnish all other materials and labor.

Try to present our ideas to the Chao Muong in such a fashion as to make him think it was his idea in the first place. Let him win full credit for the completion of any project. Do not issue orders to him or demand an instant decision. When you approach him with an idea, let him have a night to think about it. But the next day be sure to gently push him toward a decision.

Initially your weapon is talk. It must be interesting, arousing, intelligent. You are a master salesman for the United States. Some pitfalls for newcomers: drinking too much at social functions (keep your mind clear for business); getting involved with native women (creates jealousy and hate, and makes you a setup for anti-U.S. propaganda); being arrogant, sarcastic, or belittling in your conversation (these people are hypersensitive and proud, and you will come to a dead end if they dislike you). Maintain the proper team attitude of good-natured willingness and endless patience in the face of resentment to change and complete apathy.

Be tactful, be tolerant. Show exceptional tolerance to the children and the very old. Be courteous, be relaxed, and do not be in a hurry.

For success in this mission, observe the native customs. For example, when you are visiting a village, inform the villagers that you are coming so that the people can assemble. The Chao Muong always makes a political speech on these occasions. Never force your way into a village where broken branches across the trail indicate a closed celebration. Follow the native custom of removing your footgear when going into a village house. Learn the customs of your region.

Make sure the United States gets credit for all U.S. items distributed. When the Chao Muong makes a speech to the citizenry about the tools and supplies they are to receive, make sure he tells them that the equipment comes from America.

The sky is the limit in what you can achieve. You cannot make a new Laos in one day, but it only takes one day to start. Now is the time to start beating the enemy at his own game—the winning of men's minds, emotions, and loyalty to the concepts that motivate us: freedom, justice, individual human rights, equality of opportunity, and a higher living standard.

Lieutenant Colonel Little's message also discussed practical programs for medical support and sanitation; aid to education, agriculture, and transportation; improvements to marketplaces and children's playgrounds; and the like. All of these projects were in addition to the primary task of helping to train military forces.

ANOTHER legendary Special Forces officer—arguably the greatest operational Special Forces officer of them all—Lieutenant Colonel Arthur D. "Bull" Simons, also left a strong mark in Laos. Simons was a big, exceedingly unhandsome man, a magnificent leader, and a specialist in bringing the toughest jobs to a successful conclusion.* Because he was too busy mak-

---

*One of his most legendary missions occurred in November 1970, when Simons led a secret commando attack on a North Vietnamese prisoner-of-war camp called Son Tay Prison, deep within North Vietnam a few miles west of Hanoi, with the aim of rescuing better than a hundred American POWs. Fifty-six volunteer SF operators had been gathered from the 6th and 7th Special Forces Groups and from the Special Warfare Center to take part in the raid. They prepared and trained intensively for six

ing things happen in the field to punch all the tickets needed to advance to general officer's rank, he retired as a colonel. Recognition did come, how ever. Simons's statue was recently dedicated at Fort Bragg. No one deserved it more.*

In late 1961, the Pathet Lao controlled the strategic Bolovens Plateau in southern Laos. The Plateau occupies most of the Laotian panhandle region, with North and South Vietnam on the east, Cambodia on the south, and Thailand to the west; and it is mostly inhabited by Kha hill tribesmen. The Ho Chi Minh Trail ran between the plateau and the Vietnamese border. The mission of Simons and his Green Beret colleagues was to organize, arm, and train the Kha tribesmen into guerrilla bands, then to drive the Pathet Lao off the plateau, and finally to send the guerrillas into action against the Trail. They succeeded in the first two of those aims, but the attacks on the Ho Chi Minh Trail never materialized. By then the 1962 Geneva Accord had intervened, and the Special Forces had to pull back from Laos.

In 1962, various U.S. governmental agencies proposed three very different paths for achieving an acceptably stable situation in Laos: One, put forward primarily by the Joint Chiefs, argued for a full-scale conventional military intervention— slugging it out with the Pathet Lao on the battlefield—yoked with the bombing of North Vietnam; this was essentially the same plan the JCS tried in Vietnam. A second proposal put forward primarily by the CIA and the Special Forces,† argued for a counterinsurgency solution, since it seemed to be beginning to work. And

---

months (on, for example, actual-scale mock-ups of the prison), flew into Udorn Air Base in Thailand, and then helicoptered into North Vietnam on the night of November 20th and 21st. The raid went off beautifully, but for one thing: The POWs had been moved some time before. In spite of the failure to achieve its overall aim, however, the Son Tay Raid has joined the very select list of Special Forces defining moments. It's there because it shows what they can do. It also shows the cost of bad intelligence. SF troops would pay that cost many other times.

*A statue to Dick Meadows, another legendary Special Forces soldier, was also recently placed at Fort Bragg, not far from Simons's.

†The CIA and Special Forces worked very closely in Laos, and later in the early days of the war in South Vietnam. The association is natural. From time to time, Special Forces have been an action arm of the Agency. On the other hand, the association has raised suspicions. As has been noted here, some in the "big" Army, for instance, fear that Special Forces are not "real" Army but some kind of rogue or private Army. The association with the CIA does not ease those fears.

last, the diplomatic community argued for a negotiated settlement that would somehow harmonize all the major factions, turn Laos into a safe, "neutral" country, and secure the withdrawal of foreign military support. This last was the solution that was adopted, and it was codified in the Geneva Accords.

It's no surprise that the United States complied with the Accord's terms and withdrew its military forces, nor is it a surprise that North Vietnam (though a signatory) paid no attention to them. The Ho Chi Minh Trail was already far too vital to the success of its campaign against the South.

This situation continued for the remaining years of conflict in Southeast Asia. Though the United States "cheated" a little, and now and again "attacked" into the North Vietnamese border sanctuaries in Laos (and Cambodia), political and diplomatic constraints blocked the major military operations that might have ended the Trail's usefulness to the North Vietnamese. Meanwhile, the North Vietnamese never stopped expanding the Trail and making it more secure.

VIETNAM

Before turning to the role U.S. Special Forces played in Vietnam, it's helpful to review the United States' military involvement there and how the strategy for countering the Communist threat evolved.

United States military involvement in Vietnam actually goes back to 1950, shortly after the outbreak of the Korean War, when the Military Assistance Advisory Group (MAAG) was formed. This initiative resulted from a Joint Chiefs of Staff belief that Indochina was the key to holding Southeast Asia against the Communists. In those days, the MAAG's mission was relatively small—mainly liaison with the French, who were then deeply involved in fighting Ho Chi Minh's insurgents.

During the years following French withdrawal, however, when the Viet Cong gain in momentum began to place South Vietnam at great risk, the primary responsibility for the security of South Vietnam fell to the United States. No one else was eager to take the lead.

As a first step toward meeting this responsibility, the National Security Council (NSC) directed the JCS to develop a Vietnamese Defense Force capable of providing internal security. The JCS determined that a force of approximately 89,000 would be required; the mission of designing and training this force was passed to the MAAG.

In December 1954, the MAAG chief, Lieutenant General John W. O'Daniel, and the Vietnamese Minister of Defense agreed to an Army of the Republic of Vietnam (ARVN) force structure that called for the creation of three territorial and three field divisions. The territorial divisions consisted of thirteen locally recruited and trained regiments that would assist civil authorities with internal security operations. The field divisions were designed to be more "strategically mobile," and specifically to provide defense against an invasion from the north until reinforcements from the Southeast Asia Treaty Organization (SEATO) could be rushed to the scene.

Over the next five years, this force structure changed considerably. Under MAAG's direction, the ARVN evolved to a conventional force that mirrored the structure and methods of operation of the U.S. Army. In 1955, the National Security Council raised ARVN's manpower allocation to 150,000; MAAG then scrapped the three territorial divisions in favor of six new light infantry divisions, which were similar to American divisions and no longer regionally oriented. Another field division was also added, bringing the total number to ten (six light and four field). By 1959, the light divisions had been further transformed into standard heavier infantry divisions, and the field divisions had become armored cavalry regiments.

Meanwhile, the Viet Cong insurgency in South Vietnam continued to grow. Civil authorities were increasingly overwhelmed, and the ARVN was more and more called upon to assist in counterinsurgency. MAAG's mission, once simply to design and train the ARVN, now included recommending a strategy for employing those forces against the insurgents.

In 1960, Lieutenant General Lionel C. McGarr assumed command of MAAG. Faced with the formal establishment of the National Liberation Front that year, and the activation of the Peoples' Liberation Armed Forces, McGarr and MAAG began to develop a counterinsurgency plan for 1961. The plan focused primarily on offensive operations designed to destroy guerrilla forces in the field. The objective was to "find, fix, and destroy the enemy." This was even before President Kennedy blessed other, more unconventional approaches to counterinsurgency.

In spite of the growing involvement of MAAG and the ARVN in counterinsurgency operations, the guerrillas continued to gain strength, and Viet Cong infrastructures and control increased rapidly, especially in rural areas where the government had little presence or influence.

In response to the worsening situation, the Joint Chiefs of Staff sought to upgrade MAAG. In November 1961, they proposed the creation of the

Military Assistance Command, Vietnam, and on February 8, 1962, MACV was activated under the command of General Paul Harkins.* MACV's mission was the same as its predecessor's: to "assist the government of South Vietnam in defeating the Communist insurgency"; and it took the same operational approach: to destroy the enemy's field forces through large-scale operations. MACV doctrine and tactics were also conventional: making extensive use of helicopters and air mobile operations to attempt to surprise and "fix" guerrillas.

The MACV approach was not totally conventional, however. During that time MACV also attempted a pacification program (a kind of heavy-handed civil affairs operation), and in January 1962, the "Strategic Hamlet Program" was initiated. This program grew out of two distinct plans: The first had been proposed by MAAG before the activation of MACV; the other (the one preferred by the regime of South Vietnam's President Diem) had been proposed by the British Advisory Team, headed by counterinsurgency expert Sir Robert Thompson.

At that time, the insurgency had been building for approximately six years, and the six provinces near Saigon had become Viet Cong strongholds with well-established infrastructures—an obvious threat to the capital. In MAAG's view, the government had little choice but to start clearing the areas closest to home. Thus, the MAAG plan would begin with the pacification of the six provinces closest to Saigon.

MAAG's target date for the pacification of these provinces, as well as Kontum Province (approximately twenty miles to the north), was the end of 1961. Once that was accomplished, the priority would shift to the Mekong Delta and the Central Highlands; the rest of the country would follow. The target date for the pacification of the entire country was the end of 1964.

The plan proposed by Thompson and the British was based on the successful British counterinsurgency in Malaya and was focused on the implementation of strict security measures by the civil guard and the self-defense corps. They proposed to launch it initially in an area of weak VC activity, not the insurgent strongholds in the provinces surrounding Saigon, and with the ARVN playing a supporting rather than a leading role.

---

*In his book *To Move a Nation,* Roger Hilsman reports that Bill Yarborough was considered for this job but was too junior and too connected with unconventional operations to gain Army backing.

The final result, the Strategic Hamlet Program, was a compromise between the two plans. It consisted of three phases:

In the first phase, intelligence would be gathered concerning the area targeted for pacification, and the political cadre expected to administer the area would be trained. The second phase called for large-scale ARVN sweep operations in the target areas, aimed at driving out Viet Cong guerrillas. In phase three, the ARVN would hand over control of the areas to the civil guard and the self-defense corps, who would establish permanent security. At the same time, much of the local population would be forcibly resettled in fortified villages, where they could be presumed to be safe from attack.

MACV hoped that all this would somehow win over the hearts and minds of large numbers of rural Vietnamese.

On March 19, 1962, the Strategic Hamlet Program began with an ARVN sweep, code-named "Sunrise," through Binh Doung province north of Saigon. The operation was not a rousing success. The area of the sweep was close to Viet Cong support bases and heavily infested with VC. That wasn't a problem for the ARVN troops, but it turned out to be very difficult for the civil forces whose mission was to follow up and root out the VC infrastructure. After the ARVN forces conducted the sweep, the troops left, but the sweep operation had neither destroyed nor neutralized the existing VC infrastructure. This job was left to the civil forces, who simply could not do it.

Meanwhile, the local peasants were taken from their homes and the land they farmed for a living and forced into tin huts in euphemistically named "strategic hamlets," that were in reality refugee camps. The population resettlement left these people feeling more alienated from the regime, rather than less.

Despite complaints from U.S. advisers, not only were these failures repeated as the program grew, but no serious attempts were made to fix them. MACV's focus was on military operations to destroy the guerrilla forces, not on long-term pacification, the program's supposed purpose. Thus the Strategic Hamlet Program never had a unified command structure; and MACV, always primarily interested in the military sweep operations, continued to provide little support to the civil guard or the self-defense forces, whose mission was long-term security.

The South Vietnamese government, meanwhile, blatantly falsified reports: Less than a month into the program, for example, the government claimed more than 1,300 operational fortified hamlets; six months later, the number was 2,500; and when Diem was assassinated in November 1963, less than two years into the program, the total number of hamlets reported was more than 8,000. Most of these were fortified on paper only.

MACV made no serious attempt either to challenge the Vietnamese assertions or to correct the situation on the ground.

The CIA and Army Special Forces

The Strategic Hamlet Program was not the only attempt at pacification. In late 1961, Army Special Forces began to implement the CIA-conceived Civilian Irregular Defense Group (CIDG) Program, whose goal was to deny the VC access to food, supplies, recruits, and intelligence in the Central Highlands of Vietnam—and, it was hoped, to block or at least severely hinder NVA access into Vietnam from the Ho Chi Minh Trail.

The Highlands were inhabited primarily by an assortment of minority groups and primitive tribes going under the collective name of Montagnards—Mountain People (the name was supplied by the French)—though other minority groups and tribes lived in other out-of-the-way parts of the country, having long ago been driven out of the more fertile lowland plains by the Vietnamese (many of these other groups also participated in the CIDG). As in Laos with the Meo and the Kha, the Montagnards and other such groups were held in contempt by the Vietnamese, who thought of them as savages. The Vietnamese government was never enthusiastic about turning Montagnards into a counterinsurgency force, since such a force might easily turn against *any* Vietnamese.

Because of these tensions, the CIDG program was at first run solely by Americans—specifically the CIA and Special Forces—and was only loosely connected to the Strategic Hamlet Program. Although the program was conceived and funded by the CIA, the task of designing a specific strategy and implementing it fell to Special Forces. In November 1961, two Special Forces A-Detachments were deployed from the 1st Special Forces Group in Okinawa to begin the program.

The strategy developed by the SF, called the Village Defense Program, was simple and defensive in nature:

The A-Detachments would locate themselves in an area, win the trust of the people and local villages, and begin to prepare simple defenses. They would meanwhile recruit and train men from local villages with the aim of forming a small paramilitary "strike force" designed and trained to provide the villages with a full-time security force. They would provide reinforcements to villages under attack, patrol between villages, and set ambushes for the VC.

Once the SF had established an effective strike force, they would begin to organize and train "village defenses." These groups received basic training in weapons handling, were taught to defend and fortify their own villages, and fought only when their own village was under direct attack. Each village was provided with a radio, which allowed them to contact the SF teams and the strike force for reinforcement in the event of trouble.

Once the village defenders were established, the SF teams supervised programs to improve the quality of life for villagers. They established infirmaries and provided minor medical treatment, constructed shelters, improved sanitation, and generally helped in any way they could. As soon as a mutually supporting cluster of villages had been established, the process began all over again, and the perimeter was pushed out farther to include other villages.

The success of the two A-Detachments was extraordinary, and by April 1962, forty villages in Darlac Province had voluntarily entered the program. In May 1962, eight more teams were sent from Okinawa to Vietnam, and the success continued. In July, the CIA requested sixteen more SF teams, and by August, approximately two hundred villages were participating in the program. Overall, the Special Forces defensive strategy, focused on denying the Viet Cong access to the indigenous population and the resources they could provide, was working very well.

It differed markedly from the Strategic Hamlet Program in that it was able to provide an effective presence, and it involved no forced resettlement.

MACV TAKES CHARGE

As the size, scope, and effectiveness of the CIDG continued to grow, it became doubtful whether the CIA had the personnel and resources to manage the number of SF troops involved. Washington therefore decided to switch control of SF operations from the CIA to MACV. The transfer (called Operation SWITCHBACK) was completed in July 1963. Once MACV was in command, both the missions assigned to Special Forces and the execution of the CIDG program began to change.

The change was for the worse. MACV understood neither the nature of special operations nor the special requirements of counterinsurgency.

For starters, MACV viewed SF involvement in the CIDG program as "static training activities," and felt the Special Forces would be better used in more "active and offensive operations." As a result, Army SF were largely removed from their role in administering and expanding the CIDG Program and were instead assigned to provide surveillance along the Cambodian and Laotian borders and to conduct offensive, direct-action missions against Viet Cong bases.

This mission change began in late 1963, and was completed near the end of 1964. On January 1, 1965, Colonel John Speers, the commander of the newly organized and established 5th Special Forces Group, issued a letter of instruction outlining the mission assigned to the group by MACV. These were "border surveillance and control, operations against infiltration routes, and operations against VC war zones and base areas." All of these missions clearly reflected MACV's offensive strategy and focused on finding, fixing, and destroying the enemy forces in the field.

In order to free up U.S. Special Forces for offensive operations and border surveillance, the responsibility both for administering the CIDG program and for training strike forces and village defenders was transferred to the Vietnamese Special Forces (LLDB). Unfortunately, the LLDB possessed neither the skills nor the leadership of their U.S. counterparts, and worse, they came equipped with the normal Vietnamese contempt for the minority populations on which the CIDG Program had focused. As a result, many gains made earlier in "winning" the population were lost.

In a further change, the government of Vietnam integrated the CIDG Program's strike forces into the ARVN, and MACV began employing them in an offensive role, for which they had never been intended.

Before long, the strike forces were being airlifted from one place to another, in support of Special Forces raids, surveillance missions, or conventional ARVN operations. In October 1963, MACV unveiled a plan to use CIDG strike forces, in conjunction with SF, to "attack VC base camps and interdict the infiltration of men and supplies from North Vietnam."

Removing the strike forces from their local area of operations and employing them in areas unfamiliar to them drastically reduced their effectiveness. This in turn not only weakened the mutually supporting village defense system of the original CIA-SF designed program, but without detailed familiarity with the local terrain, strike forces became little more than marginally trained infantry.

Partly to exploit the success of the program and partly to make greater military use of CIDG camps and villages, MACV tried to expand the program—and quickly. CIDG camps began to be located for strictly military reasons, without regard to political or demographic realities. For example, camps were set astride suspected infiltration routes or in areas of heavy Viet Cong or North Vietnamese Army (NVA) activity. Neither served the original purpose of population control.

MEANWHILE, in spite of the best efforts of MACV, ARVN, and all the U.S. and Vietnamese government agencies involved, the situation in Vietnam worsened. By the end of 1964, the Viet Cong were conducting coordinated regimental operations. In early January 1965, the insurgents attacked and seized the village of Binh Gia, only forty miles from Saigon. In reclaiming the town, ARVN forces suffered 201 men killed in action, compared with only thirty-two confirmed VC killed. This event, and others like it, ultimately led to the commitment of U.S. combat troops to Vietnam.

The first U.S. division to be deployed as a whole was the 1st Air Cavalry Division. Once in country, in November 1965, it was immediately deployed to the Central Highlands, one of the areas of greatest VC strength, to begin search-and-destroy operations. They quickly encountered and attacked a large concentration of Viet Cong and North Vietnamese in the Ia Drang Valley. The battle resulted in 1,200 enemy killed in action, with the 1st Cav losing only a comparatively small 200. This success reinforced the Army's belief that attrition was an appropriate strategy. The victory also reinforced MACV's conviction that North Vietnam was behind the insurgency (though North Vietnam troops were not actively involved until the United States itself began sending regular troops).*

More U.S. troops followed, in ever greater numbers—and MACV continued its strategy of attrition, supported by the application of maximum firepower, until U.S. troops began to be withdrawn from Vietnam.

CARL STINER

The Army sent Carl Stiner to Vietnam in 1967. He tells us about his tour there.

Stiner:

---

*When Carl Stiner arrived in Vietnam a few years later, the North Vietnamese Army (NVA) was the main threat—not the VC.

I COMPLETED the Command and General Staff College at Fort Leavenworth in mid-June 1967, and was given a couple of weeks' leave to resettle my family (in Columbus, Georgia) before heading to Vietnam.

Half of my class had already served there; the other half was now going. Four of us, all close friends and all majors (though one was on the list for lieutenant colonel), had been assigned to the 4th Infantry Division.

We flew on a commercial chartered flight with something like two hundred other replacements, and arrived about dark at Long-Bin, the Army replacement center just outside Saigon. By midnight, after we'd been in-processed and issued our personal combat gear, and had received briefings on the general situation and the threat, we and over a hundred other replacements of all grades were loaded onto a C-130 and headed for drop-off at our respective unit locations.

Aboard the C-130, we sat on our duffel bags and held on to cargo straps stretched across the fuselage about sixteen inches off the floor. The 130 landed three or four times before reaching Pleiku in the Central Highlands, where the 4th Infantry Division Headquarters and its main support base were located, arriving just before daylight. We continued to in-process, and we received our specific unit assignments. All four of us ended up in the 1st Brigade, located at a firebase named Jackson's Hole near the Laotian Border. We were then given detailed briefings on the tactical situation in the 4th Division area of operations, and were issued weapons and ammunition. During our brief stop at Division, we had time for a welcome hot breakfast, where we were joined by a couple of staff officers who gave us a heads-up on Colonel Richard "Zoot" Johnson, our brigade commander at Jackson's Hole. We learned that Johnson was an impressive man—part Indian, a tough warfighter, and a totally dedicated "no-nonsense" officer. We looked forward to serving under him.

At 1500 hours, the four of us boarded a UH-1 (Huey) and headed about twenty-five kilometers west to Jackson's Hole.

During our in-briefing, we had been told that an intense battle was under way involving a battalion of the 1st Brigade and a *suspected* NVA regiment: *suspected,* because when the first shots are fired, you don't really know the nature and size of the enemy unit; as the battle develops, it soon becomes apparent what you are up against.

As we approached the firebase, we could see several artillery batteries firing in support of the engaged battalion. To keep out of their way, we flew through a designated "safe-fly corridor." After landing, we were ushered into a bunker, where we were told that Colonel Johnson wanted to talk to us before he made our assignments, but he was up taking part in the fighting and might not be back before morning. We were then given a C-ration meal and briefed on the current battle.

It later became clear that Colonel Johnson would not return that night, and we were told we might as well get some sleep. Sounded good to me; we hadn't had much since leaving the States. We rolled out our air mattresses and poncho liners on the dirt floor of the bunker, but didn't get much sleep: A 155mm artillery battery was firing directly over the bunker. Every time it fired (all night long) dirt fell right down on us out of the sandbags that had been placed on top of the bunker for overhead cover.

Soon after Colonel Johnson returned to the camp early the next morning, he sent his sergeant major to invite us to join him for breakfast. Meanwhile, the four of us had been discussing possible assignments. The three of us who weren't then up for promotion had agreed to ask for assignment as infantry battalion S-3's (operations officers). And we would recommend the fourth, Major(P) Maurice Edmonds, for the brigade S-3 job. Since Edmonds was about to be promoted, he was most deserving of higher responsibility. Owing to our training at Leavenworth, we all felt competent to do any job, but we wanted to be operations officers, which was in keeping with our backgrounds.

Over breakfast, Colonel Johnson welcomed us to the brigade, and then told us that he had checked our records a couple of months earlier and had picked us for the exact assignments that we wanted.

Before we left for our units, "Cherokee" (Johnson's call sign and the name we came to call him) gave us some serious advice and guidance:

"We are operating in NVA country," he told us. "They are good fighters and must be respected as such—a heck of a lot tougher and more capable than the VC, which are few in this AO [area of operations]. You can expect to encounter, and be attacked on short notice by, regimental-size units—and you must always be prepared for such action.

"Therefore:

- ✪ "All air assaults should be supported by a substantial and sufficient artillery preparation of the LZ [landing zone].
- ✪ "Never maneuver a single company by itself. Always move two together. [A month before our arrival, the 173rd Airborne Brigade

had lost the greater part of two companies moving separately into an NVA ambush at Dak To.]

✪ "Never occupy a night defensive position with only one company. One company cannot last the night against a regimental-size attack. But two with appropriate artillery fire support can.

✪ "Always have rifle companies reach night bed-down locations in sufficient time to dig defensive positions and register their DEFCONs [defensive fire concentrations] with every artillery unit in range before darkness.

✪ "Leave night bed-down locations before daylight and at varying times so as not to establish a pattern. And always recon by fire before starting your movement—just in case the NVA has moved in around your position during the night."

This sage advice reflected not only Johnson's tactical proficiency and competence, but also what he had learned in fighting the NVA. It proved very beneficial to us in fulfilling our responsibilities in our days to come.

BEFORE I move on to my unit, the 3rd Battalion, 12th Infantry, I'd like to give you a general overview of what we were facing. But please be aware that as an infantry major, I had very little knowledge of the overall strategic situation in which I found myself. My focus was very simple: to take the fight to the enemy, and to win every battle with minimum loss of life to our troops.

I can point out, however, that our position set us athwart one of the major funnel outlets for the Ho Chi Minh Trail, which explains the predominant presence of NVA rather than Viet Cong forces. The Trail had "exits" and troop staging and resupply facilities in the vicinity of the most strategically important locations. Dak To was one such location. Our mission was to deny the NVA control over this area. If we had failed to put the cork in that bottle, disaster would have soon followed. The NVA could have taken control of the Central Highlands early in the war.

I didn't have to go more than a couple of hundred yards to join my unit.

The previous year, the 4th Division had deployed as a unit from Fort Lewis, Washington, and had suffered quite a few casualties during its first year in Vietnam. Replacements had been received and integrated into my battalion throughout the year, but now it was time for the original members to complete their tour and return home. When they left, the battalion would be down to about fifty percent strength, requiring a large number of replacements (officers, NCOs, and new enlisted men) and an intensive training program to bring the entire battalion back up to combat proficiency. Most new replacements had never met one another; all of them would have to be trained and integrated into the battalion.

A fourth rifle company was also added to each battalion in order to increase its overall effectiveness.

For a month, my new unit, the 3rd Battalion, 12th Infantry, was given the mission of firebase security for the brigade headquarters. The battalion was commanded by Lieutenant Colonel Pat Volmer.

Because it was my responsibility as the battalion operations and training officer, I quickly developed a training program, which was blessed by Lieutenant Colonel Volmer. As a first step, officers and NCOs with the most experience in Vietnam were cross-leveled between companies within the battalion to create a common base of experience, and within a couple of days the program was under way.

The area around Jackson's Hole turned out to be an ideal environment for training, since just about every day each unit was likely to experience some form of low-level enemy activity—sniper activity or maybe a mortar round near where they happened to be—just enough to let everyone know they were involved in serious business.

The battalion recon platoon consisted of only twelve men. Its normal *modus operandi* involved insertion of four-man teams for a four- or five-day mission. During this time they'd observe and report, but would call for extraction if there was any risk they'd become decisively engaged. This method of operation tended to leave a large time gap between their observations of enemy activity and any possible successful response to it.

I had a somewhat different concept, which I tried out on the battalion commander, and he approved. The concept was to reorganize and train a much more capable platoon, which would function like Rangers; they would set ambushes rather than just observe and get extracted. Once the ambush was sprung, we would react immediately with on-call preplanned artillery and mortar fire, followed by the insertion of (minimally) a rifle company. This new platoon consisted of four squads of nine men each. Each squad was organized as two M-60 machine gun teams, and every man was armed with an antipersonnel claymore mine. This concept proved to be extremely effective—and the new platoon suffered very few casualties.

After six to eight weeks of day-and-night intensive training, we completed the program. We then deployed by helo to an area called VC Valley, which was located about forty kilometers east of Jackson Hole and fifteen kilometers south of An Khe (the 1st Cav Division main base).

VC Valley was a remote, desolate, and sparsely populated area, surrounded by very high mountains and controlled by an NVA cadre of squad- and platoon-size forces (its inhabitants had been impressed into growing crops for them). Our mission was to "clean it out"—an ideal mission for a newly formed and trained battalion, because the occupying NVA forces were present in only small units. In fact, the enemy did not turn out to be the biggest challenge there. Instead, it was the infection caused by the bite of a small green mite, which left boil-like sores that wouldn't heal. Everybody had them.

While conducting our operations, one of our rifle companies discovered a "lost tribe" of about 500 people living in carved-out caves in a mountainside—together with their chickens, pigs, monkeys, and water buffalo.

The Vietnamese government decided to evacuate the tribe to the Edep E Nang Refugee Center, a large camp near Pleiku, made of several hundred tin buildings. One problem: The people refused to leave without their animals. They agreed to be flown out only if we would load the chickens, pigs, and monkeys on board with them, and we had to promise to bring the water buffalo later.

Just about every Chinook (CH-47 twin-rotor helicopters) in the division was tied up for four days on this operation. And the water buffalo required special treatment. They were too mean and unpredictable to risk internal loading and hauling inside aircraft. They had to be captured, tied in cargo nets, and then sling-loaded underneath Hueys.

The battalion commander saddled me with this mission, probably because I grew up on a farm. I selected eight of our best "cowboys" and developed a technique that worked. We'd spread a cargo net on the ground and land a Huey on it. Then as the chopper lifted off to chase the water buffalo, eight "cowboys" would sit four on each side, holding the cargo net. When we were directly over one, and about five feet above its back, we'd drop the net on the buffalo, the chopper would quickly move to one side and a little lower to the ground, and we would jump out, pull the net around the buffalo, and wrestle him to the ground. Then we'd tie his legs together and arrange the net for sling-loading. Once all this was done, the Huey could fly to the refugee center with the buffalo slung underneath.

After three days, we had caught something like thirty buffalo and reunited them with the lost tribe.

By then, the division commander, Major General William Peers, had learned of the "roundup" and shown up to personally observe the action. After he watched for a while, he observed that it was the most entertaining and daring rodeo operation he had ever seen, but allowed that we had perhaps returned enough water buffalo to the lost tribe, and terminated the operation.

The successful accomplishment of the mission came at the expense of two broken arms, a broken leg, and multiple bruises. Morale was high, and I'm sure that everyone involved in the "roundup" who completed their tour will have told their children and grandchildren all about it.

After three weeks, we had also successfully accomplished our main mission of "clearing out VC Valley." We had killed, captured, or driven out NVA cadre, and destroyed all their training devices and supply storage facilities.

Near the end of October, we were ordered to move to Dak To to relieve the 2nd Battalion (Mechanized) 8th Infantry—a two-day operation involving a helicopter extraction back to Pleiku, followed by a convoy move some forty kilometers to the north. We arrived as planned at 1400 hours, which would allow the battalion we were relieving enough time to reach Pleiku before darkness. The move was uneventful.

Until recently, Dak To had been the home of a Special Forces A-Detachment, which had moved about fifteen kilometers west to a newly established campsite called Ben Het. Ben Het was only about six kilometers from the triborder area where Laos, Cambodia, and South Vietnam came together, and set astride a major infiltration artery of the Ho Chi Minh Trail. A single dirt road led from Dak To to Ben Het, and a key bridge located about midway had to be kept secured.

Dak To itself was nothing but a name; it had no facilities, no nothing, except for a short asphalt airstrip. The closest village, Tan Can, was a mile to the east; a provincial headquarters and a small U.S. advisory detachment were located there. We established our "firebase" alongside the Dak To airstrip and the road that led from Konthum to Ben Het. There was no other choice.

When we arrived at Dak To, we were greeted by the 2nd Battalion, 8th Infantry, lined with all their armored personnel carriers and other vehicles ready to go to Dragon Mountain (the 4th Division base at Pleiku). One of their mech platoons, however, still guarding the key bridge on the road to Ben Het, had to be relieved so they could rejoin their parent unit; and one of our own rifle platoons was dispatched immediately to relieve them.

We had already determined in advance the security we would have to get into position before darkness, and our teams and units were ready to assume their positions, but the other battalion was scheduled to pull out in about an hour. That didn't leave us much time to coordinate the final details of the relief operation, but everything worked out okay nevertheless.

Before the other battalion had moved out, I began to grow very concerned about the mountains to our south, which could give the NVA a significant advantage. The lower ridgeline, two or three kilometers away and a thousand feet high, was dominated by Hill 1338, which controlled the whole area, while the entire ridgeline was about eight kilometers long.

When I asked the outgoing battalion S-3 about the last time he'd had anybody up on that ridgeline, he replied, "You don't have to worry about that. Our recon platoon just conducted a sweep of that whole ridgeline a couple of weeks ago, and there's nothing up there but a lot of orangutan monkeys. And besides that, we dropped several Chinook-loads of fifty-five-gallon drums of persistent CS gas* in the valleys leading to the backside of those mountains. This should hinder any infiltration attempts. It's almost impossible to get through that stuff.

"You are really going to enjoy being the 'Lord Mayor of Dak To,' " he concluded. "It's very quiet up here, and too far away from division headquarters for them to bother you."

I did not share either his confidence or his judgment. On this same ridge, the 173rd Airborne Brigade had lost half of a battalion three months earlier. It was key terrain, if I ever saw it. Whoever controlled that ridgeline controlled the whole valley—the main avenue of approach all the way from the border to Kontum. Surely, if the NVA ever had designs on controlling the Central Highlands, they would most certainly occupy that ridgeline and Hill 1338. Why fool with the Special Forces camp at Ben Het if you could bypass it and occupy this dominant terrain as a location for your heavy-weapons firing positions?

The very next afternoon (even before I could get out to coordinate with

---

*Tear gas. When the drums hit the ground, they would burst and spread the powdery gas. It would remain inert until disturbed.

the SF team at Ben Het), a critical piece of intelligence dropped in our lap when the rifle platoon securing the bridge captured an NVA recon team. We quickly learned through interrogation that they were from the 2nd NVA Division and had in their possession sketches of the division's operations plans for taking Dak To. Hill 1338 was to be the location of the division headquarters, while the ridgeline (which we came to call 1001) was to hold the main firing positions for their heavy weapons. And we were the main target: fish down in a fishbowl.

When I told the battalion commander that we'd better get a couple of companies up on that ridgeline, and fast, he agreed. "If you can get the airlift together," he told me, "we'll do it tomorrow afternoon."

Because our parent brigade headquarters had remained at Jackson's Hole, some seventy kilometers away, we had been put directly under the control of the 4th Division at Pleiku. That's the way it works when you are operating apart from a brigade that can no longer support you.

I contacted Division and requested and got ten Hueys and six gunships for the air assault. This would give us enough lift to put eighty riflemen on the ground in a single lift. But finding a good place to put them down again proved much harder. Only one small grassy knoll on the eastern end of the ridgeline would accommodate ten Hueys landing at a time. Everything else in the neighborhood was triple-canopy jungle. It's possible to clear a landing zone in that stuff, but difficult and time-consuming: much too difficult in the time we had. In that jungle, clearing an LZ just large enough to accommodate a single Huey would take a couple of days and several air strikes of 750-pound bombs and hundreds of rounds of 155mm and 8-inch fire. And besides, our only artillery was a 105mm battery with six tubes.

That meant we were forced to use the clearing for the air assault.

On October 28, 1967, at 1500 hours, C Company began the air assault. This was preceded by an artillery prep of the landing zone, consisting of about 150 rounds of 105mm howitzer fire. When the Hueys set down, the LZ proved to be cold, and the first lift of eighty secured it, then waited for the second lift to arrive before they moved as a company toward the woodline.

The helicopters took about twenty minutes for the turnaround, and the second lift arrived with the remainder of the company. The lift was expected to continue until the second company (B Company) had also been inserted.

As soon as C company was complete, the company commander began his movement toward the woodline, which was about 100 meters away. Chest-high elephant grass provided good concealment for the formation. After advancing fifty meters inside the woodline, the point squad began receiving very heavy fire from a well-dug-in NVA position, which was concealed by spider holes with overhead cover. Although they'd been hit by artillery during the prep, they'd held their fire until the squad was inside their position, thus forcing C Company to temporarily pull back without reaching the woodline.

During the exchange, the NVA deliberately shot about half of the members of the point squad—one of their favorite tricks; they knew that U.S. forces would not leave their wounded or dead on the battlefield. Once the U.S. wounded were on the ground, the NVA would go back down into their holes to await the inevitable U.S. artillery barrage, which would be followed by the company's attempt to recover their casualties. As the company launched another attack, the NVA would attempt to shoot more, all the while holding the company forward of the NVA's main defensive position without compromising its true location. If the American attack had not been successful by darkness, the company would find itself in a very vulnerable position—not properly dug in to defend itself against an NVA attack—with the likelihood that the NVA would drag the U.S. dead and wounded off during the night (they carried body hooks for this purpose).

As a result of all this, B Company, now approaching the LZ, was waved off and returned to Dak To by the battalion commander, who was airborne and controlling the operation.

Meanwhile, the C Company commander had requested artillery fire on the enemy position, and the battalion commander had also requested immediate air strikes. After a couple hundred rounds of artillery fire, the company commander decided to make another push in order to try to recover his wounded personnel. This time he was able to reach the treeline before most of the company came under a hail of withering fire. It was now obvious that he was up against at least an NVA company and perhaps a well-dug-in larger unit.

Several flights of close support aircraft arrived shortly after that, and the airborne forward air controller began to put strikes on the enemy position. Afterward, C Company was able to advance far enough to reach the point squad and recover the dead and wounded.

During the air strikes, it proved possible to lift in B Company, and they were able to link up with C Company. By nightfall, and after hundreds of rounds of artillery and mortar fire and many more air strikes (including napalm), both companies had advanced approximately 300 meters inside the woodline, several NVA had been killed, and their position had been overrun, while our troops had suffered fifteen to twenty casualties. A couple of captured NVA soldiers revealed during interrogation that they were part of a battalion of the 2nd NVA Division. Their division had moved into the area two to three weeks earlier and now occupied the lower ridgeline.

Throughout the night, we continued to defend our two companies with close artillery support, while at the same time pounding the area farther down the ridge with air strikes and artillery fire. Throughout the night, periodic enemy mortar fire was received from Hill 1338, which dominated the ridgeline. This was the terrain over which our two companies would have to advance the next morning.

Before movement began the next morning, October 29, it was decided to send a recon patrol up Hill 1338 to determine if it was occupied. Before they'd gotten a third of the way up, the patrol was pinned down by enemy fire, but they were able to disengage and returned to report that the fire was coming from an enemy position constructed with concentric and interconnecting trench lines.

Based on this report and contact the previous evening, it was obvious that we were up against more than a battalion of NVA—and maybe a regiment. All this information was reported to Division, along with our assessment that reinforcements were definitely needed: All indications were that a major battle was in the making.

In the meantime, the best thing our battalion could do was get a third company up on that ridgeline and try to clear it far enough back to protect the airfield (where reinforcements would have to land) from direct enemy fire. While we were doing this, we could attempt to keep the NVA forces on Hill 1338 under control by fire until a major attack could be mounted against them.

Division bought our recommendation, and the next morning, October 30, the third company, A Company, was lifted up to the ridgeline. Throughout the day while the 3rd/12th pushed down the ridgeline, with two companies in the lead, advanced elements from the First Brigade, our parent brigade, began arriving, along with advanced elements from its other two organic battalions. Next day, the two companies pushing down the ridge were only able to advance a couple of kilometers, even with the assistance of continuing air strikes. Several very intense engagements were fought, some at very close range. (One sergeant won the Distinguished Service Cross when he used a shotgun with double-0 buckshot to fight off an NVA squad charging directly at the company command element.)

Searches of dead NVA revealed that some of them were carrying photos of girlfriends and canteens taken from soldiers of the 173rd Airborne Brigade that had been killed in that same area in June. These discoveries enraged our own soldiers, and increased their determination to make the NVA pay a high price for the Americans they'd killed earlier on this same battleground.

By late afternoon, the First Brigade headquarters had arrived, and they were now in charge. On the following day, another battalion from the First Brigade, the 3rd Battalion, 8th Infantry, had also closed. Convoys of heavy artillery (155mm and 8-inch) from Division were also on the way.

On November 1, the 3rd/8th Infantry was inserted farther down the ridgeline, a little farther to the south on Hill 837. This put them directly astride the infiltration route supposedly blocked by drums of persistent CS gas. During the insertion, the LZ was hot, and several soldiers were killed or wounded, including the battalion commander. Nevertheless, support from air strikes and helicopter gunships made it possible for the entire battalion to close at its new location before darkness. The 3rd/8th Infantry then found itself heavily engaged, under siege, and isolated from reinforcements for the next few days. They were unable to get replacements in or to evacuate its casualties and dead. Every helicopter that approached the LZ was either shot up or shot down.

During this period, their defensive perimeter was penetrated several times, leaving little doubt that the enemy's intent was to overrun and wipe out the battalion.

Finally, Arc Lights were brought in—flights of nine B-52 bombers dumping hundreds of tons of 500- and 750-pound bombs—and the siege was broken. This gave the battalion the opportunity to bring in much-needed replacements and to evacuate casualties (the dead had to be brought out in cargo nets slung underneath Hueys). The intensity of this action made it apparent that the 3rd/8th Infantry was likely facing another regiment-size unit from the 2nd NVA Division. In fact, the intelligence folks were saying that the entire 2nd NVA Division could well be deployed in those mountains, with the objective of taking Dak To and advancing farther down the road to Kontum. Success in this would give them control over the major routes leading through the Central Highlands, with a straight shot on to Pleiku. Once there, they'd control most of the Central Highlands.

Reinforcements continued to pour in, and by the fourth of November, three U.S. brigades, reinforced by twelve battalions of artillery, were fighting in the Dak To area. The battle for Dak To was turning into one of the largest and bloodiest battles of the war. It lasted until near Christmas.

Some of the heaviest fighting was still to come.

After clearing most of the ridgeline, our battalion was given the mission to seize Hill 1338. Our plan of attack called for A and C Companies to attack up separate ridgelines, with the Recon Platoon (approximately fifty soldiers) in the center and maintaining contact between the two companies. Operating under the assumption that the 2nd NVA Division headquarters was located there, we decided to place continuous artillery fire on the hill's summit. Our minimal hope was to neutralize its effectiveness until we could get to the top.

The attack itself turned out to be a trenchline-by-trenchline fight, lasting three days, day and night. The NVA had rung the entire mountain with interconnecting bands of trenches, dug six to seven feet deep. Inside the trenches, they'd carved out little seats of dirt so their soldiers could sit with their backs facing downhill toward the advancing companies. At each position was a case of 82mm mortar rounds. They'd take up a round, strike the fuse on the ammunition box, and fling the round back over their heads toward our advancing troops. It was literally raining mortar rounds.

These positions were so secure that artillery fire had little effect on them, unless a round by chance landed directly in one of the narrow trenchlines. The most effective weapon turned out to be napalm flown in by A-4 Skyraider propeller-driven airplanes. Skyraiders were slow, but very accurate, and the troops loved them. Much of the napalm was brought in "danger close"—fifty to one hundred meters in front of the advancing troops. This resulted in some casualties to our own troops—but by choice; the alternative was worse.

When we finally reached the summit, we discovered that a few of the NVA troops who remained there had actually been chained to trees to make sure they stayed and fought. We also discovered that, sure enough, the 2nd NVA Division headquarters had been located there. By then, what was left of the division had withdrawn down the backside of the mountain into the valley, but the area was by no means secured.

One of the more memorable experiences during my tour occurred later that evening at the Dak To airfield. For several days, a steady stream of C-130s had been landing day and night, bringing in unit reinforcements and ammo (one of them had already been destroyed by mortar fire), and I had gone down to meet and orient ten just-arriving replacements, about to go to C Company on Hill 1338—a pair of lieutenants straight out of Officer Candidate School, two new sergeants, and six privates. As they were off-loading from a C-130, a helicopter was also arriving, carrying a cargo net loaded with soldiers' bodies to a Graves Registration Collection Point near the C-130. There the casualties would be placed in body bags and then transloaded to the C-130. As the helo was maneuvering to set the load down, something went wrong and the load was accidentally dropped about eight feet onto the tarmac. The crunching of bodies and breaking of bones had to leave an indelible impression on the new replacements.

As soon as the helicopter moved off, I gathered the new replacements, welcomed them to the battalion, and gave them an orientation about on- and off-loading from a helicopter. I then wished them good luck and told them that when they arrived (after a ten-minute flight) they would be met and welcomed either by the company commander or, most likely, by the first sergeant.

Except for the two new lieutenants, and possibly the NCOs, none of them had met until three days earlier, when they'd been in-processed at brigade rear at Pleiku. There they'd received their orientations, drawn their gear, and zeroed their weapons. And now they were only ten minutes away from combat.

This was the way the replacement system worked in Vietnam. Replacements came in as individuals and not as units. In units, soldiers get to know each other well before they have to fight, and they develop relationships based on mutual respect, trust, and confidence—relationships that often endure a lifetime. Forming and completing training as a unit before commitment to combat is far more effective in every sense than an individual replacement system.

They reached their company on Hill 1338 and were integrated into its ranks as the company was preparing its night defensive positions.

Next morning, after dropping off much-needed ammunition, the first helicopter carried back the bodies of one of the two new lieutenants, a sergeant, and three of the privates to where they had arrived some twelve hours before. During their first night in combat they'd made the supreme sacrifice, even before they'd met all the members of their units.

THE next day, as we swept over the ridge and down into the valleys that led to the backside, we found some amazing things: There was a swinging bridge, at least a quarter of a mile long, built underneath the triple-canopy jungle, so it could not be observed from the air. The NVA would use it to rush reinforcements back and forth between various battle positions. A dug-in hospital complex had been constructed along a stream in a valley on the backside of the mountain. It was so well-concealed that it was discovered only when a man from the point squad fell into a covered fighting position. A search of the area revealed complete underground operating rooms and enough body parts in a pile to fill a small truck.

We also learned that the NVA had taken far more casualties in the battle than the eighty or so that we'd taken in capturing Hill 1338.

About this time came the climax of another action that was part of the fight for Hill 1338: On an adjoining ridgeline about two kilometers to the west was a dug-in NVA gun position that for a few days had been shooting at the ammunition dump down at Dak To, so far without hitting it. From its "crack," we thought it was a 57mm recoilless rifle, well-concealed and protected in a cave. The gunner would fire only six rounds or so a day, obviously hoping he wouldn't be detected.

A reconnaissance patrol had been sent to the area where he was believed to be located, but hadn't found his position. For some reason he did not fire while the patrol was in the area. After that, brigade headquarters assumed the mission of neutralizing him; they leveled an eight-inch howitzer and fired directly at the shooter's position—but had no more luck than the recon patrol.

He continued to shoot, but not daily, and he varied the time on those days he did fire, then pulled the weapon back into the cave before counterfire could be placed on his position.

After a few days of this cat-and-mouse, he finally hit an ammo bunker filled with 155mm rounds—causing an explosion of something like 1,100 tons of various calibers of ammunition, including 8-inch and 175mm.

From my location on the 1,000-foot-high ridgeline, it looked and felt like an atomic explosion, with the mushroom cloud blossoming 1,000 feet above us.

A couple of moments after it went off, I called my Leavenworth friend, Maury Edmonds, who was still the brigade S-3, and said, "Maury, did you just get nuked? It looks like it from my location."

"I don't know what happened," he answered, "but there's eight-inch and 175mm unexploded shells lying all over this area."

The explosion was so intense that it caved in many of the bunkers, and it took days to clean up the mess, and several ammunition convoys to re-stock the ammo.

AFTER the battle for Hill 1338, a lot of fighting was still going on through-out the brigade area of operation, and my battalion was given the mission to secure Hill 660, near the intersection of the Laos, Cambodia, and Vietnamese border. It also turned out to be a very hot area, and we contin-ued to be involved daily in significant contacts until the twenty-seventh of December, our first day in a long time without enemy contact.

At this time some of the reinforcing units that had arrived at the begin-ning of the battle began redeploying elsewhere within the division area of operations. The First Brigade, with its three organic battalions, would now assume responsibility for the mopping-up operation, as well as security for the entire Dak To area of operation.

All our units had fought magnificently, and we were very proud of our ac-complishments—essentially, thwarting the 2nd NVA Division's plans for taking control of the Central Highlands and the major infiltration route that would have permitted them either to cut Vietnam in two all the way to the coast or turn south toward Kontum and Pleiku.

I have never known a more dedicated and selfless group of men: men who were motivated for the right reasons and who were willing to lay their lives on the line for our freedom. We were fighting for what we believed in, what we thought was right, and I can never recall a time when a single sol-dier refused to fight or showed cowardice in the face of the enemy.

Near the end of the war, newspapers in the States carried stories of pot-smoking, rapes, and fraggings of officers and NCOs. None of that hap-pened in my unit.

After the battle, the 3/12 Infantry received a Presidential Unit Citation for its accomplishments, and many individual soldiers received medals for heroism. When General Westmoreland visited our battalion around Christmas, he told us that our battalion had seen more combat than any other battalion in Vietnam.

I N retrospect I would like to emphasize our respect for the NVA soldiers. They were outstanding fighters, who had little material support beyond what they carried on their backs. They knew how to survive, and they were tough.

On the other hand, it's hard for me to understand the ways they chose to motivate their troops to fight. Or at least their ways were alien to our culture.

If they had one weakness, it was in their noncommissioned officers' corps. They neither trained nor trusted their NCOs with enough authority to exercise flexibility in reacting to changing battlefield situations. I'm baffled by a culture whose leaders will chain their troops to trees to make sure they remain in position and fight. It is equally hard to understand a culture where political indoctrination forms the basis for motivation.

Every NVA soldier carried in his combat pack a small bag of marijuana wrapped in plastic. Before each battle, the troops would assemble to hear a lecture by the political officer (one for each company). As part of this preparation process, everyone would smoke the marijuana. You could often smell the aroma a good distance away from their attack position, and you knew they were ready and coming when you started smelling it and started hearing the bugles blowing.

Once they'd launched, they stuck to their attack plan—without any obvious ability to change it—until they had either suffered so heavily they could not continue or had been ordered to withdraw.

D U R I N G the Battle of Dak To of November and December 1967, we were involved in almost continuous daily fighting, yet we had inflicted heavy casualties on the 2nd NVA Division, forcing it to withdraw into their Cambodian and Laotian sanctuaries for refitting.

During this same period, the Special Forces detachments in the Central Highlands reaped the benefits of their Village Defense Program efforts to organize and direct the Montagnard tribesmen. Their outstanding work denied the Viet Cong supplies and recruits from the area tribes, and reduced the Viet Cong's capability primarily to small-unit activities such as occasional ambushes and weapons attacks.

The main threat, however, still remained: the NVA units using the Ho Chi Minh Trail to infiltrate into the "sanctuary" and resupply areas located in Laos and Cambodia, and from there directly into Vietnam, a one-night march.

In response to the change in mission assigned to Special Forces in 1965—"border surveillance and control, operations against infiltration routes, and operations against VC war zones and base areas"—most Special Forces camps had been relocated closer to the border near the main infiltration routes. Because their activities disrupted the NVA, they were prime targets. That meant in practice that they became vulnerable to attack by battalion- or regiment-size units at any time.

Two years earlier, there had been six SF A-Detachments (at Ben Het, Dak Pek, Dak Seang, Dak Sut, Poly Klang, and Plei Me) in what was now the First Brigade's operational area. All had been heavily involved in organizing and training the Montagnard tribesmen. But by January 1968, only Ben Het, Dak Pek, and Plei Me remained.

Although all of them had been well fortified, Dak Seang had suffered heavily during a three-week siege (all resupply had to be air-dropped), and the camp was closed. Dak Sut and Poly Klang, subjected to repeated attacks, had also been closed.

Two of the remaining three, Ben Het and Dak Pek, were close to the border astride major infiltration routes. Their exposed location made them very vulnerable. The A-Detachment at Plei Me was in better shape, since it was in a much less threatened location.

Ben Het, fifteen kilometers west of Dak To, and only ten kilometers from the triborder area, was a typical SF camp: heavily fortified bunkers with interconnecting trench lines; observation towers; rows of concertina wire fencing, interspersed with Claymore antipersonnel mines; fifty-five-gallon drums of phu gas (napalm); and a short airstrip—too short to accommodate aircraft larger than C-7A Caribous.

Two batteries of 175mm howitzers had been positioned there for support of SF teams operating across the border against NVA infiltration and base areas. A U.S. infantry company had also been placed there for additional security. With maximum charge (110 pounds of powder), the 175s could hurl a 500-pound high-explosive projectile thirty-six kilometers; they were highly effective against targets discovered by the SF teams.

Several ammunition convoys a week (including tanks for protection against ambush) were necessary to resupply the 175mm howitzers. That meant the road to Ben Het had to be swept at least twice a week for mines, with tanks covering the minesweeping teams.

Dak Pek was located on another major NVA infiltration route, forty kilometers to the north in no-man's-land. It was reachable only by air, and defended only by the A-Detachment there, mortars, and a contingent of loyal Montagnards. No U.S. artillery was in range.

ALTHOUGH these camps were located in our division's area, MACV had primary responsibility for their security (most of their support actually came from the 5th SFG). Our division commander, Major General William Peers, was neither in the SF chain of command nor responsible for the security of the camps. Even so, he recognized their vulnerability and the valuable role they were performing against the NVA, and decided on his own to augment their support. Peers took his concerns to my brigade commander, Colonel Johnson, and told him to make sure they had all available support needed for their defenses.

By January 1968, after Maury Edmonds was promoted to Division G-3, I had moved up to become Brigade S-3 (operations officer), and so I got the job from Colonel Johnson to visit each camp once a week. There I would check their defenses to determine what ammunition and artillery support they needed (this would include establishing a fire-support channel with U.S. units within range), exchange intelligence information, and establish a communications channel for operations.

The day after the Colonel gave me the mission, I set out with the brigade aviation officer and the fire support coordinator to visit the two SF camps. For the next six months, I not only ran the brigade's operations, I was also closely involved with the Special Forces camps within the area.

The first time we showed up, the SF troops were initially a little stand-offish and apprehensive. I don't know why, but they probably suspected I'd come to find faults. But when I told them I had worn the Green Beret a little over a year earlier, had trained many of the teams now in Vietnam, and was now in a position to help them with "conventional support," they really opened up and welcomed us.

We went on to check their defensive measures as if we were in our own units, and except for mortar ammunition and preregistered defensive concentrations from artillery, we found them to be in pretty good shape (since Dak Pek was beyond artillery range, they had to be supported by air).

Though in the days ahead our visits proved mutually beneficial, our biggest payoff came from the exchange of intelligence information. I was very impressed with their operational activities against NVA infiltration; these had returned with intelligence information that might reveal future NVA plans for the area.

Both camps were reporting that their "border watch teams" had heard what appeared to be road-building activities near the border. If they were not mistaken, these roads were aimed in the direction of the camps at Ben Het and Dak Pek.

By mid-February 1968, aerial reconnaissance operations had confirmed their reports: The NVA were building roads under the triple-canopy jungle; they were already two to three kilometers inside Vietnam, and were headed toward Ben Het and Dak Pek.

In coordination with both camps, the First Brigade assumed responsibility for interdiction of the road-building operations. Soon, air strikes against both roads had succeeded in delaying but not stopping the construction work. Recon teams confirmed that the NVA was using a clever tactic to deceive us. They had left the bomb craters unfilled, leaving aerial observation with the impression that our bombing had made the roads unusable. And then, at night, they had built bypasses around the craters and camouflaged them with vegetation. This could be quickly removed when the roads were needed for large-scale movement of troops and equipment, and replaced.

The NVA were putting a lot of effort into possibly taking out a couple of remote SF camps. "Why?" we asked ourselves. And this led to a larger question: "What is the real purpose of these roads? Are Ben Het and Dak Pek the final objectives? Or are they just intermediate objectives for a much larger operation?"

The answer—or at least parts of it—came as a result of a major intelligence breakthrough in mid-March.

A young Army captain, commanding a radio research unit attached to the First Brigade, succeeded in breaking the code for the NVA ground tactical operations net. For the first time, we had reliable information about near-term NVA tactical plans—that is, we were not getting strategic intelligence about the NVA master plan for Vietnam, only operational intelligence concerning our particular area of operations. But this was accurate and *very* useful.

This information was so crucial and sensitive that it was safeguarded with the highest security. Only those who had an absolute need-to-know had access. We were afraid that Major General Peers would pull our captain and his detachment back to Division, but he didn't. Instead, he would fly out to Dak To every day for a personal briefing.

As an aside: For about thirty consecutive days, brigade headquarters had been receiving a daily dose of incoming fire every afternoon—sometimes thirty rounds of 82mm mortar, sometimes fifteen to twenty rounds of 57mm recoilless rifle fire, and sometimes ten to twenty rounds of 105mm GRAD rocket fire (we feared this the most; no bunker could stop a GRAD rocket).

The weapons and gunners had reinfiltrated the area where we had earlier fought the 2nd NVA Division, and the ammunition was hauled in from Cambodia by sleds pulled by elephants. The fire was becoming more intense and accurate every day, and it was obviously coming from more and more firing positions.

Through this new intelligence source, we learned that the gun crews coming into the area were being instructed to "shoot at the Texas flag."

Only one flag flew in the whole brigade base area. Sure enough, it was the Texas flag—flying on a twenty-foot pole above the sandbagged tent where the forward air controller slept (he was a lieutenant colonel from Texas). The tent was directly above and slightly behind the brigade tactical operations center, and provided a perfect aiming point. The lieutenant colonel was awfully proud of his flag, but it had to come down. It remained inside his sandbagged tent for the rest of his tour.

FROM this new intelligence we also learned (almost daily) which units they planned to engage with fire, the coordinates of their firing positions, and how many rounds they planned to fire. Accordingly, we planned our counterfires to impact their locations about two minutes before their scheduled firing times.

We also pieced together that Dak Pek and Ben Het were both targets for major ground attacks, which would most likely be supported by armor. It was likely that Dak Pek would be hit in early April. Once it was taken out, follow-on units could move through the mountains to our north and take positions near Dak To and to our rear. From Dak Pek, they could also head south toward Kontum and on to Pleiku.

Ben Het was to be knocked off in early May. Dak To would follow.

Though we didn't know it at the time, this plan of attack would turn out to be supportive of the major attacks of the 1968 Tet campaign—a long-planned and prepared-for NVA and Viet Cong offensive throughout South Vietnam, designed to inflict heavy casualties and damage and thus achieve a major setback for the South Vietnamese government and a worldwide propaganda victory. Tet accomplished those aims—even though the Communists actually lost Tet militarily. Afterward the Viet Cong were practically destroyed as an effective fighting force, and the NVA also took a huge hit. The first recognizable Tet attacks took place at the end of January, but the campaign continued for some months after that.

What we did know was that unless we prevented the fall of Dak Pek and Ben Het, we at Dak To would be cut off and fighting in both directions.

WHILE day-and-night air strikes continued to pound both NVA road-construction operations, in early April the 5th SF Group decided to bring in a MIKE Force (composed of Vietnamese Rangers) to attack the road builders and their security battalion near Dak Pek.* Once that was accomplished, they would reinforce Dak Pek defenses.

The Rangers were lifted into Dak To by C-123 aircraft, then air-assaulted into the Dak Pek area by helicopters with gunship support. When they reached the area, they were almost immediately engaged by a superior NVA force. Two of their accompanying twelve-man advisory team (an Australian captain and a U.S. SF NCO) were killed during the first few minutes.

Faced with overwhelming firepower, the losses of key advisers, and heavy losses of their own, the Mike Force broke off the engagement, leaving the remainder of the advisory team there. We were able to extract that team before dark, together with the bodies of those KIA (the defenders of Dak Pek were not involved in the action, and remained in place at the camp).

It took three days for the disorganized and retreating remnants of the Mike unit to be assembled at Dak To and flown out.

It was obvious that the NVA would eventually lay siege to Dak Pek and was willing to pay a high price for the camp. As air strikes continued, Dak Pek was reinforced with an infantry battalion from the 1st Brigade, together with thirty preplanned Arc Lights (a total of ninety B-52 bombers), which would be employed when the attack came.

The attack came in early April—by an estimated NVA regiment sup-

---

*MIKE Forces were handpicked, specially trained, quick-reaction forces modeled along the lines of U.S. Army Ranger units. Each unit had about fifteen hundred men and an advisory detachment of twelve to fifteen U.S. and Australian Special Forces members. Each field force/corps area had its own MIKE Force. The first one to be trained was composed of Chinese Nungs, recruited for their fighting ability, but due to the shortage of Nung recruits, practically all other MIKE Forces were manned by volunteers from Vietnamese Army Ranger units.

ported by tanks—but was unsuccessful. Our preparations had paid off. The few surviving NVA withdrew back to the sanctuary from which they had come.

Ben Het would come next, and we expected the same—perhaps even more, because this infiltration route had greater strategic value. If Ben Het could be knocked off, it was a straight shot over a major road network to Dak To, on to An Khe (the division base for 1st Cav), and then to the coast and Da Nang.

Two major pieces of key terrain dominated Ben Het: a hill to the west, and another to the east—each within supporting fires distance of the other. It would be awfully tough to take Ben Het without controlling both hills. The 3rd Battalion, 8th Infantry (reinforced), was given the mission to oc cupy these hills and defend Ben Het. The plan called for air strikes on the western hill summit to clear a landing zone, followed by an artillery prep, and then by the landing of two companies. Once this hill was occupied, the rest of the battalion would occupy the hill to the east.

When the first flight, carrying a rifle platoon, touched down, they immediately came under fire from an NVA force that had already occupied the hill. Artillery fire was shifted to the hill's western back side, while the remainder of the two companies were landed at its eastern base. By nightfall they had fought their way up the hill, driven off the NVA force, and linked up with the platoon at the summit. The eastern hill was occupied without incident.

For the next two days, the two hills would be developed into defensive positions, completely bracketed by the fires of five supporting artillery battalions.

Meanwhile, the 7th/17th Air Cav conducted daily screens to the west of Ben Het to detect infiltration. When it was detected, the plan was to stop it with artillery and air strikes. But things did not quite work out that way. In spite of thousands of rounds of artillery, 846 close-air-support sorties, and 99 Arc Lights—all during a three-week period in May 1968—Ben Het and the two hills were hit by three regiment-size NVA attacks.

At first light on the mornings after each of these attacks, the 7th/17th Cav would pursue and engage the attackers all the way to the border. As one Cav commander reported back, "The foot trails through the dust of the bomb craters are three, four feet wide, and many are covered with blood and dragged body trails."

The NVA never succeeded in taking Ben Het, and their casualties must have been enormous. Yet after each attack they withdrew to their sanctuary to refit and come again.

During this same period, several smaller NVA units were also discovered in the hills only a thousand meters north of the Dak To airstrip, and Arc Light strikes had to be brought in danger-close (within 350 meters of friendly positions) to neutralize them. Somehow, at least a battalion-size unit had managed to get through, because on the night of the main Tet Offensive, this unit attacked the South Vietnamese province headquarters located in the village of Tan Can one kilometer east of the Dak To base complex. Supported by an Air Force gunship, the SF-trained CIDG defenders acquitted themselves well. At least 125 NVA bodies littered the clearing around the village.

DURING the Tet campaign, practically every unit in the 1st Brigade area of operations was attacked, yet not a single unit's defenses were penetrated, and the NVA suffered heavy casualties.

In retrospect, we can assume that the heavy fighting during the November–December '67 battle for Dak To and in the April–May '68 fight for Dak Pek and Ben Het had significantly reduced the 2nd NVA Division's capability to accomplish their part of the Tet campaign.

Though the NVA and Viet Cong suffered heavily during Tet, that did not break their will or change their designs on the Central Highlands. Nightly bombing did little to stop the convoys rolling down the Ho Chi Minh Trail. Both the glow of headlights and the green tracers from NVA antiaircraft weapons were clearly visible from the firebases our battalions occupied.

During the next two months of my tour, hardly a day passed without significant contact with at least a company-size NVA unit, and there were two or three battalion-size attacks against our battalion firebases as well.

Twice a week, a resupply convoy—usually fifty to a hundred trucks escorted by military police, helo gunships, and tanks—would run from Pleiku to Kontum, and then on to Dak To. Even though the jungle had been cleared 100–200 meters on each side of the road, the convoy was often ambushed by at least a company-size force. Sometimes the fighting was so intense that the tanks would fire on each other with beehive rounds (flechette) to clear off the NVA.

I ROTATED from Vietnam in July 1968. While I was there, the 1st Brigade, together with the Special Forces teams and their Montagnard defenders, controlled and defended the Central Highlands, never losing a battle, and never abusing, violating, or oppressing the people there.

All of us who were able to come home felt that the cause for which we fought and sacrificed was worthy, justifiable, and right—our own freedom and the freedom of those we had been sent to defend.

I have the utmost admiration and respect for all with whom I was privileged to serve, especially the soldiers of the 1st Brigade and the Special Forces teams, and for their sacrifices and accomplishments in relieving the plight of the Montagnards. I also share their sorrow over the tragedies suffered by the Montagnards after U.S. forces were withdrawn. Though all Montagnards endured terrible retribution from the NVA—many were killed, and many others died in reindoctrination camps—the extraordinary and heartfelt efforts of the SF teams who served with them saved many others, who now live in the United States as productive citizens.

Deep Reconnaissance

Tom Clancy resumes:

Reconnaissance behind enemy lines is a traditional special operations mission—to put eyes on otherwise hidden enemy activities. In Vietnam, because the enemy found it so easy to hide beneath triple-canopy rain forest or in tunnels, the need for deep reconnaissance was even more than normally pressing.

In the spring of 1964, MACV and the South Vietnamese Joint General Staff established a dedicated deep reconnaissance capability, called Leaping Lena, made up of CIDG and Vietnamese troops under U.S. Special Forces leadership. Its mission was to conduct critical, hazardous recon missions inside South Vietnam (though a few teams were also sent across the Laotian border against the Ho Chi Minh Trail, but with disastrous results). In October of that year, a control headquarters was established, called Detachment B-52, and the overall operation became Project Delta.

Throughout the war, Delta was involved in long-range reconnaissance against enemy sanctuaries and concealed enemy positions. This took many forms—reconnaissance-in-force missions (often using MIKE Force units), intelligence collection, directing artillery and air strikes, bomb damage assessment, rescue of downed pilots and allied prisoners of war, capture of enemy personnel in order to gather intelligence, deception missions, PSYOPs, photoreconnaissance, and many others—all deep within enemy territory. Teams would be inserted for several days, then brought out and debriefed. The program continued until 1970, when Detachment B-52 was deactivated.

Though Delta had a nationwide mission, other deep reconnaissance operations—Projects Omega and Sigma (Detachments B-50 and B-56)—had a more regional orientation. But their missions were otherwise very similar.

DEEP reconnaissance across borders (into Laos or Cambodia, say) was by its nature a covert operation, and initially a CIA responsibility; but later it became a MACV-directed mission (though with some continued CIA participation), under what was called MACVSOG—the Military Assistance Command Vietnam Studies and Observation Group (it was called that for cover purposes). MACVSOG was activated in January 1964, and used Special Forces, Navy SEALs, Air Force Air Commandos, and Vietnamese to conduct covert and unconventional operations throughout Southeast Asia, but of course specifically against North Vietnam, the NVA, the Viet Cong, and the Ho Chi Minh Trail.*

MACVSOG was involved in a wide range of activities, not just deep reconnaissance. A great deal of effort, for example, was put into operations against North Vietnam: Agents were inserted, with the aim of setting up intelligence or resistance cells (most were captured soon after insertion and executed or turned). There were seaborne commando raids against the North Vietnamese Navy and North Vietnam's coast. There were psychological operations and dirty tricks. And teams were sent to observe the Ho Chi Minh Trail. Later, teams conducted raids against it.

Beginning in 1961, Special Forces personnel, under CIA direction, had been involved in cross-border surveillance into southeastern Laos. For the next two years, close to fifty teams sent over the border gave the Agency eyeball proof that the NVA had a strong and growing presence in Laos and were infiltrating at least 1,500 troops a month into South Vietnam. Between 1963 and 1965, for political reasons, this surveillance was halted. For those two years, Americans were not allowed to conduct cross-border deep reconnaissance against the Trail, allowing the NVA the opportunity to greatly build up and extend their facilities and capabilities. By 1964, it was esti-

---

*For a fuller description of MACVSOG activities, see the recent and excellent *The Secret War Against Hanoi*, by Richard H. Schultz, Jr., HarperCollins, 1999.

mated that at least 45,000 troops had infiltrated south, and the numbers were growing.

In March 1965—and after considerable struggle—the JCS finally convinced the Lyndon Johnson White House to allow MACVSOG to resume covert cross-border operations into Laos, with Special Forces personnel leading the teams. The SOG operational plan was ambitious (and just maybe workable). It had three phases: (1) Short-stay, tactical intelligence missions would identify NVA headquarters, base camps, and supply dumps. These would then be attacked by air strikes. This would be followed by (2) company-size raids against NVA facilities discovered by recon teams. This would be followed by (3) the recruiting, organizing, and training of local tribesmen living near the Trail to become the nucleus of long-term resistance movements against the NVA. This phase was based on the earlier—and successful—White Star Program in Laos. The overall aim of the plan was to interdict traffic on the Ho Chi Minh Trail.

No one will ever know how well the plan would have worked. Using the preservation of the 1962 Geneva Accords as a reason, the State Department successfully opposed the implementation of the second and third phases, and severely limited the first.

The terms of the deal worked out with the State Department allowed teams into Laos to observe the Trail, but only a few of them could go in each month, their time inside Laos was extremely limited, they had to walk in (they couldn't use helicopters or parachutes), only a very small part of the border was open to them, and they could penetrate no more than five kilometers into the country (their area of operations was in all about fifty square miles). Targets that the teams identified could be bombed, but only after the American Embassy in the Laotian capital had approved the target, and the targets would have to be bombed by U.S. planes based in Thailand.

The man chosen to run this program was (by then Colonel) Bull Simons.

He quickly put together a field organization and headquarters staff, and recruited teams—usually three Americans and nine Vietnamese from one of the minority tribes, such as Nungs and especially the Montagnards.

The mission was to be totally covert, and the teams infiltrated into Laos were to be, in the jargon of the covert world, "sterile." That meant they wore non-American/non-Vietnamese uniforms that were made somewhere in Asia for SOG. The uniforms showed neither rank nor unit insignia.

In the fall of 1965, the first teams crossed the Laotian border; excellent results soon followed. After two years of unrestricted operations in Laos, the

NVA didn't expect trouble. They'd gotten overconfident. SOG teams quickly identified truck parks and fuel depots, supply caches, bridges, and other storage sites. Air strikes were called in, with the BDAs (Bomb Damage Assessments) often claiming eighty to a hundred percent destruction.

Continued success resulted in expanded missions. Thus, in 1966, helicopters were allowed for insertion of SOG missions, though they could penetrate no deeper than five kilometers inside Laos. The team inserted could now, however, go another five kilometers on foot. In other words, the limit was now ten kilometers and not five. Missions would last up to five days.

Though the SOG teams' primary mission did not change—covert teams identifying targets on the Trail for air strikes—other missions came to be added, virtually identical to those conducted by Project Delta within South Vietnam:

Teams conducted BDAs, tapped NVA land communications, captured NVA soldiers to gain intelligence, rescued U.S. personnel who were evading or escaping capture, and inserted electronic sensors along the Trail to detect targets for air strikes. Thousands of seismic and acoustic sensors were placed, most of them by air, but SOG teams also carried many in on their backs. Larger teams came to be formed and used for conducting raids, ambushes, and larger-scale rescue.

In 1967, the depth of insertion by foot or by helicopter was allowed to grow to twenty kilometers; the size of the teams was allowed to increase, as was the number of teams per month (from a high of fifteen to forty-two); and Cambodia was added to SOG's area of operations (the NVA had significant facilities and operations there, including the main NVA headquarters in the south, called COSVN—the Central Office for South Vietnam). However, operations in Cambodia would be limited to reconnaissance, and missions were limited to no more than ten per month. There'd be no air strikes, no raids, no combat except to avoid capture. Teams were expected to avoid contact, and helicopters could only be used for emergency exfiltration.

Just as in 1966, SOG had much success in 1967. They'd caught the NVA napping. "For two years," Richard Schultz writes, Bull Simons and his "SOG teams had used surprise, diversion, deception, and operational deftness to outfox the NVA on the Trail." In 1968, that began to change. The NVA started countermeasures. The NVA's Laotian defenses "had become redundant, layered, and in-depth. Hanoi knew it could not sustain its war

in South Vietnam without unfettered use of the Trail, and it took the necessary steps to defend it."*

The chief agent for this change was the Tet campaign, which consumed
enormous quantities of supplies and enormous numbers of troops. The
NVA *had* to have free movement on the Trail for Tet—and for the most part
they got it—but they needed it even more after Tet. During the next two
years, they exploited that strategic victory (though, to repeat, it was a tactical defeat). Tet convinced the White House (in both its Johnson and Nixon
years) that the war in Vietnam was not winnable. The best outcome was
thought to be a dignified withdrawal combined with help for our South
Vietnamese friends.

Tet also had a number of practical consequences:

During the offensive, the SOG teams that would have been tasked for
deep recon inside Laos and Cambodia were needed for fire brigade missions
inside South Vietnam. Observation of the Trail suffered, of course.

Meanwhile—with characteristic ingenuity and common sense—the
NVA were setting up their defenses. These were—characteristically—primitive, and terribly effective. As early as 1966, the NVA had placed spotters
at high points (ridges or treetops) along the border to listen or watch for insertion helicopters. When helicopters were detected, the observers would
communicate back to headquarters by radio—or by drums, bells, or gongs.
Later, the NVA began to scout the possible helicopter landing zones—since
there were only a finite number of these—and placed spotters to observe
them. Antiaircraft weapons began showing up in ever-increasing numbers.
(Lyndon Johnson's Tet-inspired bombing halt over North Vietnam released
large numbers of personnel and equipment for expanding the Trail's security system.) Trackers began to hunt for SOG teams; they then coordinated
their findings with follow-up military units. The NVA studied SOG operational patterns and methods (night movements, phases of the moon, and the
like) and set up traps and ambushes. A very mobile, Ranger-like unit was
formed to attack the teams. Spies in Saigon passed over plans and schedules to the NVA.

The consequences were predictable: Casualties during recon operations
in Laos and Cambodia dramatically increased, while average team time on
operations in Laos decreased from the Bull Simons goal of five days down

---

*The Secret War Against Hanoi, p. 240.

to no more than two days. That was how long teams were able to avoid the NVA searching for them.

By 1970, the magic word out of the Nixon-Kissinger White House was Vietnamization. U.S. Forces would withdraw from Vietnam, while South Vietnam's forces would be given "all the help and support they needed" in order to take over the war. (It should not be forgotten that the American buildup had originally been justified as a way to give South Vietnamese forces time to grow strong enough to take care of their own war. That never happened.)

For the next two years, SOG recon teams continued to cross over into Laos and Cambodia. Large-unit incursions went into both countries to attack the Trail and the NVA command facilities located along it: In Cambodia it was a joint U.S.–South Vietnamese effort. In Laos, it was solely South Vietnamese—and a great disaster. Bombings came and went. The reconnaissance produced valuable intelligence, and there was considerable heroism, but the end game was in motion. The final moves were already determined.

In the spring of 1972, MACVSOG was disbanded.

Not many months after that, the NVA no longer needed the Ho Chi Minh Trail.

VII

BETWEEN
THE WARS

In 1966, Special Forces had seven active component groups—the 1st, 3d, 5th, 6th, 7th, 8th, and 10th Special Forces Groups, four of which were augmented with PSYOPs, civil affairs, engineers, support, etc., to meet other special requirements.

After Vietnam, Special Forces were drastically cut back, and by 1978 their force structure had been reduced to only three active groups—the 5th, 7th, and 10th. Promotions dried up and the overall scope of activities was severely diminished. The focus of the military establishment withdrew from operations involving foreign internal defense and development, and returned to the tried-and-true conventional doctrines and procedures in which professional soldiers had long found comfort. The main emphasis now was seen as preparing for a potential major land war against the Soviets, and that called for modernized conventional forces, not the more unorthodox ways of special operations.

The survival of Special Forces itself was never in doubt, but the survival of the organization that people such as Bill Yarborough had envisaged, capable of performing a multitude of roles on a big stage, was.

This was despite the fact that SF had had many successes in Vietnam. The 5th Special Forces Group had operated long and hard there; it was the most highly decorated unit in the conflict, and had more Medal of Honor winners than any other regiment-sized unit. Many young officers who served in SF assignments in Vietnam went on to achieve flag rank, and several of them became four-star generals. Many NCOs retired with the rank of sergeant major. Nevertheless, many of the regular officers who had risen to higher positions of authority on the conventional side would see a lesser role for unconventional-type units in future conflict—and Special Forces did not have a champion in the higher levels of decision-making. There was a lot of discord between SF and the main army in Vietnam.

And it had to be said that Special Forces did not always help matters. Retired Special Forces Major General James Guest explains:

IN *Vietnam, the 5th Special Forces Group operated independently for the most part. It had a small staff section that would get missions from the field force commander, an Army three-star general. The SF units that came in to do the missions didn't work for the division commander or for the senior adviser, but for the overall commander, and were forbidden to brief lower commanders on their missions. Because of the urgency of the missions, it often happened that neither the field force commander nor the units explained them to the local division commanders, and in the process they also ran over a lot of bureaucratic staff officers. This inevitably led to bad feelings. What many division commanders and their staffs saw was uncontrolled wild men running around in the bushes.*

Now we had our characters on those kinds of missions. And they were high-stress missions. That kind of stress sometimes leads to bizarre behavior.

Some of our guys stayed on teams three and four years, running some kind of intense operation. When they came back into a base camp, they often just let it all hang out in ways that upset the others.

The A camps, whose missions were area control and interdiction of the Ho Chi Minh Trail, were particularly misunderstood. They were perceived by the conventional forces as country clubs established by SF, with all the amenities of home—refrigerators and things like that. Yet nobody stopped to think about how it would be to live in one of those places. They were exposed. The Camp at Lang Vie, for example, was overrun by North Vietnamese tanks.

A similar kind of situation went on out in the A camps themselves. They were normally out in the hills, but close to divisions, so the people in the divisions could see that the way the SF guys did things was not necessarily the way everybody else in the Army did them. And, of course, on occasion, SF might "liberate" equipment from the division—which had a lot of equipment. They needed it, so they took it.

Or one of the SF guys might come into the division, and he just didn't look like an American soldier. He might have long hair, and be wearing tiger fatigues and big, brass Montagnard bracelets (which meant a great deal to the Montagnards), and be carrying a Sten gun or other foreign weapons. In the context of the A camp, all this was perfectly appropriate (Special Forces have always trained to use foreign weapons), but to everyone else, it was bizarre—nonregulation.

FURTHERMORE, the Special Forces habit of rubbing the rest of the Army the wrong way did not end with the war in Southeast Asia. Since most of the Army distrusted them, the Special Forces tended to react accordingly, to overplay their skills, and then rub in their triumphs in a way certain to cause resentment.

In 1977 and 1978, Jim Guest was with the 10th SFG at Bad Tolz in Germany, a unit often called upon to mimic Soviet special-operations units, particularly those trying to "penetrate" secure facilities. Guest's penetration teams were almost invariably successful—to their delight and the consternation of their targets.

On one occasion, the VII Corps deputy commander had Guest run an operation against the VII Corps Tactical command posts.

Jim Guest relates what happened:

"WHAT do you want us to do?" I asked.

"I want you to attack the CP as if you were Russian operatives, Soviet Special Forces," the general answered.

"Yes, sir," I said. Then we went to work. Of course, he didn't tell the corps staff to expect us, and neither did we. Part of the game was to avoid tipping off corps headquarters.

We assigned one and a half A-Detachments to run the actual operation— ODA-6, reinforced by a six-man Ranger team from the Ranger detachment stationed at Bad Tolz, where they normally ran the USAREUR (U.S. Army Europe) survival training course. The team rehearsed in several ways. It moved into the operational area, occupied mission support sites, cached equipment, established observation on the targets, identified the critical parts of each target and selected routes into and out of the target areas. There were attacks on the targets, immediate-action drills, helicopter operations, sniper operations in which the snipers were used to secure the mission support sites and to provide overwatch for the attacking elements during attacks in the Corps areas, and finally, VII Corps field SOP—especially those items that would apply to the team as they conducted operations. The detachments were particularly interested in the way the Corps military police operated, since they planned to operate as MPs.

Meanwhile, we gathered all the open data on the corps we could find—how the Corps uniforms were worn, how their vehicles were marked, the normal separation distance between elements of the Corps field CP, how the VII Corps specifically provided security forces, and their estimated reaction time, and what kind of equipment we could expect to be confronted with. We also studied everything available about communication systems, about how to visually recognize secure facilities, and about antennas. We identified the different CP locations by the types of antennas, and we knew where the units were because of the orientation of their antennas. And finally, we made mock-ups of how the CPs looked laid out on the ground.

When the time came to run the operation, we did a little recon near the gates. I had soldiers hang around until they heard the challenge and the password, then we immediately passed the info on to the strike team. When they were ready to go, we put the strike team itself into VII Corps MP uniforms, and took our own jeeps and marked them up like MP jeeps. That's how our guys made the initial infiltration.

Once they were inside, they successfully penetrated and knocked out all the communications installations, simulated an attack on the operations complex with standoff weapons (81mm mortars carried in the trailers of our look-alike MP jeeps), and took out the critical technicians, such as the computer operators.

The teams successfully gained access to all its target elements in the Corps area, with the primary emphasis on the operational complex and on the areas with technicians.

Then, for show and tell, the team took pictures with KS 99 cameras. They photographed the antenna configurations, the operational complex, vehicles (with identifying markings prominently displayed), Corps security points, the technicians' living and working areas, helicopter pads with helicopters parked, the Generals' Mess, where all the key leaders and staff officers congregated on most nights for the evening meal, and routes in and out of the Corps areas, including the vehicle parks.

Here is how they took out the computers:

In those days, their scarcity value made computers more important than they are now; there were so few of them and they were so big and cumbersome. So our guys found the big van where they kept the ultracomputers, and went down, again dressed as MPs but carrying satchels like couriers, and banged on the hatch.

Naturally, the computer operators inside opened the hatch. "You know you can't come in," they said. "This is—"

"That's all right. We have a message from the Corps commander that they want you to send out." And it was two red smoke grenades. They chucked them through the hatch and slammed it shut.

Pretty soon, the fresh air generators cranked up, and red smoke came rolling out of the exhaust ports. It was quite a sight.

Other members of the strike team "killed" the remaining computer operators in their tents—with lipstick, their normal method of "slitting" friendly throats.

As one NCO described it: "We crawled into the tent where they were all sleeping and waited under the bunks where we could reach up with our fingertips and find them, and then we'd take the lipstick and draw it right across their necks.

"But one of them, a female, just gave me all kinds of problems. I kept trying to find the head, and I couldn't find it. Then I heard this screech: 'Eeeeeeek.' So I didn't move for a while. I just laid under her cot till she went back to sleep. But because of her eeeeek, I knew where her head was, and after she was asleep again, I found her neck."

(Incidentally, if all of this had been a real Soviet penetration, the loss would have been catastrophic for the Corps in the near term, but it would not have permanently stopped Corps operations, only significantly interrupted things for twelve to twenty-four hours until the damage could be repaired.)

When the day came for us to give the action report, the general said, "I want the team members to come up and give a debriefing to the entire Corps staff."

Soon after that, the strike team, in their regular uniforms, were setting up the debriefing in a big theater, when a suspicious colonel came in (it turned out he was responsible for security and counterintelligence operations). "What are you people doing?" he asked.

"We're up here to brief the general."

"What are you briefing the general on?"

"We're briefing the general on the infiltration of VII Corps tactical CPs in the field."

The colonel's face went white, and he turned around and left in a fury. In fact, pretty soon most of the corps staff, from colonels on down, were equally incensed—especially as the debriefing proceeded and we described in detail how we had broken into everything they had.

This led to a lot of hard feelings.

Another example of the kind of thing that would really incense the rest of the Army happened in 1978, when we were scheduled to participate in that year's REFORGER (Reinforcement of Germany). Beforehand, all the leaders had to go up to the V Corps to be briefed about what everyone was going to do.

At the end of the briefing, the commander got up and said, "As the United States V Corps commander, I will not allow the so-called elite units to disrupt the exercise. They will not be allowed to run any mission I do not directly, personally okay." He didn't want to let us operate—that is, to make him or his exercise look bad.

Well, we were sitting in the back of the room, while the big chiefs—the Corps commanding general, his G-3 and G-2, and the Allied commanders participating in REFORGER—were up front on a kind of stage looking at us get painted as black sheep. It didn't sit well with us.

So REFORGER continued down the road, and we looked like we were just cooling our heels; but what we really did was select one of the division headquarters. "Before the exercise is over, we are going to destroy the division headquarters," we promised ourselves. And then we prepared and deployed a small reconnaissance team from one of the A-Detachments to check out the operational area.

The team, which wore civilian clothes and spoke fluent German, made the initial preparation by studying the operational area and deciding on individual cover stories, in case they were stopped by German authorities or in some way became involved with American military units. To the Germans, they were Americans on leave and carried the proper documents. To the Americans, they were local Germans, and carried authentic-appearing German documents.

The division field CP was the focus of the operation, with the operations center, communications center, and computer center the primary items of interest.

The strike team then remained in isolation/mission preparation at Bad Tolz and planned/rehearsed, according to the information they were receiving from the recon team. This primarily focused on movement by helicopter, rappelling from the helicopter with operational equipment, movement to the objective area, linkup with the recon team, attacking the division CP, movement out of the area, and pickup by helicopter in an isolated area. Again, we also rehearsed snipers to cover the attack and withdrawal from the target.

Finally, the general thought he'd delayed us long enough to keep us from running an exercise against him or one of his units. So eighteen hours before the end of the exercise, he okayed us to run operations. What he didn't know was that we already had the operations set up and cut.

At that time there were storms all over Germany, but we flew the helicopters carrying the strike teams in and out of them, putting the teams about five miles away from the division headquarters. It was all a piece of cake; we came straight through: the command post, the operations center. In fact, the SF guys were taking the maps down off the wall and rolling them up when the assistant division commander came in. Here's this general standing there with a fish-out-of-water look on his face, and here are these three or four other guys, all in black paint and balaclavas, dismantling his CP.

"Well, who are you?" he asked.

"We're Special Forces," they said. "We're destroying your division headquarters." And then one of them turned around and shot him with a blank and said, "And, General, you're supposed to fall down on the floor, because you're dead."

This next story comes from a strike team member at a nuclear weapons site we'd also decided to take out. "You know," he recounts, "there was this big ol' female lieutenant—she was really pissed off. She was just going wild at the idea that we would take down her little kingdom. I thought we were going to have to handcuff her before we finished. In fact, we did handcuff her. We not only handcuffed her, we handcuffed her dog—a big German shepherd. We duct-taped his muzzle. I'm sure even today that lady still hates us, because, one, we got in her installation, and, two, we did what we were there to do."

When it was all over, we didn't actually do anything to the sites. We just went in, left them a card that said: "We would have destroyed you," and left.

At the debriefing, the commander didn't like what he was hearing—at least at first; but as the debrief continued, he began to get very interested and to participate with some energy, particularly when he realized we were just doing what we had been instructed to do by USAREUR and were not laughing at him or his unit.

"We could have done whatever we wanted to do," we told him. "We took your CP and weapons sites. We passed through the outside security force like butter, and we took it all down so quickly that we didn't set the alarms off; and that gave us a window of time to do whatever we wanted."

We then submitted a detailed report to USAREUR, as required by our instructions, and they used the report to make improvements in their operations for real-world operations.

SMALL wonder that there was friction. Playing "Gotcha" made the SF guys feel good—and they *were* doing what they were trained to do—but it's hard to blame the "big" Army for not welcoming them as brothers.

As a result, Special Forces eventually became a bill payer for the rest of the Army. Pentagon finances tend to be a zero-sum game: Your gain is my loss—a battalion less for me, a battalion more for you. Those who have power, influence, or backers at the Pentagon are happier with their budget than those who are seen as marginal or out of fashion. That was the Special Forces.

When the cutbacks first began to hit Special Forces in the early '70s, they were assigned few real-world missions outside the United States, despite the fact that "slow-burn" wars, both Communist- and non-Communist-inspired, continued to fester in the Third World. So the Special Forces had to find ways to keep themselves occupied. Major General Hank Emerson, the SF commander, conducted benign real-world SF-type missions inside the United States—missions that had the added benefit of providing needed services to poor and isolated communities, migrant farm workers, prison inmates, and especially to American Indians.

Green Berets parachuted into Arizona and linked up with Indians at Supai. Together they built a bridge across Havasu Creek, which allowed the Indians to take their farm machinery across the creek and into their fields. Later, Green Beret veterinarians checked Indian livestock for disease, gave inoculations, and offered classes in animal care.

Among the Seminoles, Green Berets taught local officers law-enforcement techniques; gave written and spoken English classes for Seminole children and adults; provided instructional programs dealing with drug and alcohol abuse, first aid, and nutrition; and provided increased health and dental services. They provided similar services for the Cheyenne and other native peoples.

None of this was their "real" mission, but the training allowed the much weakened and reduced Special Forces to keep themselves tuned up and ready for when the call came again.

AN example of the kind of challenge they faced came in 1982. The 5th SF Group at Fort Bragg had been given the assignment to support the recently created Rapid Deployment Joint Task Force (RDJTF)—which two years later became CENTCOM—in its planning for Southwest Asia. Iran was then a major focus. According to the conventional wisdom, the Soviets could possibly roll down through Iran, grab its warm-water ports, and of course, its oil, thus affording them the strategic position to control the flow of all oil out of the Gulf. The RDJTF's mission was to make sure that did not happen.

Operating in Southwest Asia meant deserts, of course, but as a consequence of the chaos after Vietnam, no one in Special Forces had desert training.

Jim Guest, then the 5th Group commander, tells the story:

THE 5th was a big group. In 1982, we had fifty-four A-Detachments, but our entire training budget was only $350,000. Major General Joe Lutz, the commander of the JFK Center, told me, "I want you to train your group to go to war in the desert."

"Yes, sir," I said. "I'll do that."

But when I started checking into the realities of desert training, I realized that nobody in SF had actually trained there. I told General Lutz that we needed a site in the desert where we could start training the troops.

"We don't have any money for that," he told me. "But go ahead and do it, and we'll find the money somehow." And he did.

So we got started.

I sent a major and a couple of captains out west, and they found a post near Fort Hauchucha, Arizona, near Tombstone, where the local desert matched up pretty closely with the deserts in the Middle East; it was the harshest desert we could find. We then put a training unit out there.

At the same time, I commissioned a desert study, which concluded, "In Vietnam, the engagement range for the enemy was usually fifty to three hundred meters. In the desert, it starts at fifteen hundred meters. To fight there, you need bigger, more accurate weapons."

Other important conclusions: First, you must prepare yourself psychologically to operate in such a strange and hostile environment. Second, mobility is a must. You need a vehicle. You can't just walk in the desert very far and survive; the rough terrain wears you out. And you need something to carry water, equipment, and survival gear. In most other operational areas, we carry all this in rucksacks. But not in the desert. Third, you must be able to navigate by the stars, like ships at sea. And then you also must know how to camouflage in the desert, how to estimate distances, how to make expedient repairs on vehicles and other pieces of key equipment (it's a long way back to your support).

Then we got the group together, and I told them right up front: "Most of you *are veterans of Vietnam, where—unfortunately—we fought in the jungle. Now you're going into the desert to learn how to fight there, because you don't know how. That means we're going to have to shift the total thinking of the group.*"

We trained for seventy-six days, and the guys learned how to survive and navigate. Navigation is damned difficult. You either have a haze, which keeps you from seeing far enough to orient yourself, or if it's clear, everything appears far closer than it actually is, and when you get off the post, it's really harsh. We had a lot of trouble getting accustomed to navigating in the desert.

After four weeks of orientation and general learning, we put them out in the desert in A-Detachments, and took everything away from them—no food, no water—and they had to survive for two weeks. Live or die, it was up to them. (Of course, we had our own outpost to watch them.)

After they'd been out for a while, somebody came up to me and said, "You know, the guys out there look like that movie, Quest For Fire" *(where cavemen roamed around a desert trying to survive). He was right; they did. In the daytime, the sun was so hot they stayed under shelter, and when they had to go out, they tied rags around their heads, like Arabs. They hunted and traveled at night, with homemade spears, slingshots, anything they could get. And they hunted anything they could find—porcupines, birds, snakes.*

Special Forces are very cunning. After they came back in, they told us, "As we wandered along the wadis, we kept seeing these little holes. 'What the hell are they?' we kept asking ourselves. And it finally dawned on us that they were rat holes. And that meant rattlesnakes were going to come out at night and hunt them. And that meant we could get them both.*

"I don't know how many rattlesnakes we killed and ate, but we depopulated some of those areas."

After we found out about the rat holes, we always put guys in areas where there was a good supply of them.

The same thing went for water. We always put the guys in areas where they could find it. Before they went out, they'd study maps, which showed where they could dig down and get water; it would seep up under dried streambeds. In some places, little springs trickled up, but they had to be careful about these, because some of them were alkaline.

After we'd been doing this for a while, we realized we needed vehicles, not only for the reasons already mentioned but to use as weapons platforms for .50-caliber machine guns and TOWs. Our area studies had convinced us that any enemy with the potential to hurt us in the desert would be mounted on vehicles—or, in some cases, camels.

We needed vehicles, but there was no money. And since we couldn't get anybody to give us anything, we took our own trucks, painted them desert brown (for camouflage), and cut their tops off. We had to do that so the trucks could be easily dismounted—but also so we could mount the weapons and have 360-degree observation on the move. In the desert, you need to see in every direction—especially for protection against surprise or helicopters.

"Cut the tops off very carefully," I told our mechanics. "If we ever have to turn one of the trucks back in, we can just set it down and weld the top back on, and nobody'll ever know."

Sometimes we went to the Property Disposal Yard (the PDO yard) and picked up vehicles the army was throwing away or selling. We would take three or four broken-down and beat-up vehicles to a place our mechanics and maintenance people had set up out in the desert, and rebuild them ourselves. We cut two or three vehicles in pieces, and welded the good pieces together to make one workable truck.

A lot of people thought we were nuts, but it was just Special Forces ingenuity once again.

The payoff came when we went on an exercise a year later with some elite Arab units, and it turned out that we were more at home in their desert than they were. We could navigate in the desert. We could live in the desert. And they couldn't. They didn't know how to live and fight there. In fact, we had to give them water. This gave us a great deal of confidence.

After the exercise, we asked them, "How do you guys get around in the desert when we're not here?"

"Oh, we get the Bedouins to help," they told us.

NEW LIFE

By the late 1970s, Special Forces funding stood at one-tenth of one percent of the total defense budget (it is now 3.2 percent)—and even this was an improvement over their earlier share of the pie. Training, tactical mobility, and optempo* suffered; and there was no significant modernization.

---

*Operational tempo—A measure of the total demands placed on a military unit, typically the number of days per year the unit is deployed away from its home base or station.

The world was changing, however. Insurgencies were spreading and international terrorism was on the rise. Operational failures, such as the Desert One tragedy and the failed *Mayaguez* rescue,* only emphasized the obvious: America was losing its ability to respond to unconventional threats, and something had to be done about it.

Actually, it *wasn't* obvious to most in the military high command, but a few people saw the writing on the wall. One of them was General Edward C. "Shy" Meyer, the Chief of Staff of the Army during the early '80s. In an article titled "The Challenge of Change," in the 1980–81 *Army Green Book,* an annual publication reflecting the opinions of the senior leadership of the Army, he wrote:

"Today, the cumulative effect we seek for the U.S. Army is the speedy creation of the following: Forces with the flexibility to respond globally, in NATO or in other more distant locations; forces capable of sustained operations under the most severe conditions of the integrated battlefield; forces equally comfortable with all the lesser shades of conflict." A graph showing the possible spectrum of conflict demonstrated why the last was particularly critical. Because "low-risk, high-leverage ventures, such as activities on the lower end of the spectrum, are the most likely military challenges to occur, [we need] forces that are created most wisely so as to make best use of our national resources."

And General Meyer was as good as his word. Putting his muscle and prestige on the line, he instituted sweeping initiatives, which led to the following:

1. Changes in the Special Operations command structure, to include all Army units with related capabilities—all Special Forces, Ranger, Psychological Operations, Civil Affairs, and Army Special Operations aviation units.
2. Immediate development of a Special Forces modernization action

---

*In 1975, the Cambodians captured the freighter *Mayaguez* and held its crew hostage. In response, the United States mounted a major rescue operation, made up of a Navy carrier task force, Marines, and Navy and Air Force special operations forces. Two hundred Marines, plus helicopters, made an assault on Koh Tang Island, off the Cambodian coast, where the hostages were being held. The assault failed—as a result of intelligence, communications, and command failures—and the Marines had to be withdrawn, after losing fifteen KIA, three MIA, and most of their helicopters.

program, a Special Operations Forces Functional Area Assessment, and a United States Army Special Forces Master Plan.

General Meyer also ordered the activation of the 1st Special Forces Group, with orientation toward the Pacific region; gave instructions to upgrade the capabilities of psychological operations and civil affairs units; and directed that the authorized level of organization (ALO) for the other Special Forces units be upgraded to ALO-1 (the highest priority). This meant they were authorized to acquire the personnel and equipment they needed.

In Carl Stiner's words: "As a result of his understanding of the complex nature of the challenges that our nation would face, as well as the capability of Special Forces for meeting these challenges, in large measure General Meyer is due the credit for bringing the SF back from their lowest point ever, as well as for the many critical missions they have performed since."

IT was a good start, but much more was needed. At this point, Congress picked up the ball.

In 1986, spurred by the same real-world concerns that had inspired General Meyer, Congress passed the Goldwater-Nichols Act. A sweeping work of military reformation, it strengthened the unified combatant commanders (such as the CINCs of CENTCOM or EUCOM) and the organization of the Joint Chiefs of Staff, made the Chairman of the Joint Chiefs the President's chief military adviser, and in general integrated the forces of the different services more effectively.

That same year, Senators Sam Nunn and William Cohen proposed an amendment to the act to provide the same kind of sweeping changes to U.S. Special Operations. It passed, too—and the effects were stunning.

First, it established the U.S. Special Operations Command (USSO-COM), which was to be commanded by a four-star general and would include all active and reserve special operations forces stationed in the United States (outside the United States, such forces would normally be under the command of the CINC of a particular area).

Second, it established an Assistant Secretary of Defense for Special Operations and Low Intensity Conflicts—ASD (SOLIC)—whose job was to supervise those areas, including oversight of policy and resources.

Third, it defined the mission requirements of special operations. These now included: direct action, strategic reconnaissance, unconventional warfare, foreign internal defense, counterterrorism, civil affairs, psychological operations, humanitarian assistance, and other activities specified by the President or the Secretary of Defense.

Fourth, it gave the new USSOCOM its own funding and control over its own resources. A new major funding category was created—Major Force Program 11 (MFP-11)—which required the Defense Department to keep special-operations forces funding separate from general service funding. USSOCOM funding could be revised only by the Secretary of Defense after consultation with the CINC of USSOCOM.

Fifth, the amendment (and later follow-up legislation) specified in unusual detail the responsibilities of the new CINC and the Assistant Secretary of Defense, the control of resources in money and manpower, and the monitoring of SOF officer and enlisted promotions.

At long last, Special Operations had arrived.

THE devil, of course, was in the details. Congress could mandate, but it was the military that would have to implement.

To begin with, a brand-new command had to be set up—created and staffed pretty much from scratch—and opinions varied on how to do it. For instance, General James Lindsay, the new commander (in late 1986) of the U.S. Readiness Command (REDCOM), had one idea. REDCOM's job was to prepare conventional forces to support the unified regional commands, a job that included deployment and contingency planning, joint training of assigned forces, and defense of the continental United States. Lindsay saw the mission of the new special operations command as similar to REDCOM's, in its own way, and reasoned, "Why not combine the commands? And make the special forces component subordinate to REDCOM?" He further refined the idea by proposing that they both be combined into a new command, called USSTRICOM (U.S. Strike Command).*

Neither his original idea nor its revision worked, because they failed to take into account the mandate of the Nunn-Cohen legislation to create a broadly service-like organization commanded by a full, four-star general— (not a three-star subordinate to a REDCOM/STRICOM commander)—but

---

*More accurately, he was proposing to resurrect STRICOM, which had been REDCOM's predecessor in the '70s and had had some contingency/strike responsibilities in places like Africa. When REDCOM was created on the bones of STRICOM, these capabilities were removed.

they got people thinking . . . and the result must have been a surprise to him.

In January 1987, Senator Cohen sent a directive to the JCS Chairman, Admiral Crowe, specifying that the new command had to be pure Special Forces and would have a "blank check." Subsequently, on January 23, the Joint Chiefs announced that it was REDCOM itself that would no longer be needed, and that SOCOM would be built on REDCOM's foundation, using its facilities, resources, infrastructure, and any staff that could handle the assignment. It was formalized by the Secretary of Defense in March of the same year, and on April 16, SOCOM was activated in Tampa, at the former REDCOM headquarters—with General Lindsay as its first commander.

Now that the infrastructure was settled, the commands had to decide exactly who was going to be in it—who *were* the "special forces"? Predictably, there was no little debate about this, too. The Army part was easy. It passed to the new command all of its Special Operations Forces—the SF groups, the special operations aviation units, and the 75th Ranger Regiment (PSY-OPs and civil affairs came later, during Carl Stiner's tenure as CINC). For the rest, it was more complicated. The Air Force special operations forces, for instance, then under the Military Airlift Command (MAC), were transferred to USSOCOM, but the Air Force hoped to retain some control. The Marines had units that were labeled special operations–capable, but they had no actual special operations units. Though the Navy had never previously shown much love for its SEALs, it suddenly discovered that the SEALs were an indispensable part of the Navy family and tried to hold on to them—and their part of the special operations budget. The Navy managed to keep that debate going for the better part of a year, but it was a lost cause, and the SEALs went to USSOCOM. Finally, there was debate about whether the Joint Special Operations Task Force should become part of US-SOCOM, or report directly to the national command authorities without the hindrance of an interim layer. In the end, it was placed under USSO-COM as a sub–unified command.

Putting The Pieces Together

Meanwhile, while all this was going on, the "Functional Area Assessment" that General Meyer had inspired was beginning to produce results.

The Army's Training and Doctrine Command (TRADOC) had been

tasked to conduct an in-depth analysis of how SF should be organized, manned, equipped, and trained. It was to answer the questions: "Where are we now? What is broken? How do we fix it? Where do we need to go in the future?"

General Maxwell Thurman, the vice chief of staff of the army, was the overseer of the analysis; the TRADOC commander, General Bill Richardson, supervised it personally; and other outside generals—Mike Spigelmire, Tom Fields, Fred Franks, and Ed Burba—headed the panels. The study was conducted by the Special Warfare Center and School at Fort Bragg.

Thurman's leadership gave the analysis particular force. Everyone involved reported to him, and everything they reported was put on the front burner. He listened to everybody, heard every problem and every solution, and put a time clock on it. This was not some committee report to be filed away somewhere and forgotten. At the end of the process, there would be an implementation plan—approved by Generals Thurman, Richardson, and Lindsay, and then *done*: no complaining, no foot-dragging.

When it was all over, the analysis proposed the following:

First, Army Special Forces could no longer exist in the wilderness; there would be a separate SF branch (like Infantry, Armor, or Aviation) and an NCO career-management field. That meant that SF troops and officers could have a career path within Special Forces itself; previously, they'd had to rotate among other parts of the military if they expected to get ahead. This goal was accomplished in April 1987; the commandant at the Special War Center and School became the chief of branch, just as the commandant at Fort Benning was the chief of branch for the infantry. "At this point," Jim Guest remarks, "we went from being looked at as something kept in the dark and under the covers to sitting up at the head table with the rest of the big shots."

Second, the Green Berets needed to become a major, three-star (lieutenant general) command. This allowed Special Forces to become masters of their own destiny, and to oversee and execute their own training and readiness programs. When a three-star commander sat down at a table with other three- and four-star commanders, he carried weight that one- and two-star commanders didn't. Army Special Forces became a major command in 1989.

Third, the academic center, schools, and training facilities were upgraded, and the selection, assessment, and training made more professional and tough.

And, fourth, an equipment-acquisition plan was instituted to upgrade all of the SF communications, weapons, aircraft, and training facilities in order to meet mission requirements.

The modern Special Operations force was now ready to go.

MAKING PROFESSIONALS

Or almost ready to go. As previously noted, one of SF's problems was that many of the generation that emerged from Vietnam, or who came into the force after Vietnam, failed to attain the high levels of professionalism expected of men who make up a force that calls itself elite. In Vietnam, they'd operated out on the end of a string without much supervision. Others—recruited after the Army drawdown in the '70s—were not the best group of men to begin with. Some of them had simply been looking for greater freedom and intrigue than they could get in conventional units, and had found their way into SF. Meanwhile, back then SF did not give a strong enough professional orientation to its younger officers. As a consequence, some of them picked up "outsider" attitudes, simply because that was what was in the air.

On the other side of the coin, it was hard for them to get promoted, and that also didn't help their attitude any. Normally, if you were good, you moved through key positions in a variety of conventional units. Your performance and potential were recognized by people who counted, and in due course you were selected for promotion and for attendance at Leavenworth and later the War College, in Carlisle, Pennsylvania, or one of the other high-level service schools. Promotion and selection boards were composed exclusively of officers with conventional backgrounds.

Back in the '70s and the early '80s, however, most officers were dead-ended in Special Forces. The personnel assignment people in Washington were content to drop them there and "forget" about them. In many ways, assignment to SF was career suicide, and so it was small wonder that some officers just figured: To hell with it. Such people simply reinforced the perception that special operators were not "real" Army.

ALL of this came to a head soon after the passage of Nunn-Cohen, during Jim Guest's tenure as head of the Special Warfare Center and School. The four-star TRADOC commander sent Guest the following message: "I'm tired of having to apologize for Special Forces," he announced in no uncertain terms. "I am tired of their reputation. I am tired of having to deal with their lack of professionalism. Are they in the Army or not?

"If you don't do something about this, I am going to relieve you. I will run you out of the Army."

Jim Guest says:

So *that caught my attention. That's when I realized that we couldn't let things go on the old way, and that's when we started saying, "Hey, we can't mess around any longer outside the Army system; we've got to do things inside it. We've got to make ourselves more knowledgeable of it. That means, first of all, that we've got to convince the senior generals that we are professionals, that we are capable of doing special missions, and that we're not just a camp of thugs."*

At the same time, we started retiring the soldiers who did not or could not meet the new standards, or who refused to meet them. Some looked at the future and decided that they did not want to be in a more structured force.

After that, we raised the standards. We wanted smarter people, so we established an IQ level—a high one. If you wanted to come into Special Forces, you had to have an IQ of at least 120.

Then we had to do something about training.

In those days, when someone volunteered for Special Forces and was chosen to take the Q Course, he received a permanent change of station to Fort Bragg. In other words, he was ours. If he dropped out, something had to be found for him at Fort Bragg. This caused problems: We had more washouts than people who made the grade, and we had to find places for all those people at Bragg. Second, we had a lot of money invested in these folks. We needed to find a way to reduce the initial investment while making sure we let the good ones come through. Finally, we were being used by a lot of people who simply wanted a ticket into the 82nd Airborne Division or somewhere else at Bragg, so they would volunteer for Special Forces and then immediately drop out of the training, some by voluntarily terminating themselves, some by just flunking it somewhere along the line. That had to stop.

What we did was persuade General Vuono, the Army Chief of Staff, to institute a new selection and assessment program that would come in before the Q Course. We'd recruit the new people, then they'd sign up and come to Bragg TDY (temporarily, not permanently) and go through a two-week selection drill that would pinpoint those men who could operate on their own but could also subject themselves to a team for a mission. "Our idea," as we explained to the Chief of Staff, "is to give them zero training—absolutely none. We want to get them out there and make them as uncomfortable as we can, put them through situations that are as ambivalent as we can make them, and stress them as much as they can bear. Then we want them to make a choice. Do I really want to be Special Forces or not?"

The course we came up with was designed by one of the men who had put together the selection course for our top special missions units. The volunteers were always in unbalanced situations. They never knew what to expect. They never knew what was going to happen to them. They'd think they were stopping for a meal break, and would get a mission two minutes before they were going to eat. "Move. Report here," which might mean five miles of hard marching with heavy rucksacks.

We never told them where or why or how far they were going. We never said, "You're going from here, and you'll end up over here." Only, "You start here and go in that direction." Then they'd march until they met somebody else, who'd send them on another leg of the journey.

People who can't deal with ambiguous situations will fall out when they're out there alone and confused in the country, particularly when we've got them under physical stress.

We didn't harass them, the way they do at places like Jump School. We didn't have to. Sure, one morning we gave them push-ups and things like that, just to show them, "yes, we can do that to you if we want to. But that's not how we're going to do it. We're going to tell you what we want you to do and then see if you attempt to do it."

At the end of the course, we had a thirty-mile forced march, and that pretty well tested them out. We had people who quit just doing that—both officers and NCOs.

Some men we flunked. Some of them could do everything we asked for physically, but we took them out for psychological reasons. Some men were loners and could not handle the stress of operating in a team.

We were looking for solid men of character and integrity, motivated for all the right reasons—men of maturity and sound judgment, with the inner strength to do whatever was required under all conditions and circumstances, and who did not have to be "stroked" to do their best.

It worked. We truly began to get the very best men. On top of that, we'd begun indoctrinating them into Special Forces right up front. They were paying a price to be in Special Forces. They'd made a real investment, and it was going to mean something to them. The result was that we were able to fill our slots with quality replacements, who were soon recognized by the

Army by receiving promotions faster than their peers in the conventional Army did.

Next, we rebuilt and upgraded our training facilities at Camp MacKall (adjacent to Fort Bragg), where we did the Q Course and some of the other courses. During World War II, the Army had trained nearly all of their airborne units there, but everything was left over from then—Navy Quonset huts, an old mess hall, and a latrine. We needed a new sewage and water system, new buildings, and new training facilities; and General Thurman made sure we got all this when he was TRADOC commander.

As for integrating an awareness of special operations into the service schools, such as the infantry school at Benning or the armor school at Knox, and at the advanced courses at Leavenworth or the War College, not as much has been done there. I don't see in their curriculum any focus on Special Forces, Civil Affairs, PSYOPs, and Special Operations Aviation and how they can be integrated on the battlefield. That was a major failure we set about to correct, and which still needs work.

We've got to put an advanced training and education slice into all those schools. We've got to make sure those folks are being taught an appreciation of SF, because sitting in those audiences are future CINCs, senior staff officers, senior planners, and senior subordinate commanders for the CINC—and they need to know what we can do.

We've done a lot to make Special Forces even more professional. Now the Army has to learn how to use them most effectively.

CARL STINER—BETWEEN THE WARS

Meanwhile, Carl Stiner was progressing through several key assignments: a tour with Army headquarters in Washington; a battalion command with the 82nd Airborne Division, where he was also division operations officer; study at the Army War College, and a Masters degree in public administration; a tour in Saudi Arabia, as the assistant project manager for training and modernizing the Saudi National Guard—a Special Forces–type assignment; brigade command at Fort Benning, Georgia; and in 1979, he and twenty-two other handpicked officers were sent to Saudi Arabia and Yemen to help the Saudis put out the civil war between North and South Yemen—another SF-type assignment.

After returning from Yemen, he was again assigned to the Pentagon to work for General Edward C. "Shy" Meyer, the Army Chief of Staff.

On a Thursday afternoon toward the end of February 1980, General Meyer called Stiner into his office. "When you come in tomorrow, Carl," he said, "I think you better wear your Class A uniform. And, oh, by the way, you better bring Sue in that afternoon. There's going to be a special ceremony."

"What kind of ceremony?" Stiner asked.

"I am going to promote you to Brigadier General," the General answered, "and you are going to be assigned as the Chief of Staff of the Rapid Deployment Joint Task Force, MacDill AFB, Florida."

The RDJTF was created by President Jimmy Carter in response to a perceived slight against the Saudis and other friendly Arabs. All major nations except the Arabs had a standing U.S. unified command to look out for their security interests. "Why not us?" the Arabs had told Carter. Two years later, the RDJTF became the United States Central Command, and assumed responsibility for U.S. security interests in Southwest Asia.

The next day, Stiner, wearing his Greens, brought Sue in for the 3:00 P.M. ceremony.

When it was over, Meyer told Stiner to report the next day—Saturday— to Lieutenant General P. X. Kelley, who was to be the commander of the not-yet-activated RDJTF.

At that meeting, Kelley told Stiner to leave for MacDill on Monday, write the activation order on the way down, and publish it when he got there. This would activate the Rapid Deployment Joint Task Force, effective March 1, 1980.

When Stiner showed up at MacDill, he was met by a total staff of four enlisted personnel, but over the next couple of months, these were augmented by 244 handpicked men—mainly officers from all the services. Stiner remained there until May 1982, during which time he and the staff formed and trained the most effective joint command in existence, and wrote and exercised three major war plans for Southwest Asia (one variant became the foundation for Operation DESERT STORM seventeen years later).

In June 1982, he was reassigned to the 82nd Airborne Division as the Assistant Division Commander for Operations, now working for Major General James J. Lindsay. In August 1983, a call came for him to report the following day to General Jack Vessey, the Chairman of the Joint Chiefs of Staff. He had another deployment.

This time, Lebanon.

VIII

THE LEBANON
TRAGEDY

In September 1983, Lebanon began a rapid and uncontrollable descent into hell.

Carl Stiner was present during the worst days of it. "What came to pass in Lebanon defies logic and morality," he says, "but it clearly exemplifies what can happen when ethnic biases, religious differences, and security interests are used as a catalyst by outside powers for achieving political gain."

In August of that year, the Chairman of the Joint Chiefs of Staff, General Jack Vessey, sent Brigadier General Carl Stiner to Lebanon as his man on the scene and to help implement the U.S. military assistance program (Stiner's experience as a military adviser in Saudi Arabia and Yemen surely was a big factor in generating this assignment). In that capacity, Stiner worked with Lebanese authorities to try to stop the nation's descent. They did not succeed, but not for want of skill, intelligence, and goodwill. The forces of chaos simply overwhelmed everyone else.

Though Stiner's assignment to Lebanon was not specifically a Special Forces mission, it shared many characteristics of such missions—including military advice at the tactical level, political management (both military and diplomatic) at the strategic levels, and the need for cultural sensitivity.

ROOTS

The tragedy of Lebanon was the result of forces long at work:

Following the breakup of the Ottoman Empire and Turkey's defeat in

World War I, the League of Nations put Lebanon under temporary French control. France promised Lebanon complete independence in 1941, but was not able to grant it until 1943, and French troops did not leave the country until 1946.

Lebanon has a complex ethnic mix. At the time of its independence, the country was more or less evenly divided between Muslims and Maronite Christians, and the Muslims were divided between Sunnis and Shiites—the Sunnis were more moderate and prosperous, while the Shiites tended to be more radical and politically volatile. There was also a large, similarly volatile sect called the Druze, whose beliefs combine Christian and Muslim teachings; about 400,000 Druze now inhabit the mountainous area of Lebanon and Syria. Add these all together, with long-simmering feuds of every kind, and it was a recipe for trouble.

In establishing the Lebanese government in 1943, the French tried to stave off ethnic conflict by setting up a power-sharing arrangement that favored the Sunnis and the Maronite Christians—the most conservative and "stable" of the Lebanese factions. The National Pact of 1943 used a 1932 census (probably the last census to reflect a near-even mix between Christians and Muslims) to determine the ethnic and religious makeup of the government. Key positions were filled by applying a formula derived from that census. The presidency was reserved for Maronite Christians, the prime minister position for the Sunni Muslims, and so on. The Shiite Muslims and Druze were left out of any position of meaningful responsibility.

By the time the government was established, the changing demographics—the sharp rise in Shiites, for instance—had already rendered the formula obsolete.

Despite the potentially unstable ethnic situation, Lebanon quickly flourished as a nation. With its two major seaports and its strategic location at the eastern end of the Mediterranean astride traditional trade routes, it soon became known as the gateway to the orient—and Beirut as "the Paris of the Middle East." Trading was the main engine of its economy. Major companies established offices, and Beirut soon became the banking center of the Middle East, with approximately eighty-five commercial banks.

In 1970, however, another chaotic element was added—the Palestinians.

In 1947, the United Nations divided Palestine in two: Part would become the home for the Jews displaced as a result of World War II; the other part would continue as the Palestinian homeland. The Jews accepted the UN decision; the Arabs rejected it.

On May 14, 1948, the Jews proclaimed the independent state of Israel, and the next day neighboring Arab nations invaded it. The invasion failed, and when the fighting ended, Israel held territory beyond the original UN boundaries, while Egypt and Jordan held the rest of Palestine. More than 600,000 Palestinians who had lived within Israel's new borders fled the Jewish state and became refugees in neighboring Arab countries, mainly Syria and Jordan.

The Palestinians, now a people without a homeland, continued their armed resistance from bases in those countries, but their presence and their military activities against Israel became a major political problem, particularly for Jordan. By 1970, the problem had gotten out of control, and the Jordanian government dealt with it violently, by forcibly expelling the PLO, the Palestinian Liberation Organization.

The approximately 10,000 PLO fighters, the fedayeen, initially settled in the southern part of Lebanon, bringing thousands of Palestinian refugees with them, exacerbating a situation which had already been particularly volatile for over a decade. In 1958, Arab nationalists (mostly Shiites, though some Druze also participated) had rebelled against the pro-Western government of Christian President Camille Chamoun. Chamoun asked the United States for help, and about 10,000 U.S. Marines and soldiers landed on Lebanon's beaches. This show of force helped the government restore order, and the troops were withdrawn.

After the 1958 crisis, the next Lebanese president, Fouad Chehab, made a serious effort to mend fences with the Arabs. He gave Muslims more jobs in the government, established friendly relations with Egypt, and worked to raise living standards.

Although the Lebanese government had always sympathized with the Palestinian cause, their sympathy never translated into strong support; nor did they welcome the new Palestinian presence—they were simply too weak to keep them out. Soon the PLO began launching attacks against the settlements of northern Israel from their base in southern Lebanon. As the Israelis retaliated against PLO strikes, the Shiites in southern Lebanon suffered greatly, aggravating the hatred that already existed.

By 1975, much of the PLO had migrated to West Beirut, where they established their main base of operations, with its own system of law and order and its own taxes. This did not sit well with many Lebanese, but especially with the Christian militia (the Phalange), and soon a full-scale civil war broke out between the Palestinians and the Phalange.

An estimated 40,000 people, mostly civilians both Lebanese and Palestinian, perished during the bitter fighting, and the Lebanese Army fell apart. It virtually ceased being an effective fighting force.

At this point, the Syrians became involved.

The Syrians had had designs on Lebanon as far back as recorded history, and they entered the fray twice, first on the side of the Palestinians and then on the side of the Christian militias. Their switch was all in the interest of their larger aim—the control of Lebanon. Their participation resulted in the Syrian occupation of the Bekáa Valley, a strategic area located between Lebanon's mountain spine and the Syrian border; they have remained there ever since, orchestrating to their advantage the large number of Shiites who migrated to that area as a result of the civil war and subsequent conflicts.

By 1978, Lebanon had become the main base of operations for the PLO. In that year, the Israelis launched a large-scale sweep of southern Lebanon against the Palestinian bases. Approximately 100,000 refugees, mainly Palestinians and Shiites, were sent fleeing to civil-war-ravaged West Beirut. By now, most of Lebanon had become a battleground, but where before it had been primarily Christian militias against the PLO, now it was just about everybody against everybody else. Long-standing hatreds, feuds, memories of atrocities, as well as ethnic and religious differences, were unleashed; each faction had its own militia—well-armed and deadly; and the various factional militias and clans began fighting each other.

✪ The Druze occupied the Chouf Mountain region, which domi-
    nated Beirut and the primary land routes leading from Beirut to
    Damascus. The Druze controlled the Peoples Socialist Party, or
    PSP, under its leader Walid Jumblatt, and operated the most heav-
    ily armed of the Lebanese factional militias (though their num-
    bers were not great). The PSP's primary enemy were Christians,
    and their support and armament were provided by Syria, but in-
    cluded Soviet advisers at firing battery locations. By mid-1983,
    their armament consisted of approximately 420 tubes of modern
    Soviet artillery, including D-30 howitzers, BM-21 rocket launch-
    ers, numerous heavy mortars, air defense weapons, and thirty T-
    54 Soviet-made tanks given to the PSP by Libya—all within range
    of Beirut and its suburbs.

✪ The Syrian army controlled both the northeastern part of Lebanon and, more important, the Bekáa Valley and its population of Shiite Muslims.

✪ Israel established a security zone in the south, where Christians, Palestinians, and Shiite Muslims lived together but hated each other.

✪ Terrorism had meanwhile "advanced" to a stage of "state sponsorship." Sponsoring states included Syria, Libya, and Iran. The most dangerous of these, Iran, developed new forms of terrorist warfare—suicide bombings and hostage-taking—aimed at spreading the Islamic revolution through subversion and terrorism. The U.S.-educated Hosein Sheikholislam, a disciple of the Ayatollah Khomeini and a veteran of the U.S. Embassy siege in Tehran and later of the TWA 847 hijacking, was the chief architect of this campaign. The militant arm formed to carry it out was called Hezbollah, "Party of God," and consisted of fanatical fundamentalist Shiites drawn from all over the world. They were trained by Iran's Revolutionary Guards in camps, then sent back to their home countries to establish revolutionary cells. These were the most dangerous of all terrorists, willing to martyr themselves for the Islamic revolution. Because Westerners, and particularly Americans, were seen as the "Great Satan," they became their primary targets. The main Lebanese base for Hezbollah operations (and terrorist training) was located at Baalbeck in Syrian-controlled territory in the Bekáa Valley, only an hour's driving time from Beirut. Hezbollah operating cells were established in West Beirut.

✪ The "Movement of the Disinherited," known as the Amal, was headed by Nabih Berri, a lawyer, born in West Africa and educated in France, and whose family lived in the United States north of Detroit. Berri's goal was to reduce the power of the Christian minority, and to allow the Shiites, who now outnumbered the Christians, to use their numbers to dominate Lebanese politics. Amal was supported primarily by Syria, while its two primary enemies were the Palestinians and the Israelis.

✪ Question: Were the Syrians and Amal friends? Answer: When it was convenient. Question: Were the Druze and Amal friends? Answer: When it was convenient. Question: Were the Syrians and Iranians friends? Answer: When it was convenient.

✪　Within Beirut itself were also several other independent militias,
such as the Maurabi Toon, who claimed to represent what was
called the Peoples Worker Party, but whose *raison d'être* was criminal: robbery, ambush, and kidnapping.

In June 1982, Israeli armed forces launched a full-scale invasion of
Lebanon called Operation PEACE FOR GALILEE. Its aim was to clean out the
PLO once and for all. In two weeks of fierce fighting, the Israelis drove
the PLO from their strongholds near Israel's northern border, destroyed a
major part of Syria's forces occupying the Bekáa Valley, including air defense
batteries, tanks, and fighter aircraft, and pushed all the way to Beirut, where
they linked up with the Christian Phalange militia and surrounded Muslim
West Beirut, the center of militant Muslim activities in the capital. The
PLO was now training their terrorists in West Beirut, as well as launching
attacks against Israel and Jordan from there. It had also become the latest
temporary refugee camp home for 175,000 Palestinians who had fled the
earlier Israeli sweep in the south. Soon the Israelis were bombing West
Beirut daily.

Israel's crushing blow to the Syrian military forces seriously humiliated
the Syrian President, Hafez Assad. In the coming months, Assad turned to
the Soviets for assistance in rebuilding his weakened forces, with payback
against Israel a primary aim.

At this point, the U.S. State Department got involved, with a long-term
goal to promote Lebanese stability—an impossibility as long as the PLO was
there. The more immediate goal was to stop the fighting and to get the
PLO, the Syrians, and eventually the Israeli forces out of the country. To
that end, the State Department proposed sending in a multinational force
to provide security for the withdrawal of the PLO to whatever Arab state
was willing to take them.

Though the Joint Chiefs of Staff were opposed to committing U.S. forces
to this venture, Defense Secretary Caspar Weinberger felt that other international partners would be reluctant to join the effort unless the United
States took the lead. He also felt that a U.S. military presence in Beirut was
the only way to stop the Israelis from destroying the city, and to obtain their
eventual withdrawal from Lebanon.

On August 25, approximately eight hundred U.S. Marines, along with
contingents from France and Italy, went ashore to position themselves between the Israelis, the Syrians, and the PLO.

Meanwhile, Tunisia agreed to accept Yasir Arafat and his PLO fighters. Their evacuation was completed by September 1. Ten days later, the Marines returned to their ships, and the French and Italians also withdrew.

Part of the PLO evacuation agreement included a promise by the American and Lebanese governments, with assurances from Israel and leaders from some (but not all) of the Lebanese factions, that law-abiding Palestinian noncombatants, including the families of evacuated PLO members, could remain in Lebanon and live in peace and security.

Two weeks later, Lebanese President-elect Bashir Gemayel, whose daughter had already been killed in an ambush meant for him, was killed by a bomb placed on top of his house (it was thought) by a Syrian agent. Gemayel, a warrior who favored military solutions to internal problems, had been the leader of the Christian Phalange militia, whose chief supporter was Israel, and the man the Israelis had counted on for a peace treaty that would best serve the interest of their security. The death of Gemayel dashed all hopes for that. It was not in Syria's interest to see such a treaty come about, since by now Syria viewed Lebanon as a strategic buffer against Israel.

The next day, in violation of their guarantee to protect the Palestinian noncombatants who had elected to remain behind, the Israeli army entered West Beirut. Their stated justification was to *protect* the refugees and to clean out PLO infrastructure and supplies left behind by Arafat.

On the night of September 16, the Israeli army allowed the Phalange militia to enter the Palestinian refugee camps at Sabra and Shatila in West Beirut to search for the source of sporadic gunfire aimed at the Israelis. It's hard to say why (local hatreds being so deeply rooted), but the Phalange went on a rampage. When the shooting was over, more than 700 unarmed Palestinians had been slaughtered.

The Lebanese government immediately requested the return of the U.S. Marines to protect the people of West Beirut.

Again, the Joint Chiefs strongly opposed it, but this time Secretary Weinberger joined the opposition. The previous Marine intervention had been a limited, short-term operation. This one looked open-ended and fuzzy—and therefore risked disaster.

President Reagan overrode their objections. He obviously felt that he had to do everything he could to prevent another massacre of Palestinians.

This time the Marine unit was close to twice the size of the one before it—a Marine Amphibious Unit (MAU) of approximately 1,500 men. The

French and Italians also agreed to return. The mission the Joint Chiefs assigned the Marines was called PRESENCE—meaning they were expected to be present and visible, to keep hostiles separate by patrolling throughout the city, and to try to be friends to all factions alike. The JCS wanted the Marines to be as impartial as possible—and *hoped* the mission would last no longer than two months.

It was an unusual mission for a military unit, but a similar operation had worked before. The problem was that not every faction respected them or their presence. And there was another problem as well: The Marines would have liked to set up their operations on terrain that dominated the city, but all dominant terrain was already occupied by one or another of the warring factions. That meant the Marines had to settle for low, flat ground near the airport; there was nowhere else to go. The building they chose for their barracks, however, provided them with easy access to many of the locations associated with their mission, including the American Embassy; and it was one of the strongest buildings in Beirut. They felt they could defend themselves there. . . .

ON April 18, 1983, a suicide car-bomber—probably a Hezbollah fanatic operating from the Sheikh Abdullah Barracks at Baalbeck in the Bekáa Valley—destroyed the U.S. Embassy in Beirut. Sixty-three people were killed, seventeen of them Americans, including the CIA station chief and all but two of his officers. This was the first car-bomb attack against American facilities.

The bombing had serious consequences, and of these the loss of intelligence was most immediately critical. The entire U.S. HUMINT (human intelligence) mechanism (i.e., the links with local agents) was practically destroyed. For several months, gaping holes existed in the U.S. ability to know what was happening on the ground, either in Beirut or in the rest of the country. This failure later came back to haunt America.

The longer-term effects of the bombing were even more serious. There is no evidence that anyone in Washington understood the consequences in terms either of the threat to Americans abroad or of its implications to future policy. Terrorism became a form of war, which ultimately forced America out of Lebanon. The United States was not prepared to deal with it.

A month later, Secretary of State George Shultz attempted to broker an agreement (known as the 17 May Agreement) whereby all foreign forces would simultaneously withdraw from Lebanon. Lebanese President Amin Gemayel, brother of Bashir Gemayel, and Prime Minister Menachem Begin of Israel, signed on to the agreement (on condition that the Syrians did also); but when Shultz went to Damascus to present the plan to Assad, Assad refused to withdraw from Lebanon under any circumstances. As far as Assad was concerned, he was orchestrating the situation from a position of strength.

Syria reinforced its refusal to cooperate by declaring Phillip Habib, the President's Mideast envoy, *persona non grata.*

Habib's replacement, Robert "Bud" MacFarlane, the President's Deputy National Security Adviser, believed that if the Syrians and the Israelis could be convinced to withdraw, then dealing directly with the leaders of the major factions might produce a solution to the Lebanese problem. Before going to Lebanon, MacFarlane met with Assad in Damascus, and left realizing that Assad was in control of the future of Lebanon—and that he was not about to relinquish that position.

MacFarlane arrived in Lebanon on August 1. Within the next couple of weeks, he recommended that Washington suspend its effort to broker a joint Syrian-Israeli withdrawal and instead concentrate on reconciling the various Lebanese factions. MacFarlane and U.S. Ambassador Reginald Bartholomew met several times with Nabih Berri and Walid Jumblatt to bring them into an accommodation with President Gemayel, but they made no progress. Both Berri and Jumblatt put the blame on Gemayel—claiming that he was more concerned with preserving the Christian presidency than with accommodating the factions. But the unspoken agenda here was that both Berri and Jumblatt were puppets of outside authority—and had little leeway to negotiate a peace agreement.

ASSIGNMENT TO LEBANON

In August 1983, then–Brigadier General Carl Stiner was the assistant division commander for operations for the 82nd Airborne Division at Fort Bragg. One day in mid-August, at four in the afternoon, he was in the field, inspecting training for the ROTC Summer Camp, which the 82nd conducted annually, when he received a call on his radio to return to headquarters immediately.

Carl Stiner continues the story:

I thought the call related to a possible brigade-size mission I'd been designated to lead aimed at preventing several thousand "peacenik demonstrators" from breaking through security fences at the Seneca Army Depot in New York State (they wanted to disrupt the shipment of nuclear weapons to Europe). The brigade had been well trained for civil disturbance operations and was standing by while civil authorities were trying to defuse the situation.

Back at Division, I learned that I'd gotten a call from the Pentagon directing me to report to General Vessey, the JCS Chairman, by nine the next morning, with fatigues packed, prepared to take a trip. Since I would probably have launched from Fort Bragg with the brigade if I was going to Seneca, I now guessed that I was most likely being sent to someplace like Honduras, since the Nicaraguans had recently been intensifying their activities in that neck of the woods.

The next morning, I caught a ride to Washington with Lieutenant General Jack MacMull, the XVIII Airborne Corps Commander. At the Pentagon, General Vessey's people told me to go around the building for the rest of the day and learn everything I could about the U.S. program in Lebanon, because the Chairman and I would be leaving for there that night. Vessey would spend three days in the country, and then I'd remain "as the Chairman's and the SECDEF's man on the ground."

For the rest of the day, I got briefings from principal staff officers of the Offices of the Joint Chiefs of Staff and the Secretary of Defense, and learned the details about why I was going: It was taking too long for orders and information to be passed over the existing chain of command from Beirut to General Vessey and Secretary Weinberger, and the information they were receiving was so filtered through the various links in the chain that it was questionable whether it fully represented what was actually happening to the Lebanese government, the Lebanese Army, the Israeli Army, and the U.S. Marines at the airport.

The existing chain of command to Lebanon ran from Washington to NATO headquarters in Mons, Belgium, to the European command in Stuttgart, to the commander of U.S. Naval Forces Europe in Naples, to the deputy commander of U.S. Naval Forces Europe in London, to the commander of the 6th Fleet in Gaeta, Italy, to the commander of the Amphibious Task Force off the coast of Lebanon, to the commander of the Landing Force also off the coast of Lebanon, and finally to the commander of the Marine Amphibious Unit at the Beirut airport. This chain was the normal arrangement for fighting the Cold War, and also for handling anything else that might occur in the European area of responsibility, but it was not an efficient arrangement for dealing with the fast-breaking and complex situation in Lebanon.

At 7:00 P.M. that evening, General Vessey and I departed from Andrews Air Force Base for Beirut. En route, we talked about the situation in Lebanon—the personalities involved, the U.S. assistance program, the impact of occupying powers, ongoing diplomatic initiatives, and so on—until about midnight, when we tried to get a little sleep before we hit Beirut and a full schedule of tough meetings on the U.S. military assistance program. If that had any serious shortfalls, we needed to find out about them.

We arrived in Beirut around midmorning, and went directly to the Ministry of Defense for a meeting with General Ibrahim Tannous, chief of staff of the Lebanese armed forces. Tannous was a soldier's soldier, revered by Lebanese fighting men for his bravery during a battle with the Syrians (he'd lost an eye in the process). Though the Lebanese army was then at best a marginal fighting force, he was doing everything possible to rebuild it sufficiently to take over security responsibilities for all Lebanon when the Syrian and Israeli occupying forces withdrew. Tannous was extremely pleased with U.S. military assistance, and specifically with the training and equipment Colonel Tim Fintel was providing. Fintel, an Armor officer, was chief of the Office for Military Cooperation. Most training for reraising the Lebanese armed forces was being conducted by U.S. Special Forces.

General Tannous had organized an ethnically balanced staff, which was functioning well together: Major General Hakim, a Druze, was his deputy commander; his director of personnel was a Sunni Muslim, Colonel Simon Quassis; a Maronite Christian was director of intelligence, Brigadier General Abbas Hamdan; a Shiite Muslim was director of operations; and his director of logistics was also a Sunni Muslim.

After eight years of atrophy while the civil war had raged in one form or another, the Lebanese army had done little but attempt to maintain order. Now Tannous was trying to build an army that represented the current ethnic mix of the population (Christian, Sunni Muslim, Shiite Muslim, and Druze), rather than the population at the time of the 1932 census. His efforts were beginning to pay off. The army, with U.S. help, was rapidly becoming a cohesive and effective force.

Three brigades had already been formed and equipped, and a fourth brigade's training was well under way. When the Israeli army withdrew, Tannous planned to achieve stability in south Lebanon and security along Israel's northern border by employing a brigade of approximately 2,400 men. He would then provide internal security by employing two brigades in Beirut. Within a year and a half, the Lebanese army was expected to grow to seven brigades and be able to take responsibility for the security of all Lebanon.

Over the next three days, Vessey and I met with Ambassador Reginald Bartholomew; President Amin Gemayel; General Moshi Levy, commander of Israeli forces; the commanders of the French and Italian forces; Vice Admiral Jerry Tuttle, commander of the Sixth Fleet; Colonel Tim Geraghty, commander of the 24th Marine Amphibious Unit; and Colonel Tom Fintel. We also visited the training camp and observed the training the SF team was conducting. They were living in the Cadmos Hotel in West Beirut and the training site was in East Beirut.

It was a very productive time. All the key leaders—*except* Syria's and the factions'—had provided firsthand insights into the complexity of the situation (the exception was significant, though we had no idea then how complex and difficult the factional situation would very soon become). The multinational forces were particularly impressive; their presence was a stabilizing influence, and for the first time in many months, Beirut was calm. The airport, banks, and restaurants had reopened; people were taking leisurely evening strolls on the Cornice.

We were particularly impressed with Tannous's leadership and his plan for building an ethnically representative army. We were convinced that given sufficient time and the opportunity for an orderly relief of the Israeli forces, Tannous and his army could likely provide the stability necessary for the Lebanese government to regain control of the country.

As time passed, General Tannous and I became close professional friends. We worked well with each other.

On the way to the airport for his departure, General Vessey laid out what he expected me to do in Lebanon: "It's obvious," he told me, "that the Lebanese army is the only effective institution of government to which we can tie our assistance program. That means I want you to work closely with General Tannous in coordinating the timing of Israel's withdrawal with the development of Tannous's forces, so the Lebanese will be able to effectively relieve the Israeli forces. We want to eliminate the possibility of a void that will encourage renewed fighting by the factions.

"I want you to report to me daily over the SATCOM and the fax machine I'll leave with you. But also keep EUCOM [U.S. European Command] informed of what's going on here.

"One other thing: You're going to be the military adviser to the President's special envoy to Lebanon [at this time Robert MacFarlane], and you'll come back to Washington every two to three months to brief the Joint Chiefs."

MacFarlane and I soon developed a very close relationship. My primary function was to be his conduit both to Tannous and to the Israeli forces in Lebanon. But this brought an even more important benefit: Tannous knew personally most of the senior leadership of the Syrian cabinet and armed forces—their backgrounds, their motivation, and their "leanings." This was vital information.

When MacFarlane visited other Arab nations, I traveled with him as part of his team. In this capacity, I provided information about current military needs and U.S. military assistance. Specifically, I would tell him what each country might ask us for—as well as how the Defense Department would view that request.

Over the next couple of weeks, I lived, like the Special Forces trainers, at the Cadmos Hotel. Each morning I went to the British Embassy in West Beirut or the Ambassador's residence at Yarze, a Beirut neighborhood, where embassy activities were also conducted. After the 1983 bombing, the British had allowed the U.S. to use their embassy, but the heavy fighting and the terrorist threat sometimes made travel unsafe for Ambassador Bartholomew, forcing some operations to be conducted from his residence.

Wherever I was, Embassy or residence, I read the latest intelligence traffic received by the station chief, Bill Buckley. (Buckley was good at his job. He was successfully rebuilding the network of agents lost in the Embassy bombing, and we got along well, but—predictably—he was not always cooperative about sharing information with anyone outside his office.) From there, I went to the Ministry of Defense to get a rundown on the security situation from General Tannous. At some point, I'd also meet with Ambassador Bartholomew (an outstanding man in every respect—always open with me and I with him) to bring him up-to-date and receive instructions from him. Each evening I sent a detailed fax message to General Vessey (the same information went to the EUCOM staff—usually to the watch officer, Lieutenant Colonel Charlie Wilhelm in the J-3 Operations Directorate).

I met frequently with Israeli intelligence officers; and at least once, but most times twice, each week, I visited the Marines at the airport to brief Colonel Tim Geraghty and his staff on these meetings and on what I'd learned from Tannous. The Marines were always eager to get intelligence and operational information about Beirut, but often complained about their vulnerable location, a situation made worse by the scarcity of accurate information about the areas around them.

After meeting the Marines, I would normally be picked up by Marine helo and flown out to Rear Admiral Jerry Tuttle's flagship, where I would brief Tuttle and his key officers. These meetings kept everybody up to speed operationally, but the truth of the matter was there was very little intelligence information available about the nature of threats to American forces.

As I went about assessing the senior leadership of the Lebanese armed forces, particularly the senior field-grade officers (lieutenant colonel and colonel), I came to realize that they were the most educated group of officers I had yet encountered. Each had recently attended practically every military course available in England and the United States, and most held master's degrees from American universities. All of this education came with a price, however: Most of them were content to be staff officers; they lacked the motivation to be troop leaders, and particularly the skills to be warfighters.

Of the senior officers, the one I came to respect most was the director of operations, Brigadier General Abbas Hamdan, a very intelligent and articulate Shiite, and a man of principle. He had been educated in France, where he had married a French woman, and had two fine children. He was loyal without question to the democratic government of Lebanon, and motivated to do everything possible to help his nation.

I was also extremely impressed with the younger officers, particularly the lieutenants and captains. Most were graduates of Sandhurst in England, and had received their commission there. They were energetic and dedicated, constantly present with their troops, and motivated toward making their units the best ones possible, regardless of their ethnic mix. The cohesion and esprit that seemed to exist there was a joy to behold.

Meanwhile, the Chairman's office and my daily meetings with Ambassador Bartholomew kept me informed about ongoing political initiatives aimed at the withdrawal of Israeli and Syrian forces.

In early August, General Tannous began to confide his concerns that a concurrent Syrian-Israeli withdrawal would be very difficult to arrange.

Assad had no reason to withdraw from the Bekáa Valley, even if the Israelis withdrew from the parts of Lebanon they occupied. On the other hand, the Israelis had every reason to leave. They had suffered heavy losses during the invasion, and pressure for a withdrawal was mounting in Israel. The problem was that it would be some time before the Lebanese army was in good enough shape to replace them. If the Israelis proved unwilling to remain in place until the Lebanese army forces were ready to conduct an orderly relief, the situation in Lebanon could become perilous.

That gave Tannous only one viable option: With President Gemayel's permission, he wanted to negotiate directly with Israel to obtain an agreement for Israeli forces to remain in place until his own forces were ready to take over from them. To that end, he asked if I would be willing to take Brigadier General Abbas Hamdan and Colonel Simon Quassis, Tannous's director of intelligence, to Israel for talks with Uri Labron, the Israeli Minister for Lebanese Affairs.

General Vessey and Ambassador Bartholomew agreed to this plan, and Bartholomew offered to provide an officer from the Embassy to accompany us.

The meetings were to be kept close-hold and conducted at night.

In fact, though I agreed with Tannous's analysis of the situation, I was never optimistic about his plan's chances for success. A relief in place was unquestionably imperative for the security and stability of Lebanon, but there was no doubt that the Israelis would do whatever they perceived was in their best interests, and the Lebanese army had better be prepared to react to the results—ready or not.

I arranged for a Marine helicopter to fly us out to Tel Aviv on the next night; it would then wait until the meetings were over and return us to Beirut before daylight. The meetings were held in Uri Labron's office, usually from nine in the evening until midnight, and were always cordial, frank, and direct.

At the first meeting, Abbas Hamdan detailed his government's concerns about the timing of the Israeli withdrawal, but indicated that three brigades were almost ready to relieve Israeli forces in place. Tannous's hoped-for plan: He would first relieve the Israeli forces in the Chouf Mountains overlooking Beirut, while keeping a brigade employed in the vicinity of Beirut. When all Israeli forces had withdrawn, he would station a brigade in southern Lebanon to provide a security zone for Israel's northern border.

Labron's reply was vague. In essence: (1) The Israeli forces had pretty well achieved their objectives in Lebanon by driving the PLO out. (2) He had no indication from his government of a timetable for withdrawal of Israeli forces. (3) We should continue the meetings next week. (4) The group should meet the commanders of the Israeli units in Lebanon in order to get to know them better and work out a plan for relief of forces in place.

The next afternoon, Hamdan, Quassis, and I met with the Israeli Defense Force director of operations and the chief of intelligence for the Israeli forces in Lebanon to discuss plans for the relief. Like Labron, they were not aware of a timetable for withdrawal, but would be willing to work with Lebanese army officials.

The message from General Tannous indicated a slight change of position: Though he desired more time to ready his units, he was now willing to risk an earlier employment in order to prevent a dangerous void that would likely occur after an Israeli pullout.

During the next meeting in Tel Aviv, Labroni seemed pleased that we were working with the Israeli officers to develop a plan for relief, but he was still not aware of a timetable. He did have something new to present, however: The Israeli government had decided to provide its own security force to man the buffer zone on the Lebanese side of the border. A mainly Jewish and Christian militia was already in the process of being formed, and it was headed by a former lieutenant colonel of the Israeli Defense Forces.

This was not exactly the news the Lebanese wanted to hear, but I could understand Israel's position relative to its own security. The Lebanese army was untested at this particular point. I communicated all this to my superiors.

Back in Beirut, Tannous was disappointed that Israel would not trust the Lebanese army to guard its northern border, but the news was not all bad. The Israeli decision would now free up another brigade for Beirut.

Around August 20, meetings with Israeli officers produced a detailed plan to position Lebanese army units to support the Israeli withdrawal. These meetings took place in the field along the route that most of the Israeli forces would be using in their withdrawal from the Chouf Mountains, and they concluded with an understanding that the plan was acceptable. Again, no definite timetable had been established for the withdrawal, but Lebanese army officials were to be notified when a date was set.

On September 2, 1983, General Tannous hosted a dinner for General Levy, the Israeli chief of staff, and General Ehud Barak, Israel's chief of military intelligence, to request more time to ready his forces and get his troops into position before a pullout by the Israelis.

It was at this meeting that Tannous learned that the Israeli government had reached a final decision on a pullout timetable: The withdrawal was to begin immediately, starting the night of September 3. According to Levy, the decision was a political one, and there would be no delay. Tannous himself was shocked and deeply humiliated. He felt he had been let down by the Israelis.

The following morning, Israeli Defense Minister Moshe Arens met with Richard Fairbanks, a senior member of the U.S. national security staff. Fairbanks requested a delay, but Arens indicated that the decision had already been made, and the withdrawal would begin as scheduled.

Around midnight, the rumble of tanks and heavy vehicles could be heard from Beirut and the Chouf Mountains. The Israelis were pulling back to Israel.

They had left the dangerous void that Tannous feared.

Chaos soon followed.

Because Lebanon had become a high-threat situation, Tannous became concerned about my personal security. I reluctantly mentioned this to General Vessey in one of my daily situation reports and was given an intelligence major to help me with my duties. He was a godsend; I already had about as much as I could handle—and besides, two have a better chance of surviving than one. Every two or three days, we moved, always at night, to a different sleeping location. And during the periods of heaviest fighting and shelling, we stayed with Tannous in the underground operations center at the Ministry of Defense—not just for safety. I could best fulfill my responsibility there. Twice, my major and I were caught in ambushes, and both times his driving skills and ability to do bootlegger spins saved us.

ESCALATION

Even before the Israelis withdrew, the Marines at the airport had come under fire from Druze positions on the ridge above the city. The Druze apparently hoped that the provocation would leverage the Lebanese government into greater power sharing.

In late July, several mortar rounds had landed inside the Marine defensive perimeter; and again, late in August, heavier shelling resulted in the death of a Marine sergeant and a lieutenant. Though the Marines had considerable firepower available to them—155mm howitzers, five M-60 tanks, and all the firepower in the fleet—they had so far refrained from using it. But this time the provocation was too great, and the Marines returned fire, using their 155mm howitzers.

We also suspected that the Christian militia took occasional shots at the Marines, in order to trick them into using their massive firepower against the Druze and the Shiites—and to draw them into the fray.

Three days before the Israeli withdrawal, the leaders of the two main Muslim militias had issued separate statements, claiming that the Marines had turned against the Muslims—a situation made far worse, they added, because of the training assistance the Marines were providing the Lebanese army (actually practically nil). Though the Marines were trying to adhere to the tenets of their mission, and were firing only in self-defense, without taking sides, it was now obvious that the factions and their militias were not following the same rules of engagement, and were trying to link the Marines to the Christian-dominated Lebanese government in the eyes of the people.

The Israeli invasion had succeeded in ridding Lebanon of the PLO, but had done little to neutralize the Muslim armed factions, which were simply biding their time and strengthening their ranks until the Israeli withdrawal allowed them to rush in, fill the void, and resume their war against the Christian-dominated government.

Within twenty-four hours of the withdrawal, the militias began rushing to stake out their territories: The Amal Shiites controlled West Beirut (large numbers of Shiites migrated to West Beirut, taking over hotels and apartment buildings at will); the Druze PSP controlled the Chouf Mountain region; the Syrians controlled the Baalbeck Valley region and the large number of Shiites in that area; the Christian Phalange controlled East Beirut and attempted to take from the Druze the ridgeline above the airport and hold it until a Lebanese army brigade could reach it; and, in the south, Israel was establishing its own uniformed militia, designed to prevent Shiite and Palestinian raids against Israel's northern region. The Sunnis, who tended to be moderate and more affluent, opted to stay out of the militia business.

After the Israeli withdrawal, Beirut was an armed camp—totally unsafe. Soon, heavy artillery and mortar fire began raining down on Christian East Beirut and the Marines at the airport. Death constantly threatened everyone—from snipers, crossfires between factions, ambushes, and indiscriminate shellings by heavy artillery and rocket fire. This sometimes involved thousands of rounds that reduced sections of the city to rubble in less than half an hour.

And in general, all hell broke loose—assassinations, hostage-taking, factional fighting, and massive shellings—designed to bring down the government, drive out the U.S., French, and Italian forces, and allow each outside sponsor (Syria and Iran) to obtain its own political and religious objectives.

Assad and the Iranians were sitting in the "catbird seats." No one had any control over them, and it was impossible to influence them—but their aims were not the same.

Syria's objective was to control Lebanon through its support of the Amal and PSP militias and of Iranian-sponsored terrorist activities, but to prevent the spread of the Islamic revolution in Syria and Lebanon.

Iran's objective was to use terrorist activities to drive Americans out of the region, while at the same time spreading in the region their brand of fundamentalist Islam.

SHORTLY after midnight, September 3, the night the Israeli withdrawal started, the Marines at the airport, now obvious targets, were hit once again by heavy Druze artillery and a rocket barrage of more than a hundred rounds, killing two more Marines. Colonel Tim Geraghty immediately dispatched a situation report through his chain of command: "The stakes are becoming very high," he wrote. "Our contribution to peace in Lebanon since 22 July stands at 4 killed and 28 wounded."

Support came three days later.

On September 7, aircraft from the carrier *Eisenhower* began flying reconnaissance missions over the Chouf Mountains in an attempt to locate the Druze artillery positions. On September 8, the destroyer *Bowen* fired its 5-inch guns at targets located by the reconnaissance flights, but achieved only minor results, due to the low apogee (flat trajectory) of the rounds, and especially since the fires were not observed and adjusted by U.S. forward observers.

On the same day, the Druze militia, backed by Syrian artillery fire, drove off the last of the Christian militia who'd tried to take the ridgeline south of the airport. Meanwhile, fighting among the militias within Beirut intensified.

Tannous was faced with a dilemma. Something had to be done to ease the situation in Beirut itself, but he also needed to take the Druze-occupied ridgeline, which was only five kilometers away from the Presidential Palace and the Ministry of Defense (MOD). He immediately ordered one of his brigades into West Beirut to "clean it out." He also sent the 8th Brigade, with approximately 2,400 men, to take the town of Souk al Gharb, located near the center of the ridgeline, to clear the Druze militia off the ridge, and then to hold it. Lebanese intelligence estimated that a force of approximately 3,000 Druze militiamen, reinforced by about 300 Palestinians and 100 Iranian Revolutionary Guards, now held the ridge; they were supported by about thirty Soviet-made T-54 tanks, and backed by Syrian heavy artillery.

During the next three days, some of the heaviest fighting of the war took place. For most of those days, the artillery falling on the 8th Brigade attacking Souk al Gharb and on the city—mainly on East (Christian) Beirut—was coming at a rate of about 1,200 rounds per hour.

The brigade that entered West Beirut successfully accomplished its mission with very few casualties. In a couple of days, it had captured approximately 250 militia fighters and supporters and collected eight two-and-a-half-ton-truck-loads of ammunition, weapons, and Soviet communications gear, including complete radio stations with fifty-foot antenna towers.

The 8th Brigade fighting for the ridgeline had a much tougher go. Pounded constantly by heavy artillery fire, the brigade suffered many casualties but performed well. The only way that it could advance under the artillery fire was by hugging buildings as it went up the ridgeline (parts of the area were urbanized). After two days of continuous fighting, it finally succeeded in driving the Druze militiamen from the town.

Tannous and I immediately went to Souk al Gharb to check the brigade and to ensure that its commander, Michel Aoun, was setting up his defenses across the entire ridgeline—which had to be held if Beirut was to be protected—not just in the town itself. Tannous wanted to see firsthand rather than trust Aoun's radio reports.

For some time, Tannous had had concerns about Aoun's ability to effectively lead the brigade. Although it had so far performed well, the brigade commander tended to be indecisive and panicky, and he was prone to "cry wolf." His panic did not indicate solid and daring leadership.

When we got up there, I was stunned. I have never in my military career seen such devastation from artillery fire. Even heavy power lines on steel towers were down—cut by shrapnel. The steel fragments were so thick on the ground you could rake it up in piles. Every one of the brigade's rubber-tired vehicles had shrapnel-caused flat tires, and virtually every soldier in the brigade had some kind of bandaged wound.

And yet, despite more than 200 casualties, the brigade was in good spirits. They had fought well together as a cohesive unit.

After we left, Michel Aoun began to report concerns about the brigade's ability to hold the ridge. He requested reinforcements and more artillery ammo.

On the night of September 10, he reported convoys approaching from Druze territory, and then unloading troops forward of his position.

Shortly thereafter, one of his companies was attacked. It suffered seven dead, forty-three wounded, and several missing, and its commander was hacked to pieces with axes. The attackers, who did not speak Arabic, were probably Iranian Revolutionary Guards from Baalbeck. Aoun was frantic.

Though the heavy fighting on the ridgeline slacked off over the next week, the Druze, with Syrian support, began targeting the officers with long-barreled sniper rifles. For obvious reasons, leadership suffered greatly, and the troops, losing confidence, hunkered down in their holes. This in turn greatly increased their vulnerability to Druze infiltration of their lines at night, which could eventually open an approach to the Presidential Palace and Ambassador Bartholomew's residence in the Yarze neighborhood of Beirut, only about four kilometers from the front. If the Druze forces could actually take the Presidential Palace and Yarze, that would likely mean the end of the Lebanese government—as well as the U.S. assistance program.

As the days passed, the Druze began to increase the pressure. Their main attacks came at night on the forward, southern slope, where the attackers were mostly protected from Lebanese artillery fire supporting the defending brigade. With each attack, Aoun became more panicky.

During this period, I was with Tannous day and night, making recommendations about tactical options and encouraging more aggressive operations.

We visited the brigade at least twice weekly—and once, as we checked frontline defensive positions, narrowly missed getting hit by sniper fire ourselves.

Meanwhile, pressure from the Lebanese government was daily growing more intense to get the Marines and the naval task force offshore to fire in support of the Lebanese army. Gemayel was becoming panicky himself.

Any night now, he saw imagined hordes of Iranian Revolutionary Guards attacking the Palace and hacking everyone to pieces.

One night—I don't recall the date—Ambassador Bartholomew asked me to accompany him to a meeting with Gemayel. When we arrived at the Palace, Tannous was already there. Gemayel was in quite a state.

"How much longer do you think we can hold out?" he asked me, visibly alarmed.

"As long as your troops are willing to fight," I told him. "Except for the Syrian artillery, you've got the advantage. But you have to be more aggressive—you've got to have your units do more patrolling, and doing to them what they're doing to you. Even if you don't have a lot of artillery, you've got an Air Force and you've got bombs—but you haven't used them."

"Our pilots don't have experience dropping bombs," he answered. "And besides, we don't have the equipment that hooks the bombs to the planes."

"We just might be able to help with that problem," I told him.

By the time the meeting was over, he had calmed down.

Afterward, Tannous thanked me. "Gemayel just wanted to hear the truth from someone other than me," he told me.

I got together with Jerry Tuttle, and with the assistance of a couple of Navy machinists, bomb mounts were made and bombing sights were fabricated (for daylight use only).

Within the next couple of days, the Lebanese Air Force bombed suspected assembly areas and buildings used by the Druze for fighting locations. Although the bombings were not greatly effective, they gave a great psychological boost to the army.

Meanwhile, Robert MacFarlane requested a change in the Marines' rules of engagement, to allow fire support for the Lebanese army on the ridgeline at Souk al Gharb. Washington okayed the change but reemphasized that the Marines' mission remained the same. The order left the actual authority to fire on Souk al Gharb to Tim Geraghty, who proved very reluctant to exercise it. Once this was done, he knew, the Marines would be drawn deeper into the conflict. Because they were supporting the Lebanese army (though by this time it was nearly sixty percent Muslim), they would seem to be supporting the Christian government, and would therefore no longer be "impartial."

On September 19, the usual daily assault on the 8th Brigade at Souk al Gharb began at two in the morning with an artillery barrage. An hour and a half later, Simon Quassis, Lebanon's chief of military intelligence, awakened U.S. Colonel Gatanas, a member of MacFarlane's staff, in a panic: "Without American help," he told him, "Souk al Gharb will fall in half an hour." Gatanas called me with this report, and indicated that he was going to the 8th Brigade command post to check with Aoun personally.

This was a good idea, I told him, because I wouldn't put it past Quassis and Aoun to cook up something like this in order to get U.S. fire support.

Gatanas reached Aoun five hours later. By then, Aoun was totally confused and distraught, and all but out of artillery shells. "Where is the main threat coming from?" Gatanas asked him.

"Everywhere."

Gatanas was later able to sort through Aoun's confusion enough to determine that hand-to-hand fighting was occurring on the brigade's southern flank, but the main threat was probably coming from the north. The Lebanese soldiers seemed to be holding, but the same could not be said for leadership at the brigade level, which was likely to come apart. It was clear they were ultimately going to require fire support. Without it, the leadership would surely break down, at which point the brigade would no longer be a capable force and could not defend the ridge.

At the MOD, where I'd been staying ever since the heavy fighting had started, Tannous confirmed all this: In his view, Aoun was unstable. Without fire support, the 8th Brigade risked being routed.

I relayed this information to Geraghty, and at 9:45 A.M., Gatanas, who was still on the ridge, received permission to call in naval gunfire. Shortly thereafter, the cruiser *Virginia* opened fire. During the course of the day, the *Virginia* and other naval ships fired a total of 360 rounds on the Souk al Gharb ridgeline. Though the psychological effect of all this firepower was probably greater than any tactical results, the brigade held and was able to resupply.

In retaliation for the American intervention, shells started falling on the Ambassador's residence at Yarze later that day, forcing its evacuation. Only the Marine guard force and the radio operators remained.

On September 23, Robert MacFarlane went to Damascus for another meeting with Assad. He was once again about to come away empty-handed when he dropped news on Assad that caught the Syrian president's attention: "President Reagan wants you to know," MacFarlane told Assad, "that the battleship *New Jersey* will be arriving off the coast of Lebanon in two days."

This escalation of resolve *and* firepower caught the attention of the Lebanese factions as well.

The next day, all sides agreed to a cease-fire.

Soon the airport and the Port of Beirut were reopened. Although much of the city had been reduced to rubble, it began to come alive again. Crews were out cleaning up the streets and restoring power and water. The banks began to reopen, and people began to go about their business. The city remained divided along factional lines, however. It wasn't safe for people to leave their own areas.

Still, the resiliency of the Lebanese people was amazing.

MacFarlane returned to Washington in early October, hoping the cease-fire would hold.

It lasted only a couple of weeks.

DURING this lull, I left Beirut and traveled first to Stuttgart to brief General Lawson, the Deputy CINC for Europe, and then on to Washington to brief the Joint Chiefs.

In the meantime, the training of the Lebanese army continued. A supply ship carrying military equipment, supplies, and ammunition, bought and paid for by the Lebanese government as part of the military assistance program, finally showed up after a two-week delay (it had crashed into a pier in Italy). It was very welcome.

Later in October, the shelling of the 8th Brigade resumed from Druze militia batteries located ten to fifteen kilometers west of the ridgeline. The firing this time was much less intense than in September, and now had a discernible pattern: There was firing in the morning, and then again later in the afternoon. This turned out to be a convenient *modus operandi* for the Druze, many of whom kept a mortar in their backyard or in their houses (they'd drag it out and quickly set it up to fire). They dropped a few rounds in the tube before going to work and again in the afternoon as they returned.

The 8th Brigade continued to hold the ridgeline. But ominously, almost every night they could see headlights of convoys resupplying Syrian artillery positions in the Chouf.

The shelling of the Ambassador's residence at Yarze and the Ministry of Defense also resumed, but also at a reduced rate, which meant that people were more or less able to conduct business as usual. You couldn't say that people were leading "normal" lives, but chances of immediate, violent death were much lessened.

Soon the Shiites in West Beirut began ambushing people traveling the coastal road—an ironic setting, since it was hardly more than rock-throwing distance from the fleet of twenty-eight American warships, including a battleship and two aircraft carriers. People were killing each other and burning the bodies in clear view of many of the ships, and nothing could be done about it.

Though I encouraged Tannous to have the Lebanese army brigade responsible for the area put a stop to it, little was done, because the brigade commander and most of the brigade were Shiites.

Meanwhile, the Navy continued its daily reconnaissance flights over the Chouf Mountains and the Bekáa Valley. Soon they were drawing antiaircraft fire from SA-7 missiles and 37mm twin-barrel antiaircraft guns.

The New Threat

As October dragged on, we began to receive credible intelligence reports of possible car bomb attacks, sometimes even giving the make and the color of the car. One of these messages indicated that a spectacular act now being planned would make the ground shake underneath the foreign forces.

A Lebanese intelligence official believed that this act could be perpetrated in one of the many sea caves that snaked underneath Beirut. Some of these caves were large enough for passage by small boats, and the PLO had already used them as ammunition storage areas during their occupation of West Beirut.

A meeting held between Tannous and the commanders of the multinational forces (who were, understandably, deeply concerned) decided to search the tunnels and use well-drilling and seismic detection equipment to determine if any of the caves ran under the multinational force positions. The seismic detection equipment was brought in from the United States and Europe; the well-drilling equipment was already present in Lebanon.

A Lebanese navy search found nothing suspicious within the known caves, while seismic detection and well-drilling failed to locate any previously unknown caverns.

During all this activity, of course, everybody was doing everything possible to determine the nature of the target, and the method and timing of the attack.

At 6:30 Sunday morning, October 23, 1983, Tannous and I were sitting over coffee in his MOD office, discussing the training activities of the Lebanese army and future employment plans. The office had a large plate-glass window, providing a panoramic view of Beirut.

WHAM!

We heard a tremendous explosion. Shortly afterward, the shock wave rocked the building. A huge black column of smoke topped by a white, rapidly spinning smoke ring—like an atomic explosion—was rapidly rising from an area approximately two miles away, near the airport.

"God willing," Tannous said, part in exclamation, part in prayer—he was a devout Christian, "I hope it's not the Marines!"

He jumped up from his desk. "Let's go," he said. "We've got to get there. We'll take my car"—instead of a military vehicle—"and go straight through West Beirut to the airport. That's the shortest route."

Before we reached the car—WHAM!—another huge explosion. And we could see a similar cloud rising over the area where the French compound was located.

The explosions had shocked West Beirut to life. As we went through town, making at least seventy miles an hour, people were already on balconies and the tops of buildings trying to see what was going on.

As Tannous had feared, the Marines' compound had been truck-bombed. When we arrived, there was almost indescribable devastation. I have never seen anything like it. Fires were burning everywhere, people were torn apart, and the building had just collapsed on top of itself. The survivors were all in a daze.

When the blast occurred, Colonel Geraghty had been working in his office about a hundred yards away. He was now doing everything possible to bring order.

"Whatever you need, you've got," Tannous told him. "We'll bring every emergency crew in Lebanon to bear on this, and I'll get you heavy construction equipment in here immediately to lift some of these layers off these people."

One of Beirut's largest construction companies, with a contract to clean up rubble from previous fighting, was quickly ordered in to help. Tannous also immediately ordered one of his army brigades to move into the airport area to provide security for the Marines.

Tannous and I spent no more than ten minutes at what was left of the Marine compound before heading to the French compound only a couple of miles away, where we found similar, but somewhat lesser, devastation. "It was a truck bomb," the French commander reported. "We have at least twenty-five dead." The number would eventually reach fifty-nine.

Tannous offered the French the same assistance he'd given the Marines, and ordered in a Lebanese army battalion to secure their area.

We returned to the Marine compound. By this time, two guards who had witnessed the bombing reported that a yellow Mercedes-Benz stake bed truck, about the size of a dump truck, had rammed through the gates and the concertina wire, smashed over the guard shack, and plunged straight into the lobby of the four-story building, where some 350 Marines were sleeping. Once inside, the driver had detonated the bomb, killing himself and 241 Marines.

It was obvious that both the Marine and the French bombs had been planned to go off simultaneously, but for some reason there had been a two- to three-minute delay. Forensic experts from the FBI later concluded that the bomb under the Marine barracks contained the equivalent of 12,000 pounds of TNT. It dug an eight-foot crater through a seven-inch floor of reinforced concrete. One of the strongest buildings in Beirut was now reduced to a pile of pancaked rubble; the heavy reinforcing steel rods in the concrete had all been sheared like straws.

Within minutes, the intelligence community intercepted this unattributed message: "We were able to perform the spectacular act, making the ground shake underneath the feet of the infidels. We also got that Army brigadier general and the CIA station chief [Bill Buckley] in the process."

It was not so, thank God, but it was the first indication that Buckley and I were on the "hit list."

Later that afternoon, a previously unknown group called "Islamic Jihad" (meaning "Islamic Holy War," a group of fanatics supported, we learned later, by Hezbollah) telephoned the following to the Beirut newspaper: "We are soldiers of God and we crave death. Violence will remain our only path if the foreigners do not leave our country. We are ready to turn Lebanon into another Vietnam. We are not Iranians or Syrians or Palestinians. We are Lebanese Muslims who follow the dicta of the Koran."

The next day, picture-posters of both "martyred" truck drivers were pasted up throughout the Shiite south suburbs of Beirut.

Soon the Hezbollah connection began to come clear: According to Lebanese intelligence, the suicide drivers had been blessed by Sheikh Fadlallah, the spiritual leader of Hezbollah, before they launched their suicide missions. And a couple of days later, we learned that messages had been intercepted from the Iranian Foreign Ministry to Mohammed Mohtashamipur, the Iranian ambassador in Damascus, urging a major attack against the Americans. We also learned that Hosein Sheikholislam, the chief Iranian terrorist, had checked into the Sheraton Hotel in Damascus. He checked out on October 22, the day before the bombing. And Lebanese intelligence officials reported that the Iranian embassy in Damascus had been evacuated early on Sunday morning, just before the bombing.

Two weeks later, a young woman on an explosive-laden mule rode into an Israeli outpost at the edge of the southern buffer zone and detonated herself, killing fifteen Israelis. Shortly thereafter, her picture-poster went up in Beirut, Damascus, and Tehran alongside those of the two suicide truck bombers.

The four bombings—the U.S. Embassy, the U.S. Marine unit, the French unit, and the mule incident—gave clear evidence that the United States was not prepared to deal with this form of terrorist warfare. Nor did our intelligence community have the capability to penetrate fanatical religious-based organizations in order to provide adequate warning to U.S. forces and agencies around the world. Thus appropriate defensive measures or preemptive action could not be taken.

Both the U.S. and the French began planning to retaliate for the truck bombings by sending air strikes against Hezbollah headquarters in Lebanon at the Sheikh Abdullah barracks in Baalbeck. Both nations attempted to coordinate the strikes to occur on the sixteenth of November, but it did not happen that way.

The French launched from their battle group flotilla on the afternoon of November 16, as planned, but to no effect. Reconnaissance photos revealed they had missed the barracks complex completely. The U.S. attack did not take place until December 4.

Jerry Tuttle, the commander of the U.S. naval forces, preferred the time of the attack to be at midday so the sun would be directly overhead and his pilots would be better able to see more clearly the Syrian radar sites and artillery gun positions, which he had targeted (and the Joint Chiefs had approved). But for political reasons, the Joint Chiefs preferred an early-morning attack time, around 7:30 A.M. on December 4. Either there was a screwup in the conversion between Washington time and Lebanese time, and/or the order was garbled as it passed over the convoluted chain of command between Washington and Tuttle, but General Lawson, now the new deputy commander of the U.S. European Command, received a call at 5:33 A.M. on December 4, ordering the strike to occur at 7:30 A.M.

When Tuttle was wakened, he was already five hours behind the curve. Planes had not been loaded with bombs, and the pilots would be flying directly into the rising early-morning sun.

Twenty-three planes—Navy A-6s and A-7s—were launched. As soon as they entered the Chouf Mountain area headed for Baalbeck, they began to draw surface-to-air missile fire. Two planes were lost, with one pilot killed and his bombardier captured by the Syrians. As with the French strike, the raid had little effect: Two Syrian gun emplacements were knocked out and a radar site was damaged. All were back in operation within a week.

EFFORTS TO FIND A SOLUTION

Meanwhile, efforts continued on two fronts to find a solution to the disaster in Lebanon:

Inside Lebanon, General Tannous continued his heroic efforts to rebuild the army and provide stability to government-controlled areas—at that time only parts of Beirut and the ridgeline to the south that dominated the capital were considered stable. Concurrently, Ambassador Bartholomew was working with the factional leaders to reach a power-sharing agreement that would be acceptable to President Gemayel and everyone else concerned.

Outside Lebanon, President Reagan's new special envoy, Ambassador Donald Rumsfeld, was visiting the leaders of the modern Arab nations in southwest Asia, looking both for support and for suggestions that might lead to peace in Lebanon. He visited, at least monthly: Syria, Jordan, Saudi Arabia, Egypt, the United Arab Emirates, Oman, Kuwait, Qatar, Algeria, Morocco, Tunisia, and even Iraq (the United States was supporting Iraq in its then-ongoing war with Iran). These efforts forged a consensus for peace among all but one of these nations. Tragically, the one exception, Syria, could exercise an effective veto. It was obvious that Assad wanted the multinational forces out of Beirut in order to secure his own political objectives in Lebanon.

"Lebanon has always been a part of Syria," he once commented. "Read your Bible."

I have never seen a man more dedicated to his mission than Ambassador Rumsfeld, but success was just not in the cards. There were too many factors he could not influence—especially Syria, the two of three major factions that Syria controlled, and the Iran-influenced Hezbollah and its new form of terrorist warfare.

The time I spent with Ambassador Rumsfeld, like my time with Bud MacFarlane, proved very beneficial to me. It gave me a chance to get to know the key leadership of the modern Arab nations, and I was able to put this experience to effective use in my next assignment as the Commander of the Joint Special Operations Command.

Meanwhile, support in the United States for the administration's policy in Lebanon was eroding rapidly, both in Congress and at the Pentagon.

The Joint Chiefs of Staff had never favored the Marines' reentry into Lebanon in 1982. To them it was a "no-win" situation, though they did not want to give the appearance of abandoning an ally by "cutting and running." During the decision-making process, they gave this advice to the civilian leadership. As always, once the decision was made, they saluted and complied.

Even before the Marines were bombed in October, Congress had only very reluctantly authorized a continued Marine presence in Beirut for another eighteen months, but *only* if the administration did not try to expand their role, relocate them, or otherwise change the mission without congressional approval. As Congress returned to work in January 1984, the majority Democrats pressed for resolutions to withdraw the Marines. But, for the sake of our allies and our own self-esteem, President Reagan rejected that course. In his weekly radio address on February 4, 1984, he maintained (hopefully) that "our efforts to strengthen the Lebanese army are making sure and steady progress."

AT the same time—January 1984—the Shiite mullahs and Nabih Berri, no doubt prompted by Assad, devised a plan to bring about the disintegration of the Lebanese army, now sixty percent Muslim. In the eyes of Berri and the mullahs, the army had been used by Gemayel to keep the Christian minority in power. They now called on the Shiites in the army to stop acting as pawns of the Christians and lay down their arms and return to their barracks.

The commander of the predominantly Shiite Lebanese 6th Brigade, which had been keeping the peace in West Beirut, immediately complied by pulling his forces out of the city and back to their barracks. The Muslim militia quickly took over the streets. At the same time, the mullahs began broadcasting from the mosques that the Shiite soldiers should return to their barracks and no longer fight for a government that did not represent their interests.

Soon afterward, the Druze deputy commander, Major General Hakim, defected to the Druze PSP in the Chouf Mountains.

The evening after his defection, a Lebanese army battalion commander operating south of Beirut took three of his Christian lieutenants out on a reconnaissance. They didn't return. The next morning, a patrol sent out to locate the battalion commander found the three lieutenants with their throats cut—and no battalion commander; he had defected. Two other Christian soldiers were later found in their foxholes, also with their throats cut.

The same day, the Shiite militia began raking the family home of the Shiite but loyal Brigadier General Abbas Hamdan with machine-gun fire. Hamdan, who had been staying at the Ministry of Defense, sent his family back to safety in his wife's native France, but he remained in Beirut until Tannous persuaded him to join his family, his chances of survival in Lebanon being effectively zero.

In a matter of days, Lebanese army units, which had fought so well and so cohesively for months, lost trust in one another and began to fission; the pieces flew off to the various factional militias. Beirut's old "Green Line"— a street that served as a demarcation line between Christians and Muslims—once again became a battle line. Daily killings returned.

Early in February, the Embassy began evacuating nonessential Americans.

Meanwhile, a big question remained: What to do about the Marines in Beirut? After the bombing, they'd brought in replacements and continued to perform their mission.

A week after the Embassy started its own evacuation, the National Security Planning Group, presided over by Vice President George Bush, concluded that it was time to withdraw the Marines. President Reagan reluctantly accepted the recommendation.

The task of informing Amin Gemayel about this decision fell to Ambassador Rumsfeld, who just a week earlier had assured him that the United States would continue to stand behind the Lebanese government.

Rumsfeld later told me it was probably the toughest thing he ever had to do.

Ambassadors Rumsfeld and Bartholomew broke the news to Gemayel in his operations center in the basement of the Presidential Palace—the upstairs having been long since destroyed by artillery fire.

The news shattered Gemayel. Though he was assured that the assistance program to the Lebanese army would continue for the foreseeable future, he understandably felt seduced, abandoned, and powerless to do anything about it.

Later, an equally crushed General Tannous told me, putting on a brave front, "I will gather together what remains of the Lebanese army and continue to fight for what I believe is right for Lebanon. We may have to make some concessions with Syria, but as long as I am in this job I will continue to do everything in my power to bring peace to Lebanon."

The next day, as the *New Jersey* blasted away with its 16-inch guns at Syrian artillery positions in the Chouf Mountains, the Marines began withdrawing to their ships. In a nine-hour period, the battleship fired 288 2,000-pound, 16-inch rounds.

The last element of the Marines left the beach at noon on February 26. At a brief ceremony to turn the airport over to the Lebanese army, as the Marines struck the American flag, the presiding Lebanese officer grabbed his country's flag and presented it to the Marines: "Well, you might as well take our flag, too," he said. He then asked the Marines to drop him off by helicopter back at the Ministry of Defense; he was a Christian and could not pass through the Muslim checkpoints. After they dropped him off, the last Marine sortie proceeded on to the ships.

Within minutes, the Shiite Amal Militia began occupying their vacant positions and taking control of the airport.

The fighting between the factions continued, making the situation for the Americans who still remained even more dangerous. The only halfway-safe place for Americans was now on the Christian side of the "Green Line" in East Beirut. Because they could no longer cross the Line, the airport had become off-limits, which meant that an Army helicopter detachment had to be brought in to Cyprus to shuttle Ambassador Bartholomew and the remaining military to Cyprus for connections elsewhere.

The remaining Muslim officers on Tannous's staff soon found themselves targets of their own factions. Though most soon paid for their loyalty with their lives, a few, like Hakim, managed to escape to other countries.

As word of the throat-cutting spread, mistrust among the remaining soldiers grew even more, and within days the army that had fought so well began to split along factional lines.

They did not fight each other during the breakup. They just slipped away with their weapons and returned to their own ethnic enclaves. The Shiites went to West Beirut and the Bekáa Valley, the Druze back to the mountains, and the Christians to East Beirut.

The 8th Brigade's losses were quickly filled by Christians, and it continued to hold the ridgeline at Souk Al Gharb. Tannous, having no other choice, quickly reorganized the army to compensate for the losses, but it was now a "Christian force," with far less capability, operating mainly from East Beirut and defending the Christian enclaves, the ridgeline at Souk Al Gharb, Yarze, and the seat of government.

Assad took advantage of the opportunity by moving Syrian regular units to take control of the northeastern sector of Lebanon and all major roads leading to the north and east. Now, with the Israelis controlling the buffer zone in the south, all that remained under Lebanese government control was the enclave of Beirut, but even that was mostly controlled by the Amal, which danced to Assad's tune.

Once his generals were in charge of all the trade routes—and lining their pockets—Assad began to stipulate conditions for reorganizing the government.

Of course, Tannous had to be replaced. When that time came, he relinquished command of the armed forces with respect, dignity, and pride, and quietly returned to his cement factory in East Beirut. However, his loyalty remained to Lebanon and its armed forces. The last I heard, he was still conducting advanced officer's classes on tactics in a training area/classroom that he'd established in the garden behind his house—an initiative he'd begun during the early phases of rebuilding the army in order to improve the tactical proficiency of midlevel combat arms officers.

A New Form of Terrorism

Flushed with their bombing successes, the Islamic Jihad raised the stakes even more by introducing a new form of terrorism—"hostage taking."

The first American was taken hostage on February 10, 1984. By the time TWA 847 was hijacked, some fourteen months later, seven Americans had been kidnapped.

Kidnapping is not a new idea, of course, and had long been commonplace in Lebanon: In the early '80s, more than 5,000 people from all sides had been kidnapped for ransom. Islamic Jihad's new tactics, however, were aimed solely at achieving political leverage—a big difference.

Their initial motivation was to capture a stable of Americans who could be used as bargaining material with the Kuwaiti government after the Kuwaitis had rounded up the seventeen Iranian-backed terrorists responsible for a December 1983 suicide bombing spree against six targets in Kuwait, in which five people had been killed and eighty-six wounded. One of those held in Kuwait was the brother-in-law of Lebanon's most feared Shiite terrorist, Imad Mugniyah, known as the "enforcer." Mugniyah was the thug responsible for the Islamic Jihad hostage-taking spree.

On February 10, 1984, the day before the trial for the seventeen terrorists was to begin in Kuwait, the first American was kidnapped, Frank Regier, a professor at the American University of Beirut. The second was Jeremy Levin, a reporter for the Cable News Network, kidnapped on March 7. The third was William Buckley, the CIA station chief in Beirut, kidnapped on March 16.

I should add a personal note here: The message claiming that Buckley and I had also been killed with the Marines should have been a warning to Buckley. I had talked to him about his vulnerability as soon as we learned of it. Though I had been in the survival mode since day one in Lebanon, and advised him to do the same, he played down the danger. "I have a pretty good intelligence network," he told me. "I think I'm secure." He remained in his apartment, and traveled the same route to work every day. As for me, I checked my car for bombs before I drove, varied my routes when possible, and when I wasn't in the MOD with Tannous, I was moving every second or third night to a different location.

SOMETIMES bad guys commit good acts. Thus the Shiite militia, who were not especially friendly to us, but even less friendly to Islamic Jihad, found and rescued Frank Regier on April 15, 1984. The whereabouts of the remaining hostages remained unknown, however, and it was ten months later, February 14, 1985, before another emerged from captivity, when Jeremy Levin escaped from the Sheikh Abdullah Barracks at Baalbeck and made his way to a Syrian checkpoint about a mile away. He was taken to Damascus and released to the American Ambassador.

During these months of captivity, Mugniyah would from time to time force the hostages to read statements aimed at the release of the seventeen terrorists imprisoned in Kuwait. The statements were videotaped and then shown over television.

When this failed to produce results, Mugniyah and his Hezbollah terrorist friends hijacked a Kuwaiti airliner flying to Iran. This also failed to budge the Kuwaitis.

Meanwhile, Buckley's kidnapping had become a major CIA concern. Not long after his capture, his agents either vanished or were killed. It was clear that his captors had tortured him into revealing the network of agents he had established—the source for most of our intelligence on the various factions in Beirut. It's thought that the Jihad eventually killed him. The United States had once again lost its primary intelligence sources in Beirut, making it even more dangerous for the Americans remaining behind.

I left Beirut in late May 1984 and returned to an assignment in the Pentagon. Saying goodbye to General Tannous, Ambassador Bartholomew, and Ambassador Rumsfeld* was one of the toughest challenges I have faced. I respected them for their tireless work to bring peace to Beirut—but it was just not to be. For my part, I hated to leave. Though it had been a professionally rewarding experience, and I had learned much that would stay with me, it was the first challenge in my military career that I had failed to complete to my satisfaction.

As I stood on top of the hill at the helipad waiting for the Blackhawk from Cyprus, my thoughts and prayers were for those I was leaving behind.

By October 1985, when the hostages from the hijacking of TWA 847 were released in Damascus, nine Americans had been kidnapped and held hostage by Mugniyah. But of these, only six remained: Bill Buckley was dead; Regier had been set free by the Shiite militia; and Jeremy Levin had escaped to the Syrians. The six remaining hostages had been in captivity for better than a year and a half—a *very* long time.

We wanted them back, very badly.

When I left Beirut, never did I imagine that I would return again. But in September 1985, I found myself with a Special Operations Task Force at a location in the eastern Mediterranean, prepared for a hostage rescue attempt. We had intelligence information indicating there might be a release of all the hostages. My orders were to set up a mechanism for their pickup and covert return to the United States. We were also prepared for a rescue operation, in case something went wrong.

---

*Bartholomew returned to Washington to become a principal deputy in the State Department. Rumsfeld is now the Secretary of Defense.

We did not know the actual release point, except that it would be some-where in the vicinity of the American University in West Beirut.

At midnight on September 14, 1985, the streets were vacant near the American University. A car pulled up, the back door opened, and a man got out dressed in a running suit. The car sped away. The man was picked up by one of our operators, brought to a predesignated point on the beach, the proper code signal was sent by the operator, and a helicopter picked the two of them up and brought them back to an aircraft carrier over the horizon. When the helicopter landed, the Special Forces operator announced, "This is the Reverend Weir."

Reverend Benjamin Weir, an American missionary, had been held captive for sixteen months by the Shiite Muslims. Weir was fed a hot meal in the Admirals' Mess, then taken to the hospital bay in the belly of the ship, where he was given a complete physical examination (he was in remarkably good shape considering what he had been through) and held for the next three days while we waited for the release of more hostages.

When he was picked up, he had with him notes from other hostages for their families and a message from his captors for personal delivery to President Reagan. We did not look at any of these messages.

Three days later, the deal for the release of the other hostages had failed to materialize, and we were told to return Reverend Weir to the United States. Reverend Weir, dressed in a flight suit, was flown to a location else-where, where a C-141 was waiting to return him to Andrews Air Force Base.

Some months after that, the intelligence community located the build-ing in West Beirut where the hostages were being held, and described it in sufficient detail to allow us to locate a similar building in the western United States. We modified this building to mirror the Beirut building's in-terior, a rescue force rehearsed the mission, and an infrastructure was es-tablished in West Beirut to support the operation.

Then disaster hit.

Two weeks before the planned launch of the rescue attempt, the Hezbollah uncovered one of the agents with access to the building; he was tortured and killed. Before he died, he revealed the names of the other agents involved, who were also killed. It was assumed then that the hostages would be split up in various locations, and so the rescue attempt was scratched. There was never again sufficient credible intelligence to support a rescue attempt, but eventually the hostages were released.

BECAUSE such anarchic violence is blessedly beyond most Americans' experience, my countrymen seem to have had a hard time grasping the complexities that led to the factional fighting and ultimately to the destruction of Beirut. Maybe this story will bring additional insight:

In December 1983, as Colonel Tom Fintel was nearing the end of his tour as chief of office of military cooperation, General Tannous arranged a going-away ceremony, complete to the presentation of a Lebanese medal on behalf of President Gemayel.

Sporadic artillery fire made an outside ceremony unsafe, so Tannous decided to hold the ceremony in an officers' club on the top floor of the Ministry of Defense, overlooking the city. Only principal staff officers and brigade commanders were invited, along with wives, but wives were not expected to show up, because of the risk.

To my surprise, two wives—Christians—actually braved the shelling to attend.

I'd never met them before, but as soon as they entered the room, they came straight to me. Without even introducing themselves, one brought her face close to mine: "Why don't you do something about this shelling that's killing our children?" she practically cried. "You've got all those ships sitting out there, with aircraft carriers. Bomb the heathens that are destroying us."

"We can't do that," I said. "The people who are shooting and shelling are also Lebanese citizens. This is a Lebanese problem, and it has to be worked out by Lebanese."

They came back at me with fire in their eyes. "They are not Lebanese citizens!" one said. "They are nothing! They don't even have a soul."

"We teach our children that they are born with a little black tail," the other said. "And it is their duty to kill them, pull their pants down and hack it off!"

Lebanon's wounds are cut deep. Healing that agony may require as many generations as it took to create it.

Two days after this ceremony, the Ministry of Defense was hit by an artillery barrage that destroyed the officers' club.

AND less than two years later, I was on my way to Sicily to deal with another hostage-taking, this time aboard the *Achille Lauro*. . . .

IX

THE *ACHILLE LAURO* STRIKE

C arl Stiner resumes the account begun in the first chapter. It is Tuesday, October 8th, at the Sigonella NATO Base, Sicily:

As soon as we arrived in Sigonella early Tuesday morning, we began refueling the planes, but we would not take off until later that day, since we had to time our departure to arrive at about dusk at Cyprus (Cyprus would provide us with coverage of the eastern Mediterranean, and a base for the takedown of the ship, if that proved feasible). Meanwhile, we off-loaded the small contingent of SEALs and the two Little Bird gunships that would remain at Sigonella.

This ground delay proved useful, since it gave me my first opportunity during the mission to talk to my commanders face to face. We had lifted off from three bases in three states, assembled en route, and landed sequentially. Now, on the ground at Sigonella, I held a commanders' conference to talk about conducting the operation.

There were blessedly only three possible scenarios:

⊘ First scenario: The ship remains on the high seas and in the vicinity of Cyprus. In that case, we could reach it from there and wouldn't need Navy platforms (ships) for staging and recovering our helicopters. Of the three scenarios, this would be the least complex for us, and would offer us the best conditions for success, since the terrorists wouldn't have a sanctuary, such as, for example, Iran, Libya, or Algeria.

✪ Second scenario: The ship finds a port somewhere. In this case our operation would be easy or hard depending on the cooperation of the host country. Yet, even if the host country consented to our operation, surprise would be difficult to achieve; we would have to be concerned about the territorial waters issue, and perhaps we'd have local police or military forces to deal with.

✪ Third scenario: The ship sails beyond the recovery range of our helicopters. In that case, we would need Navy platforms for recovery of our helicopters after our initial assault.

After the conference, I communicated these options to the Pentagon and USEUCOM. Then I talked with the U.S. commander at Sigonella, Bill Spearman, to find out if he had learned anything useful from his Italian counterparts, such as the Italian base commander. We also talked about support I might need when we returned. I knew this was prudent but, at the time, I was convinced it was unnecessary. We were focused on a takedown at sea and never imagined that the action would end up (as it did) back at Sigonella. In any event, I asked Bill to take care of my troops who'd remain at Sigonella and promised to keep in touch through my liaison team there.

By afternoon we had reached our window for reaching Cyprus at dusk.

Before boarding the plane, I decided to check with Vice Admiral Moreau (whom Admiral Crowe had designated to work the details and to keep him informed) about what was going on in Washington, to find out if we were cleared into the military base on Cyprus, and to update him on our planning options for the takedown. I did this on the SATCOM, which my radio operator carried (he was always by my side).

Moreau had three messages: Efforts to locate the *Achille Lauro* were continuing, and the Israelis had been asked to help. The decision had been made to take the ship down; I would receive the "Execute Order" soon. And approval had been granted by "our friends" to use Cyprus.* That had been expected, but it was good to know.

"We're launching now," I told him, "and are scheduled to arrive by dusk.

---

*The base on Cyprus is operated by a friendly nation that is sensitive to our using it for counterterror missions. We have therefore not identified the base or the friendly power.

If the ship can be found today, and it's within range of our helicopters, we might be able to do a takedown before daylight."

"Sounds good," he replied. "I'll pass it on."

Next I decided to check with my liaison officer in Rome. I was glad to learn that he had established contact with Ambassador Rabb and was operating from the U.S. embassy. All the pieces were moving into place.

I boarded the plane and we launched. This involved staggering our launch times, which in turn allowed us to sequence our landing in order to accommodate the available ramp space at our destination. No more than four C-141s and two C-5s could be on the ground off-loading at any one time.

ON BOARD THE *ACHILLE LAURO*

The *Achille Lauro* had set sail from its home port in Genoa, Italy, on October 3, 1985, with 750 passengers on board, for a seven-day voyage that would include a visit to Ashod, Israel. Most of the crew of 344 were Italian, while the passengers were an international mix of travelers.

On the morning of Monday, October 7, the 633-foot liner had docked at Alexandria, Egypt, to let off passengers who wanted to tour the Pyramids. The ship would loiter off the coast of Egypt and then come back that evening to pick up the passengers at Port Said before continuing the voyage to Israel.

Most of the ninety-seven passengers who had elected to stay behind were too elderly or infirm for a rigorous day among the antiquities. Among these was the sixty-nine-year-old Leon Klinghoffer, wheelchair-bound after two strokes. Klinghoffer was accompanied by his fifty-eight-year-old wife, Marilyn. There were ten other Americans.

During lunch, a pair of Arab-looking men burst into the dining room, firing machine guns in the air. Moments later, the passengers were all flat on the dining-room floor.

When they heard this commotion, the officers standing watch on the bridge were able to send the distress signal that the ship was being hijacked. This was the message received in Göteborg, Sweden, that had been monitored.

As all this was happening, two other Arab-looking terrorists were taking over the bridge. When the ship's captain, Gerardo de Rosa, arrived, the terrorist leader, Majed Molqi, ordered him to put the ship into radio silence and head for the Syrian port, Tartus, which was four-hundred miles away—punctuating his demand with a burst of machine-gun fire into the deck. Syria was a haven for terrorists, and Hafez Assad, the president, exercised considerable leverage over several terrorist organizations.

In all, there were four terrorists—not the twenty claimed by the terrorist leader. But they had the advantage of shock and surprise.

The terrorists, it was later learned, were PLO (Palestine Liberation Organization) members. Their original plan had been to wait until the ship entered the Israeli harbor at Ashod, where they would take control of the ship. They would then hold the passengers hostage, while negotiating for the release of fifty other Palestinian terrorists who had been tried, convicted, and sentenced by Israeli courts. But things had not worked out according to plan. The four men had not behaved like normal cruise-liner passengers, a fact noted by an alert ship's steward, who figured lunchtime would give him an opportunity to check out the stateroom they occupied. What he found when he entered was the four men cleaning automatic weapons. Their only choice was to make their move.

WHEN the *Achille Lauro* arrived off the port of Tartus Tuesday afternoon, the JSOTF was still flying to Cyprus. Though aircraft from the U.S. 6th Fleet were crisscrossing the eastern Mediterranean searching for it, no one other than a few on board the vessel had any idea where the cruise liner was until the terrorists announced their presence near Tartus, where they broadcast a request to land and a demand for the release of the fifty Palestinian terrorists. Their hope was that Syrian President Hafez Assad would provide them a sanctuary and a platform for negotiations. Their hope was misplaced.

Though President Hafez Assad remained friendly to terrorists, he was not at that time friendly to Yasir Arafat's Palestinian Liberation Front terrorists. Assad had fallen out with Arafat, and since Assad had by then identified the *Achille Lauro* hijackers as members of the PLO, he saw an opportunity to undermine Arafat.

Assad, taking advantage of the opportunity, refused this request.

The terrorists were now in a desperate situation, knowing that they were no longer hidden and increasingly vulnerable to an attack. To deter that, they arranged twenty hostages in a circle out on an open upper deck, visible to aircraft. One of the twenty hostages was Leon Klinghoffer. His wheelchair prevented him from ascending the stairs to the deck and joining the others. "The terrorists ordered me to leave him," his wife Marilyn reported later. "I begged them to let me stay with him. They responded by putting a machine gun to my head and ordered me up the stairs. That was the last time I saw my husband."

Majed Molqi then broadcast threats. Passengers would be killed unless he saw movement on his demands by 3:00 P.M.

At three, Molqi went to where Leon Klinghoffer had been left, moved him near the starboard rail, and shot him in the head and chest. Two of the ship's crew were ordered to throw the body overboard.

Afterward, Captain de Rosa was told to call this information to Tartus.

This message may have been picked up by the Israelis, because I was informed later that we had reason to believe someone had been killed, even though by that time the hijackers were claiming that all of the hostages were safe.

Meanwhile, the hijackers had picked another victim, Mildred Hodes.

Though Majed Molqi continued to demand action from Tartus, the Syrians continued to stall.

By this time, the PLO leadership had realized that matters were getting out of hand and it was time to institute damage control. Using a codename, "Abu Khaled," Abu Abbas, who was one of Yasir Arafat's chief lieutenants and a member of his executive council, broadcast a message over an Arab-speaking radio station, directing the terrorists to return to Port Said without harming the hostages.

The *Achille Lauro* set sail from the vicinity of Tartus somewhere around 4:30 or 5:00 P.M., to take advantage of the coming darkness. The ship again went into radio silence.

WHEN the *Achille Lauro* first broke radio silence near Tartus, the JSOTF was about midway into its flight to Cyprus, and I was being kept abreast of the intercepted communications between the terrorists and the Tartus port authorities by Vice Admiral Moreau at the Pentagon. At the same time, our liasion officer in Rome was keeping me up to date on developments within the Italian government.

What I learned was that Ambassador Rabb had met with Italian Prime Minister Craxi, Foreign Minister Andreotti, and Defense Minister Spadolini to explain that President Reagan was pleased at the Italian government's collaboration during the hostage crisis, but the U.S. government had learned authoritatively that an American citizen had been murdered and others had been threatened, and that this was "untenable." Rabb stated further that the

U.S. government was absolutely unwilling to undertake negotiations, and had decided to attempt a military rescue operation some time Wednesday night.

Meanwhile, the *Achille Lauro* had vanished again; and again, 6th Fleet aircraft lost it.

CYPRUS

The arrival of darkness also meant that JSOTF aircraft had started landing on Cyprus. We instantly raced into action.

Based on an intelligence guess that the *Achille Lauro* might not be headed for Egypt but for Larnaca, in Cyprus, which was not far away, we clandestinely rushed forces into position for a takedown, just in case the ship did show up.

Things did not in fact work out that way.

At about daylight, Wednesday, October 9, an Israeli patrol boat spotted the *Achille Lauro* off the Israeli-Lebanese border heading south—for Egypt.

Even so, the ship was still in international waters and a good distance from Egypt. Earlier we had requested two Navy ships from the U.S. European Command (USEUCOM) for platforms from which to launch our helicopters. Meanwhile, three U.S. Navy ships had arrived in the vicinity of the *Achille Lauro* and were shadowing it from over the horizon. Plans had already been made for positioning the SEAL assault forces onboard the two U.S. Navy platforms. The plan was to conduct a ship takedown just after darkness at 2100 hours, Wednesday night.

Back at Cyprus shortly after daylight, I was finalizing last-minute details for the assault with my commanders when a helicopter landed just outside our hangar. Colonel "Lou" quickly responded, "It's not one of ours; they were all back before daylight." Lou's helicopters had been conducting test flights after reassembly following offloading.

I said, "Sergeant Major, find out who that is. No one else around here has a helo that makes that sound."

The sergeant major rushed outside and quickly returned. "Sir," he said, "we have a couple of guests." Standing there with the sergeant major were two Italian officers, a lieutenant colonel and a major, in flight suits and wearing survival equipment and weapons.

"What are you two up to?" I asked them.

"We are here to recover our ship," the lieutenant colonel said.

"You gotta be shitting me," I said. "Where is the rest of your force?"

"Well, we've had a few maintenance problems on the way," he answered, "and some of my force is broken down on islands between here and our home base, and they will be coming in a little later."

Knowing that whatever he might eventually be able to gather up would be totally inadequate and untrained for ship takedown operations, I said, "We can't wait, we are up against a time crunch."

"I do have a diagram of the ship," he offered, "if that will help any."

Would it! Boy! this was welcome news. Up to that moment, we had had no clear idea of the layout of the *Achille Lauro*.

For this operation, we had drawn sketches for planning, using other ships as models, but we'd had to guess where the towers, antennas, masses, and the bridge were located on the *Achille Lauro*. Although we had the best pilots in the world, it is still risky business flying helicopters at night in an assault into the structures of a ship, placing shooters exactly where they ought to be—all under night-vision goggles—and especially on a ship that is likely to be blacked out.

"I'll make you an offer," I said. "You give us that diagram, and we'll take you along on this operation, but keep you out of harm's way. We'll recover your ship, and turn it over to you. No one will ever know that you didn't do it . . . unless you tell them. You can have all the credit."

He was ecstatic, thinking that he had made the best deal of his life, and he promptly handed me the diagram. What he didn't know was that should Captain de Rosa and his ship drivers be killed during the assault, he could have ended up driving the ship. . . . You can't just let one float by itself. Of course, we would not have let this actually happen before loaning him a trained ship driver. Yes, our SEALs had people trained for driving ships.

The diagram was a godsend. It was about four feet by eight feet and showed in detail where all the structures were that could cause us problems in darkness. Within an hour, with its help, all our assault forces were able to tweak their plans and brief their troops.

CAIRO

In Cairo, Egypt's Foreign Minister Abdel Meguid was asking the ambassadors of the various countries involved for advice: Would it be best to negotiate or refuse to negotiate? Meanwhile, Yasir Arafat sent Abu Abbas to Cairo to deal with the hijackers.

Yasir Arafat already had a working relationship with the Italian prime minister, as he did with the Egyptian government. In those days, the PLO leader had developed several "under the table" agreements—especially with governments that lay within what might be called the PLO area of influence. These governments were afraid that the PLO could bring down their governments if they did not cooperate. These agreements permitted the PLO to operate within those countries.

By Wednesday morning, Arafat claimed to have everything under control. "We have succeeded in bringing the ship back into the waters off Egypt," he announced. "I can reveal to you that we have a high degree of confidence regarding a positive conclusion to the affair."

Meanwhile, neither the Egyptians nor the Italians were eager to pursue the terrorists once they had arrived in Egypt. For various diplomatic and internal political reasons, they hoped the terrorists on *Achille Lauro* would simply disappear and the whole affair would go away unnoticed.

As far as the United States was concerned, this was not an option. To the United States, like Israel, a terrorist attack was no different from any other military attack. It could not be met by appeasement. The only option was military action.

Neither position was, strictly speaking, unreasonable, given the needs and premises from which each side started. But compromise and appeasement are not a wise long-term approach to terrorism.

By late Wednesday afternoon, actions were well under way for positioning the assault force of Navy SEALs aboard a Navy ship just out of sight of the *Achille Lauro*. Four hijackers were not enough to guard hostages, control the crew and the bridge, and maintain a watch over the entire ship. There was every likelihood the SEALs would reach the ship without detection by the terrorists. Come night, they would launch their strike. Once they were aboard, they had no doubt of the outcome.

As the rescue force prepared to strike, events were taking place in Cairo that would make the attack unnecessary.

That evening the Egyptian government announced: "At four-twenty P.M., the hijackers, whose number is four, agreed to surrender without preconditions. They surrendered at five P.M." The statement was soon amplified by the Egyptian Foreign Minister: "The four hijackers have left the ship and are heading out of Egypt." These statements had a subtext: that no harm had been done to any of the passengers. Up until this point, the murder of Leon Klinghoffer had been concealed, based on statements Captain de Rosa had been forced to make over the radio as the liner neared Egypt. "I am the captain," he had said. "I am speaking from my office; and everybody [aboard] is in good health."

As it happened, each of those statements was false. First, the Egyptian government had agreed to preconditions. They had promised the terrorists safe passage out of Egypt. Second, the hijackers were not yet heading out of Egypt, and would not do so until the next day. Finally, the terrorists had blood very much on their hands.

Even before these facts emerged, the Reagan administration was furious. As far as they were concerned, it was a lousy deal. It's not acceptable for terrorists to take Americans hostage and get away with it. In the words of White House spokesman Larry Speakes: "We believe those responsible should be prosecuted to the maximum extent possible."

ON Wednesday evening, after the terrorists had left the ship, the truth about the Klinghoffer murder came out when a distraught Captain de Rosa announced to Marilyn Klinghoffer that her husband had been shot and his body dropped overboard. The rickety structure of Egyptian and Italian whitewash and deception was tumbling down.

When Nicholas Veliotes, the U.S. ambassador to Egypt, learned of the murder, he immediately contacted Meguid to insist "that they prosecute those sons of bitches."

Meguid dodged, claiming—once again—that the terrorists were already out of the country, a claim confirmed by President Hosni Mubarak the next day. "The terrorists have already left Egypt," he announced. "I don't know where they went, but they possibly went to Tunis.

"When we accepted the hijackers' surrender," he continued, "we did not have this information. This information emerged five hours after the surrender. In the meantime, the hijackers had left the country."

This was a lie. The terrorists were then sitting in an Egypt Air 737 at Al Maza air base near Cairo waiting for a place to fly to. Nobody wanted them.

American intelligence was on the ball, however, and had the tail number of the plane—2843.

LATE in the evening of October 9, Vice Admiral Moreau informed me that the terrorists had surrendered and left the *Achille Lauro*. That meant there was no longer a requirement for an assault on the ship, he concluded, and I could begin my redeployment to home bases.

Shortly after that, I ordered Captain "Bob" to prepare for redeployment. Meanwhile, our airlift, which had remained at their dispersal bases since our arrival, began arriving at the Cyprus base; and starting at around 2200 hours, we began a phased redeployment back to home bases.

Standard operating procedure was to deploy and redeploy as combat-configured entities (task forces) should any requirement for our services develop while en route. The planes all stopped in Sigonella to refuel and then proceeded on back to the States.

By the time daylight Thursday was approaching Cyprus, only three aircraft were left—a C-5 and two C-141s. The C-5, loaded with UH-60 Blackhawks, had developed a bad hydraulic leak from a busted hose. It could not retract its main landing gear and was losing an alarming amount of fluid.

The problem was not the leak itself, but the continued presence of the aircraft at "our friends'" base in daylight, where it would be visible to Soviet spy satellites. Two colonels from our host nation were really getting nervous. They could accept a couple C-141s, but the C-5 would attract too much attention and cause political problems. They wanted it gone.

It was a touchy situation.

The only thing I could think to do was to take a look myself to see if I could come up with something that might help. I crawled up into the C-5's wheel well to look at the broken hose, and as soon as I did, I realized that the "Docs" had some surgical tubing that might work. Sure enough, they had a hose that looked about the right diameter, and the pilot, an experienced older Air Force Reserve lieutenant colonel, agreed to fly the plane if we could stop the leak.

He shut the engines down to take the pressure off the hydraulic system. Then he, a mechanic, and I climbed up in the wheel well, and with hydraulic fluid spraying all over us, repaired the hose well enough so the plane could fly with its wheels down.

They took off just at the break of day and flew at low level to Sigonella, where the plane was fixed properly.

WASHINGTON

For all of Thursday, the four hijackers remained at the air base northeast of Cairo, but now they had a destination. They were to be flown to Tunisia (the new location of the PLO headquarters after they'd been forced out of Beirut by the Israelis).

While this drama was playing out in Cairo, a few members of the NSC staff in Washington came up with a brilliant idea. They were aware, from intelligence intercepts, that the Egypt Air aircraft had not yet left the ground. So why not use planes from the aircraft carrier *Saratoga*, which was nearby in the Mediterranean, to force the plane down at some friendly airport and take the terrorists into U.S. custody?

After some discussion, the NATO base at Sigonella was chosen as the friendly location that would cause the fewest potential problems. Sicily was Italian, and so was the *Achille Lauro*. After further discussion, it was determined that intercepting a civilian airliner was indeed physically possible. The President was contacted, and Reagan gave his approval.

MEANWHILE I was still on the ground on Cyprus with my two C-141s, awaiting darkness so I could launch for home. I had with me my battle staff, my communications (including my low-level intercept capability), and my medical unit, as well as Captain Bob and two of his SEAL platoons—my reaction team, in case anything unforeseen happened en route.

I was just about to launch Bob's C-141, when I received a call from Vice Admiral Moreau, who briefed me on a concept plan—approved in principle by President Reagan—for capturing the terrorists should they be flown from Egypt to Tunisia. "F-14s from the *Saratoga* will be responsible for intercepting the Egypt Air plane and forcing it down at Sigonella. You are to follow the plane into Sigonella, capture the terrorists, and fly them back to the U.S. in chains to stand trial. Stand by for word to launch in order to link up with the F-14s that will make the intercept." And then by way of conclusion: "The Italian government has given its approval of all this, both for the landing and for our taking the terrorists."

This last proved to be over-hopeful. At this point the Italian government had no idea that we were going to do anything of the kind, and it's doubtful that they would have approved it if they had known. The mistake was a screwup—a mixed-up communication somewhere along the line. But as it turned out, it was a welcome failure, since it afforded an opportunity to capture the terrorists who had hijacked the ship and killed Leon Klinghoffer.

After my conversation with Art Moreau, I walked over to brief Bob and his men. The first thing I noticed was the look of disappointment on all their faces—disappointment that they'd missed the opportunity to conduct the ship assault and deal appropriately with the criminals who had brutally killed an American. But as soon as I got to the part of my briefing that said we had another opportunity to capture the terrorists, several of the SEALs began forcing themselves to puke out the sleeping pills they had taken so they could sleep on the way home. They were ready for the new mission.

THE INTERCEPT

A secure—and urgent—call came to Rear Admiral Dave Jeremiah on the USS *Saratoga* from 6th Fleet headquarters. They were to change course and prepare to launch what was called their "alert CAP" (the Combat Air Patrol consisted of two F-14 Tomcat interceptors and an E-2C Hawkeye radar plane, which would direct the fighters). Though the *Saratoga's* captain had no idea what was going on, or why they were changing course, he couldn't miss the 6th Fleet's urgency, and he launched the alert CAP.

At 7:10 P.M., local time, an F-14 took off, soon followed by an E-2C radar plane. Moments later, the mission came through: "To intercept and divert to Sigonella, Sicily, a Boeing 737 charter with the *Achille Lauro* hijackers on board now en route from Cairo to Tunis." More F-14s were launched. Eventually, six of them (supported by aerial tankers) made a fence over the Mediterranean between Crete and Egypt.

As I was preparing to launch from Cyprus with my two C-141s shortly after the F-14s had launched, shit once again happened: The pilot informed me that one of the engines on my plane would not start. It was probably a "glow plug" problem, he told me.

"How many glow plugs are in an engine?" I asked the mechanic (we always carried a mechanic on special operations missions as part of the crew). "And how many does it take to start it?"

"There are six per engine," I recall him saying, "but it only takes one good one to start an engine."

"So why can't we take one or two from a good engine and put them in the failed engine to get it going?" I asked.

"We can give it a try," he said.

Four or five of us then deplaned to give the mechanic a hand removing and replacing the engine cowlings, while the mechanic transferred the "glow plugs." This took about thirty minutes.

Now the engine was ready to go. However, because the earlier attempts to start it had "loaded it up" with fuel, the mechanic was concerned about chances of a fire. "Now let's get everybody off the plane," he announced, "and get ready for the fireball if it starts." Everybody quickly deplaned, and the mechanic gave the pilot the signal. The three good engines were started, and then the failed engine was given a try. Nothing happened for maybe thirty seconds, and then some smoke came, and then all of a sudden a flame jetted out as far as the tail of the airplane—or at least that was how it seemed. The pilot smiled and gave a thumbs-up to all of us outside, then we quickly reboarded the aircraft.

After launch, we remained in radio contact with the E-2C, so as not to interfere with the intercept operation. Flying time from Cyprus to Sigonella was about three or four hours.

BACK in the United States, at 4:37 P.M., Washington time, President Reagan directed Defense Secretary Weinberger to intercept the plane and its hijackers.

"National Command Authority" is two men, the President and the Secretary of Defense, who is second to the President in control of the armed forces. This means command authority passes through the Defense Secretary on the way down to, say, the 6th Fleet

Weinberger called the Pentagon and gave the Chairman of the Joint Chiefs, Admiral Crowe, the okay to proceed.

MEANWHILE, the E-2C watched for the Egypt Air 737. When they picked out likely contacts flying the route from Cairo to Tunis, F-14s then had to check the tail numbers. Around midnight, they began checking out possible radar contacts.

The first two blacked-out aircraft they examined turned out American C-141 transport planes—our team on the way to Sigonella.

The F-14s intercepted their target two tries later—tail number 2843. A pair of F-14s with lights out now flew, one on each of the commercial aircraft's wingtips. The crew and passengers of the Egypt Air plane were in total ignorance that they'd been bracketed by U.S. fighters.

The formation proceeded westward. No problem. That was where the Americans wanted them to go—for the time being.

Meanwhile, the State Department had asked the Tunisian government to deny the Egyptians permission to land, and the Tunisians had agreed.

278 ★ Tom Clancy

When the Egyptians tried Athens, they again got a negative response. Their only recourse was to return to Cairo, and Cairo control had to comply with their request.

At this point, the Egyptian pilots got a surprise: "2843, this is Tigertail 603. Over," the E-2C Hawkeye radioed. The Egyptians did not reply.

The Hawkeye repeated: "2843. Tigertail 603." It took four tries before the Egyptians got nerve enough to acknowledge.

"Tigertail 603. Egypt Air 2843. Go ahead."

"Egypt Air 2843. Tigertail 603. Be advised you're being escorted by two F-14s. You are to land immediately . . . immediately . . . at Sigonella, Sicily. Over."

This can't be, the Egyptian had to be thinking. "Say again. Who is calling?"

"Roger. This is Tigertail 603. I advise you are directed to land immediately, proceed immediately to Sigonella, Sicily. You are being escorted by two interceptor aircraft. Vector 280 for Sigonella, Sicily. Over."

"Repeat again," the Egyptian requested.

The E-2C complied: "You are to turn immediately to 280. Head 280 immediately."

The Egyptian had no choice. "Turning right, heading 280."

The F-14s had by then switched on their running lights, and the Egyptian had realized that they were only a few feet from each of his wingtips. "I'm saying you are too close. I'm following your orders. Don't be too close. Please."

"Okay, we'll move away a little bit," the Hawkeye answered (he was actually a hundred miles off). And the F-14s edged away a little. It was time for a change anyway, since the F-14s were too short-ranged to escort the 737 all the way to Sigonella. Soon, these F-14s were replaced by three others, who were to take the Egyptian airliner to Sicily.

At Sigonella, Bill Spearman was in his office in gym shorts. He'd been playing racquetball when he got word that I needed to talk to him.

"Bill, it's coming," I told him. "You are the only one that's going to know about it, and you're going to make it happen. We are coming to your location with an Egyptian 737 with the terrorists aboard, followed immediately by my two C-141s. Get hold of my people that I left there and tell them that I want the 737 to clear the runway immediately, for I will be landing blacked out seconds behind it. Tell them to block and hold that 737 and don't let anybody off or on. When I get there I'll take charge. Also, Bill, I want you to make sure that we are granted permission to land and that the Italians don't try to block us."

Spearman then went to brief the Italian base commander, Colonel Annicchiarici. As it happened, this was Annicchiarici's last day on the job. The next day, a lot of Italian brass would be on hand for his change-of-command ceremony, including an army three-star. Annicchiarici was not especially pleased at the going-away present that we had dropped on his lap; but it thankfully didn't take him long to realize that his friend Bill Spearman had been as much in the dark about it as he was.

"Beel, if you were in uniform, I would have known that you knew about this all along," Annicchiarici told him when he learned about the Egypt Air plane, "but since you are in your shorts, I believe that you didn't know anything about it either."

AT about midnight, Italian Prime Minister Craxi received a telephone call from the White House, informing him, in his words "that U.S. military aircraft had intercepted an Egyptian civil aircraft which the U.S. government believed with a reasonable degree of certainty to be carrying the four Palestinians responsible for the hijacking of the Achille Lauro. The U.S. President asked the Italian government for its consent to proceed with the landing of the civil and U.S. military aircraft at Sigonella." They were hoping that the Italians would not want the hijackers and would get themselves off the hook by agreeing to let the Americans take them.

And in fact, Craxi was not pleased to learn that he was on the hook. He wanted the whole terrorist situation as far from Italy as possible.

Craxi didn't know what to do. So he decided to punt. The Egypt Air 737 would be allowed to land at Sigonella base.

SHORTLY after midnight, my pilot informed me that if things continued to go as planned, we'd be on the ground at Sigonella in about an hour.

I called the Pentagon to give an update and to verify that my mission was to take the terrorists off the plane, place them in chains, and fly them back to the United States to stand trial. (I never could figure out the "bring them back in chains" part. In the first place, I didn't have any chains except for "cargo tie-down chains" on the C-141, and I had already decided that I would put the terrorists on the plane with Captain "Bob" and his two SEAL platoons. I couldn't think of anything more secure than that.)

By this time the Chairman and the service chiefs had assembled in a small conference room in the National Military Command Center (NMCC) at the Pentagon and were listening to my radio traffic.

Vice Admiral Moreau answered my call.

"We should be on the ground at Sigonella in about an hour," I told him. "The SEAL detachment that I left behind at Sigonella will set the trap and hold the plane until I get to it."

"Your mission is as stated," Moreau replied. "And the Italian government has agreed that you can take the terrorists."

"Roger," I said. "Then we shouldn't be on the ground long. My goal is to have everything out of here before daylight."

Craxi's okay did not in fact make much of a difference—except later for official purposes. Admiral Crowe had already directed Jeremiah to bring Egypt Air 2842 into Sigonella whether the Italians liked it or not.

In any event, Craxi's approval did not reach Italian airport approach control at Sigonella, who wanted no part of what was going down. They refused the F-14s permission to land, and told them to go to a civilian airfield nearby.

The Navy squadron commander tried one more time, but directed the Egyptian to follow him in—permission or no. Together, they began their descent toward Sigonella. Approach control's answer was again no.

At this point, the commander used the old pilots' trick. He switched his transponder to emergency mode, declared a fuel emergency (though he had plenty of fuel left), and brought the Egyptian airliner into its final approach. The trouble was, the Egyptian was coming in too low.

The commander told the Egyptian to break off his approach, which he did. He then circled around to try again.

Meanwhile, in the Sigonella tower, a Navy lieutenant pushed the Italian controller out of the way, took the mike, and radioed the Egyptian permission to land.

Once the Egypt Air plane was safely on the runway, the F-14s took aerial photos of the plane and headed back to the carrier—their part of the operation now complete.

My team took over from there.

SIGONELLA

As the Egypt Air plane rolled down the main runway to a taxiway at the end, where it was directed to stop, the SEALs who had remained at Sigonella raced to meet it in pickup trucks and set up a perimeter around it.

Soon after that, my two C-141s landed, with lights out, and stopped on the active runway where the Egypt Air had pulled off. Moments later, we added the men on the C-141s to the SEALs already surrounding Egypt Air 2843.

On the way to Sigonella, Captain Bob and I had been in constant contact, planning and coordinating what his SEALs had to do in order to secure the Egyptian plane and take control of the terrorists.

One of the two team leaders, Lieutenant "Bo," was to assemble his assault team off the tarmac behind the 737, and be prepared to assault the plane on order, should a takedown become necessary.

Lieutenant "Randy" was to establish a security perimeter around the plane, but outside the security already being provided by the team we had previously dropped off in Sigonella.

Bob also placed his snipers in firing positions where they could see what was happening inside the plane,

By about 2:00 A.M., Friday, October 11, Bob and I had established our command post under the tail of the plane. When I looked, I could see lights on inside and a couple people walking around.

Bob and I went to the nose of the 737 and plugged into the intercom jack. I identified myself and asked the pilot who he had on board. He did not answer.

"If you don't cooperate, we'll find out one way or another," I told him.

That brought an answer. "I have my crew and an 'ambassador' on board," the pilot said, leaving open the possibility that there may be additional people on the plane.

"Then come down off the plane," I told him. "And bring the ambassador with you."

Before they opened the door, Bob told me that his snipers were reporting armed men in uniform. "No sweat, boss," he told me. "They've got them in their sights."

The door opened and the pilot, followed by the "ambassador," came down the ladder. They were both very nervous, particularly the "ambassador." They got even more nervous when they saw the SEAL shooters, all in black combat gear and equipped for business.

I was very suspicious of the "ambassador." Although he was dressed in a business suit, I figured him for a general officer, perhaps from the Egyptian Intelligence Service, who had been sent along to ensure that everything went right in Tunisia.

When I met him, the "ambassador" produced an authentic-looking diplomatic passport and a letter claiming he was an authorized representative of the Egyptian government.

"My orders are to take the terrorists off the plane and fly them back to the U.S. to stand trial for killing Leon Klinghoffer," I told him.

This seemed to make him even more nervous, and he asked if anybody had an aspirin.

"We can handle that," I said.

In the air on the way to Sigonella, I'd felt a headache coming on. By then it was October 11, and none of us had had more than a couple of hours sleep since October 7. When I'd asked our team doctor for a couple of aspirin, Darrel had stuffed what felt like a handfull of aspirin into my pocket.

I accommodated the ambassador with about half of what I had, and he gulped down several of them. He then asked for a cigarette, and one of my radio operators satisfied that request. At that point he wanted to make an urgent telephone call. I told him we would escort him over to base operations (Bill Spearman's operations center) and assist him with his call.

As he was escorted to the operations center, I sent one of my intelligence officers along with a couple of our people to tap the phone. They were to stay with him as long as necessary, and keep me posted on what they were hearing.

The person he needed to talk to so urgently, as it turned out, was Abdel Meguid, the Egyptian Foreign Minister, to whom he described the terrible situation he was in and asked for guidance.

"You'll just have to sort things out as best you can," he was told, "until a decision about what to do can be reached."

He stayed on the phone most of the day with various people back in Egypt—remaining very concerned about the uncertainty of the predicament they were in. But he was even more worried about the consequences that could result from the high-level passengers they had on board (who weren't identified at this point, but it was clear he wasn't talking about the terrorists).

The intelligence information from his conversations was relayed to me, and proved very useful later.

ONCE we had the pilot and the ambassador off the plane, I decided to go aboard myself, accompanied by SEAL Lieutenant Commander "Pat," and see who was on it.

Inside, the plane had been configured in a VIP executive mode, with three "working tables." At one table on the far side of the plane sat the four terrorists, unarmed and easy to identify. Three of them appeared to be in their twenties, and one looked to be a little younger. Next to them at another table sat eight to ten members of Egypt's counterterrorist force (Force 777), all of them in uniform and all armed with automatic pistols. At another table on the right sat two men in civilian clothes—evidently big shots. One was very Arab in appearance and very tough-looking. The other was younger, redheaded and freckle-faced, and resembled no ethnic group in the region that was familiar to me. There also were the copilot, the navigator, and about four other crew members.

Although they were armed, I did not consider the 777 guards to be a threat. As it happened, we had trained the 777 Force a few years back, but we knew they had not kept up their proficiency, and now they found themselves at the mercy of those who had trained them—the best in the world. And they knew it.

After we had looked around, Pat and I left the plane.

Back at my command post beneath the tail of the plane, I was joined by Colonel "Frank" and several members of the battle staff who would add their brains and experience to mine. Bob also positioned his executive officer, Commander "Tom," with "Frank." Those two were capable of handling anything.

Meanwhile, Bob was firmly in command of security. I told Frank to manage the door and keep an eye on those still inside the plane.

About fifteen minutes after we landed and took control of the plane, Italian troops of all kinds began showing up and taking up positions outside of our positions—Army troops, Carabinieri (police), and even young green conscripts with World War II weapons (the same bunch had recently been in Bill Spearman's motor pool, shooting at birds). The whole affair was kind of comical. They were showing up in anything available to carry them— pickup trucks, motor bikes, cars, and even three-wheeled construction carts with five or six guys in their dump buckets.

The sudden appearance of armed American forces taking over part of his base had so astonished Colonel Annicchiarici, that he'd decided he had to *do something*. He immediately ordered his own troops into action.

About the same time, a couple Italian officers showed up and tried to board the plane, to see who was on it, but were turned away by Frank and Tom.

So this was the situation not too long after midnight on Friday, October 11:

We had the plane surrounded with two rings of about eighty to ninety heavily armed shooters and snipers positioned at strategic locations. However, the outer ring of our security was now directly facing the Italians—eyeball to eyeball. Though I figured they had us outnumbered by about three to one, I wasn't worried about them taking us on. They knew better than that. However, I was concerned that something unanticipated, like a vehicle backfiring, could cause one of their young, jumpy troops to open fire. If that happened, several people would die, mainly Italians.

About this time, Bill Spearman showed up at the plane with Colonel Annicchiarici, followed soon after that by an Italian Army three-star (whose name I do not recall), who had come to officiate at the change of command. As it soon turned out, we were lucky to have the three-star there. He was friendly and intelligent, and did what he could to help the two sides—his and ours—navigate a difficult situation. Over the next twenty-four hours, the two of us came to work closely together to sort out this complex situation.

After we'd been introduced, I explained our mission and my under-standing of the Italian government's position—that is, that they had agreed to turn the terrorists over to us.

"If it were up to me," he replied, "I would give them to you in a minute. But I have received no word to this effect, and you must understand where that leaves me."

"Maybe the word just hadn't gotten down to you yet," I told him. "How about you going back up the tape to check, while I check with my ambas-sador in Rome?"

He agreed.

I contacted my liasion officer and told him to get Ambassador Rabb on the horn. When Ambassador Rabb came on the radio five minutes later, I explained that we had forced the Egyptian airliner down at Sigonella with the four terrorists on board and that my orders were to take the terrorists and fly them back to the States to stand trial, and it was my understanding that the Italian government had agreed to turn them over to me.

"You've done what?" he blurted, taken aback. I could tell from his reaction that he didn't know anything about any part of this. But he said he would check.

About fifteen minutes later, the Italian lieutenant general returned. "I have gone all the way back to the Minister of Defense," he said, "and no one knows about any such agreement.

"You must understand," he added, "that it was an Italian ship that was hijacked, and this is Italian soil, with Italian jurisdiction. And we just can't afford to turn them over."

"Let me check with Washington to see if there is a misunderstanding."

Still standing by the plane, with the Italian three-star close by, I made another call to the Pentagon. I don't recall who answered, but it sounded like Admiral Moreau, and I knew that all the chiefs were listening.

"I want to bring you up to speed and to reverify my mission," I said. "Here is the situation: We have the plane. I have verified that the four terrorists are on board, along with eight to ten armed guards from the 777 Force, which I do not consider a threat. Also there are two other men, one a tough-looking Arab in his mid-forties, who has to be important, and a younger redheaded, freckled-face guy sitting at a table with him. We have not been able to identify these two. I have already taken the pilot off the plane, along with another individual who claims to be an ambassador. He is now calling back to Egypt and we are monitoring his phone conversations. Mostly he is requesting guidance to deal with the terrible situation they have ended up in.

"The Italian base commander here at Sigonella felt that he had to react," I continued. "I think more to save face than anything else. In my estimation, they have positioned about three hundred or so troops in a perimeter around us. We are eyeball to eyeball. I have an Italian three-star with me. He has called all the way back to his Ministry of Defense and can find no one with any knowledge of an agreement to turn over the terrorists to us. I have also talked to Ambassador Rabb, and he has no knowledge of such an agreement.

"I am not worried about our situation. We have the firepower to prevail.

But I am concerned about the immaturity of the Italian troops, some of whom are green conscripts, as well as the absence of anybody with the ability to control them in this tense situation. A backfire from a motorbike or construction cart could precipitate a shooting incident that could lead to a lot of Italian casualties. And I don't believe that our beef is with our ally, the Italians, but rather with the terrorists.

"Now with this picture, I just want to reverify that my mission is to take the terrorists off the plane and bring them back to the U.S."

After I finished, I got a "wait out."

About five minutes later, a response came—I thought from Secretary Weinberger, but it could have been Admiral Crowe, since I had never heard his voice over SATCOM: "You are the ranking American on the scene, and you do what you think is right."

I "rogered" the message. Which was *exactly* what I wanted to hear. It gave me the latitude to do what I thought would turn out best.

By this time it was about 4:00 A.M. We had been on the ground now for approximately two hours, trying to sort this mess out. During that time, I had occasionally overheard discussions between Italian officers, including some disagreements. There were apparently questions about which "magistrates" (judges) ought to have jurisdiction over the terrorists. The Italian justice system was complex, and there'd be plenty of magistrates involved, all with differing responsibilities. This could conceivably further complicate a conclusion that would be in the best interest of the United States.

After listening to all this for a while, and doing some thinking on my own, I'd come to my main conclusion: No matter how complex the Italian justice system was, and how many magistrates would be involved, we had to somehow find a way to fix responsibility for prosecuting the terrorists on the shoulders of the Italian government. We needed to find a way to hold their feet to the fire inescapably.

A little later, a way to do that came to me.

About that time, my counterpart, the Italian three-star, and I moved the short distance to the base commander's office, which was where he had to make his calls anyhow, to find a more suitable place to discuss the issues at hand.

When we got there, I made a proposal that I thought would be in the best interest of both governments. "The first thing we've got to do," I told him, "is un-mingle the troops, to minimize the possibility of a shooting incident between the United States and Italy that could leave a lot of dead or wounded Italians lying on this tarmac when the sun comes up—a situation you and I must avoid.

"Once we have done that, I will take the Force 777 guards off the plane, disarm them, and take them to a secure holding area. Then we will take the rest of the air crew off, leaving only the terrorists and the two unidentified individuals on the plane.

"Once that's done, I will reduce our security force to a minimum visible presence around the plane.

"Come daylight, you or whoever you designate can enter the plane and take the remainder off one at a time. Then, you, along with a two-man detail that I provide, will take them to whatever location the district attorney designates for charging and lock up; and we will assist in verification/identification." What I had in mind was to fly in some of the former hostages from Egypt and put the terrorists before a lineup, but I didn't spring this on the lieutenant general until later.

The lieutenant general seemed to like that idea and, with a nod of his head, asked for a few minutes to discuss the proposal with his higher-ups. He picked up the phone, and then about fifteen minutes later told me that the proposal was agreeable.

Soon after that, he ordered the Italian troops surrounding the aircraft to withdraw, and judging from their reaction, they were relieved to do so. But it was good to see that they left with no animosity.

MEANWHILE, the White House was calling Craxi again: The President felt strongly about bringing the terrorists to justice, the Italian was told.

The Italian prime minister claimed that he personally had no problem giving the hijackers up to the Americans; but this was an Italian legal matter, and Italian courts had jurisdiction.

DURING the next hour, we disarmed the 777 Force guards, removed them from the plane, and took them to a holding place where they could get some food and rest (under armed escort). Next, the power was shut down on the plane, and the crew was removed and reunited with the captain elsewhere on the base.

This left only the four terrorists and the two unidentified individuals on the plane.

At this point, in order to lower the anxiety level of the Italians, we reduced our guard force around the plane to six visible SEALs, but a reaction force remained nearby, if needed.

At daybreak, Colonel Annicchiarici, accompanied by several armed guards and a paddy wagon, showed up with the Egyptian "ambassador." The colonel and the ambassador boarded the plane, and after maybe two hours of negotiations, they persuaded the four hijackers to surrender. They were loaded in the paddy wagon and placed in a military jail at the air base. Later, they were taken downtown and arraigned before the local Italian district attorney.

The two remaining unidentified men, however, were by this time claiming diplomatic immunity as PLO envoys, and refused to leave the plane. The tough looking one was carrying an Iraqi diplomatic passport with a name on it that I forget, but we suspected—and could not yet positively prove—that he was the terrorist mastermind, Abu Abbas. The other one, the redhead, turned out to be the political officer of the Cairo PLO office—a functionary (as we later found out) by the name of Hassan.

If Abbas actually turned out to be on the plane, and we could bring him to trial, we would have achieved a far more significant victory in the war against terrorism than just grabbing the four hijackers. He was the mastermind and organizer; they were nothing but hit men.

Unfortunately, we had not yet identified him, and more important, he was on Italian soil. Prime Minister Craxi wanted no part in bringing Abbas to justice. The Italian prime minister stonewalled. His intention all along was to get Abbas out of Italy as fast as an aircraft could be found to carry him and a safe haven could be found to take him in (this last came from a source inside the Italian government).

Meanwhile, positively confirming whether or not the tough-looking Palestinian was Abbas became our priority. We did this using photos that the Agency sent us over SATCOM—a fairly recent technology that our people had developed.

Before we'd had this technology, photographs and additional maps had had to be flown to us at night out of Washington (or wherever) by special courier flight. Even after engineers in the corporate electronics industry had told us time and again that it couldn't be done earlier that year, a young army captain had designed the circuitry and all the necessary systems for a device that would let us send pictures and drawings over SATCOM. Captain "Rich" was at the time assigned to the our Intelligence Directorate, and he was one of the smartest and hardest-working young officers I have ever known.

After the captain* designed the system, which we called "PIRATE," industry built us two of them. We gave one to the Agency, and we had the other one with us.

By means of PIRATE, the Agency sent us the photographs of Palestinian leaders. And these permitted us to positively identify our guy as Abu Abbas.

N o w that the terrorists were in Italian custody, I decided it was a good time to reduce our signature. It was daylight now and the press had begun to show up outside the fence with their long telephoto lenses. For that reason, I told Captain Bob and his SEALs that they were released to head back to home base.

They launched at 0900 hours, feeling good about themselves and their accomplishments in the war against terrorism.

Meanwhile, I stayed behind with my assault CP and a few other essential personnel in order to see this thing through to a "satisfactory" ending.

ABBAS AND HASSAN

During the standoff between American and Italian troops, Italian officials had contacted the Egyptian Ambassador to Rome, Yehia Rifaat, stating that Italy intended to take custody of the four hijackers and prosecute them, and that the two PLO representatives would have to leave the plane and furnish testimony.

In response to this, the Egyptian government agreed to the handing over of the four hijackers to Italian judicial authorities. But the disposition of the two PLO emissaries was another thing again. The Palestinians, the Egyptians announced, were covered by diplomatic immunity; they had been brought to Sigonella against their will, and they had no intention of getting off the plane. In fact, the Egyptian government argued, the plane itself was on a special governmental mission, and benefited from diplomatic immunity under international law. As long as the two Palestinians remained

---

*His outstanding work caught the attention of the CIA Director, who asked us to give him to the Agency so he could do for the nation what he had done for Special Forces. Though I hated to lose him, I couldn't refuse.

aboard, they were on Egyptian territory, and the Egyptian government declared it was prepared to "defend, if necessary, the inviolability of the plane
with arms."

Finally, at about 0900 on Friday, October 11, Ambassador Rifaat delivered a formal diplomatic note, in which the Egyptian government sought a
clarification of the legal status of the Egypt Air plane and its occupants, and
requested that the plane be allowed to leave Sigonella immediately, along
with all its remaining passengers.

About 10:00 that same morning, a small brown executive jet landed and
parked at the end of the runway near the Egypt Air 737. Two well-dressed
middle-age men deplaned and approached the 737. One claimed to be
from Rome representing the Italian government. The other, probably an
Arab, never spoke. After their credentials were confirmed by my Italian
three-star counterpart (he told me they were both from the Italian government), we agreed to let them board the plane to talk to the two Palestinians
(no one was yet admitting that they were in fact Abbas and Hassan), and
they remained there for about an hour before returning to their plane
and departing.

I didn't actually buy the story they gave me. Their behavior made me
suspicious that they were somehow going to try to smuggle Abu Abbas
and Hassan out of Sigonella, and perhaps out of Italy. This would confirm
what I'd already learned from my Italian three-star counterpart, who'd
dropped pretty clear indications from time to time that the Italian government was trying to find an easy, no-pain way out of the dilemma they felt
they were in.

I called Vice Admiral Moreau, explained my concerns, and asked if he
could find a Navy T-39, which is a small, executive-type jet, from somewhere nearby and send it to me so we could follow them, should my fears
turn out to be accurate.

I had already selected four of my best people for my "chase team"—
Lieutenant Colonel "Dick," Major "Johnny," Command Sergeant Major
"Rick," and one of our best SATCOM radio operators—when at about 2:00
P.M., a pair of Navy lieutenants showed up saying that their squadron, VR
24, located on Sigonella, had been tapped for the mission, and they were
my pilots, reporting for instructions.

"Where's your plane?"

"In the hangar, sir," they answered, "at the end of the taxiway."

I joined the two pilots up with the four on my chase team. "What I want you to do," I told all six of them, "is to get the jet ready to launch on very short notice, but keep it hidden. Then I want you to sit in it and wait for my instructions. If they try to smuggle Abbas out of country by plane, you're to launch immediately, tuck right up under its tail, and follow it to wherever it goes. Your mission is not to recapture Abbas, but just to report to me. I'll tell you what to do."

MEANWHILE, I had continued my internal debate about the best way to pin responsibility on the Italians for bringing the terrorists to trial so that they could not wriggle out of it and strict justice would be done. The moment had come, I felt, to recommend to my Italian three-star counterpart that we fly the American hostages in from Cairo (they were then at the American Embassy). Once they were here, we'd set up a lineup under the close watch of whatever magistrates had responsibility, and let the hostages identify the terrorists.

"This should be possible," he told me. "And perhaps it's a good idea."

"Then would you contact the local district attorney and set this up some-time later in the evening?" I asked. "And I'll work on getting an airplane to bring the hostages here."

About an hour later, he reported that the district attorney had agreed to my proposal, but would like a two-hour notice to arrange the lineup in the presence of the magistrates.

I then called Vice Admiral Moreau to ask for a C-141 to bring the American hostages to Sigonella. I also pointed out to him how important it was for the hostages to positively identify the terrorists before the magis-trates who would have ultimate responsibility for their trials.

"That's a good idea," he said. "I'll work it and get back to you."

JUST before dusk, the executive jet returned, taxied to the end of the run-way, turned around, and stopped, but kept its engines running and its land-ing lights on. The two men I'd met before got off the plane, approached the 737, and again asked permission to board. They stayed on board for half an hour, then took off again.

All of this strengthened my suspicion that someone was setting up the machinery to get Abu Abbas and his partner out of the country.

Shortly after dark, the Italian base commander, the Egyptian "ambassa-dor," and the Egypt Air crew showed up at the 737. Twenty minutes later a panel truck arrived with the Egyptian 777 guard force. At about 9:30

P.M., the 737's engines were started. At the same time, the Italians began to move trucks and construction equipment to block the entrances to the main runway. The only one they left open was the one the 737 would travel.

I called the Navy T-39. "Get ready," I told them. "The 737 has cranked up. It will probably make a dash for the runway very soon."

At about 9:50 P.M., the Egyptian 737 turned around and headed toward the end of the active runway. He began his takeoff run at about 10:00 P.M.

The T-39 began his own takeoff run at the same time. Since access to the main runway was blocked, the T-39 took off down the taxiway, which paralleled the main runway; and the two aircraft passed each other going in opposite directions, with Italian officers diving in the ditches as the T-39 roared over their heads.

Just after liftoff, the T-39 made a hard right turn and took up its trail position as I'd instructed.

Meanwhile, the Italians launched four jet interceptors from another base to try to drive the T-39 off and escort the 737 to its destination. Some very heated conversations took place between the interceptor pilots and the T-39 crew, but to no avail. The T-39 crew continued their mission.

The Egyptian 737 flew to Fuciamo Airport, an auxiliary field next to Rome's main international airport, Leonardo da Vinci.

When permission to land the T-39 was denied, the T-39 pilots declared a tactical emergency and set down right behind the Egyptian 737. The Egyptian 737 taxied to a position near the VIP lounge, and the T-39 parked beside it. Abu Abbas and his companion exited the plane and went inside. About an hour later, they emerged, dressed in Italian air force officers' flight suits, and boarded a waiting Yugoslav civilian airliner which had been delayed for a scheduled flight to Belgrade, Yugoslavia.

Meanwhile, Ambassador Rabb had presented the Italian government with a request for the arrest of Abbas preparatory to his extradition. Craxi continued to stonewall. This request, he said, "did not, in the Justice Minister's opinion, satisfy the factual and substantive requirements laid down by Italian law. . . . This being so, there was no longer any legal basis . . . [for] detaining Abbas, since at the time he was on board an aircraft which enjoyed extraterritorial status."

Shortly after the plane took off for Belgrade, Ambassador Rabb arrived at the Chigi Palace, the official residence of the Italian Prime Minister, to protest the release of Abbas. As he left, Rabb told reporters, "I'm not happy about what happened here today."

The State Department scrambled to prepare another extradition request for Yugoslavia; it was actually delivered before Abbas landed in Belgrade. But it was a lost cause. Yugoslavia had diplomatic relations with the PLO, and Abbas, as a member of the PLO's executive council, enjoyed diplomatic immunity. Two days later Abbas flew on to Aden, South Yemen, and from there to Baghdad.

At about 11:00 P.M. October 11, a C-141 from Cairo landed, with twelve American hostages aboard. We took five of them, including Marilyn Klinghoffer, to the jail downtown; the others remained in the VIP lounge. At the jail, the district attorney had arranged a very professional lineup (with magistrates present, as well as my Italian three-star counterpart). The five Americans positively and without hesitation identified the four terrorists as the ones who had hijacked the ship.

When the time came for Marilyn Klinghoffer to take a close look at Majiad al-Molqi, she spat in his face, then turned to me. "Let me have your pistol," she told me, her voice cold with rage. "I want to shoot him."

"I know how you feel," I told her. "I'd want to do the same thing. But you have to understand that it would only further complicate matters. It's best to let the Italian courts handle this thing in the appropriate way."

She looked at me and said, "It hurts, but I guess you are right. Please pass my thanks to all your troops for what they have done for us."

At about midnight, I took the hostages back to their C-141, which was waiting with its engines running, and prepared to launch.

In the meantime, all our people who'd remained behind with me had loaded my C-141, and were also prepared to launch . . . except we couldn't go anywhere. The Italians had blocked the plane with construction equipment.

Meanwhile, I went over to the plane that would carry the hostages home, to say "goodbye." While I was there, the lieutenant general arrived.

After thanking him for his cooperation, I told him, "In my judgment, we've together been able to bring about the best possible ending for this complex incident.

"Shortly," I also told him, "the hostages will be taking off for the United States, and I plan to be about thirty seconds behind them."

He then looked me straight in the eyes and said, "We have decided that you're not going anywhere."

"What do you mean by that?" I said.

"You have created all this mess, and we just can't let you fly away from it."

I looked him in the eye. "Did you bring along clean underwear and a shaving kit?" I asked.

"No, why?"

"Then I hope the ones you're wearing are clean, because if you don't unblock my plane, you are getting ready to take a free ride to the United States—with me."

He looked at me for a moment, smiled, and then said, "Good luck, my friend."

Moments later, on his order, the construction equipment that blocked my plane was removed, and we took off, following the C-141 carrying the hostages.

It was a new day, Saturday, October 12, 1985.

FOR all of us in the JSOTF, as well as the Navy participants (Rear Admiral Dave Jeremiah, his staff, and all the crews of the USS *Saratoga*), things had gone very well. They had all done an outstanding job, with utmost proficiency and professional competence. We had been able to bring about a successful conclusion to a very complex and high-stakes situation.

When we landed back at Pope Air Force Base, my aide handed me a card, which indicated that although this was only the twelfth of October, we had already been on the road for 154 days that year, had been in fifteen different countries, and had flown 197,000 miles. Some of these missions had gone well, others had been frustrating; but all of them had been rewarding learning experiences in the war against terrorism, and many close relationships had been developed with our allies.

I was amused to learn later that warrants for my arrest had been issued by both Italy and Egypt. However, for the next two years I continued to travel on missions through both countries, usually in a plain flight suit, without ever being questioned or delayed.

In fact, forty-one days after the *Achille Lauro* incident, we found ourselves back in Sigonella again to deal with an Egyptian Air flight that had been hijacked to Malta.

On this mission I remained in constant radio contact with Major General Robert Weigand, who was stationed in Egypt and was accompanying the Egyptian 777 Force on an Egyptian C-130 to Malta to undertake a rescue operation for the hostages on the Egypt airliner. Bob had told me that the Egyptians had requested our assistance in breaching the airliner.

While we were readying our helicopters for assisting the Egyptians, Captain Bill Spearman showed up and said, "Your friends want to see you down at the airfield VIP lounge."

"What friends?" I said.

"Your Italian friends."

"Bill," I told him, "I don't have time to fool with them. We've got a hijacking to contend with, and the Egyptians need our assistance."

"You've got to go meet with them," he insisted.

We went back and forth for a few more minutes, until I finally consented to go with him, but only for ten minutes.

And since I was uncertain about their mood, I decided to take along a couple Special Forces escorts for company.

When I walked into the lounge, four or five Italian senior officers (though not my three-star friend) jumped up and said, "Welcome back! We knew you were coming!"

"How did you know that?"

"Because your plane used the same call sign as last time," they said, smiling.

My concerns turned out to be far misplaced. The get-together was very jovial.

And then, as I was leaving, the Italians announced, "We thought the operation with the ship went well; it was the politicians that screwed things up."

Unfortunately, after readying a Blackhawk and two of our best breachers for the flight to Malta, it turned out we were not able to assist the Egyptians

We learned later that a Libyan employee in the control tower at Malta had convinced the Maltese to stipulate that assistance could only be flown in by an Italian helicopter, knowing full well the time it would take to get clearance for such a mission from Rome. The Egyptians, meanwhile, went ahead with the operation. In the process, they used far more explosives than were necessary, resulting in the death of sixty passengers, making it the bloodiest hijacking up to that time.

CONSEQUENCES

My earlier fears about the capacity and responsiveness of the Italian judicial system proved to be misplaced. The Italian judicial authorities not only quickly brought the hijackers to trial, they widened their investigation, and were able to identify many others involved in the conspiracy that led to the hijacking of the *Achille Lauro*. The investigation was completed in record time and the cases were brought to trial before the Genoa Assize Court in l986.

The following received sentences as indicated.

PLO officials deemed ultimately responsible:

- ✪ Abu Abbas: life in absentia
- ✪ Ozzudin Badrakham (a PLO accomplice): life in absentia
- ✪ Ziad el-Omar (a PLO accomplice): life in absentia

HIJACKERS

- ✪ Magied al-Molqi: thirty years
- ✪ Ibrahim Abdel Atif: twenty-four years
- ✪ Ahmed al-Hassan: fifteen years
- ✪ Abdullah Ali-Hammad: charges dropped; he was a minor at the time

ACCOMPLICES

- ✪ Youssef Saad: six years (for furnishing funds and weapons)
- ✪ Abdul Rahim Khalid: seven years (for furnishing funds and weapons)
- ✪ Mohammed Issa Abbas: six months, added to an existing seven years (for possession of weapons and explosives)
- ✪ Said Gandura: eight months (for possession of forged passports)

Some years later, before I left active duty as Commander-in-Chief of the U.S. Special Operations Command, my wife, Sue, and I were invited to Egypt by the Egyptian Minister of Defense on behalf of President Mubarak. They invited me to review Egyptian special-operations capabilities and the assistance the United States could provide Egyptian forces in dealing with the terrorist threat then causing internal problems—terrorist attacks on tourist buses, bombings, and the like.

We could not have been treated better, and the follow-up to that visit has been beneficial to both countries.

X

Panama: Operation blue spoon

From JSOTF, Carl Stiner moved on to command the 82d Airborne Division, and from there, now a lieutenant general, he moved up to command the XVIII Airborne Corps—the Army's quick response force: Its lead elements could be "wheels-up" within eighteen hours to go anywhere in the world. At the time, the Corps contained four divisions, two separate combat brigades, and an armored cavalry regiment: The 82nd Airborne Division, 101st Air Assault Division, 10th Mountain Division, 24th Mechanized Division, the 194th Armor Brigade, the 197th Infantry Brigade, and the 2nd Armored Cavalry Regiment.

On August 5, 1989, while evaluating the 28th Infantry Division at Fort Indiantown Gap, Pennsylvania, during the division's annual summer training, Stiner took an afternoon off to fly to Fort Monroe, Virginia, for General Max Thurman's change-of-command and retirement ceremony. High-ranking officers from every service would be there, as well as key people from the Department of Defense and Congress.

Thurman, the TRADOC commander, was known as a man who got things done—who could successfully take on the toughest jobs. Some years earlier, when Thurman had been a two-star, the Army's recruiting program had been on the rocks, and a number of recruiters were facing courts-martial for untoward activities. General Shy Meyer, the Army Chief of Staff, had picked Thurman to straighten the mess out, and he had, in spades.

Since Stiner had to rush directly from the field to the aircraft, he had no chance to change out of his fatigues. This was just as well; he had to be back in Pennsylvania later that evening to supervise live-fire activities, which would prevent him from attending the evening reception; but he did not want to miss the ceremony itself, and the chance to celebrate his old friend's accomplishments. The two men had known each other since 1973, when Thurman had been the Commander of Division Artillery and Stiner the G-3 Operations Officer in the 82nd Airborne Division. They had served together again from August 1979 to March 1980, this time in the Pentagon, working for General Meyer (Thurman had been the Director for Program Analysis and Evaluation for the Army, while Stiner was the Exec for Staff Action Control).

After the ceremony ended, Stiner stood at the rear of the reviewing stand to greet General Thurman and apologize for missing the reception. "Let's step over here for a minute," Thurman replied. "I have something I want to tell you. But let me get rid of these people." He turned to other well-wishers waiting to shake his hand. "I'll see you all over at the reception," he told them, shooing them off. "I have to talk to Carl Stiner for a couple of minutes."

He led Stiner to a quiet spot about thirty feet from the reviewing stand. "What I am about to tell you is close-hold," he said. After a quick nod from Stiner, he went on. "I am not retiring. The Noriega regime in Panama has got the President very worried. For that reason, I'm being retained on active duty to take command of SOUTHCOM"—the United States Southern Command. SOUTHCOM's area of responsibility included Central and South America, and its mission was mainly security assistance and counterdrug activities. "Though I'm not the CINC yet, I have already talked to Carl Vuono and Admiral Crowe"—Vuono was the Army Chief of Staff and Crowe was Chairman of the Joint Chiefs of Staff—"and you are my man in Panama. I'm holding you responsible for contingency planning and combat operations that may have to be executed there. I want you to go down and take a look at the staff, the training readiness, and whatever else needs it."

"What about the joint task force already down there?" Stiner asked. U.S. Army South (USARSO), commanded by Army Major General Bernie Loefke, included all the forces already stationed in Panama.

"You absorb it," Thurman answered. "I'm going to hold you responsible for everything. All forces will be under your control."

"Yes, sir."

"The reason I want you is that in XVIII Airborne Corps you've got a headquarters twice the size of SOUTHCOM's, and the best communications, equipment, and trained forces in the Army for conducting contingency operations."* By that he meant that XVIII Airborne Corps was a warfighting-capable headquarters, while SOUTHCOM, by the nature of its mission, was not.

"Here is how it is going to work. You remember Admiral McCain"—the CINCPAC from 1968 to 1972, who'd operated from Hawaii. Stiner nodded yes. "There was a man in Vietnam by the name of Westmoreland, who was doing the fighting from Saigon." He gave Stiner a hard look. "Me McCain, you Westmoreland. I can't give you detailed instructions now, but when I am confirmed by Congress, that is the way it is going to be. Now get with it."

"Yes, sir," Stiner answered. There wasn't much else to say. He understood Thurman's guidance. He knew exactly what had to be done, and how to go about it.

HISTORY

The isthmus of Panama is one of the world's most strategically important pieces of real estate. At its narrowest, the Atlantic and Pacific Oceans are barely fifty miles apart, making a link between them feasible. The economic, political, and military ramifications of this fact are incalculable.

Once part of Colombia, Panama won its independence in 1903—with help from the United States, which was eager to build a canal across the isthmus on terms Colombia had opposed. That same year, the new nation signed the Hay-Bunau-Varilla treaty, which allowed the United States to build the canal. The United States also gained control over a "canal zone," extending five miles on either side of the fifty-two-mile-long waterway. The canal project was completed in 1914.

As the years passed, the Panamanian people increasingly resented U.S. control of the Canal. Eventually, the United States recognized their concerns, and President Carter negotiated an agreement whereby the United States promised to cede control by the year 2000 and, until that date, to share many U.S. military installations in Panama with Panamanian defense forces. After the handover, the United States would withdraw its troops, and revert all military installations to the Panamanian government.

None of the treaty provisions pleased the Joint Chiefs of Staff. Treaty or no, the Canal remained strategically vital to the United States.

---

*Fast response combat operations—smaller scaled than a theater war.

The U.S. Senate shared many of the Joint Chiefs' concerns. In ratifying the treaty, it inserted a provision that permitted the United States to continue to defend the Panama Canal after 1999.

NORIEGA

Manuel Antonio Noriega rose to power as an intelligence officer for the dictator, Brigadier General Omar Torrijos. After Torrijos's 1983 death in a plane crash, Noriega took over the Panamanian Defense Force (PDF), an organization that included that country's armed forces, police, customs, and investigative services. During his rise to power, Noriega had cultivated friends and patrons within the U.S. intelligence community. After Torrijos's death, he continued this practice, but broadened it, to include clients within Colombia's Medellín drug cartel and arms traffickers.

By 1985, Noriega was in total control of the country.

The first confrontation between Noriega and the United States took place in June 1987, after the former PDF chief of staff, Colonel Roberto Diaz-Herrera, had publicly accused Noriega of involvement not only in the death of Torrijos, but also in the 1985 murder of an opposition leader, Doctor Hugo Spadafora, and in electoral fraud. The Panamanian people, who had never supported Noriega, took to the streets, but Noriega's riot police ruthlessly put down the unarmed demonstrations.

The U.S. Senate promptly passed a resolution calling for the dictator to step down. After a Noriega-inflamed mob attacked the U.S. Embassy, the State Department cut off economic and military aid to Panama. Later, on February 5, 1988, federal judges in Miami and Tampa indicted Noriega and assorted henchmen on numerous counts of drug trafficking. Noriega counterattacked by organizing a harassment campaign against U.S. citizens, setting up obstructions to U.S. rights under the 1977 Panama Canal treaties, and turning to other outlaw states—such as Cuba, Nicaragua, and Libya—for economic and military assistance. Cuba and Nicaragua provided weapons and instructors to help develop "civilian defense committees," which became known as "Dignity Battalions," for intelligence collection and control of the population, while in 1989, Libya contributed $20 million in return for use of Panama as a base to coordinate terrorist activities and insurgent groups in Latin America.

As a result of this military and economic assistance, the PDF grew to a well-equipped and -armed force numbering some 14,000 men.

CONTINGENCY PLANNING:
FEBRUARY–NOVEMBER 1988

After the U.S. federal indictments against Noriega, the Joint Chiefs of Staff directed General Frederick F. Woerner, Jr., the Commander in Chief of U.S. Southern Command (USCINCSO), to revise existing contingency plans according to the following guidelines: to protect U.S. lives and property; to keep the canal open; to provide for noncombatant evacuation operations in either peaceful or hostile environments; and to develop a plan to assist the government that would eventually replace the Noriega regime.

A series of new plans followed—collectively known as ELABORATE MAZE—which would be executed by Major General Loefke, commander of U.S. Army South (USARSO), as Commander of the Joint Task Force, Panama (JTFP).

These plans envisioned a massive buildup of forces within U.S. bases in Panama. These forces would either intimidate the PDF leaders and cause them to overthrow Noriega, or failing that, invade Panamanian territory and overthrow the PDF.

Though General Woerner's mass approach offered several serious drawbacks, he favored it over the surprise strategy preferred by some planners, which was that, after a period of buildup, forces from the United States, in concert with Special Operations Forces and General Woerner's troops, would conduct a quick, hard, deliberate attack against Noriega and the PDF.

The most serious drawback to the Woerner approach: It was too slow. It gave the bad guys time to recover and respond. Thus, if Noriega escaped capture during the initial assault, he could flee to the hills and organize guerrilla warfare. The nearly 30,000 U.S. citizens living in Panama were also vulnerable to hostage-taking—or worse—not to mention the likelihood of heavy civilian casualties and property damage.

On March 16, 1988, a PDF faction staged a coup attempt at La Comandancia (the PDF headquarters), which Noriega ruthlessly suppressed. Afterward, he purged from the PDF anyone he considered undependable, declared a state of national emergency, cracked down on political opposition, and stepped up anti-U.S. harassment, in the form of severe travel restrictions, searches, and roadblocks.

AFTER reviewing Woerner's plans, the JCS Chairman, Admiral Crowe, asked Woerner to break OPLAN ELABORATE MAZE into four separate operations orders to facilitate execution. General Woerner's staff named these collectively, PRAYER BOOK. The first, KLONDIKE KEY, covered noncombatant evacuation operations. U.S. citizens located throughout Panama would be escorted to assembly areas in Panama City and Colon for evacuation to the United States (Panama City, on the Pacific side of the Canal, is the capital of the country. Colon is the Caribbean gateway).

According to the second, POST TIME, the Panama-stationed 193rd Infantry Brigade and forces deploying from the continental United States and the U.S. Atlantic Command would defend U.S. citizens and installations, and the Panama Canal. The forces from the United States would include a brigade from the Army's 7th Infantry Division, a mechanized infantry battalion from the 5th Mechanized Division, the 6th Marine Expeditionary Brigade, and a carrier battle group. These would constitute the bulk of the force that would implement the other two operations orders in the PRAYER BOOK series—BLUE SPOON and BLIND LOGIC.

BLUE SPOON called for a joint offensive operation to defeat and dismantle the PDF. It would begin with operations conducted by nearly 12,000 troops already in Panama, and would last up to eight days. During the next two weeks, they would be joined by approximately 10,000 more troops from the United States. Meanwhile, a carrier battle group would interdict air and sea routes to Cuba and provide close air support, while an amphibious task force would provide additional ground troops. In addition to U.S.-based forces listed for POST TIME, the SOUTHCOM Commander would employ a joint task force of special operations forces from SOCOM for operations against the PDF leadership, command-and-control facilities, and airfields. The special operations forces would also rescue hostages, conduct reconnaissance, and locate and seize Manuel Noriega.

The SOUTHCOM Commander would not only exercise overall command of BLUE SPOON, he would be the tactical coordinating command. Together, he, with the Commanders of Joint Task Force Panama and of the Joint Special Operations Task Force, would conduct simultaneous but separate operations.

Once the initial BLUE SPOON assaults had been completed, the joint task force would begin civil military operations under BLIND LOGIC, the fourth operations order in PRAYER BOOK. The civil affairs phase would help reestablish public safety and public health and restore other governmental services, followed by the transfer of control to civilians.

In the longer range, U.S. civil affairs troops would work with a new Panamanian government to restructure the PDF and institutionalize its loyalty to civilian authority and democratic government.

Lieutenant General Thomas W. Kelly, Director of Operations of the Joint Staff (J-3), had differences with SOUTHCOM from the beginning. He was not convinced that SOUTHCOM had enough command-and-control capability to manage, employ, and support all the forces contemplated for BLUE SPOON. Once additional forces from the United States deployed, a Corps Commander would be needed to command and control the whole operation. In his view, the XVIII Airborne Corps had the kind of staff and the rapid deployment capability needed.

During the summer of 1988, General Woerner temporarily resolved this conflict by augmenting his staff with thirteen add-ons and a handful of special operations planners. As he saw it, his staff's expertise and experience with Panama and the PDF made SOUTHCOM fully qualified to serve as the warfighting headquarters for BLUE SPOON, but he also realized that the Corps headquarters would be needed to run the overall operation if the JTFP had to be reinforced with additional major forces from the United States, and on July 5, 1988, he asked Admiral Crowe to include a Corps headquarters in the BLUE SPOON force list. In Woerner's mind, however, the Corps Headquarters would not take over tactical command and control until after the operation began, and only if Woerner decided to deploy the U.S.-based forces on the POST TIME list.

ADMIRAL Crowe approved the CINC's request on October 19, 1988, and directed the Commander of U.S. Army Forces Command,* General Joseph T. Palastra, Jr., to revise the force list accordingly. Nine days later, Palastra authorized Lieutenant General John Foss, who was at that time the commander of the XVIII Airborne Corps, to establish liaison with SOUTHCOM.

Because he would not have operational control until after BLUE SPOON was under way, and possibly not even then, Foss initially delegated the

---

*U.S. Army Forces Command (FORSCOM) was responsible for the readiness of all CONUS-based Army forces. XVIII Airborne Corps was included in his command.

planning responsibility back to the JTFP Headquarters, but for the next year, he monitored the JTFP planning for the operation.

Meanwhile, Kelly remained unhappy with what he saw as an incremental and disjointed command arrangement, and in November 1988 met with the J-3s from SOUTHCOM and FORSCOM to resolve the issue. His own preference was to deploy the Corps headquarters as a complete package before all the combat forces had deployed, but he could not budge Woerner—even though the SOUTHCOM J-3, Brigadier General Marc Cisneros, agreed with Kelly. It seems that Admiral Crowe also agreed with him, but he did not overrule SOUTHCOM.

ELECTIONS IN PANAMA

On May 7, 1989, after six years of oppression, Panamanians turned out en masse to vote in Noriega-sanctioned elections. He evidently thought his candidates, led by his nominee for president, Carlos Duque, would win easily—especially with the help he'd organized from his friends.

Despite the presence of high-level observers, such as former president Jimmy Carter, and lesser lights from the Catholic Church and the U.S. Congress, Noriega's goon squads and Dignity Battalions did their best to intimidate voters. The people had other ideas, however. The opposition, led by Guillermo Endara and his vice-presidential running mates, Ricardo Arias Calderon and Guillermo Ford, defeated Noriega's candidates by three to one.

When these results were announced, jubilant Panamanians took to the streets by the thousands.

Noriega did not like what he saw, and on May 10, he annulled the election results—blaming them on foreign interference—then sent the PDF, the national police, and his Dignity Battalions into the streets to put down the demonstrations. Many people were killed, and the opposition leaders went into hiding—after getting dragged out of their victory car and beaten.

All of this increased President Bush's concerns about the safety of the thousands of U.S. citizens in Panama, and he ordered 1,900 additional combat troops to Panama—nearly 1,000 troops of the 7th Infantry Division, from Fort Ord, California; 165 Marines of the 2nd Marine Expeditionary Force from Camp LeJeune, North Carolina; and 750 troops of the 5th Mechanized Division from Fort Polk, Louisiana. All the units arrived in Panama by May 19.

Getting Tougher

Two months earlier, on March 21, former congressman Dick Cheney had become Secretary of Defense. Cheney immediately looked for new ways to pressure Noriega. Meanwhile, members of the National Security Council staff met to discuss other actions, which resulted in presidential approval of National Security Directive 17, issued on July 22, 1989, which ordered military actions in Panama to assert U.S. treaty rights and keep Noriega and his supporters off balance.

Such actions were graded according to category, and ranged from what were called Category One (low risk/low visibility) through Categories Two and Three (low risk/high visibility and medium risk/high visibility) to Category Four (high risk/high visibility).

Category One actions would include publicizing the evacuation of U.S. dependents, expanding anti-Noriega campaigns in the media and psychological operations, and placing PDF members under escort inside U.S. installations.

In the remaining categories, U.S. troops in Panama would take more active roles.

In Category Two, military police would increase their patrols between U.S. installations, battalion-sized forces would deploy to Panama for intensive exercises, and troops stationed in Panama would practice amphibious and night combat operations.

In Category Three, U.S. forces in Panama would increase their reconnaissance and armed convoys near important PDF installations.

In Category Four, U.S. troops would take full control of several key military facilities, such as Fort Amador, Quarry Heights, and Fort Espinar. Fort Amador is located on a peninsula just southwest of Panama City. SOUTHCOM's headquarters were in Quarry Heights in Panama City, and its Operations Center was in a tunnel dug during Canal construction. Fort Espinar is in the north, near Colon. All of these were joint PDF-U.S. installations.

The President's get-tougher policy also had major policy consequences, since he had moved toward the kind of bolder strategy that General Woerner had resisted. He decided to replace General Woerner.

On June 20, Admiral Crowe recommended General Thurman as Woerner's replacement. Thurman had served in Vietnam and though he had somewhat limited warfighting experience or expertise, he was considered a man of action who could make things happen. With that in mind, Crowe asked Thurman to review the PRAYER BOOK operations orders—especially BLUE SPOON.

On August 4, the day before his scheduled change-of-command ceremony, Thurman came to Fort Bragg for a pair of briefings on BLUE SPOON: one on the JTFP concept for conventional force operations, the other on the Joint Special Operations Task Force concept of special operations.

Stiner could not attend, but he was represented by his deputy commander, Major General Will Roosma. That night, when Roosma laid out for him the substance of the briefings, along with Thurman's questions and comments, Stiner started getting inklings of what Thurman would tell him directly the next day.

BACK TO PANAMA

After his August 5 meeting with Thurman, Stiner wrapped up his duties with the 28th Infantry Division, but kept his new role in Panama uppermost in his mind. Getting up to speed on BLUE SPOON was an early priority; so far he had not personally reviewed it.

But his first priority was to get down to Panama and SOUTHCOM.

His last visit there had been a couple of years earlier, as the JSOTF Commander. This one would be very different: He was now totally responsible for the major operation that was shaping up.

His overriding concern was the 30,000 Americans, about 5,000 of whom were U.S. dependents living alongside PDF soldiers on joint military installations. This was a ready-made recipe for mass hostage-taking—or even massacre.

Back at Fort Bragg, he put together the team he would take with him—his chief of staff, Brigadier General Ed Scholes; his G-2 and G-3, Colonels Walters and Needham; and six officers from the intelligence and operations directorates who had taken part in the initial plan review process. He hoped to leave four of them in Panama (with SATCOM capabilities), so he could have daily reports.

The next night, Stiner and his team, dressed as civilians, left Pope Air Force Base in an unmarked special mission aircraft (a C-20 Gulf Stream), and landed around 9:00 P.M. at Howard Air Force Base, across the Canal from Panama City. He was met by Brigadier General Bill Hartzog, who had replaced Marc Cisneros as the SOUTHCOM J-3. Cisneros had moved over to replace Major General Bernie Loefke as commander of U.S. Army South. They spent most of the rest of the night with Bill Hartzog in Quarry Heights, in the tunnel that housed the SOUTHCOM operations center, receiving briefings on BLUE SPOON revisions. Although General Woerner still commanded SOUTHCOM, Hartzog was aware of General Thurman's and Washington's concerns, and had begun rewriting the BLUE SPOON operations order.

Stiner also learned many necessary details.

On the minus side, the tactical communications facilities in Panama were not nearly adequate for a major contingency operation. On the plus side, there was a combat service support capability—including a major hospital. Somewhat augmented, this capability would do for the initial stages of combat.

The next morning, Stiner and his party, still in civilian clothes, moved a short distance to Fort Clayton, U.S. Army South headquarters. There he linked up with Brigadier General Cisneros; Colonel Mike Snell, the commander of the 193rd brigade; and Colonel Keith Kellogg, the brigade commander who had come in with the 7th Infantry Division contingent during President Bush's May buildup, and who was now operating in the Colon area.

For the next two days, Stiner learned everything he could, about Noriega and the PDF on the one hand, and about the training and readiness of forces in Panama on the other.

Noriega had recently stepped up provocations aimed at disrupting what were called "Sand Flea" exercises—training activities allowed by the treaty. He then used the media reports of those confrontations to spread his hostile message. Though the U.S. troops involved had performed with exemplary professionalism so far, this kind of thing was a potential flash point for larger conflict and had to be closely watched.

Before Stiner and his team left Panama, Cisneros okayed the installation of Stiner's cell of four smart majors—planners—in the operations center.

His final business was to give Hartzog his assessment:

The revised BLUE SPOON, Stiner knew, was going to be considerably changed from General Woerner's original plan. In Stiner's view, any successful operation required surprise, overwhelming combat power, and the cover of darkness, to take advantage of the U.S. Army's unequaled night-fighting capabilities. It would not be a slow buildup, but a short, sharp, over-whelming shock.

Even though the commanders he'd met had shown an invaluable knowl-edge of the PDF and the local environment, Stiner had discovered holes that needed filling. Units in Panama were not as ready and proficient in urban live-fire operations at night as the forces coming in from the United States. This would require an intensified training program. Additionally, the aviation unit was short on pilots, and the majority of crews were not suf-ficiently proficient in nighttime battalion-size combat air assaults—though in a crunch, Stiner knew that, if he had to, he could make up for it with trained and ready crews already available in the XVIII Airborne Corps avi-ation battalions.

BACK at Fort Bragg, Stiner reviewed his visit to Panama with General Thurman—an experience that had left Stiner particularly unimpressed with the centerpiece of BLUE SPOON, the gradual buildup. The recent buildup in May hadn't deterred Noriega one bit, and there was no guarantee that BLUE SPOON would have more than a fifty-fifty chance of success.

"My people at Bragg," Stiner told his boss, "will get to work on a plan to neutralize Noriega's power base. We plan to take out the PDF and the na-tional police in one fell swoop, and in one night.

"With your blessing, sir," he continued, "I hope to visit Panama again in about two weeks, together with the leaders of the units that I will most likely select for this operation, and I plan to continue visiting Panama frequently until all this is over."

"Drive on," Thurman said. "And keep me informed."

ON August 10, 1989, the President nominated General Colin Powell to be the new Chairman of the Joint Chiefs of Staff, to take office on October 1. Earlier, General Powell had taken over the United States Forces Command from General Palastra, which had made him Stiner's immediate boss; but he already knew General Powell well from his days at JSOTF, when Powell had been the Executive Assistant to Secretary of Defense Caspar Weinberger.

While General Powell was still at FORSCOM, he scheduled a one-day trip to Bragg to get a firsthand look at the XVIII Corps's readiness and plan-ning initiatives for Panama. Though his visit was scheduled for only one day, bad weather kept him at Bragg, and Stiner took advantage of the opportunity to point out the revisions he had in mind for BLUE SPOON.

Powell agreed with Stiner—and Thurman—that the force buildup originally envisaged for BLUE SPOON took too long (twenty-two days) especially if a crisis hit. A quick-strike, one-night operation using the capabilities of the XVIII Airborne Corps and the Special Operations Command was the way to go. Stiner, of course, knew the capabilities of both commands better than anybody else, and he also knew how to meld them together as one fighting team.

"Continue revising the plan," Powell told Stiner.

LATER that month, Thurman, Stiner, Hartzog, and Gary Luck, the JSOTF commander, met to get up-to-date. Since April 1988, they concluded, when BLUE SPOON had been published, Noriega had grown increasingly defiant and his forces better equipped and trained. A twenty-two-day buildup could result in prolonged fighting, more casualties, and more opportunities for Noriega to take hostages or escape to the hills to lead a guerrilla war. Stiner wanted a quick strike that would lead to decisive victory.

During September, as the staffs of the XVIII Airborne Corps, SOUTH-COM, and SOCOM continued to revise the plan in that direction, Stiner made another visit to Panama, this time with the commander of the 82nd Airborne Division, the Assistant Division Commander of the 7th Infantry Division, the Ranger Regimental Commander, and Gary Luck, along with their operations and intelligence officers—including another of his best planners, to augment the four he'd already left there. Again, they traveled at night in civilian clothes, and in the same C-20 used for the first trip. At Howard AFB, they were met by Hartzog and Cisneros, and went directly to Fort Clayton for briefings.

The next day, the party broke into smaller groups and took off on clandestine reconnaissance missions, to get a better feel for the targets that had been selected, if a contingency operation was launched. Twenty-seven prime targets had been selected. Some key installations and facilities would have to be protected. Other targets would have to be "taken out"—or "neutralized."

Targets to be protected included the Pacora River Bridge, the three locks on the Canal, Madden Dam, the Bridge of Americas (crossing the Canal at Panama City), Howard Air Force Base, the U.S. Embassy, and all U.S. dependents living on military installations shared by the PDF.

Targets to be taken out included the Comandancia and all PDF military installations.

The reconnaissance gave the commanders awareness of what they would actually be facing—though no one knew yet which targets would be assigned to which commander. Stiner later made these decisions, based on his knowledge of unit capabilities. Some targets could be taken only by SOF forces, while others were better suited for conventional units.

Meanwhile, the Senate had confirmed General Thurman as CINC, and on Saturday, September 30, 1989, he took command from General Woerner at SOCOM headquarters in Panama. One day later, at midnight, Colin Powell took over as chairman of the JCS; his welcoming ceremony occurred the next day.

The October 3 Coup Attempt

On Sunday evening, October 1, a woman phoned the CIA station chief in Panama City: "Can you meet me downtown where we can talk? I have something that you need to know about." Though she refused to identify herself, the meeting was arranged.

She turned out to be the wife of Major Moises Giroldi, the commander of Noriega's security forces at the Comandancia.

"My husband is very worried about what the Noriega regime is doing to our country," she told the station chief, "and has decided to take action. Tomorrow morning at nine, as Noriega arrives at the Comandancia, my husband and others who oppose him will conduct a coup. We may need U.S. help to block PDF forces moving against the coup. We'll be back in touch."

That night, when the meeting was reported to General Thurman, he immediately went to his command post in the tunnel at Quarry Heights, where he hoped to pick up more news.

Sometime after midnight, a pair of CIA agents went straight from a meeting with Major Giroldi to Quarry Heights, where they confirmed to Thurman that the conspirators planned to grab Noriega at about nine that morning and take control of the Comandancia, thus cutting him off from communications with his field units. However, they might need U.S. help to block the major roads from the west, in case PDF units reacted to the coup.

Once in control, Giroldi planned to talk Noriega into retiring to Chiriqui Province in western Panama, where Noriega had a country house—one of his many luxury homes.

The CIA agents went on to explain that Giroldi, who had played a large part in crushing the coup attempt eighteen months earlier (he'd identified the conspirators, who had then all been jailed and tortured), was not exactly a man of conspicuous integrity, and could not be totally trusted now.

Though he had a bad feeling about the entire CIA report, General Thurman decided to pass it up to the Pentagon, just in case, and at about 2:30 in the morning, he reached General Kelly at home on his secure phone. After Thurman described what was going on, Kelly asked for his thoughts. "My advice is to wait and see what happens," Thurman said.

Soon after that, Generals Kelly and Powell met in the Pentagon with Rear Admiral Ted Shafer, the deputy director of the Defense Intelligence Agency, whose analysts were already busy trying to check out the coup information. The immediate consensus was that the whole thing was likely a trick or a deception; but if not, the plan was ill-conceived and unlikely to succeed.

By this time, Secretary Cheney was in his office for a heads-up from Powell, followed by a further review by Kelly and Shafer. All four then went to the Oval Office to update the President, where Powell recommended holding off on a decision until there was further information. "If there's a coup," Powell told the President, "we need to watch it develop before we act." The President agreed.

That day, the coup did not go off. But Mrs. Giroldi reported it was on for the next morning, October 3.

That morning, Noriega arrived earlier than usual at the Comandancia; the ceremonial guard force met the entourage in the normal way, but then took the dictator into custody—sparking an immediate argument between Noriega and Giroldi. Shots were fired, which General Thurman could hear at his quarters in Quarry Heights about a mile from the Comandancia.

Thurman immediately called Powell with a report.

By 9:00, it was clear a coup was under way, but its outcome was still far from certain. By noon, Panamanian radio announced that a coup was in progress.

Meanwhile, under the guise of a routine exercise, U.S. forces blocked the road to Fort Amador, though the Panamanian 5th Infantry Company based there had not attempted to react. At about the same time, two PDF lieu-

tenants, identified as coup liaison negotiators, arrived at the front gate of
Fort Clayton and asked to see Cisneros (now a major general), who spoke
fluent Spanish. Thurman told Cisneros to talk to them.

According to the lieutenants, the coup leaders had control of Noriega
and his staff, and were now looking for an honorable way for the dictator to
step down, yet remain in Panama; but when Cisneros offered to take him
into custody at Fort Clayton, the lieutenants refused. They had no intention
of turning him over to the United States. They still pressed for a U.S. roadblock at the Bridge of the Americas, however, to prevent Panamanian forces
from coming up from Rio Hato.

Cisneros made no promises.

TALKING Noriega into stepping down turned out to be a much more formidable undertaking than Giroldi had imagined. What the two men said to
each other, we'll never know, but we do know that Noriega out-talked
Giroldi. Rather than continue the conversation, Giroldi left Noriega in a
locked room for a few minutes, then went off to regroup. It was a fatal mistake: The room had a telephone. Noriega (it was later learned) evidently got
in touch with Vicki Amado, his number-one mistress, and asked her to contact the commanders of the 6th and 7th Companies at Rio Hato and the
PDF Mechanized Battalion 2000 at Fort Cimarron, some twenty miles
northeast of the city.

Soon, a 727 launched from Tocumen International Airport, ten miles east
of Panama City, landed at Rio Hato and began shuttling the 6th and 7th
Companies back to Tocumen. Meanwhile, Battalion 2000, ten miles farther
east at Fort Cimarron, headed to Tocumen with a convoy of trucks and V-
150 and V-300 armored cars. There they picked up the 6th and 7th
Companies and went on to the Comandancia.

The forces the coup leaders feared had merely flown over the
Comandancia, linked up with other reinforcements, and entered the com-
pound from the eastern side—actions that proved very enlightening to
Stiner and his planners as they revised BLUE SPOON.

At this point, it was obvious the coup was over. Shots from inside the
Comandancia could be heard—executions. Major Giroldi and his number
two, a PDF captain, were taken to Tinajitas (five miles north of the city, and
the home of the 1st Infantry Company), tortured until they identified the
other coup leaders, and executed.

"The PDF's response to the coup seriously demonstrated considerable military capability and resourcefulness," Carl Stiner remarks. "That day's events made it very apparent to me that if democracy was ever going to succeed in Panama, we had to clean out the whole kit and caboodle, including Noriega, his PDF force, the command-and-control structure (specifically the Comandancia)—and the national police as well. That was not all—as we came to learn. Noriega had placed his disciples in control of every key position in every institution of government, and all of them were on the take in some form or other. They would all have to go."

BOOSTING READINESS

After the failed coup, General Thurman acted to improve readiness: All personnel on duty now wore camouflage fatigues. Marksmanship training was intensified, and everyone—individuals and crews—had to be qualified in their weapon systems. Category three and four exercises were increased, and companies on Sand Flea exercises visited some of the twenty-seven planned targets daily (although the troops involved didn't know this). A nightly helicopter assault exercise was also conducted, to improve proficiency with night-vision goggles.

In order to beef up command and control, General Thurman officially designated Stiner as his war planner and war fighter; and on October 10, Stiner was named commander of Joint Task Force South.*

Stiner and his staff were already well ahead of the game with planning revisions to BLUE SPOON. In early September, Major General Will Roosma and a team of planners met with the SOUTHCOM staff to further integrate planning. On October 9, Stiner and his key staff flew to Panama for a contingency planning summit with the CINC—again wearing civilian clothes and traveling in an unmarked airplane. For the next three days, the two staffs worked in the SOUTHCOM command post in Quarry Heights, ironing out operational and tactical details.

Meanwhile, Stiner took time off to make a clandestine helicopter reconnaissance of the likely targets, which was critical for finalizing plan development. He was accompanied by Colonel Mike Snell, the commander

---

*When officially activated for combat, this would be the warfighting headquarters, and would include the XVIII Airborne Corps, all forces stationed in Panama, and everything else that would eventually be included in what became known as Operation JUST CAUSE.

of the 193rd Infantry Brigade, who was intimately familiar with the country and PDF locations.

As the meetings were concluding, General Thurman announced that Stiner would be in overall command of all U.S. combat forces in Panama, including special operations forces, and that the contingency plan for Joint Task Force South would include the following objectives, to: protect U.S. lives, key sites, and facilities; capture and deliver Noriega to competent authority; neutralize the Panamanian defense forces; support the establishment of a U.S.-recognized government in Panama; and restructure the PDF as directed by the duly-elected government.

An unwritten but high-priority mission from Washington was to rescue Kurt Muse, a CIA operative who had been arrested by Noriega and imprisoned in the high-security Modelo prison. Muse had been told that he would be executed if U.S. forces launched an attack against Panama. His executioner kept him under constant observation.

To accomplish these objectives, Joint Task Force South would have to either protect or neutralize the twenty-seven major targets. Many of them were in or near Panama City, but several, including the elite companies at Rio Hato, Battalion 2000 at Fort Cimarron, and Torrijos-Tocumen Airport, were some miles from the capital (the airport was dual-use: Tocumen was the civilian side, Torrijos the military). There were also major targets in the Colon area, on the Caribbean side of the country some forty miles northwest of Panama City.

Now that the targets had been determined and prioritized, Stiner and his commanders had to decide on the tactics and forces best suited for each.

At the end of the three days, Stiner summarized his "Commander's Intent" for the operation.*

In essence, he said: "Using electronic warfare capabilities to jam PDF communications, together with our EC-C130s (Volant Solo and Compass Call) to override civilian media stations and broadcast our message to the people of Panama, we will take advantage of surprise and darkness to attack or secure all twenty-seven targets simultaneously. A vital part of the operation is the protection of U.S. lives, beginning from H-hour and until stability

---

*A message personally written by the commander reflecting his views and priorities on the conduct of an operation, and serving as guidance to subordinate commanders and planners for developing their detailed tactical plans.

has been achieved. The key to success is surprise and the simultaneous takedown of the PDF, its command-and-control capability, and the national police. The majority of the fighting must be over by daylight, with our forces in control of the area bounded by Panama City to Colon in the north, and from Rio Hato in the southwest to Fort Cimarron in the northeast. Most Panamanians are our friends, and therefore we must minimize casualties and collateral damage. We will employ psychological operations at the tactical unit level to try to persuade each installation to surrender without a fight. If this does not achieve results, then measured force will be applied to accomplish the mission. At daylight, because there will be no law and order, the tactical units must be prepared to begin stability operations to protect life and property. To support this requirement, we will begin bringing in the rest of the 7th Infantry Division and the remainder of the 16th Military Police Brigade, beginning at H+4 hours and closing by H+24 hours. The capture of Noriega, the rescue of Kurt Muse from the Modelo prison, and other special mission requirements are the responsibility of the JSOTF. These operations are an integral part of the success of this operation, and will commence concurrently with all other operations at H-hour. I hope that the signal which will be sent by our actions at H-hour will make our job much easier as we fan out to take down PDF units in the rest of the country. If we can achieve some degree of surprise, and if we do this right, I don't expect much staying power out of the PDF."

At the same time, Stiner laid out his warfighting philosophy: "Hit first; surprise the enemy; overwhelm him with heavy combat power; use the cover of darkness to take maximum advantage of our night-fighting capabilities during the initial assault and follow-on attacks, so that our superior forces are on the objectives come dawn; and always fight under favorable conditions."

The party returned to Fort Bragg on October 11 to complete the plan.

During the next week, they worked day and night. For security purposes, planning for General Luck's special missions operations continued at his headquarters, but liaison officers were exchanged between the XVIII Airborne Corps and the Joint Special Operations Task Force to ensure continuity and integration.

The morning after their return, Stiner spoke to the planners at Fort Bragg:

"As I analyze this mission," he explained, "these are the specified and implied tasks that we must be concerned with:

- ❂ The priority is to protect U.S. lives and the key sites and facilities in Panama.
- ❂ We must capture Noriega and deliver him to competent authority.
- ❂ We must neutralize the PDF, and at the same time neutralize the command-and-control mechanism (that is, the Comandancia), as well as the national police.
- ❂ We must support the establishment of a U.S.-recognized government.
- ❂ We must be prepared to begin stability operations as soon as the fighting is over—because there will be no law and order.
- ❂ We must be prepared to engage in necessary nation-building activities to assist the new government get on its feet and begin to meet the expectations of the people.
- ❂ We must be prepared to restructure the Panamanian Defense Forces and the national police as the new government decides.

"This is a very difficult and complex mission," he continued. "We must plan to defeat the PDF and the national police in one night, and the next day raise those whom we have fought in a new image—no longer the oppressors of the people, but respected by them. We will be extending our hand to the PDF and then reraising him in a new image as a citizen or national policemen—whatever the new government decides.

"Practically all the fighting must be done in urban terrain—cities and built-up areas. We must limit the collateral damage—which translates to minimum loss of life on both sides—and limit all damage outside of what is strictly necessary to accomplish the mission.

"Accordingly, we will be forced to establish for ourselves specific rules of engagement that will limit our total combat capability. That is, we must limit ourselves to using only direct-fire weapons—individual rifles; machine guns; 66mm LAWs and AT-4 antitank weapons; Sheridan armored reconnaissance vehicles, with their large-caliber main guns; Apache helicopters with their hellfire missiles; AC-130 gunships; and artillery—the last three only in a direct-fire role for building-busting purposes. There'll be no "area fire" weapons, such as mortars and bombing.

"These rules of engagement must be very clear, so that every person involved in this operation has a clear understanding of what he can and cannot do.

"As for planning, the staff is to concentrate on the conventional aspects of this operation, leaving the special operations part to General Luck's head-quarters—specifically, the capture of Noriega and his henchmen. The Noriega gang must be neutralized in order to provide an environment where the civilian government can function without threat. All other special mission requirements will also be the responsibility of Luck's command, but when it comes time for execution, the two plans will be integrated. Luck will control the special operations side, reporting to me, the same as the other task force commanders.

"The success of this mission depends in large measure on the effectiveness of small units accomplishing their assigned missions. Therefore, I want to give them maximum flexibility and latitude in making the decisions necessary to accomplish their mission."

He continued: "I will personally begin work on structuring the command and control arrangements for this operation. These will be simple and direct—no unnecessary layering. As it stands right now, I plan to absorb the U.S. Army South headquarters into my headquarters (Joint Task Force South), making General Marc Cisneros my deputy.

"Because different forces from different services will be involved, we must have a joint CEOI [Command Communications and Electronic Operating Instructions], so we can talk to each other. I want this to be short and to the point, not a Sears, Roebuck catalog. Once it is developed, I plan to have an exercise where we can tweak all our radios and other means of communication, to ensure that we can talk to each other—and once we start this operation, we are not changing frequencies and call signs until it's over. We will conduct this operation with such momentum that it will not matter if the PDF gets hold of one of our CEOIs, because they won't be able to do anything with it anyhow."

"Finally, within four days I want to see a draft plan that I can have in the hands of my major subordinate commanders within five days, to allow them time to study it before our next meeting in Panama, when I plan to have them present."

COMMAND RELATIONSHIPS

Within four days, a draft operations plan was completed. This included command-and-control relationships:

Beginning at the top was General Thurman, CINC South.

Immediately under him was Lieutenant General Stiner, Commander

Joint Task Force South. When Stiner's headquarters absorbed the Headquarters of U.S. Army South, Major General Marc Cisneros became Stiner's deputy commander, and Cisneros's staff principals became deputies to the staff principals of the XVIII Airborne Corps.

Directly underneath Stiner were six task forces, as follows:

1. The Joint Special Operations Task Force (JSOTF) was headed by Major General Gary Luck. All special mission forces in Panama were to be under his command and control.
2. The Air Component was commanded by Lieutenant General Pete Kemph, the 12th Air Force Commander. All the planning for tactical air support would initially be handled by Brigadier General Bruce Fister, Gary Luck's deputy. After the initial assault, control of all aviation assets would revert to Pete Kemph.
3. Task Force Bayonet, headed by Colonel Mike Snell, was to be made up of the 193rd Brigade already stationed in Panama.
4. Task Force Pacific was to be headed by Major General Jim Johnson, commander of the 82nd Airborne Division and his Division Ready Brigade (DRB)—approximately 4,000 paratroopers, with all weapons and equipment, including twelve more Sheridans.
5. Task Force Atlantic would initially be commanded by Colonel Keith Kellogg, the 7th Infantry Division's 3d Brigade Commander, already in Panama.
6. Task Force Semper Fi was headed by Colonel Charles Richardson, commander of the Marine Expeditionary Battalion already brought in during the May 1989 buildup.

These officers were responsible for completing their portion of the plan, and then for rehearsing it.

The units already in Panama (12,000 troops), together with those coming from the United States at H-hour and throughout the first day, would bring the troop total to more than 26,000. By comparison, the earlier version of BLUE SPOON provided only 10,000 additional troops (total: 22,000) over twenty-two days. At H-hour there would be enough forces available to secure twenty-four of the twenty-seven planned targets. The three remaining—Panama Viejo (on the eastern side of Panama City), Tinajitas, and Fort Cimarron—would be secured by battalion air assaults conducted by the 82nd Airborne Division DRB, who would jump into Tocumen International Airport at H+45 minutes. The airport itself would be taken by Rangers, who were to jump in at H-hour. After landing, the 82nd was to assume operational control of the Rangers and take responsibility for security of the airport.

If all went as planned, the heavy fighting should be over by daylight, with all targets either neutralized or protected, as the case may be.

Later that day, the remaining two brigades of the 7th Infantry Division, commanded by Major General Carmen Cavezza, would arrive from Fort Ord, California, while the remainder of the 16th Military Police Brigade would fly in from Fort Bragg. These units would round out the forces necessary to bring stability and security to Panama City and Colon, and in time to the rest of the country.

ON Friday, October 13, Carl Stiner drove from Fort Bragg to Knoxville, Tennessee, for his daughter Carla's wedding the next day at the Ball Camp Baptist Church. Just in case he couldn't make it, he had arranged for his brother Tom to stand in; but in fact, everything worked out fine—with one hang-up. When he linked up with his wife, Sue, at the Holiday Inn, he found her sitting there with a shoe off and pain on her face.

"What's wrong?"

"I broke a bone in my foot yesterday," she answered, "and it hurts bad."

"Are you going to be able to go through with the wedding?"

"One way or another. This is my first daughter's wedding, and I'm certainly going to do my part. What I want you to do is go out and get me an ace bandage, and wrap my foot real tight. We've got to get on over to the rehearsal."

That I did, Stiner remembers. *Sue could always withstand a lot of pain, but what she did that night during the rehearsal and the next evening during the wedding was just out of sight. It was beyond me how she made it through the entire ceremony, walking without a limp, and with a beatific smile on her face.*

Talk about courage.

During the reception, at about ten in the evening, I received a call: The Chairman wanted to see me and Gary Luck the following day for a briefing on the revisions to OPLAN BLUE SPOON.

We were stuck with two cars in Knoxville. That meant Sue had to drive one back to Bragg; my other daughter, Laurie, drove the second.

At six the next morning, Sue dropped me off at Cherokee Aviation at

Knoxville Airport, where a plane was waiting to fly me to Washington. Then
she headed back to North Carolina—in pain. The next day, her foot was placed
in a cast, but that didn't do the job; and a month later she had to have screws
put in.

Meanwhile, I linked up with Gary Luck in the Pentagon, and we pro-
ceeded to the Chairman's office, where I brought General Powell up to speed
on the conventional side (pointing out our efforts to make the operation more
responsible and decisive), while Gary Luck covered the special mission part.
After we had both explained the revised command arrangements and our plans
to integrate efforts, General Powell praised the work everyone had put into the
plan, then released me to return to Fort Bragg. Gary Luck stayed overnight, and
accompanied Powell to the Oval Office to brief the President on his special task
forces' mission in Panama.

FINALIZING THE PLAN

On October 19, Stiner, his key staffers, and the commanders of his major
units made another civilian clothes visit to Panama, this time in two special
mission aircraft. For two days, the warfighting commanders met to discuss
the plan and put the final details in place. Joining them were General
Thurman and the SOUTHCOM staff; Lieutenant General Pete Kemph;
Brigadier General Robin Turnow, the commander of Howard Air Force
Base; and Rear Admiral Jerry C. Gnecknow, CINCLANT's representative
to the operation.

The meeting started with an intelligence estimate:

The Panamanian Defense Forces numbered almost 13,000 troops, including the national guard, the police, and other separate units, but only
4,000 to 5,000 of these could be counted real combat troops. The ground
forces were deployed throughout thirteen military zones, and consisted of
two infantry battalions, ten independent companies, one cavalry squadron,
a riot control company, and a special forces command, which numbered
about four hundred specially trained and equipped troops. PDF army equipment included twenty-eight V-150 and V-300 armored cars. The navy numbered about four hundred sailors and was equipped with twelve high-speed
patrol boats, all armed with cannons. The Air Force numbered about five
hundred troops and was equipped with thirty-eight fixed-wing aircraft, seventeen helicopters, and numerous air defense weapons systems. There

were, finally, up to eighteen paramilitary units—"Dignity Battalions"—but intelligence about these units and their missions was spotty.

Meanwhile, the intelligence agencies had begun to develop a most wanted list—people who would have to be removed or neutralized if there was to be a democratic environment in Panama. In addition to Noriega, up to a hundred others were expected to be on the list: Noriega's disciples and henchmen, those in key government positions, and others wanted for crimes against the people, or simply for racketeering—the whole gang was up to their eyeballs in crime.

STINER then presented his concept of operations: After an analysis of the mission statement, his "Commander's Intent," the operational command structure, the targets assigned to each major subordinate command, and the allocation of forces, he gave his thoughts on the phasing of the operation:

PHASE I

- ✪ Clandestinely deploy JSOTF Headquarters, Army Special Missions Unit, and Special Aviation assets to in-country forward staging base (FSB).
- ✪ Infiltrate other needed conventional weapons systems for H-hour activities to in-country FSB.
- ✪ Marshall other CONUS [Continental United States] forces for deployment.

PHASE II

- ✪ Begin reconnaissance and surveillance (R&S).
- ✪ Deploy rangers to CONUS intermediate staging bases (ISBs).
- ✪ Deploy selected CONUS forces to in-country FSB.

PHASE III

- ✪ Conduct pre H-hour activities—i.e., secure critical facilities.
- ✪ H-hour activities.

PHASE IV

- ✪ Conduct follow-on/stability operations.
- ✪ Handover and redeployment.
- ✪ Transition to nation building (Operation PROMOTE LIBERTY).

Stiner concluded by summarizing H-hour activities:

Fire Support: Just before H-hour, the AC-130 gunships will be in orbit with a full load of ammunition and prepared to respond to the fire-support needs of all task forces. Apache helicopters will also be ready to deliver precision fire support against all major targets.

Beginning at H-hour, the following will occur simultaneously:

In conjunction with the opening of combat activities, JTF South will use EF-111 aircraft to jam all PDF tactical communications, and use EC-130 Compass Call and Volant Solo aircraft to override all Panamanian media and broadcast this message to the people: "We are the Americans, your friends. We are here to give your freedom back. We will be attacking only those targets that are necessary for that purpose. Stay in your homes and no one will be harmed."

Task Force Red: The 75th Ranger Regiment will conduct concurrent parachute assaults to secure Torrijos-Tocumen International Airport and neutralize the 2nd Infantry Company, and at Rio Hato to neutralize the 4th and 6th PDF Companies, the Sergeant Majors Academy, and the Cadet Academy.

The Joint Special Operations Task Force will conduct operations to rescue Kurt Muse from the Modelo prison; render unusable the airfield at Paitilla (in Panama City), along with Noriega's executive jet located there; disable Noriega's presidential yacht; secure the waters of the Canal south of the Miraflores locks (that is, between the locks and Panama City and the Pacific—about five or six miles); *conduct activities as necessary to capture Noriega and other priority targets on the most wanted list; and conduct hostage-rescue operations and other special mission activities as directed.*

Task Force Bayonet (the 193rd Brigade): Will conduct operations to neutralize the Comandancia; secure Fort Amador; and neutralize the 5th Independent Company, Ancon DENI stations (PDF intelligence), PDF engineer compound, Balboa Harbor (the harbor at Panama City), *and the PDF dog compound.*

Task Force Semper Fi: Will conduct operations to secure and protect the Bridge of the Americas; Howard Air Force Base; seize the port of Voca Monte; and neutralize all PDF and Dignity Battalion units in its area of operations (AOR).

[Task Force Semper Fi had initially deployed to Panama as a battalion-size unit, but was now brigade-size after augmentation by U.S. Army attachments.]

Task Force Atlantic [elements of the 7th Infantry Division]: Will be responsible for securing most of the former Canal Zone north of those operations areas in the neighborhood of Panama City. It will conduct operations to secure Fort Sherman and the Caribbean entrance to the Panama Canal; the Gatun Locks; Coco Solo; Fort Espinar; the Madden Dam; rescue political prisoners from the Renacer Prison; and secure Cerro Tigre (a PDF supply complex).

Task Force Pacific: The 82d Airborne Division conducts parachute assault at H+45 at Tocumen Airport; assumes OPCON of 1st Ranger Battalion and security of the airport; beginning within thirty minutes, conducts air assault operations to secure in priority Panama Viejo (a primarily ceremonial cavalry squadron and a 170-man detachment from Noriega's elite and fiercely loyal special operations antiterrorist unit known as the USEAT), Tinajitas (5th Rifle Company), and Fort Cimarron (Battalion 2000).

Following my presentation, each major subordinate commander presented his portion of the plan and described how he expected to accomplish his mission.

TOWARD the end of the first day, each commander made a clandestine reconnaissance of his targets. That night, they made adjustments to their plans, and these were briefed and finalized the next day in open session, with everyone present. That way, the process was coordinated, and each commander was familiar with the overall plan and its details.

Toward the end of the second day, three fire support concerns came up:

First: The fire support systems available at H-hour were not powerful enough for the 193d Brigade's building-busting mission in and around the Comandancia. Although the 82d Airborne would be dropping twelve Sheridans at H+45, these would not be available for support of the 193d brigade as they entered the built-up area near the Comandancia.

Second: It was feared that low cloud cover could limit the effectiveness of the AC-130 gunships. Given the kind of "surgical" fighting planned for built-up areas, an additional highly accurate fire support system was needed.

Third: Colonel Buck Kernan, commander of the 75th Ranger Regiment, pointed out that the airfield at Rio Hato, the only available drop zone for the parachute assault, was close to the 6th and 7th PDF Companies, two of Noriega's best. If surprise was not achieved, his Rangers could take heavy casualties during the jump. For that reason, Kernan asked for air strikes against these two companies' barracks.

"This was a serious problem," Carl Stiner observes, "because air strikes against the PDF had been ruled out by the Secretary of Defense, on the grounds that most of them were our friends—just misguided—and if at all possible, we had to give them a chance to surrender.

"We had to find another way to deal with this threat. In fact, over the coming days, we had to come up with solutions to each of these three problems—and we did."

At the end of the conference, the commanders discussed the various employment options—the time necessary to round up all the planes and crews and get them to the right bases for loading the assault troops. BLUE SPOON would most likely be launched following a Noriega-inspired provocation. He had already stepped up the frequency of these events, a flash point was always possible.

The urgency of the provocation would determine the launch time available. The deliberate employment option was based on a forty-eight-to-sixty-hour notification—plenty of time.

However, there always remained a strong possibility that Noriega would create an incident requiring a quicker response than BLUE SPOON allowed. To cover that possibility, two corollary plans had to be worked out: a no-notice response (in case of a hostage situation or a threat to a key facility—such as the canal locks), and a short-notice response (less urgent, but still requiring action within fourteen to sixteen hours).

In either case, the initial response would have to come from forces already in place—seven U.S. combat battalions, including a Special Forces battalion, and aviation support; General Luck's forces would follow on from CONUS within twelve hours. Responsibility for both the no-notice and short-notice option was laid on General Cisneros, the U.S. Army South commander, who was tasked to develop these plans.

On the way back to Fort Bragg, Stiner worked on fire support issues: The 193rd Brigade's H-hour problem at the Comandancia was relatively easy to solve. They would clandestinely pre-position four Sheridans, with their large-caliber main guns; six Apache helicopters, with their hellfire missiles; and three OH-58 scout helicopters. A few days later, he put this into a formal request, and on November 7th, Secretary Cheney signed the deployment order.

Buck Kernan's problem with the drop at Rio Hato was tougher. They had to keep the PDF from killing Rangers when they were most vulnerable—descending in parachutes—but they also had to do all they could to avoid killing PDF, if that was prudently possible.

The answer, when it hit Stiner, was logical: "We don't have to kill PDF in their barracks. We just have to put them in no condition to fight." A way had to be found to stun them long enough—five minutes would do it—for the C-130s to get safely across the drop zone. Once the Rangers were on the ground, they could do the rest.

Offset bombing*—for shock and awe—was the solution. The question, then, was by what?

He first considered using F-111s, with their standard 750-pound bombs; then called his air component commander, Pete Kemph, to get his views. What he wanted, he explained, was to create five minutes of shock and confusion by dropping bombs maybe 150 to 200 meters from the 4th and 6th PDF Companies' barracks.

"I'm thinking of using F-111s," Stiner told Kemph.

"There is a much more accurate system," Kemph replied. "The F-117. And it can carry bigger bombs—two thousand pounds."

"But F-117s are black," Stiner said—secret.

"For something as critical as this, it could probably be brought out," Kemph pointed out. "I'll tell you what. The next time you are down in Panama, I'll send the F-117 wing commander down with bomb data, and you can decide for yourself."

Not long after that, Stiner reviewed the data with the wing commander, and there was simply no comparison. The F-117s could put 2,000-pound bombs exactly where he wanted them. With the F-111s, there was a significant risk of error. In due course, the Secretary of Defense approved an F-117 drop of two bombs at Rio Hato in support of the Rangers.

TOWARD the end of October, General Carl Vuono, Army Chief of Staff, asked Stiner and Luck to come to Washington to bring him up to date—primarily to make sure they were getting the support they needed.

"This is the most sophisticated thing I've ever seen," he announced when he'd heard the details. "Over three hundred planes and helicopters in one small area, attacking twenty-seven targets at night. You'd better rehearse this thing all you can."

"It's not going to be as messy as it looks," Stiner explained. "A lot of detailed flight planning has already gone into it. All the pilots are proficient with night-vision goggles, and the AC-130s can illuminate the key targets

---

*Bombing that aims to *barely miss* a target.

with their infrared searchlights; the night will look like daytime. We'll own the night.

"Our units can do this. We've trained them that way."

Vuono liked what he'd heard and pledged his support.

PLANNING continued until October 30, 1989, when General Thurman signed USCINCSO OPORD 1-90 (BLUE SPOON), making BLUE SPOON official—though planning did not stop there. Stiner's planners completed the Corps plan a few days later, and he signed it as ready to execute on November 4. Gary Luck's planners completed their plan the same day.

On November 3, Thurman, Stiner, and Luck gave the BLUE SPOON briefing to the Joint Chiefs in the Pentagon in a room called the Tank. Though the Chiefs were generally supportive, like Vuono, they questioned the plan's complexity. Assurances of the capabilities and readiness of the forces convinced them, and they approved it.

MEANWHILE, the Sheridans and Apaches were set to deploy on the nights of November 15 and 16. The Sheridans would go the first night on a C-5 aircraft, and the Apaches the following night on another C-5.

Stiner took advantage of the transportation to set up another commanders' conference in Panama. Accompanying him on the C-5 hauling the Sheridans were Colonels Needham, G-3 (operations), and Walters, G-2 (intelligence); Colonel Bill Mason, Corps Signal Officer; and Major Huntoon, one of the chief planners. Three days later, he was joined at Fort Clayton by his major subordinate commanders and staff officers.

The four Sheridans and their crews arrived at Howard AFB at about midnight. For the sake of operational security, the crews had removed their 82nd Airborne division patches and sewed on 5th Mech Division patches.

With their swim shrouds raised to break up their outline, the tanks were loaded on tractor trailers and taken to the mechanized battalion's nearby motor pool and placed inside large tents, where they'd remain until needed—though the crews drove them two nights a week in the motor pool to keep the seals lubricated to prevent leaking.

In order to familiarize themselves with the environment, the Sheridan crews accompanied the mechanized battalion on their daily Sand Flea exercises, which let them eyeball the targets they'd hit—though they had no idea that was what they were doing.

The C-5 carrying the six Apaches landed at Howard the next night at midnight. They were off-loaded and rolled into hangar number one for re-assembly. They remained there during the day, but the crews flew them at night—to familiarize themselves with flying in Panama and to condition the locals to the sound of Apaches.

At the commanders' conference, each commander briefed Stiner on the details of his plan. All of this was generally satisfactory, but Stiner was still uncomfortable with the level of the crew proficiency for executing battalion-size air assaults at night. A program of intensified training was initiated to correct this.

BOMB THREAT

On November 18, word came to General Thurman that the Medellín drug cartel was planning attacks against Americans in Panama in retaliation for U.S. counterdrug assistance in Colombia. The source stated that three car bombs had already been positioned in a Panama City warehouse, ready to be moved to American targets and activated, and that a three-person terrorist team, expert at fabricating false identities and gaining access to U.S. installations, was already operating within Panama. The source providing this information had been given a lie-detector test, and had passed.

"We have no choice," Thurman said to Stiner. "We have to take that kind of threat seriously. That means you are stood up, my friend"—meaning he was activating Joint Task Force South immediately for its wartime mission. "I will increase the alert status to the maximum for all installations and troops. You're in charge. So start operating now."

"Yes, sir," Stiner replied.

When Thurman told Powell what he had done, Powell was a little bent out of shape; only the SECDEF has authority to activate a Joint Task Force. But Secretary Cheney, recalling the Beirut bombing of U.S. Marines, did not contest Thurman's action.

Stiner sent his commanders back to their units in the United States to begin rehearsals, but he and his staff remained behind in Panama to oversee the increased security.

Carl Stiner continues:

All U.S. installations were "closed," checkpoints were manned by armed guards, nothing was admitted without a thorough inspection and proper identification, and SOUTHCOM flew in explosive detection dogs—not enough of them, it turned out, to suit the MPs. They started hollering for more.

328 ★ TOM CLANCY

"Shit," I told them, "you don't need a trained dog, what you need is 'deterrent' dogs to spread out among the ones you've already got. So get out and catch you some."

They did, and it was a sight to behold. As the trained dogs were crawling underneath the cars, the deterrent dogs were as often as not hosing down the hubcaps.

All our security measures quickly resulted in virtual gridlock. Traffic lined up to get on installations was sometimes over a mile long.

Meanwhile, our people had located the warehouse where the car bombs had supposedly been placed, and I'd gone to General Thurman to see if he couldn't get Panama-based FBI or DEA personnel in there to check it out; but it turned out they had no legal authority. Neither was it technically legal to use U.S. military personnel, since a deployment order for a military operation in Panama had not been published by the Secretary of Defense.

We still needed somehow to get into that warehouse, which was guarded twenty-four hours a day by an armed guard. I told Thurman that it would be unconscionable to let one of those bombs explode, and that I would take care of it. The guard agreed to cooperate and willingly unlocked the door. There were no car bombs, and no evidence there ever had been.

The whole thing was a hoax.

On November 27, with approval from Washington, the Joint Task Force was dissolved and I returned home.

The bomb hoax was not a total loss, however. The security measures had turned out to be a good exercise in readiness.

PROVOCATIONS

As units rehearsed their plans in the United States and Panama, the situation in Panama was swiftly deteriorating. Dignity Battalions were increasing their provocations, and Noriega was busy firing up the PDF with machete-waving personal appearances.

Back in the States, Stiner was involved in rehearsals or on the road, making certain that all the major commands from all the services were aware of all the details of the plan and prepared to support their part in the operation.

He made three trips to the Pentagon to brief General Powell, and he also briefed Admiral Frank Kelso, Commander of the U.S. Atlantic Command (who was responsible for providing cover for the airlift armada as it passed Cuba); General Hansford T. Johnson, the Commander of the Military Airlift

Command, who would be providing the airlift; General Edwin H. Burba, U.S. Army Forces Command Commander; and General Jim Lindsay, Commander of the U.S. Special Operations Command.

In late November and early December, conventional and special operations forces conducted detailed rehearsals at Fort Bragg and Eglin Air Force Base, and in Panama. Since operational security was a major concern, rehearsals were masked as routine training exercises. Only senior commanders and staff knew about the link with the actual contingency plan.

As the situation in Panama continued to deteriorate, Stiner grew more and more convinced that it was just a matter of time before the plan would have to be implemented. Every unit was rehearsed and ready, but training continued, to maintain unit readiness. Now came the waiting.

The National Command Authority had never wanted a preemptive strike, since the universal perception would be that it was an "invasion of a small and unprepared foe by the world's strongest nation"—taking a sledgehammer to a flea. Instead, they wanted a trigger incident that would justify the operation in the eyes of the world.

On December 15, the Noriega-appointed National Assembly voted to make him head of government and "maximum leader of the struggle for national liberation." Another resolution stated, "The Republic of Panama is declared to be in a state of war with the United States, as long as U.S. aggression in the form of economic sanctions imposed in 1988 continues."

TRIGGER

At about 9:30 P.M. on Saturday, December 16, four young officers, just off duty at SOUTHCOM headquarters, were driving downtown for a pizza, when they were stopped at a PDF roadblock near the Comandancia. The PDF soldiers began beating on the car, trying to drag the Americans out. The driver sped away. The PDF opened fire. Barely a minute later, when it was all over, one officer had been shot in the ankle and Marine First Lieutenant Robert Paz had been mortally wounded.

Shortly afterward, the PDF stopped Navy Lieutenant Adam Curtis and his wife, Bonnie, who had witnessed the shooting incident, at the same roadblock. They were taken to the Comandancia and interrogated in the presence of a PDF officer. There, Curtis was kicked in the head and groin, and his wife was threatened sexually, then made to lean against a wall. She eventually collapsed on the floor. When the lieutenant protested, the PDF interrogators shoved wads of paper into his mouth, put a gun to his head, and again kicked him several times in the groin. "Your husband will never perform in bed again," one of the interrogators told Bonnie.

After four hours of this, the PDF abruptly released them.

General Thurman learned of these incidents at 11:00 P.M., in Washington, where he'd gone for meetings. He immediately flew back to Panama.

About the same time, the liaison team in Panama got word to Stiner at Fort Bragg.

Meanwhile, Noriega had issued a communiqué that blamed the shooting incident on the four U.S. officers, alleging they had broken through a PDF checkpoint, shot at the Comandancia, and wounded three Panamanians—a soldier, a civilian, and a one-year-old girl.

The next morning, Sunday, December 17, Stiner got a secure phone call from Lieutenant General Kelley: "General Thurman is recommending the implementation of the OPLAN," Kelley told him. "The Chairman, the SECDEF, and I are about to brief the President. Is there anything you want to pass on?"

"Yes, there is," Stiner answered. "What happened is unfortunate; there is nothing we can do to bring back Lieutenant Paz or relieve the pain and suffering of the Navy lieutenant and his wife. But what we can do is clean up this mess once and for all by implementing the full OPLAN, and that is my recommendation. We are prepared to do it right."

Stiner continued:

"We need a decision on H-hour, and I'd like to have it established at 0100 hours. I have three reasons:

"First, that's when the tide is highest in Panama (it fluctuates some forty-three feet there). The SEALs have to swim to some of their targets in order to place their explosive charges. If we pick the wrong time, they'd have to walk across mudflats, thus compromising their operations, and greatly increasing the risk of not being able to accomplish these critical missions at H-hour.

"Second, we want to minimize possibilities for hostage situations. For that, we need a time when there is little chance that a wide-body civilian jet, and several hundred passengers, will be landing at Torrijos Tocumen International Airport. We have been watching the airport for a couple of months, and seldom does a large jet land after midnight.

"Third, we have three major targets that we cannot secure at H-hour. After it jumps at H+45, the 82nd Airborne Division needs four hours to make three battalion-size combat air assaults before daylight. With H-hour at 0100, we believe that most of the fighting will be over come daylight."

Kelley promised to pass this on to the President and get back to Stiner after the meeting. He called back at 5:15 that afternoon: "The President has made the decision to go," he said. "And you've got what you wanted. H-hour will be at 0100.

"The President also wants you to pass on to the commanders and troops his total trust and confidence in their ability to accomplish the mission, and that he'll be praying for them."

Stiner immediately called his stateside commanders to give them the word. A couple of hours later, he assembled his staff at the XVIII Airborne Corps Headquarters to review the sequencing of operations that would follow on the President's decision.

Shortly, the official "Execute Order" was published by Secretary Cheney. It established H-hour as 0100 hours, 20 December 1989.

That night, Brigadier General Ed Scholes, XVIII Airborne Corps Chief of Staff, left for Fort Clayton with a contingent of headquarters staff officers to establish a small command post to handle pre-H-hour details from that end.

At 0900, Monday, the eighteenth, the XVIII Airborne Corps called an emergency deployment readiness exercise (EDRE) to serve as a cover and no-notice order for executing Corps Plan 90-2. This initiated the 82nd Airborne's eighteen-hour planning-and-alert procedure, a normal routine which would cover deployment, though only key personnel knew this.

Later in the afternoon, Stiner, key members of his Corps staff, and an advance command element from the 82nd Airborne Division, led by Brigadier General Joe Kinzer, took off for Howard Air Force Base in two unmarked C-20s. The entire contingent traveled once again in civilian clothes; they did not change into battle dress until Tuesday night.

MEANWHILE, there'd been a major command change. Gary Luck was being promoted to Lieutenant General and would now command U.S. Army Special Forces Command; Major General Wayne Downing was taking over as commander of the JSOTF. Since General Downing's background was filled with Airborne, Ranger, and Special Operations assignments, including combat in Vietnam, there was no loss in command continuity. He had been completely read-in on the plan, and had participated in all the rehearsals.

By the time the Execute Order was published, a large part of the special operations forces had already clandestinely infiltrated into Panama; the rest were scheduled to be infiltrated before H-hour. At 0100 on Monday morning, General Downing left for Panama with a contingent of his forces.

The force he would command totaled approximately 4,400 and was composed of special operations, psychological operations, and civil affairs units from the Army, Air Force, and the Navy. The largest special operations component, and its principal assault force, was the 75th Ranger Regiment, dubbed Task Force Red.

Carl Stiner comments:

Gary Luck had done an outstanding job integrating the joint special operations activities into the overall plan, and now he would not have the opportunity to execute them. On that count, I had to feel sorry for him. On the other hand, his promotion was long overdue and he would do an equally outstanding job commanding the Army's Special Operations Command and go on to command the XVIII Airborne Corps in Operation DESERT STORM, *less than a year away.*

Pre-H-Hour

Maintaining operational security had from the outset been crucial to the plan. Without it, we could forget about achieving surprise. And without surprise, there would certainly be greater casualties—on both sides. The troops stationed in Panama gave me the most concern in this regard. Some lived off-base, some had Panamanian girlfriends, some of the families had maids, and all our installations had Panamanian workers—a ready-made situation for a compromise.

One of my main reasons for going down to Panama early was to meet with the commanders there to determine how to best alert the troops for the operation without compromising security. And of course, I could control the pre-H-hour activities better there than I could back at Bragg.

There was no doubt: the troops in Panama were ready. All units were already in a high state of alert and could be assembled in two hours. They'd had intensified training; they'd eyeballed every target they would take down; and commanders had even prepared handy "battle books," which provided the com-

plete tactical plan for each target. For the sake of security, however, units below battalion level had deliberately not been briefed. And now this would have to be done for real, and quickly.

After landing at Howard Air Force Base on Monday night, I went straight to Fort Clayton and assembled all my commanders down to battalion level to tell them the operation was a go, at 0100 hours, 20 December—twenty-eight hours away. We then decided to call the junior officers in for briefing at 8:00 P.M. the next day, and the troops sequestered and briefed at 9:00. This would allow four hours for detailed briefings at company level, issue of ammo, and preparation for movement to attack positions. Both Civil Affairs and Psychological Operations teams (equipped with portable loudspeakers and pre-cut scripts) had previously been assigned to all company-level combat units.

Meanwhile, General Thurman and I had one other major concern—the security of the rightfully elected government, Endara, Ford, and Calderon, in hiding since their beating in May. Although Green Berets stationed in Panama had been keeping an eye on them and had responsibility for a rescue mission (if needed), the truth was that Noriega could have taken them anytime he wanted.

The Deputy Chief of Mission, John Bushnell (the Ambassador was on home leave), solved that problem by inviting the three men to dinner at his quarters on Howard Air Force Base, Tuesday evening, December 19. After dinner, they were flown by helicopter to Quarry Heights, where they were briefed on the operation by General Thurman.

Just before midnight, a Panamanian judge was provided space in Thurman's headquarters, and there officially swore in Endara as president, and Ford and Calderon as vice presidents. After the ceremony, they were taken to a safe house on Fort Clayton, where they prepared the speeches they would deliver the morning after H-hour.

The United States immediately recognized the Endara government.

MEANWHILE, we had several people tracking Noriega, and they had a fairly good handle on where he was about eighty percent of the time. That turned out not to be good enough.

On Tuesday the nineteenth, he had spent most of the day in the Colon area. Late that afternoon, his entourage left Colon and headed for Panama City—or so we thought. We later learned that somewhere between Colon and Panama City, the convoy had split in two, one part headed east to a rest camp near Torrijos-Tocumen International Airport, where Noriega had a rendezvous with *a prostitute (arranged by his aide, Captain Gaitan—a true bad guy; he'd reportedly murdered three people). The other part proceeded on to the Comandancia, where a Noriega look-alike got out, was greeted by the honor guard, and proceeded inside.*

Based on information our people provided, Wayne Downing and I both quickly realized that this man was not Noriega.

But where was the real one? We didn't know.

BACK *in the States, marshaling had been completed and troops were loading and launching from fourteen different bases. Since the plan called for radio silence, we conducted everything up until H-hour from a Master Execution Checklist. As long as a unit was on schedule, there was no need for reports; we broke radio silence only when something happened that might keep a unit from accomplishing its mission at the specified time.*

So far, so good. Everything seemed to be on track—including command and control: I had overall control from my headquarters in Panama, while Downing provided an alternate command post in that country. He had complete communications and the ability to control the whole operation. Airborne over the Atlantic in an EC-130 was the Deputy Corps Commander, Major General Will Roosma, with a complete battle staff and all the communications necessary to control the operation. And back at Fort Bragg was another fully manned command center, also capable of controlling the operation.

A total of 253 fixed-wing aircraft and 80 helicopters were to be involved in D Day activities. On the next page is a listing by type and number.

Some of these aircraft, such as the thirty-five KC-10 and KC-135 tankers, would assume orbit positions outside the immediate operational area so as not to interfere with combat activities.

All those carrying troops or in troop support missions would assemble over the Gulf of Mexico, drop down below Cuba's radar coverage and proceed through the Yucatán Gap, and then on to Panama and their specific target areas. Just in case any were challenged by Castro's air force, twelve F-15 fighters were aloft near Cuba and ready to respond.

All crews involved in the combat operation would wear night-vision goggles. All troop-carrying aircraft, including heavy equipment drop operations, would fly blacked-out, and were to be AWADS-equipped (technology for all weather conditions). *All crews flying special operations forces would be SOLL-II qualified* (able to make blacked-out landings in total darkness).

D Day Fixed Wing

GENERAL SUPPORT		JTF-SOUTH	
KC-10	12	C-141	28 HE Airdrop
KC-135	23	C-141	3 CDS Airdrop
AC-130	9	C-141	20 PERS Airdrop
E-3 AWACS	3	C-141	43 Air Land
EC-130 ABCC	3	C-5	16 Air Land
EF-111	2		
EC-130 (Compass Call)	2		
EC-130 (Volant Solo)	2	JSOTF	
		C-141	5 HE Airdrop
F-117	6	C-141	7 PERS Airdrop
F-15	12	C-130	19 PERS Airdrop
OA-37	18	C-130	3 Air Land
A-7	5	MC-130	3 Air Land
		C-5	2 Air Land
		HC-130	7 Air Land

TOTAL: 253

THE first call from a commander came at about 6:00 P.M., an hour before the 82nd's scheduled takeoff time, from Major General Jim Johnson, Commander of the 82nd Airborne Division: A severe ice storm had hit Pope Air Force Base and it would be impossible to launch all his troops as scheduled. The twenty-eight C-141 heavy drop aircraft had been loaded and pre-positioned at Charleston. No problem as far as they were concerned. The problem was with the troop-carrying C-141s. There was not enough de-icing equipment to launch the twenty personnel birds at one time. At this point, he had only eight ready to launch, and it would be three to four hours before he could launch the rest of the force.

I was not surprised when he asked for a delay, but I denied it. "Send those eight on," I told him, "and send the rest as soon as the others can be de-iced."

Of course, I knew there was no getting around a delay, which would mean that three key targets—Panama Viejo, Tinajitas, and Fort Cimarron—could not all be taken before daylight. Two of them, probably Tinajitas and Fort Cimarron, would have to be taken in the morning, which would likely mean more casualties. You have to adjust for the unforeseen in any complex operation.

MEANWHILE, a thick fog had moved in at MacDill Air Force Base in Tampa, where the tanker aircraft had been assembled. Though it was so thick that a truck had to lead each plane to the end of the runway for takeoff, all the aircraft launched on time.

Delaying H-hour for the entire operation would have resulted in serious consequences, as I well knew. Commanders are trained and entrusted to make these kinds of judgments, and to develop alternative plans.

Accordingly, I called Johnson back ten minutes after his call. "Your first priority," I told him, "is to take Panama Viejo, and if possible Tinajitas, before daylight. Fort Cimarron," which was farther from Panama City, "can be taken later in the day. I'll take responsibility for containing Tinajitas and Fort Cimarron by keeping AC-130s nearby until you can conduct your air assaults."

We knew in advance that the PDF had established a nest of sixteen heavy mortars near Tinajitas, which could range all of Panama City and Howard Air Force Base. For that reason, they had already been targeted for AC-130 strikes at H-hour, and afterward if required.

THOSE mortars had given us other concerns: Since the nineteen C-130s carrying Rangers to Rio Hato and Torrijos would have been in the air for seven hours, they'd be practically running on fumes when they made their drop. Because they were not air-refuelable, we had to have fuel for them in Panama; the plan was to land them at Howard—about forty miles from Rio Hato. But, because the PDF mortars might be firing on Howard, an alternative plan had to be developed. We therefore planned to land two C-5s on the civilian runway at Torrijos-Tocumen, where they could serve as "wet wing filling stations" for the C-130s, if necessary. The C-5s were to land immediately after the Rangers had secured the field and cleared the runway of obstacles.

As it turned out, we had no problem using Howard, but still used the C-5s for refueling helicopters, particularly those supporting the 82nd's three air assaults.

AS we got closer to H-hour, Downing and I monitored PDF command nets to determine if they had any inkling of our operation.

And then we got a kick in the gut.

At 1830 I got a call from Bragg: Dan Rather had just announced on the

CBS Evening News, *"U.S. military transport planes have left Fort Bragg, North Carolina, home of the Army's elite 82nd Airborne paratroopers. The Pentagon declines to say whether or not they are bound for Panama. It will say only that the Bragg-based XVIII Corps has been conducting what the Army calls an airborne readiness exercise."* And on the NBC Evening News, Ed Rabel reported, *"United States C-141 Starlifters flew into Panama this afternoon, one landing every ten minutes. At the same time these aircraft were arriving, security was tightened around the air base. U.S. soldiers could be seen in full combat gear on roads around the base."* At the end of his brief report, Rabel noted, *"No one here could confirm that these aircraft were part of a U.S. invasion group, but tensions on both sides are high this evening over the possibility of a U.S. strike."*

Washington had also received a report that a PDF soldier had overheard U.S. soldiers discussing H-hour, and had sent this information up the chain to Noriega; but I didn't believe it for a minute. All U.S. servicemen were locked up and preparing for the attack at the time when this was alleged to have happened.

However they got it—from reports in our media or otherwise—the PDF apparently picked up word of the operation, now only three hours away. At 10:00 P.M., our listeners began hearing conversations among PDF commanders that indicated they knew something was up. One PDF commander told another: "Tonight is the night, the ball game starts at one o'clock"; others called in their troops and ordered weapons to be issued. There were enough such indicators to convince me to recommend to Thurman that we should advance H-hour. My plan was to attack earlier with the troops already in Panama, to gain as much advantage as possible. The Rangers and the 82nd would just have to attack as scheduled.

I had first hoped to move H-hour ahead by thirty minutes, and Thurman approved that. But after checking again with Wayne Downing, who'd be running the three concurrent critical actions—rescue Kurt Muse, attack the Comandancia, and neutralize Patilla Airfield, Noriega's jet, and the presidential yacht—he and I realized that a thirty-minute advance might be pushing the envelope a bit. So we settled for fifteen minutes, which Thurman approved.

H-hour for all units in Panama was therefore set for 12:45 A.M.

TWENTY-SEVEN MINUTES TO GO

Now everything was on track. Most of the facilities that had to be protected had already been clandestinely secured. Special Forces reconnaissance teams had

been covertly inserted in the vicinity of the major targets where they could report the latest information. Units were loaded and ready to move.
Communications hot lines had long since been established to the major supporting commands—LANTCOM, SOCOM, the Air Mobility Command, and
of course our parent headquarters, SOUTHCOM, only a short distance away
in the tunnel at Quarry Heights, where General Thurman would remain the
first night.

Though sporadic gunfire could be heard throughout Panama City, by then
that was usually the case on any night.

As all troops well know, "Shit happens."

We didn't expect airliners at Torrijos-Tocumen after midnight. This night
turned out to be an exception. At 12:40 A.M., a Brazilian wide-body landed,
with more than three hundred people on board. At 0100 hours, when the
Rangers dropped, these people would either be inside the terminal getting
fleeced by the PDF and the customs agents or still unloading. Either way, we
had problems.

I called Downing to tell him to prepare for a mass hostage situation at the
airport.

"We'll be standing by," he answered. "But remember, we have four rifle companies in that battalion, and one has responsibility for securing the terminal
and the control tower. They should be able to handle the situation."

"Let's hope so," I said.

WITH only minutes remaining, combat was fast approaching. The AC-130
gunships and Apaches were airborne and ready to start preparatory fires on key
objectives. The four Sheridan tanks brought in on October 15 were now approaching firing positions on Anton Hill. They'd engage the Comandancia
with their main guns at precisely 0045 hours. Twenty-five Special Forces soldiers from Task Force Black were aboard three Blackhawk helicopters en route
to secure the Pacora River bridge, which was critical in keeping Battalion
2000 out of the fight at the airport.

During the planning phase, we had ruled out destroying the bridge. It was
the only way for people in much of eastern Panama to get to Panama City. That
meant the bridge had to be secured and protected.

All units in Panama were "locked and loaded" (rounds chambered and
weapons cocked) and moving to their assault objectives. Once again, men had

to resort to a barbaric way of settling differences. Hopefully, the dying would last no longer than about four hours.

During the final minutes before H-hour, I learned from Thurman that the name of the operation had been changed to Operation JUST CAUSE. General Jim Lindsay of USSOCOM had called General Kelley: "Do you want your grandchildren to ask you, 'What were things like back there in BLUE SPOON?' " And Kelley had agreed: BLUE SPOON didn't sound like anything anybody would ever want to be proud of.

"I sure am glad Jim Lindsay made that call," I told Thurman, "because what we're about to spill blood over certainly is a 'just cause.'"

XI

PANAMA: OPERATION JUST CAUSE

At precisely 0045 hours, two EF-111 aircraft jammed PDF tactical communications, special operations EC-130s began to override Panamanian radio and TV stations and broadcast the U.S. message to the Panamanian people, and all units began engaging their targets.

Special Forces snipers, who had painstakingly worked their way into strategic overwatch positions, also began systematically to eliminate PDF sentries with highly accurate sniping. The sniper teams were led by Sergeant Major Pat Hurley (later killed in the Gulf War in a nighttime helicopter crash during a raging sandstorm as he was returning from a behind-the-lines mission in Iraq).

At the Modelo Prison (part of the fifteen-building Comandancia compound), the assault was under way to rescue Kurt Muse. Six operators from Task Force Green (the Army special mission unit), supported by AH-6 Little Bird gunships and OH-6 lift ships, made the short jump from the pods of their helicopters down to the rooftop. During their approach to the prison, the gunships cleaned off four .50-caliber machine guns from the roof of a high-rise in the compound that housed one of Noriega's Dignity Battalions. An AC-130 gunship blasted the Comandancia with its 105mm howitzer. Green tracers from PDF guns were flying everywhere.

The operators entered from the roof and moved through the totally dark building down to the second floor, neutralized the guards as they went, blew the cell door, and were back on the roof ready to lift off with their "precious cargo" (now outfitted with a flak vest and Kevlar helmet)—all within six minutes.

A few moments later, Wayne Downing called Stiner on the hot line. "We got our man," Downing said, "but the helicopter may have been shot down as it was lifting off the roof."

"When you get it sorted out, let me know what the situation is."

Downing called back in less than five minutes. "Don't know whether the helicopter was shot down or whether it just had too much weight to lift off the building. It appears that it sort of fell off the building and came down on the street. I am arranging a rescue operation now, and will keep you posted."

Downing had been both an armor brigade and a Ranger Regiment Commander, and brought some unique skills to the mission. As a Ranger, he emphasized surprise, agility, and cunning, but he also appreciated the speed and overwhelming firepower of armor. During the planning, he'd been assigned the mechanized infantry battalion for the assault on the Comandancia and Carcelo Modelo, and for that mission received the platoon of Sheridan light tanks and the Marine Corps LAVs. From this force, he tailored a quick-reaction element; LAVs and armored personnel carriers would carry his highly trained special mission forces—some of whom had never been in an armored vehicle. No problem, they were Special Forces and adaptable. Major Howard Humble, a former mechanized infantry company commander in Germany, and now an SF officer, got the force organized and moving into the streets of Panama City that night and led them with distinction for the next five days.

Downing called this force his "Panzer Gruppe" and positioned it as a re-action force at various places in the city. It could go faster than helicopters, hit places they couldn't, and could be broken up into several elements for greater flexibility (to find their way around Panama City, they used a map they got from a gas station). The APCs' .50-caliber and 20mm machine guns were small beer in a major war, but in fights against lightly armed forces inside a city, they provided tremendous firepower.

One of the Panzer Gruppe elements was sent to rescue Muse and *his* rescuers. Once they'd picked them up, they first took them to a junior high school for transloading to a helicopter, and then on to the field hospital at Howard Air Force Base for treatment. Here it was learned what had happened: The helicopter carrying Muse and his rescuers had been overloaded and caught a skid on a power line, causing it to crash in the street. Once down, the pilot had been able to move the helo to a parking lot, from where he'd attempted to take off. The helo had gotten about thirty feet off the ground when it was shot down, landing on its side. Three operators had been injured in the crash, including one already shot in the leg. They'd formed a perimeter to protect Muse and had been engaged in an intense firefight until they'd been rescued.

At about the same time all this was happening, heavy fire at the Comandancia brought down a second special operations helicopter, which crash-landed inside the compound and slid up against the security fence surrounding the Comandancia headquarters. Though neither pilot was injured, they knew they couldn't last long in the withering fire. They jumped out of what was left of the aircraft, threw their flight vests on the fence, climbed over, and crawled beneath a portico that covered an entranceway.

As they huddled there, a PDF soldier—perhaps the first prisoner of the war—came crawling out of the grass with his hands over his head. "I want to go with you," he called out in broken English. They took him in.

A Panzer Gruppe squad rescued all three.

The following morning, a third light observation helicopter was shot down and went into the Canal on the Atlantic side. Unfortunately the crew was lost.

At H-hour, the four Sheridan tanks and an AC-130 pounded the Comandancia's main headquarters and the PDF barracks, while the lead battalion of the 193rd Brigade moved down Fourth of July Avenue, turned left into a street dominated by high-rise buildings, and began its assault into the compound. The way ahead of them was blocked by heavy trucks and other obstacles, and most of the PDF they could see were wearing civilian clothes—mainly Levis. It was clear they'd been alerted in advance—they planned to fight for a while and then fade into the populace in civilian clothes when the going got tough.

Some of the heaviest fighting of the operation followed.

The lead battalion pushing through with their APCs instantly came under very heavy fire from windows, ledges, and rooftops, and from civilian vehicles sandbagged as fighting positions. For the next two hours, heavy fighting continued. By 3:00 A.M., the Comandancia was on fire, with smoke so thick the Sheridans could not see their targets, but the 193rd had formed a cordon around the compound and begun operations to clear each building.

As a result of a PSYOPs broadcast that designated a local street for safe passage, six truckloads of PDF had surrendered; but the three security companies remaining inside the compound were still putting up stiff resistance.

Since he had no idea what to expect once his troops got inside the Comandancia, Stiner decided to bring in a Ranger company the following afternoon to do the detailed search of the building. The company was from 3rd Ranger Battalion and had jumped the night before with the 1st Ranger Battalion for the H-hour assault on Torrijos-Tocumen International Airport.

As PDF and Dignity Battalions fled the area outside the cordoned compound, they set fire to the nearby slum of Chorillo to slow the advance of the U.S. troops.

AT H-hour, another Task Force Bayonet battalion, the 1st Battalion, 508th airborne infantry, launched an assault against Fort Amador less than two miles away, with the aim of neutralizing the PDF's 5th Infantry Company. Since Fort Amador was a treaty-designated "joint use" post—with both Panamanians and Americans living or working there—this would be a delicate operation. The PDF occupied all the buildings on the south side of the facility, near the Canal, while American military families lived directly across the golf course fairway—among them, Marc Cisneros and his family. Cisneros was well-known and respected by most Panamanians, and for this reason Noriega hated him. Cisneros played a large part in the coming action.

"This was the first time in my military career," Carl Stiner recalls, "that family members of U.S. servicemen would find themselves without warning right in the middle of a combat environment."

Because it was the Christmas holiday season, the PDF had set up life-size nativity scenes near their barracks—but nativity scenes with a difference, with machine-gun positions established directly beneath each of them. The guns pointed directly across the fairway at the quarters of the U.S. military families.

The battalion commander's attack plan called for infiltrating most of his headquarters company onto the installation before H-hour. At H-hour, two rifle companies, augmented by a 105mm howitzer, would conduct an air assault directly behind the quarters area occupied by U.S. families. As they landed, they would immediately establish a security perimeter around the U.S. housing area and then attack the PDF barracks less than a hundred yards away, one company from the north, and the other from the south.

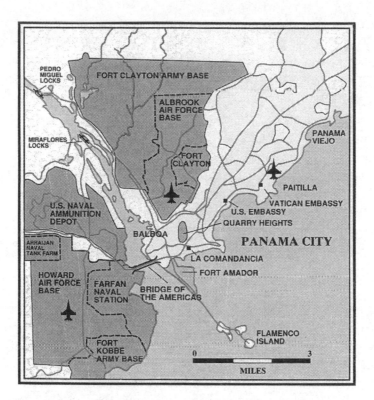

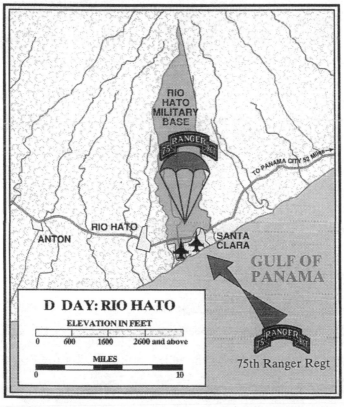

D DAY: RIO HATO

ELEVATION IN FEET

0	600	1600	2600 and above

MILES

0	10

75th Ranger Regt

OPERATION JUST CAUSE

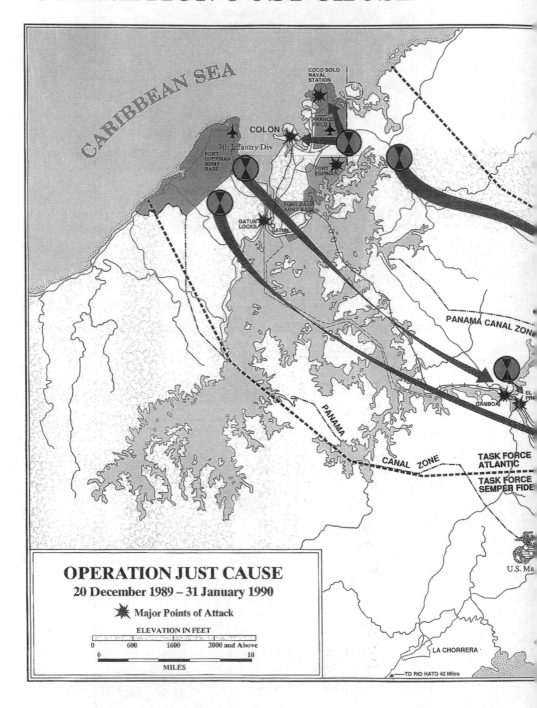

OPERATION JUST CAUSE

20 December 1989 – 31 January 1990

✸ Major Points of Attack

ELEVATION IN FEET

| 0 | 600 | 1600 | 2000 and Above |

0 ————————————————— 10

MILES

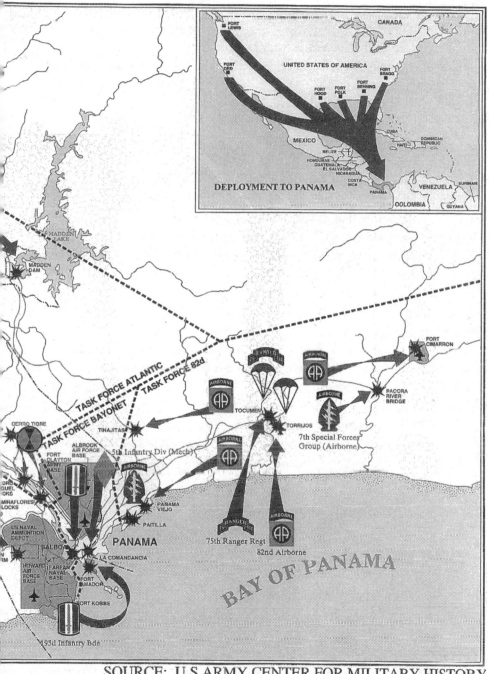

DEPLOYMENT TO PANAMA

SOURCE: U.S ARMY CENTER FOR MILITARY HISTORY

Another company from the battalion would secure the Balboa Yacht Club on the south side of the peninsula and directly behind the PDF barracks. The Club was a frequent gathering place for PDF officers, and several boats of the PDF Navy were usually docked nearby.

Once the assault troops were in position, and the families warned to take cover, the battalion commander was ready to launch his operation. He decided to hold off on building-clearing operations, however, until he'd tried PSYOPs. From time to time, he fired the howitzer on vacant buildings—to make sure the PDF knew he was there and meant business—while his broadcast teams sent out a surrender message. At first light, building-clearing operations would police up anyone left.

It didn't take much persuasion. Moments after the howitzer started firing, PDF were bolting out of their buildings and down to the water, throwing in their weapons. A total of 140 PDF surrendered or were captured. Moments after that, the night was quiet—except for the broadcasts and the occasional firing of the howitzer.

The next day, clearing proceeded, punctuated by sporadic sniping. That ended at 3:00 P.M., when Marc Cisneros talked the last sixteen holdouts in the gymnasium into surrendering. Fort Amador was secure.

During interrogations, it was learned that most PDF officers had abandoned their troops even before H-hour and left them to defend themselves. On the whole, PDF officers were a bad lot. Most were on the take and skimming the pay from their soldiers.

Meanwhile, the company securing the Balboa Yacht Club launched its operation. In attempting to escape, many PDF troops had disguised themselves as waiters, but their combat boots gave them away, and forty-seven prisoners were captured.

No one who knew anything at all about Manuel Noriega had serious questions about his character. He was a seriously evil human being—right up there with Saddam Hussein in the bad guy department. Blessedly, accidents of birth had placed him in a small, weak country, which limited his evildoing opportunities. That said, no American involved in Operation JUST CAUSE had any idea how bad Noriega *really* was until searches of his residences and offices began to reveal the depths of his degradation.

At Fort Amador, Noriega maintained a set of offices, which U.S. forces searched at about noon. Marc Cisneros was there to make sure this was done properly. Carl Stiner describes some of the "delights" it contained:

"In Noriega's desk, in the top right-hand drawer, they found some of the rawest, most hideously disgusting pornographic videos you can imagine. In the left-hand drawer were photo portfolios of PDF atrocities against political prisoners—pictures of tortures, castrations, beatings, flayings, executions, mass rapes, and much worse. On a wall was a life-size silhouette target—President Bush and Marc Cisneros with bullet holes through their heads.

"We found similar materials at the offices of many high-ranking Noriega henchmen."

TASK FORCE WHITE

Task Force White, commanded by Navy SEAL Captain "John," consisting primarily of Navy SEAL Special Boat units, was also carrying out its three major H-hour missions, to: take out of action Noriega's personal yacht and the PDF patrol boats in Balboa Harbor, at the Pacific Ocean entrance to the Canal; block the runway at Paitilla Airport in downtown Panama City; and isolate PDF forces at Flamenco Island, a mile or so out in the Bay of Panama.

Two hours before H-hour, a pair of dive teams in combat rubber raiding craft left Rodman Naval Station for Pier 18 in Balboa Harbor, where Noriega's yacht was docked. A fire support team, armed with .50-caliber machine guns and a 40mm grenade launcher, came along in another boat, just in case they ran into trouble. The boats moved slowly and quietly, without a wake, until they reached the drop-off point about 150 meters from the yacht. The divers entered the water carrying two twenty-pound charges in haversacks, then swam at a depth of twenty feet, following a compass heading. The two teams of four divers arrived beneath the yacht thirty minutes before H-hour, placed their charges on the two main propeller shafts, and connected them with det cord. They set the timers to explode at 0045—H-hour.

Just as they finished, the yacht's engine started; the divers raced away and hid behind the pilings at Pier 17. Moments later, their charges went off, and they had to hang on for dear life during the buffeting that followed. As soon as things got calm, they swam underwater back across the Canal to the rendezvous point. The yacht was out of action.

AT H-hour, three platoons of SEALs—ninety-three men—were landing at the southern end of Paitilla Airfield in combat rubber raiding craft. Moving slowly and deliberately, covering each other as they went, two platoons headed north on the western side of the field; the third and a mortar section moved on the eastern side.

As they approached the hangar where Noriega's jet was parked, the lead team, on the western side, came under intense fire from the hangars, killing one SEAL and wounding others. Worse, they were in the open and exposed, and their supporting AC-130 gunship could not fire without endangering the wounded. The second platoon on the western side was ordered in as reinforcement. When it arrived, the PDF opened up again; the SEALs' M-16s had little effect against the PDF, who were firing from concrete block buildings.

The battle lasted for another thirty minutes, but by using 66mm LAWs and 40mm grenade launchers, the SEALs finally prevailed, and disabled Noriega's jet. In the process, three SEALs had died and several others had been severely wounded.

THE third Task Force White mission was to isolate Flamenco Island, the home of the USEAT, Noriega's elite special operations force. The best way to keep the USEAT out of the fight was to block the causeway from Panama City to the island, which was done by special boat patrols.

The SEALs and special boat units accomplished other important maritime work as well, not only in the Canal but also in the anchorages in the Caribbean and Pacific where ships were waiting to transit. Several of these vessels were boarded in stirring fashion, as the SEALs chased down the Noriega infrastructure and Dignity Battalions.

On one raid, Captain "Rick's" special-mission SEALs were in hot pursuit of some Dignity Battalion thugs attempting to board a ship at anchor at the Colon dock. Supporting the SEALs were fast-attack vessels, and one of them caught the Dignity Battalion guys climbing the captain's ladder and calmly shot the ladder off its stanchion supports with highly accurate 40mm grenade fire. The thugs landed in the water and were quickly policed up by the SEALs.

TASK FORCE BLACK

Task Force Black was commanded by special forces Colonel Jake Jacobelly, an old hand in Latin America and Panama.

Major Higgins, a tall, thin West Pointer, who spoke fluent Spanish, with twenty-four special forces officers and NCOs, had the mission to secure the Pacora River bridge and block Battalion 2000.

As his troops were loading onto three Blackhawks at Albrook Air Base, intelligence came in that a convoy had left Fort Cimarron, headed for Torrijos-Tocumen. The team quickly finished loading and raced for the bridge. Fifteen minutes later, they could see the PDF convoy's headlights as the pilots swung around and landed about a hundred meters from the southwest end of the bridge. The team dismounted, climbed the bank up to the road, and ran as hard as they could to secure the bridge before the convoy began crossing.

When they reached it, the lead vehicle was no more than a hundred meters away. While the team rushed to establish security positions on each side of the road, an officer and two NCOs fired a 66mm light antitank weapon, a more powerful AT-4, and a squad automatic weapon at the lead vehicle, stopping it in its tracks.

Meanwhile, the Air Force combat controller called in the AC-130 gunship on station in their area, and it was overhead within minutes. The pilot had an easy time identifying the convoy, since it never occurred to them to turn their lights off; but even without lights, infrared equipment made the vehicles and personnel visible. Before engaging, the pilot warned Higgins that his troops guarding the southwest side of the bridge were in his marginal safety limits: Would he accept friendly casualties? Higgins told him to go ahead, and the AC-130 started blasting away. As it fired, it illuminated the area with its infrared searchlight, so the SF personnel could see with their night-vision gear.

The PDF soldiers scrambled out of the trucks and took up firing positions in a treeline.

By 0200 hours, the AC-130 was running low on fuel and had to go off station; another AC-130 immediately moved in.

In the meantime, the PDF, wearing gas masks and using riot-control gas, charged the bridge, but the fire from Higgins's men broke the charge, and a number of PDF jumped over the side in desperation.

By dawn, the fighting had subsided, and Higgins's little force were undisputed masters of the bridge—with no casualties. Meanwhile, a quick-reaction force (QRF) from Task Force Black arrived by helicopter and landed on the other side of the bridge to make a sweep of the destroyed convoy; the team that had been fighting all night remained in position as security.

On the bridge, they found eight dead and several others wounded, who were treated by Special Forces medics at the scene; they found and captured several other PDF hiding in a house off the road; and the few who escaped later ran into the Rangers and the 82nd Airborne Division at the airport.

During interrogations, it was learned that the convoy had been transporting more than fifty soldiers from Battalion 2000's heavy weapons company, led by the company executive officer, and armed with 81mm mortars, 90mm recoilless weapons, and .30-caliber machine guns. According to the executive officer, they were on their way to Panama City to put down "some sort of civil disturbance."

Later that morning, a two-and-a-half-ton truck flying a white flag arrived from Fort Cimarron to claim their dead.

At 3:45 P.M., a scout platoon from the 82nd Airborne Division on the way to Fort Cimarron linked up with Higgins and his men.

At 5:30 P.M., Higgins and his twenty-four Green Berets and twenty POWs were extracted by helicopter back to Albrook Air Force Base. Mission accomplished.

JAKE Jacobelly's Special Forces teams from Task Force Black conducted three other essential H-hour missions or follow-on activities:

Tinajitas Recon for the 82nd Airborne: At 7:00 P.M. the previous evening, a four-man reconnaissance team had started cross-country on foot to place eyes on the Tinajitas Cuartel (Barracks), the 1st Infantry company, and the nest of sixteen mortars near Tinajitas. The team was in position by 1:00 A.M., and reported their findings to General Kinser at the 82nd command post for relay to Jim Johnson as he approached his airdrop. They passed reports on the mortars directly to Stiner's headquarters.

Cimarron Cuartel: At 9:00 P.M. the previous evening, another four-man reconnaissance team had been inserted by Blackhawk five kilometers outside the Cimarron Cuartel to report on Battalion 2000. This team reported the convoy movement toward the Pacora River bridge.

Cerro Azul TV II Antennae: The jamming and override broadcast beginning at 12:45 A.M. had successfully overridden all but one TV station—TV Station II, Noriega's primary media outlet. When attempts to jam it proved unsuccessful, an eighteen-man SF team was deployed just after H-hour to disable it temporarily.

The obvious way to disable a TV station is to knock down the antenna tower, but Stiner's people only wanted the station off the air for days, not months. For that reason, the team fast-roped from helicopters onto the station compound and removed a critical electronics module.

TASK FORCE ATLANTIC

Task Force Atlantic, on the Caribbean side of the Canal, was commanded by Colonel Keith Kellogg, and consisted of two infantry battalions, a two-hundred-man aviation section with Huey helos and Cobra gunships, a Vulcan air defense weapons section, an MP company, and an engineer company. One of the battalions—the 3rd Battalion, 504th Infantry—was actually from the 82nd Airborne Division. It had arrived on December 10 to attend the Jungle Operations Training Center as part of a normal training rotation, which it was scheduled to complete before Christmas. The battalion was not aware that its graduation exercise would involve combat.

Task Force Atlantic had several complex missions, to: isolate and clear Colon; neutralize the PDF 8th Infantry Company, stationed at Fort Espinar in Colon; neutralize the PDF 1st Marine Battalion at the Coco Solo Naval Station, east of Colon; disable the multiengine aircraft on France Field, just south of Coco Solo; capture the PDF patrol boats at the ports; protect the Madden Dam; seize the electrical distribution center at Cerro Tigre; secure the vital Gatun Locks; and free political prisoners, including Americans, now held in El Renacer prison, midway across the isthmus.

None of these was easy. Fort Espinar and Coco Solo were both joint-use facilities, with U.S. military dependents living next to PDF soldiers. Coco Solo had once housed the School of the Americas and was a particularly complex target, because the Cristobal High School and the Coco Solo Hospital were also located there. The PDF force at Coco Solo, the Panamanian Naval Infantry Battalion, was noted for arrogance.

At H-hour, loudspeakers from C Company, 4th Battalion, 17th Infantry broadcast surrender messages to the PDF Naval Infantry Battalion at Coco Solo; the offer was refused, and the PDF countered with a heavy volume of fire from their barracks area. Their defiance did not last long. After they were given the chance to observe the total destruction of their headquarters buildings by the Vulcan weapons systems and realized their barracks was next, the white flag began waving.

After this demonstration of U.S. firepower, clearing Colon turned out to be far easier than expected. Instead of stiff resistance, the 3rd Brigade en-

tered the city of 60,000 on December 22 with the majority of its two battalions and was met by thousands of cheering Panamanians. Four hundred
PDF soldiers, mainly from the 8th Infantry Company, surrendered during
the clearing operation.

T H E Renacer prison, located on a peninsula in the Canal, consisted of an
outer layer of buildings, guard towers, and Cyclone fences; and an inner
layer—the actual prison—consisting of two large concrete block buildings
within an inner fence. This was guarded by twenty to twenty-five troops
from Battalion 2000, intermixed with the prisoners and living in the same
buildings—which made the prisoner rescue even more difficult.

The rescue mission was assigned to C Company of the 82nd's 3rd
Battalion, 504th Infantry: An amphibious force of two rifle platoons would
come down the Canal in a pair of Army landing craft—a two-hour ride
from Fort Sherman, near Colon—and neutralize the prison's outer ring of
defense and provide fire support for the platoon that was to be landed inside the prison compound. Cobra helicopters would take out the guard
towers, while another rifle platoon in Huey helicopters landed inside the
prison compound.

Although the plan worked perfectly, it was not easy. The defenders put
up a strong fight, using CS (tear) gas as well as light weapons, but by 6:00
A.M., the prison was in U.S. hands, and the prisoners—two American jour-
nalists, five political prisoners from the March '88 coup attempt, and fifty-
seven actual criminals—were unharmed.

Task Force Atlantic now controlled all its assigned objectives. Elements
of the Task Force handled their other assignments as planned.

TASK FORCE SEMPER FI

Task Force Semper Fi, under Colonel Charles E. Richardson, had a very
broad mission, all in the areas just west of the Canal, to: secure and protect
Howard Air Force Base, the U.S. Navy ammunition depot, Rodman Naval
Station, and the Arraijan tank farm; secure and defend the Bridge of the
Americas; block PDF reinforcements from the southwest, and neutralize
the PDF and Dignity Battalions in zone; capture the PDF stations at Vera
Cruz and Arraijan; and neutralize the headquarters of the 10th Military
Zone in La Chorrera, fifteen miles west of Panama City. The task force ac-
complished all its missions.

Torrijos-Tocumen Airport

On the military—Torrijos—side of the airfield were stationed approximately two hundred soldiers of the PDF 2nd Rifle Company, armed with three .50-caliber machine guns and a ZPU-4 antiaircraft gun, 150 men of the Panamanian Air Force, and thirty airport security guards.

Lieutenant Colonel Robert Wagner and the 1st Battalion, 75th Rangers, had the mission to neutralize these forces and secure the Ceremi PDF military recreation center at the La Siesta Military Resort hotel, a quarter mile away. Meanwhile, C Company of the 3rd Ranger Battalion would secure the civilian terminal. Because the 82nd Airborne Division brigade was jumping forty-five minutes behind them, and Battalion 2000 was only forty-five minutes up the road (if they could successfully cross the Pacora River bridge), the Rangers had a very brief time window. They had to work fast.

At precisely 0100 hours—even as the Brazilian airliner was unloading at the main terminal—an AC-130 gunship engaged the 2nd Infantry Company's machine-gun and antiaircraft positions, and an AH-6 gunship began firing at the company compound's guard shack and another guard shack in front of the civilian terminal, eliminating the PDF guards.

Five minutes earlier, five C-141s from the States had heavy-dropped twelve jeeps, twelve motorcycles, and two HMMWVs on the Tocumen drop zone. Three minutes after the AC-130 began firing, seven more C-141s dropped Wagner and his battalion, followed immediately by C Company of the 3rd Ranger Battalion, dropping from four C-130s. More than seven hundred Rangers had landed in minutes, 150 of them on the tarmac by the main terminal. Many passengers from the Brazilian jet were welcomed to Panama by their "privileged" view of parachutes falling all around their airplane.

The Ranger battalion assembled, moved on foot out to their objectives, and quickly overwhelmed the resistance offered by the 2nd Infantry Company. The psychological impact of the AC-130 was too much for the PDF defenders; most tried to escape, including forty helicopter pilots in a barracks at Torrijos. When they looked out their windows and saw parachuting Rangers, they took off to the hills. They surrendered five days later, on Christmas Day.

C Company's plan was to move three platoons into the terminal from different directions, then each platoon would cover one of the floors; their frequent rehearsals had not, however, prepared them for an airliner unloading 376 passengers. That meant their immediate priority was the passengers' safety.

The Rangers entering the building found most of the passengers in the terminal waiting area—and no PDF. The building was dark. Power was knocked out by a grenade thrown into the terminal's generator by the Rangers. The Rangers continued clearing operations wearing night-vision goggles.

Most of the doors on the first floor were locked, and the Ranger squad moved on until they found a steel door that opened. The lead element stepped inside, somebody fired a shot, and a woman started screaming in English, "Don't shoot!"

The Rangers pulled back to take stock. There were obviously hostages and PDF inside, but it was hard to tell how many.

A Ranger sergeant wearing night-vision goggles slipped back inside and saw what looked to be four hostages—two American women and a Panamanian woman and her baby—and maybe a dozen PDF soldiers.

The sergeant came out to report, just as the company commander was arriving, prepared to talk sense to the PDF, but when that didn't work, he made an ultimatum, "Come out or you'll all be killed," at which point the PDF put down their weapons and came out. None of the hostages was hurt.

As the 3rd Platoon approached the terminal, PDF fired at them through a plateglass window. The platoon raced into the building and isolated the PDF in a men's room. The squad leader moved inside to take a look, but PDF hiding in the stalls shot him three times. His troops dragged him out and tossed in two hand grenades, but the PDF were protected by the metal stall doors. The Rangers then made a concerted assault. As they entered the room, a PDF shot one of them three times in the head (his Kevlar helmet saved him); the Rangers then killed two PDF; another PDF soldier jumped out of a stall and tried to snatch a Ranger weapon; another Ranger shot him in the head and killed him; another PDF jumped out and grabbed a Ranger around the neck; they slammed each other up against the wall and fought hand to hand. The Ranger kicked the PDF through a window, and he landed one floor down in front of a Ranger private who had just taken up a firing position with an M-60 machine gun. Caught by surprise, he cut the PDF soldier in half as he tried to pull a pistol.

———

TWO and a half hours after the jump, Torrijos Tocumen airport was secured.

Inside the terminal, the Rangers separated detainees—civilian passengers from the Brazilian airliner—from the prisoners, and flex-cuffed (using flexible plastic handcuffs) the prisoners. The detainees were asked to wait in the terminal until order was restored. When some of the children became hungry a few hours later, the Rangers arranged a meal with the restaurant manager and paid for it themselves.

AT 2:08 A.M., the first 82nd Airborne troopers began dropping on their drop zones—twenty-three minutes late because of the ice storm at Fort Bragg. The rest of the drop was also delayed by the storm, but the entire 82nd was finally on the ground by 5:15 A.M.

By 10:00 A.M., the 82nd had assumed responsibility for the security of the airfield.

LATER, it was learned from one of Noriega's bodyguards that a Ranger roadblock near Torrijos-Tocumen had narrowly missed capturing the dictator—and saving the United States a lot of trouble. Here is how it happened:

The day before, after Noriega's entourage from Colon had split and a decoy had gone on to the Comandancia, Noriega had been taken to the rest camp at Ceremi for a date with a prostitute. By the time he got there, he was reportedly in less than total control, having consumed about two fifths of scotch by then.

The first inklings that his country was being invaded came when he heard the AC-130 and attack helicopters firing on Torrijos-Tocumen, soon followed by the roar of transports dropping Rangers.

Moments after the firing started, Noriega ran out of the hotel, wearing nothing but his red bikini underwear, and jumped into the back of his car. "The Americans are after me!" he cried. "Let's get out of here."

Down the road, they ran into the Ranger roadblock.

"My God," he screamed, "they know where I am! They dropped these guys right on top of me!"

When a car ahead of them hit the roadblock and began drawing fire from the Rangers, Noriega's car made a quick 180-degree turnaround and took a back road into Panama City. Afterward, Noriega was so "shook," it took a day to get him calmed down.

AT one time that first night, the JSOTF had 171 aircraft in the skies over Panama City. No one had a midair collision, and no one ran out of fuel. The AC-130 gunships kept twenty-four-hour coverage for ninety-six straight hours, using their sensors, weapons, and searchlights to intimidate the PDF and support the SF, Rangers, SEALs, and the conventional forces.

USAF special operations forces in Panama—the 1st Special Operations Wing (SOW)—were commanded by Colonel (later Major General) George Gray and composed of MH-53J Pave Low helos, AC-130 gunships, MH-60G Blackhawks with refuel probes, MC-130 Combat Talon aircraft for air-drop and penetration of heavily defended airspace, and EC-130 aircraft used for PSYOPs, radio, and TV.

RIO HATO

While the 1st Ranger Battalion was parachuting down on Torrijos-Tocumen, the other two battalions of the 75th Regiment were making a parachute assault at Rio Hato, west of Panama City.

They had launched seven hours earlier from Fort Benning, Georgia, in seventeen C-130s of the 317th airlift wing, stationed at Pope Air Force Base. Each of the first fifteen aircraft was crammed with sixty-five Rangers (C-130s normally carried fifty-two fully loaded troops), jammed tighter than rush-hour subways. Forget about moving. Forget about walking down the aisle to a "toilet." Five-gallon cans were passed around under people's legs. Because there wasn't room to rig, everyone had donned their equipment before boarding. Each Ranger carried on his lap a sixty-to-one-hundred-pound rucksack loaded with ammunition and supplies—including at least one 66mm light antitank weapon (LAW). As it turned out, the LAWs came in very handy.

At H-hour, F-117 stealth bombers dropped two 2,000-pound bombs, with time-delay fuses, 150 meters from the 6th and 7th Company barracks. For the next three minutes, Apache helicopters, AH-6 helicopter gunships, and an AC-130 gunship fired on antiaircraft weapons positions around the airfield.

At H+3 minutes, the lead C-130 crossed the drop zone at 500 feet, trailed immediately by the C-130s dropping the Rangers, followed shortly by two C-130s dropping four jeeps and four motorcycles.

As the Rangers started their descent, they could see green machine gun tracers crossing the drop zone—or worse, whizzing up toward them. Thirteen of the fifteen C-130s received multiple hits. And a few Rangers were also hit as they descended. The bombs and the preparatory fire had had an effect—two hundred cadets were later found hiding under their bunks—but not enough. Most of the PDF 6th and 7th Companies had managed to deploy around the airfield, and were coming at the landing Rangers in CG-150 armored cars and other military vehicles with machine guns blasting; a .50-caliber machine gun on the rock archway at the main gate raked the drop zone.

From all indications, they had been alerted before the attack, and they were good soldiers. They did what good soldiers do.

The Rangers did not take this quietly; Rangers are as passive as blowtorches. As they slipped out of their chutes and assembled for their assaults, they fired at the PDF vehicles with their LAWs, and knocked several out even before moving on to their assigned assault objectives. They knocked out three trucks this way, one of them a fuel tanker that burned for hours.

In one of the stranger moments of that night, a Ranger's parachute was snagged by a fleeing PDF two-and-a-half-ton truck, which dragged him across the drop zone, with the Ranger yelling for help. His call was answered when a comrade coolly put a LAW rocket into the truck cab at 150 meters—a long shot for a moving target.

While all this was happening, Colonel Buck Kernan, the Ranger regimental commander, was single-handedly shutting down power at the airfield—though not exactly on purpose.

During his descent, he'd passed through the field's power lines. When he landed, his parachute was tangled in the lines and in flames. As he pulled the chute free, he dragged a light pole onto the power lines supplying the camp—shorting out the entire airfield complex. He quickly detached from his parachute harness, and found himself on the edge of the bullfighting ring in the center of the camp.

Meanwhile, the regimental sergeant major, Chief Sergeant Major Leon Guerrero, who had jumped after Kernan, was floating down above him watching all of this, worried that the colonel was badly injured. But when he saw Kernan climb out of the ring and had determined his boss was okay, the only thing he could do was break into laughter. Kernan instantly took charge and rallied his troops.

Colonel Kernan's plan for the takedown for Rio Hato called for two AC-130 gunships, one Army Apache, and two AH-6 helicopter gunships to be orbiting near Rio Hato before the troop-carrying C-130s arrived. At precisely 0100 hours, they engaged known antiaircraft weapons positions and other preselected targets in the Rio Hato complex, with great results. The Rangers started dropping at precisely 0103 hours.

Once on the ground, 2nd/75th Ranger Battalion had the mission of neutralizing the 6th and 7th PDF Companies, while 3rd/75th Ranger isolated the airfield, cleared the NCO Academy, the camp headquarters, the communications center, the motor pool, and the airfield operating complex.

Although the complex was defended by some of Noriega's elite, these were no match for Rangers. Once on the ground, the Rangers attacking assigned objectives with platoon- and squad-size elements quickly overwhelmed the PDF, killing 34 and capturing 278, along with thousands of weapons.

After an hour and fifty-three minutes of tough, close-quarters fighting, Rio Hato was secured, resistance had ceased, and supply aircraft had started landing.

ONE Ranger mission was to search Noriega's "Farralon" beach house on the airfield's southern approach to the airfield. It was unoccupied. Rangers from Lieutenant Colonel Al Maestas' 2d Ranger Battalion found the large double-glass door locked. The Rangers debated how to enter the luxurious home. Their solution? They backed off and shot a LAW rocket into the door, shattering it into nano-pieces. (Troops in the JSOTF later called LAWs "the Ranger key.")

Again, vast quantities of pornography were found.

TURNING LAWs into an entry device is typical of Rangers. They are not subtle. Several days later, the Rangers moved into Panama City and began establishing checkpoints and traffic control.

About 10:30 one night, a Ranger squad was manning a major intersection. This checkpoint had been set up with typical Ranger efficiency, and in depth. The block was manned by three Rangers, supported in overwatch by a 90mm recoilless rifle and an M-60 machine gun.

A car approached, slowed, then accelerated and burst through the barriers.

No screwing around with the Rangers. The 90mm immediately engaged, the sedan exploded with a direct hit, and the M-60 hosed down the flaming wreck just to make sure. Inside were PDF soldiers, all dead, and several open bottles of whiskey. They'd been drunk when they ran the block.

The story quickly made the rounds of the JSOTF. Somebody drew a cartoon poster of a Ranger gunner destroying a sedan; its caption read: "RADD!—Rangers Against Drunk Drivers."

TASK FORCE PACIFIC

Though the ice storm at Pope Air Force Base had taken its toll, the twenty heavy-drop and three CDS birds (C-141s) from Charleston were unaffected, and arrived at Torrijos-Tocumen on schedule at 1:45 A.M. carrying most of the equipment the 82nd would use in Panama: seventy-two HMMWVs, most of them equipped with .50-caliber machine guns; eight Sheridan M-551 armored assault vehicles; four 105mm artillery pieces; and several pieces of engineer equipment. Twenty-six minutes later, eight C-141s arrived with paratroopers. General Johnson, his Division Assault CP, and his brigade and battalion commanders flew in with the first eight birds. An hour after that, five more birds dropped. The last seven dropped at 0515 hours, completing the Division Ready Brigade of more than 2,000 paratroopers.

The first division objective was Panama Viejo in eastern Panama City. Stationed there were the PDF 1st Cavalry Squadron, primarily a ceremonial unit with approximately eighty horses, and a 170-man detachment from Noriega's elite and fiercely loyal special operations antiterrorist unit (USEAT), equipped with V-300 armored assault vehicles and antiaircraft weapons. The job of taking this target had been given to the 2nd Battalion, 504th Infantry.

Since the entire DRB had been cross-loaded among the twenty C-141 personnel birds—normal practice in an airborne operation to spread the risk—and all the arrivals were staggered, the entire 2nd/504th did not assemble for the air assault until most of the personnel planes had dropped. And it was nearly daylight when the first lift of the 2nd/504th launched for Panama Viejo, with eleven Blackhawks carrying thirty-five troopers each, supported by two Cobra gunships and two Apaches. They landed relatively unopposed at 6:45 A.M., and quickly set about establishing a security perimeter around their landing zone.

The second lift landed just to their north, behind the barracks. As the Blackhawks approached the landing zone, they took heavy small-arms fire, and two lift ships were hit. Though the two ships made it back to the pickup zone at Torrijos-Tocumen, they were disabled and out of action. The troops on the lift were also quickly engaged by heavy small-arms fire after they hit the ground.

The third lift arrived without serious opposition and began to push outward.

A total of five hundred troops were now on the ground, and all met resistance—PDF and USEAT wearing civilian clothes, using hit-and-run tactics.

By 11:55 A.M., after suffering heavy casualties, the PDF had melted into the civilian population, and the battalion commander officially declared Panama Viejo secured; but sporadic fighting continued for the rest of the afternoon.

TINAJITAS

Tinajitas, the home of the two-hundred-man 1st Infantry Company, was located on a hilltop six miles north of Panama City and eight miles west of Torrijos-Tocumen, and was surrounded on three sides by the sprawling slum village of San Miguelito, the home of a Dignity Battalion. It was a tough target. Anti-helicopter obstacles had been set up in the garrison's large courtyard; adjacent to the compound were four 120mm mortars, six 81mm mortars, three 60mm mortars, and a ZPU-4 antiaircraft gun. An AC-130 had engaged the dug-in position three times during the night.

There was only one way to effectively attack Tinajitas, and that was by landing on a ridgeline 700 meters down the hill. The landing zone would be clearly within the range of the mortars, and the fight would be uphill all the way.

The 1st Battalion, 504th Airborne Infantry, lifted off from Torrijos-Tocumen at 8:00 A.M., preceded by two Apaches and an OH-58 helicopter to overwatch the landing zone. During their initial survey of the area, the fire support element took no ground fire, but as they broke off to lead the approaching lift ships to the LZ, they crossed over San Miguelito and received heavy and effective ground fire. Rather than risk collateral damage to civilians, they did not return the fire, but reported it to the air assault task force commander, then flew to Howard Air Force Base to check the damage.

An escort Apache immediately flew to San Miguelito, located the enemy position, and received permission to engage the target, which was neutralized by salvos of 30mm fire from a distance of 2,800 meters, leaving ten dead PDF soldiers.

The landing zone at Tinajitas turned out to be the hottest encountered by 82nd units. The delay brought on by the ice storm had given the PDF time to set up defenses and inflict casualties. (One Blackhawk took twenty-eight hits but still remained airborne, thanks to its redundant systems.)

As they approached the LZ, the first lift came under automatic-weapons and 81mm mortar fire from PDF soldiers positioned in buildings to their west and southwest. After landing, as they were deploying in their attack formation, the paratroopers came again under heavy fire, this time from the hilltop and the surrounding barrio. These troops, supported by fire from the two Apaches, attacked the PDF position; heavy fire continued as the second and third lifts came in.

The battalion then fought up the hill, but when they reached the top, the garrison turned out to be abandoned. The PDF had left a stay-behind element to counter the attack, while the rest of the company had withdrawn into the barrio to fight alongside the Dignity Battalion. The stay-behinds slipped away before the paratroopers reached the top.

The battalion later moved into the barrio and neutralized organized resistance.

The battalion commander declared the position secure at 2:30 P.M.

FORT CIMARRON

As of noon on D Day, only one major target remained to be taken—Battalion 2000. But with three companies, eight V-300 armored cars, fourteen mortars, and four 107mm rocket launchers (somewhat attrited during the attempt to cross the Pacora River bridge the night before), it was one of the most demanding targets of the twenty-seven.

At 12:05 P.M., Lieutenant Colonel John Vines, Commander of 4th Battalion, 325th Airborne Infantry, departed for Fort Cimarron in eleven Blackhawks, escorted by Cobra gunships. The assault required two lifts.

After landing, paratroops fanned out into the villages outside the encampment, where they encountered heavy PDF resistance (another consequence of the ice storm delay); five PDF soldiers were killed in the resulting firefights.

When they reached Fort Cimarron, the battalion PSYOPs team broadcast a surrender message; in reply, the PDF inside the cuartel fired on the paratroopers. The battalion commander directed an AC-130 gunship attack on the barracks complex. The gunship fired at the barracks area almost continuously for four hours.

At daylight, when the paratroopers conducted a sweep through the garrison compound, they found it empty. They prepared for a counterattack, but it never came. The survivors of Battalion 2000 had abandoned the garrison, put on their Levi's, and made their way into the city.

Battalion 2000 casualties were heavy.

STABILITY OPERATIONS

U.S. forces broke the PDF—and Noriega's ability to control his forces—during the first hour of combat. By the end of D Day, most of the fighting was over—though Panama was by no means safe. Many of the PDF had changed into Levi's and slipped into the city, where they banded together to continue making trouble.

There was no law and order.

Have-nots, armed bands of hoodlums, Dignity Battalions, and PDF displaced by the fighting—and sometimes a mix of all the above—started looting and causing mayhem.

This had been anticipated by American planners; the Task Force Atlantic and Task Force Pacific division commanders had orders to move into the city and begin stability operations to secure key facilities and mop up resistance.

By dawn of the twentieth, there were already 3,000 refugees in the Balboa High School athletic field, including many PDF who had infiltrated in civilian clothes. There were also 1,500 detainees in a camp being established on a rifle range halfway up the Canal—a number that grew to 4,600 within a week, as more detainees were brought in from the combat units.

Meanwhile, hospitals had to be reopened and sanitation services restarted.

A CBS News poll later determined that 93 percent of the Panamanian people supported U.S. operations—yet the same people had instant expectations that their new government could not soon fulfill, since the removal of Noriega's appointees had decapitated most of the vital institutions.

Though additional units from the 7th Special Forces Group and civil affairs were being brought in to handle these needs, the demand was now, and it could only be satisfied in the near term by the military personnel already on the ground.

The immediate tasks were:

- ✪ Mopping up and bringing security to the major cities, particularly Panama City and Colon.
- ✪ Neutralizing the PDF and Dignity Battalions in the remainder of Panama.
- ✪ Reestablishing law and order.
- ✪ Taking care of refugees and displaced persons.

Meanwhile, all major military objectives had been achieved: The PDF had been neutralized, the PDF command and control no longer functioned, Noriega was no longer in control, and the new government had been installed.

On the downside, Noriega had not been captured, and U.S. forces had no idea where to find him.

MA BELL

Throughout D Day, heavy-lift transports had been landing at Howard Air Force Base and Torrijos-Tucumen, bringing in Major General Carmen Cavezza and two additional brigades from the 7th Infantry Division, as well as the 16th MP Brigade from Fort Bragg, to bring stability to Panama City and Colon, while extending operations to the west to neutralize the remaining PDF main force units. The 75th Ranger Regiment could now be "freed up" to join in liberating the west and clearing the area north of Panama City.

On December 20, the new government asked General Thurman to send a force to liberate political prisoners at Penomone Prison, sixty-five miles southwest of Panama City.

Wayne Downing got the call. That morning, he had flown to Rio Hato to visit Buck Kernan and his Rangers. Later that day, Stiner called him: "I want you and Kernan's rangers to conduct a battalion-size air assault tonight to liberate the political prisoners."

Meanwhile, A Company, 1st Battalion, 7th SFG, which was already stationed in Panama, was to operate toward the west with the Rangers and the 2nd Brigade of the 7th Division. Later that afternoon, Major Gilberto Perez, the commander, flew his company to Rio Hato, where it would stage for these operations.

Downing and Kernan decided to fly out and take a look at the prison—which turned out to be located in a populated area. Taking it could easily result in collateral damage and civilian casualties. Later, as Downing and Kernan prepared the units for the assault, they kept telling themselves, "There has to be a better way to do this."

At about that time, Perez linked up with Downing and Kernan. Since he was already familiar with the country, they asked if he had any helpful ideas about liberating Penomone.

"I just happen to know the major who commands the prison," he told them. "So why don't you let me call him? I'll tell him what's about to happen and see if he'll surrender."

"That's a real gamble," Downing said after he and Kernan had talked this over. "We have to keep preparing for the assault tonight. But go ahead and call him up, and see what he says."

Perez got on the phone and called the major. "Did you see what happened to the Comandancia last night?" he asked the major in Spanish.

"Yes, it was terrible, wasn't it?" The major answered.

"You're exactly right," Perez said, "and the same thing is going to happen to you tonight."

"What do you mean?"

"The Rangers are planning to assault the prison tonight, but if you are agreeable to their terms, you can avoid loss of life."

"What do they want me to do?"

"You can send someone down here," Perez told him, "and we'll give him the terms and conditions."

"I will come myself. Where are you?"

"At Rio Hato," Perez answered.

The major showed up an hour and a half later, and Downing laid out the terms for surrender: "At eight o'clock tonight, you'll leave enough guards to keep the prisoners under control, march all the rest down to the air strip"—near the prison—"lay down your arms, and raise the white flag.

"To keep you honest, an AC-130 gunship circling overhead will see your every move, and relay back to me exactly what you are doing and if you are living up to the terms of the agreement. If you do what I said, no one will get hurt."

The major agreed to the terms and returned to the prison.

Meanwhile, Downing had told Kernan: "Even if this works, I want you to run the operation as planned—except with no gunfire—in order to send the message to the other PDF installations."

At 8:00 that night, Downing and Perez set up an observation post near the prison, Kernan prepared his Ranger battalion for the assault, and the AC-130 watched the prison. A few minutes after 8:00, prison guards were marching down the hill toward the airstrip. At the airstrip, they placed their weapons in a ditch alongside the runway, then got into a formation and raised the white flag.

Downing and Perez accepted the surrender ten minutes before the air assault hit the prison. The awed PDF watched as Little Bird gunships hovered over the prison compound and Rangers fast-roped down. Not one of them believed the major had made the wrong decision.

WHAT happened at Penomone was repeated elsewhere in western Panama, became standard operating procedure, and was known as "Ma Bell."

It worked this way: One of Major Perez's A-Detachments would make contact with a PDF cuartel to find out if the commander was willing to surrender. A rifle company from Colonel Lin Burney's 2nd Brigade, 7th Infantry Division,* would fly in to accept the surrender—but was prepared for combat. After surrender, both the A-Detachment and the company would remain as a guard and stabilizing force until the government decided what to do with the cuartel. This was their mission: (1) To secure the cuartel and ensure that no PDF got away. (2) To gather intelligence on the weapons caches of the PDF and Dignity Battalions who had not yet surrendered. (3) To help the local civilian leaders gain control of the town. (4) To assess the local infrastructure—hospital, public utilities, law and order—and establish priorities for follow-on civil-military operations. (5) To conduct joint Panamanian/U.S. patrols throughout the area.

---

*Burney's brigade had just arrived in country; two battalions were being positioned at Rio Hato when the "Ma Bell" program got under way.

The second and third "Ma Bell" missions secured the cuartels at Santiago and Chitre. Each PDF commander surrendered without resistance, and one of Burney's rifle companies took control.

On Christmas Day, Perez and his team flew into Las Tablas, the capital of Las Santos Province. Perez telephoned the local commander, who willingly surrendered. As Perez and his team were searching the cuartel, a crowd of civilians gathered outside the wall—presenting Perez with an opportunity. He assembled the PDF on the parade field and had his own troops line up beside them. He then called the combined force to attention, ordered "present arms," and had the Panamanian flag raised on the cuartel's flagpole—thus demonstrating that the United States was not a conqueror, but a liberator, and gaining civilian support for follow-on U.S. efforts.

That same day, Lieutenant Colonel Joe Hunt and his 3rd Battalion of the 75th Rangers air-assaulted into Malek airfield near David, the capital of Chiriqui Province.

DAVID was the home of Lieutenant Colonel Del Cid, who commanded its largest PDF installation. Del Cid was the second-most-powerful man in Panama and a close friend of Noriega's—the man tagged by the dictator to carry out his plan for guerrilla warfare in the mountains. Like Noriega, he had been indicted for drug trafficking.

On December 21, as the Rangers were preparing their air assault against David, Marc Cisneros phoned Del Cid and gave him unconditional surrender terms. The following day, he agreed to the terms, and a white flag appeared over his headquarters. He was picked up by the Rangers on Christmas Day, flown to Howard Air Force Base, and arrested by the DEA. He was then flown to Homestead and on to Miami for arraignment.

Meanwhile, Burney and his brigade provided security and support throughout central and western Panama. As a result of the rapport they established, civilians provided valuable intelligence that helped locate weapons caches, people on the most wanted list, and PDF and Dignity Battalion members who had not yet been captured—*and* no more than eight shots had been fired in that part of Panama.

ELSEWHERE, U.S. forces were closing the noose on armed bands of holdouts, and intensifying operations against Dignity Battalions in Panama City.

Until two days into the operation, when documents were captured during a raid on a headquarters, not much was known about this mysterious organization, except that they were baddies—Noriega's control and enforcement force—who had terrorized the people enough to make them afraid even to talk about them.

According to the captured documents, there were eighteen Dignity Battalions, and they were the best paid of Noriega's forces—including quarters for both members and their families. A list of leaders—also provided by the documents—added many names to the most-wanted list.

During the next days, Downing and his special mission units worked tirelessly to uproot and dismantle the Dignity Battalions, and track down their leaders. Their success soon inspired the locals to reveal where Dignity Battalion members were holed up. And by December 23, that threat had pretty much ended.

By then, the equivalent of four combat brigades and fifteen hundred military police had brought stability to Panama City, Colon, and most of the rest of the country, and all the PDF regional commanders had surrendered. One major task remained—capturing Noriega.

THE SEARCH FOR NORIEGA

At H-hour, Wayne Downing launched one of the most intensive manhunts in history, when he went to work to disassemble Noriega's infrastructure (the most-wanted list) and capture the elusive Noriega.

Downing's Panzer Gruppe—now two Sheridan armored reconnaissance vehicles, two U.S. Marine Corps LAVs, five Army APCs, four confiscated PDF two and-a-half-ton trucks, and an old yellow school bus—together with his air assets, would give him maximum flexibility responding to leads.

Task Force Green, commanded by Colonel "Pete," and Task Force Blue, his Navy special mission unit, commanded by Navy SEAL Captain "Rick," supported by quick reaction helicopters and AC-130 gunships, had been given the difficult job of capturing the Dictator. The first mission of both task forces was to search Noriega's plush apartments and houses scattered throughout Panama. Task Force Green operated within Panama City; Task Force Blue was assigned the Colon area and western Panama.

WAYNE Downing continues:
Rolling up the infrastructure accomplished two goals: The Noriega gang was all bad; we had to bring them to justice. And we needed to deny Noriega op-

tions. We wanted him to have nowhere to lay his head. And so we went after every Noriega crony and hangout we could find, and we rolled them up.

These people were incredible. There are so many tales, people walking around with thousands of dollars in hundred-dollar bills in their pockets—drug money. And mistresses, girlfriends—we ran into just about anything you can think of. These were dirty people.

Here is an example of how we did it—though it's not exactly typical.

There was one guy that everyone in the neighborhood feared, rich and ruthless, the baddest of the bad; no one dared to speak against him. So our guys went to his place to pick him up.

It was like a movie. They came up and the door was very heavy, very fancy, with a gold doorknob, and locked. So they put a door charge on it, to blow the door open.

Inside, the bad guy was in his living room, where he had built an enormous, 5,000-gallon aquarium; it took up an entire wall and was filled with all kinds of exotic fish. When he heard our troops outside, he panicked and started to run, crouched down and bent over, with his arms protecting his head. That was when they blew the door. The doorknob shot out across the room, drove up into his rectum, and got wedged up there.

Meanwhile, shards from the blown-down door were flying around, and some of them shattered the aquarium. So when our troops came in, they found this bad guy hopping around with a gold doorknob up his rear, and fish flopping all over the floor and stuck to the ceiling. This wasn't intentional—we were sorry for the fish—but it made a story our guys will tell their grandchildren.

A few minutes after all this, the local people were out in the street cheering. Because this guy was so bad.

After a lot of operations like this (most of them not so vivid), the SEALs and Special Forces from the special missions units broke Noriega's infrastructure. And he could not escape. Every place he went, he ran into where we had been. We'd covered every possible safe haven.

DOWNING'S people worked day and night, and they were amazingly successful.

Raids on Noriega's offices and houses had captured almost $8 million in U.S. currency, a briefcase containing a list of bank accounts in Switzerland and the Cayman Islands, and diaries laying out his involvement in witchcraft and voodoo worship. The money and documents were temporarily turned over to SOUTHCOM until a proper place could be found for securing them.

Two days after H-hour, nearly everyone on the most wanted list had been picked up and interrogated. Most of them—looking out for their own skin—cooperated with the interrogators and provided names of other key people in Noriega's infrastructure who had not yet been identified. A list of about a hundred people was developed from this information, and Downing's forces immediately set out to find them.

And yet, by the morning of December 23, Noriega was still missing.

CARL *Stiner continues:*

The first break came midmorning on December 23 when one of Noriega's inner circle of bodyguards appeared at the main gate at Fort Clayton with a proposition for Marc Cisneros: He had information about Noriega that he would exchange for protection for himself and his family. Though these guys were all real thugs, he got his guarantee, and it was his information that filled in the details of Noriega's movements on the evening before H-hour—his diversion on the way back from Colon, his rendezvous with the prostitute at the Ceremi rest camp, his escape from the Ranger's roadblock.

This was good news. It meant Noriega was still in Panama City; we would continue relentless pressure until he could be cornered. Part of the pressure involved our watching embassies where he might find asylum.

At 8:30 the next morning, another Noriega bodyguard showed up with the same proposition. When he met Cisneros, he said, "I just now slipped away from Noriega and his other bodyguards. He's at the end of his rope, he's taking drugs and alcohol, and he's crazy as hell. He'll kill us all.

"I can tell you where he is, but you have to hurry. They're about to move on. When I left, bags were packed. They're driving a blue Montero SUV."

Within minutes, Downing was on the scene with his Panzer Gruppe.

They found the place abandoned, but the coffeepot was still hot, and cigarettes were still burning in the ashtrays. A call to all units was immediately put out to watch for the Montero.

Marc Cisneros and I spent most of the day checking on stability operations, but arranged to return to headquarters at 3:00 P.M. At 3:00, I went directly to my operations center, and Cisneros went to his office on the second floor of the same building. When he got there, he learned he had an urgent phone call from Monsignor Laboa, the Papal Nuncio. This was Laboa's second call; he had something important on his mind. Cisneros took the phone.

"Noriega is here," Laboa whispered, "in the Papal Nunciatore. I called you earlier, hoping you could intercept him. Come over here. I need to talk to you." The Papal Nunciatore was the Vatican's Embassy in Panama City, and had the same immunities as any other embassy recognized by the U.S. government.

Cisneros hurried to me with the news.

"Go ahead and see Laboa," I told him. "Call me as soon as you have details. I'll tell General Thurman and Downing."

I immediately called Downing: "We've got a problem," I said. "Noriega's in the Nunciatore—a sanctuary. Get over there right away and take charge of the situation. Secure it."

Then I called Thurman.

Within minutes, Downing had surrounded the Nunciatore with his troops.

The Nunciatore, located in one of the wealthier parts of the city, was a two-story stucco building with a pleasant, well-groomed yard, all surrounded by a seven-foot-high concrete wall.

Meanwhile, I was thinking. "Why the Nunciatore?" I asked myself. "We have been watching the Nicaraguan Embassy, the Cuban Embassy, the Peruvian Embassy, and all the others where we thought he might hole up; but we never considered the Nunciatore. All the same, now we have him; it's just a matter of how to get him out."

Shortly, Cisneros phoned with the Nuncio's story:

Noriega and Captain Guitan, his aide, had called to ask for refuge. "What we want you to do," Noriega demanded, "is pick us up at an ice-cream stand," which he named, "and bring us to the Nunciatore. If you don't, we'll go to the mountains and start a guerrilla war."

Laboa felt he had no choice. He sent a car to pick them up.

"My earlier call," he explained to Cisneros, "was to let you know about the car. I'd hoped U.S. forces would intercept it before it returned to the Nunciatore—and you'd do me a favor if you took your soldiers right now and dragged him out; but unfortunately, that's impossible. We both have to recognize the diplomatic protocols."

"That's fine," I told Cisneros. "Now what I want you to do is find out from

Laboa if anyone else has taken asylum in the Nunciatore, and if they have weapons. And tell him that Downing is establishing a security perimeter around the Nunciatore and will be our man on the scene."

Forty-five minutes later, Cisneros returned to headquarters. "The Nuncio doesn't think Noriega brought weapons with him," he told me, "but he's not sure." We were fairly certain he had weapons, and this complicated matters: We were in a potential hostage situation. "Several others in Noriega's inner circle are also there," Cisneros continued, "as well as a few women, and eight to ten children."

The others turned out to be: Captain Guitan; Colonel Castergen, the Navy Commander; Lieutenant Colonel Velarde, a chaplain; Captain Castillo, Noriega's personal bodyguard; and Colonel Madrinan, Chief of the Department of National Investigation. Five Basque separatist terrorists had also come in with the Noriega gang, on the reasonable assumption that we'd want to pick them up.

By then, Downing had secured the area with Colonel "Pete" and his forces from Task Force Green, and had established his operational center in the elementary school across the street. I called him there: "Tell Laboa that he's in a very dangerous situation, and as far as we're concerned, he violated the Nunciatore's immunities when he went out and fetched an indicted criminal, then brought him inside and provided refuge.

"Advise the Nuncio that he's living in a bed of snakes who could care less about him and could kill him at any time."

We then talked about the best way to get the women and children out of there, in order to simplify the situation.

DOWNING met Laboa in the elementary school.

"I'll do what I can to help," Laboa said nervously when Downing gave him my message. It had scared him badly.

Then Downing asked, "Will you authorize a rescue operation if we hear shots from inside? We believe Noriega has weapons."

"I can do that," Laboa answered.

"Will you put that in writing?"

"Yes," the Nuncio responded.

"I have two other questions," Downing said: "Will you help us to get the women and children out?"

"Yes, of course."

"And will you and your staff leave after that?"

"No, we can't do that," Laboa replied, then went back inside the Nunciatore.

Thirty minutes later, a priest delivered an envelope with a note typed on Vatican parchment and signed by Laboa that authorized a rescue operation if shots were fired inside the Nunciatore. This was a "get out of jail free" card for Laboa if anything beyond his control happened, but it was also our trump card. If anything *did* happen, we had authority to conduct an immediate assault. And we had a plan to accomplish it.

I quickly called General Thurman to give him an update. At the same time, I asked him for a change in his rules of engagement to allow an assault if the lives of those inside were in danger. This was approved by SECDEF.

Meanwhile, Downing went to work getting the women and children out, and it turned out they were not the only ones who were eager to leave; several men wanted out as well—all demanding to be flown to Nicaragua, Cuba, or Venezuela.

"We'll see about that," Downing said.

Toward evening, Downing's old yellow Panzer Gruppe school bus rolled up, and about ten men and women and twelve children came out. They were then loaded and taken to a secure location, where they were segregated. The women and children were taken to their homes, and the men were sent to our detention camp.

"I didn't offer them asylum," Downing said when he called me. "I didn't have the authority. I just told them we'd work on it. But what I had to do is get the women and children out; it was a very dangerous situation."

Still inside were Noriega, five of his henchmen, and the five Basque separatists—all bad people, except possibly for the chaplain, who may have stayed inside out of hope to take care of Noriega's spiritual needs.

In the meantime, while we tried to figure out how to get Noriega out of there, we'd begun to discover just how bad Noriega and his crew really were. Downing's task force had added ever more fascinating evidence to what Marc Cisneros had come up with after we captured the PDF side of Fort Amador.

On Christmas Eve, I received a call from Jim Johnson: "We have secured Noriega's main residence in downtown Panama City," he said, "and found things you need to take a look at. I would recommend that you come out tomorrow."

"What did you find?"

"He's heavily involved in witchcraft, for one thing. But that's only a beginning." That caught my attention.

"I'll try to get out there tomorrow morning," I told him.

When I dropped all this on my staff at a meeting that night, the J-2 spoke up: "You won't believe this," he announced, "but I ran into a warrant officer in the MI Battalion with a master's degree in witchcraft. You need to take him along."

"I didn't even know there was such a degree," I said. "But get him ready to go, and we'll leave tomorrow about eight-thirty."

The next morning, I flew out and linked up with Johnson at Paitilla airfield. From there we were escorted to Noriega's house. When we got there, I had a hard time believing my eyes.

The house was lavishly furnished with gaudy "objets d'art." Large silver pelicans—estimated at about $25,000 each—were all over the place. In the main study was probably the biggest collection of ceramic frogs in the world. In the office was a world-class collection of busts of Hitler; he had at least twenty-five of them. Also in the office was a large poster board containing the pictures of the Catholic Church's representatives in each of the Central American countries with "X"s marked beside several names. Presumably, an "X" meant future elimination.

Behind the house was a patio, connecting the residence to what was called the "girls' dollhouse," built for his daughters when they were children; it was as large as most people's homes. On each end of the patio were two large altars set up for voodoo worship and witchcraft. Noriega had brought to Panama two "high-powered" witches from Brazil. One of them was reputed to be the world's leading witch; he lived on the causeway to Fort Amador in a house where at H-hour the SEALs had established a roadblock (I don't know what became of him).

The MI warrant officer explained each of the altars. On one was arranged containers of blood, a skull, crows' feathers, and ears of corn with multicolored kernels. All of this, the warrant officer explained, puts the "worshiper" in the right frame of mind for some kind of atrocity or evil act.

On the other altar were arranged stuffed doves, pictures of babies, and other "nice" things. The "worshiper" would cleanse his soul here afterward.

In Noriega's bedroom were several pairs of red silk bikini underwear—a Noriega trademark. We had found them just about everywhere Noriega showed his face. According to the warrant officer, the witch doctor had likely told Noriega they would protect him from physical harm.

"Maintain tight security here," I told Johnson as I left. "I don't want anything disturbed before we show it to the right people. After that, we'll turn it over to Panamanian authority." Among those whom I especially wanted to see all this—and what we had found at Fort Amador—were high-level officials of the Catholic Church. As soon as Noriega had himself brought to the Nunciatore, General Thurman started talking with the Catholic hierarchy, and of course with Washington, about ways to resolve the problem. When I got the chance, I suggested to Thurman that he invite some selected Catholic officials down to show them what we'd found.

It was an eyeful, that's for sure; but it gave us real insights into the man Noriega. It also began to give me ideas about how to get Noriega out of the Nunciatore.

THE first thing I did after I left was meet with Downing. We were particularly interested in finding a use for Noriega's red underwear. For all we knew, he was wearing a pair right then. If he ever had a need for the powers they gave, it was certainly then.

Our first idea was to hang a pair on a clothesline outside his window (Laboa had told us where it was) and shoot them full of holes to show him how empty their powers were.

"I can take care of that," Downing said, and the demonstration was carried out later that afternoon.

Meanwhile, I'd picked up an interesting detail from the warrant officer: A goat was a very bad omen. That set me thinking.

This led to an instruction to my J-2 to come up with the ugliest, stinkingest billygoat he could find, and doctor him up for Noriega. The next day the J-2 produced a goat with really impressive horns and a beard that came down just short of his knees. They decked him out in a pair of red bikini underwear, rigged him up so a remote control signal sent smoke blowing out of his nostrils and ears, and tied him outside Noriega's window.

We never knew how Noriega took all this, but it couldn't have helped his digestion.

ON the night of December 23, the media was cleared into Panama.

Well before the operation was launched, Thurman and I agreed on how we would work media affairs. Essentially, his headquarters would handle them, under his public affairs officer, an Air Force colonel; and I provided my public affairs officer, Jake Dye, an Army colonel, to SOUTHCOM, which established a media center in a large tent just outside the head-quarters. There would be two daily press briefings—one in the morning and one in the afternoon.

From the beginning the operation had been kept secret, but on the night of the twentieth, there were enough media already in Panama to cover a good part of the activities in the vicinity of the Comandancia. TVs are common in Panama; which meant civilians could watch the battles taking place live on their home screens.

On the night of the twenty-third, Panama's airspace was still closed to everything but military traffic. A call came in from Pete Kemph at Howard Air Force Base. A Lockheed L-1011 was overhead, asking permission to land.

"Who's on it?" I asked.

Kemph called back, "It's a load of media; they've been cleared from Washington."

"We have no alternative but to let them land," I said.

They were met on the ground by Thurman and taken to Quarry Heights, where they were given a complete briefing. Afterward, Thurman announced that the plan was to put them out in groups of three or four with each rifle company so they could get front-line coverage. Company commanders would be responsible for their security, food, and protection. Every day they would select a small number to travel around in a helicopter and pick up their "take," which they'd have time to file for the evening news.

The media found this arrangement totally unacceptable. Each media team wanted helicopters of its own, so they could immediately get to the action (one team had a satellite communications set it would take a Chinook to carry).

"I'm sorry," Thurman told them, "but I can't accommodate you on that. We're still involved in security operations and don't have enough helicopters to support the troops, much less give you dedicated helicopters."

They reluctantly agreed to this arrangement, but that didn't last long. Many of them began to slip away and rent cars; pretty soon they were running around all over the place.

It didn't take the press long to find out that Noriega was in the Nunciatore. Not long after that, they took over the Holiday Inn, about a hundred yards away, and were out on the balconies with their pinpoint microphones, trying to pick up what was going on.

This worried me. "We've got very sensitive negotiations going on outside

the Nunciatore between Downing, Cisneros, Michael Kuzack," the U.S.
Embassy representative, "and Laboa," I told Thurman, "and we have to find
a way to block these microphones listening in. What I'd like to do is bring
in some psychological operations loudspeakers and play music."

"Good idea," Thurman said. "Set it up."

And that's what we did.

Pretty soon, the press got teed off and started calling directly to the
White House, claiming we were violating their first amendment rights by
blasting them with rock music. That was not, in fact, true. It wasn't all rock
music. We had also selected some good country-and-western songs, like
Johnny Cash's "Ring of Fire," and "Nowhere to Run To," and "In the
Jailhouse Now."

We didn't forget Noriega in all this. We wanted to send him a clear message that the ball game was over. During the afternoons, we hooked up the
loudspeakers to U.S. Southern Command radio so he could also hear about
the surrenders of his PDF commanders and the freezing of his overseas
bank accounts.

The loudspeaker campaign didn't last long.

The White House put pressure on General Powell, who called General
Thurman and demanded an explanation. General Thurman did that, but it
apparently did not satisfy the White House, and we were ordered to stop the
music.

As we wrestled with the problem of prying Noriega out of the Nunciatore,
operations were going on throughout western Panama to bring security and
stability, and great progress had been made (looting had practically ceased),
owing in large measure to the signal sent by combat activities at H-hour.
Also contributing to the success was the surrender of Lieutenant Colonel
Del Cid. Word of his surrender had also almost certainly reached Noriega
before he'd entered the Nunciatore; this would not have lifted his mood.

All the while, intelligence reports were coming in that Noriega supporters were planning rescue attempts.

One report claimed that rescuers planned to land a small helicopter inside the Nunciatore grounds and fly him out. In response, Downing positioned Ranger stinger-missile teams on every nearby high-rise building.
There was no way a helicopter was going to get into the Nunciatore.

Another report claimed Noriega was going to slip away out the back and down an irrigation ditch. Infantry troops were brought in to secure the ditch, and surveillance cameras with infrared capability were installed for all-around security.

MEANWHILE, progress was slow on the Noriega problem—though matters were far from a standstill. Washington had been negotiating with the Vatican, and those negotiations continued. We had made suggestions to Monsignor Laboa about keeping Noriega's misery level as high as possible, and Laboa was cooperating. Noriega was not getting special privileges. Laboa had ordered his room's air-conditioning to be turned off, and Noriega, a vegetarian, was served the same food as everyone else. Of course, Laboa had also been a major factor in getting the women and children out.

At the same time, General Thurman was pursuing initiatives with Panama's Catholic leadership. Archbishop Marcus McGrath, the senior Catholic prelate, took a witchcraft-and-voodoo tour of the residence and "dollhouse"; and he also had laid out for him the pornography, the torture photos, and the poster listing several of the Catholic priests in Panama and Central America, with "X"s marked next to names.

AFTERWARD, the archbishop convened a bishops' conference, resulting in a letter from the bishops to the Pope, asking for an order to release Noriega to U.S. custody.

Movement from that direction came on December 29, when the Vatican newspaper reported: "The Vatican had never intended to hinder justice by granting Noriega refuge." On New Year's Day, Monsignor Berlocco, the Vatican's expert on Central America, arrived to help Laboa with Noriega. The next day, he confided to Cisneros that he hoped for a speedy and just resolution to the problem.

ABOUT that time, I had an idea: Back at the October 3 coup, when Noriega was being held in the Comandancia, we had pretty good evidence that he'd called Miss Vicki and asked her to get hold of the troop commanders who'd come in to rescue him.

If she was useful then, why wouldn't she be useful now?

I told Downing to have Miss Vicki brought in so we could talk to her. We picked her up that night, then sat her down and told her how she could help save her lover's life.

Vicki was a very strong woman and at first refused to cooperate, but as the night wore on, she began to talk about her thirteen-year-old daughter. The girl had a mild heart condition (it required medication, but was not life-threatening). It was obvious Vicki loved the girl very much, and had somehow gotten the impression that we "had" her; we didn't tell her any different. In fact, during the night we were able to locate her daughter—and ensure her safety.

At daybreak, Miss Vicki agreed to cooperate—with the condition that we let her see her daughter. We brought the daughter in, along with clean clothing for Vicki, and then let her take a shower and have a nice breakfast with her daughter.

After that, we gave her our message for Noriega: He had only two options. One was to come out feet first. The other was to come out with dignity—wearing his general's uniform—and surrender.

In the meantime, we were setting up for her a special phone link to the Nunciatore, which of course Wayne Downing could monitor.

We gained a tremendous amount of intelligence listening to these conversations. The lady turned out to be better informed than we thought, and laid things out straight.

She led off by explaining to Noriega that his support infrastructure had totally crumbled, the people were against him, and Del Cid had surrendered. Then it got personal. She was deeply worried about him. He was trapped in a corner with very few options, and it was obvious she cared a lot about him and wanted him to stay alive.

At first, Noriega steadfastly refused to consider surrender, but as the next couple of days passed, he began to waver.

On January 1, Panamanian radio announced that a large anti-Noriega demonstration would take place the afternoon of the third on the avenue that passed the Nunciatore. The demonstration was advertised as a "show of support for U.S. actions in Panama." On January 2, we received intelligence that anti-Noriega groups might take matters into their own hands and try to "deal with Noriega" during this "friendly" demonstration.

Security was increased. Two additional infantry battalions took up positions along the demonstration route, snipers were posted on every local high-rise roof, Sheridan tanks and a battalion of military police were brought in to establish a roadblock two hundred yards from the Nunciatore (demonstrators could not pass beyond it), and an AC-130 gunship and Apache helicopters would overwatch.

The snipers were given orders to shoot anyone who fired on the demonstration, as well as any demonstrators attempting to storm the Nunciatore; but no one was to fire on the crowd without my approval.

Early on the afternoon of January 3, thousands of people marched toward the Nunciatore, beating pots and pans and waving banners proclaiming support for the United States.

As the crowd was beginning to move, Cisneros was on the way to a meeting with Downing and Monsignor Laboa in Downing's elementary school headquarters. As he drove past the demonstrators, several of them were shouting "We want Noriega!"

Many of the demonstrators knew Cisneros, and one group stopped him: "Let us have him," they called out, "and we can solve this problem very quickly."

"No," he told them. "That's not the way to go. We're much better equipped to handle the problem. Don't look for a confrontation, or you may become casualties yourselves."

Shortly, the crowd had grown to several thousand (some estimates put it at 20,000) and could be heard from the Nunciatore a mile away.

Near the Nunciatore, Cisneros and Laboa discussed the demonstration. "Do you know about Mussolini's final days?" Cisneros asked the Nuncio.

Laboa was familiar with the story. A mob had lynched the Italian dictator, then hung him upside down, naked.

"If this mob gets hold of Noriega," Cisneros continued, "they will most certainly lynch him. But if he surrenders, we will protect him."

That seemed to motivate Laboa in a way we hadn't seen before. With a very worried look on his face, he leapt up and dashed across the street to the Nunciatore. Moments later, he had a talk with Noriega. We don't know what they said, but the Nuncio surely mentioned that Noriega's countrymen out there in the streets were in a killing mood.

Miss Vicki also had a talk with him at about that time. Their conversation lasted about ten minutes. "The decision is in your hands," she concluded.

The demonstration outside grew ever noisier, but remained "peaceful"; no shots were fired. Thousands were chanting, "Assassin! Assassin! No more! Down with Noriega! Out of the Nunciatore!" A Noriega mannequin in military uniform with a pineapple head was hung in effigy.

An hour before dark, a light rain began to fall and fog was moving in. At about the same time, we sent the demonstrators a message over our loudspeakers that it was time to break up and go home. And they did.

We'll probably never know who influenced Noriega more—Miss Vicki or the Nuncio. However, we were asked to bring one of Noriega's uniforms to the Nunciatore. Marc Cisneros had confiscated three uniforms from his Fort Amador office. We sent over one of these.

At 8:44 P.M. on the evening of January 3, 1990, "General" Noriega, accompanied by Father Vilanueva, another priest at the Nunciatore, and Monsignor Laboa, walked out of the gate and into the street, where Downing was waiting. Downing had never seen Noriega in person, but judging from pictures, had imagined he was a robust, roly-poly guy. That did not turn out to be the case. The man was small and shriveled-up. "Have they substituted another guy?" Downing instantly asked himself. "Did Noriega slip out the back gate?"

Downing grabbed Lieutenant Colonel "Jerry," his man in charge of security. "Make sure they're watching the rear," he said urgently. "This isn't Noriega."

Meanwhile, another Embassy official, standing beside Cisneros, remarked, "Don't worry, that's him."

Noriega was carrying a Bible and a toothbrush.

The party entered the school, continued through it, and walked down the steps leading to the soccer field, where two Blackhawks were waiting.

Monsignor Laboa gave Noriega a final blessing, which concluded, "My son, now I leave you."

Downing then took Noriega a little further; Laboa did not wish to be present when the dictator was handcuffed. As they neared the helicopters, two large special operators were waiting with flex cuffs. As they approached him, Noriega put up a protest. "I am a general," he announced. "I am a prisoner of war. I don't need to be treated like this."

His protests were ignored. For his own protection, he was quickly cuffed and placed in the lead helicopter, and the helo lifted into the fog. At Howard Air Force Base, an MC-130 was waiting with its engines running and two DEA agents on board, along with a special operations doctor. As the tailgate was closing, Noriega was read his rights, then placed under arrest by the DEA agents.*

En route to Homestead Air Force Base, he was made to undress for a physical examination. He pulled off all his clothes except his underwear.

---

*Guitan remained in the Nunciatore and eventually left. He is believed to be in Peru.

When he was told to take that off, too, it turned out he was in fact wearing two pair—white boxer shorts and red bikinis underneath.

The JSOTF surgeon, Lieutenant Colonel "Tony," gave him a thorough physical. He was physically fit, and no physical harm had been done to him. He was then given an Air Force flight suit and a pair of hospital sandals. After he put these on, he was handcuffed, shackled, and placed in a seat at the front of the aircraft near the bulkhead, where he slept for the next four hours.

Before landing, he asked to put on his general's uniform, and was allowed to do so. At Homestead Air Force Base in Florida, a Learjet was waiting to fly him to Miami for arraignment before a federal judge.

DURING the drama of Noriega's surrender, Senator John Warner and I monitored every detail in the operations center at Fort Clayton (Warner was there to show his support and make a personal assessment).

As the Blackhawks lifted into the fog for Howard Air Force Base, shouts went up from the seventy-five or so operations officers and NCOs who had been working practically around the clock since the start of Operation JUST CAUSE. This was *IT! The last objective had been accomplished!*

Now we could devote our full attention to getting Panama back on its feet—free from oppression. Senator Warner rushed to the big operations map and with a Magic Marker wrote: "Great job! We are all very proud of you!" Then he made a few much-appreciated inspirational comments.

The word spread quickly. Joyful Panamanians filled the streets—expressing their thanks so effusively the troops had a hard time eliminating the last pockets of resistance.

THE VETTING PROCESS

On Friday, December 22, 1989, President Endara decided to abolish the PDF, except for a two-hundred-man presidential guard force, a specially trained and equipped reaction force (whose numbers were yet to be defined), and the new Fuerza Publica (public police force), with a new chief to lead it. In the past, the functions of police, customs, and defense had all been merged into the PDF. These functions were now separated.

The task remained to sort out the PDF. Some were being held by our infantry companies in the west. Others were being held in the detention camp.

The sorting-out task was assigned to Vice President Calderon, who soon asked for our help. At a meeting with Thurman and me, the three of us agreed that U.S. forces would handle the working out of this process, and Calderon would represent the Panamanian government.

Practically, it worked this way: A team would take helicopters to the various PDF cuartels, and either I or a brigade commander would go along to assist. When we came to a cuartel, all the PDF there would be assembled, and an announcement would be made: "The new government is in charge, and the decision has been made about the future of the PDF." Then the sorting-out began: First, all those on the most wanted list were identified and segregated. Then the officers and the enlisted were separated into groups, and the members of each group were given the opportunity to take and sign an oath of allegiance to the new government.

All those who signed were paid on the spot with money that U.S. forces had confiscated, and they were sent home to buy food for their families.

Many of these volunteered for the new police force.

All those who refused to take the oath (very few, as it happened) were placed with those on the most wanted list and then flown off under U.S. guard to the detention camp.

At the detention camp, there were a total of 4,600 detainees. The truly violent were segregated in one section, looters in another, PDF members in another, and Dignity Battalion members in another, with a separate section for women. PDF members were then segregated by rank—officers in one section and enlisted in another. Though everyone was given the opportunity to pledge allegiance to the new government, those on the most wanted list, former prisoners, or anyone caught committing violent crimes were kept in confinement at the camp.

Most detainees were younger PDF enlisted members who had simply been caught up in the U.S. dragnet. They were swiftly released.

Because of past PDF oppression, enmity ran deep among Panamanians toward most PDF cuartels. This meant that U.S. forces had to guard the cuartels and work out ways to minimize reprisals against the former PDF, until the new government was fully in charge.

OPERATION PROMOTE LIBERTY

"I can handle the combat part of this operation," I remarked to General Thurman during the first planning session for Operation JUST CAUSE, "but who is going to be responsible for planning the 'nation building'?

"The combat part is the easier of the two," I told him, "because when you are shooting at someone, you are in control of the variables. But, when you enter the nation-building phase, you are not. The new government is in control, and you have to respond to their needs and priorities. For that reason, the transition from combat operations to stability to nation-building must be seamless, so there is no loss in momentum. And the planning for it must be integrated from the beginning.

"It will require a different kind of command-and-control structure, different kinds of forces—with more technical and specialized capabilities—and a different approach to psychological operations. Their objectives and themes must be focused on support for the new government. Some of the forces needed, particularly Civil Affairs, are in the Reserves and must be identified now for call-up when needed.

"It is this phase," I concluded, "and the way we leave Panama, that will form the basis for judging the success or failure of this whole operation."

"This is very important," Thurman answered. "But I want you to focus exclusively on the combat operations; and SOUTHCOM will handle the planning responsibilities for nation-building. Some work has already been done; the BLIND LOGIC plan has gone through considerable development, but it needs to be revised and made to conform with the new combat plan."

As planning progressed, the concept of operations for the critical nation-building phase was as follows:

- ✪ Transition from combat operations to stability operations to nation-building.
- ✪ Establishment of a military support group to administer nation-building programs.
- ✪ Conduct nation-building with in-country forces, plus augmentation as required.

During the transition phase, the combat units would also establish the security environment needed for nation-building, and use their own organic capabilities for food distribution, medical care, transportation, and cleanup.

Long before H-hour, Civil Affairs teams would be attached to the combat units, to assist commanders with civilians and refugees during the combat phase. Special Forces A-Detachments would also be attached to combat units during the transition phase; and as combat units were redeployed, they would remain in assigned areas of operations to assist with nation-building.

The Military Support Group for administering nation-building programs was formed as the USARSO Headquarters; I had absorbed it earlier when I had formed my headquarters, JTF South, but now it was reinstated. It would consist of three major components: 96th Civil Affairs Battalion; 1st PSYOPs Battalion; and Special Operations Forces (SOF), consisting of SOUTHCOM's Special Operations Command, 7th Special Forces Group, Naval Special Boat units, the 122nd Signal Company, and a Special Aviation Detachment. Logistical support would be provided by the 41st Army General Support Group.

Detailed planning for nation-building was completed along with the combat plan. During planning, it was determined that approximately three hundred uniquely qualified Civil Affairs personnel would be needed—sanitation engineers, medical administrators, facility planners, construction supervisors, banking, police supervisors, etc. For security reasons, they could not be notified in advance, and were therefore notified at H-hour for individual call-up; they arrived in Panama within three weeks. All active-duty units needed were force-listed to arrive as soon after H-hour as they could be flown in.

SOUTHCOM interfaced with the country team and the new government and executed nation-building activities, while I continued my efforts to bring stability and control to Panama.

On December 21, the Military Support Group was activated; and some three hundred civil military affairs reservists were called up. On December 22, the 96th Civil Affairs Battalion arrived and immediately got to work; the 7th Special Forces Group followed over the next couple of days.

The 96th's assignments were to: restore basic functions in Panama City and throughout Panama, establish a police force, provide emergency food distribution, supervise Panamanian contractors in the cleanup of the city, and restore medical services. Their commander, Lieutenant Colonel Michael Peters, immediately established an operating infrastructure. Commanders and operational detachments were assigned to Zone P (Panama City and the eastern provinces), Zone C (Colon), and Zone D (the provinces west of Panama City).

On December 22, the day the 96th arrived in country, President Endara abolished and reorganized the PDF.

The major task and challenges associated with nation-building were as follows:

- ✪ First and foremost was the restoration of law and order.
- ✪ Second was the future disposition of the PDF.
- ✪ Third was the care and feeding of the 3,500 refugees then under U.S. control.
- ✪ Fourth was the restoration of medical services.
- ✪ Fifth was to clean up Panama City and restore services to the people.

On December 20, the 16th MP Brigade was brought in from Fort Bragg, and was immediately sent into Panama City, operating under U.S. rules, to provide security for the civil affairs efforts. The plan was to conduct joint patrols using the Brigade's HMMWVs; two U.S. MPs and two Panamanian policemen would ride together. The Panamanian policemen would make actual arrests, but under U.S. supervision. The immediate challenge was to come up with enough former policemen or soldiers to meet the need. Out of the first four hundred volunteers screened by the Panamanian government, only 160 were acceptable; but this was enough to get started. The vetting process continued among the units of the former PDF.

A police academy also had to be established. By U.S. law, the training of foreign police forces is the responsibility of the Justice Department. However, since security considerations had prevented us from bringing them in on the planning of JUST CAUSE, the Justice Department had passed its authority to the Department of Defense. The 7th Special Forces Group was brought in to establish the training programs for both the presidential guard unit and the national police force. The police and security experts needed for this mission were called up from the Reserves.

BECAUSE of the surgical nature of our invasion, collateral damage throughout the country was small. The only significant damage occurred in the Chiriori slum near the Comandancia, where many homeless had built cardboard and plywood shacks. Soon after our assault on the Comandancia, many weapon-toting PDF and Dignity Battalion members, dressed in civilian clothes, took refuge there, and then set the community on fire.

Later, many tried to pose as refugees; but most were caught.

Early on December 20 (D Day), we established a refugee center on the athletic field of Balboa High School, which was managed by a Civil Affairs company and governed by the mayor of Chiriori. An average of 3,500 refugees per day were provided with adequate food, clothing, shelter, medical treatment, and security. Eleven thousand people were processed through the center, many just to get a meal, before it was eventually given over to the new government and then closed.

We knew from an early survey that Panama had adequate medical facilities, doctors, and technicians, but there was a severe shortage of medical supplies.

During combat, Task Force Bayonet captured a warehouse in the Balboa area containing 150,000 pounds of medical supplies—accessible only by means of bribes. We changed that system on the spot, and the supplies were immediately distributed to Panamanian medical facilities. Two hundred and eighteen tons of Department of Defense medical supplies were also provided to hospitals and medical clinics.

Meanwhile, U.S. aid stations and hospitals were opened to the sick and wounded; fifteen thousand Panamanians were treated at U.S. facilities.

From December 26 to January 3, Civil Affairs and Special Forces troops operated thirteen food distribution centers, handing out 1,660 tons of food—mostly meals-ready-to-eat (MREs)—and one million tons of bulk food, such as baby food, liquids, dehydrated milk, and dried beans.

Cleaning up Panama City was relatively easy. The Civil Affairs troops and the MPs used some of the less hostile detainees held at the detention camp, organized them into detachments, placed them under U.S. guard, and took them into the city to do cleanup work. This was a great morale boost for local residents.

One of the first official ceremonies performed by President Endara was to swing a sledgehammer against the wall of the now-war-ravaged Comandancia. His swings were punctuated by chants from a crowd: "Harder, harder." This hated symbol of torture and oppression was being transformed into an apartment complex for those who had lost their homes in the fire.

TRANSITION AND REDEPLOYMENT

As word of Noriega's arrest and imprisonment in the United States spread across Panama, there was no longer any reason for resistance, and it was now possible to begin redeploying our combat forces.

Downing's special mission forces meanwhile relentlessly dismantled the Dignity Battalions; people were coming forth with information on their whereabouts about as fast as Downing's forces could follow up on them. It was a matter of time before they were no longer a viable force. That moment occurred on January 10, when Benjamin Calomarko, their commander, surrendered to U.S. forces.

At 6:00 P.M. on January 11, General Thurman was notified by the Pentagon that Operation JUST CAUSE was officially terminated.

It had indeed been a just cause. All our troops had believed that from the beginning. Their reward would be an enduring feeling in their hearts that they had sacrificed for what was just and right, and that their actions had made Panama a better place.

Their victory for freedom had not been without cost:

U.S. FORCES
- Killed in action   23
- Wounded in action   324

PANAMA
- Personnel killed in action   314
- Wounded in action   124
- Other personnel, weapons, and miscellaneous:

Captured and detained	4,600
Weapons	52,009
Armored vehicles	28
Vessels/ships	18
Money	$7,857,215
Counterfeit money	$101,051
Ammunition	600 tons
Explosives	42 tons
Chemical (CS/CO)	13,392 canisters

All armored vehicles, crew-served weapons, and ammunition were evacuated to the United States.

All other weapons and ammunition, except what was needed for training and equipping the new presidential security, reaction, and police force, was either destroyed or evacuated to the United States.

All vessels/ships and aircraft were restored to operational condition and left with the new government.

All money was turned over to the new government.

All explosives and chemical weapons were destroyed.

On January 3, we began a phased redeployment (January 18–26) of the 17,000 combat troops over and above the 9,500 troops normally assigned to SOUTHCOM.

Much nation-building work still had to be done in support of PROMOTE LIBERTY. Some of its requirements could take up to two years. The units involved with longer-term programs remained in Panama, but were rotated on a scheduled basis.

For the next nine days, my headquarters, JTF South, continued stability operations while managing the phased redeployment of our forces. We were also transitioning to a headquarters, JTF Panama, commanded by Major General Cisneros, which would take over responsibility for nation-building and security. Its headquarters and Military Support Group had been activated on December 21. Soon it would take control of the 193rd Brigade, the Marine Amphibious Unit, and additional forces that would remain behind—one of Major General Carmen Cavezza's combat brigades, plus a battalion of MPs from the 16th Military Police Brigade.

JTF South passed over all responsibilities to JTF Panama on January 11.

On January 12, at 8:00 A.M., two thousand troopers from the 82nd Airborne Division, the XVIII Airborne Corps staff, and I jumped onto Sicily Drop Zone at Fort Bragg to a cheering, flag-waving crowd of five thousand family members and dignitaries, among them, General Carl Vuono, Army Chief of Staff. The troops assembled on the drop zone and marched with their colors waving in the brisk cool breeze to the bleachers area.

This is what I said there:

"Thank you—and I cannot begin to tell you what you mean to us.

"I wish you could have marched with us across that sand, and experienced our feelings as we drew closer and realized the meaning that you and these children conveyed with the flags you were waving.

"The mission to Panama was a difficult one. We literally decapitated a government, and then shook hands with the very people we had fought the night before and said, 'We want to help you now.'

"You would have been very proud of your soldiers. They're dedicated and motivated by all the things the American flag stands for, the very flags you were waving. No one ever fought more bravely or with more compassion for those they faced in battle.

"Everyone knew there would be danger, but not a single one hesitated to go, or to enter battle time and time again. They were well-trained for the mission, and they fought the way they had trained. We believe that what we were sent to do was just and right.

"Twenty-three of our comrades are at peace today, and they deserve the highest honors for their sacrifice. Our experience adds meaning to the expression 'Freedom Isn't Free.'

"To the families and all the members of this great community, we thank you for your prayers and your support. It gave us strength when strength was needed—and we thank you from the bottom of our hearts."

POST-ACTION THOUGHTS

In the days following Operation JUST CAUSE, I was asked many times, "What lessons did you learn?" and, "If you had to do it all over again, what would you do differently?"

Let me answer the second question first: "I'd have guarded the Nunciatore. That way we would either have grabbed Noriega on the way in, or we would have taken that option away from him."

As for lessons learned: JUST CAUSE was a very successful operation. There were several reasons for its success:

First, the Goldwater-Nichols Act of 1986 clearly established the chain of command down to theater level, along with the authority for fulfilling command responsibility. Under this act, the Chairman of the Joint Chiefs of Staff was made the principal military adviser to the National Command Authority (SECDEF and President), and the Joint Staff was made directly responsible and subordinate to the Chairman, not to the Joint Chiefs, as had been the case before. This does not mean that an astute Chairman does not consult with the service Chiefs; but it eliminated consensual decision-making that was sometimes influenced by service parochialism. The act also included the warfighting commanders-in-chief in the chain of command, and gave them additional authority for conducting military operations in their theaters for wartime as well as peacetime activities.

Second, clear guidance was given by the National Command Authority to General Thurman.

Third, from the start, General Thurman gave me full authority over all forces and the necessary freedom for developing the plan.

Fourth, once the plan was completed, we briefed it all the way up through the decision-making authority, and it was approved as written.

Fifth, we were allowed enough time to fully rehearse.

Sixth, when the operation was launched, we were allowed to execute it without changing the plan.

Back to the question: "What lessons did you learn?"

I can't say we really learned any lessons. In my opinion, you only learn a lesson as a result of a big mistake, or when you have failed to anticipate an event somewhere along the line—training readiness, plan development, or the like—that could effect the mission.

With that said, however, we did validate some principles and procedures that contributed to our success in Panama, which also apply to future operations:

- ✪ Integrated planning and execution are key to success for all contingency operations, particularly for joint operations when forces from other services are involved.
- ✪ A streamlined "warfighter"-oriented command-and-control structure, responsive to needs at lowest levels, is imperative.
- ✪ Overwhelming combat power results in quick victory with fewer casualties on both sides.
- ✪ Continuous review of rules of engagement, with responsive and assured dissemination, maximizes combat capability and flexibility.
- ✪ Use of Joint Communications Electronic Operating Instructions (CEOI) is crucial for successful joint operations.
- ✪ Troops fight to standards to which they are trained—and nothing more. There is no substitute for live-fire training, under the most realistic conditions, as you expect to fight.
- ✪ Maximum latitude must be allowed units at lowest level; otherwise don't expect their fullest potential.
- ✪ No force more powerful than PSYOPs can ever be brought to the battlefield. If you can influence the minds of your foe, the job is much easier and less expensive by every measure.
- ✪ Appropriately integrating Special Operations and conventional forces maximizes force potential and capability in ways not otherwise possible.

Though all of this contributed immeasurably to the success of Operation JUST CAUSE, it is no more than what is normally expected of senior commanders.

And finally, the plan the leaders create may be a thing of great beauty, yet it is only as good as the troops that execute it. The outcome is determined at their level.

I cannot praise enough the motivation, the technical and professional competence, the daring, the maturity, and the caring of our troops at all levels from all the services. Our officers and NCOs were superbly trained; they led their troops the way troops expect to be led. They and their troops did everything we asked—and then more. They have earned the credit for all that was accomplished in Operation JUST CAUSE.

One more group deserves recognition—the wives in Panama who were embroiled without warning in mortal combat, and who spent the night of December 19 and 20 huddled over their children in closets as the battles raged. These same women, two days later, opened and operated the Commissary and P.X. so families could get much-needed supplies. They were professionals of the highest order, most deserving of our deepest respect and gratitude.

YES, Operation JUST CAUSE was an occasion of deep satisfaction. We didn't rest on our laurels, though. We knew another major crisis could come any time, and we had to be prepared for it. Little did we know, however, just how soon that would be.

XII

SHADOWS IN
THE STORM

A t 1:00 A.M. on August 2, 1990, three divisions of the Iraqi Republican Guard, equipped with nearly a thousand tanks, streamed
across Iraq's border with Kuwait. Within half an hour, helicopters dropped
Iraqi commandos on rooftops in Kuwait City. By dawn, the massive invasion
of the small Arab country at the top of the Persian Gulf was well under way.
By nightfall, it was nearly complete, and Saddam Hussein could declare that
Kuwait was now his country's "19th province." By week's end, eleven Iraqi
divisions had backed up his claim.

Though early on American satellites had detected the massing of Iraqi
troops along the border, there had been mixed interpretations of Saddam's
intent, and the initial U.S. approach had been uncertain and at times muddled. In the early hours of the invasion itself, the Bush administration
seemed unsure about what to do. All that quickly changed, however, and on
August 5, President George Bush made his famous "line in the sand"
speech, declaring that the invasion "will not stand." Within hours, Bush had
put together a powerful multinational coalition, including leading Arab nations, and American troops were en route to the Gulf. The massive buildup
that followed eventually brought half a million U.S. troops to the region.

Among them would be nearly 9,000 special operations soldiers—7,705
in Saudi Arabia and 1,049 in Turkey. Special Operations Forces (SOF)
would perform a wide variety of tasks, ranging from simple language interpretation to strikes against targets more than a hundred miles behind enemy
lines. During the early stages of the American buildup, small groups of

SOF operators would be posted on the front lines, both to gather intelligence and to serve as trip wires, symbolic sacrifices in the event Saddam chose to invade Saudi Arabia.

The range of SOF missions in the Gulf amply demonstrated the potential of special operations in the post–Cold War era. It would have done so even more if their initiatives had not been blunted for several reasons—including command attitudes that would have been familiar to the earliest special operators.

WHEN news of the invasion came in, General Stiner, now the Commander-in-Chief of the U.S. Special Operations Command (SOCOM), was sitting in a room at CIA's headquarters in Langley, Virginia. Unlike some of the career intelligence officers around him, Stiner was not surprised by the news. Months before, his intelligence people had pegged Kuwait as one of the next geopolitical hot spots, and SOCOM had been working on contingency plans for possible SOF involvement since July. Even after national intelligence agencies declared that the Iraqi pre-invasion buildup amounted to mere saber-rattling, Stiner had begun mentally drawing up a list of SOF personnel who would be needed to augment the U.S. Central Command (CENTCOM) Headquarters in the event of war.

In order to better support the warfighting CINCs in planning for the employment of SOF forces, each CINC had been given his own Special Operations Command (SOC), resident in his own headquarters, and commanded by either a brigadier general or colonel, with thirty to forty officers and senior NCOs. In time of crisis, it was SOCOM's responsibility to augment the Special Operations Command as necessary to fulfill its warfighting responsibilities. Colonel Jesse Johnson, a very capable and experienced SF officer, was Schwarzkopf's SOC Commander. He required at least two hundred augmentees right off the bat—and more later as the need for SOF capabilities became more clearly identified.

Under the U.S. military's regional joint command organization, CENTCOM was responsible for all operations in Southwest Asia. In many ways, Stiner's SOCOM functioned as a service agency to the different regional commands. With the exception of individual operations directly ordered by the President, CENTCOM's four-star commander, General Norman Schwarzkopf, would direct SOF personnel in Southwest Asia, as Thurman had in Panama.

Available forces included the potent, highly trained special mission units,

Army Special Forces, Navy SEALs, Army and Air Force special aviation units, Rangers, PSYOPs, and Civil Affairs units. At the time of the Iraqi invasion, selected SOCOM special mission units had just finished an exercise simulating a mission deep behind the lines of a Southwest Asian country. The training routine would prove an eerie prelude to what they would soon face in the Gulf.

When news of the Iraqi invasion came in, Stiner immediately placed SOCOM on alert, and SOF planning cells whipped into action.

IRAQ'S rapid invasion of Kuwait presented America with a number of immediate problems, not the least of which was the capture of the American Embassy in Kuwait City. Besides Embassy personnel, many Americans were caught by surprise by the invasion and were trapped in Kuwait and Iraq itself.

SOCOM was tasked by the National Command Authority to develop a plan for rescuing embassy personnel, should that become necessary.

Getting them out wasn't going to be easy, even though the Embassy in Kuwait City presented a classic target for hostage rescue; the building could be isolated and its layout was well-known. Major General Wayne Downing, the JSOTF commander, would later recall that the risks were great: "No one wanted to do this operation," he said later. There was a high potential for casualties and collateral damage. Just as important, the operation might provoke the Iraqis into attacking Saudi Arabia and the allied coalition forces still gathering there. General Schwarzkopf worried that it would precipitate war before he was ready to fight.

By mid-August the forces of nations joining the coalition began arriving in Saudi Arabia, and as they did so, Special Forces detachments from the 5th Special Forces Group (known as coalition support teams—CSTs) were assigned to each unit from division to company level. They spoke the language, advised on training and planning, facilitated the communications for command and control, prepared for effective combat operations, and would be the units' link to U.S. fire support. They lived with their coalition units, trained with them, and later went to war with them.

This was an unsung yet critical mission in the war, one made entirely possible by the evolution that had taken place in Special Operations since the days of Bill Yarborough. SF soldiers could speak the language both of the allies and the enemy, and this key ability would eventually be hailed by General Schwarzkopf as "the glue that held the coalition together."

In addition, special operators' cultural training had taught them not only how to secure a house without killing noncombatants—but also which fork to use at a diplomatic banquet at the Embassy. Such assets made them invaluable as liaison troops.

To Carl Stiner, CSTs personified what made Special Forces special. It came down to a person "motivated by his inner strength, mature judgment, and technical competence. You put him out there maybe for four or five months or longer. And the image of the United States is resting on what he does. And you've got to know that he's going to do what's right when the time comes."

The First Gulf War—Earnest Will

Stiner's proposals for a special operations war against Iraq drew on several past Special Operations missions, not least of which were a series of operations conducted in the Gulf during the Iran-Iraq War, called Operation Earnest Will. As that war dragged on, a threat so complex and politically significant developed that it ultimately required capabilities that only SOF forces possessed.

By the fall of 1986, the ground war between those two nations had devolved into a stalemate. Iraq had devastated its adversary's economy with strikes on Iranian oil facilities, while Iran had struck back by initiating a tanker war and targeting neutral ships in the Persian Gulf. These attacks especially threatened Kuwait, who, while officially neutral, had been helping the Iraqis during the war.

Mining and attacks by small, swift patrol boats became so successful that by the winter of 1986–87, Japanese, Swedish, and Norwegian ships stopped traveling to Kuwait. This put pressure not merely on the Gulf states, but on the entire world, and oil prices began to rise to dangerous levels.

In March 1987, President Ronald Reagan took steps to end the problem. He agreed to register eleven Kuwaiti tankers as American ships, and provide them with Navy escorts. The U.S. ships would form protected convoys through the Gulf.

That portion of the mission received a great deal of media attention, and was generally successful, but it did not stop the Iranians from preying on individual ships. Contact mines were a special problem. Cheap, and hard to detect with the naked eye, such mines were easy to deploy covertly at night, and could easily cripple a tanker. Their presence alone disrupted commerce.

While the U.S. rushed minesweeping gear to the Gulf, the Navy realized that the problem had to be attacked at the source: The Iranians had to be intercepted before they released the weapons.

Two MH-6 and four AH-6 Little Bird helicopters from the Army's special aviation unit were assigned to do just that. They were placed directly under Middle East Force commander Rear Admiral Harold J. Bernsen and charged with nailing suspicious contacts identified by Navy patrols.

Their first challenge was to adapt the gear aboard the helicopters to sea duty. Just the act of landing and taking off from a rolling ship presented pilots with problems they had never encountered before. In addition, certain Army munitions, including the potent 2.75-inch rockets used by the Little Birds, could be ignited by radio bands common on Navy ships. After considerable testing, Navy experts found that special metal barrier plates, and the substitution of a Navy rocket motor, would allow the Army weapons to be safely stowed aboard ship.

By August 6, the helicopters were ready for action. Operating at night in elements of three—one MH-6 and two AH-6s—they flew with Navy LAMPS helicopters, which vectored them toward suspicious targets. Each helicopter in the operation had different capabilities. The LAMPS (special versions of the Kaman SH-2F Seasprite) were equipped with powerful surveillance radars, but were lightly armed (if at all) and not generally suited for nighttime attacks. The MH-6 and AH-6 were both variations of the Hughes/McDonnell Douglas MD500/530 series, extremely quick and agile scout helicopters. Both variants were armed. In general terms, the MH series were more optimized for transport and observation missions, and the AHs for firepower.

Meanwhile, Admiral Bernsen needed patrol craft to monitor and intercept the Iranian strike boats. Because of the mine danger, the patrols had to be made by fast, shallow-draft craft, but the Gulf's rough seas and frequent storms ruled out much of the Navy's light-craft inventory. Bernsen settled on Mark III patrol boats, sixty-five-foot fastmovers that could hit thirty knots and mounted both 40mm and 20mm cannons, as well as numerous lighter weapons. Six Mark IIIs, along with slightly smaller and less capable craft, were detailed to the operation.

SEALs began arriving in late August, giving the admiral a force he could use for several contingencies. SEAL Team Two and SEAL Team One, along with support units, were housed aboard the *Guadalcanal,* an assault ship whose helicopters were already supporting EARNEST WILL convoys. The aircraft elevator and hangar deck soon began echoing with live-fire exercises.

But there was another problem: For tactical and strategic reasons, the *Guadalcanal* had been ordered to operate in the southern Gulf, too far south for SEAL operations against the Iranians ranging in the northern Persian Gulf near Farsi Island. A land base seemed out of the question, and even if a site could be found on friendly soil, it would be far from the Iranian waters and an easy target for terrorists. Special Operations officers back in the States as well as Bernsen and the SEAL commander on the scene wanted a mobile sea base, but any American ship that far north would be an instant and obvious target for the Iranians. Not only would it be subject to mining, but it would draw considerable attention to U.S. involvement in the conflict. SOF commanders began searching for a low-profile floating home that could support the operations without drawing too much attention. In essence, they wanted a vessel with a crane, space to hoist patrol boats aboard for servicing, a helicopter landing pad, and room to house the special operators and support team.

The Military Sealift Command found two oil-rig-servicing barges, the *Hercules* and the *Wimbrown VII,* large craft previously used by civilian companies. The *Hercules* measured 400 feet, and came with a massive revolving crane designed for oil-rig construction, a helicopter pad, and plenty of space. It seemed tailor-made for the mission. *Wimbrown VII,* at about half the *Hercules*'s size, was a tighter squeeze, but it, too, met the mission requirements.

The SEALs went to work converting the craft, adding hangars and skids for the boats as well as defenses and radar. With a Navy frigate providing escort, the *Hercules* set sail from Bahrain at the southern end of the Gulf on September 21. *Wimbrown VII,* in need of more work, followed in October, though for several reasons it was not actually deployed in hostile waters until November.

As the *Hercules* put out to sea, an Iranian cargo vessel that intelligence had tagged as a possible minelayer was sailing southward from Iran. The vessel was called the *Iran Ajr.*

At about 1830 on September 21, the *Iran Ajr* veered from its normal course near Iran into international waters east-northeast of Ra'Rakan, a small island off the northern tip of Qatar. Meanwhile, the Navy frigate *Jarrett* was sailing about fifteen miles away, with three Special Ops helicopters aboard. The MH-6 and two AH-6s took off to monitor the *Iran Ajr*.

They found her forty-five minutes later. The MH-6, equipped with sophisticated night-flying and surveillance gear, took a quick pass. The Little Bird's pilot spotted "a bunch of fifty-five-gallon drums down the port side, a canvas-covered area in the middle, and a Zodiac-type boat." The Iranian vessel was apparently not carrying mines, but this was not standard cargo for a merchant ship, either. The pilot pulled back and joined the other helicopters, which shadowed the vessel for about an hour. There was no sign that the Iranians were aware of their presence.

At 2250, the *Iran Ajr* turned off its lights and reversed course. The MH-6 went in for another look. This time the pilot saw the cylindrical-shaped objects being pushed over the side and realized he was looking at mines. He radioed back for instructions.

"Take them under fire!" came the order from the frigate. The AH-6s closed in. "Inbound hot," warned the pilot, as the Little Bird's minigun opened up, spraying the deck near the mines with machine-gun fire. The attack helicopters launched 2.75-inch high-explosive rockets and raked the ship with gunfire. An exploding paint locker sent fireballs skyward. Soon, the engine room and the steering and electrical systems were disabled. The ship went dead in the water. The helicopters were ordered to cease fire.

Fifteen minutes later, the ship's crew managed to restore power; the ship began moving again. They also tried desperately to deploy the mines.

More rockets and machine-gun fire from the AH-6s changed their minds. As the flames stoked up and the lights died again, the *Iran Ajr*'s crew began to abandon ship. Their Zodiac pulled away, attempting a high-speed escape. An AH-6 pursued in the darkness. As the helicopter closed on the small boat, someone on the craft "jumped to his feet in a threatening manner," according to a SOF crew member. Unsure whether the Iranian had a man-portable antiair missile or some other weapon, the helicopter pilot fired his pistol out of the open door. Incredibly, he not only "neutralized" the Iranian but punctured the boat.

SEALs, meanwhile, were preparing to take the ship. Despite planning and communications snafus, a SEAL platoon approached it just after first light in a shallow-draft landing craft, chosen because it was unlikely to set off a contact mine. However, it exposed the assault team to other dangers.

"As we got closer, we hunkered down behind the gunwales," a team member said later. "The coxswain was inexperienced, and it took him five minutes to get us in position before we could board. One grenade lobbed into the well deck . . . and we all would have been history."

As the SEALs scrambled aboard and secured the enemy ship, they realized that all the Iranians aboard had fled. In fact, they'd left so quickly, the teletypes and radios were still on.

The capture of the *Iran Ajr* stopped its minelaying operation, and saved ships and lives. Perhaps more important, the boarding team discovered a number of intelligence documents, including a chart showing where it had already laid mines.

The *Iran Ajr* was eventually sunk by SOF personnel—but not before U.S. Secretary of Defense Caspar Weinberger, in the Gulf to inspect U.S. forces, had taken a personal tour.

THE *Hercules* and its force of patrol boats and helicopters began operations in the area of Farsi Island on October 6. Within hours, they had discovered the Iranians' patrol pattern and devised a way to disrupt it.

Using a buoy navigational aid as a precise checkpoint in the open water, the SEALs and three Little Birds set up an ambush. Vectored toward a radar contact by a Navy LAMPS helicopter, an MH-6 pilot picked up an object on his FLIR (Forward Looking Infrared Receiver, for night vision). He pressed forward for the attack.

"We've got some vessels dead in the water at twelve o'clock," he told his flight. "Approximately one-half mile, no movement, no hostile intent at this time."

The helicopters closed in fast. The image in the FLIR sharpened. A 12.7mm machine gun and its telltale tripod sat on the deck of the largest vessel in the screen.

Not an American weapon. Not an American boat.

"We have Boghammers," shouted the pilot over the radio, alerting the others to the enemy. There were actually three boats—two smaller Boston Whaler types as well as the "Boghammer," a potent and fast patrol craft forty-one feet long and displacing about 6.4 tons. Boghammers were used for a variety of purposes by the Iranians, none of them benign. The sky lit up with tracers as the Iranians spotted the Americans. The MH-6 ducked left, and an AH-6 put two rockets and a barrage of machine-gun bullets into the cluster of boats. The Boston Whalers caught fire.

The Boghammer, however, had only just begun to fight. As he closed to attack, the AH-6 pilot saw the telltale flash and spiral of a shoulder-launched SAM spitting into the air; he immediately began defensive maneuvers.

"It went right by my door, off the right side of the aircraft," he recalled. The missile proved to be an American-made Stinger heat-seeker. Fortunately, it, and probably a second, were launched without definite locks on their targets. The Little Birds were unharmed.

Obscured by the smoke from the other two boats, the Boghammer took off. But it's hard for a boat to outrun a helicopter, and the second AH-6 took it out with a rocket from extremely close range. The craft sank within thirty seconds.

Meanwhile, two American patrol boats closed in at full speed. The SEALs got to the wrecked boats just as the flames were dying out, and began picking up survivors amid six-foot swells. But the danger had not completely passed.

"Several prisoners were pulled out of the water armed," said a SEAL team member later. "One petty officer actually wrestled a guy for his gun— I mean actually wrestled him on the deck for his gun. The gun went over the side."

Meanwhile, a force of twenty or so Iranian small boats massed in the distance. Had they come forward, they might have overpowered the patrol craft; the helicopters, low on ammunition and fuel, would have been hard-pressed in the attack. The SEAL commander nevertheless turned his two patrol boats in the Iraqis' direction. The bluff scattered them.

Only six of the thirteen survivors from the three Iranian boats lived. The wounded Iranians were treated by the Americans and eventually returned home.

THE Special Forces operations demonstrated to the Iranians that further patrol boat operations would come at a heavy cost. So they turned to a new tactic—Silkworm missiles.

Essentially a Chinese copy of the Russian SS-N-2, Silkworms are relatively slow, sixties-era weapons with primitive guidance (though they use active radar on final approach), an explosive warhead of nearly nine hundred pounds, and a range of twenty-five to fifty miles. Despite their limitations, they remain a potent threat against unarmed or lightly armed ships. In

1967, the original Soviet version was used by Egyptian patrol boats to sink an Israeli destroyer, the first time in history that a ship was sunk by a surface missile.

On October 15, the Iranians launched an attack against tankers loading oil at Kuwait's Sea Island terminal. The British-owned *Sungari* suffered a direct hit, and an American-flagged Kuwaiti tanker named the *Sea Isle City* was struck the next day. Though seventeen crewmen and the American captain were injured in the attack, the vessel was not seriously damaged.

The Reagan administration ordered a retaliation. But the President, seeking to limit the conflict, ruled out a strike against Silkworm sites, which were on Iranian soil. He opted instead for the destruction of an Iranian oil platform known as the Rashadat GOSP (GOSP stands for gas and oil separation platform; this one had multiple structures). The Rashadat GOSP had two platforms 130 meters apart. At the north was an oil-drilling rig; at the south was a platform used as living quarters and equipment storage and repair. A third platform, supposedly abandoned, lay about two miles north of these structures.

Three destroyers, a frigate, and a cruiser were tagged to shell the platforms. A SEAL platoon would then board and search for prisoners before blowing them up.

The operation got under way at 1340 on October 19. Broadcasts from the destroyer *Thach* warned the Iranians to abandon the platforms; they quickly complied, and shelling began. Flames leapt up within minutes, and the fire soon spread.

Smoke and flames towered over the SEALs as their three rubber assault boats were lowered from the deck of the *Thach*. They could feel the heat as they approached the ravaged oil rig. "The surface of the water was on fire within a two-hundred- to three-hundred-foot radius around the burning platform," remembered the SEAL officer in charge.

Trying their best to ignore the heat, flames, and smoke, the SEALs set charges on the oil drilling platform, then searched the other platform, capturing cryptographic encoding devices and documents. All three platforms were eventually destroyed, with no American causalities and none known to the Iranians.

Though the Iranians did not immediately end their attacks, the U.S. Special Forces activities caused them to sharply reduce the tempo of their attacks and shift their focus to the central and southern Persian Gulf.

It was not until April of 1998, when the U.S. frigate *Samuel B. Roberts* struck a mine east of Bahrain, that another major operation was launched, this time primarily by regular Navy units. Initially targeting oil platforms, the engagement eventually included several Iranian patrol boats and aircraft, most of which were destroyed or heavily damaged.

PACIFIC WIND

That was the background when, in September, Stiner journeyed to the Gulf with Downing to get a firsthand view of the situation, brief Schwarzkopf, and finalize details on the embassy operation, which came to be called PA-CIFIC WIND. Before departing, Stiner checked with Powell to see if he had any special guidance.

"Saddam is making threats about waging a worldwide terrorist campaign," Powell told him, "and I don't want Norm worrying about this. You keep the terrorists off his back and tell him that we want his focus to be to the North."

In Saudi Arabia, Stiner linked up with Jesse Johnson, while Downing co-ordinated the details of PACIFIC WIND with Schwarzkopf's staff and component commanders.

For the next three days, Stiner and Johnson visited every coalition support team, as well as other SOF forces, including those involved in retraining and equipping the remnants of Kuwait's army that had ended up in Saudi Arabia, and the training of resistance teams for infiltration into Kuwait City.

In Stiner's mind, the contributions that SOF could make were limited only by what SOF would be allowed to do—and by Johnson's ability to effectively manage the myriad of complex mission profiles. Johnson's problem was his colonel's rank—every other component commander for Army, Navy, Air Force, and Marine conventional forces carried three stars. This just wasn't going to work. The general officers would inevitably command more resources as well as respect. He was going to have to take it up with Schwarzkopf.

Meanwhile, Downing had settled on the details of PACIFIC WIND.

The plan for taking the embassy was deceptively simple: JSOTF special mission units, supported by USAF air strikes to neutralize air defenses and isolate the embassy compound, would land at night by helicopter in the compound, take out the Iraqi guards, and rescue the personnel being held there.

If the goal was straightforward, however, the chances of achieving surprise and neutralizing the Iraqis in the occupied city was not. The invaders
had located their theater headquarters in the Hotel Safir next to the embassy. The nearby beachfront, as well as the local road network, gave the
enemy easy access to the target. Even the act of positioning the assault
group close enough to Kuwait to launch the attack was a complicated logistics matter.

Vice Admiral Stanley R. Arthur, commander of the U.S. Seventh Fleet
and the Navy component of Central Command, solved part of the logistics
problem by making a Navy LPH available for the mission. LPHs look like
World War II–era escort carriers, and in fact, the first versions of the assault
ships were converted from just such vessels. At about 600 feet long, LPHs
are only half as long as attack carriers such as the *Nimitz,* and displace less
than a fifth of a supercarrier's bulk; but they can carry a reinforced Marine
battalion and its vehicles, as well as support them once an attack is under
way. Optimized to get the assault troops on and off quickly via helicopter,
LPHs typically carry two dozen helicopters, and can make about twenty-
three knots. Though now overshadowed in the Navy by the newer Wasp and
Tarawa LHA vessels, the LPHs nonetheless offered the Special Operations
troops both a jumping-off point and floating headquarters.

At a meeting in the Gulf, Arthur assured Downing he could quickly off-
load the Marines and replace them with the Special Operations package.

Downing and Stiner were well aware that the Iraqis had to be neutralized with overwhelming firepower at the start of the operation. The most
practical method for that was to use the Air Force. Soon after their arrival,
they met with Brigadier General Buster C. Glosson, a command pilot who
oversaw all U.S. Air Force wings in the Gulf and directed planning for
Lieutenant General Chuck Horner, the CENTCOM air commander.
Downing and Colonel "Pete," one of his commanders, laid the plans out in
Glosson's small command room in Riyadh, carefully going over the assault.
When he finished, Glosson had a funny look on his face.

"Are you guys serious?" asked Glosson.

"Yeah," said Downing. "We're serious."

"You guys really think you can go in in downtown Kuwait City?"

"If we got your support the way we want it, we can do it."

Glosson looked at the map again. "You're goddamn right," he said finally.
"You got my support."

Glosson's F-117As and F-15Es—the Air Force's front-line tactical bombers—were what they wanted. As eventually perfected, the plan called for a pair of F-117A Stealth Fighters to launch laser-guided missiles at the Iraqi headquarters in the Hotel Safir precisely sixty seconds before the helos landed. The 2,000-pound warheads would reduce the hotel's eight floors to rubble, wiping out the Iraqi headquarters, as well as depriving the enemy of a fire control center. Electrical power would be cut with another F-117 attack on a nearby electrical tower. The F-15E Strike Eagles would then drop cluster bombs around the embassy, neutralizing Iraqi troops and creating a minefield to isolate the building.

Cluster bombs were a common weapon during the war. Officially called CBUs (Cluster Bomb Units), they are actually a collection of smaller bomblets, and can be configured for different missions. CBU-87s spray more than two hundred antipersonnel and antiarmor bomblets over an area, killing unprotected personnel and destroying lightly armored vehicles. CBU-89 "Gators" lay down a mix of about a hundred antipersonnel and antiarmor mines, creating an instant minefield. The word *Gator* comes from the twenty-four BLU-92/B antitank mines the CBU launches; the image of snapping alligators provides an apt metaphor for these weapons' devastating effect on vehicles.

Glosson did more than commit Air Force support for the assault. He took the plan personally to General Schwarzkopf. Though the CINC was still not enamored of an attack that might precipitate a war he wasn't ready to fight, he gave his okay.

At a meeting with Schwarzkopf, Downing briefed PACIFIC WIND. Then, with Downing and Johnson present, Stiner summarized his visit for the CINC: "I have visited all SOF teams and units in your area of operations, and in my judgment they are doing an outstanding job. The coalition support teams (CSTs) will be worth their weight in gold—they'll give you 'truth in reporting' about what the coalition units are doing.

"You already have nine thousand SOF over here," Stiner continued, "and I'm prepared to give you whatever you need. I know you have the greatest confidence in Jesse Johnson—and I do, too. But, considering the complexity of his operation, together with what SOF can do for you in the broader context, I would like to give you one of my best two-stars—maybe even two general officers—to run our part of things." He had already told Johnson the same thing privately before the meeting.

"I'll think about it," Schwarzkopf responded.

At this point, Stiner delivered Colin Powell's message about keeping terrorists off Schwarzkopf's back so he could focus his attention on Kuwait and Iraq.

"I intend to move one-third of my special mission forces to Europe," Stiner said, "but here would be better, so they can respond quicker.

"I would also like to establish a small tactical command post in Saudi Arabia or Egypt, so I can be more responsive to your needs. I'll even wear a plain flight suit with no rank. Nobody will know that I'm here."

"I'll let you know," the CINC replied.

Back in the States a week later, Stiner learned from Powell that he could forget about his small command post. According to Schwarzkopf, the Saudis didn't want another four-star command in their country. The offer of a general officer to run Schwarzkopf's special operations activities never received an answer.

Stiner thought he knew the reason. As we have often seen before, the "big" Army has traditionally been, at best, unfamiliar with special operations, and at worst, hostile. Such attitudes naturally derive from the normal machinery of internal politics, the sort of political infighting that springs up within any organization. Part of it comes from a distrust of unconventional warfare in general. In some cases, the image of Special Forces as "can-do" guys actually hurts them. Highly trained elites called on to operate clandestinely in hazardous situations risk a bad reputation. It's not a big jump from there to thinking SF guys can be evil.

One Special Forces general recalled meeting a Navy officer who told him that sitting down with Special Forces planners was like encountering "the princes of darkness." Despite the success of Earnest Will and a concerted effort by the Special Forces Command not only to increase SOF professionalism but to make others aware of it, as the Cold War wound down, such attitudes—and others even worse—were far too common.

The SOF approach to warfare called for a high degree of cooperation between different branches of service. But that cooperation wasn't always forthcoming.

General Schwarzkopf himself apparently did not trust SOF units—or if he did, he did not want them inside Iraq before his conventional forces were in place and ready to fight.

Both General Schwarzkopf's CENTCOM and General Stiner's SOCOM were headquartered at the same base near Tampa, Florida. They were next-door neighbors. While the two men got along personally, there was plenty of friction between members of the two commands. "Schwarzkopf was a good example of a senior officer who did not understand Special Operations and was afraid of it," said Major General Jim Guest, looking back on the start of the Gulf War. "Schwarzkopf's mentality was, 'I have a coiled cobra in a cage and if I open that cage, that cobra is going to get out and possibly embarrass me.'"

Many SOF officers understood Schwarzkopf's decision not to allow Stiner to move his command to the Middle East. Two four-stars in the same battle theater could cause unnecessary confusion, no matter how carefully they orchestrated their command structures. But the CENTCOM CINC's resistance to SOF went beyond that. In the opinion of Stiner, Downing, and others, Schwarzkopf handicapped the utility of Special Operations in the Gulf War by insisting that the command be represented and managed in the theater by the colonel—no matter how able—instead of a general officer. He also allotted insufficient resources and priorities for SOF units, thus hampering planning and intelligence.

Though SEALs were among the first units in the Gulf, Schwarzkopf changed deployment priorities in favor of more conventional forces, which delayed the arrival of most of the 5th Special Forces Group. This meant that, when most needed, he did not have available his main Special Forces asset, the Army Green Berets, with its broad range of special operations expertise and capabilities. That left only a few SEALs to work with Saudi forces to provide intelligence, coordinate air support, and form an American trip wire at the border at a most critical time. Combat air support (CAS) was not generally considered a SEAL mission, but the unit's inherent flexibility and its interface with different branches and services helped it do its job.

After the 5th SFG finally arrived in late August and early September, Special Forces personnel began branching out as CSTs, serving initially with Saudi, Egyptian, and Syrian units. Some 109 CST teams were eventually formed, working at all levels of command.

During September, Green Berets replaced SEALs at the border, working with Saudi paratroopers and border police along the Saudi side of the berms separating the countries. Nine reconnaissance detachments provided around-the-clock surveillance and "truth in reporting."

"You've got three missions up on the border," 5th SFG commander, Colonel James Kraus, told his men. "See, Scream, and Scoot." Special Forces units didn't always "scoot." Several snagged infiltrators and deserters during the early days of the buildup.

MEANWHILE, there was a justified fear of Iraqi-inspired terror attacks. National intelligence agencies had learned that as many as thirty Iraqi terrorist teams were positioning to conduct strikes against U.S. embassies and other allied facilities in other parts of the world. To counter this threat, SOF units provided security to vulnerable embassies and other facilities, and special mission teams were prepared to deploy instantly to handle unexpected situations.

As a result of these and other related efforts, no Iraqi terror attempts were successful—though at least two Iraqi operations, one in Jakarta and another in Manila, were foiled when terrorist bombs blew up while the terrorists were preparing or transporting them. "Iraqi bad luck," the JSOTF commander Major General Downing put it.

While all this was going on, Special Operations troops began practicing for PACIFIC WIND off the coast of Florida. They built a mock-up of the Embassy, and the Navy lent them an LPH. They worked out problems: For example, while the Army and Air Force people were used to working at night, the Navy wasn't. The assault ship's captain nearly freaked when Downing told him to turn off the deck lights.

"God, I can't do that," protested the captain.

"Yeah, we can do it," Downing responded. The lights were turned off.

Thirty helicopters, from Army Special Aviation, commanded by Lieutenant Colonel "Doug," crammed with Army special missions troops, peeled off from the deck in the dead of night without a hitch or scraped rotor blade. The Navy captain turned to Downing and said, "If I didn't know I was awake, I would think I was dreaming this."

A short time later, a pair of Air Force F-15 pilots flew in from the Gulf to help with a live-fire rehearsal at Fort Bragg. The Eagles came in low and hot; and windows broke in nearby Fayetteville. But a little broken glass seemed incidental.

MEANWHILE, SOF planners were working up other missions. The most promising involved fomenting and supporting a guerrilla movement similar to the one that eventually kicked the Soviet Union out of Afghanistan. Intelligence analysts had noted that Kurds, in the north of Iraq, and Shiites, in the south, were displeased with Saddam's regime. Encouraging dissident movements there, as well as stoking guerrilla activity in Kuwait, would weaken and disrupt the Iraqi military, whose units would be tied down dealing with dissension. A pilot team of SOF ground and air personnel flew to Turkey soon after the invasion to examine the possibilities in northern Iraq. About half of the 10th Special Forces Group would be on the ground there by the end of September, ostensibly in Turkey to help provide search and rescue support for the U.S. Air Force pilots shot down over northern Iraq. The operation was headed by Brigadier General "Richard," himself a former commando.

At least four different dissident groups were active in Kuwait, estimated to consist of about 3,500 armed personnel. Though these could have been supported and encouraged in various ways, especially since SOF troops were already on the front line as "trip wires" and well-equipped SEAL units were in the Gulf, the plans for assisting resistance movements and general sabotage failed to receive support from Washington or from Schwarzkopf, who worried about the political ramifications of losing Americans behind the lines.

As an alternative, which would also provide a source of intelligence in Kuwait City, a Special Planning Group was organized under SOCCENT, consisting of an SF lieutenant colonel, two SF warrant officers, and five SF NCOs. This group conducted specialized unconventional warfare training for selected Kuwaiti personnel, who were eventually infiltrated into Kuwait. The Special Planning Group provided operational direction and intelligence-collection requirements to the Kuwaiti resistance throughout the conflict. Ninety-five percent of the HUMINT intelligence that came from occupied Kuwait resulted from this initiative.

By the end of October, however, a systematic campaign by the Iraqis had greatly diminished the effectiveness of the Kuwaiti resistance groups; photos smuggled out of the country showed dismembered bodies hanging from lampposts—a sign to others.

SOF planners also mapped operations against Saddam.

The Iraqi dictator's normal procedure was to disguise his movements, use doubles, and move constantly among temporary headquarters (i.e., converted recreation vehicles) and permanent ones, as well as sleeping quarters. The SOF plan was to strike him in one of his rec vehicles; or, as Stiner put it, "We'd hit him one night while he was laughing at us in one of his Winnebagos."

There were a few little problems with this plan: In addition to the massive operational difficulties of such a risky operation, U.S. law forbade assassination of heads of state. True, once combat had been initiated, Saddam would become a legitimate target, but as it was, the plan withered and died.

So did others. In December, Saddam released the American hostages, including those at the Embassy he called "guests." PACIFIC WIND and similar plans were quietly shelved.

THE AIR WAR

Other plans, however, moved forward. As the buildup of allied troops progressed, the United States shaped a strategy for driving the Iraqis out of Kuwait. The war would take place in two distinct stages:

- ✪ An aerial assault was designed to neutralize Iraqi units, deprive Saddam Hussein of command and control over his forces, and weaken the country's ability to resist attack.
- ✪ A ground attack would then physically confront Iraqi ground forces and drive them from Kuwait and positions threatening Saudi Arabia.

From the very beginning, the air campaign was seen as essential to the success of the mission. The coalition planners hoped to decimate and terrorize the Iraqis before launching ground troops. Not only would that increase the odds of quick success, but it would lessen the number of casualties, an important political consideration.

The air attack itself could be broken into distinct phases. The most critical would occur at the very beginning, when the Iraqis' vast network of integrated antiair defenses had to be neutralized. Based largely on a Soviet model and heavily reliant on Russian weapons, Iraqi air defenses included a sophisticated network of advance warning and localized radars, a wide range of surface-to-air missiles, front-line fighters like the MiG-29, and a large number of antiaircraft artillery batteries that, though primitive, remained deadly. The multilayered defenses had to be neutralized as quickly as possible to give coalition aircraft freedom to operate over Iraq at will.

The first strike had to be massive and quick, but it also had to be stealthy. That meant cruise missiles and the still largely untested F-117A Stealth Fighter would have key roles in the operation. But there were too few of these to cover the vast number of Iraqi air defense units, and the sheer size of the country made it difficult to orchestrate an effective attack everywhere at once.

As plans developed, it became clear that one of the keys to the first-day mission would be the destruction of two Iraqi early-warning radars guarding the country's southwestern frontier. While most of Iraq's early-warning radars were sited to cover one another (if one went out, others made up for the loss), eliminating these two sites would provide a "black" corridor for planes flying north.

The hole would be especially useful for F-15E Strike Eagles targeted to hit Scud missiles in the first hours of the air war. Destroying those missiles had become a top priority, since their launch against Israel might prompt retaliatory raids, which in turn could threaten the fragile allied coalition.

However, striking the radars, though obviously desirable, brought serious problems. An attack on these sites would take resources from other high-priority Iraqi assets. More important, it could also warn the rest of the defense network. To avoid such a result, the sites would have to be knocked out simultaneously, but the large number of individual radars and support facilities at each site made it difficult to coordinate comprehensive, effective bombing raids that would achieve that end.

As General Glosson contemplated the plans, a Special Forces officer, Captain Randy O'Boyle, joined his staff to help coordinate Special Forces operations. An experienced flight examiner and planner, Captain O'Boyle had particular expertise with MH-53J Pave Low helicopters, which had come to the Gulf with the 20th Special Operations Squadron, part of the Air Force Special Operations Command. In September, he became the helicopter advisor in the planning cell for the air campaign.

After examining the developing plans, O'Boyle realized that the early-warning radars would be perfect targets for Special Operations ground forces. Glosson agreed. General Schwarzkopf did not. When this plan was presented to him, he exploded. The CINC was not prepared to commit ground forces across the border until he was ready. An alternative had to be found.

In the meantime, the radars were moved back about twenty miles from their original position a mile or so from the border. A ground assault became impractical.

Jesse Johnson then considered making the attack with his Pave Lows, but while the MH-53s were highly capable aircraft, they were optimized for clandestine insertion and extraction missions, not blowing things up. They were big and fast, and able to operate in bad weather and at night, but their heaviest weapons were only .50-caliber machine guns. The helicopters' commander, Lieutenant Colonel Rich Comer, believed his machine guns could destroy the large dishes, but probably not before the Iraqis had time to call their headquarters.

There *were* helicopters in the Gulf that had more than enough firepower to eliminate the dishes quickly, however—Army Apaches. Decked out with Hellfire missiles and 30mm chain guns, the AH-64s could make short work of the installations.

If they could find them. Though their pilots were well-versed in night fighting, the Apache helicopters were primarily designed for engagements with tanks and armored formations, which are easy to find, even at night. The desert in that part of the world is *empty,* landmarks are virtually non-existent, and Apaches did not come equipped with the sophisticated navigation and sensor equipment aboard the Air Force birds. The Apaches would have trouble finding the targets at night.

The obvious solution was to combine Pave Lows (for guidance) with Apaches (for firepower). And that was the solution chosen. The Pave Lows would lead the Apaches to the sites, then step aside as their smaller brethren went to work. A simple notion, yet one that had never been tried, even in training. And it wasn't simply a situation where Air Force guys would climb in their birds, take off, and let the Army guys hang on to their tails. Different service cultures had to be coordinated; likewise communications gear. There were other, even more practical, problems: The Apaches' limited range would have to be increased, and their weapons, optimized for armor attacks, would have to be tested for effectiveness against radars and their vans.

The Apache commander, Lieutenant Colonel Dick Cody, quickly came on board and adapted his unit's tactics and aircraft for the mission. He welded 1,500-gallon tanks to the bottom of his helos and conducted live-fire practice sessions with Hellfire antitank missiles to make sure they would explode when striking the comparatively soft targets.

They did. The plan—called EAGER ANVIL—proceeded.

It would be the first strike of the war.

General Schwarzkopf, suspicious as ever of special operations, somewhat reluctantly blessed it, but kept close tabs on the training. The story goes that he allowed the operation to proceed with one overriding order: "Do not screw this up."

THE Saudi desert stretched out in endless darkness as White Team skittered toward Iraq during the early-morning hours of January 17, 1991. In the lead Pave Low, Pilot Captain Mike Kingsley and his copilot took turns scanning the green screen of the FLIR. They had been flying now for just over an hour at a relatively leisurely pace—no strain for the powerful helicopter; the same could not be said for the crew. The six men—two pilots, two flight engineers, two para-rescue men, or PJs—had been practicing this gig for weeks, but even the most realistic exercise was still simply an exercise. The standard "test guns" order shortly after takeoff had blown away only a portion of the jitters. They were going to start a war and they knew it.

A few hundred yards back, the pilot in the second Pave Low, Major Bob Leonik, rechecked his navigation set, which had gone flaky shortly after takeoff when the Enhanced Navigation System (ENS) had inexplicably "dumped." The crew had had to work feverishly to reset the system. At the same time, a glitch in their SATCOM coding had deprived them of a secure way to talk to Command. Both problems had been solved, the helicopter was precisely on course, and relatively unimportant transmissions were now coming over the radio. Mission Commander Comer, listening to the SAT-COM from the left-hand seat of the Pave Low cockpit, resisted the impulse to tell them all to shut up.

Farther back, the Apaches flew in a four-ship, staggered-line formation. Each attack helicopter carried two crew members and was loaded with Hellfires, rockets, and 30mm machine-gun shells.

White Team pushed over the border, dropping to fifty feet over the shifting dunes. The pilot pulled right, ducking toward the dry bed of a large wadi that would hide the flight's approach toward its target. The crew doused the last lights in the cabin.

"We're in Iraq," said the copilot laconically. It was just past 0213. Their attack was to begin at 0238. H-hour for the war was 0300.

The west and east radar sites—called "California" and "Nevada"—were very similar. Each contained a number of Soviet-made radars and support vans. Each radar sat on its own van or truck, either buried in the sand or placed in a revetment. Antennas were either the familiar rotating dishes or else something more like fixed radio masts. Together, they scanned a wide area and covered both high and low altitudes. An assortment of support trailers or vans were arrayed around for communications and other functions, and there were also troop quarters.

Neutralizing the sites meant hitting not just radars but their control and communications facilities.

One big problem with launching a surprise attack on an early-warning site is that it is itself designed to keep such attacks from being a surprise. But no radar will give one hundred percent coverage. EAGER ANVIL's tactics had been drawn up to take advantage of known holes in California's and Nevada's capabilities. Different radars have different capabilities, but in general they have trouble picking out objects very close to the ground. Even radars designed to detect low-flying airplanes—such as the P-15M Squat Eyes at each of the target sites—have limited detection envelopes because of ground clutter and physical limitations in the equipment. In this case, the helicopters would be essentially invisible at fifty feet off the ground even at close range. If they got higher than that, however, they could be easily spotted.

They could also be heard, no matter what altitude they flew, and so the routes of both attack groups carefully avoided known Iraqi installations. When the Pave Lows in Red Team detected an unexpected Iraqi formation in their path, they doglegged around them, hoping to prevent the troops from hearing the very loud rotors of the MH-53s and AH-64s.

The Pave Lows in White Team drove up the wadi to a point about ten miles southeast of the radar sites, then swung left, the pilot pushing the throttle for more speed as White Team whipped over a road. He listened intently, hoping that the PJs in the back wouldn't see anything on the highway.

Nothing. They were ghosts, wandering across the desert undetected.

2:36. They reached the IP 7.5 miles southeast of their target—the "no-shit point," they called it. One of the crew members ignited chemical glow sticks in the back of the helicopter, waving his arm through the open doorway and dropping the bundle on the desert floor, a literal "X" marking the navigation spot. All the high-tech equipment aboard the Pave Lows notwithstanding, the success of the mission came down to a PJ's steady hand.

The Apaches sped forward at sixty knots, using the glowing sticks to orient themselves for the attack. They updated their guidance systems, then kicked on their target-acquisition computers and continued in toward the targets. A dozen buildings, clusters of command vans, radar dishes, a troposcatter radar antenna—the site began to reveal itself in their night goggles. One by one, the interphones in the helos buzzed: "I've got the target." Lasers beamed.

Lights popped on in the buildings as they closed to 5,000 meters.

"Party in ten," commanded the Apache fire team leader, Lieutenant Tom Drew.

Figures began running toward the three antiaircraft pits guarding the base.

"Five . . . four . . . three . . .," said Drew calmly.

Before he reached "one," Thomas "Tip" O'Neal pickled a Hellfire. "This one's for you, Saddam," said Dave Jones, O'Neal's copilot, as the Hellfire whisked off the left rail of the Apache. It was the first shot of the war.

Twenty seconds later, the missile hit home, incinerating a set of generators providing power for the radars. By then, a host of missiles were under way. Hellfires, then Hydra-70 rockets, then 30mm chain guns gouged a gaping hole in the Iraqi air defense systems. Less than five minutes after the attacks began, both Iraqi sites had been damaged beyond repair—"Condition Alpha," as the coded message back to base put it.

The Special Forces crews in the Pave Lows watched the destruction with fascination and some trepidation; they'd be called on if the sporadic answering fire managed to bring down any helicopters.

As the Red Team Pave Lows waited for their Apaches, Iraqi ground forces fired two SA-7 heat-seekers at one of the MH-53s. The pilot managed to duck the shoulder-launched SAMs with the help of decoy flares and some quick jinking across the sand. "We were too busy trying to dodge the missiles to see where they went," said Captain Corby Martin, one of the pilots.

Before the early-morning strike had knocked out the radars, an operator at one of the sites had apparently managed to get off part of a message indicating that they were under attack. Relayed to Baghdad, the warning seems to have caused antiaircraft units in the enemy capital to begin firing into the air willy-nilly. That turned out to be a good thing. By the time the first F-117 attack on the city actually began about fifteen minutes later, they had expended their ammunition and overheated much of their gear.

Crossing the border behind the EAGER ANVIL helos, SOF troops in Chinook CH-47s touched down to plant beacons to help guide American raiders.

American bombers were soon streaming through the hole poked by the SOF and Apache units. . . .

MH-53J Pave Lows played an important role throughout the war, inserting SOF units and flying combat and search-and-rescue (CSAR) missions.

The CSAR missions were controversial, since combat rescue was not a traditional SOF task, and the Air Force and Navy were never convinced either that it was a high enough priority or that SOF was devoting enough resources to it.

Schwarzkopf tasked Special Operations with combat rescue partly because of the hazardous conditions inside Iraq, partly because Special Forces had the deep infiltration and exfiltration capability required, and partly because the Air Force's own rescue capability had been allowed to atrophy after the Vietnam War, and there was no other alternative but to task SOCOM for assets.

Seven bases, five in Saudi Arabia and two in Turkey, were used to stage the missions. At the very beginning of the air war, the helos loitered over Iraq at night in case they were needed. But this was obviously hazardous, and Johnson soon ordered the units to scramble over the line only if they had a "reasonable confirmation" of a pilot's location. During the early stages of the war, rescues were also restricted to nighttime.

While there was no denying the capability of the SOF crews or the helicopters, some Air Force and Navy officers bristled that their service was not directly responsible for its own search and rescue. (Though they were Air Force aircraft, the Pave Lows were SOCOM assets.) Johnson's restrictions, while protecting the helicopter crews, lessened the odds of recovering pilots, especially since U.S. air crews were equipped with obsolete emergency radios, whose limited range and frequencies exposed them to the enemy. The other services also felt that not enough resources were devoted to the CSAR mission.

Nonetheless, Pave Low crews accounted for one of the most daring operations of the war, a full daylight rescue of a downed Navy pilot under fire. And they did it with help from a number of Air Force units, including a pair of A-10A attack planes (called Warthogs, because that's what they look and act like), flying far behind the lines.

On January 21, several days after the start of the air war, Lieutenant Devon Jones and Lieutenant Lawrence R. Slade were flying "Slate 46," an F-14A escorting a Navy EA-6B Prowler on a strike against a radar installation protecting the Al Asad airfield in northern Iraq, roughly fifty miles west of Baghdad. After the Prowler had completed its mission, Jones banked his plane and began heading back toward the USS *Saratoga,* his squadron's floating home in the Red Sea. As he turned, he saw a missile coming up for him. He started evasive maneuvers, but the SAM managed to detonate close enough to his Tomcat to rip its tail apart and render the plane uncontrollable.

Both Jones and Slade, his radar intercept officer, bailed out. Separated as they left the plane, the men quickly lost track of each other in the dim light of early dawn. After they reached the ground, they unwittingly headed in different directions.

Meanwhile, Captain Tom Trask was sitting with his crew in an Air Force Pave Low at Ar-Ar, a tiny base near the Iraqi border. Tired from a succession of missions, Trask's squadron had been slotted "last in line" behind some Air Force and Navy Blackhawks; their priority today was supposed to be some well-deserved rest.

But neither Saddam nor the weather cooperated. Heavy fog socked in the airfield. When the call came at about 7:15 A.M. that American fliers were down, the Blackhawk pilots couldn't see to take off. Two Pave Lows, including Trask's, took over the job.

The initial information about the shootdown came in muddled, and at first the Special Operations airmen thought they were trying to rescue crews from the A-6 as well as the F-14. Breaking with their usual tactics, the helicopters "chopped" their flight in half, each focusing on a separate crew. Though they were flying a preplanned route that snaked across Iraq and avoided the most potent defenses, Trask's helicopter was sighted by an Iraqi border unit. They escaped easily, and their luck continued when the fog lifted, allowing them to nick down to fifteen feet above the ground.

Then two Iraqi fighters took off from an Iraqi air base dead ahead.

"Snap south, snap south!" yelled an AWACS controller monitoring the area. Meaning: "Turn south and run like hell."

This would have worked fine for a fighter. But no helicopter was going to outrun a MiG. Trask hunkered his helo into a dry wadi as one of the enemy planes whipped toward him.

"We actually saw him fly over," he said later. Fortunately, the helicopter was too low to be picked up by radar and was hidden from the Iraqi by a broken cloud deck. The AWACS had meanwhile vectored in F-15C Eagles. As soon as the MiG realized he was being hunted, he turned tail and landed back at his air base.

Trask pushed northward toward the area where the F-14A had gone down. Deep in Iraq without escort or even another Pave Low to back him up, he was starting to feel pretty lonely.

There was another problem: No one had heard from the F-14 crew. Downed pilots follow very specific schedules, or "spins," which dictate when they try to contact SAR assets and what frequencies to use. The rescuers know this and follow procedures designed to minimize the chance that the enemy will find the downed pilot first. Though no one then knew this, slight but significant differences in Air Force and Navy spins made it difficult for the Air Force searchers and the Navy searchee to connect. The effort was also hampered by the survival radio Jones carried. Not only was its range limited, but the enemy could easily home in on it.

In short, the planes looking for the Navy pilot came up empty. After several hours of standing by deep in enemy territory, Trask turned his helo back toward the border to refuel.

As all this was going on above him, Lieutenant Jones had been hiking for over two hours, which brought him to a clump of low bushes and vegetation near a muddy wadi. He dug a hole with his survival knife. An hour and a half later, his bloodied and blistered hands had managed to clear a hole three feet deep and four feet long. The hole soon came in handy; a farm vehicle with some business at a water tank a thousand yards away inspired him to cover up in it.

Since air crews had been briefed that rescues would take place at night, he didn't expect to be picked up anytime soon. He passed the time by making calls for help on his survival radio—and keeping his hole clear of scorpions.

By coincidence, a flight of Air Force A-10s flying search and rescue deep in Iraq had been given a backup frequency that coincided with the Navy pilot's rescue frequency. Jones, meanwhile, had decided to transmit and then listen at times that were slightly off his normal schedule, hoping he might find his lost backseater on the air.

What he found instead were unexpected but enthusiastic American voices.

"Slate 46, this is Sandy 57. Do you copy?" said one of the A-10A Sandy (for search and rescue) pilots.

"Sandy 57, Slate 46. How do you read?" Jones answered.

His voice was so calm, the A-10A pilot thought for a moment he was dealing with an Iraqi impersonator.

As the A-10s worked to get a fix on the downed airman, Trask saddled up again for the flight north. Joined by the other MH-53J, he alerted the AWACS and sped over the desert.

"The SAMs are kind of coming up and going down, coming up and going down," recalled Trask, who did his best to follow the AWACS' directions and steer clear of the defenses.

Meanwhile, the A-10A pilot kicked out a flare so Jones could spot him and vector him toward the spot where he was hiding. The Warthog passed over the pilot's hole about a hundred feet off the deck.

Communicating this location to the approaching Pave Low proved more difficult. Unlike the helicopter, the A-10A was equipped with an ancient navigational system that tended to drift; his coordinates were as likely to send the Pave Low in the wrong direction as lead him to the pilot. Worse, there was no secure way for the two aircraft to communicate. Running out of fuel, the A-10A pilot resorted to a primitive voice code to pass the location to Trask and then took off to refuel.

Jones waited. And waited. Every minute dragged. Unknown to him or the Special Ops rescue crew, the Warthog pilot's coded coordinates had been confused; the Pave Lows were heading twenty miles south of him. Meanwhile, a fresh pair of A-10As came north to help. Jones made contact, then directed them toward the water tank and held down his mike button so the Hog "drivers" (as the pilots call themselves) could use their radios as direction-finders.

At about the time Jones heard the throaty hush of the planes' twin turbofans, he heard a closer and more ominous noise. A pair of Iraqi troop trucks were approaching in the distance, kicking dust behind them. The Iraqis had homed in on his radio signal.

Trask clicked his mike switch to alert the A-10s.

"Roger, we got 'em," said the Warthog driver. "We're in."

A few seconds later, the attack planes rolled onto the trucks. A thick stream of 30mm uranium-depleted shells smashed the lead truck to bits. Its companion turned and fled.

"Okay, where's he at?" Trask asked the A-10s from the Pave Low.

"He's right next to the truck."

By now, the truck was simply a big black hole, smoking in the desert. Trask whipped the Pave Low down between the hulk and the pilot. Within seconds, the PJs were helping one very happy Navy lieutenant aboard for the ride home.

When Lieutenant Jones had pulled the handle, he'd been flying somewhere between 25,000 and 30,000 feet; the ejection and landing had bruised him some and left him sore. But otherwise he was uninjured—and went on to fly thirty more missions in the war. His backseater, unfortunately, had been captured. He would spend the rest of the war as a POW.

SPECIAL Operations forces continued to fly combat search-and-rescue missions for the duration of the conflict.

There were other successes: A Navy SH-60B launched from the USS *Nicholas* picked up an Air Force F-16 pilot in Gulf waters two days after the Slate 46 incident; two SEALs made the actual rescue, jumping into the water to help the pilot.

After the start of the ground war, the pilot of an F-16 shot down in southern Iraq was picked up by aircraft from the Army special aviation unit. The MH-60 helicopters that made the rescue were equipped with weapons and an avionics set roughly comparable to those in the larger MH-53J.

All in all, a total of 238 rescue sorties were flown by Special Operations aircraft, accounting for about a third of their overall mission flights. By comparison, the Air Force flew ninety-six rescue sorties; the Navy and Marines, a total of four.

The allied air forces lost thirty-eight aircraft to hostile action over Iraq and Kuwait. While that is a staggeringly low percentage of casualties compared to the total number of combat sorties—64,990 by all allies—the majority of the downed airmen who survived their crashes were captured by the Iraqis. This was caused in great part because they had bailed out into hostile territory many miles from American forces.

After the war, emergency equipment and procedures were upgraded. A radio with better range and security was introduced (which, ironically, ground SOF units already carried). Efforts were also made to improve procedures and information-sharing between the services, so locating a downed pilot wouldn't again depend on a lucky frequency assignment.

SPECIAL Operations aircraft performed a variety of missions beyond combat rescue. Within a few days of their arrival in the Gulf, they were supporting SEAL reconnaissance teams, and Air Force AC-130 Special Operations "Spectre" gunships were to play a critical role when ground action began—as they had in Panama.

Two slightly different versions operated in the Gulf during the war, the

AC-130A and the AC-130H. While most of the basic armament and equipment sets in the planes are similar, the H models feature more-powerful engines—and a howitzer. The gunships make terrific high ground for firing artillery, but they are vulnerable. Typical operations call for night-fighting over extremely hostile territory.

Depending on the model, Spectre weapons include a 105mm howitzer, two 40mm cannons, and miniguns. The weapons are controlled by an array of radar and targeting systems, and are very accurate.

AC-130Hs from the Air Force Special Operations Squadron arrived at King Fahd International Airport on September 8, 1990.

Some months later, on January 29, after the start of the air phase of the war, the gunships were called out to help Marines repel a raid by Iraqi forces on Khafji, a small desert village in northeastern Saudi Arabia. The raid, conducted by several mechanized brigades (its aims were unclear—possibly to provoke Schwarzkopf into starting ground action before he was ready), caught the Americans off guard. As the small Marine unit in the village dropped back to a more defensible position, two six-man teams found themselves isolated on rooftops amid a sudden flood of enemy troops. The Marines stayed in the city, quietly directing artillery and air strikes via radio.

Next day and during the following night, more Iraqis streamed forward to reinforce the town.

U.S. Marine and Saudi units struck back. Three AC-130Hs provided firepower in what turned out to be one of the hottest engagements of the war. The Spectres blasted Iraqi positions and tank columns in and around Khafji. As daylight on January 31 approached, the planes were ordered to return home. The black wings and fuselages of the slow and relatively low-flying planes made them easy targets against the brightening sky.

One of the gunships—69-6567, called Spirit 03—was backing a Marine unit that had come under fire from an Iraqi missile battery when the call came to go home.

They stayed on station to help the Marines.

Another order to break off came in.

"Roger, roger," acknowledged the copilot.

A few seconds later, an Iraqi shoulder-launched SAM slammed into the wing and sheared it off. The Spectre spiraled into the Gulf; all fourteen crew members died.

This was the worst SOF loss of the war.

A SPECTRE'S firepower is awesome, but that pales in comparison with the weapon a C-130 deployed a few days after the Khafji battle.

The plane was an MC-130E Combat Talon, designed for low-level missions behind enemy lines. Typically, Combat Talons insert and supply Special Forces troops with long-range clandestine parachute drops. Some are also equipped with Fulton STAR recovery systems and can literally snag commandos from the ground in areas too dangerous for helicopter pickups.

The MC-130E's unique ability to carry a large cargo and deliver it at a very specific time and place also allows the propeller-driven craft to drop skid-mounted BLU-82s, or "Daisy Cutters" (because they work like very destructive lawn mowers). Consisting of 15,000 pounds of high explosive, the "Blues" are about the size of a Honda Civic hatchback. A long sticklike fuse in the squat nose triggers the explosion before the bomb buries itself in the ground, maximizing the explosion's force.

BLU-82s were used during the Vietnam War to flatten jungle areas for use as helicopter landing zones.

After that war wound down, the BLU-82s were largely forgotten until Major General Stiner—in his days as commander of the JSOTF—remembered his experience with the bomb in Vietnam as he was searching for a weapon that might be used effectively against terrorist-training camps. What he needed, he realized, were BLU-82s. But when he went looking for any that still remained, he found only four BLU-82 shells in a bunker at Tuello Army Depot. He also managed to locate a couple of Vietnam-era Air Force sergeants who still knew how to mix the slurry (explosive). None of his air crews had ever dropped one.

With his own funds, he brought the number of the weapons to eight, and had two crews trained. The investment paid off big-time in the Gulf War.

While nowhere near as accurate as laser-guided or other "smart" bombs, they don't need to be: The Blues' sheer size makes a considerable impact. (For comparison's sake, the most common iron bombs dropped from B-52s and other aircraft are five hundred pounds.)

Minefields posed a problem for the Marines scheduled to invade Kuwait. MC-130 crews—aware of this—suggested that the Blues could be used to clear them: Pressure from the explosion would set off the mines.

At least, they thought they would. The tactic had never been tried with the BLU-82. After some debate, the allied commander approved the mission. A pair of MC-130s, escorted by SAM killers and Air Force Raven EB-

111s to help fend off radars, lumbered over the target area at about 16,000 feet. As the bombs slid out the back of the planes, the pilots had to work hard to hold the suddenly unbalanced MC-130s steady.

The first explosions were so massive (the story goes) that a British commando operating in Iraq more than a hundred miles away grabbed his radio. "The blokes have just nuked Kuwait!" he is said to have told his commander.

Whether the story is apocryphal or not, the bombs devastated the minefields. They also killed anyone within 4,000 yards of the explosion who wasn't in a protected position. Eleven were dropped during the conflict.

The Blues were also potent psychological weapons. When an Iraqi unit was told they were due for a BLU-82 bombing, most of its men promptly came across the lines and surrendered.

PSYOPs

Surely the least publicized major effort of the war was the Psychological Operations (PSYOPs) campaign. This was a comprehensive effort with several aims: to build coalition support for the war, counter Iraqi propaganda, unnerve Saddam's troops, and loosen the Iraqi resolve to fight.

Planning for the campaign began very early in the American buildup. The head of the 4th Psychological Operations Group, Colonel Tony Normand, prepared for General Schwarzkopf a comprehensive PSYOPs campaign with strategic (aimed primarily at populations) as well as tactical (aimed primarily at enemy military forces) operations. Normand, who had shaped the highly successful PSYOPs campaign in Panama, drew up a broad plan with the help of his staff, under the direction of Lieutenant Colonel Daniel D. Devlin, who had just relinquished command of a 4th Group battalion. By contrast with his attitude toward SOF operations, Schwarzkopf turned out to be a big PSYOP booster from the start.

"PSYOP is not really a difficult subject to understand, but many try to make it overly complex, and in the end, fail to understand it at all," noted Devlin, who served as deputy commander of the 4th PSYOPs Group after it deployed to the Gulf. "First, any political, military, legal, informational, or economic action can be psychological in nature, and therefore part of a strategic PSYOP plan at the national level. Second, any military or informational action in the combatant Commander's (CINC's) sphere of influence can be psychological in nature as a part of the CINC's operational PSYOP plan. Third, any military action on the battlefield can be a part of the tactical PSYOP plan. Really good military minds understand the psychological nature of the battlefield."

After the plan was completed, Normand waited for two days to get in to brief the CINC. Called away before he could make the presentation, he told Devlin to give the briefing.

Devlin recounts:

"He said not to be concerned if I had to give the briefing before he returned. He told me, 'The success of the briefing will only determine whether we take part in this operation, or return home to Fort Bragg to rake pine needles.' That's kind of the essence of our relationship. We were always direct with each other, but with a great deal of friendship and humor. He was my boss. He knew he could count on me."

The CINC's office called for Devlin twice, but then sent him back when more pressing matters delayed the meeting. "The numerous overlapping demands on the CINC's time were amazing," Devlin recalls. Finally, General Schwarzkopf had time for the briefing.

"I went in and gave General Schwarzkopf a personal, one-on-one briefing from a three-ring binder," Devlin continues. "About a half-dozen staffers followed me in and stood in the corner waiting to see me dismembered, because the majority of the CINC's staff didn't think much of us being there. At the conclusion of my briefing, General Schwarzkopf pounded his right fist on the table and said, 'This is exactly what we need. There's an information war going on right now and we're losing it! What do I need to do to make this happen?' The staff's acceptance of us changed amazingly following the briefing."

Schwarzkopf personally edited a draft message, making it much stronger, and then authorized its transmission to Colin Powell. The message requested PSYOP assistance, and, as a result, the 4th PSYOP Group began deploying to the Gulf on August 25. The first group to deploy included Normand, Devlin and the planning staff, and a few others. Once there, as additional PSYOP assets came in from Fort Bragg, Normand and his immediate staff prepared more detailed operational plans covering a wide range of strategic, operational, and tactical missions. But even with the CINC's backing, most of Normand's PSYOP plans sat for months at the Defense Department, apparently stymied because of geopolitical sensitivities in Washington.

"We're afraid of cross-border operations," explained Colonel Normand later. Cross-border operations—from Saudi Arabia, say, over the border into

Iraq—were in many cases inherently dangerous and always carried a potential to backfire and cause embarrassment. Thus they were likely to be
sidetracked by Washington. This meant that a strategic campaign aimed at
telling Iraqi citizens why the war was evil couldn't be launched. But it also
hamstrung the tactical operations aimed at Iraqi soldiers.

"A leaflet is a cross-border operation," said Normand. "You're told to start
targeting the Iraqi soldiers. Well, you can't do that because they're not on
your side of the border. You can't do cross-border operations."

The official resistance led Normand to shuttle between Washington
and Riyadh with one plan after another, seeking approval from the Joint
Chiefs and a myriad of other military brass, as well as Defense and State
Department officials. After several weeks of this, he finally received approval to proceed.

After a fashion: Washington had split the plan into two halves—overt and
covert. "Overt" PSYOP actions were okay, but covert actions were put on
hold. The catch-22: Nearly everything Normand wanted to do was considered "covert," much of it simply because it required cooperation from another organization or country. With the exception of a film called *Line in the
Sand*—which had to be reedited because the delays made parts of it out of
date—the major PSYOP initiatives against Iraq were put on hold. The film
would later be smuggled into Iraq and distributed freely around the rest of
the world; but little else in the way of a "strategic" PSYOP campaign—targeting common Iraqi citizens and telling them why their country was being
attacked—would ever be implemented.

Carl Stiner has views about this kind of thing: "Certain lawyers get in the
act, and you've got certain people that don't want their thumbprint on anything that might have risks associated with it. That's the way they've survived; they limit their exposure. And when you run into that, you've got to
get the Chairman or the CINC to override all these birds and get their
asses out of the process or they'll delay it to eternity."

Finally, Normand went to Schwarzkopf in mid-December, shortly before he was scheduled to relinquish command of the 4th PSYOP Group for
another assignment. Standing in front of the CINC in disgust, he told him,
"We need to send a message back to Washington that if we don't get approval soon we can't execute." He handed the general a piece of paper. "I
recommend you send this message."

Normand had carefully prepared a "Let's Go" message, a masterwork of
diplomatic language, politely requesting Washington to "relook" the issue.

"Bullshit," said Schwarzkopf. He ripped up the paper and began writing his own message. It began with the words "Bungling bureaucrats in Washington," and then got really nasty.

"What do you think about that?" the CINC asked, handing it back to Normand.

"If you'll sign it, I—"

"It's signed," Schwarzkopf broke in.

The PSYOP tactical campaign aimed at Iraqi troops suddenly hit the fast track. The campaign took off with the start of the air war a few weeks later.

MUCH of the DESERT SHIELD/STORM PSYOP mission was aimed simply at countering the propaganda Saddam was spreading. The PSYOP warriors were trying to set the record straight. Arab countries were a vital part of President Bush's carefully constructed coalition, and so it was vital that their citizens, and in fact the Islamic world in general, know the truth about why the coalition was fighting Saddam.

Cairo is the Arab media center, the Arab "Hollywood." The highly regarded Radio Cairo is there, many Arab and international news organizations have offices in the city, and Arab intellectuals tend to congregate there. If you want to get the word out to the Arab world—and to the entire Islamic world—you want to work through these facilities. At the same time, Egypt was an ally in the coalition. Government officials as well as media members were receptive to American-inspired suggestions and information.

Normand sent Devlin to Cairo at the end of October.

Here are Devlin's thoughts on the experience:

"The extensive Iraqi propaganda machine required countering with factual information that Saddam was in every way a despicable human being—a horrific leader who did not care about his people, an unjust Muslim, a terrible neighbor, an untrustworthy Arab and Muslim, and a liar in everything he said." The PSYOP operation, therefore, aimed to point out these truths and strip him of support from the Islamic world and elsewhere, while eliciting increased Islamic and world support for the coalition forces. With strong backing by the American ambassador, who provided entry to the Egyptian government and military, and by American embassy officials, Devlin organized a cooperative effort out of Cairo to counter the continuous Iraqi propaganda.

"Because the invasion was literally a television news event, it was important to point out to the entire world exactly what a brutal dictator he was. But we wanted to point out specifically to the Islamic world that Saddam had attacked his Islamic brothers without justification, or the support of the rest of the Islamic world.

"According to Islamic law, you can be a bad Muslim and an evil man who does not follow the law. But then you can have a change of heart and convert to a follower of the law. Once you have done that, you can proclaim the right to call a Jihad." Saddam claimed he was a good Muslim in calling for a justified Jihad. "But also according to Islamic law, Muslims don't attack other Muslims. So Saddam's claim had this fundamental flaw."

Both the Arab world and the Islamic world as a whole had to pay attention to this truth, but it obviously could not come directly from Americans.

"We wanted to get word out to the Islamic world that noted Islamic clerics faulted his reasoning and justification, according to the Koran and Islamic law. Our goal was not to get them to say what we wanted; we wanted them to say, print, and transmit what they were already saying as Islamic experts, recognized as such by the Islamic world: Saddam's claims were not true, according to Islamic custom and law."

This message went out: Devlin's team and their Egyptian colleagues found ways to insert it into plays, radio and TV shows, soap operas, and magazines and newspapers. Islamic conferences held for world Islamic leaders condemned Saddam. The end result was a chorus of voices in all media denouncing Saddam from recognized Islamic sources.

"I never told them what to write. The suggestion would be that an article (or program, or conference, etc.) stating their beliefs would be useful. They would take it from there. One result was a book, written very quickly, by a noted Islamic scholar.

"Effective PSYOP is not always preparing the message; it is extremely effective when already available materials, programming, or information are properly directed."

Another aspect of the PSYOP war saw the 4th Group working like a political campaign's media advisers, suggesting talking points for U.S. officials and others who would counter Saddam's propaganda. "We suggested four or five information points every few days for leaders of the United States, Egypt, and other allies, such as Great Britain, to use in public interviews, press conferences, and statements. This showed that the coalition force re-

ally spoke with one mind. Every day, ideas would float back and forth between governments and leaders. From these, we'd take four or five points
for all to use.

"It was magic to watch all of this unfold. Following agreement on the
points by the leaders, and their dissemination through the Ambassador and
the CINC, we would watch them come back through the media over the
course of a week."

Very few people outside of military circles are aware of PSYOP campaigns. And even the military . . .

"You have to be satisfied with accomplishment, because you sure as hell
don't get any recognition," Devlin concludes.

BY the time the war got under way, Colonel Layton Dunbar had taken over
as the 4th Psychological Group's commander. The unit's efforts varied:

In December, stickers began appearing on buildings in Kuwait City encouraging resistance to Saddam—a PSYOP project. Two days after the first
bombs fell in the air war, PSYOP troops—predominantly members of the
Pennsylvania Air National Guard—launched the Voice of the Gulf, a radio
program broadcast on both AM and FM bands from three ground stations
and an airborne EC-130. Subtle PSYOP appeals played in rotation with
music and news programs.

B-52s can carry a very large load of bombs, and when the load hits, it
wastes a lot of territory and makes lots of noise. In other words, B-52s are
not only strategic and tactical weapons, they are psychological weapons.
Ground troops who have seen what they can do are not eager to repeat the
experience—or be subjected to it.

Six Iraqi military units were targeted for treatment that combined
PSYOP leaflets with B-52 strikes. The operations unfurled over several
days. On day one, leaflets were dropped on the unit, warning that it would
come under B-52 attack at a specific time. The soldiers were urged to flee.
At the specified moment, the B-52s would arrive with their loads of bombs.
Afterward, a fresh round of leaflets would arrive, reminding them of the
strike and warning that a new one would soon follow. Neighboring units
nearby would receive their own warnings. Mass defections often followed.
Or as Carl Stiner put it, "They ran like hell."

The Air Force was at first reluctant to sign on to this approach (who
warns the people they're going to bomb?), but they eventually became big

boosters. These operations conveyed a sense of overwhelming superior force, while filling the enemy with dread.

You don't have to kill the enemy to win a war. It's enough that the enemy does not choose to fight.

Later, the Air Force adopted a PSYOP campaign that targeted SAM sites, warning them that they would be bombed if they turned on their radars. "It kept bad guys from shooting at Air Force aircraft," Normand comments. "So they turned out to be among our strongest proponents."

One feature of PSYOP leaflets was the positive portrayal of Iraqi soldiers. As a unit historian pointed out later: "He was always portrayed as a decent, brave fellow who had been misled by his leaders, but who would be received by the coalition forces with the dignity he deserved." Coalition soldiers were depicted in unthreatening ways.

This portrayal was not accidental. PSYOP planners market-tested their products. Among other things, they discovered that Iraqi soldiers responded better to simple leaflets with primitive illustrations and poor-quality paper; slicker efforts were too Western. They also discovered the kinds of content that worked and the kinds that didn't.

"We had some Iraqi POWs who had surrendered," said Normand. "We laughed and joked with them and found out that the thing they miss the most over there was bananas. Over and over, for some reason, that kept coming up."

So PSYOP leaflets began to feature a fruit bowl with bananas.

The subtle touches took time; a single leaflet could involve as many as seventy-five people and a week and a half to develop. The leaflets were then dropped by a variety of aircraft, including B-52s, F-16s, F/A-18s, and MC-130 Combat Talons. The 8th SOS dropped approximately 19 million leaflets from MC-130s alone.

PSYOP troops also used specially prepared balloons, relying on carefully charted weather patterns to target specific areas with leaflet drops, and they paid smugglers in Jordan and off the Kuwaiti coast to distribute leaflets in Iraq.

A PSYOP survey of many of the 86,743 Iraqis prisoners found that 98 percent had seen a leaflet; 80 percent said they had been influenced by it; and 70 percent claimed it had helped them decide to give up. Radio messages were found to have reached 58 percent of the men; 46 percent had found these messages persuasive; and 34 percent said they had helped convince them to surrender. Loudspeaker broadcasts reached fewer, and affected fewer still: Thirty-four percent had heard them; 18 percent had found them persuasive; and 16 percent claimed the messages had helped convince them to give up. These numbers, have to be considered with skepticism, since they were supplied by prisoners of war probably eager to please their captors, but even so, the vast number of Iraqi defections indicate the PSYOP campaign helped demoralize a large part of the Iraqi army.

Demoralizing the enemy was not, in fact, the main PSYOP goal.

"PSYOP basically has two functions," Colonel Normand comments. "To persuade and to inform. Persuasion is important. But supplying information is most of what we did. A lot of times, it's questionable whether you are going to get an enemy soldier to surrender. So your main task may not necessarily be to persuade him, but to let him know what he has to do. If the situation reaches a point where you can't go on, then here are the things you need to do to save yourself."

Accordingly, the PSYOP warriors gave soldiers in Kuwait and Iraq very clear maps to allied lines, where they could go to surrender or wait to be repatriated.

Supplying maps to the enemy, and warning units that are about to be attacked, seems an odd military tactic. Even more, an odd SOF tactic. These are *shadow* warriors. But in fact the goal is also a traditional one for the SOF: to affect people's hearts and minds. Successful PSYOP operations share another SOF principle as well: Think creatively. For example, PSYOP planners recognized that the goal of a particular bombing raid is to make the targeted unit ineffective, as opposed to simply killing as many men as possible— which meant that a good propaganda campaign could actually accomplish much more than bombing alone. The leaflets helped make the allies seem overwhelmingly powerful.

No wonder so many Iraqis deserted as the war progressed.

PSYOP units also worked with ground troops near the front, in campaigns designed either to confuse the enemy or to trick him into revealing his position.

In one celebrated example, a Marine unit's Light Armored Vehicles, or LAVs, were tape-recorded. The PSYOP team then used loudspeakers to convince an Iraqi unit that LAVs were maneuvering near the border. When the Iraqis began firing at them, Marine air and artillery zeroed in on the enemy positions.

Sixty-six loudspeaker-equipped teams accompanied advancing armies during the ground war to encourage surrender and direct enemy prisoners of war. The teams helped herd and control the large number of EPs (enemy prisoners) taken by coalition forces.

Some nine hundred PSYOP soldiers took part in various facets of the campaign; most were highly educated and many were language specialists. The 4th Psychological Operations Group (Airborne) included nearly fifty Ph.D.s. Normand had a B.A. in political science and two master's degrees, one in international affairs and the other in strategic planning. Devlin earned a B.S. in history education, and two master's degrees in national security affairs and international relations. Both were trained and experienced U.S. Army foreign area officers (FAOs), army strategists, and joint service officers (JSOs).

Interestingly, clinical psychologists play a very small role in PSYOPs. They're too narrow. "Their focus is on an individual's thinking processes, but they don't go beyond that into the effects of that thinking. They don't consider what that thinking causes to happen in a society and in a culture," explained Normand.

THE WAR AGAINST SCUDS

Saddam had his own psychological weapons, as well. After the air war began, Saddam struck back with "Scud" missiles.

Scuds were not an effective tactical weapon. They were obsolete and inaccurate. The original Scud design had been introduced in 1957, but even then it looked back more than it looked forward: It was a near-descendant of the Nazi V-2s that had terrorized London in the latter part of World War II. A modern military commander actually had little to fear.

Stock versions of the Soviet SS-1 mobile missiles (as they were officially designated) could send a 1,000-kg warhead of conventional high explosives just under 300 kilometers. The Iraqis had increased their range by welding additional fuel sections to some of the rockets. Two Iraqi variants used during the war had ranges of just over 400 and 550 miles. Achieving this, however, came at a considerable price. Payloads had to be reduced, and worse, shoddy welding often meant that the missiles ruptured as they flew, decreasing their already poor accuracy. This defect actually made it harder for antimissile systems, like Patriot MIM-104 missiles, to target them effectively.

There was considerable concern that the Scuds might carry nuclear, bi-ological, and chemical warheads. While Iraq had chemical—and probably biological—weapons, there was debate over whether they could be used on the missiles, and though the Iraqis had a program to develop nuclear weapons, they were years away from a working warhead in 1991.

In the end, no chemical, nuclear, or biological agents were launched on Scuds during the war.

Because the Scuds were not seen as a serious tactical threat to American forces, they were mostly ignored by the early Air Force war plan (except to knock out known Scud sites during the first moments of the war). But the Air Force made a serious error in estimating their strategic importance: Like the German V-2s, they had a potent psychological effect.

Saddam's targeting during his first salvo of the war, January 18, made his strategy obvious. Eight Scuds were launched toward Israel that night; the most serious strike injured a dozen people. The injuries were light—mostly cuts and bruises from shattered windows. In all, about sixty people in Tel Aviv and Haifa were hurt. But Saddam's goal wasn't so much to kill Jews as to provoke Israel into a military response. Israeli action, he believed (prob-ably correctly), would drive the Arab nations arrayed against him from the allied coalition.

A switch from support to opposition by the leading Arab nations would have subjected American forces to innumerable difficulties, encouraged terrorist attacks, and greatly complicated logistics.

Saddam did very nearly get his wish: A flight of Israeli air force jets were reportedly scrambled for a retaliatory raid but were called back. The Israeli government tottered for weeks on the brink of ordering a revenge raid, yet the go-ahead blessedly never came. President Bush and his administration worked feverishly to calm the Israelis with assurances that stopping the Scuds was a top priority. It *was* a top priority. But stopping them wasn't easy. The attacks continued. By the end of the first week of the war, more than thirty Scuds had been launched against Israel. Another eighteen were fired at Saudi Arabia.

Meanwhile, the U.S. Air Force changed targeting priorities to concen-trate on the missiles, but the Iraqis had put enormous effort and ingenuity into making the Scuds mobile, and into deception and camouflage. They had adapted transport vehicles to use as primitive launchers, drastically cut the arduous launch preparation procedure, and produced convincing decoys. Hitting such missile units at night from 15,000 feet in the air was problematic. Even with well over fifty sorties a night, the United States failed to stem the Scud attacks.

In September, and again in late December, Carl Stiner had recommended deploying a Joint Special Operations Task Force to Saudi Arabia, consisting of more than one-third of his special mission forces, to be readily available for counterterrorist operations as well as deep-strike missions, but he had been turned down. Even so, his planning continued.

When Scuds became a critical political issue in Israel, Stiner and Downing quickly developed a plan for dealing with the threat by putting special missions forces deep inside Iraq.

On January 22, while Stiner lobbied Powell by phone, Downing met with Lieutenant General Thomas W. Kelly, director of operations for the Joint Chiefs, to present the plan. Intelligence had narrowed the launching positions against Israel to three areas, or "kill boxes," in western Iraq. The Amman-Baghdad highway ran through one; the other two were on the Syrian border near Shab al Hiri and Al Qaim. Downing outlined a force that would stalk the kill boxes and locate the Scuds so they could be destroyed by air, or attacked by the patrols themselves if air was not available. Augmented by Rangers and other special operators and supported by special mission aircraft, teams could spend several days north of the border accomplishing their mission.

Ground forces, Downing argued, had a much better chance of locating the Scuds than the fighter-bombers, which had to fly at relatively high altitude (to avoid antiaircraft defenses), often in bad weather. Kelly liked the plan enough to take it to Colin Powell.

"Interesting, but not yet," Powell said.

The same day, a Scud landed in a Tel Aviv suburb. Ninety-six people were injured. While none of the direct injuries was fatal, three Israelis died of heart attacks, possibly caused by the raid.

Israel continued to pressure the Bush administration, which in turn pressured the SECDEF and the Chairman. On January 30, Powell called Stiner and Downing to his office. Downing briefed essentially the same plan he had given Kelly. He proposed three possible force packages—small, medium, or large.

"All right," said Powell, when the briefing ended. "I'll go up and get the Secretary of Defense. Give me those slides."

Powell disappeared with the briefing slides. A few minutes later, he returned with Secretary of Defense Dick Cheney.

Downing and Stiner hit the key points again.

"Every night you see Saddam Hussein sitting in his doggone Winnebagos with his war council, laughing at the United States," Stiner said to the Secretary of Defense. "The air war has been ongoing for a week, and he is still very much in control. The Scuds are continuing to fall on Israel, and we can do something about it, if we're allowed to get in theater and do our thing."

Cheney looked at Downing.

"General, when can you depart for Saudi Arabia?" the Secretary asked.

"We can go tonight," said Downing.

"Why don't you do that?"

"You know Norm doesn't want these guys over there," Powell told Cheney.

"I don't care what Norm wants," replied the Secretary of Defense. "He's had seven days to shut this thing off and he hasn't done it. They're going."

Downing left immediately with a force package of about four hundred personnel, especially tailored for the mission. Operating out of Ar-Ar in western Saudi Arabia near the border, the package was the middle-size of the three attack options he had outlined.

When the general arrived in Riyadh the next day, Schwarzkopf was trying to catch a quick nap. Downing, who'd known the CINC for almost his entire time in the Army, went down to meet him in his bedroom.

"You work for me, not Carl Stiner," Schwarzkopf barked in greeting. "I don't care if you talk to General Stiner, but I don't want you reporting to him."

"I won't do that," Downing answered.

"I don't want you going into Iraq and getting captured, you understand that?" Schwarzkopf added. "The last thing I want is a damn general paraded on Iraqi television."

"Okay," said Downing.

Schwarzkopf had nothing to worry about on either count. Downing wasn't a cowboy, and in any event he was well aware of the devastating effect a captured general might have on both morale and public opinion. Likewise, Stiner never interfered with Schwarzkopf or his chain of command.

Before leaving for his new base, Downing went to see British Special Air Service Colonel Andy Massey, whose 22nd SAS Regiment commandos were already conducting anti-Scud operations north of the border. During the course of the Scud war, about 250 SAS men would work in the southernmost kill box along the Amman-Baghdad highway.

"Currently, we have twenty-seven guys unaccounted for—they are missing in action," Massey told Downing. "I want to tell you everything we've done right, and everything we've done wrong."

The extreme cold and the openness of the desert had caused major problems. Two British commandos had already died of hypothermia. And there was simply nowhere to hide during the day.

"The place is covered with Bedouins," Massey said. "You meet a Bedouin and you've got a fifty percent chance he is going to turn you in."

Though some of his own troops were on foot, Massey also made it clear that the patrols needed to be mounted. Without vehicles they were easy prey.

It was an important lesson.

EVEN before they left the States, Downing and his planners realized the critical mission wasn't to destroy Scuds; it was to stop Scud missiles from shooting into Israel. That realization meant they didn't have to find the missiles themselves; any of the facilities necessary for launching them would do just as well.

"When you focus on that as a mission, a whole bunch of other things open up to you," Downing explains. "All of a sudden, you start after things like the logistic system, the fuel system, the communications systems, people, barracks, roads. I mean, it's not just the missiles.

"A target list that was very, very small and very, very vague became an enormous target list that let us be very, very smart."

Field-level troops and commanders formulated the specific tactics, not the generals. Downing and Stiner saw their jobs as primarily answering the question "How do we support this?"

"The guys who are going to do the mission plan it," said Downing. "Generals don't plan it."

The Special Forces Scud missions began February 7, when sixteen SOF troopers and two vehicles were helicoptered into Iraq by MH-53J Pave Low and CH-47 Chinook helos. They were supported by armed Blackhawk helicopters, called defensive armed penetrators, as well as regular Air Force and Navy airplanes, including F-15Es, F-18s, and A-10As. A week after the operation began, the original anti-Scud forces were augmented with additional special missions units, a reinforced Ranger company, and additional special operations helicopters.

About fifteen anti-Scud SOF missions were undertaken during the course of the war. More would surely have been launched if the war had not ended. The mission lengths and sizes varied; at one point, at least four different American SOF units were looking for Scuds inside Iraq.

The insertions were made by helicopters, whose movements were coordinated with large packages of bombers heading across the border to attack Iraqi installations. Personal, up-front leadership was exercised by commanders at every level, a trademark of special operations. "Doug" and "Rich" personally flew the lead on every critical air insertion; "Eldon," "Ike," and "John," and their troop commanders and sergeant majors, led every ground patrol. The Ranger raid against a command-and-control node near the Jordanian border was led by "Kurt," the Ranger company commander. While the Iraqi defenders concentrated on the high-flying bombers, the helicopters zipped undetected across the open desert at sand-dune level.

While specific procedures varied according to the situation, in general, the ground units would hide during the day, while reconnaissance and attacks took place at night. Fighter-bombers and attack planes detailed to Scud-hunting would be vectored to their targets by the SOF teams. The Strike Eagles worked mostly at night, the A-10As mostly during the day.

One of the keys to the Scud operations were special all-terrain vehicles and humvees, which could be carried inside special operations helicopters. Machine guns, grenade launchers, and antitank missiles gave the vehicles considerable firepower. Besides the driver and up to ten passengers, gunners could sit on elevated swivel-seats at the rear.

Transporting the vehicles and combat teams across sometimes two hundred miles of hostile territory presented a problem, however. The fuel required for the long-range missions also weighed the helos down. All that weight meant they couldn't hover: They had to literally land on the fly. Twenty-knot rolling touchdowns on a smooth landing surface are one thing—and they are quite another in sand dunes at night. The uneven terrain—not to mention rocks—could easily destroy the fuel-laden helos.

As soon as the operations began, the special operators realized that their aerial and satellite intelligence photos—used by the Air Force for their earlier attacks—in many cases missed the desert roads the Scud transports were actually using. And even when the targets were pointed out, hitting individual missile launchers from 15,000 feet and above was a difficult proposition.

Back behind the lines, Downing met with Buster Glosson to discuss the possibility of using CBU minefields on the newly discovered Scud routes and rear staging areas. Glosson liked the idea. So Downing asked him to come along to discuss the plan with Schwarzkopf, who still insisted on signing off on every covert mission. The CINC tended to trust the Air Force general more than he did SOF officers. After hearing the plan, the always skeptical Schwarzkopf turned to Glosson, who of course gave it his thumbs-up. The boss was convinced.

"Once we figured out what the logistics flow was, we went in and put these minefields in," said Downing. "And they were devastating."

Cooperation between SOF and Air Force units was very high, and probably saved the lives of a number of operators behind the lines. On at least two occasions, Air Force F-15Es intervened when Iraqis attacked the special operations teams. In one case, a Strike Eagle pilot switched on his landing lights and plunged toward a patrol of nine armored vehicles, scattering them so a SOF helo could rescue a four-man SOF contingent. In another, an Eagle weapons officer used a smart bomb as an antiaircraft weapon, wiping out an Iraqi helicopter.

As part of the SOF Scud campaign, Blackhawk helicopters conducted armed reconnaissance missions, flying their specially equipped MH-60s at night with the aid of night-vision goggles. On their first night out, they nailed a Scud.

When they reported this to Downing, he was skeptical. Downing was a Vietnam veteran with two tours as a junior infantry officer; he knew better than to trust the first reports back from the field.

"Yeah, right," he told them. "Let's see the videos."

Like most U.S. military aircraft, the sophisticated helicopters included equipment that recorded attacks. His men dutifully brought the tape in, and set it unseen in the viewer. Downing frowned through the fast forward with obvious disbelief.

Then the pilot slowed the tape just as a Scud missile came into focus on the screen. A few puffs appeared; an Iraqi soldier ran past the camera.

"Holy shit!" said Downing, as the Scud exploded.

He grabbed the phone and called General Schwarzkopf. "They got some Scud missiles," he told the general when he came on the line.

"Yeah, right."

"No, we really did."

"Okay, that's good," said Schwarzkopf, hanging up, still clearly unconvinced.

Downing turned to his staff. "Get me an airplane," he said. The general grabbed "Dave," one of the warrant officers who had flown the mission. Three and a half hours later, the two men walked into General Schwarzkopf's war room in Riyadh.

"What are you doing here?" demanded Schwarzkopf.

"Sir, I want to talk to you about these Scud missiles," Downing told him.

"Yeah, right."

"We've got a video I'd like to show you," said Downing.

Glosson was standing nearby. "I'd like to see it," said the Air Force general, who was himself taking a lot of the heat for the Scud launches.

Sweeney set up the video. Schwarzkopf hunched over the monitor— then began dancing like a kid as the screen lit up with flames.

"Holy shit! That's a Scud missile. Hey, where'd you get this?" he asked Downing. "Can we transmit this back to the States?"

For Downing, it was a particularly sweet moment. Several years before, Schwarzkopf had cornered him in a Pentagon hallway, and lambasted him for pushing a proposal to outfit Special Operations helicopters with rockets, miniguns, and cannons. The helicopters Schwarzkopf had scorned had just scored a big kill.

Downing didn't bother mentioning it.

IRAQI Scud launches peaked on January 21, when fourteen were fired; ten were launched on January 25 and another six on January 26. By then, the missiles had become a priority for the Air Force. The British SAS, and then American Special Forces units, took up the operation soon afterward. Firings dropped off precipitously during the second, third, and fourth weeks of the war, dwindling off to nothing by war's end.

U.S. and British efforts to stop them had had an effect, but the Iraqis were clever and resourceful, and going after the missiles was something like trying to figure out a shell game.

The Scud campaign didn't achieve its intended aim of breaking up the allied coalition—but it did tie up considerable American resources. And though Scuds were tactically negligible, they could hurt, and hurt bad. An attack on Dhahran in late February, for example, killed twenty-eight U.S. soldiers and injured ninety-seven others.

Assessments after the war concluded that attacks on the missiles by fixed-wing aircraft were only very marginally effective. Most searches and attacks from the air took place at night (to protect the aircraft), but at night, even when an attacking aircraft flew directly on top of a missile site, the limits of airborne sensors and the vagaries of weapons made the site hard to hit. The ability of the Iraqis to modify the missiles and their tactics added further problems.

It might have made a difference if SOF had made a concerted effort against the Scuds from the beginning of the war, but that is speculation. The Iraqis were operating a small number of highly mobile launchers across a vast area.

The Scud campaign was probably the most successful Iraqi effort of the war.

GOING DEEP

As the Allied Command prepared for the ground war, Special Forces units prepared special reconnaissance (SR) missions to coincide with the attack. These were classic SF operations, providing mission commanders with information about enemy movements and capabilities.

And in at least one case, enemy dirt.

Two teams went into Iraq in the area through which Lieutenant General Fred Franks, the VII Corps commander, intended to sweep, testing soil conditions and analyzing the terrain in order to determine whether the desert soil would be able to support tanks and other heavy vehicles.

Inserted by Pave Lows, the teams included engineers who tested the soil with penetrometers. They also used still and video cameras to give commanders a visual record of what they'd be facing once they crossed into Iraq.

The overall thrust of the allied plan depended on a wide maneuver, or "left hook"—the famous "Hail Mary" that sent American troops racing north into Iraq before turning back east in the direction of Kuwait. While the strike would hit the Iraqis on their flank, the maneuvering American troops would themselves be vulnerable on their flanks. Real-time intelligence on the ground beyond the flanks was critical for both the XVIII Airborne Corps and VII Corps, the two allied groups charged with the forming the hook.

The XVIII Airborne Corps, which included the American 101st and 82nd Airborne Divisions, started farther west and would charge to the Euphrates before turning east. The VII Corps would head roughly toward Al Busayyah and then swing right for Kuwait.

SF teams were assigned to each Corps to provide intelligence. Team members spent roughly a month prior to their jump-off occupied with training and developing techniques for the mission. The general game plan for each team was similar. They'd be inserted by helicopter at night, then hand-dig large holes, called "hide sites," where they would stay during the day. The missions usually broke down to six or eight men, split into two hide sites. The two elements might locate several miles from each other, or they might be close together, depending on the particular circumstances. (There were at least six teams.) The teams were equipped with a variety of communications gear and armed with MP-5 submachine guns, grenade launchers, a variety of other light weapons, and a variety of communications gear.

The sites themselves, in areas as much as 165 miles inside enemy territory, were to be located near highways the Iraqis were expected to use to move troops, and the plan called for the SF teams to observe and radio back information day and night. Teams spotting armored concentrations and Scud missiles were to call in immediately; otherwise they would call at regular intervals. Generally, the plans called for the units to stay in place until "picked up" by approaching ground troops.

The SF SR teams were sent out on the evening of February 23.

It turned out that many were plagued by bad luck—and far worse, lousy intelligence. Information provided to the teams indicated that most of the areas into which they were to be dropped were sparsely populated; several teams found this wasn't the case. Additional snafus, including delays that upset mission timing, caused severe complications.

Two of the SR missions supporting the VII Corps remained undetected and provided important intelligence until they were joined by elements of the 1st Cavalry Division on February 27. A third team had to be exfiltrated early because of the presence of Iraqi forces.

But things proved to be much more difficult in the XVIII Airborne area, where three missions ran into problems.

On one, the operators discovered their target site was a Bedouin camp. As they scouted for another site in their helicopter, they came under attack from antiaircraft artillery and SAMs and had to abort the mission.

SR 008B, a three-man team drawn from 5th SFG A-Detachment 523 and led by Master Sergeant Jeffrey Sims, was infiltrated by Blackhawk to a location near Qawam am Hamzal, where they would monitor vehicles for the XVIII Airborne Corps. Though the approach of the helicopters set local dogs barking, Sims and his men, Sergeant First Class Ronald Torbett and Staff Sergeant Roy Tabron, ignored them, and moved quickly to their hide site four kilometers away. Each man packed about 175 pounds; besides food, ammunition, weapons, communication gear, and equipment to construct their hide site, the Green Berets carried ten quarts of water apiece. Though they were armed with a variety of weapons, their ammunition stocks were relatively light. Their job was to stay out of sight, not shoot people.

The next morning, Bedouins appeared in the field where the Green Berets were hidden. The team lay low, hoping they might somehow be overlooked. No such luck: Around midday a little girl and her father stuck their heads into the rear exit hole of the hide site. The shocked Iraqis quickly backed away. As a pair of team members moved to grab them, they saw about twenty other Bedouins nearby. Loath to harm the civilians, the three SF operators grabbed their essential gear and moved down the drainage ditch.

The Bedouins closed in, perhaps believing they might earn the reward the Iraqi government had posted for captured pilots. Several began firing small arms. The SF team called in air support and asked to be extracted.

A long firefight followed. At one point, an F-16 pilot had to back the Iraqis off by dropping a thousand-pound bomb and CBUs. But such measures proved temporary; the team was trapped in the relatively open terrain. Buildings near the highway provided Iraqis a vantage to pin them down, while others tried to flank them. Despite efforts to conserve their ammunition, their small stock quickly dwindled.

About an hour and a half after the firefight began, another F-16 managed to hold off the attackers with another bomb strike, then circled above while a Special Forces Blackhawk rushed in to try a broad daylight rescue. Enemy troops were now closing in. Disregarding his flight plan, Warrant Officer "James" blew right over an Iraqi division, leaving the startled Iraqis unshouldering their rifles.

On the ground, Sims and his men grimly thought about the grenades they'd clipped to their belts as last-resort weapons. The grenades were meant for themselves.

Suddenly, Sims heard a helicopter approaching. "He was screaming down the road, going around 140 knots, on one side of the power line, six feet off the deck," Sims remembers. The team popped a small white flare to mark their position. The helicopter pitched its nose up, swung around in a circle, and then slapped down nearly on top of them.

Team member Sergeant First Class Ronald Torbett's mouth dropped. He thought the helicopter had been hit by the fusillade of rifle fire from the Iraqis—not an unreasonable assumption, given the hail of bullets from the enemy troops nearby. But he was wrong. The difficult maneuver had been controlled, a piece of master aircraft driving between power lines and Iraqi gunfire. As the helo's door gunner laid down suppressing fire, the three Green Berets jumped inside. The Iraqis continued to rake the helicopter; miraculously, no one inside was seriously hurt, and the pilot managed to re-peat his aerobatics, dodging bullets and power lines to get away. Flying at top speed no more than twenty feet off the ground, the Blackhawk barreled back toward coalition lines.

It made it home safely, but was so badly damaged it didn't fly again dur-ing the war.

DECEPTION ON KUWAIT BEACHES

Even though the main allied ground attack came from the west, General Schwarzkopf's plan included a direct attack on southern Kuwait, a mission tasked to the Marine Corps 1st and 2nd Divisions, along with Kuwaiti and Arab units. This attack would tie down Iraqis as the "hook" was launched; it would also aim to eventually capture Japer airfield, Kuwait International Airport, and Kuwait City, all strategically and symbolically important.

One option that was also seriously considered was a Marine amphibious landing on Kuwait.

However, reconnaissance of the beaches during the fall and winter months by SEALs, as well as by Marine and Navy units, made it clear that an amphibious landing would be bloody, and result in the destruction of a considerable amount of Kuwait's infrastructure. Reluctantly, the Marines settled on a land assault from the south, itself no picnic. To make it work, the Iraqis had to be convinced the Marines were coming from the sea.

Special Forces SEALs played an important role in the deception. Lieutenant General Walter E. Boomer, the Marine Corps CENTCOM commander, asked Navy Special Warfare Task Group commander Captain Ray Smith to develop a plan to help divert Iraqi armor in the Kuwait area. Boomer wanted to draw the Iraqis tanks and guns away from his own units and tie them down near the coast. The general suggested a diversionary landing operation; the SEAL leader quickly accepted.

After the air war began, the SEALs began looking for a beach where they could stage their mock invasion. Fifteen reconnaissance missions were un-dertaken in the area between the Saudi border and Ra's al Qulay'ah on the Kuwaiti coast. Pave Lows supported some of these missions, inserting the SEALs on "soft duck" operations; the others were made from patrol boats. On at least one occasion, the Iraqis fired at the Special Forces troops, but no casualties were sustained. But neither could the SEALs find the right kind of beach.

One night, on patrol, Lieutenant Tom Dietz and his men spotted three Iraqi patrol boats near the naval base at Ra's al Qulay'ah. Excited, they called for air support. But the controller informed them that no airplanes were available. While no doubt tempted to take them out themselves, that would have potentially compromised their own mission. So they turned their patrol craft southward toward Mina Su'ud. Looking out toward the dark Kuwaiti shore, Dietz saw something he'd been hoping to spot for days—a long, empty beach. He made a note to come back as soon as possible. They did so a few nights later.

THE winter water off the Gulf was cold, but the SEAL swimmers were used to dealing with considerably worse. They slipped off their rigid-hull inflatable boats quickly, pulling themselves quietly through the water to the Kuwaiti shore. Lieutenant Dietz saw a low-slung shadow as he paddled; he kicked for it, then made his way out of the water onto a boat ramp.

For an hour, he lay at the waterline, watching in the darkness. There were buildings nearby, and the beach was littered with obstacles and other Iraqi defenses. But there were no patrols.

"I have a good feeling," he told himself when he slipped back into the water. Mina Su'ud would be the perfect beach to hit.

The plan was approved on February 19, and the SEALs conducted a dress rehearsal on February 22. Time was of the essence: The ground war, and thus the SEALs' mission, was set to begin on the night of February 23 and 24.

Leaving Ra's al Mish'ab in four small, fast Special Operation Crafts (powered by twin 1,000-hp Mer-Cruiser engines), the SEAL platoon sped through the mine-filled sea on the evening of February 23. Mines and the Iraqi shore defenses weren't the only hazard; the Special Operations boat crews were going to be extremely exposed to potential "blue on blue," or friendly-fire incidents. For that reason, they'd been supplemented with communicators who were assigned to help fend off their friends who might bomb them by mistake.

Twelve and a half miles off the target areas, the crews cut their engines. Four abreast, they drifted toward their launch point, while the SEALs broke out and inflated their rubber Zodiacs. At 2100, a six-man SEAL demolition team boarded its Zodiac. The coxswain then fired up the small, quiet motor.

Trailed by two of the patrol boats, the rubberized assault craft headed toward the beach.

Precisely forty minutes later, Lieutenant Dietz and five of his men slipped into the water. Each swimmer's weight had been augmented by twenty pounds of C-4, the charges already prepared. Their emergency gear included bottles of air for use in escaping underwater, pistols at their belts—and MP-5Ns and M-16s in case things got truly hairy. The six SEALs paddled steadily toward the beach, then crawled up on the sand in the shallow water. The timers were affected by the water temperature, and so Dietz had to consult a chart to work out when to set them. They pulled the pins at exactly 2247 for the planned 0100 detonation. The charges were set to go off in the shallow water as the tide rolled out, maximizing the effect of the explosions.

The swimmers were back aboard their rubber boats by midnight. The speedboats came forward and placed orange buoys, as if marking the boundaries of a landing area. Then they dashed toward shore, machine guns blazing at a building on the left bank of the target area. Intelligence believed that it was used for weapons storage.

Soon Navy ships and airplanes were delivering bombs and shells to the general area, heating up the show. As they turned away from the beach, boat crew members tossed off four-pound floating charges timed to go off at various intervals. The planted C-4 packets went off at 0100.

As far as the Iraqis knew, the Marines were on their way.

Elements of two Iraqi divisions rushed to man defensive positions near the beach. While the Iraqis waited for an attack that would never come, the Marines and their Arab allies blasted into Iraq and Kuwait.

The SEAL deception was part of an overall disinformation campaign that drew attention away from the main areas of attack. The campaign included everything from PSYOP leaflets in bottles supposedly dropped from ships offshore to commanders' "leaks" to news media. All this helped convince the Iraqis that the "real" invasion would come from the sea.

SEAL tcams were involved in several other actions during the war, including the boarding and capture of seven oil platforms in the Durrah oil field after U.S. helicopters had come under fire there on January 18.

Eight special boats supported a contingent of thirty-two Kuwaiti Marines during an operation on February 8–14, when the Kuwaitis seized Qaruh, Maradim, and Kubbar Islands. These were nonetheless the first reclamations of Kuwaiti territory by coalition forces, and therefore symbolically important.

FROM January 30 to February 15, SEALs used their Swimmer Delivery Vehicles (SDVs—wet submergibles) to conduct six major mine-hunting missions in hostile Iraqi waters, ten-hour dives using the vehicles' onboard sonar. Because the vehicles are literally full of water, SOVs require SEALs to wear scuba gear. Though they cleared twenty-seven square miles of water, the Iraqi mining operations were so pervasive that amphibious operations in those waters were still considered high risk.

Throughout the campaign, explosive- and detonator-equipped Navy SEALs also conducted mine countermeasures by helicopter—flying on a total of ninety-two helo sorties. They were dropped into the water to place charges directly on the mines. Twenty-five Iraqi mines were destroyed in this manner.

ON the night of February 22–23, a SEAL team landed a group of CIA-trained Kuwaiti guerrillas near Kuwait City in preparation for the start of the ground war.

SEALs, working with Marines and British forces, also helped enforce United Nations trade sanctions in the Gulf. A total of eleven "takedowns"—forced boardings of ships that refused to submit to inspections—were initiated during the war; all were successful.

Captain Smith's men also helped restore and train crews for three Kuwaiti navy ships that had escaped the invasion. All told, the Navy Special Warfare Task Group brought two hundred and sixty people to the Gulf, the largest SEAL deployment since the Vietnam War.

ON TO THE END

As U.S. and coalition forces closed on Kuwait from the west, the reconstituted Kuwaiti forces that the 5th Special Forces had helped train and equip (four brigades) were entering Kuwait City from the south. For political and symbolic reasons, the Kuwaitis and other Arab units formed the liberating spearhead designated to take Kuwait City, their maneuver and air support being coordinated by the accompanying SF personnel that had trained them.

By the time the Kuwaiti troops roared into the city on pickup trucks with .50-caliber machine guns mounted on the back, the Iraqi units guarding Kuwait's capital had already fled.

The ground war quickly turned into a rout, as the battered and hopelessly outclassed Iraqi army fell back toward Basrah. Pounded from the air and in many cases cut off from retreat, vast numbers of Iraqis surrendered or were captured. The Republican Guard and other Iraqi units had been decimated and suffered heavily as they fled in disarray toward Baghdad.

The allied objective of freeing Kuwait had been achieved, with relatively little loss of American life.

Acting on the recommendation of the Chairman, the SECDEF, and others, President Bush ordered American troops to halt the attack one hundred hours after the ground war had begun.

At the time of the cease-fire, somewhere between two and three hundred Special Operations personnel were behind the lines, with at least one patrol north of the Euphrates. Some SOF units had to drive out on their own; others were picked up by helicopter at night.

DESERT STORM had been a resounding success and a complete victory over a formidable foe. But no one had anticipated the end would come as abruptly as it did.

As with all conflicts, many things still needed to be done after the last shot had been fired. Unfortunately, the Civil Affairs units that would play the major role in helping Kuwait get back on its feet had not begun arriving in Saudi Arabia until after the start of the air war. Despite their inadequate planning time, CA did play an important role in post-liberation Kuwait. Working as part of the combined Civil Affair Task Force, CA personnel provided relief operations in the city and throughout the liberated country. Within two months, the task force distributed 12.8 million liters of water, 125,000 tons of food, and 1,250 tons of medicine.

Though after the war senior CA leadership came under criticism for a lack of initiative and "ill-coordinated" initial planning, CA's problems resulted from its late arrival and the unanticipated early end of the war—both beyond its control.

POSTWAR OBSERVATIONS

Carl Stiner will conclude:

> DESERT STORM *was a brilliantly conceived and executed military operation from beginning to end that achieved the desired result—the liberation of Kuwait. There is no question that the President—after considering*

all the involved factors and consulting with all the concerned allies—made the right decision. He was right to stop the war when he did.

Monday-morning quarterbacks will always question decisions—particularly people with neither responsibility nor accountability.

With regard to Special Operations support to the operation, I offer the following observations:

- ✪ *Special Operations forces performed all missions outstandingly and contributed significantly to the victory. When SOF capabilities are integrated appropriately with those of conventional units, the result is a capability not otherwise achievable.*

- ✪ *CINCs need the best available advice and experience for most effectively employing and supporting Special Operations forces. All CINCs now have flag rank officers as commanders of their Special Operations Commands (SOCs). This was not possible during* DESERT SHIELD/DESERT STORM, *because USSOCOM was not authorized to have a flag rank officer at CENTCOM headquarters.*

- ✪ *Better intelligence support is needed for reconnaissance teams operating deep in hostile territory—particularly current maps and overhead photo coverage. The Grenada invasion produced a similar finding.*

- ✪ *SOF units need to be "flowed," so as to arrive in sufficient time to prepare appropriately for mission assignments; otherwise their potential is proportionately limited.*

- ✪ *Could SOF have done more? The answer is yes! But the CINC is the one who is responsible and accountable. He calls the shots as he sees them. Once he has made up his mind, all other CINCs fall in line to support. That's the way it is according to Goldwater-Nichols. And the way it should remain.*

XIII

BULLDOG AND HIS PACK: AN INCIDENT IN THE WAR

*T*here's a story from the war that merits a chapter in itself, so Carl Stiner *and I have pulled it out and presented it here.*

With something like nine thousand Special Forces personnel in the Gulf, there is no "typical" SF story. However, the best-known deep recon account to come out of the war involved a team led by CW2 Richard "Bulldog" Balwanz. Their experiences illustrate not only the difficulties of SR missions in general, but the challenges (many of them unnecessary) that Special Operators faced during the war.

The warrant officer arrived in the Gulf with the first SF units at the end of the summer. Posted to the border area for surveillance, he also served as one of the "trip wires" in case Saddam attacked Saudi Arabia. He'll now take up the story:

DESERT STORM was a defining moment for SOF, in that it validated the Nunn-Cohen Amendment to the Goldwater-Nichols Act in setting up US-SOCOM. This was really the second time that SOF was deployed in its entirety, covering the full spectrum of their missions.

In the early part of the war, I was up on the border doing surveillance just outside of Khafji. Anyplace that I ran into coalition forces, I always found SF guys with them. We had SF teams down to brigade levels, sometimes to battalion levels, with every coalition force in theater—including the Syrians and the Moroccans. We would traditionally consider those fellows unfriendly toward U.S. interests; but there we were, working side by side with them.

About half a dozen teams covered the entire border between Kuwait and Saudi Arabia. I was with an SF team working with a Saudi Arabian counterpart—their equivalent of a Special Forces team—but they were border guards as well. We'd patrol the border at night; and the Iraqis were obviously doing the same thing just across on the Kuwaiti side. We'd have visual contact with them; and we could see the buildup and the fortifications over there. Every so often, we'd actually get deserters coming over, waving their white flag, particularly after the bombing campaign kicked off.

If you can picture the border, a big berm ran along the Saudi side and one also on the Kuwaiti side. It was like a tank trap, so if the tanks started to come, they'd drive up over the top and drop in a ditch. We had standing orders not to cross that berm.

There was also a space of maybe one to two miles between the berms that we called No-Man's-Land. The border proper was out there somewhere in the center. When the Iraqis invaded Kuwait, the Kuwaitis just came across with anything they had, and a lot of the vehicles broke down; so there were bone piles of these vehicles. One night, we were looking around with NVGs, when we noticed a glow in one of the vehicles out on a little knoll in No-Man's-Land. We figured there must have been a short in the battery.

Obviously, the Iraqis had seen the same thing; and one morning they came up in an armored vehicle—the first time we had seen any type of armored vehicle out there. He came right out into No-Man's-Land up on a knoll just north of Khafji.

My team commander ordered me to get out there and see what they were doing.

I didn't feel comfortable about it, but he's my boss, so okay. We jumped in a humvee, and the Saudis lifted the gate to let me cross the Saudi berm. As soon as I got to the other side, I hung right and hugged the berm, just kind of looking. Meanwhile, the captain was standing on top of the border station directing me through the radio. "No, no, turn left, turn left, get out there."

Well, about that time the Iraqis had hooked a chain to the abandoned vehicle and were dragging it off. They must have thought we were using it, because they dragged it off the knoll. The captain kept insisting, "Get out there, get out there." I figured, well, it's safe to go out there now; they're gone. So I topped the knoll.

But it turned out the Iraqis were there. They swung their guns around on us, and I thought, *Man, I'm dead.* It was real tense for a brief moment. And then they just continued doing what they were doing, and we drove off.

I had a discussion with my counterpart, the Saudi commander.

"They came into Saudi Arabia," I told him.

"Oh, no, they didn't," he said. He was telling me he wasn't going to go out there to check.

I said, "Yes, they did. I can see the tire marks on the border territory. They have been inside just a hundred meters, but they were in Saudi." And we had a discussion. I said, "Look, I'll tell you what we'll do. The tracks are still there in the sand. We'll go out there. We'll turn on the GPS, take a reading, come back, and we'll plot it on the map. And if it plots on the Saudi side, then that proves that I'm correct. If it doesn't, then I'm wrong."

So he agreed to that, and we did. We drove back out there, did the GPS, came back, and plotted it; and sure enough, it plotted out about a hundred meters into Saudi Arabia. We thought that was significant, because up to that time, there had been no Iraqi incursions into Saudi Arabia.

A little later, all of a sudden, a heat round came back down from battalion, saying, "Hey, what are you doing crossing that berm? You've got standing orders not to cross the berm." It kind of got to be a case of who said what, me or my captain. It wasn't good for anybody.

Later, the battalion commander came up and sat down and talked to me and I didn't know what to expect. I thought I might be in deep shit. But he surprised me. "Well," he said, "I'm going to tell you what. I have a team that's sitting back in the rear down at the Bat Cave"—that was our nickname for the SF base at King Fahd Airport, where the SOC had a team, ODA525.

You have to understand that every team in 5th Group was deployed into the war effort except this one team. Before they'd flown out of the States, their captain had just left for special mission tryouts, so the team had deployed to Saudi without an officer. The company sergeant major had stayed back to run the rear area, and their team sergeant had been picked to move up to the company sergeant major, which left the team without its leadership. As a result, they were basically being choggie boys.* The battalion used them to run errands. They're very proud individuals, and they wanted

---

*A slang term heard mostly in Korea: someone who runs around doing menial work for some organization—"an errand boy."

to get involved in the war effort, but they were left out of it. They called them the Catholic girls: They were saving it for the big one.

So the battalion commander offered that up to me when he came up to the border. "I've got this team back there that's sitting in the Bat Cave; and they're really not involved in the war effort, and they need a strong leader. I'd like to offer that to you. I want you to think about it."

Of course, I wanted to kiss the guy. I got in touch with him and with my company commander and said, "Look, I would like to have that team, but if I'm going to have any credibility as a leader, I've got to get them involved in the war effort immediately. I can't go back there and then have things not change. If they stay being choggie boys for the battalion, there's no value to me being there, so I need your assistance in getting these guys involved. We'll gear up, and I think we should get some of the first missions that come down."

So that's what set the groundwork.

WHEN I got to the Bat Cave, what I found was really something else.

The guys in 525 had been back there for several months. They'd been there so long they'd built furniture. They had a putting green. They had cable TV. I don't know where they'd gotten it, but they had it. And—like many other units at King Fahd and elsewhere—they'd set up stills for moonshining. I'm not saying that these guys were bad soldiers; anytime good soldiers have time on their hands and are idle and are not challenged—well, let's just say they're very resourceful.

When I got there, they really had a bad attitude. They were underused.

Not that they didn't benefit the war effort: They taught all the teams in the fifth group how to conduct close air support (which came in handy later), and the guys were also *really* physically fit, because they spent a lot of time in the gym.

So when I took over, the first thing I did was get them out and involved. We went clear out almost to the Jordanian border, way up in the northwest part of Saudi Arabia, and conducted operations in support of teams that were preparing for some activities. We were doing long-range cross-country movement using humvees and the GPS system.

GPS is a great system, one of the best things we had in DESERT STORM, because navigating in the bare desert can be close to impossible. With the GPS, you just set it up in the windshield and it told you which way to go. It was important to be able to use GPS across hazardous or rough terrain at night, or driving under blackout conditions with NVGs.

After we came back, about mid-January, we got the special reconnaissance mission.

About the same time, they called me in and said, "We want you to look into hide sites." At that time, we had no hide site kit, no standard equipment. There was also no SOP on how you developed and did a hide site, so we had to conduct some research and development on our own.

We went out and actually dug hide sites, to determine the best way to go about it. What's the ideal size for four guys to live in there? How are you going to sleep? How are you going to eat? Because once you go into the ground, you stay in there, for a week, ten days. You're sleeping in there. You're shitting and pissing in there. We had to figure out how to do all that. . . .

The hide kits we developed weighed about a hundred pounds apiece with all the poles and the tarps. You have to keep in mind that all this was carried on our backs.

But then we got the mission, and we went into isolation; we prepped, we studied, we got all the current intel, and we brought in the SOAR guys that were going to fly the mission for us, to do route planning.

The mission was actually for us to get into a hide site and place eyes for real-time intelligence up on Highway 7, a major north-south highway that came out of Baghdad, went south down to An Nasiriyah, and then southeast over to Basrah. It was a major line of communications. We'd be in direct support of the XVIII Airborne Corps commander. Our reports would go directly back to the SFLO, or the liaison officer—the SOCOR they called it, the Special Operations Coordinator that worked at the Corps headquarters. And he was in direct contact with the Corps commander.

The Corps commander wanted to know what the enemy was doing. Were they reinforcing the front? If they were reinforcing, what type of equipment and what type of troops? What sort of tanks?

The mission statement also said that we had to be able to identify signature items of equipment—equipment that is organic to certain units, and which will identify them. The T-72 tanks, for example, were used only by the Republican Guards. If you saw a T-72, you knew that you were dealing with them.

We got our plan together, and were sitting there, waiting and wondering, when the Battle of Khafji broke out—the Iraqis came across the border, and so we got called up there. The main Iraqi units had already pulled out, but our commanders felt there were still some isolated people left who may have been gathering intel, so we went building to building and door to door, kicking doors, clearing buildings. We really got boned up on our urban warfare, if you will. We never did find anybody, but every door you kicked down, you didn't know.

We were in Khafji when we got the call: "We're going to execute." So we came back down to the Bat Cave, got all our gear together, and went up to King Khalid Military City, KKMC, where our task force was located. We spent a couple of days there, waiting.

One of the things we were waiting for was some special boots we'd ordered. American jungle boots leave a telltale print in the soft loam soil through which we were going to be walking, and we didn't want to leave any tracks like that. Finally, the evening before we were supposed to go in, the brand-new boots arrived. Some of the guys said, "I'm not going to wear them. They're not broke in." So I took plastic MRE boxes, cut them to the shape of the boots, and taped them to the bottom of our old boots, so they wouldn't leave a print.

We were scheduled to go to a place about two hundred meters off Highway 7 and near a small river, the Shatt al Gharraf. There were also agricultural fields and canals and ditches. The ditches were dug by hand, so the dirt was piled up on the sides. Our intention was to use them for moving around, so if people were out there, we'd be able to get down the ditches and walk if we had to.

We were going to put in two hide sites. One of them would watch northbound traffic, the other southbound. Periodically, about every four or six hours, we had to report back to headquarters, but if we saw something significant—Scud launchers or a company of armor or such—we reported it immediately.

It's now February 23, 1991.

From KKMC, we loaded onto two Blackhawk helicopters, four guys on each one.

We had some really great SOAR pilots, the greatest pilots in the world. The SOAR guys had proven themselves time and time again. We knew they would get us in there. More important, I knew they would come and get me.

A guy named Kenny Collier, a chief warrant officer, flew the mission lead on my helicopter. I went up to him and kind of pulled him close. "Kenny, I have no doubt that you'll get me in there," I told him. "But if I need you, I need you to come and get me. Don't leave me in there." He got a big smile on his face. "I told you, Dawg, you call, we haul."

We took off out of KKMC and flew to Rafhah, an air base up on the border, for refueling. We were going about 150 miles across the border into Iraq—a long way for a Blackhawk. The SOAR guys determined that by the time they flew us in, dropped us off, and returned, they'd have about ten minutes of fuel remaining.

We wanted to be actually crossing the border at about eight that evening. We were all hyped up, camouflaged: We're ready, we're going to war, we're going in there. The guys are excited. We had trained our entire career for this, to support our country and do these types of missions. We had rehearsed. We had gathered all the intel. We had done very thorough mission planning.

We crossed the border at about eight—and then for some reason, we got recalled. They said, "Abort the mission. Return to station." So we turned around.

To this day, I don't know the reason for that recall, but whatever it was, we hadn't even gotten back yet, when they said, "No, no, execute, execute."

We couldn't just turn around, because of the fuel, so we had to get off and refuel the helicopters, all of which put us behind our planning curve. The timing was very tight. If we took too much time on this end, that put us in a potential white-knuckle situation at the other end.

Kenny Collier had been a Special Forces soldier, so he knew the importance of time. They tried to make up some for us. They flew very low and they flew very fast. They may have been twenty feet off the desert floor and just streaming 160 knots or so, going across that desert floor.

I was on the headset with the pilot when I felt the helicopter jump up, and a big thump. I felt her shudder and I didn't know what it was. It scared me half to death.

"What is that, Kenny? What is it?" I asked over the headset. And he was calm as could be, which really impressed me. We'd hit a sand dune and ripped the rear wheel off the back landing gear. "Oh, don't worry about it," he said. "We just hit a sand dune. We're all right." Which calmed me right down.

Because of the delay, the helicopters lost their GPS satellite coverage for a time.* They had to use some sort of backup navigational system.

---

*In those days, there weren't enough GPS satellites to cover the world; and that meant there were periods without GPS coverage.

"I can't guarantee you that I'll put you on the exact spot where you wanted to go," the pilot told me.

I said, "Well, Kenny, you get me as close as you possibly can, and we're going to go on with the mission."

As we approached the target area, he made a few "false insertions"—that is, he would lift, come up high, and intentionally get picked up on radar, then he would touch down and sit there for ten seconds or so, so if the enemy came out to find out what was going on, they'd find nobody there. We did a couple of those, and then finally, he stayed low and swooped in, and we rolled out. And then they were up and gone.

It was an eerie feeling as they were going away, because you could hear the blades propping quieter and quieter, and you realized that you were one hundred and fifty miles in the enemy's backyard.

ONE of the questions we'd asked intel was, "Are there dogs in that area?" They'd told us there weren't. The Arabs don't like dogs. They consider them filthy animals and they don't own them.

However, while this is true for Arabs who live in the city, the country Arabs—the Bedouins and the farmers—have dogs for the same reason our farmers do. They use them for security. So there *were* dogs out there. As we rolled off the helicopter and they flew out of sight, I thought we'd landed in a pound. You could hear dogs howling all over the place.

Once the helicopters were out of earshot, though, the barking faded, and we realized they were reacting to the sound of the helicopters and not necessarily to our presence.

The first thing we did was to move off maybe a hundred meters and set up a little defensive perimeter and just listen. It's a tactic to take in the night sounds, to let your eyes and ears adjust to your environment. There was nothing but silence, which is what I wanted to hear.

I turned to my weapons sergeant: "Bring out your GPS. Let's see if we have some coverage now." We did. We were actually north of the area in which we wanted to be, but not far, maybe a mile or two. However, each individual on my team had a rucksack that weighed in excess of 175 pounds, which is extremely heavy. That included our two hide-site kits, twenty-five pounds for each guy. Every team member had five gallons of water—that's forty pounds. Each guy was carrying radio equipment.

I went on a leader's recon with my weapons sergeant. We found the area we wanted, determined where we would put our hide sites, went back,

picked up the team, and brought them into the area. We pulled out our dehandled shovels and started to dig, and the first thing we realized was that
though we had rehearsed in Saudi Arabian sandy loam, this soil up here was
agriculture soil. It was hard. There was no way we were going to dig a hide
site before dawn with just a dehandled shovel.

The other team, under team sergeant Charles Hopkins, moved back a little bit, found some softer soil, and dug down, but when we tried to do it,
too, it became apparent we were going to run out of time. Since we had to
get under cover, we decided to put our hide site in one of the ditches that
crossed the area. We laid our supports and used that ditch as our hole; we
camouflaged it with sandbags up the front as best we could; got some vegetation to put on top of it, and brush, too; and did what else we could in the
time we had.

We knew traffic going up and down the highway would never be able to
see anything out of the ordinary. It blended in.

Now, we thought that the farmers in Iraq operated the way they do in the
States. A farmer plants his fields, then goes out once in a while to check his
crops to make sure things are going on. But he's not out there every day
looking. However, in this part of Iraq we failed to take into consideration the
fact that their technology is very far behind ours. The kids don't sit in the
house and watch TV and play video games. They don't have TVs and computers. They play out in the fields. We didn't realize that.

So we were inside the hide sites at first light, four of us in each hide. One
guy was on watch at a peephole (Sergeant James Weatherford); one guy
recorded what was going on; and the other two guys basically rested. I was
one of the guys resting. I had my eyes closed; but I was aware of what was
going on, and heard Weatherford say, "Man, there's a lot of activity out
there. There's people along the road."

There was a lot more going on than we had anticipated.

About nine o'clock in the morning, we started hearing children's voices.
And Weatherford said, "There's kids out there. They're out there playing."

They got closer and closer, and as they started getting louder, I got concerned. And then all of a sudden, the sounds stopped. It got quiet. The children came up; and they actually looked into the peephole where
Weatherford was on watch. They looked inside and they saw this guy all
camouflaged up, looking back at them, and they gave a little scream and
jumped back.

At the same time, two of my soldiers came out of the back side of the canal, carrying silenced MP-5 submachine guns and silenced pistols. The kids saw them and took off.

"Chief, what do we do?" my guys asked. "What do we do?"

Now, there's no doubt in my mind that if I had told them, "Don't let those kids get away. Shoot them," they would have done it. And we'd been cleared to do that, if any civilian came in and compromised the mission.

Two of them were girls, maybe seven or eight years old, and one was a boy, younger. It was an instant decision. "No, don't shoot them," I said.

I was not going to shoot children.

Several things probably went into that. I have a Christian background. I had children of my own about that age. It just wasn't in me to shoot children. Whatever happened to us, I was willing to accept that. If they were going to bring in forces, I could defend myself. We had weapons, and I knew we could bring in close air support and that we could get out of there. But I wasn't going to shoot children.

The kids ran off toward a little village not too far away. We brought up our SATCOM radio and called for immediate extraction. We said, "Hey, we've been seen. We got caught. We need to get out of here. Our positions have been compromised."

While our guys were working on the exfiltration, nobody from the village came back to investigate. I had no idea if the kids had told somebody about us—or if maybe they thought they had seen a boogey man. But after they ran off, nobody came to check us out. At that point, we determined that even though the hide positions were compromised, maybe the mission itself wasn't.

So we moved back up this canal to another area, and set up again. When nobody came, we canceled the emergency exit.

"Look," I said, "I feel pretty secure. Nobody's come. We moved out of the area. We're going to continue with the mission. At nightfall, we're going to find another area and get in and continue on."

All day, we continued to watch, to monitor the highway, to report the traffic. At 1200, we sent back information based on what we'd seen.

Shortly afterward, I was lying on a mound of dirt, watching the road with some binocs, and I caught something out of my peripheral vision back to the side. I looked back and there were two kids, but this time they had an adult with them. I slid back into the ditch real quick, but I knew in my heart that they'd seen me. Even so, I was hoping, well, maybe they didn't. And I told the guys, "Look, I think we just got . . . somebody's just seen me." And

Buzzsaw (Robert) DeGroff scurried up on the side and checked things out. By that time, the folks were moving toward us. "Yes," Buzzsaw whispered, "here they come."

I came out of the hide to talk to them. The adult had on a Palestinian-type checkered headdress, and they were all looking at me; and so I gave them my best "*Salaam ala'ikum*," and spoke to them in Arabic, thinking of what the intel guys told me: They may be friendly, they may be indifferent. I was thinking hard, hoping in my heart that that was the deal.

Again, the thought of killing these people—that wasn't going to happen. They were unarmed, they were civilians, there were two kids.

Then they took off real fast, moving backward. This time, we weren't as lucky as before. It was just a matter of twenty minutes or so when people started coming.

All of a sudden, these teenagers started approaching, a gang of them, maybe fifteen or twenty getting close to us. They were just teenage kids and were ignorant of what was going on. So I spoke to them in Arabic. I told them to stop, to get away, to leave us alone. And finally I held up my gun, and when they saw that, they scattered.

I decided to move out.

By this time, other civilians were coming, a lot of them, and pulling up on the road were five vehicles—three deuce-and a half military transport–type trucks, a Toyota Land Cruiser, which served as a command-type vehicle, and a bus. The next thing we knew, an Iraqi company was unloading from them, probably a hundred plus people. Pretty soon, all of them were out there on the road, talking.

At this time, we were all looking at each other: "Hey, we're in deep shit."

We called for immediate exfiltration, but they said, "Well, it's going to be a while before we can get extra birds in there. We're going to line up close air support for you."

I said great.

It was time to implement our emergency destruction plan—to make a pile of all the stuff we couldn't take with us and get rid of it. The engineer already had a block of C-4 made up with a one-minute time fuse on it. He reached in, pulled out the igniter, and we put it down. I saved one radio from the pile, an LST-5, because it was a SATCOM radio, but it also did double duty as a UHF radio for talking to aircraft. You screwed a whip antenna about the size of an ink pen into the top of it and it went to UHF. I could call close air support on it.

All the other equipment went into the rucksacks.

Meanwhile, the Iraqi army guys were starting to maneuver on us—coming up this side and that side—and some civilians had armed themselves, farmers with their hunting rifles and such. If somebody came into your backyard, you'd go out to defend it. That's what they were doing.

At this point, the ground war had started, but we didn't know it. We hadn't been told when we went in, "Hey, the ground war is going to start at midnight."

But the Iraqis did know it, and that's what must have gotten them so excited.

They were also probably overconfident. They didn't realize what they were up against. They probably thought we were a downed air crew—easy pickings—and they could just come out there and grab us.

Anyhow, we set the charge on all our sensitive and classified equipment, and then threw the rest of our rucksacks on top of that to lighten the load. All we had on was load-bearing equipment—just the nylon straps on which you clip your ammo pouches, your canteens, and so forth. I stuffed an MRE into my pocket and had a night-vision device hanging around my neck. We kept a single GPS system that contained our egress route; all our way points were in it.

Then we pulled the time fuse on the C-4 and ran as quickly as we could back up one of the canals. Suddenly, we hit an area where the canal got shallow, and there was a turn. We were basically stuck in this elbow in the canal.

When the charge went off, the Iraqis were less than a minute behind us, and close air support was twenty minutes out. I knew we were in some deep shit. A company-sized element was maneuvering on us, trying to outflank us.

As soon as the charge went off, we came under heavy fire. We waited. We held our fire.

It wasn't easy, though. The most accurate fire didn't come from the soldiers. The Bedouins were hunters, and they were good. . . . I mean, kicking the dirt around our heads.

As the soldiers came in, they moved in groups of four or five, walking upright, looking and holding their guns up to the ready. They had on low-quarter shoes, office shoes. These were not front-line troops, combat soldiers; they were office workers. They'd been told to grab their guns and go out and get us.

A U.S. infantry squad would have kept a low profile, doing fire-maneuver and bounding and going off to position, but these guys were just standing upright. That was to our benefit.

Buzzsaw said, "Do we fire? Do we fire?"

Finally, I said, "Yes, open fire."

Nobody did anything for a while, because everybody was sort of reluctant to get it going. They knew that once we started shooting, we were in deep trouble. So I gave it again: "Fire."

Buzzsaw opened up with his 203 (a 40mm grenade launcher attached to an M-16). The other 203s opened up. The grenades went out and landed among the Iraqis. All of a sudden, a guy'd be out there with tattered clothing staggering around. The rest of them had dropped. You wondered what in the world was going on.

My guess is that in that opening volley, we eliminated probably forty of them.

All of a sudden, we were in a hell of a firefight, but holding our own, desperate for close air support.

We had to set our SATCOM radio back up in the UHF mode so we could talk to the aircraft. We set up the SATCOM dish, then went to put in the whip antenna. We had lost it.

It seems that when things go bad, they go really bad. We were in the midst of a firefight, and we didn't have any way to talk to the aircraft.

But sometimes you get lucky. Sergeant DeGroff just happened to be carrying a PRC-90 survival radio. He pulled it out, turned to Weatherford, my communications sergeant, and said, "Hey, will this thing work?"

Weatherford looked at it. "It's a line-of-sight radio," he said. "I don't know if it'll work or not. I doubt it. Not unless somebody's in the area to pick it up."

The air support was out there. We could hear them over our SATCOM; they were calling for us, but we couldn't get them back. So they flew around without finding us.

After a while, one of the sorties took out a nearby bridge over the river because he didn't have anything better to do, and that actually helped us. A lot of civilians had come out for the show, and there were women and children out there, but once things started blowing up and they realized bombs were being dropped, the civilians fled.

About that time, we moved over into what I guess you'd call Plan B. We had school-trained snipers on our team, good-quality people; and as the

Iraqi troops got up and tried to maneuver, we'd drop them. And we just stayed down in the ditch, which was probably the most secure place we could be. Had we gone up out of it, it would have been the end of things.

For a little while, things got quiet enough for DeGroff to pull out the PRC-90. He made a call over it and picked up an AWACS. And I'll tell you, when that voice came back over it, it was just miraculous. I can't use any other word. It was miraculous that we had a PRC-90 radio—fifties-vintage technology. But it worked, and it saved our skins.

Pretty soon, they got a forward air controller to talk to us, and then they started sending sorties of F-16s. F-16s are not your ideal close air support platform, but they were the ones that could get there the quickest. So the -16s got on the Guard net, and we could talk to them directly on the PRC-90 radio. We used it to call close air support the rest of the day.

We still had a problem: We were in the midst of a firefight. We were taking fire from the flanks. We had to direct the planes in for close air support—there were a pair of them. But they couldn't spot our position.

We didn't bring smoke. We had pin flares, but it was the middle of the day, so pin flares didn't work. We did have signal mirrors, so we did what we could with them. The two F-16s flew over, and we were huddled down there in the ditch, trying to flash them with the signal mirrors.

That's when it came in handy that these guys had just taught close air support to the entire theater.

Buzzsaw said to the F-16 pilots, "Look, this might sound strange, but I want you to fly from the moon to the sun." Though it was about one o'clock in the afternoon, the sun and the moon were both out there at the same time. "When you're above me, I'll tell you."

So they came around, and that's exactly what they did. One of the aviators picked us up, identified our position, and relayed it to the other. They went through a long conversation about our precise position, but once they'd done that, we were in business.

Meanwhile, some of the Iraqis had gone out there on the highway and were flagging down other vehicles, trying to get more people into the fray. It happened that an entire convoy of military vehicles, mostly deuce-and-a-halfs, was passing about then, and they got them to stop. So when our first strikes came in, they also destroyed the convoy—a lot of secondary explosions came off those deuce-and-a-halfs.

After that, vehicles would come down the highway, and people would try to flag them down, but they'd see bodies burning and wouldn't stop. They'd keep on going. They'd say, "I'm not going to get involved in that."

Later, I found out that one of the F-16 flights had picked up a column of armor coming into the area and had taken them out on the road before they came close to us.

However, that still left us with a lot of folks out there on one flank that was real hot, and other folks on the other flank, and I was up directing the fire, shifting back and forth. It was working very effectively, and I was very pleased: The guys were doing a tremendous job knocking off targets, keeping calm, saving the ammunition. Nobody stood up, like you see in movies, shooting full automatic from the waist. It was very calculated—lowering the barrel, taking a sight picture, pulling the trigger, and dropping the target.

But still, one of the flanks was very hot. We were really getting a lot of fire off it. We had to call in a close air support mission with cluster bombs. It was going to be close—what we call danger-close, which is anything within a thousand meters. It was maybe two hundred meters—not far at all.

We knew there was a risk—there always is, particularly with cluster bombs—that those cluster bombs would get the friendly forces. And that scared the shit out of me as much as the enemy soldiers did, getting blown up by our own Air Force.

But we called in the close air support on the flank. They came in, and again, it was almost miraculous. It was such an effective strike. The cluster bombs came down—looking like they were going to drop right on top of us—and then the clam shells opened up, and we could hear the bombs from down in the ditch.

When cluster bombs hit, they start *ba-ba-bu-bu-bu-ba-ba*; it works into a crescendo, then tapers back down. And that's what happened. The bombs came right across and eliminated probably a platoon-worth of folks over on the flank that had been giving us so much trouble.

We did the same on the other side.

Then what worried me most was the ditch itself. It wasn't straight. It was twisty. If you tried to look down it, it wasn't like looking down a railroad track. You could only see maybe ten meters before it twisted out of sight.

By that time, I knew they couldn't come in on the flanks unless they started using fire maneuver and maybe brought in heavier support—but if they wanted to, they could come in force down the ditch and overrun us in really quick time.

Another air strike was coming in, and we called it right down this ditch. As soon as they lifted, my intel sergeant, Sergeant Robbie Gardner, and I went shoulder to shoulder (that was about the width of the ditch) back down the ditch, hoping to catch them by surprise. And we did.

We went maybe fifty meters and came up on the Iraqi point element coming up the ditch, but they weren't going anywhere just then, because the strike had got them down; and their guns were lying by their sides.

We came around, at the ready, and then we were face-to-face. Before they could pick up their guns, we were able to eliminate them.

We then walked all the way back down to the place where we had loaded up our rucksacks, and we found bodies all through the ditch. I recall coming up on one guy in particular. His leg was mangled and blown off, and he was about dead, but he was still breathing heavily. We got close to him and moved the gun away. He took his last breath, and that was it, he was gone. It was profound. It didn't strike me so much then as later, when I looked back.

We went all the way down to where we'd blown the rucksacks because it was getting into evening now and it gets cold in the desert. We dragged out some Gore-Tex jackets and any kind of chow that we could find. Although the jackets had been blown up by cluster bombs and our own explosion, it would still provide some warmth. We grabbed some stuff, moved back up into our fighting position, and hooked back up with the guys. By this time, the firefight had become less intense.

There was a kind of rhythm. A sortie would come in and then leave, and there'd be a lull when we didn't have air cover. At that point, the fireworks would pick up. Once a squad-size element—maybe five or six people— stood up and actually charged us, giving out this crazy battle cry: "Hey tetetetetete." It was just suicidal for them, because we were able to pick them off as they were coming in.

The Iraqis were actually pretty game early on, but as we got into the evening and the F-16s had hit them a few times, I think we destroyed their morale. They'd thought this was going to be easy pickings, this air crew out there, and all of a sudden they ran into heavy resistance. There're the M-203s. There're expert marksmen. And there's close air support, with F-16s coming in. And so the later it got, the more the battle died down.

After nightfall, I put on my night-vision goggles, looked out into the battle area, and didn't see any movement whatsoever.

Then we got word that our exfiltration was twelve minutes out.

I couldn't help but think of Vietnam then. One lesson we'd been taught was that the North Vietnamese, knowing there'd be a rescue attempt, would lie in wait. That way they had a bigger target.

Thinking of that, I decided not to give the Iraqis the chance to do the same thing.

Back behind us, maybe another three hundred or four hundred meters, was a berm that I had identified. We moved out and did a retrograde operation across to the other side of the berm. I wanted to put some cover between the Iraqi force and the helicopters when they landed, to prevent the Iraqis from stepping up.

Because the helicopters were flying low, we couldn't talk directly to them. We had to talk through the F-16 that was above us, and he would relay to the helicopter. The F-16 guy came through: "Give me your exact location so that the birds can pick you up." I turned to the weapons sergeant, who had the GPS, to get a reading. But when he pulled it out, it turned out that it was ruined. It had gotten busted up when he had fallen during the fight.

In my mind, I was seeing these guys coming in and getting the shit shot out of them. But then I remembered that that old PRC-90 radio had a beacon on it. So I said, "Can they pick up that beacon?"

They said, "Well, turn it on."

Buzzsaw kicked on that beacon, and within a few minutes we heard the *wok-wok-wok* and they swooped, and almost landed on top of us. I bet it didn't take us ten seconds and we were off the ground.

And it wasn't until then that it struck me that we were very fortunate. We had had an Iraqi company on top of us, and we had been able to get out of there. It was a tribute to the Special Forces A Team, and to the training that we had gone through.

Later, it struck me exactly what had happened to us and what we had done. I'm sure that battle is still on the minds of those people in that village today. One thing that personally satisfies me is that somewhere there are some kids, probably teenagers now, who are leading productive lives and don't know how close they came, just a decision away, to being shot.

Just before we got ahold of these F-16s, two of the guys, DeGroff and Dan Kostrzebski, one one side of the ditch, one on the other, turned around and waved good-bye to each other. It was like: This is it, we're not going to get out of here.

And one of the things that struck me at the time, and particularly later—

one of the gravest responsibilities of a ground commander—is that you are responsible for the lives of men, both losing them and taking them. Losing your own and taking from the enemy.

It's a grave responsibility, and I remember thinking, "We're gonna get overrun here, and if we do, I hope I'm one of the first guys that you're taking out, because I'm not gonna be able to stand it, fighting in this ditch and watching my guys die in front of me." But thankfully it never got to that.

XIV

THE FACE OF
THE FUTURE

C<i>arl Stiner:</i>

One of the proudest moments of my tenure as Commander in Chief of USSOCOM occurred during the spring and early summer of 1991, in the aftermath of the Gulf War. It was called Operation PROVIDE COMFORT. Within a few short weeks, special operations forces, allied with many other wonderful organizations, saved thousands of lives. Our Special Operations troops used their soldier and special operator skills to bring peace, order, and stability instead of war, destruction, and violent change. In the end, the better part of an entire population of hundreds of thousands of men, women, and children, all of whom had been dispossessed from their homes, were able to return to their farms, towns, and villages.

These people were Muslims, but that is only marginally important. These people were people.

The story of how they were saved is important for all the reasons mentioned above. But it is also important for reasons that are more immediately relevant. In the war against terrorism, any Special Forces troops ordered into countries to root out terrorists and their bases will need the exact skills and training that stood them in such good stead in PROVIDE COMFORT. They will need to gain the trust, respect, and support of some significant part of the local population. They'll need the locals to help them, and the locals will have to be shown that the SF teams are necessary to their own future well-being.

The difference between peacetime and wartime operations is always radical, and yet the similarities are greatly enlightening.

It will happen again and again: Our special forces will have to shoot at people at night and shake their hands in friendship the next day.

REBELLION

Tom Clancy:

As the Gulf War came to an end in the winter of 1991, Saddam Hussein faced rebellions in both his south and his north—continuations of deep- and long-running conflicts. Though President Bush gave these rebellions verbal support, actual American aid was limited.

In the south, Shiite Muslim groups, long at odds with the regime and the country's Sunni majority, rebelled, with Iranian help. Mutinying Iraqi army units and the Shiite majority in several southern towns formed the backbone of the revolt, which began in Nasiriyeh on March 2, 1991, and reached its peak around March 7, when Shiite groups controlled Basra, Amara, Kut, Hilleh, Karbala, Najaf, and Samawa. By then, Saddam had already organized a counterattack, reassembling Republican Guard units that had escaped the coalition onslaught in Kuwait. By March 16, the tide had decidedly turned against the rebels; a week later, the revolt had all but ended.

While Saddam's attention was in the south, in northern Iraq the Kurds renewed their own rebellion. For generations the long-oppressed Kurdish tribes had considered their homeland to include parts of southern Turkey, northwest Iran, and northeastern Syria, as well as northern Iraq—Kurdistan. In the 1980s, they rebelled to make this homeland a reality. In a brutal counterattack, Saddam's forces used nerve gas and defoliants, together with more "conventional" forms of massacre, to suppress this attempt at self-determination.

The always-fractious Kurds were too splintered among tribal and political groups to present a common front against the Iraqi leader, but continued oppression brought the different groups together, and the allied campaign against Iraq provided them with another opportunity to assert their independence. On March 4, 1991, a rebellion by the Kurdish Democratic Party under Masud Barzani liberated the Kurdish town of Ranya in northern Iraq, igniting a freedom movement across the region. On March 11, the major Kurdish factions met in Beirut under the banner of the Joint Action Committee of Iraqi Opposition to discuss a coordinated rebellion. On March 14, a day after the conference ended, 100,000 members of the Fursan—a Kurdish-manned Iraqi army auxiliary in northern Iraq—rebelled. In a series of firefights with regular units, the Kurds captured a dozen major towns and a hundred-mile arc of territory. By March 21, the insurgents controlled the provinces of Suleimaniya, Arbil, and Dahuk—the so-called Autonomous Region of Kurdistan. They also controlled much of Tamim and its capital city of Kirkuk, a region with considerable oil resources. The rebel guerrilla forces called themselves "Pesh Mergas," or "those who stand in the face of death."

Just as in the south, Saddam reorganized his army and his civilian administration and launched a drive to regain control. Backed by helicopter gunships and heavy artillery, Iraqi armored and infantry units struck Kirkuk on March 28. Lacking heavy firepower and air cover, the Pesh Merga fell back in disarray.

It was the beginning of a rout. Civilians and guerrillas alike rushed into the snow-covered northern mountains, sometimes taking nothing with them but the clothes on their back. The roads north were jammed with buses, trucks, tractors hauling trailers, donkey carts, and people on foot. Earlier Iraqi actions against the Kurds had resulted in widespread atrocities; the civilians didn't stick around to see if history would repeat itself. Somewhere between half a million and one and a half million Kurds—a little less than half the prewar population—fled toward the Turkish and Iranian borders.

By April 6, the rebellion had been completely crushed, but the exodus continued. Thousands of Kurds died from starvation and disease. At the same time, Turkey—fearing its own Kurdish minority—moved to keep the refugees from crossing their border.

America and its other allies were slow to respond.

Meanwhile, on April 5, the UN passed Resolution 688, demanding that Iraq immediately end repression of civilians in the Kurdish areas and elsewhere. The UN also directed Iraq to allow humanitarian agencies to aid the civilians who had fled.

Soon after the vote, U.S. Air Force Special Operations cargo aircraft began dropping emergency supplies into the region, but Iraqi artillery and helicopter attacks on civilians continued. More fled; the narrow band of mountainous terrain near the Turkish border became crowded with people in hellishly squalid camps.

On April 10, America warned Iraq to cease operations north of the 36th Parallel (roughly the line separating Kurdish from Arab Iraqi territory). The next day, the UN announced it would send a peacekeeping force to the area.

SOF ground units shipped out to Turkey to help survey and stabilize the air-relief operation.

On April 16, the United States, Great Britain, and France declared that Resolution 688 gave them authority to send troops into Iraq to help the refugees. A task force spearheaded by American Marines and U.S. fighter jets pushed back the Iraqis, preventing further atrocities. By that point, the death toll among refugees in the makeshift border camps was estimated at several hundred a day.

PROVIDE COMFORT, the allied relief mission, combined the efforts of thirteen nations under the direction of Lieutenant General John Shalikashvili. It had three aspects:

✪ Air interdiction to prevent Iraqi aircraft from operating above the 36th Parallel. This was primarily handled by U.S. Air Force fighters operating out of Turkey.

✪ A ground presence to secure northern Iraq and the refugees from attack, as well as prepare resettlement camps in Iraq. The Marine Corps 24th MEU (SOC)—Marine Expeditionary Unit (Special Operations Capable)—spearheaded this effort, with its 3,600 members operating approximately five hundred miles inland from their support craft in the Mediterranean.

✪ A rescue operation to bring supplies and medical attention to the displaced Iraqi civilians. Army Special Forces soldiers from the 10th SFG played a key role in this phase of the operation, as did the Air Force's 39th Special Operations Wing, which flew MC-130 cargo aircraft and MH-53J helicopters. Civil Affairs troops and members of the 4th Psychological Operations Group joined the effort by the beginning of May. Numerous helicopters from Army, Navy, Marine, and Air Force units also played a vital role in the supply effort, as did a range of U.S. and allied C-130 and support aircraft.

Brigadier General Richard W. Potter, commanding general of Special Operations Command Europe, headed the SF task force charged with bringing relief to the Kurds. Potter's "Joint Task Force Alpha" would eventually add British and Italian forces, as well as small groups from other nations. A second task force organized around the 24th MEU, called "Joint Task Force Bravo" and headed by Major General Jay M. Garner, operated farther south in Iraq, preparing camps and assisting refugees near the front lines of the guerrilla war (the mission and resources of the two task forces overlapped to some extent, especially in the early and closing days). At its peak, 11,936 U.S. servicemen were involved.

GENERAL *Potter provides an overview of the operation:*

In November and December of 1990, in talks with the Turkish General Staff to establish the second front for Desert Storm, Major General James Jamerson, Admiral Leighton "Snuffy" Smith, and I (as commanding general of SOCEUR—Special Operations Command Europe) had represented CINCEUR in support of U.S. Ambassador to Turkey Abramowitz. These talks resulted in the establishment of Task Force Proven Force, commanded by Jim Jamerson, and my supporting JSOTF, which operated into northern Iraq out of bases in southern Turkey.

In the spring of 1991, the EUCOM staff that had put together the European reinforcement of the VII Corps for DESERT STORM was still in existence. I had stood down the JSOTF and returned to EUCOM headquarters, but the relationships we had developed before and during DESERT SHIELD/DESERT STORM turned out to be of tremendous benefit as we put the relief effort together and as I stood up what General Shalikashvili later designated as Combined Task Force Alpha. We returned to Turkey on April 6 to work the relief effort. Within a week, Brigadier General Tony Zinni joined us as the deputy commander.

EARLY on, the relief effort focused on air resupply, marking of DZs, and distribution of relief supplies. Within days of our arrival, extensive reconnaissance of the camps and border areas, as well as discussions with the (always fragmented) Kurdish leadership on the Iraqi side of the border, and with the Turks on the Turkish side, had made it glaringly obvious that much more was required.

General Jamerson and I stressed the enormity of the situation to the EUCOM staff, which resulted in a confirmation visit by the DCINC, General Jim McCarthy. What the task force faced was literally hundreds of thousands of Kurds in makeshift camps clinging to the mountains along the entire Turkish/Iraqi border. Those in the camps confronted harsh weather, starvation, and exposure, which prompted a death rate of more than a thousand a day. The child mortality was horrific.

When General Shalikashvili was designated overall task force commander in mid-April, the humanitarian mission was changed from airdrop and distribution of supplies to on-the-ground relief.

On April 17, as the remaining SOF forces were moving into the area, General Shalikashvili stated his Commander's Intent and gave me the following stated missions:

1. Get into the mountains and stabilize the situation by all necessary means.
2. Organize the camps.
3. Get the Kurds under cover and safe from the elements.
4. Work food supply and humanitarian supplies into the camps.
5. Establish potable water distribution.
6. Improve the sanitation, bury the dead bodies—both humans and animals.
7. Stop the dying, especially the child mortality.
8. Convince the Kurds to return to their villages.
9. Turn the press around.

For the entire operation, General Shalikashvili never changed this overall mission set. Each time he met with me during the next three months, he simply inquired about the status of our efforts and asked how he could support them.

In fact, thinking back to General James Galvin's words as CINCEUR as Jamerson and I were deploying on the sixth—"The answer is yes, now what do you need"—I can only say that it was marvelous to have two such men in the chain of command. Direct, succinct orders, no bullshit: "Here is your mission, now get on with it." No one telling you how to suck eggs. As a Special Forces officer, I do appreciate such a command relationship.

AFTER receiving the order, Colonel Bill Tangney, 10th Group Commander, was designated ground force commander, Task Force Alpha. Bill had command not only of his own group, but operational command of all U.S. Army personnel and units in the designated AOR, and of a British Commando Battalion and elements of the Luxembourg Army, and oversight responsibility of Canadian and French military hospitals in the AOR. Colonel Hoot Hooten, commander of the 39th SOW out of Alconbury, England, was my air component commander, and established a marvelous relationship with Major General Jim Hobson, PROVIDE COMFORT air component commander.

Jim Hobson, with bags of previous AFSOC assignments, was most supportive of our mission set.

The international border between Turkey and Iraq split the AOR, with camps on either side of the border. On more than one occasion, the border split the camp. On the Turkish side of the border, the companies and teams of Special Forces had to understand the political nuances of dealing with the Kurds, Turkish sovereignty issues, Turkish military concerns, NGOs, IOs, private organizations, and subtly with Kurdish political structure and tribal affiliations. Once you crossed the border, a different relationship existed with the Kurds, the Pesh Merga, the various representatives of the various Kurdish political establishments (both structural and family/tribal affiliated), and remnants of the Iraqi governmental structure and military. While doing this political and cultural maneuvering, the SF teams and companies had to continue to work their mission: to relieve the suffering, stop the dying, and organize the camps.

Within seventy days, the camps had been vacated, death was due only to natural causes, the child mortality rate was under control, and the Kurds had either returned to their villages or were in resettlement camps established by Major General Jay Garner's Task Force Bravo. Unlike my command, which was a standing command with permanently assigned units who habitually worked together on operations and exercises, Jay Garner had to put his task force together from scratch, using 24th MEU as the base element.

This operation confirmed what I have long known: Special Forces is a Renaissance force. During my career, I had supervised, led, and commanded SF troops in the Meo Tribesman program and Khmer Series programs in Indochina, in the attempt to hold the Lebanese Army together in the early eighties, and in the aftermath of the collapse of the Soviet Union and Warsaw Pact. Give them the mission, put them in a difficult political situation, locate them in isolated outposts in rugged terrain, issue them a myriad of missions, both stated and implied, provide them top cover and the proper support, and they will accomplish any mission they've been given.

There are literally hundreds of stories of children being saved, of the birthing of babies, of food getting delivered at the critical time, of potable water being provided, of adroit handling of conflicts between Kurds and Turks, Kurds and Iraqis, and every other imaginable conflict—family feuds, tribal animosities, disputes between tribal elders, and local political haggling. The constant in all of this is the professional Special Forces officer and NCO. In the camps and in the countryside, the Special Forces soldier kept the lid on volatile situations—always keeping in mind his principal mission of saving the Kurds.

The simple fact is that no other brigade-size element could have gone into the mountains of northern Iraq and southern Turkey in early spring 1991; taken responsibility for 600,000 Kurds; organized a relief effort; stabilized the situation; dealt with the international political and cultural ambiguities; and produced success with no compromise or embarrassment to the United States.

As the task force commander, I knew that our doctrinal manuals did not prescribe how to run a humanitarian operation of that size and complexity; nonetheless it was done in camp after camp in the spring of 1991, and the intelligence, maturity, and adaptability of the Special Forces soldier were the keys. Like the Confederates' Bedford Forrest, we could get to any location in our AOR "Firstest with the Mostest." And Colonel Bill Tangney masterfully transitioned his units from combat operations to humanitarian endeavors and turned seemingly hopeless situations into success stories. That is the acme of Special Forces leadership.

THE BATTLE FOR LIVES

Tom Clancy:

Many of the 10th SFG troops called in to PROVIDE COMFORT during the second week of April 1991 were returning to an area they had only recently left. Lieutenant Colonel Stan Florer had deployed to Turkey at the beginning of the air war against Iraq. His unit's mission was to help provide combat air rescue for downed allied fliers; fortunately, they were called out for only one sortie. Soon after the end of the ground war, the 1st Battalion returned to its base in Germany, where it was assigned as part of SOCEUR.

Within two weeks, Florer was heading back to Inçirlik, Turkey, to accompany General Potter as he surveyed the situation.

"We made a visit to the main camp, Shikferan, and it was absolute disaster. The Turks were overwhelmed," he recalls. "The mountains were as serious as you can get. They were up there at eight thousand to ten thousand feet on the tops, and there was a lot of snow; it was just absolutely brutal."

Civilians were living in crude tents and hastily constructed shelters, or no shelter at all. Food was almost nonexistent, drinking water was polluted, and cholera and other diseases were rampant. The Turkish border troops had orders to keep the refugees out of Turkey—orders that were followed by whatever means necessary.

The battalion moved to Silopi in extreme southwestern Turkey, not far from the Syrian border. There, Florer split his men into small groups, distributing them in the camps all along the frontier toward Iran in the east. The SF forces, often operating in three-man teams in areas that could only be reached by air or foot, extended across a 3,600-square-mile security zone established in northern Iraq near the borders of Syria, Turkey, and Iran. The camps were on both sides of the borders, which in the remote, mountainous areas were not well defined (the Turks allowed some camps to be set up just over the line, but only as a temporary measure).

Bill Shaw, then a captain commanding ODA 063 of Charlie Company, 2nd Battalion, headed a unit airlifted to Turkey as soon as the emergency was declared. Shaw and his team greeted the deployment with mixed emotions. Specialists in military freefall—parachuting into hostile territory—they had spent the war in Massachusetts, much to their chagrin. Next to combat, which they had missed, this assignment seemed a letdown.

"We were excited to have a mission," Shaw observes. "However, humanitarian assistance just did not seem very important at the time."

Attitudes soon changed. ODA 063 landed in Incirlik for a brief rest, then moved with a large headquarters group via helicopter to Pirincikin, a remote border settlement held by about 150 Turkish border guards and surrounded by thousands of refugees. Ten minutes after their arrival at the camp, a Kurdish woman approached the Turkish military commander, crying and begging for assistance. When the commander dismissed her, Shaw and the company commander intervened. They sent two medics to help the woman, whose husband had been shot in the hip. The medics soon had him patched up (Shaw never found out how the man had been wounded).

"Their action gave our unit instant rapport," Shaw remembers. "By the next day, all twenty thousand refugees in the camp had heard the good news: Forty to fifty U.S. Army doctors had arrived."

"They thought we were *all* doctors when we got there," adds Colonel Mike Kershner, who was operations officer for the 3rd Battalion of the 10th SFG. "It was a little disconcerting to my weapons men at first, because they didn't want to be associated with that."

As it happened in fact, when the Americans arrived in several of the camps, the Kurds kept their ill children and other family members hidden. Medics began going from tent to tent, looking for sick kids. "They didn't really want you, because they didn't trust the medics or anybody else at first," says Florer. "The medics literally had to convince these women to bring their kids out and to help them. Otherwise, they would just die. They would just bury them where they could find a little spot and dig kind of a shallow little grave and put these little kids in it. They were dying by the dozens when we first got there."

For the first few days, SF medics tried to cope with the incredible array of health problems with their own supplies—which were, of course, designed to help a six- or twelve-man team in a combat situation. They were quickly overwhelmed.

Once the units established secure landing zones and road routes to the camps, however, medical supplies began to arrive in large quantities. World Health Organization packages—which typically include medicine, antibiotics, and other necessities for thousands of people—helped stabilize the health situation.

THE CAMPS

Calling the refugees' makeshift collection of shelters "camps" is a wild overstatement.

Pirincikin was typical. Thousands and thousands of people were packed into a one-hundred- to three-hundred-yard-wide valley. Observers compared it to the scene at a rock concert—without any of the good stuff, and more bad than anyone could imagine.

"The ground was covered with the detritus of their flight," Shaw remembers, "including clothing, feces, and vomit." Trees had been stripped and used for firewood. Most tents were simple tarps four or five feet high. A dozen or more people—children to elderly—could be living in each one. Ground unoccupied by tents was covered with waste and the remains of butchered animals.

As soon as they arrived, SF soldiers generally set up secure areas for sleeping away from the main camp. They stayed in canvas tents, either in small two-man tents or "GP mediums"—general-purpose medium-sized tents that could house several people. In some cases, soldiers set up one-man "poncho hootches" and bunked there. As soon as their perimeters were established—and often before—they went to work.

While the chaos in the camps seemed to invite terrorists (and, of course,

Iraqi secret agents bent on mischief), the vastly outnumbered Americans were actually relatively secure. According to SF security analysts, part of the reason had to do with the mission: The Kurds generally recognized that the Americans were there to help; they were grateful for it, and in many cases protective. Various other factors, including close ties with the civilian leadership and local guerrillas, the presence of Turkish military, and not least of all the SF's own firepower, also helped prevent attack.

On another front: The SF units included a range of foreign-language experts, yet not one spoke Kurdish. The troops had to rely on Kurds who spoke English, sometimes surprisingly well, sometimes haltingly. Since the refugees included a number of doctors, lawyers, schoolteachers, and other professionals, they often served as translators.

THE SUPPLY EFFORT

U.S. Air Force Hercules transports had been dropping supplies to the Kurds since April 7, at first aiming to provide the refugees with a thirty-day supply of food, water, and other necessities. But the difficult flying conditions and the unfamiliarity of the refugees with airdrop procedures had led to waste and tragedy. Harsh winds in the mountains and foothills blew ordinary parachutes off course; high-speed parachutes could defeat the winds, but often meant the pallets would smash on landing and ruin the contents.

The Kurds were so desperate to get the supplies, they would often run under the falling chute, not realizing that a pallet could crush them. An unknown number of civilians died this way. Other Kurds were killed when they tried to retrieve the supplies from minefields.

SF troops began organizing the supply effort from the camp site, clearing roads for trucks and establishing helicopter landing zones. The first few helicopters in were mobbed by anxious Kurds, creating unmanageable chaos. The SF troops ended that quickly.

"We figured out where the LZs were that we needed to create and then we barbwired them off," Florer remembers. "That was the way to start to bring order." The Kurds' leaders, meeting in camp councils with the SF commanders, helped allocate supplies, so resources could be distributed in a somewhat organized fashion.

Coordinating the supply pipeline was more difficult. As the relief operation got into high gear, supplies from thirty nations had to be processed and shipped to the front line. The Military Traffic Management Command off-loaded cargo at three Turkish ports, shipping cargo and pallets to a string of bases that supplied the camps. But even as a routine developed and more roads were opened, the sheer size of the operation and the involvement of nearly one hundred relief agencies with their own agendas complicated the effort. Getting any supplies to the camps in the first few days was difficult, but getting the right supplies to the right places was for a while nearly impossible, a classic case of catch-22s complicated by misinformation and a lack of resources.

Kershner's SF unit took to setting up "air guards" to spot approaching helicopters. They'd contact the aircraft, find out what they were carrying, then direct them to the camp that needed that particular supply, often countermanding the pilot's original orders. They also diverted the helicopters for medical transports. And they convinced civilian organizations to give supplies to those who needed them, rather than to the people originally intended.

"Somebody will show up representing some church organization with food or something, with instructions that it goes only to a specific group," Carl Stiner recalls, "when you're trying to treat everybody equally. Our troops had to try to redress the imbalance. The charitable groups all had the best of intentions, but preconceptions and conditions on aid added greatly to the chaos and delay."

The first wave of food rations came from the military in the form of MREs. Though this prepackaged food had been designed for American palates, the Kurds were so hungry they ate it gratefully. As days went on, food began arriving from donor countries that seemed inappropriate at best and bizarre at worst. Large two-gallon-sized cans of corn were plentiful—but to Kurds, corn was animal food. They would open a can, discover what it was, and dump it. Cheese balls were everywhere. And then there was the plum pudding—tons of the stuff were delivered by airplane, helicopter, and truck. Not even the Americans would eat that.

Packaging of the food presented another problem in the mountain wilderness. "Can openers were not supplied, so the Kurds used large rocks to open the cans," Shaw reports. The smashed cans—and in many cases the ruined contents—littered campsites for weeks.

Lentils, rice, flour, and other staples were preferred by the refugees, who could turn them into foods with which they were familiar. As these arrived in bulk, diseases caused by malnourishment ebbed.

THE HEALTH EFFORT

Water and sanitation were no less concerns. When the troops arrived, most camps had no latrines. "Everyone had amoebic dysentery," Shaw recalls, "and would go to the bathroom wherever they wanted. The river and creeks were used for a water source, bathing, dish-washing, cleansing the dead, and, worst of all, as a depository for dead animals. Our medics took water samples and found the microorganisms too numerous to count."

"In late April," Dick Potter recalls, "the press was hitting us hard about our inability up to then to stop what appeared to be cholera in Cukurca Camp. A lot of children were dying.

"We had sent samples to Louis Pasteur Hospital in Paris and to Landstuhl Military Hospital in Germany, with the same findings: no cholera, but what I would call acute dehydration and diarrhea. I was reminded of the rice water diarrhea we had in Vietnam, and the resultant child mortality. I traveled to Cukurca Camp, and by this time the camp's medical systems were organized: The Free Irish Hospital, Doctors Without Borders, Medicine Lamonde, German Red Cross, and Red Crescent Tent Hospitals were in the center of the camp. SF medics were in the surrounding hills and subcamps, tending to the sick; anyone requiring advanced treatment was sent to the center of the camp and one of the IO field hospitals.

"When I arrived, about six hundred infants had been triaged in three areas, and the doctors believed they could probably save two or three hundred of them.

"To Americans, leaving the others to die was completely unacceptable.

"Bill Tangney organized the response: He sent for six hundred cots, cut holes in the cots so the children could defecate through the hole without reinfecting themselves, brought in IV apparatus for all of the children, and convinced the elders to have the wives and mothers attend the children with Special Forces soldiers present.

"We called Landstuhl and had them send us powder to mix with water; it locked up the kids tighter than Dick's hatband.

"Bill ordered the battalion commander to reinforce the troops on the ground. After receiving a quick refresher on the use of IV apparatus, a Special Forces soldier was assigned to about three sets of mothers and children.

"Bottom line, the powder worked, the IV worked, the cots worked, the constant attention to the children by the wives, mothers, and SF worked; and I believe only two infants were lost."

Gradually, order was imposed. The security provided by the SF troops, as well as the Marines and other units closer to the Iraqis, allowed civilian relief agencies to set up makeshift hospitals. Latrines and trash piles were established; dead animals were removed from water sources. Clean water was air-dropped and trucked in. Hastily dug graves were moved from the main camp areas to better ground. New camps and hospital areas were established along roads where they could be better supplied and maintained.

Doctors Without Borders helped provide emergency medical care throughout the region; the doctors would simply show up at a camp and get to work.

There was occasional friction with (or among) the volunteer groups, or with Turkish officials, or the UN, but this tended to be generated by administrators. On a personal level in the camps, people tended to get along to get things done—though at times this came after initial distrust. "At first there was a great distance, particularly with Doctors Without Borders and some of these more liberal organizations," Florer recalls. "But it only took a matter of days and the typical SF soldier, or the officers, or whatever, would schmooze their way into their hearts, because we were really making things happen."

Now and again, working with civilians turned out to be pleasant from the start—especially when the civilians were female. One group of Irish nurses showed up in a camp just secured by SF personnel. "Fellows, could you give us a hand?" one of the women asked when their truck pulled up. Twenty men fell out, tents were up quickly, and generators were soon humming.

Special Forces units became an unofficial supply conduit for volunteer organizations. "They'd come to us and say, 'We need more fuel. Do you have more batteries? Do you have this? Do you have that?'" Florer remembers. "And of course we took care of all that stuff for them. And what we didn't have, they'd call back (to the bases in Turkey) and say, 'Hey, sir, our credibility's at stake here. You've got to get us this thing.'" SF supply sergeants practiced their time-honored tradition of begging and borrowing to supply the front lines, which in this case were refugee camps. "It was schmooze your way to victory," Florer adds.

One group that proved fairly resistant to schmoozing was the Turkish military. Threatened with its own Kurdish minority, the Turkish government did not want Iraqi Kurds within its borders. The government and military at times looked on the relief operation with suspicion, and there were a number of clashes between the Turks and refugees throughout the operation—though most occurred in the early days. In one case, a driver for the Turkish Red Crescent pulled a handgun and shot at refugees trying to overrun his bread truck. The local Turkish military unit moved in with weapons blazing to control the crowd. American SF troops responded in a helicopter to calm the scene, and came back with a half-dozen refugees the Turkish army had shot. One victim was a child.

"There were a lot of incidents," recalls Lieutenant Colonel Chris Krueger, who helped coordinate operations for the 10th Special Forces. "There just wasn't any love between the Turks and the Kurds."

As one might expect, emergencies were almost normal.

Bill Shaw and Green Beret medic Doug Swenor were in a guerrilla camp late one afternoon when a four-year-old got too close to a campfire, which set her nylon dress in flames. In seconds, she sustained third-degree burns over most of her body. Swenor emptied his medic's bag trying to clean and dress her wounds, and gave her morphine to ease her pain, but there was little else he could do.

In the meantime, Shaw got on the radio and tried to arrange a medical evacuation—nearly impossible to do; night was falling.

And yet, somehow, help came.

Though he was extremely low on fuel, a British Chinook pilot heard the distress call and diverted to the camp. The girl and her mother were loaded aboard. Shaw watched the helicopter disappear into the darkness, wondering if it had enough fuel to make it through the mountains back to Turkey.

A week later, Shaw met the pilot when he returned to drop off supplies. He had made it home to his base, but it had been very close: The helicopter's engines had coughed dry as they touched down.

Had the girl lived?

The pilot didn't know. It seemed doubtful, given the extent of her injuries. And yet none of the men—the pilot, Shaw, Swenor—could have lived with himself if he hadn't done all he could to save her.

Just a few days earlier, Shaw had complained about the mission. It was a long way from what he'd trained for. But that afternoon, its meaning—and its frustrations—hit Shaw hard. It was *exactly* what he had trained for.

The Office of the United Nations High Commissioner for Refugees, generally referred to as UNHCR or simply the UN, gradually took a more active role running the camps. At times there was considerable friction between the UN, Turkey, the SF forces, and the Kurds. It often took several days to build a working relationship. In some cases, rapport came only in the face of danger. At one camp, female members of UNHCR were attacked by Iraqi secret service agents; they retreated to their tent and were surrounded. SF personnel managed to get the women out to safety without firing a shot.

Iraqi secret agents were a problem throughout the region, but it was difficult for Americans to ferret them out and deal directly with the problem. At one point, Florer was presented with ID cards belonging to Iraqi secret service agents in Zakhu, a Kurdish stronghold. But the Americans were in no position to play detective, and Florer couldn't promise action.

"No problem," the Kurds assured the Americans—leaving what that meant to the imagination. The SF troops later learned that the guerrillas had attacked the secret police station with grenades, then gunned down the survivors.

PESH MERGA

American policy favored the Pesh Merga guerrillas for practical as well as political reasons. The resistance infrastructure represented the Kurd leadership, and like the Americans, they opposed Saddam Hussein. But having a common enemy did not ensure rapport; the American units had to sell themselves on the ground, day after day.

Soon after their arrival, Shaw and one of his men ventured from their camp to an area controlled by Pesh Merga guerrillas to meet other refugees. They were led by their guide about ten miles from the Turkish border, passing patrols of well-armed guerrillas, until they came to the camp in the ruins of an old village—destroyed during the 1980s in an attack that included both nerve gas and defoliants, which had wiped out the once-elaborate orchards.

About five to eight hundred people now lived there. The guerrillas used it as a supply and rest area for troops fighting farther south. "Things here were organized," Shaw recalls. "Family areas were separated. There was a community meeting area under a slot-ring parachute canopy and stacks of weapons and supplies everywhere."

The two Americans were greeted by heavily armed men and led to

Rasheed Hadgi, the small, elderly man who headed the camp. Hadgi, a many-times-injured hero of the Kurdish uprising, offered them food and drink—damaged MREs and Kool-Aid, obviously made from the contaminated water.

Though Shaw and his sergeant didn't want to catch dysentery, they didn't want to insult the guerrillas either; they had no other choice but to accept their hospitality. "It was the right thing to do to build rapport, but later that night we both paid the price from both ends. At the time, I personally wished I had taken the bullet."

Kershner attended several meetings with the Pesh Merga leadership, generally by car supplied by the guerrillas. "No matter what kind of car we got in, we were always at 125 percent of capacity," Kershner remembers. "Everybody was jammed in together.

"I carried a pistol; everyone else in the car had an AK-47 or a machine gun; none of these weapons had been placed on safe within memory. I spent the entire, bumpy ride in these vehicles just watching for the muzzles of all these rifles to make sure I did not get shot by accident."

The guerrillas wanted more than just medical and food support from the Americans; they were looking for massive military assistance—which they couldn't have. "It was the usual ballet dance," Kershner continues. "Two boxers circling each other in the ring trying to figure out what they're going to give and what you're going to give."

The politics between different bands of guerrillas generally followed clan lines, and sorting it all out was often a nightmare for the Americans. The different groups rarely coordinated with each other; each had to be approached separately.

Since there were no Kurdish speakers among the SF units, first contacts were often creative. In one case, a group of SF soldiers came under sporadic fire as they approached a guerrilla position. Trying to reassure the Kurds that they meant no harm, they tried yelling that they were Americans. The gunfire continued. They yelled the name of the camp; that didn't work either. Finally, one of the soldiers yelled, "George Bush."

The entire guerrilla contingent jumped up from their positions and began chanting the name of the American president, who had become a hero because of the Gulf War victory. "George Bush! George Bush!" The troops were welcomed as brothers.

Small SF elements eventually set up camps within the guerrilla strongholds as part of the effort to maintain good relations. Since the rebels controlled much of the countryside, this greatly increased security as well as built rapport. In general, the U.S. attitude toward the Pesh Merga was lenient and cooperative throughout the operation. But the British had different ideas. They set up checkpoints in their areas and often would not allow armed guerrillas to pass.

THE COMMUNICATIONS EFFORT

Reliable communications over such a far-flung operation were vital. There were no telephone lines in the mountains, and the terrain made communication by conventional radios difficult, but U.S. SF troops had brought SATCOM radios with them, so geography and terrain were no longer barriers.

Though SATCOMs accounted for as much as ninety-five percent of the communications, the devices were not without drawbacks—capacity was limited and communication had to be rationed, because there was only so much "space" on the satellite frequencies.

The relief effort also required a great deal of hands-on command attention. General Potter would "work the camps" every day—flying in and out to check with the commanders in the field. Planning sessions later in the day would allocate resources, trying to anticipate needs for the next days and weeks.

As conditions became more stable, the job of distributing supplies was gradually handed over to civilian agencies. A ration card system was instituted in many of the camps. Water-purification and -distribution systems were created. Dental clinics were established, with SF medics—and in some cases others; Bill Shaw got his first chance to practice basic dental skills he'd learned in training—pulling rotted teeth, supplying more basic care, or even acting as midwives.

"That made us nervous," Kershner recalls. "We did not want to be in a position where we were responsible or could even be peripherally involved with a dead baby or something. Fortunately, every case we had like that turned out okay. But it made us extremely nervous.

"Our guys were very concerned about the Islamic prohibitions against hanging out with their women, or even looking at their women; and here they're going to ask a woman to lie down on this camp cot and hike up her skirts. . . . Invariably the guy that was with her always had a rifle."

In fact, the Kurds took the pregnant women to the medics—a sign of enormous trust.

The trust the SF troops created was everywhere; the rapport was extraordinary.

In one camp, Major Rick Helfer built a particularly strong working relationship with its Kurdish leaders. One day, the leaders decided to honor him. A thousand kids suddenly ringed the SF perimeter and began chanting, "Helfer! Helfer! Helfer! USA! USA! George Bush! George Bush!"

"My people!" yelled Helfer, hamming it up to the other Americans' amusement. Later, he repaid their praise by dressing head-to-toe in the clothing of a Kurdish tribal elder.

LIFE in the refugee camps could turn hellish in seconds. A few days after the children's demonstration for Helfer, the same kids were throwing rocks at Turkish soldiers who had come to their camp to steal some of the refugees' supplies. The Turks locked and loaded, and lined up in firing positions. SF personnel, their own weapons at the ready, rushed between the Turks and the refugees and faced off the Turks—preventing a possible massacre.

Mines—a constant, deadly danger—had been laid along the roadways and in many flat, open areas, stepping off a well-trod path could bring death.

Some children saw them as toys.

"They would go out and collect mines," says Krueger, "then go to the top of a hill and roll the mines down to see how far they would go before they went off."

Mines caused many injuries, mostly to kids who wandered into a mined area without knowing it. "I remember an SF soldier running up to the LZ carrying a little boy with a leg that had just been severed," says Krueger, who gave up his helicopter so the kid would be evacuated to a hospital. "That big burly SF soldier with that little bitty body in his arms. His entire focus was to get him medical attention."

The danger wasn't only to Kurds; an SF soldier had to have his leg amputated below the knee after stepping on a mine.

Even relief operations could injure people. CH-47 Chinooks are powerful helicopters, capable of delivering large amounts of food and other supplies. Their massive rotors, powered by huge engines at either end of the aircraft, generate immense downdraft as they land. "It would blow little kids over. They would just go flying like tumbleweeds," Kershner recalls. "It was no fault of the helicopter. That's just physics."

The SF found safer "games" for the kids than collecting mines or watching helicopters land. One favorite involved policing the area. "The guys would give them candies from the MREs," Kershner continues, "for whoever picked up the most trash or something.

"I went to a camp and there was a medic walking through it, and a little four-year-old kid would follow this medic around everywhere. And if the medic had a free hand, the kid was holding it. I finally asked what the deal was. It turned out that the kid had choked and the medic had done the Heimlich maneuver on him. That had changed his life, and this kid was just attached to the medic."

It was hard to find a Kurd who was not grateful in some measure to the Americans. One Kurd leader offered Kershner a fourteen-year-old daughter as a wife. "It took me quite some time to convince him that it probably would not be a good idea for me to take a second wife home."

CULTURE

Americans and Kurds have vastly different cultures. The Kurds' attitudes to women, children, the elderly, and to male privilege make most Americans uncomfortable—and of course that goes the other way around.

To the Kurds, for example, children counted for very little. Adults certainly valued the youngest members of their society—if the kids needed help, they helped them when they could—but they clearly put a much higher priority on helping other adults, especially the very old. Children were often the last to get food, water, and medical attention. A dead child would generally be buried in a shallow, mass grave; an adult would receive a much more elaborate funeral and separate burial.

"They would abandon the children that were too young or too weak— they would just leave them out to die," Kershner remembers. "It was a cultural problem for the Americans to accept that they took care of the old people first. But you have to understand the old people were their corporate history—the institutional memory. They were the decision makers. So that was where their emphasis was."

Attitudes toward women also shocked Americans. It was not uncommon to see a woman carrying heavy loads while men carried nothing at all. Girls were expected to marry as soon as they were old enough to bear children. And when SF personnel tried to show the women how to make a substitute formula for children from rice water, they nearly came to blows with Kurdish men, who resented their dealing directly with the women. Such techniques had to be shown to the men first, who would then teach it to the women—if they decided the women should know it.

While some Kurdish attitudes bothered the Americans, their strong family structures provided a base for organizing relief efforts. The elders were the primary decision makers, and their decisions were normally accepted without dissent. They were therefore the first people with whom to deal.

"If you told an older Kurdish guy, 'Hey listen, why don't you get your family together, 'cause this is what we're going to do,' generally speaking he'd get his family together to do whatever you wanted him to do," Kershner recalls.

"In fact, the Kurds seemed to enjoy working with our guys. And we had real good relationships with them. Whenever you met with them, they enjoyed hearing about your family. They wanted to find out how many kids you had, what they did for a living. . . . They were very generous people. They would share their last bits with you."

Or even on occasion offer to make the ultimate sacrifice:

"One day," Dick Potter recalls, "I was involved with the tribal and camp elders in Cukurca Camp, the largest camp located entirely in northern Iraq [125,000 population]. The meeting was heated. The elders were ready to move south, but only if the town of Dahuk was under CTF PROVIDE COM-FORT control. At that time, I could not make such a commitment, and so the debate went on for hours.

"As I was leaving, the elders took me out of the tent and introduced me to two young Kurdish men, in excellent health and in their mid-twenties. The elders had heard of President George Bush's heart problems, and with great solemnity told me that if President Bush, their dear brother in Washington, needed a new heart, these two men were ready to travel to the United States to be heart donors. I thanked the elders, told them that our President had healed, and passed the message back to General Shalikashvili, who I am told passed it to the Chairman, who in turn informed the President."

The loyalty and generosity went both ways. "Big loyalties were created," Kershner continues. "If you could have told the SF guys, 'Well, we are going to leave you in place and you are just going to carve out the country, and we're going to call it Kurdistan and let all the Kurds live there,' they would have done it in a heartbeat."

GOING HOME

As the situation was stabilizing in the camps, diplomatic and political progress was also being made elsewhere. The allied occupation of Kurdish cities attacked by the Iraqis helped stabilize the political situation, and a second round of negotiations began May 7 between Iraq and the Iraqi Kurdistan Front, led by Kurdish Democratic Party leader Barzani. By this time, roughly 16,000 allied troops were involved in the relief and security operations.

Several firefights between Iraqi and Kurd forces during the first weeks of May led to planning for an allied assault on Dahuk, one of the trouble spots. But the Iraqi-Kurd negotiations—and possibly a U.S. show of force as the Marines prepared to engage the Iraqis—led to a tentative agreement on May 18, and lessening hostilities.

Refugees began returning to their homes in the northern regions of Iraq.

"First, the Kurdish leadership had to be convinced that it was safe for them to go back home," says Chris Krueger. Meetings with the various leaders and top American generals, including General Shalikashvili, laid the groundwork. Then came the job of getting the word from the leaders to the refugees, and especially to the Pesh Merga guerrillas guarding the roads and passes.

"Colonel Bill Tangney and I and the chief Kurd in the area got on an MH-60 helicopter and we started just outside of Silopi at the very first camp," recalls Krueger. "We put the Kurdish leader on a monkey strap and we would fly over the checkpoints, do a hard bank, and kind of hang him out the door, and he would wave at them and they would signal us to land." On the ground, the leader would tell the guerrillas that it was now time to return home. The trio would then board the helicopter and travel to the next site. They spent the entire day and several hundred gallons of fuel visiting camps and checkpoints.

Within twenty-four hours, the Kurds were on the move. SF units had established about a half-dozen safe routes south and supplied easy-to-read maps showing checkpoints and highways. Among the most important messages on the maps: Don't leave the roadways, because of the mines. Thousands of maps were handed out and air-dropped in the camps.

Way stations on the southern routes home included hospitals, often staffed by Doctors Without Borders, as well as military personnel. The refugees would stay there perhaps overnight, then move on. Food and water, as well as medical supplies, were available at the checkpoints. "Logistically, we didn't want another humanitarian disaster, a trail of tears, moving back to their homes and people dying en route," says Florer.

The way stations helped maintain the Kurds as they returned.

Many simply walked back home. Americans moved many others south by truck on the treacherous mountain roads. Krueger remembers that among the refugees were Kurdish construction firms, whose heavy equipment was used to rebuild—and in some cases, create—roads. The rough roads were hell on the vehicles; U.S. deuce-and-a-half transports would quickly blow out their tires, running through their duals and spares as they navigated south. Tires were often more difficult to come by than fuel, and the troops had to borrow and occasionally beg for spares. A French offer of twenty-five tires was greeted with an offer of canonization by one grateful crew.

"As we went through towns somebody would beat on the roof of a truck and say, 'Hey, a bunch of us live here,'" Kershner remembers. "And they'd stop and eight people would get out of the truck and then they'd drive on."

"We'd just truck the people back and drop them off wherever they said they needed to be dropped off."

According to Kershner, as many as fifty-six Kurds could crowd into the back of a deuce-and-a-half—a space American troops would call crowded at twenty-five. Families tended to stay together when they moved, so fitting upward of fifty people in the back of a truck—or sometimes even more than a hundred in a Chinook—was a necessity.

"They packed everything very nicely and many of them hauled it on their backs," says Florer. "And just overnight we would look out across the camp and there'd be thousands less people."

SF units from the camps escorted many of the refugees back into their hometowns, sometimes remaining for a few days. At times, disputes broke out with squatters who had moved into vacant homes; the Americans tended to stand back as the locals sorted out those problems. In the meantime, disputes between the Kurds and Iraqis continued.

As it became clear that the United States intended to pull most if not all its troops out of northern Iraq, Kurds protested. The Americans were their shield against Saddam. But by the end of June, SF units were pulling back to Inçirlik, then restaging to their home bases. For many, Inçirlik gave them their first opportunity for a shower in weeks.

BEYOND COMFORT

Ground operations connected with PROVIDE COMFORT were effectively concluded July 15, 1991, when the last Marine unit in northern Iraq hauled down its colors and prepared to pull out. Seventeen thousand tons of relief supplies had been delivered; at least half a million people had been helped.

Coalition air units continued to patrol the northern stretches of Iraq from Turkey, enforcing the cease-fire and UN agreements, and some ground units remained in the region to monitor events and deliver additional aid when necessary. Operating under the auspices of Operation COMFORT, over the next five years, allied units delivered another 58,000 tons of supplies to Kurds in their home villages.

On June 22, 1991, Barzani announced that he had agreed with Baghdad on a settlement that gave the Kurds military and political authority over the Kurdistan Autonomous Region. Though other Kurdish leaders were divided over this agreement, an uneasy peace settled temporarily over the region.

Meanwhile, a simmering, low-key war continued between Turkey and Kurds within Turkish borders, but at times this flared into large-scale Turkish actions against the Kurdistan Workers' Party—the PKK. The Marxist Kurdish group had actively opposed the Turkish government since at least 1984 and continues to do so.

In Iran, the Kurdish Democratic Party (KDP) and the Patriotic Union of Kurdistan (PUK) vied for domination in the northern areas of Iraq. In a complicated three-way conflict with the PKK, the KDP eventually aligned itself with Saddam Hussein's regime. In the summer of 1996, the KDP and Iraqi forces captured Irbil, a prominent Kurdish city in northern Iraq. The KDP and PUK, which has received support from Iran, still struggle for domination in the Iraqi Kurdish region.

A tragic coda to Operation PROVIDE COMFORT was written in 1994, when two American helicopters were accidentally shot down by American F-15s. The helicopters were ferrying a variety of officials involved in relief and peace work. Though humanitarian efforts continued, changes in the Turkish government eventually forced the United States to disband the relief effort on December 31, 1996.

Air interdiction of Iraqi flights continues under NORTHERN WATCH, paralleling efforts in the south under Operation SOUTHERN WATCH.

DEBRIEF

"Why do we need Special Forces guys to do this?" Stan Florer asks.

"Because nobody else has all it takes to do the job—the capability to organize and direct, together with the security edge. Civil Affairs guys don't have all that. Our solders are packing an advantage, and they know how to use it."

Or to put it another way: Fifty armed Americans add an eloquence of persuasion to any suggestion. It's not so much "You better get your act together or we're going to shoot" as "Here is a strong, steady, and secure structure within which you can operate. With that in place, you can begin to take charge of your own needs."

Similar conditions apply in dealings with external relief organizations. These are all fine people, but they tend to run off every which way, and tending to horrendously complex needs in an utterly chaotic situation requires focus, direction, and order.

Carl Stiner points out that the Army's—and especially the SF's—streamlined command structure facilitates getting things done, and getting cooperation from such organizations. "We obviously won't use force on them, but if they persist in wanting to do their own thing, the CINC can step in and say, 'I am responsible for this whole area and you are going to comply. And here is the schedule you're going to operate under if you want security, and if you don't, you are on your own.'"

"What was interesting about this was its relationship to the larger political picture, a larger connection to DESERT SHIELD/DESERT STORM obviously, and the combat relationship," Florer comments. With more than two dozen government and nongovernment relief agencies involved, Special Forces' ability to work with a variety of groups under difficult conditions proved to be critical. While strict discipline is necessary for any military operation, PROVIDE COMFORT demonstrated what Bill Yarborough and others long ago foresaw, that flexibility and creativity are a major force multiplier.

The same attributes that make Special Forces soldiers so valuable in combat actions—the ability to adapt to unexpected situations, to use cutting-edge technology to its fullest, to think creatively, to act quickly, decisively, and independently—turned out to be the qualities most needed to help the Kurds in the free-flowing crisis following the war with Iraq.

Training for war goes hand in hand with the battle to save lives. Tomorrow's SF soldier will continue to find his role in a shadowy territory, where there are few boundaries between armed conflict with bad guys, on the one hand, and working closely and productively with local friendlies, on the other.

"In a way," Dick Potter recalls, "the Special Forces legacy lives on in that part of the world. If you travel in northern Iraq and visit a Kurdish settlement, you're likely to encounter children in the ten-to-eleven-year group. Ask the parents and the elders their names. If they were born in the camps on the Turkish border during the great migration, you will find a middle name of Smith, Jones, Swicker, or Gilmore—the Kurds' tribute to men of the 10th Group, a living honor to the men that saved them."

FACING FORWARD

During the next ten years, special operations optempo greatly increased, with many more humanitarian assistance missions, and many more missions across the broad range of SOF capabilities. From Somalia, Haiti, and Afghanistan to Southeast Asia, Africa, South America, they were busy men.

A small sample of what they were doing during that busy decade:

SOMALIA During the '90s, SOF missions called on them to prevent fighting—or keep the lid on it—more often than to engage in combat. Through no fault of their own, their peacemaking efforts did not necessarily yield freedom from strife, most notably in Somalia, where several special operators on a UN-sponsored peacekeeping and humanitarian operation sacrificed their lives in the fiercest close combat engaged in by American forces since the Vietnam War. Two of the men earned Medals of Honor.

This incident took place in Mogadishu in October 1993, and generated much press and a bestselling book. Its notoriety has tended to overshadow the genuine successes of American and UN operations in that benighted country. In the early 1990s, many Somalis were starving, and anarchy is too kind a word to describe the chaos. The country was divided among warring tribal factions; many of these were ruled by warlord-thugs, most were engaged in "civil wars" with the others, and some were fundamentalist Muslims, hostile to the United States.

Mending Somalia—like mending Afghanistan—will not be a quick fix.

Nevertheless, during the period from 1992 to 1995, SOF made a positive difference there. They conducted reconnaissance and surveillance operations (SOF elements drove more than 26,000 miles); assisted with humanitarian relief (bringing an end to starvation); conducted combat operations; for a time tamed many of the warring factions; and protected American forces (capturing hundreds of weapons and destroying thousands of pounds of ordnance). PSYOPs troops hired and trained thirty Somalis as a nucleus for radio broadcasting and newspaper publishing. They put out a newspaper, *Rajo*—"Truth"—set up a radio station, and distributed millions of leaflets. Civil Affairs troops helped coordinate overall UN and NGO humanitarian efforts, and were involved in great and small projects—from rebuilding the Mogadishu water supply system to setting up playgrounds in the city in order to give children something better to do than throwing rocks at military vehicles.

HAITI   In 1990, after hundreds of years of corruption and oppression, Haiti—always in a bad way—seemed about to lurch at last into the twentieth century. In their first free election, the Haitian people selected a civilian president, Jean-Bertrand Aristide.

The new freedom did not last long. In September 1991, the legitimate government was thrown out by a military government, headed by General Raoul Cedras. After diplomatic efforts and a UN mandated embargo failed to force the Cedras clique to step down, and with thousands of Haitians fleeing the impoverished country in rickety, leaky boats (many perished at sea), a U.S. invasion was planned—Operation UPHOLD DEMOCRACY, modeled on Operation JUST CAUSE (Panama).

As in Panama, the XVIII Airborne Corps would run the operation, with extensive support from Army, Air Force, and Navy SOF. Special operators would take down key governmental sites, followed by linkup with conventional forces. Special Forces teams would then fan out and secure the countryside.

In September 1994, former president Jimmy Carter, Senator Sam Nunn, and retired General Colin Powell negotiated a last-minute deal with Cedras that aborted the invasion. Cedras stepped down in favor of Aristide, and the

U.S. forces were quickly reconfigured for peaceful entry. The invasion meta-morphosed into a large-scale humanitarian mission.

Lieutenant General Henry Shelton, the XVIII Airborne Corps commander, used conventional forces (most of the from the 10th Mountain Division) to secure Port-au-Prince, the capital. To secure the rest of the country, he called on Brigadier General Dick Potter to form an SF task force (called Joint Task Force Raleigh). A-Detachments fanned out into the villages and countryside, and became the only source of law and order until the Haitian civilian government could move in and take over.

The PSYOPs campaign used leaflets, radio broadcasts, and airborne loudspeakers to send the message that cooperating with American forces and staying out of bloody conflicts with the remnants of the illegal regime would be the quickest route to a restoration of democracy. Civil Affairs troops made a start on restoring Haiti's long-wasted civilian infrastructure. For example, in an operation they called LIGHT SWITCH, they brought electricity back to Jeremie, Cap Haitien, and other northern cities and towns—places that hadn't had electricity in years.

THE BALKANS   In the early 1990s, Yugoslavia fractured into rival independent states, each striving to attain some dream of ethnic-religious purity—Eastern Orthodox, Muslim, or Roman Catholic. An impossible dream—the different ethnic groups were scattered pretty much all over the map. Tragedy followed, when the ethnic factions tried to bring about ethnic purity by force—and acted out age-old hatreds in the process. Thousands of people were driven from homes their people had lived in for centuries—or worse, they were massacred.

From 1992, the UN and NATO sent forces to the region in order to impose peace, but it took a coordinated bombing of Serb targets (Operation DELIBERATE FORCE—August to September 1995) to bring about a cease-fire among the warring factions. This in turn led to the Dayton Peace Accords of November 1995 and the Paris Peace Agreement of December 1995. The peace agreements were to be implemented by Operation JOINT ENDEAVOR (December 1995 to December 1996).

SOF had an important mission in support of JOINT ENDEAVOR—primarily to interact with foreign military forces, as they had done in DESERT STORM and Somalia. But other missions included personnel recovery (such as downed pilots) and fire support.

For their primary mission, Special Operations Command on the scene sent out Liaison Coordination Elements (LCEs) to both NATO and—far more important—to non-NATO battalion or brigade commanders within each area of operations. The LCEs made certain that the intent of information and instructions passed on to the battalion or brigade commander was understood.

LCEs conducted daily patrols with their assigned units, maintained communications, assessed the attitudes of the local populace and the various warring factions, provided accurate information about violent incidents, and made general reconnaissance. Since they had their own vehicles, they were not tied to the transport of their assigned units.

Civil Affairs coordinated reconstruction of the civil infrastructure and organized relief—a big job; there were better than five hundred UN, government, and nongovernment organizations to harmonize. Civil Affairs units helped in several ways: coordinating the repatriation of refugees; restoring public transportation, utilities, public health, and commerce; and organizing elections and setting up new national and local governments.

PSYOPs got out factual information through print and broadcast media, and conducted a mine-awareness campaign, aimed mostly at children.

Operation JOINT ENDEAVOR gave way to further stabilization efforts (Operations JOINT GUARD and JOINT FORGE— December 1996 through 1999). Most SOF personnel were involved with PSYOPs and Civil Affairs specialists.

In March 1999, NATO initiated Operation ALLIED FORCE to bring an end to Serbia's violent ethnic-cleansing campaign against ethnic Albanians (primarily Muslim) in Kosovo. The nineteen-nation NATO coalition heavily bombed Serbia for seventy-eight days, at the end of which the Serbian President, Milosevic, threw in the towel and agreed to stop the ethnic cleansing. By then, the better part of a million refugees had been forced out of Kosovo.

During ALLIED FORCE, Civil Affairs units coordinated large-scale humanitarian relief with other U.S. agencies and international relief organizations. SOF aircraft airlifted food and supplies. PSYOPs EC-130E Commando Solo aircraft broadcast Serb-language radio and TV programs to inform the people of their government's genocidal policies and to warn them against committing war crimes in support of those policies.

SOF Combat Search and Rescue MH-53 Pave Low and MH-60 Pave

Hawk helicopters rescued two U.S. pilots (one from an F-117, the other from an F-16) downed in Serbia. These two missions each took less than a minute on the ground.

During the follow-up Operation JOINT GUARDIAN, SOF liaison teams initiated street patrols throughout their operational area in Kosovo. In the process, they arranged meetings between local Albanians and Serbs, to defuse ethnic violence, searched for illegal weapons caches, and helped war crimes investigators find massacre sites. Though SOF teams did not end violence, they managed to establish rapport with both ethnic factions, and their on-the-scene eyeball reports gave the leadership a clear view of local conditions.

HUMANITARIAN DEMINING OPERATIONS   In 1988, millions of mines left over from the Soviet invasion remained in Afghanistan, stopping millions of refugees from returning to their homes. Troops from the 5th SFG deployed to Pakistan to work with UN personnel and Afghan refugees to find a way to remove this tragic legacy safely. The results became a prototype for other SOF and UN humanitarian demining programs.

It was not an easy job. There was then no effective Afghan government, and there was a multitude of organizations to coordinate. The SOF troops had to more or less invent the program on the spot, and then sell it to everyone else involved. The fractious and suspicious Afghan tribes and factions did not make things easier. Special Forces had to use their political even more than their technical skills.

Practically, SOF training programs taught millions of Afghans how to identify, avoid, report, or destroy mines—and how to set up training programs they could run themselves. When SOF troops left Afghanistan in 1991, the Afghans were able to manage demining without further outside help.

Other SOF demining training programs were later set up in Cambodia, Laos, the former Yugoslavia, Central America, and elsewhere—with PSYOPs and Civil Affairs units playing a large part in making local people aware of the danger from land mines, as well as showing them how to clear them.

AFRICAN CRISIS RESPONSE INITIATIVE   After the 1994 genocide in Rwanda, and unrest the following year in its neighbor Burundi that pointed to a similar outcome, the U.S. Defense Department worked out a plan to deal with the situation—and others like it—based on training battalion-sized units from free and democratic African states to conduct peacekeeping operations within the continent. This plan matured into the African Crisis Response Initiative (ACRI), which the State Department launched in the fall of 1996.

Though military assets from the United States and its allies were used in the ACRI program, Special Forces troops soon found themselves at its heart.

The 3rd SFG, under EUCOM's command and control, developed an instruction program and sent teams to work the training. SF planners developed common peacekeeping tactics, techniques, and procedures. Training the African battalions in common doctrine and standards allowed the multinational forces to work effectively together.

The 3rd SFG-designed ACRI training came in two phases: First there was an intensive sixty-day training for individuals, platoons, companies, leaders, and staff. This was followed by exercises to practice what they had learned.

At the end of 1999, SF teams had trained ACRI troops in Malawi, Senegal, Ghana, Mali, Benin, and the Ivory Coast.

NEOs   SOF troops also took part in a number of noncombatant evacuation operations (NEOs)—usually Embassy personnel in danger during revolutions or civil wars.

In April 1996, SEALs and SF troops provided security for the American Embassy in Liberia during the evacuation of Americans and third-country nationals. Using Air Force SOF MH-53J—and later Army MH-47D—helicopters, 436 Americans and nearly 1,700 foreign nationals were safely flown out of the country.

SOF also took part in NEOs in Sierra Leone, Congo, and Liberia (again).

PEACEKEEPING AND TRAINING   SOF troops continue to be deployed in many countries in peacekeeping and/or training roles. Examples include many African nations, Kuwait, Venezuela, Bosnia-Herzegovina, Albania, and Macedonia.

And then, in September 2001, a new mission came to SOF. . . .

XV

TUESDAY,
SEPTEMBER 11, 2001

Carl *Stiner:*

Tom Clancy and I began this story with an account of a terrorist assault on an ocean liner more than fifteen years ago. We are ending it in the aftermath of another terrorist attack—the September 11, 2001, assault on New York's World Trade Center and the Pentagon in Washington. A score of fanatics commandeered ordinary civilian machines—fuel-laden airliners—and turned them into weapons of destruction. The differences between the two events are striking.

Both involved careful planning and wanton disregard of human life, but the greatest distinction is in the scale—not only in the sheer magnitude of the devastation, loss of life, and horror, but also in the obvious size and skill of the organization that let loose such savagery. In the past, you needed governments for that. But apparently no longer.

It's far too soon after these acts to predict possible long-term consequences, and we won't presume to attempt it. However, several implications are worth exploring, even at this early date.

Terrorism has been with us for a long time, and it will stay with us as long as men find cause to rage against an establishment they view as oppressive. Terrorist tactics were bad enough before, when they blew up shops and buses, hijacked planes, held people hostage. But now we are under attack by men who wreak havoc on a scale earlier terrorists could only dream about. We no longer just face single individuals with a gripe, or small groups bent on changing a political system. These new terrorists are bent on purging civilization of all those who do not share their beliefs.

The new terrorists have created an organizational web of cells operating in many different countries, but outside of any country's laws—cells that can be called upon to wage war on a scale much larger and more complex than ever before. What they have become, in fact, is their own virtual—or shadow—government, powerful enough to intimidate and strike fear into many actual governments. They are directly supported—financially, militarily, or otherwise—by sympathetic "legitimate" governments, and receive support from sympathetic wealthy individuals or organizations.

Islam is one of the world's great faiths, one that brings great riches to all the world's human community. Most of these new terrorists proclaim their total and undying faith in Islam, yet they justify their actions by their own interpretation of their religion. Their Islam is not the true Islam. In effect, they have hijacked their own religion.

On September 11, without warning, they committed the most barbaric act ever carried out against the United States, one specifically designed to kill as many innocent people as possible. The most powerful nation in the world could do nothing but watch. All our military might stood passive.

Such scenes and our feelings of helplessness will remain etched in our minds forever.

Their objective was to cause us to lose trust in one another and in our government's ability to protect its citizens, to cause us to imprison ourselves. We won't do that. But if we're smart, this will serve as a wake-up call.

For years, many of us have been concerned about our vulnerability to terrorism. To us, this attack was no surprise—though the form it took was. In fact, it could have been even worse—and maybe someday it will be.

We have all had many questions in the attack's aftermath:

"Why is the United States a target?"

"How did such an attack happen here?"

"Will there be more attacks?"

Let us begin to answer them.

WHY IS THE UNITED STATES A TARGET?

Most nations and people respect the United States. Our freedoms, and the help we have given to oppressed and impoverished people, have made us a beacon and a model for much of the rest of the world. But not for everyone. Certain groups hate us so deeply that they dream of violently destroying us.

Their hatreds come from several sources: religious differences; a culture they see as promiscuous and sinful; our foreign policies, particularly our support of Israel (an especially large grievance among Shiites); the U.S. support of Iraq during the four-year Iraq-Iran war; our support for the Christian-dominated government of Lebanon in the early to mid-eighties; the Gulf War and its aftermath, the embargo of Iraq, which has harmed many innocent Arabs; and the continued presence of our troops on the sacred territory of Saudi Arabia. All of these perceptions, and many more, combine to make the United States a magnet for attacks by extremist groups.

The terrorist war against the United States probably began as far back as November 4, 1979, when militant Iranian students took over the American Embassy in Tehran and held sixty-six Americans hostage for 444 days. This event turned into a major political crisis for the United States, but far more important, it served as a catalyst for other states to sponsor terrorist organizations that could be used to pursue their own political objectives.

Thus the 1980s were dominated by terrorist attacks against U.S. interests abroad, carried out by state-supported fundamentalist extremist groups. Terrorism quickly became a calculated, formalized, and cheap means of warfare. Attacks increased in frequency and complexity, and suicide attacks (self-induced martyrdom) grew more and more common.

Iran's Ayatollah Khomeini declared a holy war against the United States. His objectives were to drive the United States out of the Middle East (particularly Lebanon) and to spread his Islamic revolution throughout the area.

Syria's president Hafiz Assad, a secular leader of a Muslim state, hoped to use terrorism to attain one of his chief foreign policy goals—to gain dominance over Lebanon as a strategic buffer against Israel.

In April 1983, the U.S. Embassy in Beirut was bombed and sixty-three people were killed, among them the CIA station chief and all but two of his staff, neutralizing the U.S. intelligence apparatus in that part of the world. Six months later, in October 1983, the U.S. Marine Barracks in Beirut was bombed, killing 241 U.S. Marines. Shortly thereafter, all peacekeeping forces were withdrawn from Lebanon. Khomeini and Assad had each achieved major objectives.

The United States was not prepared to deal with this form of warfare, and acts of hostage-taking, hijacking, and bombings against U.S. interests increased. In 1986, Libya's Muamar Qaddafi joined the fray by launching a campaign in Europe against U.S. targets.

The disintegration of the Soviet Union changed all this for the worse. Until then, the Soviets had considerable leverage over states and organizations that sponsored terrorism, and were reluctant to sanction acts that could draw them into a confrontation with the United States. The end of the Soviet Union opened up a Pandora's box, and turned former puppet states and organizations loose to pursue their own interests, most of which were hostile to those of the United States. To make matters even worse, many Soviet scientists and technicians who had been involved in developing or producing weapons of mass destruction were now without jobs. Many were sucked up by renegade states and put to work developing advanced capabilities that could be used for attacks against the United States.

Terrorism finally reached U.S. shores in 1993, with the bombing of the World Trade Center by a group of Islamic extremists. I have never been able to learn whether this event was state-sponsored or only the work of an Islamic extremist group.

In the same year, the wealthy Saudi expatriate Osama bin Laden emerged as a mastermind and organizer of terrorism, with an especially virulent hatred of the United States. His organization, called Al-Qaeda (The Base), was a network of terrorist organizations and cells around the world, united in a holy war against the United States.

Bin Laden is believed to be responsible for the bombings of the Khobar Towers in Saudi Arabia and the U.S. Embassies in Kenya and Tanzania in 1998, as well as the suicide attack on the USS *Cole* in 2000, in the harbor of Aden, Yemen. And he is considered the prime suspect in the attack of September 11, 2001.

In other words, a war has been waged against the United States for several years. It took the attack of September 11 to wake us up to it.

How Did Such an Attack Happen Here?

The answer is simple: Our intelligence services failed us massively in the days before September 11, 2001. They must be much improved.

Let's look at a few facts:

The infrastructure necessary to support operations of such magnitude and sophistication had to be very sizable. The terrorists had to operate abroad as well as here in the United States. And these operations had to have been launched long before the act itself was committed.

The attack was extraordinarily efficient. Agents had to case airports to determine security operations. Support cells and infrastructures had to rehearse their parts so they could perform efficiently at the appropriate time. The hijacking teams probably rode on flights like the ones they would actually hijack when the code signal came.

Such a vast organizational and operational effort inevitably leaves traces that should have been apparent to our intelligence agencies—but weren't.

Many other reasons will eventually be given for the failure; these will all be examined in congressional hearings, and fixes will be made—unfortunately too late. They'll be closing the barn door after the horse has already bolted.

Fundamental to our vulnerability is our current lack of what is called HUMINT (human intelligence). We have had that deficiency for years. HUMINT is necessary to penetrate clandestine religious-based terrorist organizations.

Overhead systems (satellites) can't do that job. Neither will the hiring of agents from other countries bring a quick fix.

Unfortunately, it takes years to train operatives and to establish an effective HUMINT intelligence capability—and we are way behind the time curve in this war.

WILL THERE BE MORE ATTACKS?

As long as fanatical groups and the forces of darkness continue to exist, we are vulnerable to attack. The real question is: Will we be able to prevent it?

As I said before, the attack of September 11 could have been even worse. Terrorist organizations have become much more sophisticated and may soon have access to weapons of mass destruction—if they don't have them already—not to mention chemical and biological warfare. As always (like Mao's guerrillas), they will attempt to maximize fear and terror by hitting us where we are most vulnerable, and at a time and place of their choosing. We face an enemy like we have never faced before, who does not operate on a linear battlefield, his forces in mass. It is called "asymmetrical warfare"— assaults on our weaknesses rather than on our strengths.

So, yes, even after we have spent billions improving our security, there will most likely be another attack, but in another form—if for no other reason than to show us they can still do it.

I doubt that we will ever eliminate terrorism. It will be with us as long as there are men who dream of bringing down a nation. But we can eliminate the leaders and the resources it takes to sustain them and their operations. Hopefully, too, as with Noriega, we can eliminate the places where they lay their heads. But this will take a lot of time.

Resolve, Action, and Justice

What must we do?

First, I believe that President Bush's strategy for combating terrorism—the application of all available national options concurrently—is right on the mark.

Second, I would recommend one more arrow in the President's long-range quiver (and I'm sure it is being considered at the national level), and that is a PSYOPs campaign. The goal is not to change the minds of terrorists—which is probably impossible—but to deny them the population they need for their support and recruits. We must—to use an old phrase—win their "hearts and minds." Far too many in the Islamic world look up to the new terrorists as heroes and saviors. We have to bring the truth to these people, and to all the peoples of Islam that these men represent a perversion of Islam and not its highest expression; and in the meantime we have to show them by our actions that we respect them and their faith. But this job could take years, or decades.

In the near term, we must clean out all the terrorist cells and sympathizers in the United States. We must also improve our security systems and procedures. As the President has indicated, unilateral action by the United States will not solve this problem. We must build a strong multinational coalition that will cooperate in every way possible, and this coalition *must* include the modern Arab nations. We must have the help of other governments' intelligence services. We must stand behind the President and not become complacent.

Success will be a long, drawn-out process. Victory will be ambiguous; and there will be few victory parades. We will lose good people in the struggle, but we must not weaken in our resolve.

Our strength is in our unity and in that resolve. For both our sake and our children's sake, we must be willing to make the sacrifices necessary to win this war. We have invested too much in the defense of our freedoms to be cowed by such as bin Laden.

WHEN WILL WE STRIKE? WHEN WILL WE GO GET HIM?

In the time that has passed since the tragic September strike, I have been asked both of these questions hundreds of times—by all kinds of people, from ordinary citizens to those in the media. My usual answer has been "We will strike when it is to our advantage, and when we are ready. But it is just not 'him' we will be after; we are after the leadership and infrastructures of terrorist organizations around the world."

At the beginning of this book, our Authors' Note indicated that concerns for the safety of operational forces and their families, as well as security concerns, would prevent me from discussing some matters in which readers will legitimately be interested. That restraint applies now more than ever.

The national media, for example, has announced that U.S. and British Special Operations forces have already been inserted in Afghanistan. I cannot confirm the truth of this report, but if special operations forces *are* there, the announcement most certainly increased the risk associated with their mission.

I can say, therefore—without revealing details of how special operations forces will be used in the war against terrorism—that they will most certainly be involved. This has already been announced by our national command authorities. Because of their cultural orientation and language capabilities, and their unique skills, which span the entire spectrum of warfare, they will most certainly play a key role. All other forces will surely bring important capabilities into the mix, but it is the versatility of special operations forces that will make them the forces of choice at the point of the spear.

When Special Operations forces are committed to the campaign, we can also expect that they will conduct actions related to all their assigned mission areas of responsibility: Direct Action, Special Reconnaissance, Unconventional Warfare, Foreign Internal Defense, Psychological Operations, Civil Affairs, Counterproliferation, Coalition Support, and Combat Search and Rescue—specifically choosing and tailoring each applicable capability for the most effective mission accomplishment.

It can also be expected that most SOF operations will be covert—meaning that the American public will rarely hear of them. In far-reaching operations like these, media reports could not only mean increased risk for the forces involved, but affect political and tactical options for future operations. Information will therefore be released only by the National Command Authority, and only after coordinating with coalition partners.

It is common knowledge that Special Operations forces played unique roles in our operations a few years ago in Panama, Kuwait, Iraq, and Somalia, and contributed greatly to them. They will most certainly draw on these experiences. But there are major differences.

In Operations JUST CAUSE and DESERT STORM, the recognized governments of Panama and Kuwait supported our actions. We knew the enemy, we had selected the targets in advance, and we had rehearsed the operations to the extent necessary for success. The majority of the civil populations of both countries were friendly to the United States and supported our actions.

The war against terrorism will be in stark contrast to any threat we have faced before, and carries with it greater challenges and risks. In the first place, we will not be focusing our efforts on just one individual or target, or even on several—as in Panama, where we had twenty-seven. We will be focusing on all key personnel and infrastructures associated with the Al-Qaeda and other terrorist organizations, and will attack several targets embedded covertly in many nations throughout the world. We have yet to identify most of these cells; critical intelligence is not available, and in many cases forces will have to produce their own.

Numerous sovereignty issues will also have to be worked out at the national level. We will encounter hostile governments and hostile populations, and most operational environments are likely to be nonpermissive.

We will be required to operate in very rugged terrain and in urban areas, and we will be at great distances from our logistical bases. The enemy is elusive; he does not stand and fight on our terms. He has better field intelligence than we do. He knows the terrain, has his own support infrastructures, and uses civilians as shields. He does not recognize treaties, our principles of warfare, or our ethics. The organizations we will face do not take prisoners.

There will be many necessary missions, and each will be unique. Tactical, "cookie cutter" solutions will not be available from past military studies. The solutions to such tactical challenges are best left to those who will fight the battles. Therefore, the most effective solutions for dealing with this enemy will have to be unconventional.

All this will take time. Our enemies believe that the United States has no "staying power"—as demonstrated by our "abandonment" of Somalia and Lebanon after terrorist onslaughts. They will learn a different lesson in the coming months—or, if necessary, years.

As a nation, we are very fortunate to have special operations forces of such quality. We must give them the necessary latitude to deal with the challenges they will face. They have the judgment and skills to react appropriately and do what must be done.

The least we can do as a nation is to be patient and to stand behind them. We have no other alternative.

Appendix I:

The United States Special Operations Command: A Brief History

Before the book concludes, a quick overview of USSOCOM is in order.

President Reagan approved the establishment of the U.S. Special Operations Command on April 13, 1987, and on April 16, the Department of Defense activated USSOCOM and nominated General James J. Lindsay to be the first commander in chief. The Senate accepted him without debate.

USSOCOM had its activation ceremony on June 1, 1987. Guest speakers included William H. Taft IV, Deputy Secretary of Defense, and Admiral William J. Crowe, both of whom had opposed the Nunn-Cohen Amendment. Admiral Crowe's speech cautioned General Lindsay to integrate the new command into the mainstream military: "First, break down the wall that has more or less come between special operations forces and the other parts of our military, the wall that some people will try to build higher. Second, educate the rest of the military—spread a recognition and understanding of what you do, why you do it, and how important it is that you do it. Last, integrate your efforts into the full spectrum of our military capabilities." Putting this advice into action, General Lindsay knew, would pose challenges (a "sporty" course, he called it) considering the opposition the Defense Department had shown to the creation of SOCOM.

THE mission assigned to USSOCOM by the Joint Chiefs of Staff was "to prepare SOF to carry out assigned missions and, if directed by the President or Secretary of Defense, to plan for and conduct special operations." Mission responsibilities included to:

- Develop SOF doctrine, tactics, techniques, and procedures
- Conduct specialized courses of instruction for all SOF
- Train assigned forces and ensure interoperability of equipment and forces
- Monitor the preparedness of SOF assigned to other unified commands
- Monitor the promotions, assignments, retention, training, and professional development of all SOF personnel
- Consolidate and submit program and budget proposals for Major Force Program 11 (MFP-11)
- Develop and acquire special-operations-peculiar equipment, materials, supplies, and services

These last two tasks, managing MFP-11 and developing and acquiring special-operations-peculiar items, made USSOCOM unique among the unified commands. These responsibilities—dubbed "servicelike"—had heretofore been performed exclusively by the services. Congress had given the command extraordinary authority over SOF force structure, equipping, and resourcing.

The Command's mission evolved with the changing geopolitical environment. The fall of the Soviet Union and the rise of regional instability put SOF's capabilities in ever-greater demand, and this increased operational tempo (optempo) and called for a large SOF involvement in peacekeeping and humanitarian operations. USSOCOM later added counterproliferation and information operations command-and-control warfare to its list of principal missions, and expanded the counterterrorism mission to include defensive measures (antiterrorism).

SINCE 1987, there have been six CINCSOCs: General James J. Lindsay served from April 16, 1987, to June 27, 1990; Carl W. Stiner from June 27,

1990, to May 20, 1993; Wayne A. Downing from May 20, 1993, to February 29, 1996; Henry H. Shelton from February 29, 1996, to September 25, 1997, Peter J. Schoomaker from November 5, 1997, to October 27, 2000; and Charlie R. Holland from October 2000 to the present. Each CINC-SOC left his mark on the SOF community as he responded to significant changes on the military landscape. The collapse of the Soviet Union, the downsizing of the U.S. military, the appearance of new aggressor states, heightened regional instabilities, highly organized international terrorism, and the proliferation of weapons of mass destruction—all led to an increased use of SOF by conventional U.S. military commanders, ambassadors, and other governmental agencies.

General Lindsay's greatest challenge was to make the command the driving force behind the congressionally mandated revitalization of SOF without alienating conventional military leaders. This was no easy task, given the opposition in many military circles to the command's mere existence. As the first CINCSOC, he developed priorities to get the command functioning. They were to: organize, staff, train, and equip the headquarters; establish the necessary operating systems, including intelligence, as well as information and logistical support; develop the relationships necessary to discharge his roles and missions; create Major Force Program 11 (MFP-11) to ensure SOF controlled its financial destiny; build command-and-control relationships with the components, the Assistant Secretary of Defense for Special Operations and Low Intensity Conflict, and the special operations commands assigned to the theater CINCs; define worldwide SOF requirements; and plot the future of the command. General Lindsay also faced two major operational tests—for which he provided trained and ready forces—Operation EARNEST WILL/PRIME CHANCE ONE in the Persian Gulf, and Operation JUST CAUSE/PROMOTE LIBERTY in Panama. The use of SOF by the theater CINCs increased significantly during General Lindsay's tenure.

The creation of MFP-11 was a special and unique priority for both General Lindsay and Congress. Like the services, USSOCOM was to have its own budget and would be responsible for determining its own funding needs, including research and development, and equipping and training all the Special Operations forces of all the services.

Although the Nunn Cohen Amendment had created MFP-11 to reform SOF funding, the wording of the law permitted varying interpretations, and some Defense Department officials argued that the new command should not submit its own Program Objective Memorandum (POM), which defines and justifies all programs and initiatives necessary for readiness, including the spread of funding over time (the POM thus serves as the basis for building the budget). The services wanted to keep control of the budgeting process for SOF forces so they could use the money on things other than SOF, as they had always been accustomed to doing.

This debate lingered until September 1988, when Senators Nunn and Cohen clarified congressional intent, saying that the sponsors of the law "fully intended that the commander of the Special Operations Command would have sole responsibility for the preparation of the POM." Congress enacted Public Law 100-456 that same month, which directed USCINCSOC to submit a POM directly to the Secretary of Defense.

Four months later, on January 24, 1989, the Assistant Secretary of Defense, William H. Taft IV, signed a memorandum giving USCINCSOC budgetary authority over MFP-11. Soon afterward, the Office of the Secretary of Defense (OSD) gave USSOCOM control of selected MFP-11 programs on October 1, 1990, and total responsibility in October 1991.

By law, the services are responsible for training, equipping, and modernizing their respective forces. The CINCs are not. They take the forces they are given and employ them. The services had long been "robbing" SOF by transferring previously approved money to other requirements. Giving financial control to SOF was the fundamental basis for the Nunn-Cohen Amendment.

For the first time ever, a CINC had been granted authority for a budget and POM.

THE complex, politically sensitive process of establishing a new unified command extended into Carl Stiner's tenure as CINCSOC. He pushed the command to fulfill the provisions of the Nunn-Cohen Amendment; oversaw the implementation of developing and acquiring "special-operations-peculiar" equipment, matériel, supplies, and services; and watched over the command's submission of fully supported budgets based on SOF mission requirements.

After DESERT STORM, he devoted much of his time to raising awareness about SOF capabilities and successes in and out of the military. Supporting the theater CINCs and maintaining SOF combat readiness were also top priorities. Finally, he convinced the Secretary of Defense to designate Psychological Operations (PSYOPs) and Civil Affairs as part of SOF. This enabled USSOCOM to command and control these units in peacetime as well as war, which greatly improved the command's ability to fund, train, equip, and organize these forces.

During his time in command, SOF optempo rose 35 percent. USSO-COM supported a number of operations worldwide, most notably DESERT SHIELD / DESERT STORM, PROVIDE COMFORT (support to Kurdish refugees), PROVIDE RELIEF, and RESTORE HOPE (Somalia relief operations).

THE main challenges of General Downing's tenure were to continue the re-vitalization of SOF and to prepare the SOF community for the twenty-first century. To these ends, General Downing streamlined the acquisition of SOF-specific equipment, increased the command's focus on new emerging threats, and realigned SOF budget requirements with the reduced Defense Department's budget. His changes in the allocation of resources resulted in a far more efficient strategic planning process.

During his watch, SOF optempo again increased, with SOF participation in UNISOM II (Somalia), SUPPORT and UPHOLD DEMOCRACY (Haiti), and JOINT ENDEAVOR (Bosnia-Herzegovina), as well as many smaller contingencies and deployments.

GENERAL Henry H. Shelton guided the command through a time of greatly constrained resources and extraordinary worldwide demand for SOF support. SOF operations increased by more than 51 percent, and person-nel deployments increased by 127 percent. In 1996 alone, SOF deployed to a total of 142 countries and engaged in 120 counterdrug missions, 12 demining training missions, and 204 joint combined exchange training exercises with other nations. General Shelton's largest SOF operations com-mitment was to Operation JOINT ENDEAVOR/JOINT GUARD, the peacekeeping mission in Bosnia, and special operators assisted in noncombatant evacua-tions from such crisis areas as Liberia, Sierra Leone, and Albania.

GENERAL Peter J. Schoomaker's top priority was to organize SOF in ways that kept it relevant to national security requirements. To that end, he ini-tiated or accelerated numerous projects—headquarters reorganization; planning, programming, and acquisition enhancements; and the integration of SOF's components into one resourcing and acquisition team.

On his watch, SOF took part in the transition from JOINT GUARD to JOINT FORCE in Bosnia-Herzegovina, DESERT THUNDER in Kuwait and Saudi Arabia (to thwart Saddam Hussein's restrictions on UN inspectors' freedom of movement), and numerous contingencies and peacetime engagements. SOF played crucial roles in ALLIED FORGE, the operation that forced Serbian forces out of Kosovo, and JOINT GUARDIAN, which enforced the Kosovo Peace Agreement.

GENERAL CARL STINER, CINC USSOCOM

Carl Stiner describes his time in command:

In my thirty-five years of service, I have never known anyone who faced a challenge of greater complexity than General Jim Lindsay's in the standing up of the United States Special Operations Command, nor do I know an officer who could have done the job better. If you had the choice of whom to succeed in command, it would certainly be Jim Lindsay. Not only did he turn over a well-trained and functioning staff, but all operating systems were in place as well.

Because he had kept me constantly in the loop on his challenges and decisions, very little transition was needed when I assumed command. My challenge became to take what he had given me and move it forward.

Two major objectives remained in achieving Congress's intent: developing a new Planning, Programming, and Budgeting System (PPBS) process to structure a SOCOM POM and budget, and bringing under the command the major weapons development programs that were still being managed by the services.

Even with a congressional mandate, the Command found itself in a very difficult position to establish MFP-11. The command was still "standing up," and some 100 key personnel short of reaching its manning objective, when the Chairman directed USSOCOM to take personnel cuts proportionally equal to other commands, as part of the downsizing of the military resulting from the fall of the Soviet Empire. The Command had to take a measured approach to assuming its budget tasks.

DEVELOPING THE **POM**   The POM was the first step. The initial one was completed and submitted in 1988 during Jim Lindsay's tenure—but through the Department of the Air Force (which was USSOCOM's executive agent for budgeting issues at the time). The Command only assumed budget execution authority by October 1990.

Meanwhile, many critics at OSD level who resented the decision to give USSOCOM its own budget argued that the Command would never be able to submit a POM. They believed USSOCOM didn't have the intelligence and expertise to develop it. Nevertheless, in 1991, the Command submitted its first fully supported POM, totaling $3.2 billion—and it was the first one in, ahead of all the services. This was the first time USSO-COM had researched SOF mission requirements and developed the analysis for the POM justification instead of "cross-walking" requirements to other services.*

The establishment of MFP-11 set up a more focused resource process and insured a balanced review of special operations requirements and programs.

CONTROL OF PROGRAMS   USSOCOM also worked to take control of its major weapons programs.

On December 10, 1990, the Deputy Secretary of Defense authorized the Special Operations Development and Acquisition Center (SORDAC). Owing partly to manpower cuts, in 1992 Stiner consolidated the Command's acquisition and contracting management functions into a new directorate under a deputy for acquisition, who was named the Command's acquisition executive and senior procurement executive.

The Command's procurement strategy emphasized a streamlined acquisition process—by modifying existing weapons or buying "nondevelopmental" (off-the-shelf technology) systems. This approach permitted quick, economical improvements to operational capabilities.

Since 1987, USSOCOM has fielded a number of modified or new systems, affecting nearly every aspect of special operations. Some of the more notable are the MC-130H Combat Talon II long-range insertion aircraft and a state-of-the-art intelligence system (the most advanced in any command), both of which were used in DESERT STORM; and the *Cyclone*-class patrol coastal ships, used in Operations SUPPORT and UPHOLD DEMOCRACY. Other significant acquisitions included the MH-47E Chinook, a medium-range heavy-lift helicopter designed to conduct insertion operations under all weather conditions; the AC-130U Spector gunship, used for close air support and reconnaissance; the Mark V special operations craft, a high-

---

*In making budgets for their SOF forces in the past, the services had allocated—"cross-walked"—monies to SOF programs as they saw fit. In most cases, they "shorted" them, keeping the majority of approved funds for conventional programs.

performance combatant boat capable of being transported over land or aboard C-5 aircraft; and the rigid inflatable boat (RIB) for the Naval Special Warfare Command, which provides a long-sought capability for a high-speed SEAL insertion-and-extraction craft. The RIB program, completed under cost and months ahead of schedule, exceeded every performance objective and won the 1998 Defense Department's Packer Award for excellence in acquisition.

Another major program now coming to fruition is the Advanced SEAL Delivery System. The CV-22 Osprey aircraft program will also give the Command's forces much greater capability for long-range insertions and extractions under all weather conditions.

BY completing the POM and establishing control of major programs, US-SOCOM had complied with all the provisions of the Nunn-Cohen Amendment. Six years after President Reagan approved the Command, USSOCOM now controlled all SOF forces, its own budget, and its modernization programs.

USSOCOM has used its acquisition capability a number of times during contingencies to provide SOF with the latest technology or to accelerate modifications. During DESERT STORM, for example, the Command modified Chinooks with aircraft survivability equipment before they deployed to the Iraqi area of operations.

EDUCATING CINCs AND AMBASSADORS Following the Gulf War, I spent a great deal of my time educating commanders, particularly regional CINCs and serving ambassadors, in the capabilities of SOF—showing the CINCs how to integrate SOF into their theater engagement plans, and showing the ambassadors how to integrate SOF into their country-security plans.

A theater engagement plan is based on the national security strategy for each of the world's regions, and it is the responsibility of the regional CINC. The plan, which is country-specific, is developed with each ambassador, and details the security-assistance needs for that country.

We also educated newly appointed ambassadors on SOF capabilities before they took their posts. Every couple of months, in coordination with the State Department, we brought a new crop of ambassadors to Fort Bragg for a detailed orientation. Afterward, the ambassadors were far better prepared to use SOF forces to their fullest.

UPGRADING THEATER SOCs   I also devoted a lot of effort to upgrading the Special Operations Commands (SOCs) assigned to the regional CINCs. A special-operations-qualified flag officer was placed in charge of each SOC, and it was staffed with qualified SOF personnel. The SOCs exercised both operational control (for the CINCs) of SOF forces involved in peacetime engagements and command of SOF forces in times of crisis.

COMBAT READINESS TRAINING   Training is the most important thing we do—we must always train as we will fight. It was therefore my highest continuing priority.

Training should always be based on potential mission scenarios (including peacetime engagement missions) and serve as a rehearsal for what may ultimately become a no-notice contingency requirement. As such, it needs to cover all the bases: individual, collective, multi-echelon, and joint. Proper training—tough, realistic, demanding, and designed to develop and sustain individual and special skills—builds highly motivated individuals and units that function as an efficient, effective, and professional team. The primary focus of any training program must be the development of:

- Technically / tactically proficient leaders, sound in judgment, who will exercise initiative within the commander's intent
- Disciplined, mature troops, physically and emotionally prepared to withstand the hardships and dangers of combat
- Troops highly skilled in individual tasks, and mature beyond their years
- Small units / crews well grounded in basic technical tactical tasks and drills

There are three fundamentals to successful mission accomplishment:

1. Disciplined, competent leaders with high ethical and professional standards are the key element of any training program—and any effective combat unit. The central focus of all SOF-related training must be to develop leaders.
2. Language skills and culture training make SOF uniquely suited to our assigned mission and is fundamental to success.
3. We must focus our training on joint requirements, and we must train as we expect to fight. We will fight jointly in the future.

MEDICAL TRAINING   In the past, each service trained its own medics—
to varying levels of technical proficiency.

With the assistance of the surgeons general of all the services, we established a medical university at Fort Bragg to train all the medics of all
Special Operations units—an innovation that greatly improved medical
proficiency and readiness, and at considerable savings.

FOREIGN AVIATION TRAINING   In 1992, we established a Special
Operations Aviation Foreign Internal Defense training capability. Many nations that we help had outdated, practically useless air forces. By developing a SOF training cadre proficient in both vintage aircraft and native
languages, we have been able to help them greatly upgrade their air capability for meeting their own security needs.

COUNTERPROLIFERATION   One of USSOCOM's primary responsibilities
is to anticipate the unanticipated, and then to develop the capability to deal
with the potential threat. With the fall of the Soviet Union and the increased
sophistication of state-sponsored terrorism, the threat of an asymmetrical attack with a weapon of mass destruction (WMD) has increased significantly.

Advanced information technology allows extremists to communicate
widely and efficiently; publicly available databases serve as repositories for
technical information relating to weapons production; and materials and
technology used to make WMDs are increasingly available. Many of these
materials are widely used for legitimate commercial purposes.

The disintegration of the former Soviet Union, and the potential unem-
ployment and proliferation of thousands of skilled scientists, increased concerns about the protection, control, and accountability of WMD-related
materials and technologies. Transnational threats by terrorist organizations
have increased the potential for attacks against nonmilitary targets within
our borders.

Non-nuclear WMDs are relatively easy to manufacture and deliver.
Facilities to produce biological and chemical weapons are small and hard
to detect.

As far back as 1991, USSOCOM took high-priority actions to deal with
this threat. There are two primary requirements for success:

   ✪   Timely and accurate intelligence information for predicting the
       threat, the likely target, the type of weapon, and its general loca-

tion is a responsibility of our national intelligence agencies (for threats abroad), and the FBI (for threats within the United States).

❂ The capability to recover the weapon (in either a permissive or nonpermissive environment), to render it safe, and to evacuate it to a safe area for turnover or destruction was the focus of USSOCOM's efforts.

These efforts continued as an assumed mission requirement, and much progress was made with the cooperation and help of national agencies—though at our initiative. When Wayne Downing replaced me, he invited Secretary of Defense Bill Perry to observe firsthand the capability that had been developed. The Secretary was impressed. "Who should have this mission?" he asked.

"We'll take it," Downing answered.

"You've already got all these other high-priority missions," Perry replied, doubtfully.

"True," Downing said. "But as you can see, we have very capable and smart forces, and we can do this thing."

"What should the mission for counterproliferation say?" Perry asked.

"We'll send you a draft."

When Perry received the proposed mission statement, he signed it, and counterproliferation became an official USSOCOM mission. Along with that came funding and formalized cooperation and support from other agencies of government.

Since then, enormous progress has been made not only in developing and fielding essential technologies but in training special operators in all the skills needed to accomplish this mission. USSOCOM special mission forces have made vast strides in that direction, but that is not enough. The critical key is accurate intelligence for timely warning.

FORCES OF CHOICE   Since 1987, SOF has become the force of choice for theater CINCs and ambassadors; and SOF forces have been involved in virtually every contingency operation, as well as thousands of joint training exchanges, peacetime engagement activities, and humanitarian relief operations. I've already mentioned several contingencies and training activities. Some other significant operations, involving all elements of SOF, include: Somalia (1992–1995), Haiti (1994–1995), Bosnia-Herzegovina (1995–

present), Kosovo (1999–present), and Macedonia (1999–present). Many others cannot be mentioned for security reasons.

During the same period, SOF forces have performed a wide variety of missions under the category of "Operations Other Than War" (OOTW). OOTWs include a wide range of missions, such as humanitarian assistance, disaster relief, noncombatant evacuation, humanitarian demining, peacekeeping, crisis response, combating terrorism, enforcement of sanctions or exclusion zones, and show of force.

During the 1990s, these increased significantly.

For the UN's first forty years, only thirteen OOTWs were conducted, but from 1988 to 1994 their numbers more than doubled—with far greater scope and complexity. U.S. Special Operations forces have served in most nations of the globe, performing as instruments of U.S. national policy, executing missions, and providing assistance possible only through their unique skills, language capabilities, and cultural orientation—missions that conventional units could not perform, and in many cases where a U.S. military signature was unacceptable to the host.

SOF takes up less than 1.4 percent of the total force structure and only 3.5 percent of the DOD budget; yet the increase in optempo is ample evidence of their usefulness. During 1993, USSOCOM averaged 2,036 personnel deployed away from home station each week, serving in 101 countries. By 1996, the number had climbed to 4,613; and by 1999, it had climbed to 5,141, deployed to 149 countries and foreign territories.

This is an incredibly small investment compared to the payback.

There are significant intangible benefits as well. Enduring personal relationships with the militaries and government officials of host nations will serve our national interests for years to come.

These deployments also benefit SOF—providing training in foreign cultures and languages and knowledge of potential operational areas.

APPENDIX II:

LEADERSHIP

Carl Stiner:

The Army does a better job producing leaders than every other institution of which I am aware. This achievement derives primarily from the Army's institutionalized education system, which is designed to provide each officer and noncommissioned officer the technical and tactical proficiency necessary for every level of command: from second lieutenant all the way through general officer, and from sergeant E-5 through sergeant major.

Leadership is the fundamental "core" subject throughout all the curriculums of the schools in the "system."

Leadership and professional training for officers begins with the Reserve Officer Training Corps (ROTC) or service academy. The basic-level course for newly commissioned lieutenants is the Basic Officers Course, which is designed to develop the technical and tactical proficiency essential for leading at the platoon level. The Advance Course prepares captains for command at the company level. The Command and General Staff College prepares majors for duties and responsibilities as principal staff officers at the brigade level, as well as the essential prerequisites for commanding at the battalion level. The War College is designed to prepare officers at the colonel level for commanding at the brigade level, as well as for serving as a principal staff officer at division and higher levels of responsibility.

Other subjects increase the officer's breadth of knowledge: politico-military affairs, the Army's programming, planning, and budgeting system, and so on. For those fortunate enough to be selected for flag rank, each service runs its own two-week-long general officer orientation course, followed by the seven-week-long CAPSTONE Course, which is mandatory within the first year of promotion for all flag-rank officers of all services. This course broadens the officers' knowledge and understanding of responsibilities and joint warfighting at the unified command levels.

Other courses, such as at the Armed Forces Staff College, primarily for majors and lieutenant colonels of all services, are required for those who have been selected for joint assignments, and focus on developing proficiency in joint operational techniques and procedures.

The "Army's Educational System" is not limited to the "schoolhouses"; there is other specialized training as well—advanced degrees at civilian education institutions in appropriate technical fields; master's courses in advanced executive-level management; and branch specialized courses, like the Special Forces Qualification Course.

Credit for bringing the Army back from its post-Vietnam downturn is due to the vision and efforts of General Shy Meyer, who institutionalized the Army's education system; to General Carl Vuono, who established our national "Maneuver Training Centers"; and to General Gordon Sullivan, who gave priority to the training process by providing necessary resources and updating doctrine. These great leaders made training and combat readiness their number-one priority and spent vast amounts of time personally supervising training. The results were manifested in Operations JUST CAUSE and DESERT STORM.

WHAT MAKES A LEADER?

Some people claim that leaders are born. That may be so in some cases, and leaders certainly share basic characteristics; but not everyone with those characteristics becomes a leader—or becomes a good one. Leadership is primarily acquired. It has to be learned. I have a number of thoughts about how this should be done, based on my own experience learning leadership.

No one all of a sudden realizes, "Hey, I'm a leader." It doesn't come out of the blue. A person becomes a leader because he has a sincere desire to lead, he is willing to give it whatever it takes, and he has within him the fundamental attributes and professional qualities that all leaders must possess:

When an officer is commissioned, he takes an oath, inherent in which is the sacred responsibility for the lives and well-being of those entrusted to his leadership. This responsibility transcends normal duty hours—it is twenty-four hours a day, seven days a week—and includes the "whole person." We must not only make the soldiers we lead the best soldiers possible, but also take care of their families, and develop each soldier to be a productive citizen.

Other fundamental qualities are also required:

A leader should be physically fit (soldiers will not respect a physically sloppy commander). He must be confident in his own abilities. He must be mentally tough, particularly on himself. He must be courageous. He should be willing to take risks. He should train his subordinates by providing them with an environment in which to grow—expecting mistakes and acting as a "heat shield." He should not serve for his own personal ego, but for those entrusted to him and for his unit. A leader should never need to be told what to do; he must be a man of vision, always looking ahead and planning ways to take his unit to higher levels. A leader should never take credit for his own successes or the successes of his unit. He should give all the credit to his men—for this is all the credit that most may ever receive. We should always remember that it is squads, platoons, and crews that win battles and ultimately wars.

A leader must create within his unit "a healthy environment," and I don't mean by that mere physical health. He must make an environment that promotes the total health and growth of the whole person. In such an environment, each person will believe that what he or she is doing at this particular time—serving their country—is the most important thing they could possibly be doing. Great honor and self-respect come with this; these can never be taken away.

A leader must develop for his unit a "spiritual soundness program" that meets the spiritual needs of both soldiers and their families (you will find that many soldiers come from an unhealthy environment).

A leader must cause his troops in whatever type of unit to believe that their mission is vital, and that they must prepare for it to their utmost. Soldiers must also understand that those serving beside them have the same motivation and dedication, and they should therefore respect and take care of each other. If your objectives in developing this environment are appropriately understood, every soldier should look forward to each day and expect it to be a rewarding and fulfilling experience. He will, as a corollary, believe his unit is the best unit in the Army, and will want to be nowhere else. He wants to be here serving with his buddies.

A leader must talk to his troops. They must clearly understand the unit's mission and training objectives. They must understand the leader's goals and objectives, as well as his expectations in terms of professional standards, conduct, and duty performance.

A leader must get his troops started off right. He should have a formal program to personally welcome and orient all new replacements. They get to know him, they come to understand the importance of their mission, and they learn what is expected of them and what they can expect of the leader. If this is done right, they should leave the orientation with the conviction that they are in the best place they can be—serving their country as members of the right unit, where they are going to be taken care of.

Another important part of the command welcome program is "sponsorship"—especially for married personnel. Each couple should be assigned a sponsoring couple, who should arrange for quarters, have the refrigerator stocked with food, and meet and welcome them. Company commanders, first sergeants, and the unit chaplain should oversee this program. The company commander and chaplain should visit the new couple within the first week of their arrival.

A leader should never leave his troops "on their own" on weekends—especially unmarried troops. He should require subordinate commanders to establish positive programs to keep the troops constructively occupied and involved over the weekends.

A leader is responsible for morale, good order, and discipline. He must know what is going on in the barracks and have a system of inspections executed by the chain of command, for which they are held accountable.

Every soldier is important. I have always given my subordinates this charge: "You should put into every soldier the same love, devotion, and caring you would want someone someday to put into your own son or daughter." But after you've done this, if they still fail to perform to standards—if you can't depend on this soldier in combat—then get rid of him soonest.

A leader is responsible for the training of his unit, and mission training should be his first priority. All training activity should be oriented toward maximizing combat readiness for the mission. Training programs should be as realistic as possible, including live fire. The only exceptions are for the safety of the troops. This builds not only proficiency but confidence in both individuals and units. The proficiency required at the small-unit level cannot possibly be obtained through simulations.

A cadre training program, unique to the unit, is necessary to ensure the proficiency of subordinate leaders and staffs. Certain units have unique mission requirements for which subjects are not adequately taught in institutionalized service schools (for example, "anti-armor defense of the airhead"* for airborne units). It is the commander's responsibility to know what these are and to structure training programs to ensure unit proficiency by all subordinate leaders.

A leader must have the respect of his troops. This respect is earned—created not only by the programs I've already mentioned, but also by sharing the troops' hardships. As a division commander, I made it a practice to participate in every battalion-size operation. I would often slip into the rear ranks of a company and walk with them all night to assess their readiness and discipline, and to listen to what they were talking about. You must assess for yourself what the troops are capable of doing and where additional training is needed. That way the troops will come to trust you and talk to you—and "tell it like it is." They will also have faith in you and know you will take care of them. They have no one else to look to for their security and well-being.

Training must be your first priority. Training for combat. No soldier ever complained to me about tough, realistic training. Soldiers know this is life insurance. You can't fool a soldier.

A commander should maintain a constant state of readiness in his unit. It must be able to accomplish its combat mission *whenever* called upon. If it is not ready, the commander should correct the problem immediately. If the problem is beyond his control, then the cause should have been ferreted out a long time back and brought to the attention of the next-higher-level commander, who should take action to fix the problem.

Competition both within and among units is healthy—so long as it is not at the expense of another individual or unit. Competition for the Expert Infantryman's Badge or Expert Medical Badge is a good example. These should benefit each individual as well as their units, and should include formalized training programs to ensure that each person and each unit emerges as a winner. There is no glory or pride in second place—and no alternative to defeat in battle.

---

*An "airhead" is the airborne equivalent of a "beachhead."

LEARNING FROM OTHERS

When I entered the Army in 1958, I do not remember hearing the words "role model" or "mentor." But, as I gained experience, several people distinguished themselves above others. I learned from these men things that were not taught, and which I did not read about in a field manual.

The first officer I came to respect as a "role model" was Colonel Jim Bartholomees, the rock-solid Commander of the 3rd Special Forces Group. I joined the 3rd SFG as a captain in July 1964, when it was forming as part of President Kennedy's Special Forces buildup. Colonel Bartholomees knew how to get the most out of people, while "taking care of them" in the process. He created a command environment that provided the latitude and encouragement for subordinates to use their own initiatives and abilities. I never heard him raise his voice or belittle anyone.

In the years ahead I worked for several other outstanding leaders—each with maybe a little different leadership style; yet all were role models, and worthy of emulation and application to my own leadership style and abilities. A leader should never try to be something—or choose a style—that he is not. He should take from the gifts of his teachers / mentors and apply them to his own abilities.

To the following men, in the positions they held then, I owe more than words can say:

GENERAL ROSCOE ROBINSON: *My brigade commander, 82nd Airborne Division*

GENERAL GEORGE BLANCHARD: *Commanding General, 82nd Airborne Division*

GENERAL EDWARD C. (SHY) MEYER: *ADCO, 82nd Airborne Division; Chief of Staff, U.S. Army*

GENERAL FREDERICK KROESEN: *Commanding General, 82nd Airborne Division*

LIEUTENANT GENERAL DICK LAWRENCE: *Project Manager, Saudi Arabian National Guard Modernization Program*

GENERAL BILL LIVSEY: *Commanding General, U.S. Army Infantry Center*

GENERAL P. X. KELLEY: *Commander, Rapid Deployment Joint Task Force*

GENERAL BOB KINGSTON: *Commander in Chief, U.S. Central Command*

GENERAL JIM LINDSAY: *Commanding General, 82nd Airborne Division; Commanding General, XVIII Airborne Corps; Commander in Chief, U.S. Special Operations Command*

GENERAL JOHN FOSS: *Commanding General, XVIII Airborne Corps*

GENERAL CARL VUONO: *Chief of Staff, U.S. Army*

GENERAL JACK VESSEY: *Chairman, Joint Chiefs of Staff*

AMBASSADOR DONALD RUMSFELD: *President's Special Envoy for Middle East Affairs*

GENERAL COLIN POWELL: *Chairman, Joint Chiefs of Staff*

Over the last decade, the services have greatly improved their education systems by taking advantage of the talents and experience of the likes of those above—making them "senior mentors" in intermediate and senior-level service schools. Their talents are also used in the CAPSTONE Course and in senior-level joint warfighting exercises.

As I said at the beginning, I do not know of any institution that puts more into the training of its leaders, or any institution that produces better leaders. This is only fitting, considering that the responsibility for preserving our freedom rests squarely on the shoulders of our armed forces. It is indeed a most worthy and essential national investment.

ACKNOWLEDGMENTS

Thanks to all the people of the SOF, who have performed such magnificent feats over the years, and whose work, in this age of new warfare, is far from done. Thanks especially to Carl Stiner, a quiet hero if there ever was one, and a man you definitely want on *your* side.

—*Tom Clancy*

This book would not have been possible without the help of many great people, and to them I owe so much. Above all, to Tom Clancy, a great American and longtime friend, for making the opportunity possible to tell this story. To Neil Nyren, editor extraordinaire, for keeping us on track and focused on the end-state objective throughout the process. To Tony Koltz, for whom I have the greatest respect as a friend and professional; he showed patience and perseverance in producing the information needed by knowing what questions to ask. Without his writing and editorial skills, this book would not have been possible. To Marty Greenberg, for his advice, counsel, and assistance. To our original agent at William Morris, Robert Gottlieb, for all his help in bringing the book to fruition.

Writing this book has been a demanding challenge, lasting almost two years . . . and not just for me—trying to remember all the details and put them in context—but for my wife, Sue, who has typed and retyped so much material many times over. Without her help day and night, we would never have made it. I also thank my daughters, Carla and Laurie, for their encouragement and help. In the midst of all the demands of this period, there was a miraculous happening, the birth of our first grandchild—Jackson Wade Reel, a gift from the divine power that gives life and sustains us every day.

These people were also helpful in the development of the book:

MAJOR CONTRIBUTORS

Bigadier General Frank Akers, USA (Ret.)
Lieutenant General Clay Bailey, USAF
CW4 Richard "Bulldog" Balwanz, USA (Ret.)
Lieutenant General Mark Cisneros, USA (Ret.)
Lieutenant Colonel Daniel D. Devlin, USA (Ret.)
Jim DeFelice
Colonel (P) John DeFritas, USA
General Wayne Downing, USA (Ret.)
Colonel Stan Florer, USA
Rudi Gresham
Major General James A. Guest, USA (Ret.)
Colonel Michael R. Kershner, USA
Colonel Chris Krueger, USA
Colonel Tony Normand, USA (Ret.)
Dr. John Partin, USSOCOM Command Historian
Colonel David B. Plummer II, USA (Ret.)
Major General Richard Potter, USA (Ret.)
Major General Richard A. Scholtes, USA (Ret.)
General Peter J. Schoomaker, USA (Ret.)
Lieutenant Colonel Bill Shaw, USA
Colonel Joseph R. Simino, USA (Ret.)
Major General John K. Singlaub, USA (Ret.)
Captain W. R. Spearman, USN (Ret.)
Lieutenant General William Yarborough, USA (Ret.)

BACKGROUND BRIEFINGS

Brigadier General Heinie Aderholt, USAF (Ret.)
Master Sergeant Sandy Atkinson, USAF

Brigadier General Michael W. Beasley, USA
Major General Ken Bowra, USA
Major General Jerry Boykin, USA
Master Sergeant Chris Crane, USA (Ret.)
Master Sergeant Jimmy Dean, USA (Ret.)
Lieutenant Colonel Francis Gabreski, USAF
Lieutenant Colonel Tony Gies, USA (Ret.)
Randy Gingrich
George Grimes, USSOCOM Public Affairs
Command Sergeant Major Jim Hargraves, USA (Ret.)
Lieutenant Colonel Charles Judge, USA (Ret.)
Lieutenant Colonel David W. Kinder, USA (Ret.)
Jerome Klingaman
Staff Sergeant Andy Kublik, USAF
Command Sergeant Major Joe Lupyak, USA (Ret.)
Herbert A. Mason, AFSOC Command Historian
Clay T. McCutchan, AFSOC Assistant Command Historian
Colonel Lee Mize, USA (Ret.)
Major Paul A. Ott, USA
Command Sergeant Major Paul Payne, USA (Ret.)
Colonel Kenneth Poole, USAF
Major Jon Peck, USAF
Major General Richard V. Secord, USAF (Ret.)
Major General Sidney Shacknow, USA (Ret.)
Lieutenant Colonel Joseph Smith, USA
Major Dave Snider, USA
Lieutenant General Michael Spigelmire, USA (Ret.)
Brigadier General Joe Stringham, USA (Ret.)
Lieutenant General William Tangney, USA
Lieutenant Colonel Thomas Trask, USAF
Senior Master Sergeant William Walter, USAF

—*General Carl Stiner (Ret.)*

BIBLIOGRAPHY

Atkinson, Rick, *Crusade: The Untold Story of the Persian Gulf.* New York: Houghton Mifflin, 1993.

Bado, Captain Christopher M., *Integration of Special Operations and Conventional Forces in Conventional Warfare.* Master's Thesis, Naval Postgraduate School, 1996.

Bank, Colonel Aaron, USA (Ret.), *From OSS to Green Berets: The Birth of Special Forces.* Novato, California: Presidio Press, 1986.

Beckwith, Colonel Charlie A. (Ret.), *Delta Force: The Army's Elite Counterterrorist Unit.* New York: Avon, 2000 (first printed in 1983).

Brown, Lieutenant Colonel Ronald J., *Humanitarian Operations in Northern Iraq 1991 with Marines in Operation Provide Comfort.* History and Museums Division, HQ, U.S. Marine Corps, 1995.

Bucci, Lieutenant Colonel Steven, Interview with General Carl Stiner (Ret.) for the U.S. Army Military History Institute, 1999.

Carroll, Major Douglas E., *Special Forces Doctrine and Army Operations Doctrine.* Master's Thesis, Fort Leavenworth, Kansas, 1993.

Chinnery, Philip D., *Air Commando.* New York: St. Martin's Press, 1997.

Churchill, Lieutenant Colonel Charles W., *Interview with Lieutenant Colonel Kenneth R. Bowra.* U.S. Army Military History Institute, 1989.

Dunnigan, James F. and Bay, Austin, *From Shield to Storm.* New York: William Morrow & Company, 1992.

Flanagan, Edward M., Lieutenant General USA (Ret.), *Battle for Panama*, Washington, D.C.: Brassey's, 1993.

Gordon, Michael R. and Trainor, Bernard E., *The General's War.* New York: Little, Brown & Company, 1995.

Hilsman, Roger, *To Move a Nation: The Politics of Foreign Policy in the Administration of John F. Kennedy*. Garden City, NY: Doubleday, 1967.

Hilton, Lieutenant Colonel Carson L., *United States Army Special Forces: From a Decade of Development to a Sustained Future*. Military Studies Program Paper, U.S. Army War College, 1991.

Hiro, Dilip, *Desert Shield to Desert Storm—the Second Gulf War*. London: HarperCollins (U.S. edition by Routledge), 1992.

Hutchinson, Kevin, *Operation Desert Storm/Desert Shield Chronology & Fact Book*. Westport, Conn.: Greenwood Press, 1995.

Jones, Major Gregg D., *A Historical Perspective of Special Operations Forces As an Instrument of Strategy*. Master's Thesis, Fort Leavenworth, Kansas, 1991.

Keaney, Thomas A. and Cohen, Eliot A., *Revolution in Warfare?* Annapolis, Maryland: Naval Institute Press, 1995.

Kelly, Orr, *From a Dark Sky*. New York: Pocket Books, 1997.

Marquis, Susan L., *Unconventional Warfare*. Washington, D.C.: Brookings Institute Press, 1997.

Martin, David C. and Walcott, John, *Best Laid Plans: The Inside Story of America's War Against Terrorism*. New York: Harper & Row, 1988.

Morse, Stan (editor), *Gulf Air War Debrief*. London: Aerospace Publishing, Ltd.

Office of the Chairman of the Joint Chiefs of Staff, Joint History Office, *Operation Just Cause, The Planning and Execution of Joint Operations in Panama, February 1988–January 1990*. Washington, D.C., 1995.

Parker, James E., Jr., *Covert Ops: The CIA's Secret War in Laos*. New York: St. Martin's Press, 1995.

Plaster, John L., *SOG: The Secret Wars of America's Commandos in Vietnam*. New York: Onyx, 1998.

Scales, Brig. Gen. Robert H., Jr., *Certain Victory: The U.S. Army in the Gulf War*. Washington, D.C.: Brassey's, 1994.

Shultz, Richard H., Jr., *The Secret War Against Hanoi: Kennedy's and Johnson's Use of Spies, Saboteurs, and Covert Warriors in North Vietnam*. New York: HarperCollins, 1999.

Singlaub, Major General John K., USA (Ret.), with Malcolm McConnell, *Hazardous Duty: An American Soldier in the Twentieth Century*. New York: Simon & Schuster, 1991.

Smallwood, William L., *Warthog*. Washington, D.C.: Brassey's, 1993.

Stanton, Shelby L., *Green Berets at War*. New York: Ballantine Books, 1985.

Trest, Warren A., *Air Commando One: Heinie Aderholt and America's Secret Air Wars*. Washington: Smithsonian, 2000.

U.S. Department of Defense Plan, *Integrating National Guard and Reserve Component Support for Response to Attacks Using Weapons of Mass Destruction*. January 1998.

United States Special Operations Command History, 1999. Headquarters, U.S. Special Operations Command, MacDill AFB, Florida.

U.S. Army Special Operations Command, Directory of History, Archives, Library, and Museums, *"Cease Resistance: It's Good For You"*: *A History of U.S. Army Psychological Operations*. Fort Bragg, NC, 1996.

U.S. Army Special Operations Command, Directory of History, Archives, Library, and Museums, *Sine Parl: The Story of Army Special Operations*. Fort Bragg, NC, 1997.

U.S. Army Special Operations Command, Directory of History, Archives, Library, and Museums, *To Free from Oppression: A Concise History of U.S. Army Special Forces, Civil Affairs, Psychological Operations, and the John F. Kennedy Special Warfare Center and School*. Fort Bragg, NC, 1996.

Walker, Greg, *At the Hurricane's Eye: U.S. Special Operations Forces from Vietnam to Desert Storm*. New York: Ballantine Books, 1994.

Waller, Douglas, *The Commandos*. New York: Simon & Schuster, 1994.

Woodward, Bob, *The Commanders*. New York: Simon & Schuster, 1991.

Yarborough, Lieutenant General William P. (Ret.), Selections from his published papers, speeches, and interviews.

XVIII Airborne Corps Public Affairs Office, *A Compendium of Articles Appearing in Various Publications, 20 December 1989–13 January 1990 Detailing Fort Bragg's Participation in Operation Just Cause*.

XVIII Airborne Corps, Organizational History Files, 1989–90. *Operation Just Cause. Corps Historian's Notes. Notebook #1*.

INDEX

Abbas, Abu, 269, 271, 288, 289–95
A camps, 206
Achille Lauro (cruise ship), 27–32, 265–67
    Abbas and Hassan, 289–95
    on board, 267–70
    Cairo, 271–75
    consequences from, 295–96
    Cyprus, 270–71
    the intercept, 276–80
    Sigonella, 281–89
    Washington, 274–76
A-Detachments, 64–65, 69–70, 93–94,
    172–73, 385
    training, 129, 132–34
Advance Course, 523
Advanced SEAL Delivery System, 518
Afghanistan, 498
African Crisis Response Initiative, 498–99
Airborne units, 74, 107, 112
Air Component, 318
Aircraft, 143–44
Airlift, 28
Akers, Frank, Col., 28
Algeria, 17–19, 22–25
ALLIED FORCE, 497
ALO (authorized level of organization), 217
Al-Qaeda, 504, 508
Amal, 20–21, 231, 244, 258, 259
Ambassadors, 518
Americans, 78
Annicchiarici, Col., 284, 288
Antoine, Col., 43, 45, 47, 49, 53–55

Aoun, Michel, 246–47, 249
Apaches, 414
Arabs, 228–29
Arafat, Yasir, 3, 233, 268, 271–72
Arc Lights, 186
Area B-1, 39
Area fire weapons, 316
Arens, Moshe, 243
Aristide, Jean-Bertrand, 495
Armed Forces Staff College, 524
Army, 4–5, 58, 64, 70–71
    game-conservation programs,
      127
    headgear, 69
    institutional symbols, 74
    officers, 107–8
    social culture in, 130–31
    training in, 523–24
Army Green Book, 216
Arthur, Stanley R., Vice Adm., 406
ARVN (Army of the Republic of Vietnam),
    169–71, 174
AS (Armée Secrete), 41, 43–45
ASD (SOLIC), 217
Assad, Hafiz, 20–21, 26, 232, 235, 245, 255,
    259, 268, 503
Asymmetrical warfare, 505–6, 520
Attrition rate, 87
Atwa, Ali, 22–23
Austrians, 78
Avoiding detection, 118
AWADS-equipped, 334

Bad Tolz, Germany, 207
Balkans, 496–98
"The Ballad of the Green Beret," 76
Balwanz, Richard "Bulldog," CW2, 451–68
Bank, Aaron, 56–58, 62–66
Bartholomees, Jim, Col., 528
Bartholomew, Reginald, 25, 235, 238, 240–41,
    248, 255, 257–58, 261
Barzani, Masud, 470, 490, 492
Basic Officers Course, 105–7, 523
"Bat Cave" (King Fahd Airport SF base),
    453–54
Battalion recon platoon, 179
Battle of Dak To, 191
BDAs (Bomb Damage Assessments), 202
B-Detachments, 154, 159
Begin, Menachem, 235
Beirut, 3, 11, 24–25, 228, 503
Ben Het, 195, 197
Benjedid, Chadli, 19
Bernsen, Harold J., Rear Adm., 399
Berri, Nabih, 231, 235, 256
Bin Laden, Osama, 504
Black Hats, 108–9
Blackhawk, 9
BLIND LOGIC, 302
"Blues," 424–25
BLUE SPOON, 302–3, 337–39. See also JUST
    CAUSE
    bomb threat, 327–28
    command-and-control relationships, 317–20
    finalizing, 320–27
    pre-H-hour, 332–37
    provocations from Noriega, 328–29
    revisions to, 313–17
    shooting incident, 329–32
Boghammer, 402
Boomer, Walter E., Lt. Gen., 444
Bowen (destroyer), 245
Bowie knife, 75
British, 78, 170
Buckley, William "Bill," 25, 239, 253, 260, 261
Burba, Edwin H., Gen., 329
Burney, Lin, Col., 367–68
Bush, George, 257, 304, 395, 428, 434–35,
    448, 470, 489
Bush, George W., 506
Bushnell, John, 333

Cadre training program, 527
Cairo, Egypt, 271–75, 428
Cambodia, 79–81, 161, 191, 200–4
Camp MacKall, 134–35, 224

CAPSTONE Course, 524, 529
Carney, John, Maj., 7
Carter, Jimmy, 6, 9, 225
CAS (combat air support), 409
Castro (Mohammed Ali Hamadi), 15–16, 18,
    21
Cavezza, Carmen, Maj. Gen., 319, 365
C-Detachments, 65
Cedras, Raoul, Gen., 495
CENTCOM (U.S. Central Command), 212,
    396, 408, 449
Center of gravity, 61
CEOI (Command Communications and
    Electronic Operating Instructions), 317
Chain of command, 217, 391
Chehab, Fouad, 229
Cheney, Dick, 305, 311, 324, 327, 331,
    435–36
CH-47 Chinooks, 487–88
Chiang Kai-shek, 91
Christian Phalange, 233, 244, 257
CIA, 57–58
    and Special Forces, 172–73
CIDG (Civilian Irregular Defense Group),
    172–75, 199
CINCEUR, 473, 474
CINCLANT (Commander in Chief, Atlantic),
    10
CINCs, 449, 493, 518
CINCSOCs, 512–16
Cisneros, Marc, Maj. Gen., 304, 307, 312,
    317–18, 344, 368, 371–74, 381–82
Civil Affairs, 59, 385–86, 448, 497, 514
Clancy, Tom, 470–73, 476–78
Clandestine entry, 136–38
Clark, Mark W., Lt. Gen., 77
Clifton, Chester V. "Ted," Maj. Gen., 67–73
Cluster bombs, 407, 465
Cody, Dick, Lt. Col., 414
Cohen, William, 217, 219
Cold War, 237
Collateral damage, 316, 387
Collier, Kenny,(CWO), 456–58
Colombia, 97
Colonialism, 82
Combat readiness training, 519
Combat Talons, 424
Combined Task Force Alpha, 473
Command and General Staff College, 523
Commander's Intent, 314, 321
Communists, 36, 55, 82–84
Competition, 527
Confidence course, 115

Contact mines, 398–99
Coriolan, 52–53
COSVN (Central Office for South Vietnam), 202
Counterinsurgency, 88–98
Counterproliferation, 520–21
Craxi, Prime Minister, 269, 279, 287–88, 292
Cross-loading, 136
Crowe, William, Adm., 29–30, 266, 277, 298, 302–6, 511
Cruise ships, 28
CSTs (coalition support teams), 397–98, 409
Cuba, 300, 334
Curtis, Adam, Lt., 329–30
CV-22 Osprey, 518
Cyprus, 32, 265, 270–71

"Daisy Cutters," 424–25
Dak Pek, 192–96
Dak To, 181–84, 192, 196
Dayton Peace Accords, 496
Deep reconnaissance, 199–204
DEFCON (defensive fire concentration), 178
Defections, 430
DeGroff, Robert "Buzzsaw," Sgt., 461, 463–64, 467
Del Cid, Lt. Col., 368, 378, 380
Demining operations, 498
Democratic capitalism, 82–83
Denied territory, 136
Dennau, Tony, Sgt., 35–37, 40, 53
Derickson, Uli, 15–16, 19, 21
De Rosa, Gerardo, Capt., 267, 272–73
Desert One, 7–8, 216
DESERT SHIELD/DESERT STORM. See also PROVIDE COMFORT
    air war, 412–25
    deception on Kuwait beaches, 444–47
    postwar observations, 448–49
    PSYOPs, 425–33
    result of, 447–48
    Scud missiles, 433–41
    special reconnaissance missions, 441–44
    SR mission account by Richard Balwanz, 451–68
Desert training, 213–15
Detachment B-52, 199
Devlin, Daniel D., Lt. Col., 425–26, 428–30, 433
Dien Bien Phu, 161
Dietz, Tom, Lt., 445, 446
Dignity Battalions, 300, 304, 321, 328, 350, 363, 367–69, 384

Diplomatic immunity, 289
Direct-fire weapons, 316
Discipline, 92
Dominique Leb, Lt. (Jacques Le Bel de Penguilly), 35–37, 42–43, 45–49, 51, 53–55
Domino Theory, 164
Donovan, "Wild Bill," Gen., 37–38
Downing, Wayne, Maj. Gen., 513, 515, 521
    in Kuwait, 397, 435–40
    and Operation PACIFIC WIND, 405–7, 410
    in Panama, 331–32, 334, 337, 342, 365–67, 369–74, 376, 379–80, 382, 389
Drug trafficking, 300
Druze, 230
    PSP, 243–48, 250, 257
Dunbar, Layton, Col., 430

EAGER ANVIL, 414–17
EARNEST WILL, 398–405
Edmonds, Maurice, Maj., 177, 193
EDRE (emergency deployment readiness exercise), 331
Egypt, 271–73, 289–90, 294–96
Egypt Air 2843, 273, 276–81, 292
XVIII Airborne Corps, 297–300, 303, 308–9, 331, 441–42, 455, 495
Eisenhower (aircraft carrier), 245
ELABORATE MAZE, 301, 302
Emerson, Hank, Maj. Gen., 212
Endara, Guillermo, 304, 383, 386, 388
End state, 60
Entebbe Airport rescue, 4, 6
EUCOM (U.S. European Command), 239, 473

Fairbairn, William, Maj., 39
Fairbanks, Richard, 243
Fall, Bernard, 89–90
FFI (Force Francaises d'Interieur), 40
Fintel, Tim, Col., 237–38, 263
Fister, Bruce, Brig. Gen., 318
FLIR (Forward Looking Infrared Receiver), 402
Florer, Stan, Lt. Col., 476–79, 482, 484, 491, 493
Flynn, Mike, Col., 1
F-117s, 325
Force package, 28
Force 777, 283, 285, 287
Foreign aviation training, 520
FORSCOM, 304
Fort Benning, 104, 113–14
Fort Bragg, 222, 518, 520

Fort Cimarron, Panama, 363–64
Foss, John, Lt. Gen., 303
Franks, Fred, Lt. Gen., 441
Free French, 36, 54
French, 78, 161, 228
Friendly-fire incidents, 445
From the OSS to Green Berets: The Birth of Special Forces (Bank), 58
F-16s, 464, 467
FSSF (First Special Service Force), 59
FTP (Franc Tireurs Partisans), 41, 43–49, 51, 55

"Gabriel Demonstration," 69
Galvin, James, Gen., 474
Game-conservation programs, 127
Gardner, Robbie, Sgt., 466
Garner, Jay M., Maj. Gen., 472, 475
Gatanas, Col., 249
"Gators," 407
Gemayel, Amin, 235, 238, 248, 257–58, 263
Gemayel, Bashir, 233
Geneva Accords, 168
Geraghty, Tim, Col., 240, 245, 248, 252
German commandos, 61–62
Germans, 41, 52–55, 78
Giroldi, Moises, Maj., 310–12
Glosson, Buster C., Brig. Gen., 406–7, 413, 438–40
Gnecknow, Jerry C., Rear Adm., 320
Gobbler Woods, 135, 147–52
Goldwater-Nichols Act (1986), 217, 391, 451. *See also* Nunn-Cohen Amendment
GPS (global positioning system), 114, 454, 457
Graduation exercise, 147–52
Gray, George, Maj. Gen., 358
Green beret, 68–69
Green Berets, 66, 75, 92–98, 212, 220, 409, 443
The Green Berets (Moore), 75–76
Grenada, 10–13
Guadalcanal (assault ship), 400
Guam, 13
Guerrero, Leon, Chief Sgt. Maj., 359–60
Guerrillas, 59–60, 63, 83–85, 471, 475, 484–86
Guest, James, Maj. Gen., 206–11, 213–15, 220–24, 409
Gulf War. *See also* PROVIDE COMFORT
  air war, 412–25
  deception on Kuwait beaches, 444–47
  end of, 447–48
  first, 398–405

postwar observations, 448–49
PSYOPs, 425–33
Scud missiles, 433–41
special reconnaissance missions, 441–44

Habib, Phillip, 235
"Hail Mary," 441
Haiti, 495–96
Hakim, Maj. Gen., 257, 258
Hamdan, Abbas, Brig. Gen., 240–42, 257
Harkins, Paul, Gen., 170
Hartzog, Bill, Brig. Gen., 307
Hassan, 290
Hay-Bunau-Varilla Treaty, 299
Headgear, 68–69
Helfer, Rick, Maj., 487
Hercules, 400, 402
Hezbollah, 15, 20–21, 231, 253–54, 256, 262
Hide sites, 455
Higgins, Maj., 350–52
Hill 660, 190
Hill 1338, 183–190
Hilsman, Roger, 79, 89
Hip-pocket training, 125
Hitler, Adolf, 57
Hobson, Jim, Maj. Gen., 474–75
Ho Chi Minh Trail, 161–63, 168, 172, 178, 181, 191, 198–201, 204
Holland, Charlie R., 513
Holloway, James L., Adm., 9
HONEY BADGER, 9
Hooton, Hoot, Col., 474
Hopkins, Charles, Sgt., 459
Horner, Chuck, Lt. Gen., 406
Hostage-taking, 231, 259–63
Hoyt, Lt. Col., 156–58
Hubert, Capt., 42–46, 52–54
Huff, Paul B., Sgt., 77
Humble, Howard, Maj., 342
HUMINT (human intelligence), 234, 505
Hunt, Joe, Lt. Col., 368
Hurley, Pat, Sgt. Maj., 341
Hussein, Saddam, 395, 405, 410–12, 428, 433–34, 470–71, 484, 492

Indochina, 168
IQ requirement, 222
Iran, 15, 212–13, 231, 245
  hostage crisis, 5–9
Iran Ajr, 400–402
Iran-Iraq War, 398–405, 503

Iraq, 9, 410, 475–76, 503
  and Gulf War, 412–48
  invasion of Kuwait, 395–97
Islam, 502
Islamic Jihad, 253, 259–60, 429
Islamic revolution, 231
Isolation area, 148–52
Israel, 229, 232–33, 434, 503
Israelis, 4, 6, 228–33
  and *Achille Lauro* takedown, 266
  withdrawal from Lebanon, 235–44, 259
Italy, 269, 284, 286, 291, 293, 295–96

Jacobelly, Jake, Col., 350, 352
Jamerson, James, Maj. Gen., 473
Japan, 63
JEDBURGH, 40–55
Jedburgh Teams, 35, 40, 45, 62, 64
Jeremiah, Dave, Rear Adm., 276, 294
Jews, 228–29
JOC (Joint Operations Center), 2, 27–31
Johnson, Hansford T., Gen., 328–29
Johnson, H. K., Gen., 96–97
Johnson, Jesse, Col., 396, 405, 407, 413, 418
Johnson, Jim, Maj. Gen., 318, 335–36, 361,
  374
Johnson, Lyndon, 201, 203
Johnson, Richard "Zoot," Col., 176–78, 193
Joint Task Force Alpha, 472
Joint Task Force Bravo, 472, 475
Jones, Devon, Lt., 418–22
Jordan, 229
JSOTF (Joint Special Operations Task Force),
  1–2, 14, 17–18, 318, 322, 473
  evolution of, 3–14
JTFP Headquarters, 304, 306
JTF South (Joint Task Force South), 314, 390
J-3, 29–30
Jumblatt, Walid, 230, 235
Jump boots, 75
Jump mission, 136–38
Jump School, 107–12
JUST CAUSE, 341–44, 348–49, 508. *See also*
  BLUE SPOON
  Ma Bell missions, 365–69
  maps, 345–47
  Rio Hato, 358–61
  search for Noriega, 369–83
  stability operations, 364–65
  Task Force Atlantic, 353–54
  Task Force Black, 350–53
  Task Force Pacific, 361–64
  Task Force Semper Fi, 354
  Task Force White, 349–50
  Torrijos-Tocumen Airport, 355–58
  vetting process, 383–84

Kelley, P. X., Gen., 225
Kelley, Thomas W., Lt. Gen., 303–4, 311,
  330–31, 339, 435
Kellogg, Keith, Col., 318, 353
Kelly, Frank, Brig. Gen., 28
Kelso, Frank, Adm., 328
Kemph, Pete, Lt. Gen., 318, 320, 325, 377
Kennedy, John F., 67–73, 81, 84, 88, 96, 163,
  169, 528
Kernan, Buck, Col., 323–24, 359–60, 365–67
Kershner, Mike, Col., 477, 480, 485–86,
  488–89, 491
Khomeini, Ayatollah, 503
Kidnapping, 259–63
Kingsley, Mike, Capt., 415
Kingston, Robert "Bob," Maj. Gen., 4
Kinzer, Joe, Brig. Gen., 331
Klinghoffer, Leon, 267–69, 272, 275, 282
Klinghoffer, Marilyn, 268–69, 273, 293
KLONDIKE KEY, 302
Korean War, 63
Kostrzebski, Dan, 467
Kraus, James, Col., 409
Krueger, Chris, Lt. Col., 483, 487, 490, 491
Kupperman, Robert, 4
Kurds, 410, 492
  culture of, 488–90
  health effort for, 481–84
  Pesh Merga, 484–86
  rebellion after Gulf War, 470–76
  refugee camps of, 478–79
  return home, 490–92
  supply effort for, 479–80
Kuwait, 260–61, 508
  and Gulf War, 412–48
  invasion by Iraq, 395–97
Kuwait City, 447–48

Laboa, Monsignor, 372–74, 379, 381–82
Labron, Uri, 241–42
LAMPS helicopters, 399
Land navigation, 114, 138–40
Language proficiency, 134
Lansdale, Edward, Col., 90–91
Laos, 10, 161, 163–68, 191, 200–204
"La Violencia," 97
LAVs (Light Armored Vehicles), 432
LAW (light antitank weapon), 358–60
Lawson, Gen., 254–55

LCEs (Liaison Coordination Elements), 497
Leadership, 523–29
Leadership Reaction Course, 131–32
Lebanon, 3, 21, 227, 503, 509
    efforts at finding a solution, 255–59
    escalation of violence in, 243–51
    Israeli withdrawal from, 235–43
    new form of terrorism, 259–63
    new threat from suicide bombers, 251–55
    roots of tragedy of, 227–35
LeBlanc, Maj., 129
Left hook, 441
Leonik, Bob, Maj., 415
Levin, Jeremy, 260, 261
LHAs, 406
Libya, 231, 300
Lindsay, Jim, Gen., 218, 329, 339, 511–13, 516
Little, John T., Lt. Col., 164–66
LLDB (Vietnamese Special Forces), 174
Lodge Act, 62
Loefke, Bernie, Maj. Gen., 298, 301, 307
Long, David, 24
LPHs, 406
Luck, Gary, Lt. Gen., 309, 315, 317–18, 320,
    324, 331–32

MAAG (Military Assistance Advisory Group),
    168–70
MAAG Laos (Military Assistance Advisory
    Group Laos), 164
MAC (Military Airlift Command), 219
MacArthur, Douglas, Gen., 63
McCarthy, Jim, Gen., 473
McClure, Robert, Brig. Gen., 63, 65, 66
MacFairlaine, Robert "Bud," 30, 235, 239,
    248–50
McGarr, Lionel C., Lt. Gen., 169
McGrath, Marcus, Archbishop, 379
MACV (Military Assistance Command,
    Vietnam), 170–75, 199, 200
MACVSOG (Military Assistance Command
    Vietnam Studies and Observation
    Group), 200–204
Magsaysay, Ramon, 90
Malta, 294–95
Maneuver Training Centers, 524
Mao Tse-tung, 83–84, 91
Maquis, 36, 40–41, 52
Marines, 11, 234, 256, 258
Maronite Christians, 228, 230
Martin, Corby, Capt., 417
Massey, Andy, Col., 436–37
MAU (Marine Amphibious Unit), 233

Maurabi Toon, 232
Mayaguez (merchant ship), 4, 216
Meadows, Dick, Maj., 7
Medellín drug cartel, 327
Medical expertise, 93–94
Medical training, 520
Meguid, Abdel, 271, 282
Metcalfe, Adm., 11–12
METL (Mission Essential Task List), 124
MEU (SOC) (Marine Expeditionary Unit—
    Special Operations Capable), 472
Meyer, Edward C. "Shy," Gen., 4, 216–17,
    224–25, 297, 524
MFP-11 (Major Force Program 11), 218, 512,
    516–17
MIKE Force, 196
MILES devices, 124
Military Support Group, 386, 390
Milosevic, Slobodan, 497
Mines, 398–99, 487, 498
Miss Vicki (Noriega girlfriend), 379–80
Modelo Prison, Panama, 341–43
Mogadishu, Somalia, 494
Molqi, Majed, 267, 269, 293
Montagnards, 172, 191, 198–99
Moore, Robin, 75
Moreau, Arthur "Art," Vice Adm., 30, 266, 269,
    273, 275, 280, 290, 291
MREs (meals-ready-to-eat), 388, 480
Mugniyah, Imad, 21, 260–61
Munich Olympics massacre, 4
Muse, Kurt, 314, 322, 341–43
Mussolini, Benito, 62

Napalm, 187
National Command Authority, 329, 391, 397,
    508
National Security Directive 17, 305
Nation building, 384–88
NATO, 497
Navy, 219
Nazis, 36, 40, 44
NCOs, 87, 157
NEOs (noncombatant evacuation operations),
    499
New Jersey (battleship), 249, 258
Newlin, Michael, 19, 22, 23
New terrorism, 501–2
Nicaragua, 300
Night boat drop, 12–13
Night parachute jump, 138
Nimitz (aircraft carrier), 7, 406
Nine Rules of Conduct (Mao), 91, 93

Nixon, Richard, 204
NMCC (National Military Command Center), 280
Noriega, Manuel Antonio, 300–302, 304–5, 307–8, 310–17, 321, 328–30, 333–34, 344, 348–49, 357–58, 369–83, 506
Normand, Tony, Col., 425–28, 431–33
North Vietnam, 161, 168–99, 467
Norwegian Princess (cruise liner), 10
Nunn, Sam, 217
Nunn-Cohen Amendment, 221, 451, 511, 513–14, 518
NVA (North Vietnamese Army), 176–78, 180, 182–87, 189–204

O'Boyle, Randy, Capt., 413
Officers, 88
Offset bombing, 325
OGs, 64–65
On War (von Clausewitz), 60, 61
OOTW (Operations Other Than War), 522
Operations
    ALLIED FORCE, 497
    BLUE SPOON, 302–39
    DESERT SHIELD/DESERT STORM, 412–49, 508
    EAGER ANVIL, 414–17
    EARNEST WILL, 398–405
    HONEY BADGER, 9
    JEDBURGH, 40–55
    JUST CAUSE, 341–84, 508
    PACIFIC WIND, 405–12
    PROMOTE LIBERTY, 384–88
    PROVIDE COMFORT, 469–94
    SWITCHBACK, 173
    URGENT FURY, 10–13
OPLAN, 330
OSG (operational subgroup), 29–30
OSS (Office of Strategic Services), 35, 37–39, 46–47, 57, 63, 64

PACIFIC WIND, 405–12
Palastra, Joseph T., Gen., 303
Palestinians, 228–33, 289
Panama, 298, 306–10, 508
    Canal Zone, 299–300
    1989 elections, 304
    Noriega, 300
        search for, 369–83
    October 3 coup attempt, 310–13
    Operation BLUE SPOON, 302–39
    Operation JUST CAUSE, 341–84
    Operation PROMOTE LIBERTY, 384–88

post-action thoughts, 391–93
    transition and redeployment, 388–91
Panzer Gruppe, 369, 371, 374
Parachute Battalion (movie), 75
Parachute landing falls, 109
Paratroopers, 69, 74
Paris Peace Agreement (1995), 496
Pathet Lao, 163, 167
"Patrick," 42–43, 52
Patrolling, 113–14, 118–22
Patton, George, Gen., 44
Pave Lows, 413–21, 441, 444
Paz, Robert, 1st Lt., 329
PDF (Panamanian Defense Force), 300–301, 309–10, 312–313, 316, 320, 328–30, 336–37, 341–69, 383–87
PEACE FOR GALILEE, 232
Peacekeeping, 499
Peers, William, Maj. Gen., 181, 194
Penetration teams, 207
Pentagon, 280, 501
    finances, 212
Perez, Gilberto, Maj., 366–68
Perry, Bill, 521
Perry, Lt. Col., 130
Pesh Merga, 471, 475, 484–86, 490
Peters, Michael, Lt. Col., 386
Philippines, 90
PIRATE, 289
PLO (Palestinian Liberation Organization), 229, 232–33, 242, 244, 251, 268, 272, 275, 289, 293
Poindexter, John, Vice Adm., 30
POM (Program Objective Memorandum), 513–14, 516–17
Porr, Darrel, Maj. Dr., 32
POST TIME, 302, 303
Potter, Richard W., Brig. Gen., 472–73, 481, 486, 489, 494, 496
Powell, Colin, Gen., 308–11, 327–28, 378, 405, 407–8, 426, 435
PPBS (Planning, Programming, and Budgeting System), 516
PRAYER BOOK, 302, 306
PRC-90-radio, 464
PRESENCE, 234
Project Delta, 199–200
PROMOTE LIBERTY, 384–88
Propaganda, 428–33
PROVIDE COMFORT, 469
    battle for lives, 476–78
    communications effort, 486–88
    debriefing, 493–94

health effort, 481–84
Kurdish culture, 488–90
Pesh Merga guerrillas, 484–86
rebellions in Iraq, 470–76
refugee camps, 478–79
refugee return to homes, 490–92
supply effort, 479–80
PSYOPs (psychological operations), 59, 151,
    497, 506, 514
in Gulf War, 425–33

Q course, 129, 134–35, 147, 152–53, 222
Quassis, Simon, Col., 241–42, 248–49

Rabb, Ambassador, 269–70, 284–85, 292
Radar site neutralization, 415–16
Raff, Edson D., Lt. Col., 79
Rangers, 62–64, 66, 69, 87, 355–61
Ranger School, 107, 112–23
Rappelling, 117–18
Rashadat GOSP, 404
RDJTF (Rapid Deployment Joint Task Force),
    212, 225
Reagan, Ronald, 9, 233, 249, 255–57, 269,
    273, 277, 398, 404, 511
Red Army, 91
REDCOM (U.S. Readiness Command),
    218–19
REFORGER (Reinforcement of Germany),
    210
Refugee camps, 478–79
Regier, Frank, 260, 261
Renacer prison, Panama, 354
Republican Guards (Iraq), 448, 455, 470
Reserve chute, 137–38
Resolution 688, 471–72
Resupply, 140–45
RIB (rigid inflatable boat), 518
Richardson, Bill, Gen., 220
Richardson, Charles, Col., 318, 354
Ridgeway, Matthew, Maj. Gen., 77
Rifaat, Yehia, 289, 290
Ringers, 38
Rio Hato, Panama, 358–61
Robin Sage, 135, 147–52
Rock work, 117–18
Roosma, Will, Maj. Gen., 306, 313, 334
ROTC (Reserve Officer Training Corps), 523
Rumsfeld, Donald, 255–57, 261
Russians, 78

Sadler, Barry, Sgt., 76
Said (Hassan Izz-al-din), 15–16

Samuel B. Roberts (frigate), 404–5
Sand Flea exercises, 307
SAS, 35–36, 49, 52
SATCOM radios, 30, 288, 460–61, 463, 486
SATRAN, 32
Saudi Arabia, 224, 395–96, 405, 412, 435, 503
Saudi National Guard, 224
Scholes, Ed, Brig. Gen., 306, 331
Scholtes, Richard "Dick," Maj. Gen., 9–10,
    14
Schoonmaker, Peter J., Gen., 513, 515–16
Schultz, Richard, 202
Schwarzkopf, Norman, Gen., 396–97, 405,
    407–9, 413–14, 418, 425–28, 436,
    439–40, 444
Scud missiles, 433–41
Sea Isle City, 404
SEALs, 12–13, 27–28, 219, 265, 271–72,
    349–50, 399–405, 409, 444–47
Search-and-rescue (CSAR) missions, 418–22
Sea Stallion helicopter, 7, 9
Sensory deprivation, 132
September 11, 2001, 501–9
SERE (Survival, Escape, Resistance, and
    Evasion), 146–47
17 May Agreement, 234–35
VII Corps, 441–42
Shafer, Ted, Rear Adm., 311
Shalikashvili, John, Lt. Gen., 472–74, 489
Shaw, Bill, Capt., 477, 481, 483–86
Sheikholislam, Hosein, 231, 254
Shelton, Henry, Gen., 496, 513, 515
Shiite Muslims, 503
    in Iraq, 410, 470
    in Lebanon, 18, 228, 230–31, 244, 251, 253,
        256–58, 260–62
Ship takedown, 28, 266, 270
Shultz, George, 234–35
Sigonella (NATO base), 17, 30, 32, 265, 275,
    278–91
Silkworm missiles, 403–4
Simons, Arthur D. "Bull," Lt. Col., 166–67,
    201, 202
Sims, Jeffrey, Master Sgt., 442–43
Singlaub, Jack, Lt., 35–37, 40–42, 44–55
Skyraiders, 187
Slade, Lawrence R., Lt., 418–22
Smith, Leighton "Snuffy," Adm., 473
Smith, Ray, Capt., 444
Snell, Mike, Col., 313–14, 318
SOCCENT, 411
SOCEUR (Special Operations Command
    Europe), 473, 476

SOCOM, 219, 302, 309, 396–97, 408, 418, 451
SOCOM POM, 516
SOCOR (Special Operations Coordinator), 455
SOE (Special Operations Executive), 39
SOG, 200–204
SOLL-II, 29
  qualified, 334
Somalia, 494–95, 509
Souk Al Gharb, Lebanon, 246, 259
SOUTHCOM (U.S. Southern Command), 298, 302–4, 307, 309, 313, 385–86, 390
Southwest Asia, 213
Soviet Union, 4, 504, 512, 520
Speakes, Larry, 273
Spearman, Bill, Capt., 30, 278–79, 283–84, 295
Special Operations Forces (SOF), 1–2, 58, 128
  adaptation of, 493–94
  A-Detachments, 64–65, 69–70, 93–94, 129, 385
  African Crisis Response Initiative, 498–99
  in Balkans, 496–98
  between the wars, 205–26
  Bible of, 55–56
  change in 1980s, 216–19
  and CIA, 172–73
  demining operations, 498
  early, 84–98
  as force of choice, 521–22
  funding, 215
  graduation exercise, 147–52
  in Haiti, 495–96
  in Iraq, 469–94
  in Kuwait, 395–468
  mission, 65
  NEOs, 499
  operations, 65
  in Panama, 297–393
  peacekeeping and training, 499
  professionalism of, 221–25
  in Somalia, 494–95
  training, 131–47, 222–24
    modern, 152–54
    Q course, 129, 134–35, 147, 152–53, 222
  in Vietnam, 159, 161, 168–72
Special reconnaissance (SR) missions, 441–44
  account by Richard Balwanz, 451–68
Special Warfare Center and School, 65
"Spectre" gunships, 422–25
Speers, John, Col., 174
Stanley, Leroy, Col., 156

State-supported terrorism, 3, 231, 520
Stealth Fighter, 412
Stiner, Carl, Gen., 1, 13–14, 18, 22, 98, 217, 424, 427, 493, 512, 514–15
  and Achille Lauro, 265–67
  call to Special Forces, 127–31
  as CINC USSOCOM, 516–22
  early years, 99–107
  graduation of, 147–52
  as Green Beret, 154–59
  and Jump School, 107–12
  on leadership, 523–29
  in Lebanon, 227, 235–43
  and Operation BLUE SPOON, 297–300, 306–10, 312–39
  and Operation DESERT SHIELD/DESERT STORM, 396–408, 411, 435–37, 448–49
  and Operation JUST CAUSE, 344, 371–73
  and Operation PACIFIC WIND, 405, 407–8
  on Operation PROVIDE COMFORT, 469–70
  and Ranger School, 112–23
  on September 11, 2001, 501–9
  training of, 131–47
  on training principles, 123–26
  and TWA Flight 847, 24–32
  in Vietnam, 175–99
Strategic Hamlet Program, 170–72
Street Without Joy (Fall), 89
Suicide bombings, 231, 260
Sullivan, Gordon, Gen., 524
Sungari, 404
Survival, escape, and evasion, 145–47
Swenor, Doug, 483
Swing landing fall trainer, 109
SWITCHBACK, 173
Syria, 268
  and Lebanon, 230–31, 238, 244–45, 248, 255–56, 259

Taft, William H.,IV, 511, 514
Takedowns, 28, 266, 270
Tangney, Bill, Col., 474, 476, 481, 490
Tannous, Ibrahim, Gen., 237–43, 245–49, 251–53, 255, 258–59, 261, 263
Task Force Atlantic, 318, 322–23, 353–54, 364
Task Force Bayonet, 318, 322, 388
Task Force Black, 350–53
Task Force Blue, 369
Task Force Green, 341, 369, 373
Task Force Pacific, 318, 323, 361–64
Task Force Proven Force, 473
Task Force Red, 322, 332
Task Force Semper Fi, 318, 322, 354

Task Force White, 349–50
Team James, 35, 41, 45
Terrorism, 2–3, 231, 259–63, 501–2
Testrake, John, 14–15, 20–21, 24
Tet offensive, 195–96, 198, 203
Thach (destroyer), 404
Thayer, Charles M., 89
Theater SOC upgrades, 519
Third World, 82, 93
Thompson, Robert, Sir, 170
Thurman, Maxwell, Gen., 220, 224, 297–300,
    305–6, 308–11, 313, 317, 320, 326,
    330, 337–39, 376–78, 384–85, 389
Tinajitas, Panama, 362–63
Tojo parachutes, 136–37
Torbett, Ronald, Sgt. FC, 442–43
Torrijos, Omar, Brig. Gen., 300
Torrijos-Tucumen Airport, Panama, 355–58
TRADOC (Training and Doctrine Command),
    219–20
Training, 499, 526–27
  in Army, 523–24
  combat readiness, 519
  foreign aviation, 520
  medical, 520
  modern, 152–54
  principles, 123–26
  Special Forces, 131–47, 222–24
Trask, Tom, Capt., 419
Tunisia, 233, 274–75
Turkey, 395, 470–72, 475–77, 482–83, 487,
    492
Turnow, Robin, Brig. Gen., 320
Tuttle, Jerry, Rear Adm., 240, 248, 254–55
TWA Flight 847, 14–27
28th Infantry Division, 297

Unconventional warfare, 33, 58–66, 81–86,
    131
UNHCR (United Nations High Commissioner
    for Refugees), 484
United States, as target, 502–4
URGENT FURY, 10–13
USAREUR (U.S. Army Europe) survival
    course, 207, 211
USARSO (U.S. Army South), 298, 386
USEAT, 350, 361
USEUCOM (U.S. European Command), 18,
    31, 270

USS *Nicholas*, 422
USSOCOM (U.S. Special Operations
    Command), 217–19, 449, 511–22
USS *Saratoga* (aircraft carrier), 31, 275–76, 294
USSTRICOM (U.S. Strike Command), 218
U-10 Helio Courier, 143

Vaught, James, Maj. Gen., 6–7
Veliotes, Nicholas, 273
Vessey, Jack, Gen., 14, 227, 236–38, 241,
    243
Viet Cong, 161, 169–71, 191, 198
Vietnam, 159, 161, 168–72, 175–99, 221, 467
Village Defense Program, 172–73, 191
Vines, John, Lt. Col., 363
Virginia (cruiser), 249
Volckmann, Russell, Lt. Col., 63–66
Volmer, Pat, Lt. Col., 179
von Clausewitz, Carl, 60
Vuono, Carl, Gen., 298, 325–26, 390, 524

Wagner, Robert, Lt. Col., 355
War College, 523
Warner, John, 383
Wars, 3
Wauthier, Capt., 35, 42, 47–49, 51, 53, 54
Weapon of mass destruction, 520
Weapons programs, 517–18
Weatherford, James, Sgt., 459, 463
Weigand, Robert, Maj. Gen., 294
Weinberger, Caspar, 232, 277, 402
Weir, Benjamin, Rev., 262
White Star Program, 163–68, 201
White Team, 415
Wilderness survival, 118
Wimbrown VII, 400
Woerner, Frederick F., Gen., 301–3, 305, 307,
    310
World Trade Center, 501, 504
World War II, 35–66

Yarborough, Bill, Brig. Gen., 67–81, 85–88,
    90–98, 164, 205, 493
Yemen, 224
Yugoslavia, 293, 496

Zawodny, Jay, Dr., 89
Zimmerman, Christian, 14, 24
Zinni, Tony, Brig. Gen., 473